Lecture Notes in Artificial Intelligence 1585

Subseries of Lecture Notes in Computer Science
Edited by J. G. Carbonell and J. Siekmann

Lecture Notes in Computer Science

Edited by G. Goos, J. Hartmanis and J. van Leeuwen

Springer
Berlin
Heidelberg
New York
Barcelona
Hong Kong
London
Milan
Paris
Singapore
Tokyo

Bob McKay   Xin Yao   Charles S. Newton
Jong-Hwan Kim   Takeshi Furuhashi (Eds.)

Simulated Evolution and Learning

Second Asia-Pacific Conference
on Simulated Evolution and Learning, SEAL'98
Canberra, Australia, November 24-27, 1998
Selected Papers

 Springer

Series Editors
Jaime G. Carbonell, Carnegie Mellon University, Pittsburgh, PA, USA
Jörg Siekmann, University of Saarland, Saarbrücken, Germany

Volume Editors

Bob McKay
Xin Yao
Charles S. Newton
School of Computer Science, University College, UNSW
Australian Defence Force Academy
Canberra, ACT, Australia 2600
E-mail: {rim/xin/csn}@cs.adfa.edu.au

Jong-Hwan Kim
Department of Electrical Engineering
Korea Advanced Institute of Science and Technology
373-1, Kusung-dong, Yusung-gu, Taejon-shi 305-701, Republic of Korea
E-mail: johkim@vivaldi.kaist.ac.kr

Takeshi Furuhashi
Department of Information Electronics, Nagoya University
Furo-cho, Chikusa-ku, Nagoya 464-8603, Japan
E-mail: furuhashi@nuee.nagoya-u.ac.jp

Cataloging-in-Publication data applied for

Die Deutsche Bibliothek - CIP-Einheitsaufnahme

Simulated evolution and learning : selected papers / Second Asia
Pacific Conference on Simulated Evolution and Learning, SEAL '98,
Canberra, Australia, November 24 - 27, 1998. Bob McKay ... (ed.). -
Berlin ; Heidelberg ; New York ; Barcelona ; Hong Kong ; London ;
Milan ; Paris ; Singapore ; Tokyo : Springer, 1999
  (Lecture notes in computer science ; Vol. 1585 : Lecture notes in
  artificial intelligence)
  ISBN 3-540-65907-2

CR Subject Classification (1998): I.2, F.1.1, I.6, J.3, J.2

ISBN 3-540-65907-2 Springer-Verlag Berlin Heidelberg New York

Typesetting: Camera-ready by author
SPIN 10703189   06/3142 – 5 4 3 2 1 0   Printed on acid-free paper

Preface

This volume contains selected papers presented at the Second Asia-Pacific Conference on Simulated Evolution and Learning (SEAL'98), from 24 to 27 November 1998, in Canberra, Australia. SEAL'98 received a total of 92 submissions (67 papers for the regular sessions and 25 for the applications sessions). All papers were reviewed by three independent reviewers. After review, 62 papers were accepted for oral presentation and 13 for poster presentation. Some of the accepted papers were selected for inclusion in this volume. SEAL'98 also featured a fully refereed special session on Evolutionary Computation in Power Engineering organised by Professor Kit Po Wong and Dr Loi Lei Lai. Two of the five accepted papers are included in this volume.

The papers included in these proceedings cover a wide range of topics in simulated evolution and learning, from self-adaptation to dynamic modelling, from reinforcement learning to agent systems, from evolutionary games to evolutionary economics, and from novel theoretical results to successful applications, among others.

SEAL'98 attracted 94 participants from 14 different countries, namely Australia, Belgium, Brazil, Germany, Iceland, India, Japan, South Korea, New Zealand, Portugal, Sweden, Taiwan, UK and the USA. It had three distinguished international scientists as keynote speakers, giving talks on natural computation (Hans-Paul Schwefel), reinforcement learning (Richard Sutton), and novel models in evolutionary design (John Gero). More information about SEAL'98 is still available at `http://www.cs.adfa.edu.au/conference/seal98/`.

A number of people have helped to make the conference a great success. They include our secretaries: Alison McMaster, Jodi Wood and Kaylene Tulk, and students: Ko-Hsin Liang, Jason Bobbin, Thomas Runarsson and Chi-Wu Chou. We would like to take this opportunity to express our sincere thanks to them.

December 1998

Xin Yao
Bob McKay
Charles Newton
Jong-Hwan Kim
Takeshi Furuhashi

Conference Committee

General Chair: Professor Charles S. Newton
Organising Committee Chair: Dr Bob McKay
Programme Committee Co-Chairs: Takeshi Furuhashi, Jong-Hwan Kim and Xin Yao
Conference Secretary: Miss Alison McMaster
Special Sessions Chair: Professor Kit Po Wong
Sponsorship Chair: Dr Graham Williams

Programme Committee Members

Alan Blair (University of Queensland, Australia)
Terry Bossomaier (Charles Sturt University, Australia)
Jong-Chen Chen (National Yunlin University of Technology, Taiwan)
Shu-Heng Chen (National Chengchi University, Taiwan)
Sung-Bae Cho (Yonsei University, Korea)
George Coghill (University of Auckland, New Zealand)
David Fogel (Natural Selection, Inc., USA)
Tamas D. Gedeon (University of New South Wales, Australia)
Mitsuo Gen (Ashikaga Institute of Technology, Japan)
David Green (Charles Sturt University, Australia)
Tetsuya Higuchi (Electrotechnical Laboratory, Japan)
Tim Hendtlass (Swinburne University of Technology, Australia)
Robert Hinterding (Victoria University of Technology, Australia)
Hitoshi Iba (Electrotechnical Laboratory, Japan)
Tadashi Iokibe (Japan)
Lishan Kang (Wuhan University, P. R. China)
Nikola Kasabov (University of Otago, New Zealand)
Osamu Katai (Kyoto University, Japan)
K. S. Leung (The Chinese University of Hong Kong, Hong Kong)
Huan Liu (National University of Singapore, Singapore)
Jiming Liu (Hong Kong Baptist University, Hong Kong)
Jiyin Liu (University of Science and Technology of Hong Kong, Hong Kong)
Yong Liu (UNSW, ADFA, Australia)
Zhi-Qiang Liu (University of Melbourne, Australia)
John McDonnell (SSC-San Diego, USA)
Bob McKay (UNSW, ADFA, Australia)
Masoud Mohammadian (Monash University, Australia)
Akira Namatame (National Defence Academy, Japan)
Bill Porto (Natural Selection, Inc., USA)
Robert Reynolds (Wayne State University, USA)
Simon Ronald (University of Adelaide, Australia)
N. Saravanan (Ford Motor Company, USA)
Henry Selvaraj (Monash University, Australia)

Stephen Smith (Central Queensland University, Australia)
Russell Standish (University of New South Wales, Australia)
Russell Stonier (Central Queensland University, Australia)
Yasuhiro Tsujimura (Ashikaga Institute of Technology, Japan)
Brijesh Verma (Gri th University, Australia)
Donald Waagen (Lockheed Martin Tactical Defense Systems, USA)
Peter Whigham (CSIRO, Australia)
Kit Po Wong (University of Western Australia, Australia)
Xingdong Wu (Monash University, Australia)
Toru Yamaguchi (Utsunomiya University, Japan)
Xinghuo Yu (Central Queensland University, Australia)
Byoung-Tak Zhang (Seoul National University, Korea)
Chengqi Zhang (University of New England, Australia)
Qiangfu Zhao (University of Aizu, Japan)

Additional Reviewers

Syed Nadeem Ahmed
Hussein Aly Abbass Amein
Nick Barnes
Michael Blumenstein
Jinhai Cai
Jirapun Daengdej
Honghua Dai
M. Dash
Zhexue Huang
Md. Farhad Hussain
Jun Jo
Yuefeng Li
Man Leung Wong
Jingtao Yao

Table of Contents

Natural Computation*

Hans-Paul Schwefel

Chair of Systems Analysis
Department of Computer Science
University of Dortmund
D-44221 Dortmund, Germany

Abstract. The idea of mimicking processes of organic evolution on computers and using such algorithms for solving adaptation and optimization tasks can be traced back to the Sixties. Genetic Algorithms (GA), Evolutionary Programming (EP), and Evolution Strategies (ES), the still vivid di˘erent strata of this idea, have not only survived until now, but have become an important tool within what has been called Computational Intelligence, Soft Computing, as well as Natural Computation. An outline of Evolutionary Algorithms (EA the common denominator for GA, EP, and ES) will be sketched, their di˘erences pinpointed, some theoretical results summarized, and some applications mentioned.

---

* Abstract only.

X. Yao et al. (Eds.): SEAL'98, LNCS 1585, pp. 1–1, 1999.

Multiple Lagrange Multiplier Method for Constrained Evolutionary Optimization

Hyun Myung and Jong-Hwan Kim

Dept. of EE, KAIST, 373-1 Kusong-dong,
Yusong-gu, Taejon, 305-701, Korea
Tel: +82-42-869-8048, Fax: +82-42-869-8010
{myung, johkim}@vivaldi.kaist.ac.kr

Abstract. One of the well-known problems in evolutionary search for solving optimization problem is the premature convergence. The general constrained optimization techniques such as hybrid evolutionary programming, two phase evolutionary programming, and Evolian algorithms are not safe from the same problem in the "rst phase. To overcome this problem, we apply the sharing function to the Evolian algorithm and propose to use the multiple Lagrange multiplier method for the subsequent phases of Evolian. The method develops Lagrange multipliers in each subpopulation region independently and "nds multiple global optima in parallel. The simulation results demonstrates the usefulness of the proposed sharing technique and the multiple Lagrange multiplier method.

1 Introduction

This paper addresses the general constrained optimization problem for continuous variables defined as:

Minimize $f(\boldsymbol{x})$ subject to constraints

$$g_1(\boldsymbol{x}) \le 0, \cdots, g_r(\boldsymbol{x}) \le 0, \quad h_1(\boldsymbol{x}) = 0, \cdots, h_m(\boldsymbol{x}) = 0 \tag{1}$$

where f and the g_k's are functions on R^n and the h_j's are functions on R^n for $m \le n$, and $\boldsymbol{x} = [x_1, \cdots, x_n]^T \in R^n$.

One of the well-known problems in genetic search for solving general optimization problem is the phenomenon called genetic drift [1]. In multimodal functions with equal peaks, simple evolutionary algorithms converge to only one of the peaks, and that peak is chosen randomly due to the stochastic variations associated with the genetic operators. Evolutionary algorithms have been criticized for this premature convergence where substantial fixation occurs at genotype before obtaining su ciently near optimal points [2]. In the same context, the main problem associated with the constrained optimization techniques such as hybrid evolutionary programming (EP) [3], two phase EP (TPEP) [4], and Evolian algorithms [5] is the premature convergence in the first phase.

To overcome the above problem, Goldberg and Richardson proposed a method based on sharing in Genetic Algorithms; the method permits a formation of stable subpopulations (species) of different strings   in this way the algorithm investigates different peaks in parallel [2].

Recently, Beasley, Bull, and Martin proposed a new technique, called sequential niching [6], for multimodal function optimization, which avoids some of the disadvantages associated with the sharing method (e.g., time complexity due to fitness sharing calculations, population size, which should be proportional to the number of optima). The sequential niching method is based on the following idea: once an optimum is found, the evaluation function is modified to eliminate this (already found) solution, since there is no interest in re-discovering the same optimum again. In some sense, the subsequent runs of genetic algorithm incorporate the knowledge discovered in the previous runs.

However, the comparison results of sequential niching methods and parallel approaches by Mahfoud [7] indicate that parallel niching methods outperform sequential ones with respect to parallelization, convergence speed, and population diversity. Parallel methods, such as sharing function, form and maintain niches simultaneously within a population, and seem to have potential to escape extraneous attractors and to converge to the desired solutions.

Consequently, an improvement is expected if the sharing technique is incorporated into the first phase of Evolian. In Evolian, the first phase is equivalent to the usual exterior penalty method, since Lagrange multipliers are set to zero. When there are constraints, the subsequent phases of Evolian should be applied. The existence of multiple peaks implies the need for multiple Lagrange multipliers since different local optima conveys different Lagrange multipliers. Thus, for subsequent phases, the Lagrange multipliers should be initialized in each potential local optimum region.

In this paper, we investigate the usefulness of the sharing function in Evolian and propose the multiple Lagrange multiplier method for constrained optimization.

2   Sharing function

A sharing function determines the degradation of an individual's fitness due to a neighbor at some distance d. A sharing function sh is defined as a function of the distance with the following properties:

- $0 \leq sh(d) \leq 1$, for all distances d
- $sh(0) = 1$ and $\lim_{d \to \infty} sh(d) = 0$.

There are various forms of sharing functions which satisfy the above conditions. In [2], a sharing function is defined by a sharing parameter $_{share}$ for controlling the extent of sharing, and a power law function $sh(d)$ having a distance metric d between two individuals as a parameter:

$$sh(d) = \begin{cases} 1 - (\frac{d}{\sigma_{share}})^{\alpha}, & \text{if } d <   _{share} \\ 0, & \text{otherwise} \end{cases} \tag{2}$$

where   is a constant determining the degree of convexity of the sharing function. The sharing takes place by derating an individual's fitness by its niche count. The new (shared) fitness of an ith individual $\boldsymbol{x}^i$ is given by: $eval'(\boldsymbol{x}^i) = eval(\boldsymbol{x}^i)/m(\boldsymbol{x}^i)$, where $m(\boldsymbol{x}^i)$ returns the niche count for a particular individual $\boldsymbol{x}^i$:

$$m(\boldsymbol{x}^i) = \sum_{j=1}^{2N_p} sh(d(\boldsymbol{x}^i, \boldsymbol{x}^j)), \tag{3}$$

where N_p is the parent population size and the sum is taken over the entire population including itself. Consequently, if an individual $\boldsymbol{x}^i$ is all by itself in its own niche, its fitness value does not decrease ($m(\boldsymbol{x}^i) = 1$). Otherwise, the fitness function is decreased in proportion to the number and closeness of the neighboring points. As a result, this technique limits the uncontrolled growth of particular species within a population. As a side benefit, sharing helps maintain a more diverse population and a better (and less premature) convergence [2].

Since the EP procedure deals with the minimization problem, the use of fitness sharing in the EP loop is implemented as follows:

$$
\begin{aligned}
'(\boldsymbol{x}^i) &= (\boldsymbol{x}^i) + (t)(m(\boldsymbol{x}^i) - 1), \\
(t) &= r_s(\bar{\ } - (\boldsymbol{x}^1))/2N_p, \\
\bar{\ } &= \tfrac{1}{2N_p}\sum_{j=1}^{2N_p}(\boldsymbol{x}^j),
\end{aligned}
$$

where $m(\boldsymbol{x}^i)$ returns the niche count for a particular individual $\boldsymbol{x}^i$ calculated by (3). The adaptive parameter (t), which depends on the population statistics at generation t, controls the rate to increase an objective function in proportion to the niche count normalized by the total population size $2N_p$. The scale factor, $r_s < 1.0$ is a positive constant, $\bar{\ }$ is the average objective function of the current population, and $\boldsymbol{x}^1$ is the best individual in the population. In case where an individual $\boldsymbol{x}^i$ is all by itself in its own niche (niche count $= 1$), the last term in equation (2) disappears and the shared objective function is the same as the original one.

This shared objective function used for the stochastic tournament selection (step 5) in the standard EP implementation in [3,4,5] is as follows:

A selected number of pairwise comparisons over all individuals are conducted. For each solution, N_c randomly selected opponents are chosen from the whole population with equal probability. In each comparison, if the conditioned solution offers less *shared objective function value* than the randomly selected opponent, it receives a win.

It should be noted that this shared objective function applies only to the first phase because of the computational burden in calculating all the niche counts. In the calculation of the niche count of an individual, $2N_p$ number of evaluations of the Euclidean distance and sharing function are needed at each generation. In addition, the number of competing opponent N_c are set to $\min(2N_p - 1, 10)$ to fit into the total population size $2N_p$ and to restrict the maximum competition size to 10.

To investigate the usefulness of this sharing technique, let us consider the two functions presented in [2].

Problem #1:
Minimize $f_1(x) = -\sin^6(5.1 \ x + 0.5)$.

Problem #2:

Minimize $f_2(x) = f_1(x) \cdot e^{-4\log 2 \frac{(x-0.0667)^2}{0.8^2}}$.

With a population size of $N_p = 30$ and a maximum generation of 30, the plots of resulting individuals, where only the first phase of Evolian is used, are shown in Figure 1. The procedure of Evolian is omitted for brevity and the interested reader is referred to [5].

As can be seen in Figure 1, without sharing, the first phase of Evolian, which is simply an exterior penalty function method, can not locate multiple optima. With the help of the sharing function, it can locate individuals at local minima in the search space. It is worthy to note that the number of individuals in each peak is approximately inversely proportional to the objective value of the peak [2].

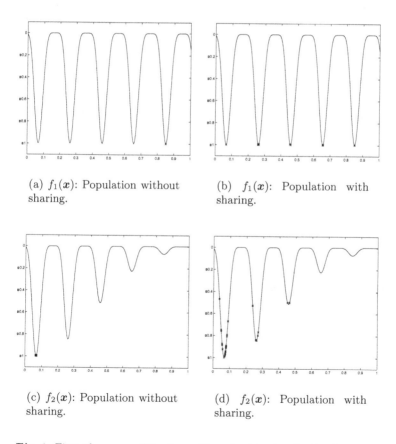

(a) $f_1(\boldsymbol{x})$: Population without sharing.

(b) $f_1(\boldsymbol{x})$: Population with sharing.

(c) $f_2(\boldsymbol{x})$: Population without sharing.

(d) $f_2(\boldsymbol{x})$: Population with sharing.

Fig. 1. First phase run of Evolian with and without a sharing function.

3   Multiple Lagrange multipliers

When there are constraints, the subsequent phases of Evolian should be applied. The existence of multiple peaks implies the need for multiple Lagrange multipliers since different local optima conveys different Lagrange multipliers. Thus, for subsequent phases, the Lagrange multipliers should be initialized in each potential local optimum region (see Figure 2).

For this purpose, Evolian has a routine to determine the multiple peaks in the current population space. Since we are interested only in the global minimum, only the peaks having the global optimum are to be calculated by the peak determination algorithm. To ease this determination process, the individuals are sorted in an ascending order of the objective function value. The high ranked individuals are determined to be peaks if they have objective values near the best one and also have a distance of at least less than the sharing parameter $share$ from the earlier arrived at peak(s).

The peak determination algorithm correctly determined multiple peaks for the function f_1. It should be noted that this algorithm draw out multiple peaks with almost the same objective values as that of the best peak. For the function f_1, the algorithm correctly determined multiple peaks, while only one peak was determined for the function f_2 as it has only one global minimum. After the determination of local peaks, Lagrange multipliers are assigned to each local peak and are updated at the peak point according to the following update rule:

$$\lambda_k[t+1] = \lambda_k[t] + s_t g_k^+(\boldsymbol{x}[t]) \quad \text{and} \quad \mu_j[t+1] = \mu_j[t] + s_t h_j(\boldsymbol{x}[t])$$

where s_t is a small positive constant. Each local region undergoes, in parallel, subsequent phases of Evolian until it meets the stopping criteria.

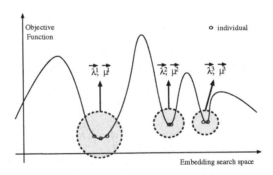

Fig. 2. In Evolian, the Lagrange multipliers are updated in parallel in local optimum subpopulation space.

Now let us consider the following nonlinear constrained optimization problem [8]:

Problem #3:

Minimize $f_3(\boldsymbol{x}) = x_1^2 + (x_2 - 1)^2$
subject to $h(\boldsymbol{x}) = x_2 - x_1^2 = 0$.

This problem has two global optima $(x_1, x_2) = (\pm 1/\sqrt{2}, 1/2)$. With specific parameter settings for Evolian as given in Table 1, the results for 100 trials are summarized with bar graphs in Figure 3.

Table 1. The speci"c parameter values for Evolian used for the function f_3.

Parameter	Value	Meaning
N_p	30	Population size
ρ	10^{-3}	Error tolerance for EP
N_g	7	Generation tolerance for EP
s_0	1.0	Initial penalty parameter
s_{max}	10^5	Maximum penalty parameter
γ	3.0	Increasing rate of penalty parameter
σ_{share}	0.1	Sharing parameter
r_s	0.1	Sharing scale factor
σ_{tol}	0.05	Peak determination similarity parameter

The results for 100 trials are summarized with bar graphs in Figure 3. From Figure 3, the frequency of forming stable subpopulations is found to be about 60% in both the cases of with and without using the sharing function. It can be seen that the use of a sharing function in the first phase has no significant improvement compared with the case where the sharing function is not used. The use of subsequent phases in Evolian leads to the formation of multiple subpopulation regions, regardless of the use of sharing function.

By investigating the bar graphs, it can be seen that the more the number of peaks determined in the first phase, the more the frequency with which the solution converges to the optima. Thus the search for multiple subpopulation regions is critical in finding the multiple global optima.

It can be said that the use of multiple Lagrange multipliers in multiple subpopulation regions effectively searches for multiple global minima in parallel.

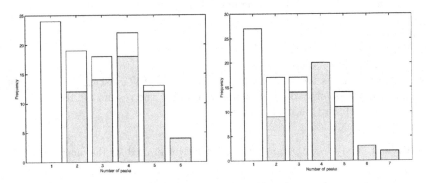

(a) Frequency versus number of peaks in 100 trials using Evolian without sharing.

(b) Frequency versus number of peaks in 100 trials using Evolian with sharing.

Fig. 3. Results obtained by Evolian with or without sharing. The white bar indicates that the solution converges to one optimum, while grey bar to two optima.

4   Summary

After the first phase of Evolian algorithm, the local minimum regions are determined using the peak determination algorithm. By applying the multiple Lagrange multipliers to these subpopulation regions, the globalness of a local solution can be improved. In addition, this subpopulation scheme is inherently parallel so that the computation time would be greatly reduced if it is implemented on a parallel machine. It is investigated that the use of multiple Lagrange multipliers in multiple subpopulation regions effectively searches for multiple global minima in parallel.

References

1. C. Hocaoglu and A. C. Sanderson, Multimodal function optimization using minimal representation size clustering and its application to planning multipaths, *Evolutionary Computation*, vol. 5, no. 1, pp. 81 104, 1997.
2. D. E. Goldberg and J. Richardson, Genetic algorithms with sharing for multimodal function optimization, in *Proc. of the Second International Conference on Genetic Algorithms* (J. J. Grefenstette, ed.), (Hillsdale, NJ), pp. 41 49, Lawrence Erlbaum, 1987.
3. H. Myung and J.-H. Kim, Hybrid evolutionary programming for heavily constrained problems, *BioSystems*, vol. 38, pp. 29 43, 1996.
4. J.-H. Kim and H. Myung, Evolutionary programming techniques for constrained optimization problems, *IEEE Trans. on Evolutionary Computation*, vol. 1, pp. 129 140, July 1997.

5. H. Myung and J.-H. Kim, Evolian: Evolutionary optimization based on Lagrangian with constraint scaling, in *Proc. of the Sixth Annual Conference on Evolutionary Programming / Lecture Notes on Computer Science (LNCS) 1213* (P. J. Angeline, R. G. Reynolds, J. R. McDonnell, and R. Eberhart, eds.), (Indianapolis, USA), pp. 177 188, Springer-Verlag, April 1997.

6. J. E. Beasley, D. R. Bull, and R. R. Martin, A sequential niche technique for multi-modal function optimization, *Evolutionary Computation*, vol. 1, no. 2, pp. 101 125, 1993.

7. S. W. Mahfound, A comparison of parallel and sequential niching methods, in *Proc. of the Sixth International Conference on Genetic Algorithms* (L. J. Eshelman, ed.), (Los Altos, CA), pp. 136 143, Morgan Kaufmann, 1995.

8. C. Y. Maa and M. A. Shanblatt, A two-phase optimization neural network, *IEEE Trans. Neural Networks*, vol. 3, no. 6, pp. 1003 1009, 1992.

Robust Evolution Strategies *

Kazuhiro Ohkura, Yoshiyuki Matsumura and Kanji Ueda

Faculty of Engineering, Kobe University
Rokkodai, Nada-Ku, Kobe, 657, JAPAN
FAX: +81-78-803-1131   TEL: +81-78-803-1119
E-mail: {ohkura,matsumu,ueda}@mi-2.mech.kobe-u.ac.jp

Abstract. Evolution Strategies(ES) are an approach to numerical optimization that shows good optimization performance. However, according to our computer simulations, ES shows di˘erent optimization performance when a di˘erent lower bound of strategy parameters is adopted. We analyze that this is caused by the premature convergence of strategy parameters, although they are traditionally treated as self-adaptive parameters. This paper proposes a new extended ES, called RES in order to overcome this brittle property. RES has redundant neutral strategy parameters and adopts new mutation mechanisms in order to utilize the e˘ect of genetic drift to improve the adaptability of strategy parameters. Computer simulations of the proposed approach are conducted using several test functions.

Keywords: Evolution Strategies, Numerical Optimization, Strategy Parameters, Neutrality, Robustness

1   Introduction

Evolutionary computation has been widely recognized as a robust approach to various kinds of engineering optimization problems. There are three main streams in this field, i.e., Evolution Strategies(ES) [1], Genetic Algorithms(GA) [5] and Evolutionary Programming(EP) [3]. Especially, when we consider numerical optimization, ES gives us better results than the other two in many problems (for instance, [2]). Although ES has several formulations, the most recent form is $(\mu,)$-ES, where $> \mu \geq 1$. $(\mu,)$ means that μ parents generate offspring through recombination and mutation in each generation. The best μ offspring are selected deterministically from the offspring and replace the current parents. Elitism and stochastic selection are not used. This paper uses ES without recombination, following Yao and Liu [12].

ES considers that strategy parameters, which roughly define the size of mutation, are controlled by self-adaptive property of their own. However, they often converge before finding the global optimum so that individuals cannot practically move to any other better points. Therefore, to avoid this behavior,

---

* The authors acknowledge "nancial support through the Methodology of Emergent Synthesis project(96P00702) by JSPS (the Japan Society for the Promotion of Science).

strategy parameters are conditioned to be larger than a certain small positive value , i.e., the lower bound. However, according to our computer simulations, which will be described in Section 4 in detail, ES not only shows strongly dependent performance with respect to   but also has a different optimal   for each problem. This suggests that ES should be applied to an optimization problem with   that is carefully tuned to it.

Recently, Liang, et al. [6] observed the same phenomena on EP and pointed out the importance of careful setting of the lower bound.

This paper focuses on how to overcome this brittleness which comes from the insu cient self-adaptive property of strategy parameters. Thus, we propose a new design of individual representation that has redundant *neutral* strategy parameters for each *active* strategy parameter so that they can accumulate various genetic changes through generations using the effect of genetic drift [8]. In addition to this, new genetic mechanisms associated with the above individual representation are also introduced in order to replace the current active strategy parameter with one of those neutral strategy parameters stochastically. We call the proposed approach as Robust-ES(RES) . This original idea comes from the basic concept of operon-GA [9, 4, 10]. Operon-GA uses redundant genotype and new genetic operations so that each individual can generate adaptive size of genetic change, which contributes to autonomous diversity control in a population.

The rest of this paper is organized as follows. Section 2 formulates the optimization problem and ES. Section 3 describes the proposed approach in detail. Section 4 shows the results of our computer simulations. Finally, Section 5 concludes this paper.

2   Function Optimization by ES

A global minimization problem can be formalized using a pair (S, f), where $S \subseteq R^n$ is a bounded set on R^n and $f : S \mapsto R$ is an n-dimensional real-valued function. The objective is to find a point $x_{min} \in S$ such that f_{min} is a global minimum on S. That is to say:

$$f_{min} = \min_{x \in S} f(x), \quad x_{min} = \arg f_{min} \tag{1}$$

According to the description by Bäck and Schwefel [2], the computational procedure of ES can be described as follows:

1. Generate the initial population of μ individuals, and set $g = 1$. Each individual is taken as a pair of real-valued vectors $(x_i, \ _i), \forall i \in \{1, \ldots, \mu\}$, where x_i and $_i$ are the i-th coordinate value in R^n and its strategy parameters larger than zero, respectively.
2. Evaluate the objective value for each individual $(x_i, \ _i)$, $\forall i \in \{1, \ldots, \mu\}$ of the population based on the objective function $f(x_i)$.
3. Each parent $(x_i, \ _i), i = 1, \ldots, \mu$, creates $/\mu$ offspring on average, so that a total of   offspring are generated. At that time, offspring are calculated as follows: for $i = 1, \ldots, \mu$, $j = 1, \ldots, n$, and $k = 1, \ldots, $,

$$\sigma'_k(j) = \sigma_i(j)exp(\tau'N(0,1) + \tau N_j(0,1)) \tag{2}$$

$$x'_k(j) = x_i(j) + \sigma'_k(j)N(0,1) \tag{3}$$

where $x_i(j), x'_k(j), \sigma_i(j)$ and $\sigma'_k(j)$ denote the j-th component values of the vectors x_i, x'_k, σ_i and σ'_k, respectively. $N(0,1)$ denotes a normally distributed one-dimensional random number with mean zero and standard deviation one. $N_j(0,1)$ indicates that the random number is generated anew for each value of j. The factors τ and τ' have commonly set to $\left(\sqrt{2\sqrt{n}}\right)^{-1}$ and $\left(\sqrt{2n}\right)^{-1}$ [2]. Notice that, when $\sigma'_k(j)$ calculated by Equation (2) is smaller than a small positive value ϵ, i.e., *the lower bound*, ϵ is assigned to $\sigma'_k(j)$.

4. Calculate the fitness of each offspring (x'_i, σ'_i), $\forall i \in \{1, \ldots, \lambda\}$, according to $f(x'_i)$.
5. Sort offspring (x'_i, σ'_i), $\forall i \in \{1, \ldots, \lambda\}$ in a non-descending order according to their fitness values, and select the μ best offspring out of λ to be parents of the next generation.
6. Stop if the halting criterion is satisfied; otherwise, $g = g+1$ and go to step 3.

A key to successful optimization in any evolutionary computation (EC) is in the diversity control. However, the appropriate diversity is strongly dependent on the current state of a population and the landscape of a problem. If its population is converged too fast compared with the ruggedness of its landscape, a method cannot often find the global optimum: on the contrary, if the converging speed is too slow, a large computational cost is required to find a global optimum. The diversity control in EC is generally achieved by adjusting the balance between reproduction and selection. However, we consider here only the reproduction at Step 3, because ES treats the selection at Step 5 as a deterministic process.

Since ES uses not recombination but mutation as a primary operator, the calculation of mutation step size ($\sigma_i(j)N(0,1)$), which is traditionally considered to be "self-adaptive", can be modified for improving the optimization performance. Kappler [7] investigated the replacement of Gaussian mutation with Cauchy mutation in (1+1)-ES, although no clear conclusions were obtained. Yao and Liu [12,11] proposed to replace Gaussian mutation with Cauchy mutation for (μ, λ)-ES, where Cauchy mutation uses the following Cauchy distribution function:

$$F_t(x) = 1/2 + (1/\pi)\arctan(x/t) \tag{4}$$

where $t = 1$. They conducted empirical experiments using many test functions to show the improvement of performance, especially on multimodal function optimization problems. They called their approach Fast-ES(FES) in order to distinguish from classical ES(CES). The success of FES can be explained such that the population does not easily lose the global search ability by the convergence of strategy parameters into local optima, because Cauchy mutation generates longer jumps more frequently than Gaussian mutation. However, the brittle property with respect to the change of ϵ still remains as shown in Section 4.

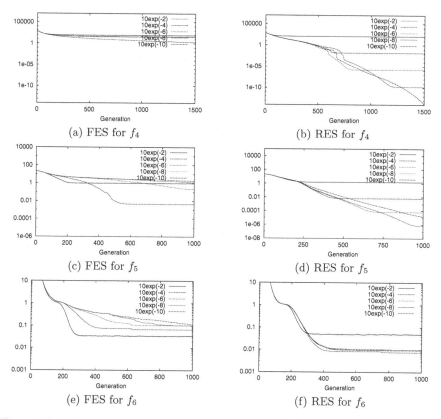

Fig. 1. The averaged best results of FES and RES for multimodal functions when the lower bounds are 10^{-2}, 10^{-4}, 10^{-6}, 10^{-8} and 10^{-10}.

3   Robust ES

When we apply ES to an optimization problem, it shows a similar evolving behavior to the other evolutionary algorithms: a simple search focus shift from a global region into a local region, which is derived from the gradual convergence of the population. This convergence is the direct effect of natural selection which, in a practical sense, makes strategy parameters small monotonically. This change has been considered as the process of self-adaptation . However, we assume here that this behavior is not adaptive enough to perform a robust search and thus ES can be extended from the viewpoint of giving more adaptability to strategy parameters.

Based on this idea, we propose a following individual representation x_i:

$$x_i = (x_i(j), \{ _i(j,p)\}) \tag{5}$$

where, $j = 1, \ldots, n, p = 1, \ldots, m$. Notice that each $x_i(j)$ has m strategy parameters, where the traditional ES has only one strategy parameter. Then, its offspring $x'_k = (x'_k(j), \ _k(j,p))$ is calculated in the following way. The component values $x'_k(j)$ are calculated in the same manner as FES, as follows:

$$x'_k(j) = x_i(j) + \ '_k(j,1) \ _j \tag{6}$$

where $\ _j$ is a random number calculated anew for each j based on Cauchy mutation. An individual x_i has $n \times m$ strategy parameters, although only $\ _i(j,1)$ is used when its $x'_k(j)$ is calculated. Thus, we call $\ _i(j,1)$ as *active* strategy parameters and $\ _i(j,p), p = 2, \ldots, m$ as *inactive* strategy parameters. They are replaced each other and are modified by the following three operations which are applied stochastically:

$$O_{dup} : \ _i(j,1) = \ _i(j,1) \tag{7}$$
$$: \ _i(j,p) = \ _i(j,p-1), \forall p \in \{2, \ldots, m\}$$
$$\ '_i(j,p) = D(\ _i(j,p)), \forall p \in \{1, \ldots, m\}$$
$$O_{del} : \ _i(j,p) = \ _i(j,p+1), \forall p \in \{1, \ldots, m-1\} \tag{8}$$
$$\ _i(j,m) = min(\ _{max}, \sum_{p=1}^{m-1} \ _i(j,p)),$$
$$\ '_i(j,p) = D(\ _i(j,p)), \forall p \in \{1, \ldots, m\}$$
$$O_{inv} : \ _i(j,1) = \ _i(j,p), \exists p \in f\{2, \ldots, d\} \tag{9}$$
$$\ _i(j,p) = \ _i(j,1))$$
$$\ '_i(j,p) = D(\ _i(j,p)), \forall p \in \{1, \ldots, m\}$$

where, D is the same mutation as Equation 2 with the lower bound , and $\ _{max}$ is a constant. That is to say, O_{dup} shifts all of $\ _i(j,p)$ into the adjacent position of $(p+1)$ then modifies with D. O_{del} discards $\ _i(j,1)$, shifts all the other $\ _i(j,p)$ into the adjacent position of $(p-1)$ and inserts the smaller value either $\ _{max}$ or $\sum_{p=1}^{m-1} \ _i(j,p)$ then modifies with D. O_{inv} swaps $\ _i(j,1)$ with one of $\ _i(j,p)$ and then modifies with D.

The proposed RES has the same computational steps as those of CES or FES concerning the other parts. The difference is only that offspring are generated by Equation 6 after applying O_{dup}, O_{del} and O_{inv} stochastically to each individual.

4   Computer Simulations

4.1   Test functions and Conditions

Six test functions are listed on Table 1. They are hypersphere function, Schwefel's problem 2.22, step function, Rastrigin's function, Ackley's function and Griewank's function, respectively. Functions f_1 to f_3 are unimodal functions and the other three, f_4 to f_6, are multimodal functions. All the functions are defined in a 30 dimensional search space and have the global minimum $f_{i,min} = 0$

Table 1. Six test functions

Expression$(n = 30)$	Range
$f_1(x) = \displaystyle\sum_{i=1}^{n} x_i^2$	$-100 \le x_i \le 100$
$f_2(x) = \displaystyle\sum_{i=1}^{n} \lvert x_i \rvert + \prod_{i=1}^{n} \lvert x_i \rvert$	$-10 \le x_i \le 10$
$f_3(x) = \displaystyle\sum_{i=1}^{n} (\lfloor x_i + 0.5 \rfloor)^2$	$-100 \le x_i \le 100$
$f_4(x) = \displaystyle\sum_{i=1}^{n} \{x_i^2 - 10\cos(2\pi x_i) + 10\}$	$-5.12 \le x_i \le 5.12$
$f_5(x) = -20\exp\left(-0.2\sqrt{\frac{1}{n}\sum_{i=1}^{n} x_i^2}\right)$ $-\exp\left(\frac{1}{n}\sum_{i=1}^{n}\cos 2\pi x_i\right) + 20 + e$	$-32 \le x_i \le 32$
$f_6(x) = \frac{1}{4000}\displaystyle\sum_{i=1}^{n} x_i^2 - \prod_{i=1}^{n}\cos(\frac{x_i}{\sqrt{i}}) + 1$	$-600 \le x_i \le 600$

at $(0, \ldots, 0)$. The main purpose of our computer simulations is to show the effect of lower bound of strategy parameters   to the optimization performance of FES and RES. The both ESs use $(\mu, \ ) = (30, 200)$, no correlated mutations and no recombinations. The upper bound of strategy parameters $_{max}$ is set at 1.0 for f_4 and 3.0 for the other functions. In the case of RES, O_{dup}, O_{del} and O_{inv} are applied to an individual with the probabilities of 0.6, 0.3 and 0.1, respectively. The number of strategy parameters m for each variable is set at 6. The six function were solved 50 times under the same initial conditions.

4.2   Results

Figure 2 compares the results of FES and RES for the unimodal functions f_1, f_2 and f_3. Figure 2(a), (c) and (e) show the results of FES. The effect of the lower bound is observed for all the functions. For f_1, the best results were obtained when   was 10^{-2} at generation 200, 10^{-4} at 500 and 10^{-6} at 1000. The better results were not obtained for the cases of smaller lower bounds, i.e., 10^{-8} and 10^{-10}. In case of RES shown in Fig. 2(b), better performance was obtained when the smaller lower bound was adopted. A clearer difference between FES and RES was observed for f_2 and f_3 as shown in Figures 2(c) and (d) or (e) and (f). FES for f_2 showed the stagnation of performance for every case. As a result, the best performance was 2.5×10^{-4} when $= 10^{-6}$. In case of RES, better results were obtained as the smaller   was adopted. Especially, RES reached 3.9×10^{-8}

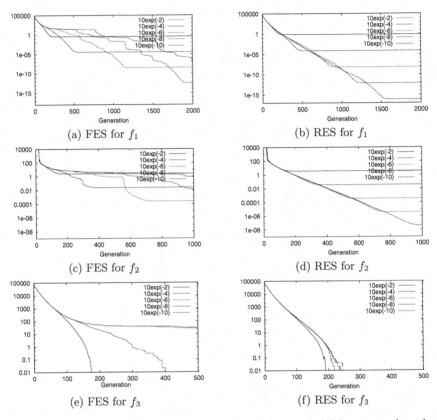

Fig. 2. The averaged best results of FES and RES for unimodal functions when the lower bounds are 10^{-2}, 10^{-4}, 10^{-6}, 10^{-8} and 10^{-10}.

when $= 10^{-10}$. FES for f_3 found the global minimum only when $= 10^{-2}$ and 10^{-4} as shown in Figure 2(e), while RES with any successfully optimized the function without a large difference in computational cost.

Figures 1(a) to (e) show the results for multimodal functions, f_4, f_5 and f_6. Similar results to those of unimodal functions were obtained. As shown in Figure 1(a), FES showed stagnation for all the cases, although the best result of 1.9 at generation 1500 was obtained when $= 10^{-4}$. In the case of RES, the better results were obtained according to the use of smaller as shown in Figure 1(b). The results for f_5 in Figures 1(c) and (d) show the same tendency as that for f_4. Figures 1(e) and (f) show the results for f_6. RES obtained the better and robust results than those of FES, although the both ESs showed the stagnation after about generation 300 and 500, respectively. However, by looking at 50 trials when $= 10^{-10}$, no trials of FES found the global optimum, while RES found it successfully in 24 trials.

Therefore, what these results are suggesting to us is that FES should adopt a carefully selected lower bound for each problem to obtain the best performance, but RES can use a smaller lower bound without worrying about the decrease of the performance.

5   Conclusions

This paper proposed an extended ES, called RES, that shows robust performance against the lower bound of strategy parameters. Computer simulations were conducted using several test functions in order to investigate the performance of RES. The robust performance was confirmed in all six functions. The future work will be directed to the detailed analysis of the evolving behavior in RES and the application of the proposed approach to evolutionary programming.

References

1. T. Bäck (1996), *Evolutionary Algorithms in Theory and Practice*, Oxford University Press
2. T. Bäck and H.-P. Schwefel (1993), An Overview of Evolutionary Algorithms for Parameter Optimization , Evolutionary Computation, Vol.1, No.1, pp.1-24
3. D. Fogel (1995), *Evolutionary Computation Toward a New Philosophy of Machine Intelligence*, IEEE Press
4. T. Gohtoh, K. Ohkura and K. Ueda (1996), An Application of Genetic Algorithm with Neutral Mutations to Job-Shop Scheduling Problems , Proc. of International Conference on Advances in Production Management Systems, pp.563-568
5. D. Goldberg (1989), *Genetic Algorithms in Search, Optimization and Machine Learning*, Addison-Wesley
6. K.-H. Liang, X. Yao, Y. Liu, C. Newton and D. Ho˘man (1998), An Experimental Investigation of Self-adaptation in Evolutionary Programming, Proc. of the Seventh Annual Conference on Evolutionary Programming, Lecture Notes in Computer Science, Springer-Verlag, Berlin, pp.291-300
7. C. Kappler (1996), Are Evolutionary Algorithms Improved by Large Mutations? , H.-M. Voigt, W. Ebeling, I. Rechenberg and H.-P. Schwefel, eds., Proc. Parallel Problem Solving from Nature IV, Vol.1141 of Lecture Notes in Computer Science, Springer-Verlag, pp.346-355
8. M. Kimura (1983), *The Neutral Theory of Molecular Evolution*, Cambridge University Press
9. K. Ohkura and K. Ueda (1995), Solving Deceptive Problems using Genetic Algorithms with Neutral Mutations , C. H. Dagli, et al. edited, Intelligent Engineering Systems Through Arti"cial Neural Networks, Vol.5, ASME Press, pp.345-350
10. K. Ohkura and K. Ueda (1997), An Extended Framework for Overcoming Premature Convergence , Proc. the Seventh International Conference on Genetic Algorithms, Morgan Kaufmann, pp.260-267
11. X. Yao and Y. Liu (1997), Fast Evolution Strategies , Control and Cybernetics, 26(3) pp.467-496
12. X. Yao and Y. Liu (1997), Fast Evolution Strategies, , Proc. of the Sixth Annual Conference on Evolutionary Programming, Lecture Notes in Computer Science, Vol. 1213, Springer-Verlag, Berlin, pp.151 161.

Hybrid Genetic Algorithm for Solving the p-Median Problem

Vladimir Estivill-Castro[1] and Rodolfo Torres-Velázquez[2]

[1] Department of Computer Science & Software Engineering, The University of Newcastle, Callaghan, 2308 NSW, Australia. vlad@cs.newcastle.edu.au

[2] Institut d Investigació en Intelligencia Arti"cial (IIIA), Spanish Scienti"c Research Council (CSIC), Campus Universitat Autónoma de Barcelona, 08193 Bellaterra, Barcelona, Spain. torres@iiia.csic.es

Abstract. The p-median problem is an NP-complete combinatorial optimisation problem well investigated in the "elds of facility location and more recently, clustering and knowledge discovery. We show that hybrid optimisation algorithms provide reasonable speed and high quality of solutions, allowing e˘ective trade-o˘ of quality of the solution with computational e˘ort. Our approach to hybridisation is a tightly coupled approach rather than a serialisation of hill-climbers with genetic algorithms. Our hybrid algorithms use genetic operators that have some memory about how they operated in their last invocation.

1 Introduction

The p-median problem is a central facilities location problem that seeks the location of p facilities on a network of n points minimising a weighted distance objective function [10]. The problem is NP-complete and has a zero-one integer programming formulation [23] with n^2 variables and $n^2 + 1$ constraints and many techniques have been developed to heuristically solve instances of the problem [4,25,26,27,28,30]. For finding high quality approximate solutions, hill-climbing variations of an interchange heuristic [4,9,16,30] are considered very effective, but they risk being trapped in local optima. Other alternatives have been also explored; amongst them, Lagrangian relaxation [3,18,32], Tabu search [25] and Simulated Annealing [16]. Recently the p-median problem has been identified as a robust method for spatial classification, clustering and knowledge discovery [5,17,19]. While facility location problems may involve perhaps hundreds of points, knowledge discovery applications will face thousands of points.

Genetic Algorithms (GAs) have been suggested as a robust technique for solving optimisation problems. However, progress towards solving the p-median problem displays a chronology analogous to the efforts to use GAs for solving other combinatorial optimisation problems. One side, we have the recent records on optimally solving instances of the Travelling Salesman Problem (TSP) with linear programming and local cuts [24,12] that dim the efforts to solving TSP with GAs [15,31]. On the other side, we see GAs providing very good solutions for the bin packing problem [7,22].

For the p-median problem, early attempts with GAs used direct binary encoding and the results were discouraging [11]. It was then accepted that GAs could not compete with the e cient and well designed hill-climbing approaches used for heuristically solving the p-median problem. More recently, the use of integer encoding [1,2] and some theory of set recombination [6] has shown that genetic algorithms could potentially become competitive. Although it is now clear that integer encoding is better than binary encoding for the p-median problem, none of the at least 5 crossover operators has been identified as the most appropriate. Also, the adequate balance between quality of the approximate solution (proximity to optimality) and computational effort has not been established.

This paper argues that although GAs for the p-median problem have improved, they hardly outperform hill-climbers. The trade-off of effort vs quality slightly favours hill-climbers. However, occasionally, GAs happen to identify solutions which are closer to optimality. In order to incorporate the e ciency of hill-climbers and the potential higher quality solutions of GA an approach to hybridisation is proposed. We will discuss why this hybridisation is challenging and present result that illustrate the benefits of this hybrid approach.

2   The p-Median Problem

In real D-dimensional space, the p-median problem is concerned with selecting p stations out of $S = \{s_1, s_2, \ldots, s_n\}$ points so that the sum of the distances of all s_i in $\Re^D$ to their nearest station is minimum. The problem is motivated by the 2D scenarios where the points are sites that must be serviced by p stations selected from the sites. Naturally, the distance from every site to its nearest station should be as small as possible. In fact, the p-median problem has a formulation where the assignment of stations minimises the expected distance for servicing a site from its station. As an example, say that S are positions in the plane of potential fires and we are to place p fire-fighting stations. Let w_i be the probability that site s_i has a fire. Then, we seek to minimise

$$E[d(s_i, \text{station for } s_i)] = \sum_{i=1}^{n} Prob(s_i \text{ has a fire})d(s_i, \text{station for } s_i)$$

$$= \sum_{i=1}^{n} w_i d(s_i, \text{station for } s_i).$$

The distance d could be the Euclidean metric or any other metric.

Note that, for any $C \subset S$ of size p, the station for s_i is the site in C nearest to s_i and we will denote it as $rep[s_i, C]$. That is, $rep[s_i, C]$ is the *representative* for s_i in C and it satisfies that $\min_{s_j \in C} d(s_i, s_j) = d(s_i, rep[s_i, C])$. In this context, the p-median problem is a problem of finding the best set C of representatives, so every site is as similar as possible to its representative. This is how the p-median translates into a clustering formulation where the sites are partitioned into p groups. Each group is a set of sites with a common representative. The expected dissimilarity between a site and its representative is minimum. We write the p-median problem in this context as

$$\text{Minimise } {}_{C \subset S \& |C| = p} M(C) = \sum_{i=1}^{n} w_i d(s_i, rep[s_i, C]). \tag{1}$$

3   The Solution Methods

There have been several formulations of the p-median problem as a 0/1-integer programming problem. A trade-off between the type of constraints in the for- mulation and the frequency by which integer solutions occur when solving the relaxed linear programming problem allows problem to be solved to optimality when n is small (a few hundred sites) [28]. However, when n is moderately large, the NP-completeness of the problem requires the use of heuristics to obtain approximate solutions.

In what follows we discuss the most effective approaches from the litera- ture emphasising similarities, rather than the differences, since we want to com- bine their features to obtain methods that integrate their advantages. The most popular type of heuristics are hill-climbers rediscovered in many contexts and best known as interchange heuristics [16,30]. The hill-climbing nature of these heuristics is clearly revealed if we structure the search space of the p-median problem as a graph with $\binom{n}{p}$ nodes. The nodes of this graph are all $C \subset S$ with $|C| = p$. The edges of the graph are defined as follows, two nodes C and C' are adjacent if and only if $|C \cap C'| = p - 1$; that is, if they differ in ex- actly one representative. So, every node in the graph is a feasible solution, we seek to find the node that minimises $M(C)$ in Equation (1). The hill-climber interchange heuristics start on a random solution C_0 (a random node in the graph). Iteratively, the heuristic explores a set $N(C_t)$ of adjacent nodes and moves to the best alternative in this neighbourhood if the alternative is an improvement (i.e. $M(C_{t+1}) < M(C_t)$). Thus, the new node C_{t+1} is such that $M(C_{t+1}) = \min_{C \in N(C_t)} M(C)$. The search halts when no better solution is found in the neighbourhood $N(C_t)$. The interchange hill-climbers offer different vari- ants in how they define the set $N(C_t)$ of adjacent nodes to explore. Complete hill-climbers and other hill-climbers [14,29,9,13] have been shown not to be as e cient [25] in finding a local optimum of high quality as an original heuristic proposed in 1968 by Teitz and Bart [30]. We will refer to this heuristic as TAB.

In an amortised sense, in the TAB search only a constant number of neigh- bours of C_t are examined for the next interchange [5]. When searching for a profitable interchange, it considers the points in turn, according to a fixed circu- lar ordering $(s_1, s_2, \ldots, s_n)$ of the points. Whenever the turn belonging to a point s_i comes up, if s_i is currently a representative, it is ignored, and the turn passes to the next point in the circular list, s_{i+1} (or s_1 if $i = n$). If s_i is not a represen- tative point, then it is considered for inclusion in the set of representatives. The most advantageous interchange C^j of non-representative s_i and representative s_j

is determined, over all possible choices of $s_j \in C_t$. If $C^j = \{s_j\} \cup C_t \setminus \{s_i\}$ is better than C_t, then C^j becomes the new current solution C_{t+1}; otherwise, $C_{t+1} = C_t$. In either case, the turn then passes to the next point in the circular list, s_{i+1} (or s_1 if $i = n$). If a full cycle through the set of points yields no improvement, a local optimum has been reached, and the search halts. The TAB heuristic forbids the reconsideration of s_i for inclusion until all other non-representatives points have been considered as well. The heuristic can be therefore be regarded as a local variant of *Tabu search* [8]. TAB's careful design balances the need to explore a variety of possible interchanges against the 'greedy' desire to improve the solution as quickly as possible.

The time required to compute $M(C')$ on an adjacent node C' of C is $O(n)$ time $O(n)$ steps to find $rep[s, C']$ for all $s \in S$ ($rep[s, C']$ is either unchanged or the new representative s_i), and $O(n)$ to compute $M(C')$ as defined in Equation (1). Therefore, the time required to test points of C_t for replacement by s_i is $O(pn)$ time. In most situations, p can be viewed as a small constant, and thus the test can be considered to take linear time.

Simulated Annealing can be considered a hill-climber that may accept solutions C_t with $M(C_{t+1}) > M(C_t)$. It also starts with a random C_0 and iteratively redefines a current solution C_t. All $p(n - p)$ neighbours of C_t are not explored, but they are sampled. A temperature T works as a tolerance parameter for accepting a $_t = M(C_{t+1}) - M(C_t)$. When $T > _t$ a worse solution may be probabilistically accepted as the current solution. The value of T decreases as more solutions are explored ($t \to \infty$). Although Simulated Annealing opens the possibility to better approximation because it escapes local optima, its computation time is much larger than hill-climbers [16] and it demands tuning of more parameters.

Genetic algorithms maintain a population of chromosomes (encodings) of feasible solutions. New populations are built from previous ones by genetic operators. Simulated Annealing is very similar to a genetic algorithm with population size 1 and a specific mutation operator. However, populations provide implicit parallelism . This means that the solutions in the current population are simultaneous samples of subspaces of the search space. Thus, the GA is exploring combinations of subspaces simultaneously and balances allocating chromosomes in subspaces of observed good performance with exploring other regions of the search space. We can see a progression of robustness in the methods.

4   The Structure of the Hybrid GA

The GA proposed here seeks to find a set C of representatives that optimises Equation (1). Thus, Equation (1) defines the objective function. Genetic operators and the encoding of feasible solutions are tightly related. The literature [1,2,6] has reached consensus that because feasible solutions are subsets $C \subset \{s_1, \ldots, s_n\}$ with p elements and $p << n$, the chromosomes are strings of p different positive integers less than n. This encoding has some redundancy since the same integer values in different order represent the same feasible solution.

However, empirical evidence [1,2,6] shows that no significant improvement in performance is obtained by choosing some canonical form (for example, keeping the integer values sorted by ascending order within the chromosome), but the extra bookkeeping slows down the search. Moreover, some genetic operators depend on this redundancy for preserving diversity in the population. For example, the *Template Operator* [2] would produce offspring identical to their parents if a canonical form is enforced; however, when representing subsets C as strings of p integers, the operator can produce offspring that encode a different phenotype of its parents despite the parents have equal phenotype. Simple crossover on integer strings [1] does not guarantee different integer values in the offspring (thus a penalty is applied when evaluating unfeasible solutions). B. Bozkaya et al [2] define 4 crossover operators, none of which is a definite winner. They are progressively more complex versions of simple crossover on integer strings that ensure that values are not replicated within a chromosome. As the operator's complexity increases, there is a small improvement in the search but at more computational effort per crossover. Since crossover occurs in the inner-most loops of the GA's program, slightly more complex crossover operators rapidly raise the demand on computational effort. Also, all these crossover operators mentioned earlier have a strong physical bias. That is, the possible offspring of two parents do not have uniform probability and the distribution is closely related to the encoding, rather than to the semantics of the chromosome in the problem. Operators that use the theory of Random Assorting Recombination [20,21] have also been proposed [6]. These operators balance two desirable properties of crossover in GAs, assortment and respect.

The goal here is not to argue in favour of one or another crossover operator, because besides using chromosomes that are integer strings it is not clear that the added complexity of more sophisticated crossing is worth it. Moreover, typically more complex operators imply more parameters that the end user must properly set at the start of the optimisation (a challenging task in itself). We argue that a more effective search is obtained by a hybrid optimisation algorithm with a rather simple and fast crossover that a GA whose genetic operators are complex, heavily parameterised and di cult to use. The operator provided by the TAB hill-climber takes a feasible solution C_t and improves it to a new solution C_{t+1}. We consider this a mutation operator and incorporate it as such in the GA. This mutation operator may appear computationally costly at first sight, but as we discussed in the analysis of TAB, it typically requires $O(n)$ time (or $O(n^2)$ time if a local optima is reached). However, evaluating the objective function requires $O(n)$ time, thus $O(n)$ time is required every time an unseen individual comes into play. Since the rate of application of this TAB mutation assures it occurs sparingly per generation, its cost is well amortised in the genetic program.

The second aspect is that the hybridisation must be a tight integration that must preserve those aspects of TAB that make it the most effective hill-climber. Thus, a non-representative s_i that fails to become a representative must be banned until all other non-representatives have also been attempted. Our mutation operator remembers the index i where the last promotion of a s_i to a repre-

Table 1. TAB and GA optimisation with respect to objective function evaluations.

Method	Values of solution found	Average	Evaluations
TAB	11.75 (3 times) 11.77 11.78 (4 times) 11.86 12.08	11.89 ± 0.23	804 ± 14
Hybrid GA	11.67 (6 times) 11.68 11.71 (3 times)	11.68 ±0.01	5,897 ±35

sentative took place. Moreover, it can detect local optima, and in this case, they are typically of high quality. By adjusting the mutation rate (and the population size) the hybrid can be configured to resemble TAB or to be more independent (TAB is the case population size 1 and mutation rate 1).

Table 1 shows the performance of TAB and a GA on a p-median problem with 100 data points and $p = 5$. The computational effort is measured as the number of evaluations of the objective function, a uniform measure of resources required. Since TAB and the GA are randomised, we show results over 10 executions. TAB is typically much faster that the optimisation with GAs, but risks getting stuck on local optima. The best solution with TAB is worst than the poorest solution with the hybrid GA. The GA has a population of 25 chromosomes. For the test problem, smaller population sizes result in poor performance of the GA. As we already mentioned, hybridisation is complicated because TAB's operation as a mutation that does a hill-climbing step needs to remember how it operated in its previous invocation. However, even if we remember the last point attempted to be promoted, this may be for a very different chromosome than the one who is now being mutated. Remembering the context of mutation per chromosome is not a successful alternative because it makes the GA work as many concurrent TAB searches, each disrupted (rather than helped) by crossover. We have found that this results in much computational effort and no better search.

Another problem that complicates hybridisation is that the chromosome mutated by TAB may exhibit an above average fitness with respect to the rest of the population, moving sharply in the direction of a local optima. This has the effect that the chromosome dominates the population and the GA converges early to local optima. This is a problem of diversity loss. Thus, we found that the population size of our hybrids can not be very small. In the results of Fig. 1, the hybrid improves the performance GA, the hybrid's population size is 15 while the GAs is 50. Smaller population sizes in the hybrid result in poor optimisation performance of the hybrid and larger population size result in as many or more function evaluations than the simple GA. We also found that although the mutation rate of the TAB mutation must be small, it must be of some impact when it occurs, otherwise it just looks like a costly random mutation. For this, when a TAB-mutation occurs, two hill-climbing steps on the chromosome are performed (and not just one). More hill-climbing steps over-fit one individual with respect to the population.

5   Final Remarks

We have presented a hybrid genetic algorithm that incorporates exploitation characteristics of a hill-climber into the GA program. This approach applies with all cross-over operators but it demands delicate balancing of the impact of hill-climbing so the hybrid GA avoids early convergence. As a result, the hybrid GA optimisation is robust and effective and balances effort/quality of solution better than the plain GA.

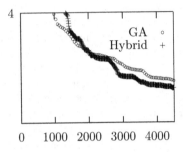

Fig. 1. Hybrid GA and GA optimisation with respect to objective function evaluations. Final average for hybrid GA is 3.54 with a standard deviation of 0.03 while the "nal average for the GA is 3.60 with a standard deviation of 0.07.

References

1. G. Bianchi and R. Church. A non-binary encoded GA for a facility location problem. Working Paper, 1992. D. Geography, U. California, Santa Barbara.
2. B. Bozkaya, J. Zhang, and E. Erkut. An e˜ective genetic algorithm for the p-median problem. Paper presented at INFORMS Conf. in Dallas, October 1997.
3. G. Cornuejols, M. Fisher, and G. Nemhauser. Location of bank accounts to optimize "oat: An analystic study of exact and approximate algorithms. *Management Science*, 23:789 910, 1977.
4. P. Densham and G. Rushton. A more e cient heuristic for solving large p-median problems. *Papers in Regional Science*, 71:307 329, 1992.
5. V. Estivill-Castro and A.T. Murray. Discovering associations in spatial data - an e cient medoid based approach. In X. Wu, R. Kotagiri, and K.K. Korb, *Proc. of the 2nd Pacific-Asia Conf. on Knowledge Discovery and Data Mining (PAKDD-98)*, 110 121, Melbourne, Australia, 1998. Springer-Verlag LNAI 1394.
6. V. Estivill-Castro and A.T. Murray. Spatial clustering for data mining with genetic algorithms. *Int. ICSC Symp. Engineering of Intelligent Systems EIS-98*. 1998.
7. E. Falkenauer. A new representation and operators for genetic algorithms applied to grouping problems. *Evolutionary Computation*, 2(2):123 144, 1994.
8. F. Glover. Future paths for integer programming and links to arti"cial intelligence. *Computers and Operations Research*, 5:533 549, 1986.
9. M Goodchild and V. Noronha. Location-allocation for small computers. Monograph 8, U. of Iowa, 1983.
10. L. Hakimi. Optimum locations of switching centers and the absolute centers and medians of a graph. *Operations Research*, 12:450 459, 1964.

11. C. Hosage and M. Goodchild. Discrete space location-allocation solutions from genetic algorithms. *Annals of Operations Research*, 6:35 46, 1986.
12. R.C. Johnson. Record travelling salesman solution. TechWeb, June 29th 1998. http://www.techweb.com/.
13. L. Kaufman and P.J. Rousseuw. *Finding Groups in Data: An Introduction to Cluster Analysis*. John Wiley & Sons, NY, US, 1990.
14. J.E. Maranzana. On the location of supply points to minimize transport costs. *Operational Research Quarterly*, 15:261 270, 1964.
15. H. Mühlenbein, M. Gorger-Schleuter, and O. Krämer. Evolution algorithms in combinatorial optimization. *Parallel Computing*, 7:65 85, 1988.
16. A.T. Murray and R.L. Church. Applying simulated annealing to location-planning models. *J. of Heuristics*, 2:31 53, 1996.
17. A.T. Murray and V. Estivill-Castro. Cluster discovery techniques for exploratory spatial data analysis. *Int. J. of GIS*, 12(5):431 443, 1998.
18. S. Narula, U. Ogbu, and H. Samuelsson. An algorithm for the p-median problem. *Operations Research*, 25:709 713, 1977.
19. R.T. Ng and J. Han. E cient and e˘ective clustering methods for spatial data mining. In J. Bocca, M. Jarke, and C. Zaniolo, *Proc. of the 20th Conf. on Very Large Data Bases (VLDB)*, 144 155, 1994. Santiago, Chile, Morgan Kaufmann.
20. N.J. Radcli˘e. Genetic set recombination. In L. D. Whitley, *Foundations of Genetic Algorithms 2*, 203 219, San Mateo, CA, 1993. FOGA-92 Morgan Kaufmann.
21. N.J. Radcli˘e and F.A.W. George. A study of set recombination. *Proc. Fifth Int. Conf. Genetic Algorithms*, 23 30, San Mateo, CA, 1993. Morgan Kaufmann.
22. C. Reeves. Hybrid genetic algorithms for bin-packing and related problems. *Annals of Operations Research*, 63:371 396, May 1996.
23. C. ReVelle and R. Swain. Central facilities location. *Geographical Analysis*, 2:30 42, 1970.
24. Rice News. Researchers forge new optimal path for traveling salesman problem. Rice University, June 25th 1998.
25. D. Rolland, E. Schilling and J. Current. An e cient tabu search procedure for the p-median problem. *European J. of Operations Research*, 96:329 342, 1996.
26. K. Rosing. An optimal method for solving the (generalized) multi-Weber problem. *European J. of Operations Research*, 58:414 426, 1992.
27. K. Rosing, E. Hillsman, and H. Rosing. A note comparing optimal and heuristic solutions to the p-median problem. *Geographical Analysis*, 11:86 89, 1979.
28. K.E. Rosing, C.S. Revelle, and H. Rosing-Voyelaar. The p-median and its linear programming relaxation: An approach to large problems. *J. of the Operational Research Society*, 30:815 823, 1979.
29. P. Sorensen. Analysis and design of heuristics for the p-median location-allocation problem. MSc s thesis, D. Geography, U. California, Santa Barbara, 1994.
30. M.B. Teitz and P. Bart. Heuristic methods for estimating the generalized vertex median of a weighted graph. *Operations Research*, 16:955 961, 1968.
31. N.L.J. Ulder, E.H.L. Aarts, H.-J. Bandelt, P.J.M. van Laarhoven, and E. Pesch. Genetic local search algorithms for the travelling salesman problem. H.-P. Schwefel and P. Manner, eds., *Proc. of 1st Workshop on Parallel Problem Solving from Nature*, 109 116, Berlin, 1991. Springer Verlag.
32. J. Weaver and R. Church. A median location model with nonclosest facility service. *Transportation Science*, 19:107 119, 1985.

Correction of Reflection Lines Using Genetic Algorithms

Binh Pham and Zhongwei Zhang

School of Information Technology and Mathematical Sciences
University of Ballarat, PO Box 663 Ballarat, VIC 3353, Australia
Phone +61 3 5327 9286 Fax +61 3 5327 9289
Email: {b.pham, z.zhang}@ballarat.edu.au

Abstract. The method of smoothing surfaces by correcting re"ection lines which is commonly used in the car design industry, relies heavily on the experience of designers and often involves very tedious work. This paper discusses how genetic algorithms can be used to alleviate this problem by providing alternative solutions under suitable constraints set by designers. Strategies for designing genetic codes, "tness functions, crossover and mutation methods, are investigated, with the aim to make the surface smoothing process more intuitive and yet leave designers with a greater choice.

Keywords: surface smoothing, re"ection line, genetic algorithm, aesthetic constraints

1 Introduction

The problem of smoothing free form surfaces is very important in many industries where it is essential to produce surfaces which are visually pleasing. In particular, in car body design, undesirable bumps, oscillations or wiggles should be identified and corrected to obtain smoother lines. One common method deployed by the automobile industry uses re"ection lines which are obtained by re"ecting a family of light sources along parallel straight lines on a surface and viewing from a fixed position (e.g. [2,3]). Irregularities on these re"ection lines are then examined and corrected, and the surface becomes smoother as a result.

A common practice for a designer is to identify the part of the surface with irregularities and to manually correct re"ection lines along some specific directions. The resultant changes to this part of surface are then calculated. These tasks may be performed iteratively until the designer is satisfied. This process is often very tedious and since it is di cult to predict the effects that corrected re"ection lines have on the surface, the decision on how to perform the corrections relies heavily on the experience of the designer. Another drawback is that this process does not produce a unique solution, nor a number of alternative solutions. What would be desirable is an automated scheme that can generate different corrections to re"ection lines to produce possible solutions that are capable of satisfying not only smoothness but also other constraints specified by the designer (e.g. orientations and maximum distance for correction vectors).

These alternative solutions would allow the designer freedom to choose the one with surface characteristics that is perceived as the most optimal in some way, for example, in terms of aesthetics. We propose to achieve this by using evolutionary programming methods based on genetic algorithms.

Genetic algorithms (GA) which simulate the evolution of a population of living beings through the mutation of their genetic codes of chromosomes, does not aim to provide an exact or the most optimal solution, but rather, to produce potential solutions that satisfy specified constraints. The simulation is based on the assumptions that offsprings inherit some characteristics of their parents and that only those who are fit would survive. How to define and evaluate the degree of fitness depends on the application domains. Thus, to apply GAs to a problem, one firstly needs to decide how best to construct the genetic codes that can represent appropriately the essence of the problem. A suitable method for mutation together with a fitness function and a penalty function must be devised to ensure that survival individuals through evolution would depict faithfully possible solutions to the problem. GAs have been applied successfully to numerous complex problems that cannot be solved easily by analytical or numerical methods. In particular, alternative solutions in computer-aided design problems such as smoothing curves [4] and bridge design [1], have been generated using this approach.

This paper explores how GAs can be used for correction of re"ection lines in an intuitive way. The aim is to remove some tedious tasks from designers, yet provide them with further "exibility and control over the ways corrections are performed. Section 2 discusses how the fitness function is designed and gives a brief description of the overall algorithm. Section 3 covers implementation details and Section 4 analyses the results.

2   Design of Genetic Algorithms

2.1   Reflection Line

There are a number of alternative methods for generating re"ection lines (e.g. [2,3]). For the first evaluation of our approach, we choose to use a more simple definition of re"ection lines proposed by Kaufmann and Klass [2], instead of the physical re"ection lines defined by Klass [3].

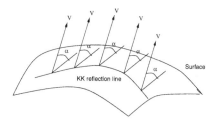

Fig. 1. KKRL: Re"ection lines de"ned by Kaufmann and Klass

The latter case will be dealt with in a future paper. To distinguish the two types of re"ection lines, we denote those proposed by Kaufmann and Klass as KKRL. We use parameter spline curves that represent a surface and construct their corresponding re"ection lines as follows. Given a fixed vector V and an angle , we look for a point on each spline where the angle between the tangent vector to the curve and V equals . The line segment formed by connecting these points is the re"ection line corresponding to angle . Thus, a family of re"ection lines can be constructed for a set of equally distributed angles (see Figure 1).

2.2 Genetic Algorithms

To design the first set of genetic algorithms to produce possible smoother surfaces, we choose the most simple assumption and constraints, and plan to carefully analyse their performance before proceeding to more complex cases. Although it is generally possible to correct the points on the re"ection lines in any direction, it appears that the most simple and natural way is to correct these points along the direction perpendicular to the curve tangent vector. In addition, we need to incorporate the following constraints which are considered desirable by the automobile industry:

- the amounts of correction should be kept to the minimum;
- the re"ection lines must be as smooth as possible;
- local convexity is retained in the adjusted splines, obtained after the re"ection splines are corrected.
- the angle between the tangent vector of the adjusted splines and V remains unchanged;

The first constraint ensures that the essence of the design has not been altered significantly after the smoothing process. It also keeps the cost to the minimum. The second and third constraints ensure that surface smoothness be achieved and oscillations be avoided. The fourth constraint obeys the definition of the re"ection lines.

Representation scheme The population of individuals in our simulation are re"ection lines, while the genetic codes are formed by sequences of corrected distances at points on each re"ection line. Thus, the genetic codes can be represented as a 2D array of corrected distances.

Genetic operations and parameters As the current practice is to correct re"ection lines directly, while the adjustments to the surface is only implied, in our first design of GAs, we choose to use a fixed point crossover and random point mutation strategy along only each re"ection line. This will facilitate comparative analysis of our method to existing ones. However, this strategy will be later extended to use variable crossover points (e.g. at points where the re"ection line is least smooth), and to allow crossover along parameter curves as well as along re"ection lines. Although there is no sound theory of selecting GA parameters such as population size, crossover rate and mutation rate, there are some empirical results indicating that the optimal performance can be achieved for the cases where population size is between 20 and 30, while crossover rate and mutation rate are between 0.75 and 0.95 and 0.005 and 0.01, respectively [5].

Selection of fitness function As stated above, a genetype and a chromosome are designed respectively as a single corrected distance and a set of corrected distances. Fitness function f provides a mechanism to evaluate a set of re"ection lines with respect to constraints. The selection of the fitness function is even more application-oriented. In our case, the better fit to the constraints, the more possibility for a chromosome to be selected for use to generate new chromosomes from which new re"ection lines are obtained. In the context of industrial design, these constraints can be interpreted in terms of position and smoothness as follows:

- positional constraints
    - each KKRL must lie with a strip specified by a designer after inspecting the original RL;
    - displacements of the points on RL to be minimum.
- smoothness constraints of KKRL
    - sum of squares of curvatures must be small as possible;
    - sum of second derivatives must be as small as possible.

Then the fitness function $f = f(Sc^2, Sh^2, N)$ is defined as

$$f = \frac{w_1}{Sc^2} + \frac{w_2}{Sh^2} - w_3 \times N \tag{1}$$

where w_1, w_2, w_3 are the coe cient and Sc^2, Sh^2 respectively are summation of the squared curvatures, and the squared distances at all points determining re"ection lines, while N represents the number of points which have violated the curvature constraints.

2.3   Description of the Genetic Algorithms

```
(1) Given a vector V and a surface, compute parametric spline curves
(2) Compute KKRL corresponding to these spline curves
(3) Ask user to specify area surrounding each KKRL within which
    the corrected one must lie
(4) Generate an initial population of chromosomes (40 X 2D arrays of
    randomly chosen displacement of KKRL points)
(5) For each chromosome (ie each set of displacement of KKRL points)
        1. evaluate its fitness and its probability of crossover and mating
        2. only display those KKRL that satisfy positional constraints
(6) Generates offsprings from each pair of parents
(7) Perform crossover and/or mutation on the selected pairs of parents
```

(8) Repeat steps 5-7 until one of the following conditions are satisfied:
    1. a number of chromosomes acquire a specified degree of fitness;
    2. a number of chromosomes satisfy visual requirement;
    3. the population is uniform.

3   Implementation

On a SGI workstation, a GUI which uses X-Windows and Motif, has been developed in C++ for doing experiments, while the display of 3D curves or surfaces is based on OpenGL.

3.1   The Overall System

To obtain a set of the re"ection lines, users have to provide the system with a set of 3D control points and a constant vector V. The system is currently able to display a set of re"ection lines. After the users specify a set of parameters for the GA, the system will correct the re"ection lines, and then display the corrected surface.

3.2   Data Structure

Non-Uniform Rational B-Splines (NURBS) have become the de facto standard for CAD surface representation in car body design, and a NURBS representation of a surface can be determined by a set of control points. Such a representation may be found in many textbooks (see, for example [6])

Following the definition of re"ection line described in section 2.1, a few re"ection lines with respect to a vector $V = (0.2, 0.2, 0.8)$ are displayed in Figure 2(a).

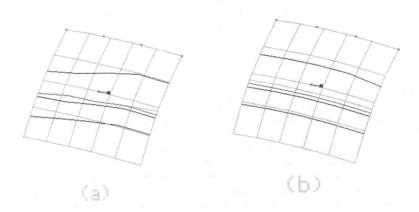

(a)   (b)

Fig. 2. KK re"ection lines: (a) original; (b) corrected

Whenever the corrected offsets and the directions of change are given, a new re"ection line can be determined by a series of scalar parameters, and a family of new re"ection lines can be determined by a 2D array of scalars, h_{ij}. Such a set of 2D array of "oating points is encoded as a chromosome, and used as a representation of a family of re"ection lines. Figure 3 describes a family of re"ection lines with their changing direction vectors, W_{ij}, displacements, h_{ij} and encoded representation at the bottom.

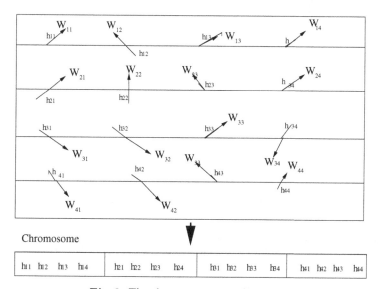

Chromosome

h_{11} h_{12} h_{13} h_{14}	h_{21} h_{22} h_{23} h_{24}	h_{31} h_{32} h_{33} h_{34}	h_{41} h_{42} h_{43} h_{44}

Fig. 3. The chromosome encode schema

As a basis of the developing GA, the data has been structured into classes and four major classes are B_Spline, Ref_Line, RLine_Surf and GA_RLine (see Figure 4). The B_Spline are used to structure B-splines, Ref_Line are for the single re"ection line and RLines for a set of re"ections lines. Finally GA_RLine is designed for the genetic algorithms. These classes are designed as a cascade relationship, represented in Figure 4, i.e. the GA_RLine is based on the Rline_Surf combined with their operations and fitness function, while Rlinc_Surf is a derived class of Ref_Line, and so on.

3.3   Curvatures and Fitness

The calculation of curvatures on the corrected splines is obtained by adding the curvature of each original spline and that of its difference spline.

$$\bar{s}(u,v) = s(u,v) + d(u,v) \tag{2}$$

$$\bar{s}_u'(u,v) = s_u'(u,v) + d_u'(u,v) \tag{3}$$

$$\bar{s}_u''(u,v) = s_u''(u,v) + d_u''(u,v) \tag{4}$$

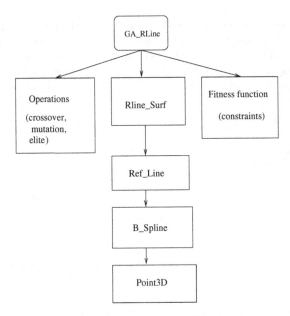

Fig. 4. The implementation of the system

where s, s' and s'' are the parameteric representation of NURBS and its first and second derivative along u direction, while d, d' and d'' are the difference spline and first and second derivatives of the difference spline along u direction.

4   Analysis of the Results

We ran the genetic algorithm on the re"ection lines with a population size of 30 generated at random, crossover rate 0.8 and mutation rate 0.08. The coe cients w_1, w_2 and w_3 selected for (1) to measure their fitness in experiments are 100.0, 15.0 and 10, respectively.

The corrected KKRL can be seen in Figure 2 at right side. Figure 5 shows the fitness changes of the best solution at generations.

The convergence of the genetic algorithm is qualitatively interpreted in terms of the speed of the optimal solutions can be generated. From Figure 5, it can be seen that the convergence of the genetic algorithm used in our experiments is slow at the beginning, but gains a dramatic increase at the later stage. One reason could be that initial random solutions are too far from potential solutions.

The amount of computation involved in our approach is proportional to the number of points on the re"ection lines to be corrected. This compares favourably with the traditional approach which has a linear relationship to the squared number of control points in terms of computations.

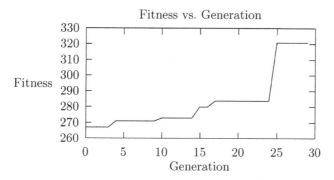

Fig. 5. The "tness change along generations

5 Conclusion

A new approach to correcting the re"ection lines based on the evolutionary technique has been proposed and implemented. Comparing with other methods, our approach has the advantages that corrections on all re"ection lines can be performed simultaneously and users can in"uence the results by modifying the fitness function.

We plan to explore this approach further in the following aspects:

- using a variable crossover point at positions where curvature is less than a specified value;
- performing fixed point crossover along parametric lines as well as re"ection lines;
- correcting re"ection lines along different directions;
- using physical re"ection lines as defined by Klass [3];
- including other aesthetic constraints in the fitness function.

References

1. Furuta H., Maeda and Watanabe E.: Application of Genetic Algorithm to Aesthetic Design of Bridge Structures, Microcomputers in Civil Engineering 10 (1995), pp.415-421.
2. Kaufmann E. and Klass R.: Smoothing surfaces using re"ection lines for families of splines, Computer-Aided Design 20 (6), 1988, pp.312-316.
3. Klass R.: Correction of local surface irregularities using re"ection lines, Computer-Aided Design 12 (2), 1980, pp.73-77.
4. Markus A., Renner G. and Vancza: Genetic Algorithms in Free Form Surface Curve Design, in Mathematical Methods for Curves and Surfaces, M. Daehlen, T. Lyche and L.L. Schumaker (Eds.), Vanderbilt University Press, 1995, pp.343-354.
5. Mitchell, M.: An Introduction to Genetic Algorithms, The MIT Press, London, England 1996.
6. Rogers, D. F. and Adams, J. A.: Mathematical Elements for Computer Graphics (2nd ed.), The McGraw-Hill Publishing Company, 1990.

Adaptation under Changing Environments with Various Rates of Inheritance of Acquired Characters:
Comparison between Darwinian and Lamarckian Evolution

Takahiro Sasaki[1] and Mario Tokoro[2]

[1] Department of Computer Science, Faculty of Science and Technology, Keio University 3-14-1 Hiyoshi, Kohoku-ku, Yokohama 223-0061, Japan
[2] Sony Computer Science Laboratory Inc., 3-14-13 Higashigotanda, Shinagawa-ku, Tokyo 141-0022, Japan
E-mail: sasaki@mt.cs.keio.ac.jp, mario@csl.sony.co.jp

Abstract. In this paper, we study the relationship between learning and evolution in a simple abstract model, where neural networks capable of learning are evolved through genetic algorithms (GAs). The connective weights of individuals neural networks undergo modi"cation, i.e., certain characters will be acquired, through their lifetime learning. By setting various rates for the heritability of acquired characters, which is a motive force of Lamarckian evolution, we observe adaptational processes of the populations over successive generations. Paying particular attention to behaviours under changing environments, we show the following results. The population with the lower rate of heritability not only shows more stable behaviour against environmental changes, but also maintains greater adaptability with respect to such changing environments. Consequently, the population with zero heritability, i.e., the Darwinian population, attains the highest level of adaptation toward dynamic environments.

1 Introduction

It is obvious that the adaptational processes of natural organisms consist of two complementary phases, each taking place at different spatio-temporal levels: 1) *learning*, occurring within each individual's lifetime, and 2) *evolution*, occurring over successive generations of the population[4,9,1]. Here, a simple question arises: How should these processes of adaptation at the different levels be connected with each other for a greater advantage? The main goal of this paper is to point to a possible direction for the answers to this question.

In the history of evolutionary theory, there have been two major ideas that give different explanations for the motive force of natural evolution and the phenomenon of genetic inheritance: *Lamarckism* and *Darwinism*. The former regards the effect of inheritance of acquired characters as the motive force of evolution. Through interactions with the environment or learning, individuals may undergo some adaptive changes that will then somehow be encoded in their genes and direct the evolutionary process. On the other hand, the central dogma of Darwinism is that the motive force of evolution is (non-random) natural selection following on random mutation ; mutation itself has no direction, but some individuals with advantageous mutations will have more chance of survival and reproduction through natural selection. It claims that evolution is nothing but these cumulative processes of natural selection. As we know, the mainstream of today's evolutionary theory follows Darwinism, and Lamarckism is regarded as wrong or as a heresy.

In spite of the biological background mentioned above, from the viewpoint of engineering it is not necessary to consider only Darwinian evolution models. Indeed, the possibility of using the heredity of acquired characters would be quite attractive[3,5]. For this reason, we compared Darwinian and Lamarckian evolution using a simple abstract model in our previous paper[10]. We showed that, under changing environments, the population with Darwinian evolution not only showed more stable behaviour against environmental changes, but surprisingly, could also maintain greater adaptability with respect to such dynamic environments than could the Lamarckian population. While Lamarckian populations could adapt themselves quite quickly to a certain single situation, they had di culty in leaving the specific state of adaptation once it had taken place owing to their extremely greedy strategy for genetic inheritance. That is why the Lamarckian population in [10] performed poorly under changing environments. Therefore, in this paper, we introduce a new parameter, *heredity rate*, into our Lamarckian model to control the amount of inheritance of acquired characters. We discuss whether there is any appropriate value range of the heredity rate that enables Lamarckian evolution to cope appropriately with changing environments while maintaining quick adaptability toward each single condition.

With other researchers who have recently considered adaptational processes under changing environments[2,8,7], we also believe that any evolutionary computation for real-world application must be equipped with adaptability toward dynamic situations. For this reason we have concentrated especially on changing environments.

2   Experimental Model

Here we present our experimental framework and settings. A hundred individuals come into a virtual world, with 500 units of initial life energy for each. Each individual has a feed-forward neural network that serves as its brain, meaning that the individual takes action based on the network outputs (Figure 1). We take an array of real numbers as a chromosome from which the neural network is developed. The chromosome directly encodes all the connective weights of the network[6]. Values of the chromosomes in the initial generation are set randomly, from the range $-0.30 \sim 0.30$.

The world contains two groups of materials, food and poison, both of which have distinctive features, i.e., patterns of bits. For example, in Figure 2,

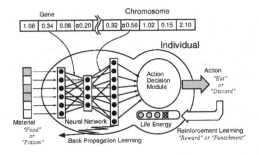

Fig. 1. The architecture of an individual.

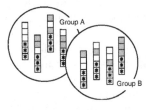

Fig. 2. The materials in the virtual world.

materials in group A are food, and those in group B are poison. The symbol * means *don t care* whether the cell is black or white. Thus, food and poison are discriminated by the upper three bits, and the lower three bits are noise.

On each occasion when given any material, an individual inputs the pattern of the material into its neural network and stochastically determines whether to eat or discard it according to the network outputs. These actions are not mapped directly from the outputs themselves. The network outputs are fed once as signals to an Action Decision Module (Figure 1), which then finally determines the action of the individual stochastically according to a Boltzmann distribution. This type of stochastic mechanism is necessary to maintain the possibility of seeking more advantageous behaviours, even if an individual has already acquired a certain adequate behavioural pattern[10].

If what the individual ate was food, it receives 10 units of energy and tries to train itself to produce the eat action with a higher probability for that pattern. Conversely, if the individual ate poison, it loses a comparable amount of energy and tries to train itself to produce the discard action with a higher probability for that pattern. When the individual discards the material, no learning is conducted. The aim of each individual is to maximize its life energy by learning a *rule* that discriminates food and poison, which in this case corresponds to a parity problem of three bits. We use the *Back Propagation Learning (BP Learning)* algorithm, in combination with a *Reinforcement Learning* framework, to train each individual. The coe cients of learning and inertia of BP Learning are set at = 0.75 and = 0.8, respectively.

Each individual is repeatedly offered a certain number of materials, 400 in the current experiments, and learning occurs. We regard this number of repeated events as the length of an individual's lifetime. At the end of each generation, some of the individuals are selected as parents by a stochastic criterion proportional to the level of their energy, i.e. their fitness. Parents re-encode their network connective weights, that suffered modification through their lifetime learning, into their chromosomes according to a given *heredity rate* τ (Figure 3). In Figure 3, w_0 and w_L represent the vectors of connective weights at the time of birth and at the time of reproduction, i.e., after the lifetime learning, respectively. Chromosomes c_e and c_i represent the one from which an individual

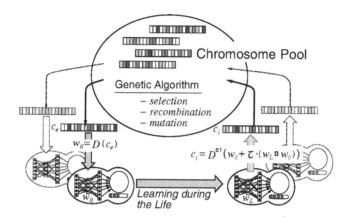

Fig. 3. The mechanisms of genetic inheritance

develops and the one which the individual produces after learning, respectively. D is a mapping from genotype to phenotype, and D^{-1} is its inverse. Individuals with $= 0$ do not re-encode any acquired characters into their chromosomes, but just hand the chromosomes that they inherited from their parents to the process of GAs. On the other hand, with $= 1$ all the acquired characters are re-encoded into the chromosomes. Therefore, we refer to the populations with $= 0$ and those with $0 < < 1$ as *Darwinian* and *Lamarckian*, respectively, and especially refer to those with $= 1$ as *full-Lamarckian*. Chromosomes of the selected individuals undergo the genetic processes of recombination and mutation. Here, the number of crossing-over points is set randomly from the range $0 \sim 4$. Each mutation occurs at the rate of 5%, with a variation range between ± 0.5. Thus, the selected parents reproduce new offspring, which then undergo lifetime learning in the following generation. Although the parameters in this paper are set heuristically according to some preliminary experiments, we have confirmed that changing these values within a moderate range results in qualitatively similar outcomes.

3   Experimental Evaluations

Now consider a world where food and poison are characterized by arrays of six bits, as shown in Figure 2. At any given time, one group of the two is set up as food and the other as poison. We referred to an environment where group A is food as Env A, and the other where group B is food as Env B. To consider changing environments, we make the world switch between Env A and Env B, so that food and poison swap their roles repeatedly at each particular interval, which is here set at 20 generations. Although a situation such as this may seem to be rather arbitrary or unrealistic, it can actually happen that characters advantageous to survival are totally overturned. A well-known example is the *industrial melanism* of certain moths in the Industrial Revolution

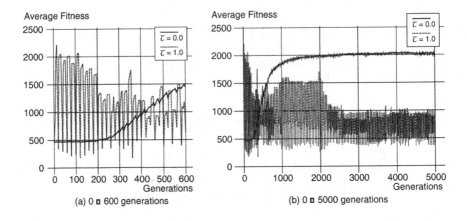

Fig. 4. The average "tness: Darwinian ($\tau = 0.0$) vs. full-Lamarckian ($\tau = 1.0$)

era in England[11]. Although we obtain qualitatively similar results even if we use a more di cult and random situation, we show here the results for this type of simple case, where the environment is repeatedly overturned, for clarity. All the experimental results, shown hereafter, are the average of 20 runs.

3.1 Darwinian ($\tau = 0.0$) versus full-Lamarckian ($\tau = 1.0$)

Let us first compare the two extreme cases: Darwinian (= 0.0) and full-Lamarckian evolution (= 1.0). Figures 4(a) and (b) show the changes in the average fitness of the populations. As is evident from the figures, the fitness of the full-Lamarckian population oscillates violently as the environment is overturned, while that of the Darwinian population hardly oscillates and is more stable. The point that we should especially emphasize is that the fitness of the Darwinian population rises over successive generations. This suggests that a population that can cope with both the rules of Env A and Env B is formed through Darwinian evolution. To confirm this practically, we let four groups of populations (an initial generation, 500*th*, 2000*th*, and 5000*th* generation) conduct learning under each of the two environments. Figures 6(a) 6(d) show the learning curves of both populations under each environment. The figures show the changes in average output errors for the discrimination ability learned during their lifetime. The mean squared error is used to measure the difference between the actual outputs and the ideal outputs. We can confirm that the Darwinian mechanism forms a population of individuals that learn both rules more appropriately as the generations proceed. In contrast, full-Lamarckian evolution produces individuals that cannot appropriately learn either rule. The two learning curves for Lamarckian individuals in the later generation differ from each other, which means that they cope with one rule better than the other. However, even if the preferred rule is given, the Lamarckian population cannot learn it better than the Darwinian one.

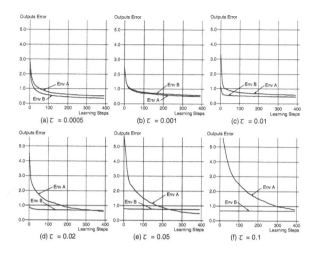

Fig. 5. Learning curves with various heredity rates

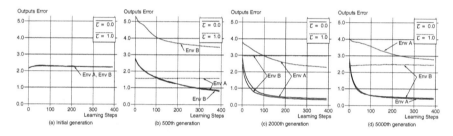

Fig. 6. Learning curves: Darwinian ($\tau = 0.0$) vs. full-Lamarckian ($\tau = 1.0$)

3.2 Controlling Heredity Rate (τ) of Acquired Characters

We now control the amount of heredity by setting   at various values and observe the evolutionary processes of the populations. Figures 7(a)   7(f) show the changes in the average fitness of the populations with the heredity rate set at 0.0005, 0.001, 0.01, 0.02, 0.05, 0.1, respectively. As shown by the figures, populations with a higher heredity rate become more unstable than those with a lower rate. The fitness oscillations of the populations with heredity rates smaller than 0.02 are within a rather tolerable range, while the oscillations grow intolerable with larger heredity rates. Figures 5(a)   5(f) show the learning curves for each environment of the $5000th$ populations with the heredity rate set at 0.0005, 0.001, 0.01, 0.02, 0.05, 0.1, respectively. As we can see from the figures, the two learning curves become more different from each other as the heredity rate gets higher, which indicates that the evolutionary processes with lower heredity rates produce individuals that can learn both rules more appropriately.

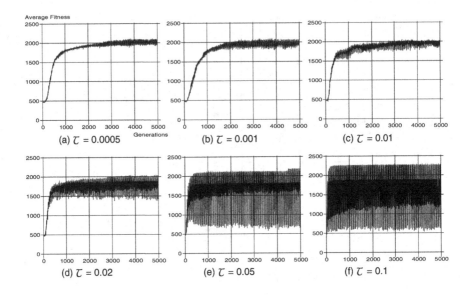

Fig. 7. The average "tness with various heredity rates

4   Discussion

Under a dynamic environment, the ability to cope with various situations becomes more important than the ability to cope appropriately only with a specific one. The direct Lamarckian effect that greedily transmits the ability to perform something is not only useless but also harmful under a changing environment. On the other hand, the indirect *Baldwin e ect* that transmits the ability to learn something plays a crucial role. Thus, the Darwinian population became most adapted toward the changing environments in our experiment.

In the real biological world, while a phenotype is developed dynamically through quite complex chemical processes according to the information of a genotype, it is very di cult to do the reverse, that is, to determine and compose the corresponding formation of the genotype for a certain phenotype. This is why Lamarckian inheritance is generally said to be infeasible. However, from our experimental results we may suggest another explanation for the essential reason why creatures selected the Darwinian strategy of genetic inheritance in the earlier stages of their evolution. The real world is an environment with strong dynamic characteristics; therefore Darwinian inheritance itself has been an advantageous strategy for adaptation to the real world.

5   Conclusions

We evaluated on a simple abstract model how learning with inheritance of acquired characters affects the evolution of the population, especially under changing environments. By controlling the amount of inheritance, we have shown that populations with lower heritability not only showed more stable behaviour against environmental changes, but also maintained greater adaptability with respect to such changing environments.

Although it must be considered whether our experimental model and results are su ciently general, we have clarified possible fundamental characteristics that are required for adaptation toward changing environments. Therefore, we believe that the results obtained here may give helpful suggestions in, for example, designing artificial intelligence systems or software agents that will be brought into play under dynamic environments.

References

1. David H. Ackley and Michael L. Littman. Interactions between Learning and Evolution. In *Artificial Life II, SFI Studies in the Sciences of Complexity, vol.X*, pages 487 509. Addison-Wesley, 1992.
2. Helen G. Cobb and John J. Grefenstette. Genetic Algorithms for Tracking Changing Environments. In *Proceedings of 5th International Conference on Genetic Algorithms and their applications (ICGA-93)*, pages 523 530, 1993.
3. John J. Grefenstette. Lamarckian Learning in Multi-agent Environments. In *Proceedings of 4th International Conference on Genetic Algorithms and their applications (ICGA-91)*, pages 303 310, 1991.
4. G. E. Hinton and S. J. Nowlan. How Learning Can Guide Evolution. *Complex Systems*, 1:495 502, 1987.
5. Akira Imada and Keijiro Araki. Lamarckian evolution of associative memory. In *Proceedings of 1996 IEEE The Third International Conference on Evolutionary Computation (ICEC-96)*, pages 676 680, 1996.
6. David J. Montana and Lawrence Davis. Training Feedforward Neural Networks Using Genetic Algorithms. In *Proceedings of the 11th International Conference on Artificial Intelligence (IJCAI-89)*, pages 762 767, 1989.
7. Naoki Mori, Seiji Imanishi, Hajime Kita, and Yoshikazu Nishikawa. Adaptation to Changing Environments by Means of the Memory Based Thermodynamical Genetic Algorithm. In *Proceedings of 7th International Conference on Genetic Algorithms and their applications (ICGA-97)*, pages 299 306, 1997.
8. Stefano Nol" and Domenico Parisi. Learning to adapt to changing environments in evolving neural networks. Technical Report 95-15, Institute of Psychology, National Research Council, Rome, 1995.
9. Domenico Parisi, Stefano Nol", and Federico Cecconi. Learning, Behaviour and Evolution. In *Toward a Practice of Autonomous Systems: Proceedings of the First European Conference on Artificial Life*, pages 207 216. MIT Press, 1991.
10. Takahiro Sasaki and Mario Tokoro. Adaptation toward changing environments: Why Darwinian in nature? In *4th European Conference on Artificial Life (ECAL-97)*, pages 145 153, 1997.
11. John Maynard Smith. *Evolutionary Genetics.* Oxford University Press, 1989.

Dynamic Control of Adaptive Parameters in Evolutionary Programming

Ko-Hsin Liang, Xin Yao, and Charles Newton

Computational Intelligence Group, School of Computer Science
University College, The University of New South Wales
Australian Defence Force Academy, Canberra, ACT, Australia 2600
Email: {liangk, xin, csn}@cs.adfa.oz.au

Abstract. Evolutionary programming (EP) has been widely used in numerical optimization in recent years. The adaptive parameters, also named step size control, in EP play a signi"cant role which controls the step size of the objective variables in the evolutionary process. However, the step size control may not work in some cases. They are frequently lost and then make the search stagnate early. Applying the lower bound can maintain the step size in a work range, but it also constrains the objective variables from being further explored. In this paper, an adaptively adjusted lower bound is proposed which supports better "ne-tune searches and spreads out exploration as well.

1 Introduction

Evolutionary programming (EP) [1] has been applied to many optimization problems successfully in recent years [2,3,4]. A global optimization problem can be formalised as a pair (S, f), where $S \subseteq R^n$ is a bounded set in R^n and $f : S \to R$ is an n-dimensional real-valued function. The problem is to find a vector $x_{\min} \in S$ such that $f(x_{\min})$ is a global minimum on S. More specifically, it is required to find an $x_{\min} \in S$ such that

$$\forall x \in S : f(x_{\min}) \leq f(x)$$

Here f does not need to be continuous, but it has to be bounded.

According to the description of Fogel [1] and Bäck and Schwefel [5], EP is implemented in this study as follows:

1. Generate the initial population of μ individuals, and set the generation $=$ 1. Each individual is taken as a pair of real-valued vectors, $(x_i, \ _i)$, $\forall i \in \{1, \cdots, \mu\}$, where $\ _i$ is an adaptive parameter. Each x has n components $x(j), j = 1, \cdots, n$.
2. Evaluate the fitness score for each individual $(x_i, \ _i)$, $\forall i \in \{1, \cdots, \mu\}$, of the population based on the objective function, $f(x_i)$.
3. For each parent $(x_i, \ _i)$, $i = 1, \cdots, \mu$, create a single offspring $(x'_i, \ '_i)$ by :

$$\ '_i(j) = \ _i(j) \exp(\ 'N(0,1) + \ N_j(0,1)),$$
$$x'_i(j) = x_i(j) + \ '_i(j)N_j(0,1), \tag{1}$$

$x_i(j)$, $x'_i(j)$, $\eta_i(j)$ and $\eta'_i(j)$ denote the j-th component of the vectors x_i, x'_i, η_i and η'_i, respectively. $N(0, 1)$ denotes a normally distributed one-dimensional random number with mean 0 and standard deviation 1. $N_j(0, 1)$ indicates that the random number is generated anew for each value of j. The factors τ and τ' have commonly been set to $(\sqrt{2\sqrt{n}})^{-1}$ and $(\sqrt{2n})^{-1}$, respectively [6].

4. Calculate the fitness of each offspring (x'_i, η'_i), $\forall i \in \{1, \cdots, \mu\}$.
5. Conduct pairwise comparisons over the union of parents (x_i, η_i) and offspring (x'_i, η'_i), $\forall i \in \{1, \cdots, \mu\}$. For each individual, q opponents are chosen randomly from all the parents and offspring with an equal probability. For each comparison, if the individual's fitness is no greater than the opponent's, it receives a win.
6. Select the μ individuals out of (x_i, η_i) and (x'_i, η'_i), $\forall i \in \{1, \cdots, \mu\}$, that have the most wins to be parents of next generation.
7. Stop if the halting criterion is satisfied; otherwise, $k = k+1$ and go to Step 3.

The adaptive parameter, η_i, also called the step size control in Step 3, is expected to adaptively adjust the step size for each objective variable. The ideal result is to have a larger step size for the objective variable at the beginning of the evolutionary process to speed up the search, and become smaller at the later stage for better fine-tuning. Eq. 1 is the update rule for the adaptive parameters at the component level [7]. An adaptive parameter value can survive to the next generation when its corresponding variable value leads to higher fitness. However, it can also survive to the next generation when the higher fitness is caused by other objective variables.

In evolution, some of the adaptive parameters are reduced too fast which cause the affected variables to lose their usefulness in maintaining diversity [8]. If the distance from x_j to the minimum x_j^* for the j-th component has, for example, $|x_j - x_j^*| \geq 1$, and the adaptive parameter $\eta_j < 0.001$, the probability for x_j reaching x_j^* will be very small. We expect that the selection procedure can expunge those individuals with the phenomenon. In fact, some individuals with the phenomenon have even better performance than others in the population. These individuals survive and generate offspring with similar characteristics. When all individuals have the feature after a certain number of generations, the stagnation happens. This problem has been studied in detail in an early paper [8].

In evolution strategies [6,9] the lower bound $\bar{\eta}$ is used to keep the step size controls from being lost. One implementation of evolutionary programming applies a small value 0.001 to replace the negative adaptive parameters when using the Gaussian update rule [10]. The empirical study in [8] has shown that a proper selected $\bar{\eta}$ can improve EP's performance significantly.

However, applying a lower bound may constrain the objective variables from finer exploitation. Different problems also need different lower bounds which can only be determined empirically [8]. In this paper, we propose a scheme to apply a dynamic lower bound on the adaptive parameters for each individual. The use of such a dynamic scheme has improved the performance of EP significantly. The rest of this paper is organised as follows. Section 2 provides a mathematical and empirical analysis of the adaptive parameters in (1+1) EP. The scheme of applying a dynamic lower bound to the adaptive parameters is presented in Section 3. Section 4 presents the main results of this paper. It compares EP with different lower bound schemes on the adaptive parameter of a set of benchmark functions. Finally, Section 5 concludes the paper with some remarks.

2   Analysis

In this section, we use a (1+1) EP as the optimization algorithm. Given an n-dimensional real-valued function $f(x)$, using one parent in each generation, the adaptive parameter η'_j is created by:

$$\eta_j^{(i+1)} = \eta_j^{(i)} \exp(\tau N_j(0,1))$$

Here j denotes the j-th component and $\tau = \frac{1}{\sqrt{n}}$ [11]. This is a modified version of Eq.1 . Given initial $\eta_j^{(0)}$, we can find $\eta_j^{(\kappa)}$ after running κ generations of successful mutations. Note that the actual generation number will be greater or equal to κ as the success rate of generating the offspring is no more than 1. Therefore, through the sequence

$$\{ \eta_j^{(1)}, \eta_j^{(2)}, \eta_j^{(3)}, \cdots, \eta_j^{(\kappa)} \}$$

we get

$$\eta_j^{(\kappa)} = \eta_j^{(0)} \exp\left(\tau \sum_{i=1}^{\kappa} N_i(0,1) \right)$$

The probability that the adaptive parameter $\eta_j^{(\kappa)}$ will be smaller than an arbitrary small number η is:

$$P_\eta = P\left(\eta_j^{(\kappa)} < \eta \right)$$

$$= P\left(\eta_j^{(0)} \exp\left(\tau \sum_{i=1}^{\kappa} N_i(0,1) \right) < \eta \right)$$

Since the sum of κ independent $N(0,1)$ random variables has the distribution [12, pp.267]:

$$\sum_{i=1}^{\kappa} N_i(0,1) \sim N(0, \kappa),$$

we get

$$P_\eta = P\left(\eta_j^{(0)} \exp\left(\tau N(0, \kappa) \right) < \eta \right)$$

$$= P\left(N(0, \kappa) < \ln\left(\frac{\eta}{\eta_j^{(0)}}\right) / \tau \right)$$

$$= \int_{-\infty}^{C} \frac{1}{\sqrt{2\pi}} \exp\left(-\frac{t^2}{2}\right) dt$$

$$= \Phi\left(\frac{C}{\sqrt{\kappa}}\right)$$

where $C = \ln\left(\frac{\epsilon}{\eta_i^{(0)}}\right)/$. For sufficiently large $\frac{C}{\sqrt{\kappa}}$, the following approximation [13] can be used:

$$\Phi(x) \simeq 1 - \frac{1}{\sqrt{2}}\exp\left(-\frac{1}{2}x^2\right) \cdot \frac{1}{x}$$

The derivative $\frac{\partial}{\partial\kappa}(P_\eta)$ can be used to evaluate the impact of κ on P_η.

$$\frac{\partial}{\partial\kappa}(P_\eta) = -\frac{\partial}{\partial\kappa}\left(1 - \frac{1}{\sqrt{2}}\exp\left(-\frac{C^2}{2\kappa}\right)\cdot\frac{\sqrt{\kappa}}{C}\right)$$

$$= -\frac{1}{\sqrt{2}}\frac{1}{C}\exp\left(-\frac{C^2}{2\kappa}\right)\left(\frac{1}{2\sqrt{\kappa}} + \frac{C^2}{2}\kappa^{-\frac{3}{2}}\right)$$

For $C = \sqrt{n}\ln\left(\eta/\eta_j^{(0)}\right)$, it is apparent from the above equation that

$$\frac{\partial}{\partial\kappa}(P_\eta)\begin{cases} > 0, & \text{if } \eta < \eta_j^{(0)} \\ < 0, & \text{if } \eta > \eta_j^{(0)} \end{cases}$$

From the trend of the adaptive parameters, we intuitively know that $\eta < \eta_j^{(0)}$ after several generations, then we get $\frac{\partial}{\partial\kappa}(P_\eta) > 0$. Thus, the larger the number of generations κ, the larger P_η. In other words, the probability that the adaptive parameter $\eta_j^{(k)}$ becomes smaller than an arbitrary small number ϵ will be higher if κ is larger.

To make a further evaluation of the impact of κ on the adaptive parameter η_j, we conducted a preliminary experiment with $(1+1)$ EP. The benchmark function tested was:

$$f(x) = -20\exp\left(-0.2\sqrt{\frac{1}{n}\sum_{i=1}^{n}x_i^2}\right) - \exp\left(\frac{1}{n}\sum_{i=1}^{n}\cos(2\pi x_i)\right) + 20 + e,$$

$f(x)$ is a multimodal function with many local minima. The function dimensionality n was set to 3 and all components x_j were initialized uniformly at random over the range $[-32, 32]$. The total trials were 100, the maximum generation was 2000, the initial adaptive parameter $\eta_j^{(0)}$ was 3. We randomly selected one vector of η to observe the variation and only the η with successful mutations were recorded. Figure 1(a) shows the average variations of the adaptive parameter η_j. At random, the third component η_3 was selected. All η_3 on each successful generation were averaged over the trial number. Only trial numbers over 40 were drawn. For large κ, less trials can generate more successful mutations.

It is clear that the larger κ becomes, the probability to get the smaller adaptive parameter becomes larger. The examples of the $(1+1)$ EP have shown that the smaller adaptive parameters were preferred after several generations. That is, through the mutation and selection, the evolutionary process is working at large step sizes in the early stage and smaller ones after certain generations.

When the adaptive parameters decrease, the best situation is when the objective variables are very close to the global optimum. Thus, the smaller step

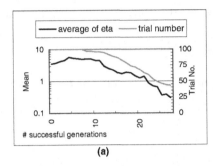 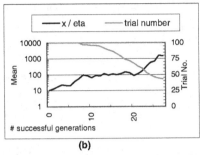

(a)   **(b)**

Fig. 1. (a)The average variations of η_3 are shown. The start of $\eta_j^{(0)} > \eta_j^{(\kappa)}$ is found at $\kappa = 12$. (b)The average relation pairs $(\frac{x_j}{\eta_j})$ are shown. At $\kappa = 25$, for example, after average of 49 trials, the worst pair has $\frac{x_j}{\eta_j} = 588$

sizes are preferred. If any of the step sizes decrease faster than the objective variables approach to the optimum, the process may be stagnated by the unbalanced component pair. That is, the step size becomes very small while the objective variable is still far away from the global optimum. In figure 1(b), the worst relation pair $(\frac{x_j}{\eta_j})$ in each generation is shown. The average per trial number and the experimental data are obtained from the same results. The stagnation largely begins when $\frac{x_j}{\eta_j}$ is over 1000.

To prevent the unbalanced phenomenon, a lower bound $^-$ is definitely needed [8]. However, the fixed lower bound creates a limitation on the search. The choice of the lower bound is problem dependent. In the next section, we propose a dynamic lower bound to improve the situation.

3   Dynamic Lower Bound

The implementation of the dynamic lower bound includes two steps. First, set up an index to measure the adaptation of the lower bound. Then, adjust the lower bound accordingly. The method used to evaluate the performance of the lower bound is similar to 1/5 success rule [9, pp.110]. If the number of successful mutations is larger than 1/5 of all mutations, increase the step size. Otherwise, decrease the step size. We calculate the number of offspring selected for the next generation, and decide the ratio of successes to all offspring. Then, apply the following rule to update the lower bound:

$$^{-\prime} = {}^- (\frac{S_\kappa}{A}),\qquad(2)$$

where S_κ is the success rate at generation and A is a reference rate, which has been set between 0.25 and 0.45 in our experiments. It is worth pointing out that our dynamic lower bound differs significantly from the 1/5 rule. The 1/5 rule is based on the component level adaptation, while our dynamic lower bound is based on the whole population, i.e. S_κ is calculated across the entire population.

Applying the dynamic lower bound, we expect to eliminate the early stagnation, support the finer exploitation, provide the adaptively adjusted lower bound, and most essentially, spread out the population for extensive search. This scheme uses the lower bound to indirectly control the mutation step size to optimize the evolutionary process. When the success rate is over the reference point, the step size will increase to encourage the offspring aggressively to extend the search range. On the contrary, the step size will be smaller for the closer range search.

4 Results

Six benchmark functions were tested as shown in Table 1. The functions were numbered as in [3], f_1, f_2, f_5 are unimodal functions and f_9, f_{10}, f_{11} are multimodal functions with many local minima. The EP algorithm used in our study was the improved fast evolutionary programming (IFEP) [14]. The difference between IFEP and classical EP (CEP) is in Step 3 of the algorithm described in Section 1. Instead of generating one offspring using Gaussian mutation, IFEP creates two offspring, one by Gaussian mutation and the other by Cauchy. The better one is then chosen as the offspring. The population size $\mu = 50$, the tournament size $q = 10$ for selection, the reference rate $A = 0.3$, and the initial standard deviations 3.0 were used. Two different IFEPs were tested, one with the dynamic lower bound initialized to 0.1 and the other with the fixed $^- = 0.0001$. The dynamic lower bound in IFEP was updated every 5 generations using eq. 2.

Table 1. The 6 benchmark functions used in our experimental studies, where n is the dimension of the function, $f_{\min}$ is the minimum value of the function, and $S \subseteq R^n$.

Test function	n	S	$f_{\min}$
$f_1(x) = \sum_{i=1}^{n} x_i^2$	30	$[-100, 100]$	0
$f_2(x) = \sum_{i=1}^{n} |x_i| + \prod_{i=1}^{n} |x_i|$	30	$[-10, 10]$	0
$f_5(x) = \sum_{i=1}^{n-1} [100(x_{i+1} - x_i^2)^2 + (x_i - 1)^2]$	30	$[-30, 30]$	0
$f_9(x) = \sum_{i=1}^{n} [x_i^2 - 10\cos(2\pi x_i) + 10]$	30	$[-5.12, 5.12]$	0
$f_{10}(x) = -20\exp(-0.2\sqrt{\frac{1}{n}\sum_{i=1}^{n} x_i^2})$ $- \exp(\frac{1}{n}\sum_{i=1}^{n}\cos(2\pi x_i)) + 20 + e$	30	$[-32, 32]$	0
$f_{11}(x) = \frac{1}{4000}\sum_{i=1}^{n} x_i^2 - \prod_{i=1}^{n}\cos(\frac{x_i}{\sqrt{i}}) + 1$	30	$[-600, 600]$	0

Table 2 summerises the experimental results of comparing IFEP with and without a dynamic lower bound. All results have been averaged over 50 runs. IFEP with the dynamic lower bound has much better performance on f_1, f_2, f_{10} and f_{11} because it maximised the IFEP's capability to keep searching for a better function value from the beginning. However, a worse result was observed on f_5 and f_9. Both of these cases lead to early stagnation of search. The experimental data showed that the lower bound decreased too fast on certain generations and could not be recovered by eq. 2. This happened when all the individuals were trapped into a local optimum. The success rate of the generation could not provide any useful information about the search in this situation. The IFEP with the fixed lower bound stagnates when the function value approaches the lower bound value. Our experimental results appear to indicate that the dynamic lower bound we proposed is quite e cient in finding a near optimal solution, but has a weak ability in escaping from a local optimum once trapped. There is a trade-off between e ciency and optimality here. In general, we feel the dynamic lower bound provides a good balance between the two. We are currently investigating methods for escaping from a local optimum once the algorithm is trapped.

Table 2. Comparison between IFEP with the "xed and dynamic lower bound on functions f_1, f_2, f_5, f_9, f_{10}, f_{11}. All results have been averaged over 50 runs. dLB and fLB mean the dynamic and "xed lower bound respectively. Mean Best indicates the mean best function values found in the last generation.

Function	number of generation	IFEP w/dLB Mean Best	Std Dev	IFEP w/fLB Mean Best	Std Dev	dLB-fLB t-test
f_1	2000	2.00e-17	3.10e-17	3.33e-7	4.05e-8	$-58.22^\dagger$
f_2	2000	6.56e-10	6.97e-10	2.31e-3	1.61e-4	$-101.56^\dagger$
f_5	20000	1.83	1.43	3.58e-1	5.77e-1	$6.76^\dagger$
f_9	5000	7.50	3.67	2.48	1.60	$8.88^\dagger$
f_{10}	2000	2.15e-9	2.47e-9	4.16e-4	1.99e-5	$-147.74^\dagger$
f_{11}	2000	1.27e-2	1.76e-2	1.17e-1	1.64e-1	$-4.46^\dagger$

†The value of t with 49 degrees of freedom is signi"cant at $\alpha = 0.05$ by a two-tailed test.

5   Conclusions

Lower bounds for adaptive parameters in EP and evolution strategies are an important issue which have been overlooked by most researchers. This paper analyses the variation phenomenon of the adaptive parameter using (1+1) EP through mathematical and empirical approaches. They both demonstrate the necessity to add a lower bound to the adaptive parameters. This paper also proposes a scheme to apply a dynamic lower bound to indirectly control the search step size. This combines population-level adaptation of the success rate with component-level self-adaptation of the adaptive parameters to optimise evolutionary performance. The experimental results have shown that this dynamic lower bound can provide better performance in IFEP for most numerical functions we tested.

The mathematical analysis of (1+1) EP in this paper did not consider selection. The selection also has an impact on the step size. The proposed update rule of the dynamic lower bound does not work in some cases. However, this scheme provides a good direction to promote and maximise the performance of the evolutionary algorithm.

References

1. D.B. Fogel. A comparison of evolutionary programming and genetic algorithms on selected constrained optimization problems. *Simulation*, 64(6):397 404, 1995.
2. D.B. Fogel. Applying evolutionary programming to selected control problems. *Computers & Mathematics with Applications*, 27(11):89 104, 1994.
3. X. Yao and Y Liu. Fast evolutionary programming. In L.J. Fogel, P.J. Angeline, and T. Bäck, editors, *Evolutionary Programming V: Proc. of the Fifth Annual Conference on Evolutionary Programming*, pages 451 460, Cambridge, MA, 1996. MIT Press.
4. K.-H. Liang, X. Yao, C. Newton, and D. Hoˇman. Solving cutting stock problems by evolutionary programming. In V.W. Porto, N. Saravanan, D. Waagen, and A.E. Eiben, editors, *Evolutionary Programming VII: Proc. of the Seventh Annual Conference on Evolutionary Programming*, volume 1447 of *Lecture Notes in Computer Science*, pages 755 764, New York, 1998. Springer.
5. T. Bäck and H.-P. Schwefel. An overview of evolutionary algorithms for parameter optimization. *Evolutionary Computation*, 1(1):1 23, 1993.
6. T. Bäck. *Evolutionary Algorithms in Theory and Practice: Evolution Strategies, Evolutionary Programming, Genetic Algorithms*. Oxford University, New York, 1996.
7. P.J. Angeline. Adaptive and self-adaptive evolutionary computation. In Y. Palaniswami, R. Attikiouzel, R. Marks, D. Fogel, and T. Fukuda, editors, *Computation Intelligence: A Dymanic System Perspective*, pages 152 163, Piscataway, NJ, 1995. IEEE Press.
8. K.-H. Liang, X. Yao, Y. Liu, C. Newton, and D. Hoˇman. An experimental investigation of self-adaptation in evolutionary programming. In V.W. Porto, N. Saravanan, D. Waagen, and A.E. Eiben, editors, *Evolutionary Programming VII: Proc. of the Seventh Annual Conference on Evolutionary Programming*, volume 1447 of *Lecture Notes in Computer Science*, pages 291 300, New York, 1998. Springer.
9. H.-P. Schwefel. *Evolution and Optimum Seeking*. Wiley, New York, 1995.
10. D.B. Fogel, L.J. Fogel, and J.W. Atmar. Meta-evolutionary programming. In R.R. Chen, editor, *Proc. of the 25th Asilomar Conference on Signals, Systems and Computers*, pages 540 545, San Jose, CA, 1991. Maple Press.
11. H.-G. Beyer. Toward a theory of evolution strategies: Self-adaptation. *Evolutionary Computation*, 3(3):311 348, 1995.
12. H.J. Larson. *Introduction to Probability Theory and statistical Inference*. Wiley, New York, third edition, 1982.
13. W. Feller. *An Introduction to Probability Theory and Its Applications*, volume 1. Wiley, New York, third edition, 1968.
14. X. Yao, G. Lin, and Y Liu. An analysis of evolutionary algorithms based on neighbourhood and step sizes. In P.J. Angeline, R.G. Reynolds, J.R. McDonnell, and R Eberhart, editors, *Evolutionary Programming VI: Proc. of the Sixth Annual Conference on Evolutionary Programming*, volume 1213 of *Lecture Notes in Computer Science*, pages 297 307, New York, 1997. Springer.

Information Operator Scheduling by Genetic Algorithms

Takeshi Yamada, Kazuyuki Yoshimura, and Ryohei Nakano

NTT Communication Science Laboratories,
2-4 Hikaridai, Seika-cho, Soraku-gun, Kyoto 619-0237, Japan
{yamada, kazuyuki, nakano}@cslab.kecl.ntt.co.jp
http://www.kecl.ntt.co.jp/as

Abstract. In this paper, we discuss an approach to an operator scheduling problem in a large organization over time with the aim of maintaining service quality and reducing total labor costs. We propose a genetic algorithm (GA) with a parameterized "tness function inspired by homotopy methods and with null mutation to handle a variable number of operators. The proposed method is applied to the practical problem of scheduling operators in a telephone information center. Experimental results show that the proposed method performs consistently better than a GA method previously developed.

1 Introduction

In the operator scheduling problem for customer service operations at a telephone information center, we are given a set of working shifts with known start and end times and number of short breaks to be taken during the work session. The primary objective is to minimize staff shortages against number of customer calls over time. This objective is so important to maintain service quality that it is treated as a constraint such that the shortage must be zero. The secondary objective is to minimize labor costs or a surplus of operators for actual needs. Other objectives such as overtime and employee satisfaction are not considered. This problem re"ects the very significant needs of a large organization such as an information service center for telephone directory assistance. Constructing a good schedule by hand, however, can be very di cult. Nippon Telegraph and Telephone Corporation (NTT), for example, has more than one hundred such centers all over Japan and currently suffers huge deficits. There is urgent demand to automatically supply e cient schedules in a short time corresponding to frequently changing work shift patterns and distribution of customer calls.

Genetic algorithms (GAs) have been successfully applied to a variety of scheduling problems including jobshop and "owshop [2,7,4,6,8]. Yoshimura and Nakano [9] first applied GAs to the information operator scheduling problem. They proposed a GA with mutation especially dedicated to the problem and a partial reinitialization method with good success. The more general form of the problem is discussed in [3] under the name of the employee scheduling problem,

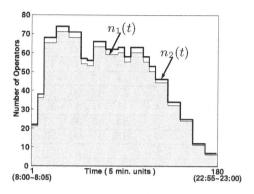

Fig. 1. Time distribution of required information operators

where they proposed tabu search approach to solve the problem and compared with other methods.

The organization of this paper is as follows. Section 2 explains the information operator scheduling problem and its objective functions. In Section 3, we brie"y review the GA approach previously proposed by Yoshimura and Nakano [9] and then modify their mutation to handle a variable number of operators. In Section 3.4 a GA with ranking based selection, duplicate elimination and local search is proposed. A new approach using a parameterized fitness function is proposed in Section 4. Experimental results using real data supplied by NTT are reported in Section 5.

2   The Information Operator Scheduling Problem

The number of human operators required to deal with inquiry calls from customers changes over time, and its time distribution is given based on statistical data at each center. Figure 1 shows such an example sampled at one of NTT's largest centers. The service starts at $t = 8:00$ and ends at $t = 23:00$. The time interval is measured in units of five minutes, therefore the total service time interval of 15 hours corresponds to $T = 180$ time units. The vertical axis represents the number of required operators for each time unit and is denoted by $n_1(t)$. A solid line at the top of the $n_1(t)$ histogram represents tolerable surplus $n_2(t)$: an acceptable margin of at most 5 % at each time unit to absorb daily "uctuations.

A *shift type* specifies the work starting and ending times and the number of breaks to be taken during the work session. The number of breaks depends on the length of the shift type, and the length of one break is fixed at 10 minutes (= 2 time units). A *break pattern* is a placement of breaks under a given *shift type*. A *working pattern* of an operator can be represented by specifying its *shift type* and *break pattern*. An operator can choose any shift type from a list of admissible

Table 1. List of admissible working shift types

No.	Shift Type	Breaks	No.	Shift Type	Breaks
1	$8:00 \sim 12:00$	4	9	$14:00 \sim 18:00$	4
2	$8:30 \sim 12:00$	3	10	$14:00 \sim 19:00$	5
3	$8:30 \sim 12:30$	4	11	$17:00 \sim 20:00$	3
4	$8:30 \sim 13:00$	4	12	$17:00 \sim 21:00$	4
5	$9:00 \sim 13:00$	4	13	$17:30 \sim 22:00$	4
6	$9:00 \sim 14:00$	5	14	$17:30 \sim 23:00$	5
7	$13:00 \sim 17:00$	4	15	$19:00 \sim 23:00$	4
8	$13:00 \sim 17:30$	4			

shift types and any break pattern under the constraint that the length of any continuous working period must be between 30 and 60 minutes. Table 1 shows an example set of admissible shift types and the number of breaks. For example, a shift type with starting time 8:00 and ending time $12:00$ has four breaks.

Let us assume there are a total of D operators available per day, and each of these operators is assigned a shift type selected from Table 1 and a break pattern. A schedule is obtained by finding a combination of D working patterns with possibly different shift types and break patterns. Each chosen working pattern corresponds to a (partial) schedule of one operator. Please note that even though the total number D is fixed, the total labor costs differ depending on the total length of the chosen shift types. In a center, operators must work in pairs, thus a working pattern is shared by two operators. To avoid confusion, however, we simply assume that one working pattern corresponds to one operator.

Let $n(t)$ be a number of operators working at time t under a schedule S. Total shortage of operators f_1 and total surplus f_2 are defined in Equation (1), where $\lfloor x \rfloor = x$ if $x > 0$; otherwise $\lfloor x \rfloor = 0$.

$$f_1 = \sum_{t=1}^{T} \lfloor n_1(t) - n(t) \rfloor, \qquad f_2 = \sum_{t=1}^{T} \lfloor n(t) - n_2(t) \rfloor. \qquad (1)$$

The objective of the information operator scheduling problem is to minimize f_2 under the constraint that f_1 must be zero. In [9], a single f with a constant $a \in [0,1]$ in Equation (2) is used as a fitness measure. Another type of fitness function shown in Equation (3) can also be considered where the constant must be small enough to satisfy $f_1 = 0$.

$$f = \frac{a}{f_1 + 1} + \frac{1-a}{f_2 + 1} \qquad (0 \le a \le 1). \qquad (2)$$

$$f^{\alpha} = \frac{1}{1 + F^{\alpha}}, \qquad F^{\alpha} = f_1 + \quad f_2 \quad (0 \le \quad \le 1). \qquad (3)$$

3   Genetic Algorithms

3.1   Solution representations

A schedule S consists of a set of partial schedules of all the operators and is denoted by $S = \{s_1, s_2, \ldots, s_D\}$. Each partial schedule s_i is a working pattern of an operator and is represented by a string of 10 integer-valued genes as $s_i = a_1 a_2 \ldots a_{10}$, where a_{10} represents its shift type number given in Table 1 and a_9 the number of breaks, whereas $a_1 a_2 \ldots a_8$ represent continuous working length before and after the breaks, thus a break pattern altogether. Each $a_1 a_2 \ldots a_8$ must be between 30 ($= 6$ time units) and 60 minutes ($= 12$ time units) as described in Section 2, and only $a_1, \ldots, a_m (m = a_9 + 1 \leq 8)$ is actually used. For example, an operator who starts working at time t_s and ends at t_e as specified by a shift type a_{10}, first works for a duration specified by a_1, then takes the first ten-minute ($= 2$ time units) break, and resumes work for a duration specified by a_2 and so on. The following equality must be satisfied (for more details, please refer to [9]):

$$t_s + a_1 + 2 + a_2 + 2 + \ldots + a_m = t_e \ (6 \leq a_j \leq 12, m = a_9 + 1). \qquad (4)$$

3.2   Mutation

For each s_i probabilistically selected for mutation with probability p_{mut}, one of the following **M1** to **M4** is applied with the probabilities p_1, p_2, p_3 and p_4 ($p_1 + p_2 + p_3 + p_4 = 1$), respectively.

M1   Two genes a_{j_1} and a_{j_2} are randomly selected and their values are exchanged.
M2   A gene a_{j_1} with a value greater than 30 minutes is randomly selected and decreased by 5 minutes, another gene a_{j_2} with a value smaller than 60 minutes is randomly selected and increased by 5 minutes.
M3 $a_1, \ldots, a_m$ are randomly regenerated under the constraint Equation (4), while a_9 and a_{10} remain the same.
M4 a_{10} is probabilistically changed to the next ($a_{10}+1$) or the previous ($a_{10}-1$) type in Table 1, a_9 to the corresponding number of breaks, and then $a_1, \ldots,$ a_m are randomly generated with the new a_9, a_{10} under Equation (4).

The mutation defined above assumes the number of genes and the total number of operators D are fixed. However, it is desirable to extend the mutation to allow D to be varied within an upperbound D_0 during the search to find a solution of higher quality. A special gene *null* for a_{10}, meaning that the operator is o duty, is introduced for this purpose. The following mutation **M5**, called null mutation, is applied with probability p_5.

M5   (null mutation) : a_{10} is probabilistically changed to *null*.

The mutation **M4** is slightly modified to incorporate this change such that if a_{10} is *null*, it is changed to any type in Table 1 at random.

1. **Initialize population:** randomly generate a set of P schedules.
2. Repeat Step 2a to Step 2d L_1 times:
   (a) Select two schedules S_1, S_2 from the population with probabilities inversely proportional to their "tness ranks.
   (b) Apply **crossover** with probability p_{cross} and obtain T_1 and T_2, otherwise just copy S_1 and S_2 to T_1 and T_2.
   (c) For $i = 1, 2$, repeat as follows L_2 times:
   Apply **mutation** to T_i and obtain $\overline{T_i}$. If $\overline{T_i}$ is at least as good as T_i, replace T_i with $\overline{T_i}$.
   (d) For $i = 1, 2$, if T_i is better than the worst in the population, and no member of the current population has the same "tness as T_i, replace the worst individual with T_i.
3. Output the best member in the population and terminate.

Fig. 2. Genetic local search for information operator scheduling problem

3.3 Crossover

A partial schedule-wise uniform crossover is employed as follows. Let two parent solutions be $S_1 = \{s_{11}, s_{12}, \ldots, s_{1m}\}$ and $S_2 = \{s_{21}, s_{22}, \ldots, s_{2m}\}$. Before applying crossover to S_1 and S_2, their partial schedules s_{ij} are sorted first by a_{10} and then by $a_1, \ldots, a_m$ in the case of ties. Let us denote the results by $S_i = s_{i1}^* s_{i2}^* \ldots s_{im}^*$ $(i = 1, 2)$. A new schedule T_1 is generated by selecting s_{1j}^* or s_{2j}^* randomly for each j $(1 \leq j \leq m)$. Similarly T_2 is generated by selecting a s_{ij}^* for each j that is not selected for T_1.

3.4 Genetic local search

It is well known that there are some problem classes in which GAs are not well suited for fine-tuning structures that are very close to optimal solutions and that it is essential to incorporate local search methods into GAs. The result of such incorporation is often called *Genetic Local Search (GLS)* [5]. In this framework, an offspring obtained by a recombination operator is not included in the next generation directly but is used as a seed for the subsequent local search. The local search moves the offspring from its initial point to the nearest locally optimal point, which is included in the next generation.

The mutation discussed in Section 3.2 is used for local search here. Instead of applying mutation only once to each individual generated from the crossover, it is applied repeatedly and the results are accepted only when they are improved (or at least the same). Figure 2 shows the outline of our GLS algorithm based on the steady state model with ranking selection. The reinitialization method introduced in [9] is substituted by the duplicate elimination technique in Step 2d to avoid premature convergence even under a small-population condition.

Table 2. Performance comparison under various parameter conditions

No.	parameters		results			
	"tness	D	$f_1(avg.)$	$f_2(avg.)$	$f_2(best)$	$D(avg.)$
I	f in [9]	105	0	173.5	135	-
II	$f^{\alpha=1}$	105	9.7	118.1	-	-
III	$f^{\alpha:1\to 0}$	105	0	143.1	123	-
IV	$f^{\alpha:1\to 0}$	100	3.0	102.5	-	-
V	$f^{\alpha:1\to 0}$	≤ 120	0	128.7	107	103.2
VI	$f^{\alpha:1\to 0}$	≤ 105	0	119.9	97	102.8

4 Parameterized Fitness Function

Yoshimura and Nakano use f in Equation (2) with $a = 0.7$ as a fitness function [9]. They observe that their GA finds a solution with $f_1 = 0$ effectively as long as $a > 0.3$, while the quality of f_2 is not always excellent. In their experiments, f_1 and f_2 start from large values, then f_1 quickly decreases to zero and does not increase again, while f_2 decreases very slowly. Once a solution S with $f_1(S) = 0$ is found, a new solution S' with $f_1(S') > 0$ is di cult to survive because $f(S')$ is inferior to $f(S)$ in many cases. Thus only a limited region where f_1 is always 0 is searched. On the other hand, if f^α with = 1 in Equation (3) is used, both $f1$ and f_2 decrease smoothly, but f_1 does not reach zero or close to zero. One may be able to overcome this dilemma by finding an optimal in Equation (3), but this itself is quite di cult.

As a possible remedy, we treat as a parameter, which decreases from 1 to 0 throughout the search. For our purpose, the algorithm in Figure 2 is slightly modified to use the parameterized f^α in which is first initialized as = 1 in Step 1, and is changed as := $(1 -)$ in Step 2b after the crossover is applied, where > 0 is a small constant.

The idea of a parameterized fitness function is inspired by a far more sophisticated approach known as the homotopy method, which has been used for decades to find solutions of nonlinear equations [1]. By initializing = 1, we start from a relaxed problem in which minimizing f_2 is easier at the cost of violating the constraint $f_1 = 0$. is then gradually decreased to enforce $f_1 = 0$ and finally a schedule with $f_1 = 0$ and reasonably small f_2 is obtained.

5 Experimental Results

Numerical experiments based on the data given in Figure 1 and in Table 1 are carried out under various conditions. Figure 3 shows the average time evolutions of f_1 and f_2 over 40 runs each on a SUN Ultra30 workstation. The programs are written in C language, and each run takes about 25 minutes of CPU time. All experiments were conducted under these conditions: the population size $P = 9$, the crossover and mutation rate $p_{cross} = 0.2$ and $p_{mut} = 0.02$ respectively,

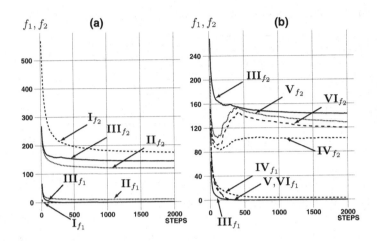

Fig. 3. Time evolutions of f_1 and f_2 under (a) "xed and parameterized "tness functions, and (b) di˜erent D settings

probabilities for each mutation: $p_1 = 0.2$, $p_2 = 0.45$, $p_3 = 0.1$ and $p_4 = 0.25$, $L_1 = 250$, $L_2 = 2000$ and $= 0.99$ are used. These values are determined based on preliminary experiments. Results are summarized in Table 2. In Figure 3(a), the number of operators D is fixed to 105 as in [9]. In the figure, the results of three different fitness functions are compared: (**I**) the same fitness function used in [9], (**II**) f^α with $= 1$, and (**III**) the parameterized f^α with decreasing from 1 to 0. It is clear that by using the parameterized fitness function, the quality of f_2 greatly improves while the constraint $f_1 = 0$ is satisfied at the end of the computation.

In Figure 3(b), the null mutation **M5** is applied as well as **M1**,...,**M4** to make D changeable. D is initialized as $D_0 = 120$ under (**V**) and $D_0 = 105$ under (**VI**) respectively, and can be varied during the search with D_0 the upper bound. p_4 is modified from 0.25 to $0.25 \times (1 - 1/N_s)$, and $p_5 = 0.25 \times 1/N_s$ with N_s number of shift types. The results of fixed D with (**III**) $D = 105$ and (**IV**) $D = 100$ are also shown for comparison. It can be seen that changing D dynamically results in better performance, with the optimal D around 102 103. The results under (**IV**) suggest that it is quite di cult to find a good solution with $f_1 = 0$ when $D \leq 100$. The best results are obtained when the perameterized fitness function and the modified mutation is used. Figure 4 shows one of the best schedules obtained under (**VI**). The picture on the right in Figure 4 shows the schedule, where the x axis represents time and the y axis the chosen working patterns. The filled block indicates that an operator is at work, while each small white block is a ten-minute break. Among 105 operators initially assigned, a total of 102 operators were found to be actually necessary, and the total surplus is 97, meaning that only 0.54 operators on average are redundant per time interval. The picture on the left shows the corresponding time distribution of the operators.

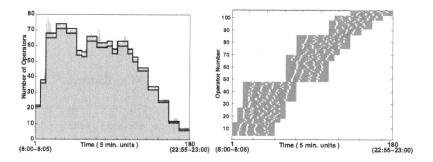

Fig. 4. Example of a solution with $D = 102$, $f_1 = 0$ and $f_2 = 97$

6   Conclusions

We have developed a genetic algorithm with local search for the information operator scheduling problem. The experimental results show that the use of a parameterized fitness function and null mutation improves the solution quality with a smaller number of total operators, while satisfying the given constraints. Future research will be to investigate the better control of   rather than decreasing it monotonically.

References

1. E.L. Allgower and K. George. Numerical Continuation Methods: An Introduction. Springer-Verlag, 1990.
2. C. Bierwirth, D. Mattfeld, and H. Kopfer. On permutation representations for scheduling problems. In 4th PPSN, pages 310 318, 1996.
3. F. Glover and C. MacMillan. The general employee scheduling problem: An integration of MS and AI. Computers and Operations Research, 13(5):563 573, 1986.
4. S. Kobayashi, I. Ono, and M. Yamamura. An e cient genetic algorithm for job shop scheduling problems. In 6th ICGA, pages 506 511, 1995.
5. N.L.J. Ulder, E. Pesch, P.J.M. van Laarhoven, H.J. Bandelt, and E.H.L. Aarts. Genetic local search algorithm for the traveling salesman problem. In 1st PPSN, pages 109 116, 1994.
6. T. Yamada and R. Nakano. Job Shop Scheduling. Chapter 7 in A.M.S. Zalzala and P.J.Fleming (Ed.) Genetic algorithms in engineering systems. The Institution of Electrical Engineers, London, UK, 1996.
7. T. Yamada and R. Nakano. Scheduling by genetic local search with multi-step crossover. In 4th PPSN, pages 960 969, 1996.
8. T. Yamada and C.R. Reeves. Permutation "owshop scheduling by genetic local search. In 2nd IEE/IEEE Int. Conf. on Genetic ALgorithms in Engineering Systems (GALESIA 97), pages 232 238, 1997.
9. K. Yoshimura and R. Nakano. Genetic algorithm for information operator scheduling. In Proc. of 1998 IEEE Int. Conf. on Evolutionary Computation (ICEC 98), pages 277 282, 1998.

Solving Radial Topology Constrained Problems with Evolutionary Algorithms

P. M. S. Carvalho[1], L. A. F. M. Ferreira[1], L. M. F. Barruncho[2]

[1]Instituto Superior Tecnico, Energy Section, Av. Rovisco Pais, 1096 Lisbon, Portugal
Phone: 351-1-841 7706, Fax: 351-1-841 7421, Email:{pcarvalho, lmf}@hertz.ist.utl.pt
[2]Edinfor—Grupo EDP, Av. Duque de Avila, 79, 1096 Lisbon, Portugal
Phone: 351-1-312 1260, Fax: 351-1-312 1201, Email: lb@edinfor.pt

Abstract. We report key algorithmic specific features involved in the evolutionary radial network problem solution. We focus on the dimensionality problem of large-scale networks and on the singularities of the radial topology search space. We (1) report the difficulties of the canonical genetic algorithm in handling network topology constraints, and (2) present both the genotype information structure and the recombination operator to overcome such difficulties. The proposed recombination operator processes genetic information as meaningful topological structures, and turns radiality and connectivity into genetic transmissible properties. Results are presented to illustrate the difference between the canonical approach and the approach taken.
Keywords. Evolutionary computation, network planning, radial topology constraints.

1 Introduction

A large class of important optimization problems has yet no reasonably fast and robust algorithmic solution: large-scale network planning problems belong to such class when the objective function is non-convex. Network planning comprehend a set of different problems whose solutions are subsets of arcs from a given graph. Those are important problems in fields like electric power and gas distribution, and telecommunications. The problem differences rely on the solution topology requisites.

Network planning has been approached in the past by mathematical programming. Branch-and-bound applications can be found in [1-3]. Mixed-integer programming approaches can be found in [4], together with Bender's decomposition [5], and with branch-exchange [6]. Tabu search [7], simulated annealing [8], and dynamic programming [9] approaches have also been taken. More recently, evolutionary techniques have also been proposed [10-12]. A motivation to take evolutionary approaches comes from the possibility to address complex objectives—the objective function is sometimes difficult to define as well behaved. However for large networks the combinatorial nature of decision-making precludes the canonical genetic algorithm (cGA) approaches. In the following we will spring out some difficulties related with the canonical string genotype (in §2). We will notice that the string genotype approach is not adequate to represent network topological relationships. A new genotype information structure is then proposed together with a recombination algorithm (in §3). In the proposed genotype approach the problem topological requisites are genetically transmitted by recombination. Illustration is provided in §4.

2 Problem Formulation and the cGA Difficulties

Many of the real-world network planning problems are characterized, as an optimization problems, by (1) a non-convex non-separable objective function of the arc decisions, and (2) topological constraints like radiality and connectivity. Take (q) as a possible subproblem formulation.

(q)   minimize $f(T)$ over all $T \in \mathbf{R}(G)$

     where
             f: objective function
            G: set of graph arcs
            T: set of tree arcs
      $\mathbf{R}(G)$: space of radial trees for graph G

The (q) problem can be stated as connecting all nodes by selecting a spanning tree T (out of graph G) to minimize f. In the following we refer to network planning as a (q)-like problem. For several reasons, such as simplicity of analysis and definition of genetic operators, the binary or bit string representation of solutions has dominated the genetic algorithm research. A conceivable canonical genotype approach defines a graph as an array of arcs, and takes binary bits to select the arcs to form a solution tree. However, the problem requires satisfaction of non-trivial constraints, such as radiality and connectivity, which the canonical crossover cannot transmit to the offspring. We point out two difficulties for the canonical approach.

D1. Topological properties such as connectivity and radiality are not genetically transmitted to the descendants by one-point crossover—the descendant populations get a significant number of non-feasible solutions.

D2. Important similarities about solutions can hardly propagate by crossover—the one-point crossover operator destroys meaningful network building-blocks, as graph adjacent arcs are generally impossible to place close to each other in a string.

D1 have been reported before [12]: corrective procedures are possible if non-feasible solutions are rare occurrences, which is not the current case. D2 have not been reported in such a context, although it represents a crucial obstacle to the success of large-scale optimization processes [13,14]. One could think of improving the representation by developing a complex coding function. However, that is difficult to do without introducing non-linearities or other kind of bias search into the process

[14,15]. We use a more natural problem-related representation, described in the following.

3 Evolutionary Approach

We take a genotype space to be a partially ordered set $(A, \leq)$ [16], i.e. a set where: (*i*) $a \leq a$; (*ii*) $a \leq b$ and $b \leq a$ implies $a = b$; (*iii*) $a \leq b$ and $b \leq c$ implies $a \leq c$, for every $a, b, c \in A$. The element a is called the *direct precedent* of the element b in A, iff: (*i*) $a \neq b$; (*ii*) $a \leq b$; (*iii*) there is no element $c \in A$ such that $a \leq c$ and $c \leq b$. The relation is denoted by $b \lrcorner a$. Similarly, an element b is called the *direct follower* of an element a in A, iff a is one of its direct precedents.

Trees are particular partially ordered sets: each tree element is directly preceded by one and just one single element; an exception is made for the first element (tree root), which is not preceded. Take g as a tree T genotype coding function.

$$g : T \rightarrow \{b \lrcorner a : \forall \text{arc}(ab) \in T \text{ with } a \leq b\}$$

Suppose we want to change tree information by changing T elements direct precedence. If we want to keep T as a partially ordered set after the change, we must guarantee that the three above mentioned properties (i), (ii) and (iii) hold for elements precedence changing. If the properties hold, we say the change is *consistent*. Let $p(b)$ be the b direct precedence element in T, and $F(b)$ be the set of b direct followings elements in T. Take Lemma 1 to identify non-consistent changes.

Lemma 1. A b direct-precedence change $b \lrcorner a$ taken over a tree ordered set (T) violates order (*i-ii-iii*) iff $b \leq a$.
Proof: Sufficiency — If $b \leq a$ there exists in T a direct ordered sequence like, $a \lrcorner x \lrcorner y \lrcorner ... \lrcorner b$. A change $b \lrcorner a$ forces a circulation $a \lrcorner x \lrcorner y \lrcorner ... \lrcorner b \lrcorner a$, and thus an order violation (property-*ii*). *Necessity* — If $b \leq a$ does not apply, either (1) $a \leq b$, or (2) no order exists between a and b. In case (1), a change $b \lrcorner a$ eliminates the order relationships between every $x : a \leq x \leq b$ and $y : b \leq y$ by eliminating the existent b-precedence. The x-elements order is not changed, they remain as followers of a. Similarly for the y-elements, they remain as followers of b, and by change $b \lrcorner a$, also followers of a. In case (2), a change $b \lrcorner a$ forces b to become a follower of a, and thus every $y : b \leq y$ become a follower of a, instead of being a follower of the existing $p(b)$.
□

Lemma 1 permits to classify precedence changes as consistent or non-consistent. When consistent, precedence changing is a possible way to change tree information guaranteeing network radiality and connectivity. Moreover, information can be easily changed in a simple exchanging procedure over the set of precedence elements, i.e. the genotype. Precedence change resolves D1.

It is known that a recombination procedure must be able to interchange important similarities about solutions (meaningful building blocks)[14]. A tree meaningful building-block is a set of adjacent arcs: a possible simple one is a path between two network elements (nodes), i.e. a sequence of direct precedence relationships. As a sequence of precedence changes, a path can be successfully submitted to a tree. Note that a path should not be rejected just because some of the constituent precedence relationships fall, as isolated, into the conditions of Lemma 1: a path is not just a set but a partially ordered set, and thus precedence change consistency must be also tested orderly. Path interchange resolves D2.

Path interchange algorithm
(Submit a path P to a tree T)
Denote by $F(x \in P)$ the set of followers of x in the path P. Name a the path smallest element ($a \leq x \; \forall x \in P$).

Step 1. Change T by changing every x-precedence to $x \llcorner a$ iff (i) $x \in F(a \in P)$ and (ii) $x \llcorner a$ is consistent.

Step 2. Update T, and repeat Step 1 taking $F(a \in P)$ as the followers of x elements, i.e. $F(a \in P) = \cup F(x \in P)$.

□

Recombination algorithm
(Interchange paths between solutions T^i and T^{ii})

Step 1. Randomly select two nodes, a and b.

Step 2. Find the paths P^i and P^{ii} between a and b: P^i in T^i and P^{ii} in T^{ii}.

Step 3. Submit P^i to T^{ii}, and P^{ii} to T^i.
□

Recombination example
(Recombination of solutions T^i and T^{ii})
Solutions T^i and T^{ii} are represented in Fig 1 (a) and (b) respectively. The descendants are represented in (c) and (d) respectively. P is the path between the two randomly selected element b and d. Take a as the solutions smallest element. The procedure is summarized in the following:

Step 1. Represent the solutions as tree ordered sets
$T^i = \{c \llcorner a, b \llcorner c, d \llcorner c, e \llcorner d, f \llcorner e\}$ and $T^{ii} = \{b \llcorner a, e \llcorner a, c \llcorner e, d \llcorner e, f \llcorner e\}$ and the paths P^i in T^i and P^{ii} in T^{ii} as $P^i = \{b \llcorner c, d \llcorner c\}$ and $P^{ii} = \{b \llcorner a, e \llcorner a, d \llcorner e\}$

Step 2. Submit $P^i = \{b \llcorner c, d \llcorner c\}^i$ to $T^{ii} = \{b \llcorner a, e \llcorner a, c \llcorner e, d \llcorner e, f \llcorner e\}$
Element c is the path P^i smallest element. $F(c) = \{b, d\}$. Both $b \llcorner c$ and $d \llcorner c$ are consistent changes in T^{ii} as no order relation exists between such pairs. Changing precedence results in the tree $\{b \llcorner c, e \llcorner a, c \llcorner e, d \llcorner c, f \llcorner e\}$.
Submit $P^{ii} = \{b \llcorner a, e \llcorner a, d \llcorner e\}$ to $T^i = \{c \llcorner a, b \llcorner c, d \llcorner c, e \llcorner d, f \llcorner e\}$. Element a is the path P^{ii} smallest element. $F(a) = \{b, e\}$. Both $b \llcorner a$ and $e \llcorner a$ are consistent changes as in T^i: $a \leq b$ and $a \leq e$. Changing precedence results in the tree update $\{c \llcorner a, b \llcorner a, d \llcorner c, e \llcorner a, f \llcorner e\}$. Only element e has a follower in P^{ii}: $F(e) = d$. The change $d \llcorner e$ is now consistent (note that it was not before the update). The change results in the tree $\{c \llcorner a, b \llcorner a, d \llcorner e, e \llcorner a, f \llcorner e\}$.

□

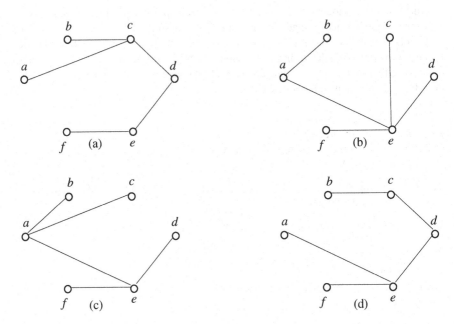

Fig. 1. Solutions T^i and T^{ii} are represented in (**a**) and (**b**) respectively. The descendants are represented in (**c**) and (**d**) respectively. Descendants result from path interchange between elements b and d.

4   Illustration

We take a complete graph problem as a theoretical example—it maximizes building-block diversity over a fixed number of nodes. That makes the correct combination of building-blocks unlikely as a random event. We took G as a 10 nodes-45 arcs complete graph. To better illustrate the rule of recombination we produce a favorable environment for the discrimination of the best building-blocks: we took f to guarantee a small building-block cost variance, or so-called small *collateral noise* [17] ($f(T) < f(T')$ for every: T with N correct arcs; and T' with N-1 correct arcs). Convergence is illustrated in Fig 2-a,b.

We also took a canonical approach to address the same problem, Fig 3-a,b. Note that for the canonical approach feasibility (i.e. radiality and connectivity) can drop considerably in the process. The results concern a 60 solutions population, and non-elitist binary tournament selection [18]. We did not use mutation.

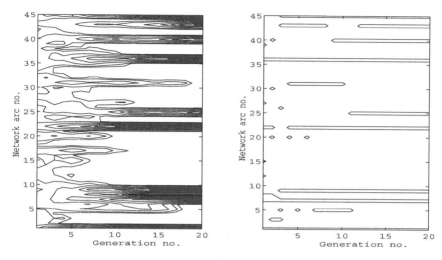

Fig. 2. Evolution of the genotypes along 20 generations: convergence to the optimum (proposed approach). Plots of contour lines show the evolution of arcs-frequency along generations. The inner lines refer to a higher frequency. (a) Full population—note that in the first generations all arcs are present with a low frequency. In the last generations only nine arcs are present, with a high frequency. (b) Best solution—note that the optimal solution is found after 12 generations (four correct arcs in gen-1, five in gen-2, six in gen-3, seven in gen-4, eight in gen-11, and all nine arcs in gen-12)

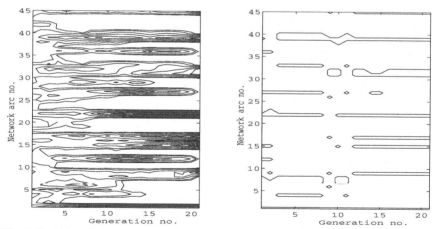

Fig. 3. Evolution of the genotypes along 21 generations: convergence to a non-optimum (cGA approach). Plots of contour lines show the evolution of arcs-frequency along generations. (a) Full population—note that (1) the population presents an important number of solutions with optimal arcs (36,40) at the latest 10 generations, and (2) those are not present in the last-generation solution (they are lost). (b) Best solution—the optimal solution is not found. The cGA is not able to find a solution with more optimal-arcs: the best first-generation solution presents four correct arcs (1,7,22,36), as well as the best last-generation one (1,9,22,45)

The results illustrate some differences between the proposed genotype approach and the string canonical one. Namely, that the optimum is found by the proposed approach after 12 generation, and that the canonical approach was unable to make any solution improvement in 21 generations, despite having access to important number of easy-to-discriminate building-blocks. These show how GA performance can be enhanced by effectively combining important solution building-blocks and ensuring feasibility.

5 Conclusion

We reported key specificities of the taken genotype space and recombination algorithm involved in the development of an evolutionary approach to radial topology constrained problems. The major innovations of our proposal are that: (1) the tree genotype information be taken as a partially ordered set of nodes instead of taken as an array of arcs; and (2) the recombination process be to change network path information between trees instead of swapping string segments between solutions.

References

1. R. N. Adams and M. A. Laughton 'Optimal Planning of Power Networks using Mixed-integer Programming Part 1—Static and time-phased network synthesis' *Proceedings IEE*, Vol 121, No 2 , 1974, pp. 139-148
2. G. T. Boardman and C. C. Meckiff 'A Branch-and-Bound Formulation to an Electricity Distribution Planning Problem' *IEEE Trans. PAS,* Vol 104, No 8, 1985, pp. 2112-2118
3. R. H. Jan, F. J. Hwang, S.T. Cheng, 'Topological Optimization of a Communication Network Subject to a Reliability Contsraint' *IEEE Trans. Reliability*, Vol. 42, 1993, pp. 63-70.
4. M. A. El-Kady 'Computer-aided Planning of Distribution Substation and Primary Feeders *IEEE Trans. PAS,* Vol 103, No 6, 1984, pp. 1183-1189
5. N. Kagan and R. N. Adams 'Application of Benders Decomposition Technique to the Distribution Planning Problem' *Proc. 10th Power System Computation Conference,* Graz, Austria, 1990
6. G. J. Peponis and M. P. Papadopoulos 'New Dynamic, Branch Exchange Method for Optimal Distribution System Planning' *IEE Proc. Gener. Transm. Distrib.,* Vol 144, No 3, 1997, pp. 333-339
7. F. Glover, M. Lee, J Ryan, 'Least-cost Network Topology Design for a New Service: An Application of a Tabu Search', *Ann. Oper. Research,* Vol 33, 1991, pp. 351-362
8. S. Pierre, M.-A. Hyppolite, J.-M. Bourjolly, O. Dioume, 'Topology Design of Computer Communication Networks Using Simulated Annealing', *Eng. Application Artificial Intelligence,* Vol 8, 1995, pp. 61-69

Solving Radial Topology Constrained Problems with Evolutionary Algorithms   65

9. J. Partanen 'A Modified Dynamic Programming Algorithm for Sizing, Locating, and Timing of Feeder Reinforcements', *IEEE Trans. Power Delivery,* Vol 5, No 1, 1990, pp. 277-283.

10. V. Miranda, J. V. Ranito, L. M. Proença, 'Genetic Algorithms in Optimal Multistage Distribution Networks Planning', *IEEE Trans. Power Systems,* Vol 9, No 4, 1994, pp. 1927-1933.

11. P. M. S. Carvalho L. A F. M. Ferreira F. G. Lobo and L. M. F. Barruncho 'Optimal Distribution Network Expansion Planning Under Uncertainty by Evolutionary Decision Convergence', *International Journal of Electrical Power & Energy Systems* (Special Issue on PSCC' 96), Vol. 20, No. 2, 1998, pp. 125-129.

12. Berna Dengiz, F. Altiparmak, Alice E. Smith, 'Local Search Genetic Algorithm for Optimal Design of Reliabe Networks', *IEEE Trans. Evolutionary Computation,* Vol 1, No. 3, 1997, pp. 179-188.

13. Z. Michalewicz, *'Genetic Algorithms + Data Structures = Evolution Programs'*, (Berlin, Germany: Spriger, 1996).

14. D. E. Goldberg, *Genetic Algorithms in Search Optimization and Machine Learning,* (Reading, MA, Addison-Wesley, 1989).

15. Thomas Bäck, Ulrich Hammel, Hans-Paul Schwefel, 'Evolutionary Computation: Comments on the History and Current State', *IEEE Trans. Evolutionary Computation,* Vol 1, No 1, 1997, pp. 3-17

16. Seymour Lipschutz, *General Topology*, McGraw-Hill (1965).

17. D. E. Goldberg, K. Deb and J. H. Clark 'Genetic Algorithms, Noise and the Sizing of Populations', *Complex Systems*, 6, 1992, pp. 333-362

18. D. E. Goldberg and K. Deb 'A Comparative Analysis of Selection Schemes Used in Genetic Algorithms' pp. 69-93 in *Foundations of Genetic Algorithms,* edited by G. Rawlins (San Mateo, CA, Morgan Kaufman, 1991).

Automating Space Allocation in Higher Education

E.K. Burke, D.B. Varley[12]

Automated Scheduling and Planning Group,
Department of Computer Science,
University of Nottingham, UK.

Abstract. The allocation of office space in any large institution is usually a problematical issue, which often demands a substantial amount of time to perform manually. The result of this allocation affects the lives of whoever makes use of the space. In the higher education sector in the UK, space is becoming an increasingly precious commodity. Student numbers have risen significantly over the last few years and as a result, university departments have grown in size. In addition, universities have come under increasing financial pressure to ensure that space is utilized as efficiently and effectively as possible. However, space utilization is only one issue to take into account when measuring whether or not a particular allocation is of a sufficient high quality. The problem of space allocation is further complicated by the fact that no standard procedure is practiced throughout the higher education sector. Most institutions have their own standards and requirements, which are often very different to other institutions. Different levels of authority control the domains of rooms and resources in different institutions. The most common situation is where a central university office controls a number of faculties, each managing a number of departments. This paper will focus specifically on applying optimization methods to departmental room allocation for non-residential space in the higher education sector. It will look at the use of three methods (hill-climbing, simulated annealing and genetic algorithms) to automatically generate solutions to the problem. The processing power of computers and the repetitive search nature of this problem means that there is great potential for the automation of this process. The paper will conclude by discussing and comparing these methods and showing how they cope with a highly constrained problem.

Keywords. Space Allocation, Hill-Climbing, Simulated Annealing, Genetic Algorithms

1. Introduction

The problem of space allocation affects the lives of almost everyone in some way or another, whether it is the size or layout of their office or work environment, limited parking space or even the organisation of their homes. This paper will deal with the problem of efficiently allocating space within academic institutions.

As student numbers increase and university departments expand, there is significant pressure on estate managers and departmental heads to ensure space is utilised as efficiently as possible. Due to the varied requirements and constraints, this task is not simple. Obtaining just an acceptable solution often takes a large amount of man-hours.

---

[1] The author's names are listed in alphabetical order

There have been few papers which have addressed the problem of space allocation within academic institutions. Giannikos et al.[1] states that space allocation has received little attention in their paper on using goal programming for academic space allocation. Rizman et al.[2] presented a goal programming model to reassign 144 offices for 289 staff members at the Ohio State University. At a facilities level, Benjamin et al.[3] used the Analytical Hierarchy Process to determine the layout of a new computer laboratory at the University of Missouri-Rolla.

The size of the space allocation process is related to the number of resources that need to be allocated and the number of rooms available. In the education sector, sizes vary from 1600 rooms in 30 buildings to 20000 rooms in 600 buildings[4].

The organisation of most working environments exhibits specific structural properties, such as members of staff being grouped into departments. As such the large problem of university wide space allocation lends itself well to decomposition. This allows us to partition the problem into smaller clusters, which it is possible to deal with in a reasonable time-scale. In real life, the domain of rooms and resources within a university are managed by differing authorities, with each level managing a subset of the overall domain. These authorities may be at different levels of abstraction with a central authority administrating the whole domain. All this occurs with communication between the different levels, with lower levels regularly requesting more space and competing with other groups on the same level. It is a continually evolving problem, made more difficult by the addition and/or removal of resources/rooms all the time.

The actual allocation of resources to areas of space happens in two ways. The first being the initial allocation of a set of resources to a group of empty rooms. The second being the addition or removal of resources from a previous allocation. This paper will concentrate on the first problem of allocating resources to empty rooms, as all the principles discussed in the first problem hold for the second.

2. The Space Allocation Process

There are two different levels to the problem of space allocation, a space utilisation level and a constraint satisfaction/optimisation level.

2.1   Space Utilisation

The main requirement for the higher education sector is to find working space for all staff and students. This involves allocating specific areas/rooms for each individual resource. The amount of space required is dependent on the level, numbers and functionality of each resource. Space guidelines are published by the various education authorities and are used within this decision process. However, it is usual for universities to adapt these guidelines to suit their own requirements. The Full Time Education (FTE) 1987-space standards are the most widely adapted guidelines, with square metre values for each type of resource.

With a listing of all-available rooms and sizes, a listing of all resources, their type (e.g. Professor, Lecture Hall, Secretary, etc.) and these space guidelines it is possible to allocate resources to rooms while attempting to maximise the utilisation of the rooms.

The problem is complicated by the fact that not all resources are capable of sharing rooms with other resources, a majority actually requiring their own rooms. The problem then is to maximise the utilisation of the rooms without violating any of the sharing limitations.

2.2 Constraint Satisfaction

The most efficient utilisation of space is one which allocates all resources while minimising the amount of rooms and space wasted by these resources. However, space utilisation is simply the first part of an efficient space allocation process. There are additional constraints which need to be taken into account:

- **Resource specific requirements**
  Unique facilities that are required by certain resources impose a limit on which rooms that resource can be allocated to. For example, lecture theatres may require disabled access or Audio Visual Aid (AVA) facilities, etc. The option of modifying rooms through building work may be available, but it is more practical (and less expensive) to use rooms which already have the facilities required.
- **Ensuring grouping and close proximity of resources**
  There are two types of spatial grouping requirements: Adjacency and proximity. There is always a requirement to place resources belonging to the same group in close proximity, (e.g. members of the same department should not be widely spread over many buildings). Likewise, resources, which are highly dependent on each other, must be adjacent or at least close to each other (e.g. Wash Rooms must be adjacent to Operating Theatres etc.).
- **Ensuring distance between conflicting resources**
  This is the direct opposite to the previous requirement. It is often desirable that resources which conflict in some way should be kept at a distance from each other. For example, library space should not be located next to engineering workshops due to noise problems.

Each university will have its own constraints and opinions as to what requirements should be satisfied to make a good allocation of space.

The constraints that cause the most complexity as far as optimisation is concerned are the ones involving spatial locations. The ability to cope with these types of constraints requires information regarding the location and distance of all the rooms within the university. These graphs (fig. 1) of rooms and distances can be decomposed into subsets of buildings and floors, but even floors can hold many rooms which all require distances from each other. Obtaining this information, which is unlikely to be available at all universities, is a major task. It could be obtained through floor plans or Computer Aided Design (CAD) drawings, but would require substantial work.

To reduce the amount of information required in making decisions upon proximity information, optimisations could be made to reduce the number of proximity links between rooms such as subset grouping[5][6]. By grouping adjacent rooms together tightly and then obtaining and storing information regarding the distances of groups of rooms from each other, the amount of information can be dramatically reduced.

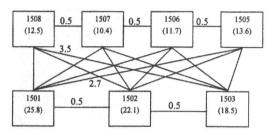

Fig. 1. Example of Room ID, size and distance information required

The same subset grouping method can be applied to the resources requiring allocation making the decision process one of overlaying the resource subsets onto the best matchin room subsets. The minimal method of satisfying proximity and adjacency constraints is t only hold information about room adjacencies, not distances. Knowing which rooms ar adjacent to each other, allows the adjacency constraints to be easily satisfied, whereas th proximity constraints can be approximated by finding out whether two rooms are linke (by following adjacencies) and by how many rooms. This method allows for compromise between excessive data gathering and constraint satisfaction and is used b the algorithms discussed in this paper.

2.3 Evaluation of the space allocation process

In order to ascertain the quality of a space allocation solution, a measure of the overall resource allocation, space utilisation and constraint satisfaction is needed. The following equation represents a generalised penalty function for any algorithmic method:

$$Penalty = \mathrm{Re}\,sourcesUnscheduled + \sum_{i=0}^{NoOfRooms-1}\left(Wastage(i) + SpacePenalties(i)\right)$$

$$+ \sum_{x=0}^{NoOf\,\mathrm{Re}\,sources-1}\;\sum_{y=0}^{NoOf\,\mathrm{Re}\,sources-1} \mathrm{Re}\,sourceConflicts(x, y)$$

Applying weights allows certain constraints to be considered to be more important than others and therefore have differing penalties associated with them. Table 1 shows the weighting functions used by the algorithms, for each of the sections of the equation above. Each constraint has an exponent and factorial weighting allowing greater versatility in applying penalties. An exponent of one represents a consistent penalty, i.e. each resource that is unscheduled increases the penalty by 5000. An exponent of greater than one represents an increasing exponential weighting depending on the size of the violation, i.e. exceeding room capacity by 2.0m² increases the penalty by 4, exceeding by 15.0m² increases the penalty by 225.

Constraint	Exponential	Factor
Resources Unscheduled – resources not allocated to rooms	1.0	5000.0
Space Wastage (per m^2) – not using full capacity of room	1.0	2.0
Space Penalties (per m^2) – exceeding room capacity	2.0	2.0
Sharing Violations – resources sharing when not allowed	1.0	2000.0
Grouping Violations – members of different groups sharing	1.0	1000.0
Adjacency Requirements – resources requiring adjacent placing	1.0	500.0
Grouping Requirements – resources requiring same/adjacent room placing	1.2	50.0
Proximity Requirements – resources requiring proximity placing	1.0	750.0

Table 1. Constraint types and penalties used in all algorithms

3. Three Methods for Automating the Problem

The methods analysed in this paper have been run using real allocation data from the School of Computer Science at the University of Nottingham. This school is moving to new premises next year due to expansion and serious space limitation of the current building, therefore this test data gives a true example of a difficult, highly constrained problem. The data consists of 83 resources, 52 rooms with 69 specific constraints. The 83 Resources consist of 1 Lecture Room, 4 Laboratories, 2 Meeting Rooms, 6 Storage Rooms, 3 Professors, 4 Senior Lecturers, 11 Lecturers, 3 Teaching Assistants, 6 Technical Staff, 8 Secretaries and 35 Researchers. The constraints consisted of 42 Resources requiring sole occupancy of a room, 7 Research groups unable to share with other groups and requiring same or adjacent rooms, 3 Secretaries needing to be adjacent/close to a manager, 3 Technical staff needing to be adjacent/proximity to laboratories/workshops and 7 Group supervisors needing to be adjacent/close to research groups.

3.1   Hill-Climbing

The hill-climbing algorithm consisted of three functions: Allocate Resource, Move Resource and Swap Rooms. Allocate resource took an unallocated resource and allocated it to a room using the appropriate fit method. Move resource took an already allocated resource and reapplied the fit method to find another room. Swap rooms took a room and swapped all the resources in that room with the resources in another. All functions chose a random source unit to work on and applied one of two fit methods to choose the target unit. The first fit method used random selection of rooms (random fit), the other chose the room with the greatest reduction in penalty (best fit).

Algorithm: Hill Climbing

1.   Evaluate Current Allocation
2.   Loop until the current allocation has not improved in n iterations
    a)   Select one of Allocate Resource, Move Resource or Swap Rooms
               in that order and apply it to produce a new allocation
    b)   Evaluate the new allocation
             i)   if it is better then make it the current allocation
             ii)   It if is not better, continue

Table 2 shows the results from 20 runs of both variations of the hill-climbing algorithm, broken down into the main groups of penalties. The average entry is a calculation of the average of all 20 runs.

Random fit managed an average utilisation of 76.5% whereas best fit managed 78.5%.

Constraints	Random Fit			Best Fit		
	Worst	**Ave**	**Best**	**Worst**	**Ave**	**Best**
Space Wastage (per m²)	997.8	929.4	508.4	553.2	540.6	512.2
Space Penalties (per m²)	5225.5	3502.4	177.9	932.5	738.9	184.2
Resource Penalties	10272.7	5544.12	500.0	8500.0	4700.0	0.0
Unscheduled Resources	10000.0	5000.0	0.0	0.0	0.0	0.0
Approx. Time Taken	1 minute 20 seconds			1 minute 6 seconds		
Total Penalty	26496.0	15538.4	1186.3	9985.7	5979.6	696.4

Table 2. Results from Hill Climbing algorithm tests

3.2   Simulated Annealing

Simulated Annealing is an extension to hill climbing, reducing the chance of converging at local optima by allowing moves to inferior solutions under the control of a temperature function $\exp(-\Delta/T) > R^7$, where Δ = the change in the evaluation function, T = the current temperature and R = a random number between 0 and 1

The initial temperature value and the rate of cooling affects how the simulated annealing algorithm performs. Through extensive tests, the combination of a 2200 initial temperature, a 300-iteration interval with a 100 decrement performed best.

The simulated annealing tests managed an average utilisation figure of 78.9%.

Constraint	2200 temp /300 interval		
	Worst	**Ave**	**Best**
Space Wastage (per m²)	555.2	507.9	475.8
Space Penalties (per m²)	695.56	281.7	0
Resource Penalties	2539.14	1307.6	0
Unscheduled Resources	0	0	0
Approx. Time Taken	7 minutes 46 seconds		
Total Penalty	3777.3	2097.2	475.8

Table 3. Results from Simulated Annealing algorithm tests

3.3   A simple Genetic Algorithm

Genetic algorithms (GA's) use progressive generations of potential solutions and through Selection, Crossover and Mutation, aim to evolve solutions to the problem through the principles of evolutionary survival of the fittest.

The GA in this paper consisted of a data encoding structured so that each gene represents a room, with a linked list of all the resources allocated to that room.

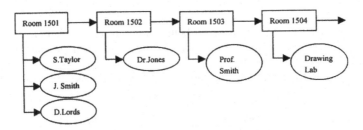

Fig. 2. Graphical representation of Genetic Algorithm encoding

The Roulette-Wheel method was used in the Selection process and the Mutation operator simply moved a resource from one room to another. However, the Crossover operator required more consideration as the standard methods frequently result in invalid solutions, i.e. a resource being allocated to two rooms. The method implemented into the GA involved checking each room in the parents and where both parents had the same resource-to-room allocation, copy that to the child. Otherwise, take a resource-to-room mapping from one parent, as long as that resource has not already been allocated.

The GA was tested with various population sizes and with various initial populations, the first of random room allocations, the second using the best fit hill climbing algorithm and the last using the simulated annealing (S.A.) algorithm. Table 4 summarises the results for a population size of 50, using elitism to ensure the best result so far is not lost.

Constraints	Best in Initial Population			Best Individual after GA run		
	Random	**Best Fit**	**S.A.**	**Random**	**Best Fit**	**S.A.**
Space Wastage (per m^2)	997.8	725.6	536.0	733.2	725.6	536.0
Space Penalties (per m^2)	3265.7	254.6	234.2	1532.5	254.6	234.2
Resource Penalties	40251.3	1265.5	500.0	7565.3	1265.5	500.0
Unscheduled Resources	15000.0	0.0	0.0	0.0	0.0	0.0
Total Penalty	59514.8	2245.7	1270.2	9831.0	2245.7	1270.2

Table 4. Results from Genetic Algorithm tests

4. Conclusions

The analysis of the figures for the space utilisation layers throughout the tests shows exactly how the different requirements and constraints of the space allocation problem conflict and work against each other. The more highly constrained a problem is, the less likely it is to ensure an acceptable level of utilisation. The methods analysed show that the automation of this process can help balance utilisation and constraint satisfaction.

Applying a polynomial-time approximation scheme bin packing algorithm[8] on the problem showed how the additional constraints affect the space utilisation. Removing all the constraints except the space wastage and space penalty constraints, allowed the binpacking algorithm to obtain 97% utilisation. Applying the sharing constraints reduced this to 82.5%. This related to the other three methods (taking into account the constraints), managed around 76-79%.

On the full space allocation problem, the three methods all performed in a reasonably acceptable manner. The Simulated Annealing algorithm performed the best with a minimum penalty of 475.8 allocating all 83 resources with zero room capacity penalties and zero resource penalties, and a small variation between worst and best. Random Fit Hill Climbing performed the worst with an approximately 25309.7 penalty variation between best and worst. In this case, 10000 was the penalty for being unable to allocate two of the 83 resources. Best Fit Hill Climbing performs better with a 9289.3 variation, never failing to allocate all 83 resources. However, Best Fit still has problems allocating all those resources without exceeding room capacities. These results, specifically the variations in best to worst, emphasise the benefit of simulated annealing over hill-climbing methods which regularly get stuck in local optima.

The results however, are offset by the amount of time taken by each method. The hill climbing methods took around 1 minute to finish, whereas the simulated annealing method took nearer 8 minutes. Improvements on the simulated annealing algorithm can be obtained by halving the cooling interval to 150. This results in a negligible increase in the average result (+839.7) and an approx. 50% reduction in time taken

The genetic algorithm managed to obtain reasonable results from the random initialisation data, however, it failed to improve on the hill-climbing and simulated annealing initialised populations. Variations on the operators used may produce more productive results, specifically the crossover operator. It may prove effective to rely completely on the mutation operator or a combination of mutation operators, as crossover consistently required more work to ensure legal solutions are produced.

Further work is required to analyse potential improvements from further testing, specifically the possible hybridisation of the three methods with each other and with other methods such as Tabu-Search.

5. References

1. I Giannikos, E El-Darzi and P Lees, *An Integer Goal Programming Model to Allocate Offices to Staff in an Academic Institution* in the Journal of the Operational Research Society Vol. 46 No. 6. 713-720.
2. L Rizman, J Bradford and R Jacobs, *A Multiple Objective Approach to Space Planning for Academic Facilities* in the Journal of Management Science, Vol 25. 895-906.
3. C Benjamin, I Ehie and Y Omurtag, *Planning Facilities at the University of Missouri-Rolia.* Journal of Interfaces, Vol. 22 No. 4. 95-105.
4. EK Burke and DB Varley. *An Analysis of Space Allocation in British Universities,* in Practice and Theory of Automated Timetabling It, Lecture Notes in Computer Science 1048, Springer-Verlag 1998. Pg 20-33
5. KB Yoon. *A Constraint Model of Space Planning.* Topics in Engineering Vol. 9, Computation Mechanics Publications, Southampton, UK.
6. F Glover, C McMillan and B Novick, *Interactive Decision Software and Computer Graphics for Architectural and Space Planning,* Annals of Operations Research 5, Scientific Publishing Company, 1985.
7. E Rich and K Knight, *Artificial Intelligence,* international Second Edition, McGraw-Hill, Ine, 1991. Pg. 71.
8. S Martello, P Toth. *Knapsack Problems.. Algorithms and Computer Implementations.* Wiley Interscience Series in Discrete Mathematics and Optimization. Pg. 50-52

Application of Genetic Algorithm and k-Nearest Neighbour Method in Medical Fraud Detection

Hongxing He[1], Warwick Graco[1], and Xin Yao[2]

[1] Health Insurance Commission, 134 Reed Street, P. O. Box 1001 Tuggeranong ACT 2900, Australia
[2] School of Computer Science, University College, University of New South Wales, ACT 2600, Australia

Abstract. K-nearest neighbour (KNN) algorithm in combination with a genetic algorithm were applied to a medical fraud detection problem. The genetic algorithm was used to determine the optimal weighting of the features used to classify General Practitioners (GP) practice pro"les. The weights were used in the KNN algorithm to identify the nearest neighbour practice pro"les and then two rules (i.e. the majority rule and the Bayesian rule) were applied to determine the classi"cations of the practice pro"les. The results indicate that this classi"cation methodology achieved good generalisation in classifying GP practice pro"les in a test dataset. This opens the way towards its application in the medical fraud detection at Health Insurance Commission (HIC).

1 Introduction

The Health Insurance Commission (HIC) of Australia is responsible for administering the Medicare Program for the Federal Government. Medicare provides basic medical cover for all Australian citizens and residents and in Financial Year 1995/96 it dollar paid benefits of 6.014 billion. The HIC has a responsibility to protect the public purse and ensure that taxpayers' funds are spent wisely on health care.

The HIC uses a number of supervised-learning systems to classify the practice profiles of practitioners who participate in Medicare to help identify those who are practising inappropriately and those who are involved in fraudulent practice. Inappropriate practice includes those who are over-servicing their patients by performing more services than is necessary for their medical condition or who see their patients more often than is warranted. Fraudulent practice includes claiming for services not performed or mis-itemising services to attract a higher benefit. An example is up-coding where a practitioner charged for a long consultation when a short consultation was conducted with a patient.

One or more expert consultants, who are pre-eminent in the speciality, such as GP, are used to identify features, or indicators, which discriminate between good and bad practice in the speciality for which supervised-learning system is developed. Once the features are selected, the consultants then classify the practice profiles of a sample of practitioners from the speciality using a risk classification scale ranging from a high risk profile to a low risk one. The classified sample is then used to train the supervised-learning system.

One challenge the HIC faces is to achieve a high level of unanimity between the classifications given by the supervised-learning system and those given by the one or more expert consultants. This is necessary to ensure that the system emulates the judgements of human experts by learning the classified patterns in the training data set. The results of the supervised-learning system are likely to be ignored if they tend to be inconsistent with those the expert. The HIC has tested different supervised-learning techniques [6,3,5] for classifying practitioners' practice profiles to see which ones give the highest agreement rates between machine-based judgements and those of human experts. The results of these studies revealed that no one supervised-learning system (e.g. rule based versus backpropagation neural network) was clearly superior to the others. One method that can be used to improve the classifications given by various supervised learning techniques is the genetic algorithm. Genetic algorithms are ideal for optimisation problems and can be applied to improve the matches between the classifications of a system and those of human experts. The aim of this research was conducted to see to what extent using a genetic algorithm to optimise the weights of features improves the classifications of a supervised-learning system above that obtained from using equally weighted features.

Genetic algorithms have been used in conjunction with other supervised-learning methods[6,3,5]. In this study a genetic algorithm is applied to improve the classifications obtained using a K-nearest neighbour (KNN) algorithm. The KNN was selected for this study because it is a widely used profile-matching technique and it bases its classifications of each case on those of its nearest neighbours using different decision rules. Two rules are examined with this study and they include the majority rule and the Bayesian rule. These rules are tested to see what effect they have on the classifications of cases, while the genetic algorithm is applied to find the optimal, or near, optimal weights for each features using the distance metric employed in this study.

A sample of GP's practice profiles is used in the research. GPs are responsible for the primary medical care of patients and account for two-thirds of the general population of medical practitioners in Australia. The aim of this paper is to report the results obtained using the KNN algorithm in combination with a genetic algorithm to classify GP practice profiles.

2   Methodology

Each GP practice profile contains a number of features which summarises aspects of a GP's practice over a year. An example is the total number of medical services performed in a year. As described previously, the features were selected by one or more expert consultants based on ability of the features to discriminate between good and bad GP practice. For legal and professional reasons it is not possible to list the features used to identify practitioners who are practising inappropriately. There were 28 features used in the GPs' practice profiles reported in this study.

Each GP profile was given a risk classification of either 1 or 2 by the consultants with 1 signifying a high-risk profile and 2 a low-risk profile. A sample of 1500 GP profiles from a HIC database was selected and divided into three data sets including a training set, a validation set and a test set. The profiles in the training set were used to provide nearest neighbour examples to train the KNN classifier. The validation set was used to optimise the weight values and the test set was used to test the generalisation of the trained KNN classifier. The training set consisted of 738 profiles, validation set 380 profiles and test set 382 profiles.

The statistic used to gauge the effectiveness of the KNN classifier and variants was the agreement rate which is simply the percentage agreement between the classifications of the expert consultants and classifications of the KNN classifier divided by the total number of cases in the dataset.

3   K-Nearest Neighbour Classification Technique

The K Nearest Neighbour classification[1,2] of a sample is made on the basis of the classifications of the selected number of k neighbours. The following two methods were used in this study to decide the classification of nearest neighbouring GP practice profiles using the KNN algorithm:

3.1   Majority Rule:

The classification of the nearest neighbours was decided by the number of class 1 (n_1) compared to the number of class 2 (n_2) of all k nearest neighbours. If $n_1 > n_2$ then the classification was 1 and visa versa for situations where $n_2 > n_1$. To avoid situations where $n_1 = n_2$, the value k was selected as an odd number.

3.2   Bayesian Rule:

The classification of a sample was based on the Bayes rule. With this approach, a normal probability distribution function was applied in the neighbourhood of each nearest neighbours whose identification is assigned:

$$P_i^1(x_i, x) = e^{-d(x_i,x)/2\sigma^2} \qquad (1)$$

$$P_i^2(x_i, x) = 0$$

if sample at x_i is class 1

$$P_i^1(x_i, x) = 0$$

$$P_i^2(x_i, x) = e^{-d(x_i,x)/2\sigma^2}$$

if sample at x_i is class 2, where $P_i^k(x_i, x)$ is the probability being class k at position x given classification at site i. The x and x_i are position vectors in multi-dimensional space. The $d(x, x_i)$ is the squared weighted distance between two positions and is calculated as follows:

$$d(x, y) = \sum_{j=1}^{n} w_j^2 (x_j - y_j)^2 \tag{2}$$

where n is the number of features, w_j is the weight of the jth feature. The probability of being class 1 or class 2 at site x given the known k nearest neighbours' classification is as follows:

$$P^1(x) = \frac{M_1(x)}{M_1(x) + M_2(x)} \tag{3}$$

$$P^2(x) = \frac{M_2(x)}{M_1(x) + M_2(x)}$$

where $M_1(x)$ and $M_2(x)$ are defined as follows:

$$M_1(x) = P_1 \sum_{i=1}^{K} P_i^1(x_i, x) \tag{4}$$

$$M_2(x) = P_2 \sum_{i=1}^{K} P_i^2(x_i, x)$$

where P_1 and P_2 are the probability of being class 1 and 2 respectively.

Because of the number of features used, intuitively it can be seen that the importance of the features cannot be the same and therefore it is inappropriate to use Euclidean or other distance measures which give the equal weighting to all features. Therefore different weights were applied to the features in the distance equation (equation 2) and the optimal values were derived using a genetic algorithm.

4   Genetic algorithm

The genetic algorithm developed by John Holland and associates[4] at the University of Michigan is a search algorithm based on the mechanics of natural selection. The algorithm is used for searching for the optimal, or near optimal, solution in a multi-dimensional space using Darwinian natural selection. In this study the genetic algorithm was used in the following manner:

4.1   Selection

At each iteration, two individuals in the population were selected to produce two offspring for the next generation. In what is called the 'steady state' approach to generating offspring, the population was kept static with most individuals retained in the next generation and only two individuals were replaced by two created offspring. The two new individuals were created through crossovers and mutations from two parent individuals. Crossovers and mutations used in this study are explained later below in subsections b and c. The two individuals that were replaced were the least optimal ones in the total population.

The selection of the parent individuals was random with the optimal ones having a higher probability of being selected than the less optimal ones. To do this, the whole population of offspring was ranked in ascending order in terms of their cost function value. The derivation of the cost function is explained later below in subsection d. A geometric series was created with common factor q. With total population N, the series was as follows:

$$a, aq, aq^2, ...aq^{N-1}(q < 1) \quad \text{where} \quad a = \frac{1-q}{1-q^N} \tag{5}$$

The probability of selecting the most optimal individual is a, the second is aq and the third aq2 and similar. This selection procedure favoured the more optimal strings being selected for reproduction.

4.2   Crossover

In the crossover, the two new individuals were formed using both parents which had been selected in the selection process. The n1 weight values from one individual father individual) and n - n1 from another individual (mother individual) were selected. The n1 was chosen randomly. The crossover procedure ensured that the new individuals took some values of weights from the father individual and some from the mother individual.

4.3   Mutation

After two offspring were formed, the small changes in values of selected parameters were added or subtracted. Weight value for each feature had a certain probability of being changed. The extend of the change x was decided by a random number which had a normal probability distribution as shown in equation 6 with a mean value μ and deviation

$$P(x) = e^{-\frac{(x-\mu)^2}{2\sigma^2}} \tag{6}$$

4.4   Cost Function

The cost function was defined as the number of mis-classified cases Nmis plus a
regularisation term which is used to avoid the problem of in"ation of the weights.
The cost function is shown in equation 7:

$$F = N_{mis} + \sum_{i=1}^{n} w_i^2 \qquad (7)$$

where the constant a is the regularisation coe cient, wi (i = 1, 2, ...n) are
the weights for all n features.

The data sets are normalised to be between 0.0 and 1.0 so that all features
used will follow to the same range. The parameters used in the genetic algorithm
and k nearest neighbour are as follows:

The ratio of geometric sequences used for selection of parents in equation (5)
is q = 0.8. Values m and s in normal distribution for mutation in equation (6)
are 0.2 and 1 respectively, and the mutation probability is 0.5.

The values m and s for normal distribution used in Bayesian rule in equation
(1) are 0.0 and 0.5 respectively.

5   Results

The results of using a genetic algorithm combined with the KNN for classifying
general practitioners' practice profiles are listed in the table 1. The results are
the average over 50 runs where each run terminate at the 2000th generation. The
last column lists the agreement rate using Euclidean distance with all weights
are equal to 1. The common difference for the series is taken as three. The graph
in Figure 1 depicts the cost reduction process for a run using k = 3 and Bayes'
rule in making the decision.

Number nearest neighbour	Regularisation Coe cient	Decision Rule	Agreement Rate Validation	Agreement Rate Test Dataset	Agreement Rate Test Dataset Euclidean Distance
1	0	Nearest Neighbour	83.16	76.96	69.1
3	0	Majority Rule	83.68	73.82	69.37
3	0.1	Majority Rule	83.95	78.8	69.37
3	0.2	Majority Rule	83.16	76.44	69.37
3	0.3	Majority Rule	83.95	76.18	69.37
3	0.1	Bayes Rule	82.63	75.39	70.68
3	0.1	Bayes Rule	83.16	78.27	70.68
5	0.2	Majority Rule	82.63	77.49	71.21

Table 1. The results of a series of runs using genetic algorithm and KNN.

The results shown in Table 1 an Figure 1 indicate that:

The KNN using the weights optimised by using a genetic algorithm improves the classification results using the Euclidean distance.

High agreement rates were obtained using the KNN with both the majority and the Bayes' rules for the validation dataset. The obtained agreement rates were in the range of 82 to 84 percent regardless of the number of nearest neighbours selected and regardless of the regularisation coe cient used.

The genetic algorithm was very e cient in this application with only 2000 generation needed to achieve desired agreement rate for the validation dataset.

The agreement rates with the test dataset were in the range of 73 to 79 percent with some variations in results for different classification rules. The best result of 78.8 percent agreement rate was obtained with the majority rule using three neighbours with regularisation. The worst result of 73.82 percent agreement rate was obtained with the majority rule without regularisation. These results are better than those obtained with the features having the equal weights.

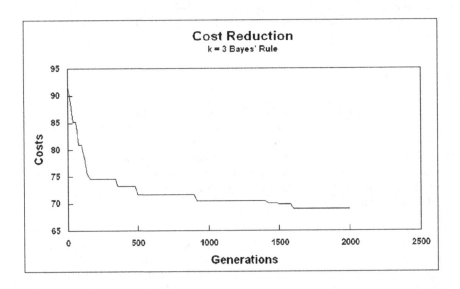

Fig. 1. An Example of the Cost Reduction as a Result of Training Using k = 3 and Bayes Rule.

6   Discussion

The results show that the genetic algorithm is very effective in finding a near optimal set of weights for the KNN classifier. The results also show that the addition of the regularisation term in the cost function helps to prevent large values being derived for variable weights, as shown by the test dataset results which show good generalisation from the validation dataset using genetically trained weights with KNN. The other factors, such as the number of nearest neighbours and the classification rule, do not appear to be critical in improving the classification results.

The agreement rates for the KNN used in combination with a genetic algorithm are comparable to those obtained from using a ripple-down rule and other approaches to classify GP practice profiles.[6] For example, the agreement rates for the KNN were in the range of 73 to 79 percent, while those for the ripple-down rules which is case-based classification system were in the range of 70-74 percent. This suggests that KNN approach discussed in this paper is at least as good as the ripple-down rules for classifying GP practice profiles.

7 Conclusions

The results in this study indicate that KNN used in combination with a genetic algorithm achieved good generalisation with classifying GP practice profiles in a test dataset. This opens the way for its application in solving a real world problem namely medical fraud detection. A further refinement of the method and the tuning of its parameters are needed to make it a routine application in the Health Insurance Commission.

References

1. D. Aha, D. Kibler, and M. Alber. Instance-based learning algorithm. *Machine Learning*, 6(1), 1991.
2. B. V. Dasarath. *NN(Nearest Neighbour) Norms: NN pattern Classification Techniques.* IEEE CS Pre, Los Alamito, 1991.
3. H. He, W. Graco J. Wang, and Simon Hawkins. Application of neural networks in medical fraud detection. *Expert Systems with Application*, 13(4):329336, 1997.
4. J.H. Holland. *Adaptation in Natural and Artificial System.* MIT Pres, Massachusett, 1992.
5. F. Luan, H. He, and W. Graco. A comparison of a number of supervised-learning techniques for classifying a sample of general practitioners practice pro"lil. In Laurie Lock Lee and John Hough, editors, *AI95,Eighth Australian Joint Artificial Intelligence Conference*, pages 114133, Canberra, Australia, November 1995.
6. J. C. Wang, M. Boland, W. Graco, and H.He. Classifying general practitioner practice pro"les. In P. Compton, R. Mizoguchi, H. Motoda, and T. Menzies, editors, *PKAW96: The Pacific Knowledge Acquisition Workshop*, pages 333345, Coogee, Sydney, Australia, October 1996.

Evolution of Reference Sets
in Nearest Neighbor Classification

Hisao Ishibuchi and Tomoharu Nakashima

Department of Industrial Engineering, Osaka Prefecture University,
Gakuen-cho 1-1, Sakai, Osaka 599-8531, Japan
Phone: +81-722-54-9354   FAX: +81-722-54-9915
E-mail:{hisaoi, nakashi}@ie.osakafu-u.ac.jp

Abstract. This paper proposes a genetic-algorithm-based approach for
"nding a compact reference set used in nearest neighbor classi"cation.
The reference set is designed by selecting a small number of reference
patterns from a large number of training patterns using a genetic algorithm. The genetic algorithm also removes unnecessary features. The
reference set in our nearest neighbor classi"cation consists of selected
patterns with selected features. A binary string is used for representing
the inclusion (or exclusion) of each pattern and feature in the reference
set. Our goal is to minimize the number of selected patterns, to minimize the number of selected features, and to maximize the classi"cation
performance of the reference set. The e˘ectiveness of our approach is
examined by computer simulations on commonly used data sets.

Key words: Genetic algorithms, pattern classi"cation, nearest neighbor
classi"cation, combinatorial optimization, multi-objective optimization,
knowledge discovery.

1   Introduction

Nearest neighbor classification (Cover and Hart [1]) is one of the most well-
known classification methods in the literature. In its standard formulation, all
training patterns are used as reference patterns for classifying new patterns.
Various approaches were proposed for finding a compact set of reference patterns
used in nearest neighbor classification (for example, see Hart [2], Wilson [3],
Dasarathy [4], Chaudhuri [5]). In those approaches, a small number of reference
patterns were selected from a large number of training patterns. Recently genetic
algorithms were employed in Kuncheva [6,7] for finding a compact reference set
in nearest neighbor classification. Genetic algorithms were also used for selecting
important features in Siedlecki and Sklansky [8] and for weighting each feature
in Kelly and Davis [9] and Punch et al.[10]. In Knight and Sen [11], genetic
algorithms were used for generating prototypes.

   This paper proposes a genetic-algorithm-based approach for simultaneously
selecting reference patterns and important features. Let us assume that m training patterns with n features are given in an n-dimensional pattern space. Our

problem is to design a compact reference set by selecting a small number of reference patterns from the given m training patterns and removing unnecessary features from the given n features. In this paper, we first formulate our pattern and feature selection problem as a multi-objective combinatorial optimization problem with three objectives: to minimize the number of selected patterns, to minimize the number of selected features, and to maximize the number of correctly classified training patterns by the reference set. Next we explain how a genetic algorithm can be applied to our pattern and feature selection problem. In the genetic algorithm, a reference set is coded by a binary string of the length $(n+m)$. Each bit value of the first n bits represents the inclusion or exclusion of the corresponding feature. The other m bit values represent the inclusion or exclusion of each of the given m training patterns. A fitness value of each reference set (i.e., binary string) is defined by the weighted sum of the three objectives. Finally we examine the effectiveness of our approach by computer simulations on commonly used data sets. Simulation results show that a small number of training patterns are selected by our approach together with a few important features.

2   Problem Formulation

In general, the main goal of pattern classification methods such as statistical techniques, machine learning and neural networks is to maximize the prediction ability for unseen patterns. Thus their performance is usually measured by error rates on unseen patterns. When pattern classification methods are used in the context of decision support, knowledge discovery and data mining, it is required to present understandable classification knowledge to human users. While the classification mechanism of nearest neighbor classification is easily understood by human users, the understandability of classification knowledge is not high because a large number of training patterns are stored as classification knowledge. Our goal in this paper is to extract a small number of reference patterns together with important features in order to show classification knowledge to human user in an understandable form.

We assume that m training patterns $\mathbf{x}_p = (x_{p1}, x_{p2}, \ldots, x_{pn}), p = 1, 2, \ldots, m$ with n features are given in an n-dimensional pattern space where x_{pi} is the attribute value of the i-th feature in the p-th pattern. Let P_{ALL} be the set of the given m training patterns: $P_{\mathrm{ALL}} = \{\mathbf{x}_1, \mathbf{x}_2, \ldots, \mathbf{x}_m\}$. We also denote the set of the given n features as $F_{\mathrm{ALL}} = \{f_1, f_2, \ldots, f_n\}$ where f_i is the label of the i-th feature. Our problem is to select a small number of reference patterns from P_{ALL} and to select only important features from F_{ALL}. Let F and P be the set of selected features and the set of selected patterns, respectively, where $F \subseteq F_{\mathrm{ALL}}$ and $P \subseteq P_{\mathrm{ALL}}$. We denote the reference set by S. Since S is uniquely specified by the feature set F and the pattern set P, the reference set is denoted as $S = (F, P)$. In the standard formulation of nearest neighbor classification, the reference set is defined as $S = (F_{\mathrm{ALL}}, P_{\mathrm{ALL}})$ because all the given features and patterns are used for classifying a new pattern $\mathbf{x} = (x_1, x_2, \ldots, x_n)$. In our nearest neighbor classification with the reference set $S = (F, P)$, the nearest neighbor $\mathbf{x}_{\hat{p}}$ to the new pattern $\mathbf{x}$ is found from the pattern set P as

$$d(\mathbf{x}_{\hat{p}}, \mathbf{x}) = \min \{d(\mathbf{x}_p, \mathbf{x}) \mid \mathbf{x}_p \in P\}, \tag{1}$$

where $d(\mathbf{x}_p, \mathbf{x})$ is the distance between $\mathbf{x}_p$ and $\mathbf{x}$, which is measured based on the feature set F as

$$d(\mathbf{x}_p, \mathbf{x}) = \sqrt{\sum_{i \in F} (x_{pi} - x_i)^2} \ . \tag{2}$$

If the class of the nearest neighbor $\mathbf{x}_{\hat{p}}$ is the same as that of the new pattern $\mathbf{x}$, $\mathbf{x}$ is correctly classified. Otherwise the new pattern $\mathbf{x}$ is misclassified.

Since our goal is to find a compact reference set that is easily understood by human users, the number of selected patterns and the number of selected features are minimized. The maximization of the classification performance is also considered in the design of the reference set. Thus our pattern and feature selection problem is written as follows:

$$\text{Minimize } |F|, \text{minimize } |P|, \text{and maximize } NCP(S), \tag{3}$$

where $|F|$ is the number of features in F (i.e., the cardinality of F), $|P|$ is the number of patterns in P, and $NCP(S)$ is the number of correctly classified training patterns by the reference set $S = (F, P)$. In (3), $NCP(S)$ is calculated by classifying all the given m training patterns by the reference set $S = (F, P)$.

3   Genetic Algorithms

For applying a genetic algorithm to our pattern and feature selection problem, a reference set $S = (F, P)$ is coded as a binary string with the length $(n + m)$:

$$S = a_1 a_2 \cdots a_n s_1 s_2 \cdots s_m, \tag{4}$$

where the first n bits denote the inclusion or exclusion of each of the n features, and the other m bits denote the inclusion or exclusion of each of the m patterns. The feature set F and the pattern set P are obtained by decoding the string S as follows:

$$F = \{f_i \mid a_i = 1, \ i = 1, 2, \ldots, n\}, \tag{5}$$

$$P = \{\mathbf{x}_p \mid s_p = 1, \ p = 1, 2, \ldots, m\}. \tag{6}$$

The fitness value of the binary string $S = a_1 a_2 \cdots a_n s_1 s_2 \cdots s_m$ (i.e., the reference set $S = (F, P)$) is defined by the three objectives of our pattern and feature selection problem in (3). We use the following weighted sum as a fitness function:

$$fitness(S) = W_{NCP} \cdot NCP(S) - W_F \cdot |F| - W_P \cdot |P| \tag{7}$$

where W_{NCP}, W_F and W_P are non-negative weights.

Since the three objectives are combined into the above scalar fitness function, we can apply a single-objective genetic algorithm to our pattern and feature selection problem (We can also handle our problem by multi-objective genetic algorithms [12] without introducing the scalar fitness function). In our genetic algorithm, first a number of binary strings of the length $(n + m)$ are randomly generated to form an initial population. Let us denote the population size by N_{pop}. Next a pair of strings are randomly selected from the current population. Two strings are generated from the selected pair of strings by crossover and mutation. The selection, crossover and mutation are iterated to generate N_{pop} strings. The newly generated N_{pop} strings are added to the current population to form the enlarged population of the size $2 \cdot N_{pop}$. The next population is constructed by selecting the best N_{pop} strings from the enlarged population. The population update is iterated until a pre-specified stopping condition is satisfied. The outline of our genetic algorithm is similar to Kuncheva's algorithm (Kuncheva [6,7]).

In our genetic algorithm, we use the uniform crossover to avoid the dependency of the performance on the order of the n features and the m patterns in the string. For e ciently decreasing the number of reference patterns, we use the biased mutation (Nakashima and Ishibuchi [13]) where a larger probability is assigned to the mutation from $s_p = 1$ to $s_p = 0$ than the mutation from $s_p = 0$ to $s_p = 1$. That is, we use two different mutation probabilities $p_m(1 \to 0)$ and $p_m(0 \to 1)$ for the last m bits of the string, each of which represents the inclusion or exclusion of the corresponding pattern in the reference set. Since $p_m(0 \to 1) < p_m(1 \to 0)$, the number of reference patterns is e ciently decreased by the biased mutation during the execution of our genetic algorithm. The biased mutation is the main characteristic feature of our genetic algorithm. We use the biased mutation because the number of selected reference patterns is to be much smaller than that of the given patterns (e.g., $1/20 \sim 1/40$ of the given patterns in computer simulations of this paper). It has been demonstrated in Nakashima and Ishibuchi [13] that the number of reference patterns could not be e ciently decreased without the biased mutation. Note that we use the standard unbiased mutation for the first n bits of the string, each of which represents the inclusion or exclusion of the corresponding feature. This is because usually the number of given features is not as large as that of given patterns. In this case, the biased mutation is not necessary for the feature selection.

4   Computer Simulations

In this section, we first illustrate the pattern selection by a two-dimensional pattern classification problem. Next we illustrate the pattern and feature selection by the well-known iris data. The iris data set is a three-class classification problem involving 150 patterns with four features. Then the applicability of our approach to high-dimensional problems is examined by wine data. The wine data set is a three-class classification problem involving 178 patterns with 13 features. Finally the performance of our approach on large data sets is examined by

Australian credit approval data. The credit data set is a two-class classification problem involving 690 patterns with 14 attributes. We use the iris data, wine data and credit data because they are available from the UC Irvine Database (via anonymous FTP from *ftp.ics.uci.edu* in directory */pub/machine-learning-databases*). In our computer simulations, all the attribute values were normalized into the unit interval [0,1] before applying the genetic algorithm to each data set for the pattern and feature selection.

4.1 Computer Simulation on a Numerical Example

Let us illustrate our approach by a simple numerical example in Fig. 1 (a) where 200 training patterns are given from two classes. In Fig. 1 (a), we also show the classification boundary by the nearest neighbor classification based on all the given training patterns.

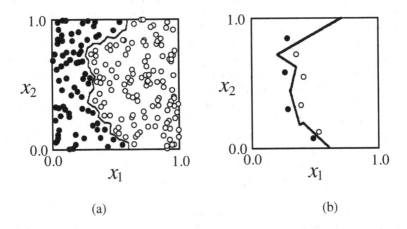

(a)   (b)

Fig. 1. Simulation result for a numerical example. (a) Nearest neighbor classi"cation by all the given patterns. (b) Nearest neighbor classi"cation by selected reference patterns.

We applied our approach with the following parameter specifications to the two-dimensional pattern classification problem in Fig. 1 (a) with 200 training patterns.

String length: 202 (2 features and 200 training patterns),
Population size: $N_{pop} = 50$,
Crossover probability: 1.0,
Mutation probabilities: 0.01 for features,
$$p_m(1 \rightarrow 0) = 0.1 \text{ and } p_m(0 \rightarrow 1) = 0.01 \text{ for patterns,}$$
Weight values: $W_{NCP} = 5$, $W_F = 1$, $W_P = 1$,
Stopping condition: 500 generations.

After 500 generations, eight patterns were selected by the genetic algorithm. Both the given two features were also selected. In Fig. 1 (b), we show the classification boundary by the nearest neighbor classification based on the selected eight patterns. From this simulation result, we can see that a small number of reference patterns were selected by the genetic algorithm from a large number of training patterns.

4.2   Computer Simulation on Iris Data

In the same manner as in the previous subsection, we applied our approach to the iris data. Since the iris data have four attributes and 150 training patterns, the string length was specified as 154. The computer simulation was iterated 10 times using different initial populations. The following average result was obtained:

Average number of selected features: 2.1.

Average number of selected patterns: 6.3.

Average classification rate on training patterns: 99.3%.

From this result, we can see that compact reference sets were obtained by the genetic algorithm. For example, six reference patterns with two features (the third and fourth features) were selected in nine of the ten trials. An example of the selected reference sets is shown in Fig. 2 in the reduced pattern space with the selected features x_3 and x_4. We also show the classification boundary by the nearest neighbor classification based on the selected patterns and features. This reference set can correctly classify 149 training patterns (99.3% of the given 150 training patterns). For the iris data, it is well-known that the third and fourth features are important. These two attributes were always selected in the ten independent trials.

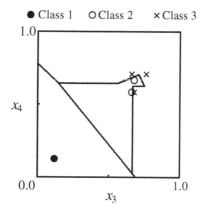

Fig. 2. Selected patterns and features for the iris data.

4.3   Computer Simulation on Wine Data

We also applied our approach to the wine data in order to demonstrate its applicability to high-dimensional classification problems. Computer simulation was performed in the same manner as in the previous subsections. Since the wine data have 178 patterns with 13 features, the string length was specified as 191. The computer simulation was iterated 10 times using different initial populations. The following average result was obtained:

Average number of selected features: 6.9.

Average number of selected patterns: 5.4.

Average classification rate on training patterns: 100%.

From this result, we can see that compact reference sets were obtained by the genetic algorithm for the wine data with many features.

4.4   Computer Simulation on Credit Data

We also applied our approach to the credit data in order to demonstrate its applicability to large data sets with many training patterns. Since the credit data have 690 patterns with 14 features, the string length was specified as 704. Much longer strings were used for the credit data than the iris data and the wine data. This means that the search space of the genetic algorithm for the credit data is much larger than the cases of the other data sets. In the application to the credit data, we used the following parameter specifications to handle such a large search space:

Population size: $N_{\mathrm{pop}} = 50$,

Crossover probability: 1.0,

Mutation probabilities: 0.01 for features,

$$p_{\mathrm{m}}(1 \to 0) = 0.1 \text{ and } p_{\mathrm{m}}(0 \to 1) = 0.005 \text{ for patterns,}$$

Weight values: $W_{NCP} = 5$, $W_F = 1$, $W_P = 1$,

Stopping condition: 2000 generations.

The computer simulation was iterated five times using different initial populations. The following average result was obtained:

Average number of selected features: 6.8.

Average number of selected patterns: 38.6.

Average classification rate on training patterns: 92.6%.

Since there is a large overlap between two classes in the credit data, the average classification rate is smaller than the cases of the other data sets. The average classification rate can be increased by assigning a large value to the weight for the classification performance (i.e., W_{NCP}). For example, we had a 94.2% average classification rate by specifying the weight values as $W_{NCP} = 20$, $W_F = 1$ and $W_P = 1$. In this case, the number of selected patterns was increased from 38.6 to 76.0. As we can see from these simulation results, there is a trade-off between the classification performance of the reference set and its compactness.

5 Conclusion

In this paper, we proposed a genetic-algorithm-based approach to the design of compact reference sets in nearest neighbor classification. In our approach, feature selection and pattern selection are simultaneously performed by a genetic algorithm. That is, a small number of reference patterns with only important features are selected. The effectiveness of our approach was demonstrated by computer simulations on commonly used data sets. The number of selected patterns was $1/20 \sim 1/40$ of the given training patterns in our computer simulations of this paper. About half features were also removed in our computer simulations.

References

1. Cover, T. M., and Hart, P. E.: Nearest neighbor pattern classi"cation, *IEEE Trans. on Information Theory.* 13 (1967) 21-27.
2. Hart, P.: The condensed nearest neighbor rule, *IEEE Trans. on Information Theory.* 14 (1968) 515-516.
3. Wilson, D. L.: Asymptotic properties of nearest neighbor rules using edited data, *IEEE Trans. on Systems, Man, and Cybernetics.* 2 (1972) 408-420.
4. Dasarathy, B. V.: Minimal consistent set (MCS) identi"cation for optimal nearest neighbor decision systems design, *IEEE Trans. on Systems, Man, and Cybernetics.* 24 (1994) 511-517.
5. Chaudhuri, D., *et al.*: Finding a subset of representative points in a data set, *IEEE Trans. on Systems, Man, and Cybernetics.* 24 (1994) 1416-1424.
6. Kuncheva, L. I.: Editing for the k-nearest neighbors rule by a genetic algorithm, *Pattern Recognition Letters.* 16 (1995) 809-814.
7. Kuncheva, L. I.: Fitness functions in editing k-NN reference set by genetic algorithms, *Pattern Recognition.* 30 (1997) 1041-1049.
8. Siedlecki, W., and Sklansky, J.: A note on genetic algorithms for large-scale feature selection, *Pattern Recognition Letters.* 10 (1989) 335-347.
9. Kelly, J. D. Jr., and Davis, L.: Hybridizing the genetic algorithm and the k nearest neighbors classi"cation algorithm, *Proceedings of 4th International Conference on Genetic Algorithm.* University California. San Diego (July 13-16, 1991) Morgan Kaufmann Publisher. San Mateo (1991) 377-383.
10. Punch W. F., et al.: Further research on feature selection and classi"cation using genetic algorithms, *Proceedings of 5th International Conference on Genetic Algorithm.* University of Illinois at Urbana-Champaign (July 17-21. 1993) Morgan Kaufmann Publisher. San Mateo (1993) 557-564.
11. Knight, L., and Sen, S.: PLEASE: A prototype learning system using genetic algorithm, In: *Proceedings of 6th International Conference on Genetic Algorithm.* University of Pittsburgh (July 15-19. 1995). Morgan Kaufmann Publisher. San Francisco (1995) 429-435.
12. Ishibuchi, H., Murata, T., and Turksen, I.B.: Single-objective and two-objective genetic algorithms for selecting linguistic rules for pattern classi"cation problems, *Fuzzy Sets and Systems.* 89 (1997) 135-149.
13. Nakashima, T., and Ishibuchi, H.: GA-based approaches for "nding the minimum reference set for nearest neighbor classi"cation, *Proceedings of 5th IEEE International Conference on Evolutionary Computation.* Anchorage (March 4-9. 1998). 709-714.

Investigation of a Cellular Genetic Algorithm that Mimics Landscape Ecology

Michael Kirley, Xiaodong Li and David G. Green

School of Environmental and Information Sciences,
Charles Sturt University,
PO Box 789 Albury New South Wales 2640 - Australia
(mkirley, xli, dgreen)@csu.edu.au

Abstract. The cellular genetic algorithm (CGA) combines GAs with cellular automata by spreading an evolving population across a pseudo-landscape. In this study we use insights from ecology to introduce new features, such as disasters and connectivity changes, into the algorithm. We investigate the performance and behaviour of the algorithm on standard GA hard problems. The CGA has the advantage of avoiding premature convergence and outperforms standard GAs on particular problems. A potentially important feature of the algorithm s behaviour is that the "tness of solutions frequently improves in large jumps following disturbances (culling by patches).

1 Introduction

Genetic algorithms (GAs) are search and optimization techniques that are based on the analogy of biological evolution [4], [9], [10]. One of the great attractions of this approach is that natural selection has succeeded in producing species that solve the problem of survival and are often highly optimized with respect to their environment. However the traditional GA approach is only a simplified version of what really occurs in nature. For instance genes and chromosomes are organized differently, and population dynamics in landscapes introduces added complexity. An important question, therefore, is whether algorithms that more closely mimic the evolutionary process convey any advantages over simple GAs. In this study we begin to address this question by investigating the performance and behaviour of a GA that embodies features of evolution in a landscape.

Traditional GAs evolve a population of individuals over time by selecting mates from the entire population (either at random or based on some fitness measure). Loss of population diversity (*convergence*) reduces the quality of many solutions. Many *ad hoc* schemes have been introduced to continually change genetic parameters in order to preserve diversity [10].

Parallel genetic algorithms (PGAs) attempt to improve the performance of GAs by restricting mating to subpopulations of individuals [3], [11]. The spatial population structure employed by PGAs helps to maintain diversity in a more natural manner. Typically PGAs utilise static population structures that are specified at the beginning of the run and remain unchanged. Here we develop an approach to PGAs in which changes in topology, brought about by varying the proportion of individuals *alive* in the population, play a crucial part in the operation of the algorithm. This approach is based on recent findings about evolution in a landscape [6] and builds on findings into the critical nature of connectivity [5], [6] and especially for cellular automata models of landscapes. The proposed cellular genetic algorithm (CGA) highlights the importance of a spatial population structure for the evolution of solutions to complex problems.

2   Parallel Genetic Algorithms

The PGA is a parallel search with information exchange between individuals within a spatially distributed population. There are two categories of PGAs; coarse or fine grained PGAs. In coarse-grained PGAs subpopulations are introduced that work independently with only occasional exchanges of individuals - *migration*. They are also known as distibuted GAs or island models [1]. In fine-grained PGAs the spatial distribution of the population is defined, and selection and crossover are restricted within the individual's neighbourhood [8].

As a consequence of local selection in PGAs, there is less selection pressure and tendency towards more exploration of the search space. Critical parameter settings include migration rate and interval, topology and the ratio of the radius of the neighbourhood to the radius of the whole grid [3].

Various PGAs have been proposed to tackle optimisation problems. Manderick and Spiessens [8] described a fine-grained PGA that uses a local selection scheme where a mate was randomly selected based on the local fitness values. The algorithm was implemented on a sequential machine, therefore it is not a truly parallel algorithm. Muhlenbein *et al* [11] use local selection too, but it is limited to a small neighbourhood (only 4 neighbours). Muhlenbein also uses hill-climbing for each individual. In recent work by Rudolph and Sprave [13], a self-adjusting threshold scheme was used to control the selection pressure. Branke *et al* [2] described a number of global selection schemes for PGAs, but they require global knowledge. Lin *et al* [7] introduces a hybrid PGA that incorporates both coarse and finegrained PGAs for job shop scheduling problems. Yao [15] also describes global optimisation using parallel evolutionary algorithms as well as the possibility of using hybrid algorithms to improve performance.

3   A Cellular Genetic Algorithm

The algorithm we explore here embeds the evolving population of the GA in a cellular automaton (CA). Computationally this is a fine-grained PGA, but with certain biologically inspired modifications. Whitley [14] introduced the term cellular genetic algorithm (CGA) for this sort of model. However one important difference in our approach is that the individuals only occupy cells in the grid; they are not identified with them. We treat the grid as a model of a pseudo-landscape, with each cell corresponding to a site in the landscape. At any given time each cell may be *active* (occupied) or *inactive*.

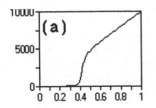 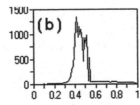 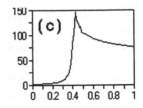

Fig. 1. Phase changes in connectivity within a genetic landscape . In each case the x-axis represents the proportion p of cells in the grid that are occupied. (a) Change in the size of the largest connected patch of cells. Note the phase change at p = 0.4. (b) Variance in the size of the patch in (a) over repeated trials. Note the extreme variance at the phase change. (c) Time for an epidemic process to traverse the largest patch.

Our approach draws on ideas from population dynamics and landscape ecology. Its rationale derives from findings of our previous research on the nature of evolution in a landscape [6]. We have shown that the structure change of a cellular automaton model plays a critical role in many ecological changes and species evolution [5] [6]. For example, a phase change occurs in the connectivity of grids as the proportion of *active* cells changes (Fig. 1).

The above result has a crucial implication. Simply by changing the proportion of active cells within the model (so that the number crosses the connectivity threshold), we can induce phase changes in genetic communication within a population. For example if we randomly assign a certain proportion of the population as *alive*, and the remaining as *dead*, the population of living individuals fragments into many patchy subpopulations (Fig. 2). Although the same fine-grained local interaction rules apply, the use of patchy subpopulations in this case resembles the coarse-grained PGA approach. This enables refinement of solutions within a subpopulation as well as the accumulation of variations between subpopulations. When individuals from different subpopulations spread out and mate, fitter hybrids often appear.

The CGA uses a toroidal grid in which the state of each cell consists of a binary chromosome as well as a value indicating fitness. The length of the chromosome is problem dependent. Each generation consist of upgrading the status of each cell in a series of steps. These steps follow the basic pattern for GAs except that the spatial arrangement of cells modifies the process in the following important ways.

1. On each generation each active cell produces an offspring to replace itself. In doing so it carries out crossover of its genetic material with one of its neighbours. A mate is selected based on its fitness value relative to the local neighbourhood.
2. Varying proportions of individuals are removed at random using a disaster option. Normally the disaster is small, but occasionally large numbers are

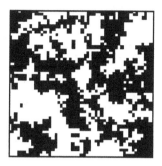

Fig. 2. Patchy subpopulations of a PGA model. Active cells are shaded, while inactive cells are represented by white cells on the 2-dimensional grid. The black area shows the extent of the single largest patch of connected active cells in this system. The proportion of active cells in this case is set at the critical level (cf Fig. 1)

wiped out. Control parameters include the rate at which disasters strike a generation and the maximum radius of the disaster zone.

3. Wherever a cell is cleared, the neighbouring cells compete to occupy it. Thus, it will take a number of generations to fill the vacant zone after a disaster.

4   Experiments and Results

Initial investigations focussed on three different selection schemes within the neighbourhood model: (a) a mate is selected at random; (b) a fitter mate is randomly selected; and (c) the fittest individual in the local neighbourhood is always selected as a mate. The size of the neighbourhood is set to one (eight nearest neighbours) in all models.

For performance evaluation De Jong's standard test functions F1, F2, F3 and F5 were used [4]. F4 was excluded due to the stochastic nature of the function. The configurations described have been implemented in C* and run on a Connection Machine CM-5. The 2-D grid size was set to 10 (100 individuals). In all runs the crossover and mutation rates were 0.6 and 0.1 respectively.

The CGA was able to find optimum solutions for all test functions. Table 1(a) lists the number of generations to reach the optimum solution for each function for a given selection technique averaged over ten runs. For all test functions, there is a significant reduction in the number of evaluations required to find the optimal solution when the fittest selection technique is adopted. Table 1(b) lists performance statistics for each function, based on the fittest selection strategy after 100 generations. Here we compare the performance of the CGA with the Manderick and Spiessens model [8] in column FG1. There does not appear to be any significant improvement in performance for F1 or F2. However, the results for F3 and F5 suggest that the CGA not only alleviates the premature convergence problem and improves results, but also finds solutions in a shorter time.

Table 1. CGA performance measures

(a) Selection Technique			(b) Comparison			
Function	Selection	Generation	Function	Performance	CGA	FG1
F1	Random	-	F1	Online	12.3358	2.8333
	Fitter	155.0		Offline	0.1659	0.0192
	Fittest	64.0		Best-so-far	0.0001	0.0000
F2	Random	136.8	F2	Online	128.789	47.7812
	Fitter	131.5		Offline	0.1597	0.3032
	Fittest	39.8		Best-so-far	0.0901	0.2573
F3	Random	141.0	F3	Online	8.3120	22.1863
	Fitter	120.5		Offline	3.8200	11.0415
	Fittest	40.3		Best-so-far	0.0000	10.8500
F5	Random	83.0	F5	Online	111.071	168.9408
	Fitter	52.3		Offline	3.4192	14.4214
	Fittest	50.6		Best-so-far	1.0021	9.2834

Next we investigated the CGA performance using a GA-hard problem. The function used is a generalised version of the Rastrigin function.

$$f(x) = nA + \sum_{i=1}^{n} x_i^2 - A\cos(2\ x_i)$$

$$-5.12 < x_i < 5.12 \text{ and } A = 3, n = 20$$

This function is predominantly unimodal with an overlying lattice of moderately sized peaks and basins. The min f(x) = f(0, 0......0) = 0.

The CGA introduces a disaster option, which allows the grid to be broken up into patches. The dynamic nature of connectivity allows interactions to be restricted to small neighbourhoods which means that good alternative solutions can persist by forming small clumps. All individuals can be considered to be continuously moving around within their neighbourhoods, so that global communication is possible, but not instantaneous. Wherever a cell is cleared, the neighbouring cells compete to occupy it.

The 2-D grid size was set to 100. The large grid is needed to achieve a more realistic model. The parameter settings for the preliminary investigations include the fittest selection strategy, with crossover and mutation rates 0.6 and 0.1 respectively. The disaster rate and maximum disaster zone radius (the range or neighbourhood size of the disaster) values were systematically altered to determine the effects of spatial disturbances on solution quality. The results are summarised in Figs. 3 and 4.

As the disaster configuration parameters are altered the ability of the CGA to find good solutions also changes. The results shown in Fig. 3 indicate that there is variation in performance when the spatial population is disturbed. The best results occur consistently with disaster rate in the range 0.1 - 0.2 and disaster zone radius value of 30. As expected disturbances of too great a severity destroys the variability of the population, and thus the basis of further advances.

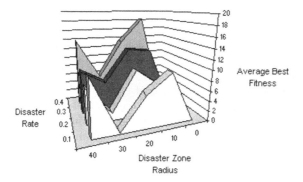

Fig. 3. CGA average best "tness after 500 generations for the Rastrigin function using di˜erent combinations of disaster rates and disaster zone radius values.

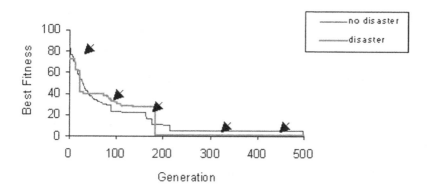

Fig. 4. A comparison of CGA performance. The best individual "tness value *vs* generation for the CGA without disasters averaged over "ve runs compared to a typical run with disaster rate = 0.1 and disaster zone radius = 30. Disasters shown here as an arrow.

If the disaster option is disabled the CGA functions as a typical fine-grained PGA. Other performance measures examined included the average and standard deviation of the solution fitness values at the end of the run as well as the time to reach the best solution. There does not appear to be significant variation, with or without disasters, based on these measures in the CGA.

Fig. 4 shows the average best-ever results of the CGA with the disaster option turned off and an example with disaster rate = 0.1 and disaster zone radius = 30. Typically we have rapid progress at the beginning, followed by a more gradual improvement in solution quality. In the CGA with disaster trial, there is often an increase in solution quality following disasters. For example, the graph shows that a significant jump in fitness occurred at approximately generation 180 following a disaster.

5   Discussion

To summarise the results brie"y, the version of the CGA that we have introduced here works well on all the standard problems with which we have tested it
with, especially De Jong's function F5 and the Rastrigin function. Improvement
in performance is attributable to the use of local neighbourhoods (i.e. the fine-
grained PGA approach) which reduces the tendency of premature convergence.
The introduction of disasters into the algorithm produces some interesting behaviour. In particular we saw that there is a strong tendency for the best fitness
in the population to increase in jumps following a disaster. This is something
that we anticipated by analogy with biological systems. Our earlier work [5], [6]
had shown that disasters in a landscape can lead to explosions of small populations that were previously suppressed by their competitors. The jumps in fitness
arise from hybridisation of these populations when they are able to spread and
come into contact with each other.

Lin *et al* [7] obtained best results for the job shop scheduling problem using a
hybrid PGA model consisting of course-grained PGAs connected in a fine-grained
PGA style topology. The CGA with disasters effectively achieves the same thing.
That is the regular operation of the algorithm, with mate selection confined to a
local neighbourhood is a straightforward fine-grained PGA. Disasters break up
the grid into isolated patches that are still locally communicating but isolated
from other patches - i.e. a coarse-grained PGA. The results support the concept
that emulating biological processes more closely holds the potential to produce
better algorithms. In this study we have tested the CGA only on standard test
problems. However, its ideal application is likely to be problems that involve
optima and criteria, which vary in time and space and correspond to the sorts
of circumstances faced by natural populations.

Acknowledgements

The CGA was implemented on the CM5 at the South Australian Centre for High
Performance Computing.

References

1. Belding, T.C. The Distributed Genetic Algorithm Revisited. In Eschelman, L.
   (Ed.), Proceedings of the Sixth International Conference on Genetic Algorithms,
   San Francisco, CA: Morgan Kaufmann (1995) 114-121.
2. Branke, J., Andersen, H.C. and Schmeck, H. Global Selection Methods for Mas-
   sively Parallel Computers. In Proceedings of AISB 96 workshop on Evolutionary
   Computing, ed. Fogarty T.C., Lecture Notes in Computer Science 1143, Springer
   Verlag (1996) 175-188.
3. Cantu-Paz, E. A Survey of Parallel Genetic Algorithms. IlliGAL Report No.97003,
   Illinois Genetic Algorithms Laboratory (1997).

4. Goldberg, D.E. Genetic Algorithms in Search, Optimization and Machine Learning. Reading, Massachusetts: Addison-Wesley Publishing Company, Inc. (1989).

5. Green, D.G. Emergent Behaviour in Biological Systems. In Green, D.G. and Bossomaier, T.R.J. Complex Systems - from Biology to Computation, Amsterdam: IOS Press (1993) 24-35.

6. Green, D.G. Connectivity and the evolution of biological systems. Journal of Biological Systems 2 (1) (1994) 91-103.

7. Lin, S., Goodman, E. D. and Punch, W. F. Investigating Parallel Genetic Algorithms on Job Shop Scheduling Problems. In Angeline, P. J. et al., (Eds) Evolutionar Programming VI, Proc. Sixth Internat. Conf., EP97, Springer Verlag, NY,.,Indianapolis, (1997) pp.383-394.

8. Manderick, B and Spiessens, P. Fine-Grained Parallel Genetic Algorithms, In Scha˘er, J.D. (Ed) Proceeding of 3rd International Conference on Genetic Algorithms.. Morgan Kaufmann, (1989) pp.428-433.

9. Michalewicz, Z. Genetic Algorithms + Data Structure = Evolution Programs - Third, Revised and Extended Edition. New York: Springer-Verlag Berlin Heidelberg (1996).

10. Mitchell, M. An Introduction to Genetic Algorithms. Cambridge, Massachusetts: The MIT Press (1996).

11. Muhlenbein, H. Parallel genetic algorithms, population genetics, and combinatorial optimisation. In Scha˘er, J.D. (Ed.), Proceedings of the Third International Conference on Genetic Algorithms, San Matteo, CA: Morgan Kaufmann, (1989) pp.416-421.

12. Muhlenbein, H., Gorges-Scheuter, M. and Kramer O. Evolution Algorithms in Combinatorial Optimisation. Parallel Computing, 7, (1988) pp.65-88.

13. Rudolph, G. and Sprave, J. Signi"cance of Locality and Selection Pressure in the Grand Deluge Evolutionary Algorithm. Proceeding of PPSN 96 (1996).

14. Whitley, D. Cellular genetic algorithms. In S. Forest, (Ed). Proceedings of the 5th International Conference on Genetic Algorithms. Morgan Kaufmann, (1993) pp.658-662.

15. Yao, X. Global optimisation by evolutionary algorithms. Proceedings of the Second Aizu International Symposium on Parallel Algorithm/Architecture Synthesis, Aizu-Wakamatsu, Japan, Society Press,.IEEE Computer (1997) pp.282-291.

Quantifying Neighborhood Preservation: Joint Properties of Evolutionary and Unsupervised Neural Learning

Ralf Garionis

University of Dortmund, Department of Computer Science XI,
44221 Dortmund, Germany

Abstract. Unsupervised learning algorithms realizing topographic mappings are justi"ed by neurobiology while they are useful for multivariate data analysis. In contrast to supervised learning algorithms unsupervised neural networks have their objective function implicitly de"ned by the learning rule. When considering topographic mapping as an optimization problem, the presence of explicitly de"ned objective functions becomes essential. In this paper, we show that measures of neighborhood preservation can be used for optimizing and learning topographic mappings by means of evolution strategies. Numerical experiments reveal these measures also being a possible description of the principles governing the learning process of unsupervised neural networks. We argue that quantifying neighborhood preservation provides a link for connecting evolution strategies and unsupervised neural learning algorithms for building hybrid learning architectures.

1 Introduction

A mapping being topographic is able to transform neighboring points in some space into neighboring points in another space, while the neighborhood relation is retained by means of the transformation. There exist several unsupervised learning algorithms performing topographic mappings (some of which we will consider in section 3). However, there is no generic framework subsuming the different learning dynamics. Identifying the principles underlying such a learning process becomes important when designing new learning schemes.

We will investigate empirically if the quantification of neighborhood preservation is suitable as a black box description of neural learning dynamics by calculating these measures in parallel to the neural learning process. By using evolution strategies for optimizing the measures of neighborhood preservation, we will see if these measures can be considered as objective functions describing topographic mappings.

2 Quantifying neighborhood preservation

A recent work by Goodhill and Sejnowski [5] identifies several methods for quantifying neighborhood preservation in topographic mappings and provides a taxonomy of these measures. The authors have also calculated the values assigned by these measures to a set of four static mappings (square to line problem) and have done some analysis on parameter variation.

Here, we will make use of those non-stochastic measures named in [5], which do not need additional parameters or target values for a mapping and which do not yield binary relationship values. Therefore, we will consider the most universal measures. These are brie"y explained in the following, where x_i (y_i) names point i in input (output) space of the mapping, while N is the number of points mapped and $^{(x)}$ ($^{(y)}$) is a function quantifying similarity of points in input (output) space.

The C measure

The cost functional C [4] measures the correlation between the distance $^{(x)}$ in input space and the distance $^{(y)}$ in output space:

$$C = \sum_{i=1}^{N} \sum_{j<i} {}^{(x)}(x_i, x_j) \, {}^{(y)}(y_i, y_j) \tag{1}$$

Metric Multidimensional Scaling

Metric multidimensional scaling (metric MDS) [14] is used to match a given set of dissimilarities of measurements with the dissimilarities of points resulting from a transformation of the initial measurements. The objective function defining the quality of matching is the summed squared differences of dissimilarities:

$$mMDS = \sum_{i=1}^{N} \sum_{j<i} [\, {}^{(x)}(x_i, x_j) - {}^{(y)}(y_i, y_j)]^2 \tag{2}$$

Sammon mappings

Although similar to metric MDS, Sammon mappings [10] are nonlinear by the use of normalization. The Sammon function emphasizes differences involving small $^{(x)}$ values:

$$S = \frac{1}{\sum_{i=1}^{N} \sum_{j<i} {}^{(x)}(x_i, x_j)} \sum_{i=1}^{N} \sum_{j<i} \frac{[\, {}^{(x)}(x_i, x_j) - {}^{(y)}(y_i, y_j)]^2}{{}^{(x)}(x_i, x_j)} \tag{3}$$

Spearman coefficient

The idea of metric topology preserving (MTP) maps presented in [1] is that it preserves the relative positions (ranks) of pairwise similarities among points.

For calculating the deviation from an optimal MTP mapping the Spearman coe cient s_p is used, which is the correlation coe cient of the ranks [9]:

$$s_p = \frac{\sum_{i=1}^{N}(R_i - \bar{R})(S_i - \bar{S})}{\sqrt{\sum_{i=1}^{N}(R_i - \bar{R})^2}\sqrt{\sum_{i=1}^{N}(S_i - \bar{S})^2}} \tag{4}$$

[1] proved that a map is metric topology preserving if $s_p = 1$.

3   Self-organizing topographic mappings

Unsupervised learning rules for topographic maps transform points in some continuous input space into discrete lattice points in neuron space. Each neuron carries a reference (weight) vector mapping its lattice position back into input space. We will now brie"y explain a selection of learning algorithms fitting in this framework.

Kohonen's self organizing maps

The self-organizing feature-mapping algorithm developed by Kohonen [7] became a synonym for unsupervised learning algorithms providing topographic mappings. Within the one- or two-dimensional lattice of neurons the algorithm has to find the neuron that is closest to some network input of arbitrary dimension. The reference vector of the neuron found (the winner) is moved by some distance in direction towards the input vector. The neurons neighboring the winner are moved by a value decreasing with growing neighborhood size.

The Folk and Kartashov elastic network model

Based on elastic interaction between neurons, the network model of Folk and Kartashov [2] moves the neuron reference vectors according to the forces acting on neighboring neurons. These forces are calculated by using the input signal density inside the Voronoi cells defined by the neurons' weight vectors, which are also considered in terms of distances. The network can perform all weight adaptations required for a single learning step in parallel.

Linsker's maximum mutual information network

The idea of maximizing the Shannon information rate (average mutual information) of an input-output mapping was used by Linsker for deriving a learning rule that performs gradient ascent in the information rate [8]. The algorithm explicitly addresses lateral connections and requires the calculation of distances from input vectors to reference vectors. While Linsker uses Euclidian exponentially weighted distances, distance measurement has to recognize that opposite side neuron grid borders are connected to each other and therefore form a torus.

4   Evolution strategies

Evolution strategies are known to be well suited for solving diﬃcult real valued optimization problems [12]. For our numerical experiments we have chosen a particular instance of parallel evolutionary algorithms, the neighborhood evolution strategy (NES) [11].

The neighborhood model of the NES places the individuals of the population on a grid being folded in such a way as to form a two-dimensional torus. Therefore, the grid defines the neighborhood relations among individuals. A particular neighborhood encloses all individuals surrounding an individual within some fixed distance in the maximum norm.

As local selection operator we used mating selection successfully. The two best individuals are selected from the neighborhood in order to generate the successor of the current individual in the next generation. Therefore, the communication among individuals within a certain neighborhood is purely local.

Both, the NES and the neural network models considered here, share similar properties: They are inherently parallel and they are based on local interactions. This is a useful prerequisite for hybrid learning systems.

5   Simulations

For calculating the measures of section 2 in parallel to the neural learning process, we used random points drawn from the bivariate uniform distribution over the range $[0, 1]$ and mapped them into a 8×8 two-dimensional neuron lattice (initially configured randomly) by using the algorithms described in section 3. The rules' parameters were chosen such that the lattice unfolds properly, while the number of input presentations required depended on the learning algorithm used (note: Linsker's rule uses batch learning). At each pattern presentation, we calculated on-line the measures of section 2 for the last 64 input-output mappings (initially less than 64) for approximating the mapping of 64 input points each addressing another neuron of the 8×8 neuron lattice. Because we consider Eucledian spaces, Eucledian distances were used for the $^{(\cdot)}$.

We used the same measuring code for optimizing the point to lattice mappings by the neighborhood evolution strategy. The NES controlled the real valued two-dimensional coordinates of 64 points in input space. The measuring functions kept the real valued coordinates of the 64 reference vectors constant while the neighborhood relation of these vectors was defined by the equidistant spaced discrete 8×8 two-dimensional grid in output space. Each of the reference vectors coordinates were set to $\frac{i}{9}$, $i = 1 \ldots 8$ for representing the topologically correct mapping of the discrete output space grid into input space. Therefore, the NES had to find under control of the measures considered the points in input space which map perfectly into the output space grid. (Due to this method the absolute values calculated by the measuring functions in the NES do not match the values of the neural network simulations.) As boundary restrictions imposed on the optimization the variable values had to stay within the interval $[0, 1]$.

For solving this 128 real valued parameter optimization problem we combined the NES with a line search algorithm (Hooke-Jeeves, [6]) ran at different frequencies within the evolution strategy's evaluation loop.

Note that it is di cult to compare the neighborhood measures gained by the neural network models and the NES among each other since the NES operates on a fixed set of input points and therefore calculates the optimum of the various measures. Because the neural network models use changing input points, they calculate the mean of the topographic distortion among the inputs. The presence of wrap around neighborhoods (Linsker's network) and border neurons (elastic network) in"uences the measure values for the neural mappings. Therefore, the slope of the measure curves is most informative regarding the learning process.

6   Discussion

We have simulated the learning algorithms (realizing topographic mappings) of section 3 which differ regarding the principles underlying the learning rules. In parallel to the learning process, we have calculated the neighborhood preservation measures of section 2 for quantifying the process of learning. Figures 3 to 5 show that at least metric MDS and Sammon mappings can be considered as Lyapunov functions describing the learning dynamics of the three network models: These functions are clearly minimized. The results for metric MDS and Sammon values are confirmed by the topology preserving mappings gained by the NES (figures 6 to 7) using local mating selection (as described in [13]) and a population size of 100 individuals.

In the neural network simulations, the on-line calculated values for the C measure and the Spearman coe cient s_p do not show changes significant enough to characterize the learning process (figures 3 to 5). In addition, the NES was not able to generate a topology preserving mapping under control of the C measure and the Spearman function. This gives rise to the assumption that the signal for directing the process of learning topological mappings provided by these two functions is too weak and that the values they calculate do not provide a strong causal relation to the development of topological mappings.

The mapping obtained for Sammon's measure (fig. 7) takes longer to learn (fig. 2) than the mapping evolved for the mMDS case (fig. 6). Some preordering of the initial grid configuration could speed up learning.

Furthermore, the line search optimization algorithm used for supporting the NES failed to converge to a valid solution at any function used.

7   Conclusions

Summarizing, metric MDS and Sammon mappings are suited for guiding the evolutionary learning process of an evolution strategy and for explaining the topology preserving learning process of a variety of neural network learning algorithms by means of a Lyapunov function. As combined result of the simulations,

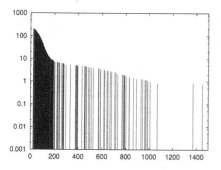

Fig. 1. Fitness values for metric MDS

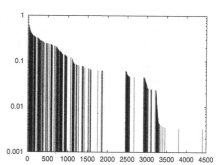

Fig. 2. Sammon s measure: "tness

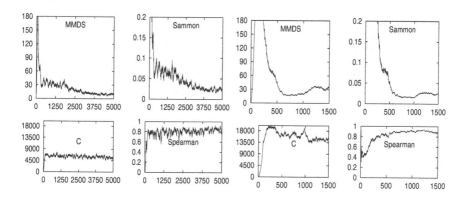

Fig. 3. Kohonen s SOM

Fig. 4. Elastic network

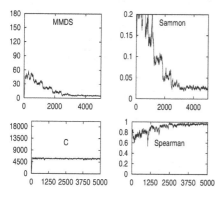

Fig. 5. Linsker s network

Figures 1 and 2: The "tness values returned by the NES are plotted as bars for each generation. A missing bar indicates that the corresponding generation does not carry an improved individual conforming to the boundary restrictions.

Figures 3 to 5: Each of the graphs show the values for metric multidimensional scaling (top left), Sammon s measure (top right), C measure (bottom left), and for the Spearman coe cient ρ_{Sp} (bottom right).

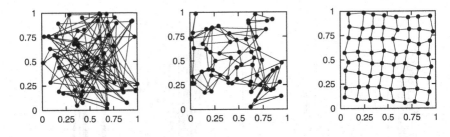

Fig. 6. Topographic mapping evolved using metric MDS as objective function: initial random con"guration, typical intermediate, and "nal mapping. Ordered intermediate con"gurations are reached much faster compared to the S-measure case.

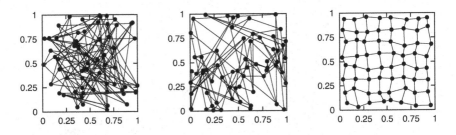

Fig. 7. Topographic mapping evolved using Sammon s measure: initial random con"guration, intermediate, and "nal mapping. Intermediate con"gurations are less stable than those for the mMDS case ("g. 6).

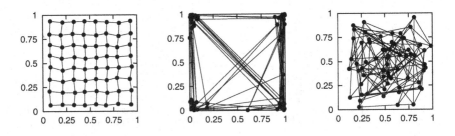

Fig. 8. Topographic mappings found by the Kohonen network (left) and by the neighborhood evolution strategy for the C measure (middle) and ρ_{Sp} (right) case.

we argue that metric MDS and Sammon mappings do characterize adequately the essential properties of topology preserving mappings.

Considering the joint characteristics of the NES and the neural network models used, hybrid architectures employing topology preserving mappings are within reach.

Acknowledgements

We thank J. Sprave for useful discussions and supplying his code for the NES. Thanks to M. Fellenberg for software support. We gratefully acknowledge support by the Deutsche Forschungsgemeinschaft (DFG) under grant Schw-361/10.

A preliminary version of this paper was published as [3].

References

1. J. C. Bezdek and N. R. Pal. An index of topological preservation for feature extraction. *Pattern Recognition*, 28(3):381 391, 1995.
2. R. Folk and A. Kartashov. A simple elastic model for self-organizing topological mappings. Network: *Computation in Neural Systems*, 5(3):369 387, 1994.
3. R. Garionis. Quantifying neighborhood preservation: Linking evolutionary and unsupervised neural learning. In X. Yao, R. I. McKay, C. S. Newton, J.-H. Kim, and T. Furuhashi, editors, *Proc. Second Asia-Pacific Conf. on simulated Evolution and Learning (SEAL'98)*, volume 2, Canberra, 1998. University College, The University of New South Wales, Canberra, and Australian Defence Force Academy, Canberra, Australia. ISBN 0-7317-0500-9.
4. G. J. Goodhill, S. Finch, and T. J. Sejnowski. Optimizing cortical mappings. In D. S. Touretzky, M. C. Mozer, and M. E. Hasselmo, editors, *Advances in Neural Information Processing Systems*, volume 8, pages 330 336. MIT Press, Cambridge, MA, 1996.
5. G. J. Goodhill and T. J. Sejnowski. Quantifying neighbourhood preservation in topographic mappings. In *Proceedings of the 3rd Joint Symposium on Neural Computation, University of California, San Diego and California Institute of Technology, Pasadena*, volume 6, pages 61 82, Pasadena, 1996. California Institute of Technology.
6. R. Hooke and T. A. Jeeves. Direct search solution of numerical and statistical problems. *JACM*, 8:221 229, 1961.
7. T. Kohonen. Self-organized formation of topologically correct feature maps. *Biological Cybernetics*, 43:59 69, 1982.
8. R. Linsker. How to generate ordered maps by maximizing the mutual information between input and output. *Neural Computation*, 1(3):402 411, 1989.
9. W. H. Press, S. A. Teukolsky, W. T. Vetterling, and B. P. Flannery. *Numerical Recipes in C, 2nd Edition*. Cambridge University Press, 1992.
10. J. W. Sammon. A nonlinear mapping for data structure analysis. *IEEE Trans. Comput.*, 18:401 409, 1969.
11. M. Schütz and J. Sprave. Application of parallel mixed-integer evolution strategies with mutation rate pooling. In L. J. Fogel, P. J. Angeline, and Th. Bäck, editors, *Evolutionary Programming V – Proc. Fifth Annual Conf. Evolutionary Programming (EP'96)*, pages 345 354, San Diego CA, 1996. The MIT Press, Cambridge MA.
12. H.-P. Schwefel. *Evolution and Optimum Seeking*. Sixth-Generation Computer Technology. Wiley, New York, 1995.
13. J. Sprave. Linear neighborhood evolution strategy. In A. V. Sebald and L. J. Fogel, editors, *Proc. Third Annual Conf. Evolutionary Programming (EP'94)*, pages 42 51, San Diego, CA, 1994. World Scienti"c, Singapore.
14. W. S. Torgerson. Multidimensional scaling: I. theory and method. *Psychometrika*, 17:401 419, 1952.

Neural Networks and Evolutionary Algorithms for the Prediction of Thermodynamic Properties for Chemical Engineering

Martin Mandischer[1], Hannes Geyer[2], and Peter Ulbig[2]

[1] Department of Computer Science XI, University of Dortmund, Germany
[2] Institute for Thermodynamics, University of Dortmund, Germany

Abstract. In this paper[1] we report results for the prediction of thermodynamic properties based on neural networks, evolutionary algorithms and a combination of them. We compare backpropagation trained networks and evolution strategy trained networks with two physical models. Experimental data for the enthalpy of vaporization were taken from the literature in our investigation. The input information for both neural network and physical models consists of parameters describing the molecular structure of the molecules and the temperature. The results show the good ability of the neural networks to correlate and to predict the thermodynamic property. We also conclude that backpropagation training outperforms evolutionary training as well as simple hybrid training.
Keywords: Neural Networks, Evolution Strategies, Hybrid-Learning, Chemical Engineering

1 Introduction

In chemical engineering the simulation of chemical plants is an important task. Millions of chemical compounds are known yet and experimental data are often not available. For this reason there is a need for calculation methods which are able to predict thermodynamic properties. Usually models are developed, which have a physical background and where the model parameters have to be fitted with the aid of experimental data. This leads usually to nonlinear regression models with a multi-modal objective function where evolution strategies are successfully used. In contrast to models with physical background simple so-called incremental methods are widely used, too. Each functional group of a molecule gives a contribution to the thermodynamic property and the sum of all contributions have to be calculated. A new way for the calculation and prediction of thermodynamic properties is the use of neural networks. Descriptors, which can be derived from the molecular structure, have to be defined for the input layer. Then experimental data for a specific thermodynamic property can be used for training. Predictions of this thermodynamic property are then possible by using the molecular structure for a chemical compound, where no experimental data

[1] **Acknowledgments:** The work presented is a result of the *Collaborative Research Center SFB 531* sponsored by the Deutsche Forschungsgemeinschaft (DFG)

are available. In this investigation the enthalpy of vaporization was taken. In section 2 we give a brief overview of the models used and continue in section 3 with an experimental comparison of physical models, networks trained with backpropagation, networks trained with evolutionary algorithms and a combination of the latter two.

2   Models for the enthalpy of vaporization

2.1   Physical models

The physical background for the enthalpy of vaporization H_v consists of electrostatic interactions forced by the atoms of the molecules. Equations can be derived from statistical thermodynamics in order to describe the interactions between molecules (first level) and between functional groups of these molecules (second level). Physical models, such as UNIVAP[2] (UNIversal enthalpies of VAPorization) which summarizes the interactions between functional groups of the molecules within a pure liquid were developed [8]. This model consists of sums of exponential terms, which include the interaction parameters and the temperature. The interactions are weighed by the surface fractions of functional groups of a molecule. The interaction parameters can be fitted to experimental enthalpy of vaporization data. This leads to a non-linear regression problem with a multi modal objective function. This function consists of the mean absolute error (MAE) over all experimental data points N between the calculated values (physical model) and the experimental data: $MAE = \frac{1}{N} \sum_N \left| H_v^{calc.} - H_v^{exp.} \right|$

Due to the complex structure of the physical model, especially the exponential terms, multi-modality occurs. An evolution strategy for solving this problem was developed [3,8,9]. Another theoretical approach is the so-called EBGVAP model (Enthalpy Based Group contribution model for enthalpies of VAPorization) which was used in our investigation, too.

2.2   Neural Networks

Neural networks are able to acquire an internal model of a process by learning from examples. After successful training the network will be a model for the process which led to the experimental data. Theoretical results show that feedforward networks are capable of arbitrary exact function approximation, given an unlimited number of free parameters or infinite precision [4].

In our experiments we used simple feed-forward networks with non-linear sigmoid activation functions. As training algorithms we employed the standard Backpropagation algorithm [6] and various $(\mu,)$ evolution strategies [7,1] as well as a combination of both.

---

[2] For the UNIVAP model it was di cult to reach the critical point, where the enthalpy of vaporization reaches null. A modi"ed temperature dependence was used in this investigation to improve the performance at critical points (UNIVAP2).

3   Experiments and Results

Comparing different methods or models is at least two-fold. On the one hand a fair comparison should allow all models the same number of free parameters to adjust to the problem. On the other hand, one can say that it is su cient if a model performs good on formerly unseen data regardless of the number of parameters it needed.

Some of our experiments were designed to find good neural models under the most similar conditions for the calculations as the physical models. Here the number of adjustable parameters was almost the same for all models. In other experiments we searched for good results independent of the number of free parameters (weights) used. One di culty is to find the optimal structure of the neural network and the optimal structure of the temperature dependent equation of the physical model. Here we only investigated the structure of the network. Another important issue is to have the same input information for all methods, which can be derived from the structure of the molecules.

3.1   Generation and Description of the Data

Selection of data. The experimental data concerning the enthalpy of vaporization were taken from data handbooks. Data for three different classes of chemical compounds were used: normal alkanes, 1-alcohols, and branched alcohols. These data were chosen for the investigation of three different functional groups, the so-called main groups: CH_3, CH_2 and CH_nOH. The group CH_nOH contains the functional groups CH_3OH, CH_2OH and $CHOH$. The experimental data cover a temperature range from 92 K to 776 K. The number of carbon atoms in the n-alkanes goes from 2 (Ethane) to 19 (Nonadecane), for the 1-alcohols from 1 (Methanol) to 14 (Tetradecanol) and for the branched alcohols from 4 (2-Methyl-2-propanol) to 6 (2-Methyl-2-pentanol).

Selection of descriptors. There are several possibilities for the definition of descriptors as input variables for a neural network: number of atoms, number of single bonds, molar mass, dipole moment and topological parameters concerning the connectivity between atoms [2]. In our investigation the descriptors for the input layer are the surface fractions of the functional groups within a molecule and the temperature. Therefore a definition of functional groups is necessary. Here the definition of the UNIVAP model [8] shall be used.

Partitioning into subsets for cross validation. After generating the data set it was subdivided into 3 classes: training (50%), validation (25%) and test (25%) set. The training set was used to adapt the parameters for all our models. The validation set could be used during the adaption process to evaluate the algorithms performance on unknown data and stop the adaption process if the error on the validation set increases. Validation and test set therefore measure the generalization ability of our models. However, 50% of the data were used only for comparison, i. e. for a test of the prediction of the enthalpy of vaporization. The distribution of the data can be seen in Table 1.

Group interaction	parameters	data points (total)	data points (training)
CH_3CH_3	3	110	53 (48.18 %)
CH_3CH_2 / CH_2CH_2	9	138	75 (54.35 %)
CH_nOHCH_nOH	3	19	10 (52.36 %)
CH_3CH_nOH / CH_2CH_nOH	12	162	76 (46.91 %)
total:	27	429	214 (49.88 %)

Table 1. Number of experimental data for the different group interactions

Transformation. For the use with the neural network the data were normalized via separate linear transformations of main-groups, temperature and enthalpy to the interval [0.1 .. 0.9]. Network responses outside of this interval were mapped onto the boundaries and then re-transformed to the original scale.

3.2 Physical Model Experiments

The training set was used for the regression of the interaction parameters and the training of the neural network. First the parameters were computed successive, i. e. first the 3 parameters for the interaction CH_3/CH_3 were calculated and with these parameters the next 9 parameters (corresponding to Table 1) were calculated and so on. These sequential experiments for the physical models were done with the aid of an encapsulated evolution strategy without a correlated step-length control [3]: $\left[GG\ 3 + 8(GG\ 7 + 19)^{200}\right]^{40}$

Three different runs with each $1.2 \cdot 10^6$ function calls of the evolution strategies gave similar results. These results were optimized by the simplex-method with 30 different runs of 1000 iterations each. The best result for UNIVAP2 (seq) and EBGVAP (seq) can be found in Table 2. In contrast to this sequential regression of the model parameters a simultaneous regression (sim) of all 27 parameters was investigated by using a similar encapsulated ES as for the sequential experiments. The results of these runs were improved by a simplex-method, too and can be seen in Table 2.

	UNIVAP 2 (seq)	EBGVAP (seq)	UNIVAP 2 (sim)	EBGVAP (sim)
Train	0.914	0.635	1.128	3.784
Valid	1.190	0.867	1.353	4.436
Test	0.948	0.613	1.209	3.863
All	1.017	0.705	1.230	4.028
	NN-A	NN-B	NN-ES (best)	NN-ES (avrg)
Train	0.652	0.570	0.612	1.143
Valid	0.566	0.878	0.876	1.536
Test	0.686	0.703	0.747	1.357
All	0.635	0.717	0.745	1.345

Table 2. Mean absolut error per pattern for different data sets and models

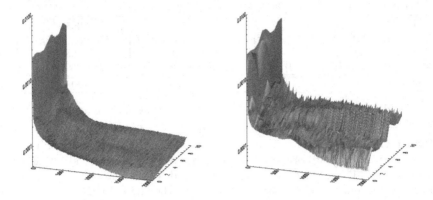

Fig. 1. Training error (η=0.8)   **Fig. 2.** Validation error (η=0.8)

3.3   Neural Networks Experiments (Backpropagation)

The learning rate   and the architecture of the network (number of hidden units and connections) have the biggest in"uence on the performance of the network [5]. To find good neural network solutions we did a primitive parameter study. We first varied the learning rate with a fixed architecture which had approximately the same number of free parameters (connections) as the UNIVAP methods. With the best learning rate found, we searched for a good number of hidden units. All runs were performed 10 times.

Variation of the learning rate. We fixed the architecture of the network at 4 input, 4 hidden and 1 output units (4-4-1) to have approximately the same number of free parameters (25) as the UNIVAP method. We started with a very low learning rate   = 0.001 and ended with a far too high rate   = 10.0. The momentum term   was fixed to 0.2. A training run was stopped after it reached the error limit or exceeded a maximum number of 100,000 pattern presentations (epochs). The error is defined as: $tss = \frac{1}{2} \times \sum_{i=1}^{n} (\ _i - o_i)^2$. With   as target vector and o as output activation of the network.

Figure 1 and 2 show the curves for 10 different runs with the best learning rate which was used throughout all other experiments. The left-hand side figure gives the error on the training set and on the right-hand side we see the validation error. If an error curve reaches the base of the graph it satisfied a specified error limit ($tss \leq 5 \times 10^{-5}$) for the whole training set. Networks with very low learning rate never reached the specified error limit, due to the very slow learning progress. A too high rate, resulted in oscillating error curves.

Variation of the number of hidden units. After variation of   we used the best rate, as constant for the hidden unit search[3]. The number of hidden units were varied between 1 and 40. Networks with less then 3 units failed to learn the task. Up to 40 units the results on training as well as validation data were

---

[3] This does not mean that both parameter are independent of each other. We consider this value to be a "rst estimate to start with.

almost independent of the number units employed. We therefore used our initial 4-4-1 network. This is an additional advantage because it can now be directly compared to other methods which use the same number of free parameters.

3.4   Neural Networks Experiments (Evolution Strategy)

In this experiment we substituted the Backpropagation algorithm with an evolution strategy. Some authors [10] reported good results when training a network with an ES. Again we systematically searched for a good parametrisation of the (15,100) ES. Parameters under consideration were the number of mutation step-sizes σ_i and the recombination scheme used on the object variables x_i (the network weights). Each parameter setting was run for 10,000 generations (1,000,000 pattern presentations) and repeated 10 times to have some statistical validity. All of the following variations of the bisexual recombination scheme were done with 1 and 25 σ : no recombination of x_i and σ_i, discrete recombination of x_i and discrete of σ_i discrete recombination of x_i and intermediate of σ_i intermediate recombination of x_i and discrete of σ_i intermediate recombination of x_i and intermediate of σ_i. For details on ES see [1,7].

None of the parameter settings lead to good and reliable results. Only one out of all ES trained network performed comparable to Backpropagation. All other networks give rather poor results. The quality of the average result did improve when using backpropagation as local search procedure (an additional training of 250,000 epochs) after ES optimization but was not as good as Backpropagation alone. Figure 3 shows the best run, which we regard as a very rare event, with a (15,100) ES.

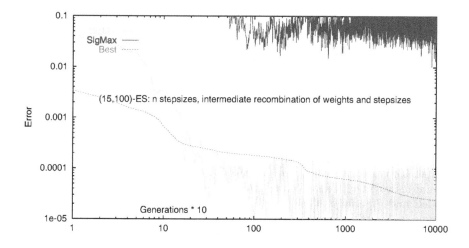

Fig. 3. (15,100) ES (error during training)

3.5   Comparison

For a comparison, we took two network architectures with learning rates gained by the previous experiments. Architecture A has 4 hidden units and the nearly the same number of free parameters (25 weights) as the UNIVAP models (27). Architecture B performs alike and has 6 hidden units (37 weights). Table 2 gives on overview of all experiments.

1. Parameters for NN-A (4-4-1): =0.8, epochs=250,000
2. Parameters for NN-B (4-6-1): =0.8, epochs=250,000
3. Parameters for NN-ES (4-4-1): best (15,100) ES # $ = n$, intermediate recombination of x_i and $_i$ (100,000 generations)
4. Parameters for NN-ES (4-4-1): average (15,100) ES # $ = n$, intermediate recombination of x_i and $_i$ (100,000 generations)

As an additional test for generalisation ability, we used all data of an ethane molecule. In figures 4 and 5 we compare all models on the enthalpy prediction for ethane. It can be seen that the physical model and the neural network performs equally well on this task, except for the critical regions near $T \rightarrow T_{cr}$ and $H_v(T_{cr}) = 0$ J/mol, where the network outperforms all other models. Almost all networks trained with an ES and the UNIVAP model give only a poor linear approximation of the enthalpy curve.

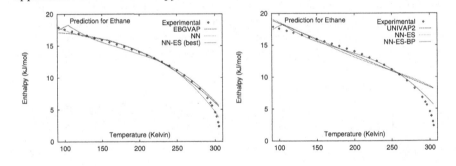

Fig. 4. Performance on ethane (good)   **Fig. 5.** Performance on ethane (poor)

4   Discussion

The most important result of this investigation is the good ability to correlate as well as to predict the enthalpy of vaporization with neural and physical methods. Neural networks with simple Backpropagation training are as good as physical models and especially at critical temperatures even slightly better, but their computational effort is much lower. The comparison of the results for UNIVAP2 and EBGVAP show the in"uence of the structure of the model itself. Further investigations could use evolutionary algorithm to optimize the structure of the models with regard to the temperature dependence. For the neural networks it can be stated that the use of surface fractions of functional groups as descriptors for a neural network leads to good results for both correlation and prediction. The big advantage of this new procedure is, that the molecules can easily be divided into functional groups, which makes it easy to use in engineering applications and allows the direct comparison of neural networks and physical models, due to the same input information. The investigations concerning the architecture of the neural networks show, that a simple network structure is su cient and a more complicated network does not give better results. In this context evolution strategies as training algorithm and combinations of ES with backpropagation failed to deliver useful models in almost all experiments.

From a thermodynamic point of view, it is interesting that a simple method like a neural network can give similar results in comparison with much more complicated physical motivated models. If a physical model gives results with a quality less than a neural model, the physical model should be improved. However, in chemical engineering there are many thermophysical properties, which are usually not described by physical methods, but by incremental methods. These methods, for example, for critical data, normal boiling points and so on, could be replaced by neural networks. However, these results are first steps in developping e cient network structures for our purpose and especially investigations with more functional groups will give a better comparison between physical models and neural networks.

References

1. T. Bäck. *Evolutionary Algorithms in Theory and Practice*. Oxford Univ. Press, New York, 1996.
2. L. M. Egolf and P. Jurs. Prediction of boiling points of organic heterocyclic compounds using regression and neural network techniques. In *J. Chem. Inf. Comput. Sci. 33*, pages 616 625. 1993.
3. H. Geyer, P. Ulbig, and S. Schulz. Encapsulated evolution strategies for the determination of group contribution parameters in order to predict thermodynamic properties. In *5th Int'l. Conf. on Parallel Problem Solving from Nature*. Amsterdam, 1998.
4. K. Hornik, M. Stinchcombe, and H. White. Multilayer feedforward networks are universal approximators. *Neural Networks*, 2:359 366, 1989.
5. M. Mandischer. Evolving recurrent neural networks with non-binary encoding. In *Proc. Second IEEE Int'l Conf. Evolutionary Computation (ICEC '95), vol. 2*, pages 584 589, Perth, Australia, 1995. IEEE Press, Piscataway NJ.
6. D. E. Rummelhart and J. L. McClelland. *PDP: Explorations in the Microstructure of Cognition*, volume 1. MIT Press, Cambridge, MA, USA, 1986.
7. H.-P. Schwefel. *Evolution and Optimum Seeking*. Sixth-Generation Computer Technology. Wiley, New York, 1995.
8. P. Ulbig. *Gruppenbeitragsmodelle UNIVAP & EBGCM*. Dr.-Ing. Thesis, Univ. of Dortmund, Institute for Thermodynamics, 1996.
9. P. Ulbig, T. Friese, H. Geyer, C. Kracht, and S. Schulz. Prediction of thermodynamic properties for chemical engineering with the aid of Computational Intelligence. In *Progress in Connectionist-Based Information Systems*. Springer, 1997.
10. W. Wienholt. Minimizing the system error in feedforward neural networks with evolution strategy. In S. Gielen and B. Kappen, editors, *Proc. of the Int'l. Conf. on Artificial Neural Networks*, pages 490 493, London, 1993. Springer-Verlag.

Evolving FPGA Based Cellular Automata

Reid Porter and Neil Bergmann

Cooperative Research Centre for Satellite Systems,
Queensland University of Technology, Brisbane, Australia
r.porter//n.bergmann@qut.edu.edu,
Ph: +61 7 3864 1987, Fax: +61 7 3864 1361

Abstract. Cellular Automata architectures are attractive due to their
"ne grain parallelism, simple computational structures and local routing resources. Some researchers have used genetic algorithms to "nd CA
that perform *useful* computations. The inherently parallel cellular automata model as well as the genetic algorithm are poorly suited to implementation on general purpose microprocessor based systems. Field Programmable Gate Arrays are an alternative that can provide signi"cant
speedup. This paper describes the Xilinx XC6216 Field Programmable
Gate Array and how it is used to e ciently search a *hybrid* 2-state, 5-
neighbour cellular automata rule space that exhibits computation universality. Its application to an image processing application, binary texture
analysis, is discussed.

Keywords: FPGA, Cellular Automata, Genetic Algorithm

1 Introduction

Cellular Automata (CA) have been considered as a model for general purpose
computation by several authors. Several works describe CA capable of universal
computation (computational power equivalent to a universal Turing machine [1]).
Field Programmable Gate Arrays (FPGA) can provide a programmable, max-
imally parallel implementation of CA but can only e ciently implement small
CA. Large CA require multiple FPGA and/or time multiplexing where array
initialisation and result reading soon dominate the computation time. Searching
CA rule spaces is one application which typically uses small test examples and
therefore small CA.

Papers by Richards et. al[2], Mitchell[3] and Sahota[4] describe the use of
genetic algorithms to search CA rule spaces where fitness is a function of how
well the CA behaviour matches a desired algorithm output. We suggest that
CA individuals be implemented in a FPGA so that the time consuming fitness
evaluation task can be reduced. By using rapid reconfigurability individuals can
then be swapped in and out of hardware as required by the genetic algorithm [5].

Cellular Automata have long been considered as an ideal architecture for
spatially distributed/inherently parallel image processing applications [6]. We
are particularly interested in the application of small CA for block based image
processing applications such as local feature identification. In this paper we

propose the use of XC6200 series FPGAs to accelerate exploration of CA rule spaces to find solutions to such problems.

Previous work in this area has applied genetic algorithms to fixed size CA rule tables. We consider a unique XC6200 *hybrid* CA model and search a hardware dictated rule space based on the FPGA structure. This rule space has the advantage of computation universality as well as ease of implementation.

Section 2 will introduce Field Programmable Gate Arrays and the Xilinx XC6216 device. Section 3 describes the XC6216 *hybrid* CA model and discusses the allocation of hardware resources and universal computation. Application of genetic algorithms and issues of representation are discussed in Section 4. Section 5 presents the CA Evolver experimental apparatus and its application to a block based image processing application: binary texture analysis. Results and observations will be presented in Section 6 followed by a summary and discussion of future work in Section 7.

2   Field Programmable Gate Arrays and the XC6216

Field Programmable Gate Arrays are now a popular implementation style for digital logic systems and sub-systems. These devices consist of an array of un-committed logic gates whose function and interconnection is determined by downloading configuration information to the device. When the programming configuration is held in static RAM, the logic function implemented by those FPGAs can be dynamically reconfigured in fractions of a second by rewriting the contents of the SRAM configuration memory.

The XC6216 FPGA by Xilinx, depicted in Figure 1(a), has a regular 64 by 64 two-dimensional array of function blocks. These function blocks, depicted in Figure 1(b), contain a function unit capable of implementing any 2 input logic gate or 3 input multiplexer as well as a d-type "ip-"op. Each block also

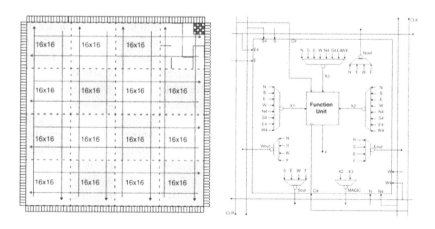

Fig. 1. (a) The XC6216 FPGA and (b) The XC6216 Cell

contains local routing resources to adjacent neighbours ($N_{out}, S_{out}, E_{out}, W_{out}$ multiplexers).

Function blocks are grouped hierarchically for routing purposes. At the lowest level blocks are interconnected to the nearest neighbours in four directions. These blocks are grouped into four and supplemented with length 4 fastlanes. These 4x4 groups then form part of larger 16x16 groups which are further supplemented by length 16 wires and chip-length interconnects. The configuration memory of Xilinx XC6216 FPGA is mapped directly to the host processor enabling partial reconfigurability where part of an FPGA device can be programmed at high speed without affecting the rest of the design. Readers are referred to [7] for a more detailed description of the XC6216 device.

3   The XC6216 *hybrid* Cellular Automata

In their simplest form Cellular Automata can be considered a homogeneous array of cells in one, two, three or more dimensions. Each cell has a finite discrete state. Cells communicate with a number of local neighbours and update synchronously according to deterministic rules [8]. One of the simplest CA models has 5 neighbours and 2 states. The state of each binary 0/1 cell depends on the state of the cell at the previous time step, plus the state of the four north, south, east and west neighbours at the previous time step.

To implement this CA model, we need to be able to implement any logic function of 5 variables. This can be achieved with a look up table, or alternatively with the logic tree of Figure 2(a). This logic tree is implemented in a 4 by 4 group of XC6216 function blocks illustrated in Figure 2(b). The function block outputs, which implement the logic tree structure are illustrated by solid arrows. The CA cell state is stored in function block 5. This function block output is routed back throughout the 4 by 4 group and to all north, south, east and west faces of the cell. Its path through the local routing resources is illustrated by dashed arrows.

State information from a CA cell's north, south, east and west neighbours is routed across all function blocks through the XC6216 length 4 *fastlanes*. This means that every function block has access to all 5 boolean state variables. The 4 by 4 group of Figure 2(b) is replicated across the XC6216 to form a 15 by 15 two dimensional Cellular Automata. The North/South and East/West ends of the array are wrapped around via the XC6216 chip length routing resources.

Codd in [8] proved that a 2-state 5 neighbour CA capable of universal computation did not exist with a finite initial configuration. Several authors achieved computation-universal CA models by adding more states or larger neighbourhoods [9]. We enhance the computational power of Figure 2(a) by including the additional memory resources ("ip-"ops) that are freely available in each XC6216 function block. This allows us to consider a CA model based on neighbourhood information from further back in time. With this in mind, unbounded but boundable propagation is easily demonstrated. We have also demonstrated the computation universality of this *hybrid* CA model by simulating Minsky's two register machine [9].

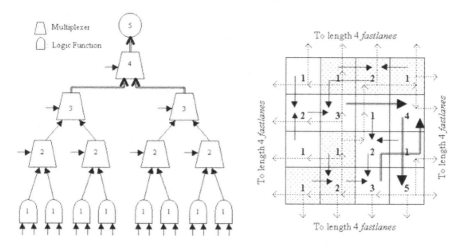

Fig. 2. (a) Flexible Logic Tree (b) Function Block Assignment

4   Searching the XC6216 *hybrid* CA rule space

To search the XC6216 *hybrid* CA rule space with a genetic algorithm several choices must be made concerning representation. In similar experiments, based in software, individuals represent fixed size rule tables. Ease of implementation leads us to consider a hardware dictated rule space with individuals based on the XC6216 configuration bit string. We consider two different hardware representations.

FPGA Bitstring: The first is based on the raw configuration bitstring of the 4 by 4 group of XC6216 function blocks. Connectivity between each group is pre-defined (to implement the 15 by 15 two dimensional CA array) but all routing and functionality within the group varies according to the genetic algorithm.

Logic Tree: The second representation is based on the "exible logic tree of Figure 2(a). In this case the routing resources both between and within each 4 by 4 group of function blocks are pre-defined and we evolve only function. A performance comparison of the *FPGA Bitstring* and *Logic Tree* hardware representations, as well as a software based CA rule table representation is presented in Section 6.

The function unit in each XC6216 function block is illustrated in Figure 3(a) and defined by two eight bit configuration bytes of Figure 3(b). CS defines whether or not the function unit will make use of the "ip-"op resource. The X1, X2 and X3 configuration bits define the input signals to the logic gate or multiplexer. Y2 and Y3 define the gate or multiplexer type. RP sets the "ip-"op as read-only and M defines additional routing resources.

When using the *Logic Tree* representation a CA individual is completely specified by defining these two bytes for each function block within the 4 by 4 group. The effective genetic string length for the *Logic Tree* GA is therefore

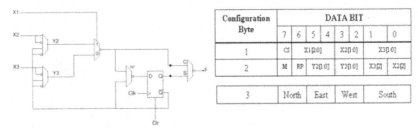

| Configuration | DATA BIT | | | | | | | |
Byte	7	6	5	4	3	2	1	0
1	CS	X1[2.0]		X2[1.0]		X3[1.0]		
2	M	RP	Y2[1.0]		Y3[1.0]		X3[2]	X2[2]
3	North		East		West		South	

Fig. 3. (a) XC6216 Function Unit and (b) Con"guration Bytes

32 bytes or 256 bits. The *FPGA Bitstring* GA requires an additional byte per function block. Configuration byte 3, illustrated in Figure 3(b), defines the local $N_{out}, S_{out}, E_{out}, W_{out}$ multiplexers of Figure 1(b). The effective genetic string length for the *FPGA Bitstring* GA is therefore 48 bytes or 384 bits.

5   The CA Evolver Experimental apparatus

Our experiments are based on the HotWorks development system. This system incorporates a Xilinx XC6216 FPGA that communicates to a host processor through a 32 bit PCI bus. The main genetic algorithm loop and genetic operators are implemented on the host processor. A population of CA individuals are held in memory and downloaded into the XC6216 as required to perform the fitness evaluation task.

The reproduction scheme is similar to that used in [3]. The fittest 100 CA individuals from a population of 300 are copied directly to the next generation. The remaining 200 are generated by application of the cross-over and mutation operators on parents chosen with replacement from the *elite* 100.

For the *FPGA Bitstring* GA a one point cross-over is applied to the 384 bit configuration bit string. For the *Logic Tree* representation a specialised cross-over that constrains the structure of CA offspring to the logic tree of Figure 2(a) is used. A cross-over branch is randomly selected and then a sub-tree formed by all child nodes and branches. This sub-tree is then exchanged between two parents similar to genetic programming [5]. In both cases offspring are mutated in exactly four randomly chosen positions.

The XC6216 CA Evolver system is applied to a binary texture analysis problem which involves identifying a particular pattern within a 15 by 15 pixel area. The binary pattern chosen in this experiment is diagonal lines. Two screenshots of the CA Evolver system, each with training image on the left and ideal image on the right, are depicted in Figure 4. Each training image is *segmented* either horizontally as in Figure 4(a) or vertically 4(b).The non-patterned segment is filled with noise of a density randomly selected from a uniform distribution between 0 and 1.

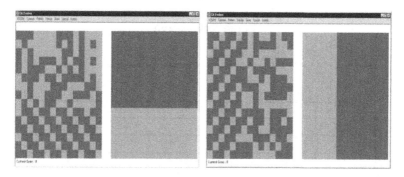

Fig. 4. (a) Horizontal and (b) Vertically segmented: input image left/ideal image right

The state of each CA cell is first initialised with the corresponding point in the 15 by 15 training image. The XC6216 is then clocked for 200 cycles at 33Mhz to iterate the CA array. The fitness of the CA individual is calculated by a bit by bit comparison of the state of CA cells and the ideal image. A fitness counter is incremented for each CA cell in correspondence with the ideal image. While the counter is greater than zero it was also decremented for each cell that is not in correspondence. As in [4] CA individuals that lead to collapsed images (the state of the CA array ends up all 1's or all 0's) are penalised and receive a fitness score of 0. Each individual within the population is evaluated against 300 training images at each generation. As in [4] the overall fitness for an individual is calculated as the root mean square over the 300 images.

6   Performance Comparison

The computation times for the XC6216 based genetic algorithms were estimated from the CA Evolver experiments. A software based experiment that searched the XC6216 *hybrid* CA rule table was also implemented and is compared in Table 1. The computation time for the genetic algorithm can be calculated as:

$\mathbf{T_{total}} = \mathbf{T_{pop}} + Generations * (\mathbf{T_{fit}} + \mathbf{T_{ga}})$ where $\mathbf{T_{pop}}$ is the time to generate a population, $\mathbf{T_{fit}}$ is the time needed to evaluate the fitness of a population and $\mathbf{T_{ga}}$ is the time to generate a new population with the GA operators.

Measurements were based on non-optimised code and it is expected that execution time could be significantly reduced. The relative measurement of speedup can be considered accurate and is summarised in Table 1.

Measurement in Seconds	Software Rule table	FPGA Bitstring	Logic Tree	Relative Speedup
T_{pop}	0.1	0.1	0.1	1
T_{it} per generation	1987.9	34.22	34.17	58
T_{ga} per generation	0.05	0.06	0.08	1

Table 1. Estimation of Speedup

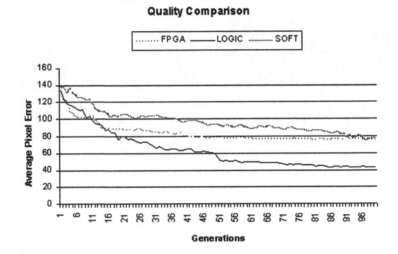

Fig. 5. Average pixel error in experiments

We also make a qualitative comparison of the two FPGA based GA, *FPGA Bitstring* and *Logic Tree* representations as well as the software based rule table GA. For each experiment run the GA had 100 generations in which to find a CA to correctly classify the diagonal line pattern. Figure 5 illustrates the average pixel error as a function of GA time (generations). The *Logic Tree* representation outperformed the *FPGA Bitstring* representation in all experiments. We conclude that constraining connectivity and evolving only function avoids strange feedback loop/analog circuit behaviours and allows a more detailed exploration of a smaller, more relevant rule space.

In several runs individuals of note appeared that performed well for images segmented in one direction (eg. vertically) but poorly in the other direction. To encourage the GA to find solutions in both directions the *Logic Tree* search space was further constrained. The multiplexer selector of node 4 in Figure 2(a) was pre-defined as the cell's current state in order to reduce the size of the non-symmetric rule space. Due to the close spatial relationship between training and ideal images, two nodes of type 1 (one in each half of the logic tree) were also pre-defined to store the initial training image data. The best of run CA from these experiments had an average pixel error of 40 pixels, lower than any other CA found. We conclude the *Logic Tree* GA can implement problem specific constraints more easily than raw FPGA bitstring and rule table based approaches.

7   Summary and Future Directions

The CA Evolver is a powerful tool with which to investigate genetic algorithm 'programming' techniques of cellular automata architectures. When searching XC6216 *hybrid* CA rule spaces speedup in the order of 10-100 times can be achieved compared to software implementations. Our initial experiments applied this tool to a binary texture analysis problem and investigated the role of representation. The FPGA based search space allowed problem specific constraints to be implemented easily leading to improved performance of the genetic algorithm.

Questions yet to be addressed include the role of non local CA neighbourhoods, extension to practical application and issues of scale. Eventually our work hopes to redefine these questions in terms of how best to 'program' XC6216 architectures as massively parallel machines and investigate a range of cellular automata models including random boolean networks.

Acknowledgement

This work was carried out in the Cooperative Research Centre for Satellite Systems with financial support from the Commonwealth of Australia through the CRC program.

References

1. J. E. Hopcroft and J. D. Ullman,   Introduction to Automata Theory, Languages and Computation , Addison-Wesley, 1979, Reading, Massachusetts.
2. F. C. Richards, T. P. Meyer, N. H. Packard,   Extracting Cellular Automaton Rules Directly from Experimental Data , Cellular Automata: Theory and Experiment, H. Gutowitz, ed., 1st MIT Press ed., 1991, Massachusetts.
3. M. Mitchell, J. P. Crutch"eld and R. Das,   Evolving Cellular Automata with Genetic Algorithms: A Review of Recent Work , First International Conference on Evolutionary Computation and Its Applications (EvCA 96), Moscow, Russia.
4. P. Sahota, M. F. Daemi, D. G. Elliman,   Training Genetically Evolving Cellular Automata for Image Processing , International Symposium on Speech, Image Processing and Neural Networks, 13-16 April, 1994, Hong Kong.
5. J. R. Koza, F. H. Bennett III, J. L. Hutchings, S. L. Bade, M. A. Keane, D. Andre   Rapid Recon"gurable Field-Programmable Gate Arrays for Accelerating Fitness Evaluation in Genetic Programming , Late Breaking Papers at the Genetic Programming 1997 Conference, J. R. Koza, ed., pp. 121-131, 1997, Stanford.
6. A. Rosenfeld,   Parallel Image Processing Using Cellular Arrays , Computer, No. 16, pp. 14-20, 1983.
7. Xilinx Inc.   XC6200 Field Programmable Gate Arrays   Product Description, Version 1.10, April 24, 1997.
8. E.F. Codd,   Cellula Automata , Academic Press, 1968, New York.
9. E. R. Banks,   Universality in Cellular Automata , IEEE 11th Annual Symposium on Switching and Automata Theory, pp. 194-215, 1970, Santa Monica, California.

Asynchronous Island Parallel GA
Using Multiform Subpopulations

Hirosuke Horii, Susumu Kunifuji, and Teruo Matsuzawa
{holly, kuni, matuzawa}@jaist.ac.jp

Japan Advanced Institute of Science and Technology
Tatsunokuchi, Ishikawa, 923-1292, JAPAN

Abstract. Island Parallel GA divides a population into subpopulations and assigns them to processing elements on a parallel computer. Then each subpopulation searches the optimal solution independently, and exchanges individuals periodically. This exchange operation is called *migration*. In this research, we propose a new algorithm that migrants are exchanged asynchronously among multiform subpopulations which have diˇerent search conditions. The eˇect of our algorithm on combinational optimization problems was veri"ed by applying the algorithm to Knapsack Problem and Royal Road Functions using parallel computer CRAY-T3E. We obtained the results that our algorithm maintained the population s diversity eˇectively and searches building blocks e ciently.

1 Introduction

There are two typical problems in Genetic Algorithms (GAs). First, GAs require huge calculation time for their genetic operations, such as selection, crossover, mutation, and individuals' fitness evaluations. Secondly, maintenance of the population's diversity is necessary to avoid the premature convergence which spreads local optimum solution and stagnates the evolution.

Island Parallel GA divides the population into subpopulations and assigns them to processing elements on a parallel computer to improve the prosessing speed. Then it performs *migration*, in other words, it exchanges individuals, so that it can maintain subpopulations' diversity.

To implement this migration, there are two possibilities, synchronously exchange individuals, synchronous migration model, and asynchronously exchange individuals, asynchronous migration model. Tanese's model called *Distributed GA* [1] is the typical synchronous migration model. It synchronously exchanges individuals among neighboring subpopulations to every fixed generation which called *migration interval*. If individuals are introduced before the search converged, it is di cult to generate superior schemata because good schemata will be destructed. Thus it is effective to introduce individuals after the search converged. However the progress of the search situation differs both the objective problems and every subpopulation, and it makes di cult to set optimal migration interval.

Munetomo's model [2] is the typical asynchronous migration model, where migration is performed asynchrounously when its genetic construction's diversity is lost. The loss of the diversity is judged by the ralative reduction rate of the fitness distribution's standard deviation. Migrants are introduced from other subpopulation which has the most different genetic construction. The differences among subpopulations' genetic constructions are measured by the differences among their fitness distributions' average values and standard deviations. However it is di cult to grasp the search situation correctly in the problem where the similarities of a gene and a fitness do not correspond such as combinational optimization problems.

Considering the problems in both models, we propose a new algorithm which performs migration asynchronously and a new migration scheme which is more suitable for combinational optimization problems.

2 Asynchronous Island Parallel GA

This section describes the feature and the aim of our algorithm. We propose a new migration scheme and a cooperative search by the subpopulations which have different search conditions.

2.1 Migration

In order to maintain the diversity of the genetic construction, migrants must be introduced from the subpopulation which has the most different genetic construction. Then we face the problem. We need scales to grasp the search situation and to measure the genetic construction of each subpopulation. As a solution for this problem we propose to use *Bias* and *Temporal Schema* [4].

Bias and *Temporal Schema* are defined as follows. The population is expressed by a matrix $P(t)$, using the bit string of each individual as a row vector, where p_{ij}^t means i-th individual's j-th locus at t generation. Diversity of the population, which has population size N and gene length L, is measured as *Bias* B^t ($0.5 \leq B^t \leq 1.0$). *Temporal Schema* TS^t is a binary string of length L and shows on which each locus has converged to 1 or 0 at t generation. K_{TS} is a parameter of the schema detection threshold which is set up in the range ($0.5 \leq K_{TS} \leq 1.0$). In each locus, when the individuals of the rate more than K_{TS} has 1 or 0, it is considered that the locus converged.

$$P(t) = (p_{ij}^t) \tag{1}$$

$$B^t = \frac{1}{N \times L} \sum_{j=1}^{L} \left[\left| \sum_{i=1}^{N} p_{ij}^t - \frac{N}{2} \right| + \frac{N}{2} \right] \tag{2}$$

$$TS^t = (ts_1^t, ts_2^t, ..., ts_L^t)$$
$$ts_i^t = \begin{cases} 1 : \sum_{j=1}^{N} p_{ij}^t \geq N \times K_{TS} \\ 0 : \sum_{j=1}^{N} (1 - p_{ij}^t) \geq N \times K_{TS} \\ * : otherwise \end{cases} \tag{3}$$

Each subpopulation judges whether the diversity of the genetic construction is lost or not by the comparison between *Bias* B^t and the fixed threshold K_B. When *Bias* B^t exceeds the fixed threshold K_B, migration is performed. Hamming distances among the *Temporal Schema* of the subpopulation which performs migration and the other subpopulations' are made into the measure which judges the degree of difference of the genetic construction. By introducing migrants, it not only recovers the diversity of the genetic construction, but also it can obtain superior schemata generated by the other subpopulations.

2.2   Cooprative Search Using Multiform Subpopulations

In Island Parallel GA, since a population is divided into small subpopulations, the random genetic drift affects each subpopulation's evolution strongly. So, even if the parameters of each subpopulation's genetic operations are set up equally, each subpopulation's genetic construction becomes various. Thus Island Parallel GA is cooperative search using multiform subpopulations tacitly.

We propose making multiform subpopulations clearly by setting the parameters for the genetic operations different values, aiming to improve the adaptability of the algorithm to object problems.

Ishikawa's model [3] performs the cooperative search using four subpopulations whose the generation gaps are set to 1.0, 0.7, 0.4 and 0.1. In his algorithm, the cooperative search is performed among the subpopulations which search the circumferences of high fitness individuals intensively by setting low generation gap, and supply new individuals by setting high generation gap.

3   Applying APGA to Knapsack Problem

We compare Asynchronous Island Parallel GA (APGA) with Synchronous Island Parallel GA (SPGA) by applying them to Knapsack Problem, which is the typical combinational optimization problem.

Knapsack Problem is defined as follows. Knapsack Problem stuffs the loads, which have weight and value as their parameters, into a knapsack, and searches for the optimum combination which maximizes the total value within the weight limits. In N loads, weight and value of the j-th load are set to w_j and v_j, and the weight limits of the knapsack is W. It is referred to as $x_j = 1$ when stu ng j-th load, and as $x_j = 0$ when not stu ng. Knapsack Problem is formulized as follows.

$$\left.\begin{array}{l} maximize \ \sum_{j=1}^{N} v_j x_j \\ subject \ to \ \sum_{j=1}^{N} w_j x_j \leq W \\ \qquad x_j \in \{0, 1\}, j = 1, ..., N \end{array}\right\} \qquad (4)$$

3.1 Experiment

The population of 512 individuals is divided into 16 and 32 subpopulations. APGA's migration is performed asynchronously, when Bias B^t exceeds the threshold of Bias K_B for 20 generations. On the otherhand, SPGA's migration is performed synchronously every 20 generations. Both APGA and SPGA are applied to Knapsack Problem which has 300 loads. Every trial is performed for 1000 generations. The results are evaluated by the average of 10 times trials.

3.2 Results and Discussion

Fig.1 shows the comparison between APGA and SPGA. Fig.1 indicates that APGA's fitness is lower than SPGA's in the early generations. However, APGA's fitness overtakes SPGA's in the later generations.

Fig.2 and Fig.3 show the changes of Bias in one of the subpopulations of APGA and SPGA in applying to Knapsack Problem. Fig.2 and Fig.3 indicate that APGA's genetic construction is maintained more diverse than SPGA's.

In APGA, although the search e ciency falls, the genetic construction's diversity recovers successfully, because migrants are introduced from the subpopulation which has the most different genetic construction. On the other hand, in SPGA, local optimum solutions spread in the whole population gradually, all subpopulations' genetic constructions become uniform, and the effect of migration is lost.

4 Applying APGA to Royal Road Functions

In this section, we apply APGA to Royal Road Functions, R_1 and R_4, which are evaluation functions proposed by Mitchell [5,6]. Royal Road Functions are given the feature of building block hypothesis specifically.

Royal Road Functions are defined as follows. R_1 uses one 8-bit binary string as one building block, and one individual consists of 8 building blocks, that is one individual consists of one 64-bit binary string. Fitness value is obtained when 8 loci, which constitute one building block, are set to '1'. Optimum value is obtained when all of the 64 loci, which constitute one individual, are set to '1'.

R_4 is an extended function of R_1 which uses 128-bit binary string as one individual. 8-bit binary string constitutes the lowest order building block, and two adjoining building blocks constitute a high order building block, that is one second order building block consists of 16-bit binary string and one third order

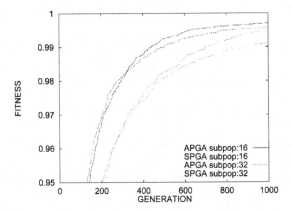

Fig. 1. The comparison between APGA and SPGA by applying to Knapsack Problem

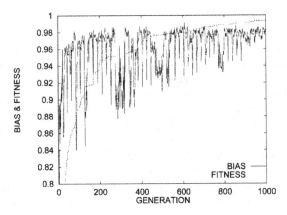

Fig. 2. The change of *Bias* in one of the subpopulations of APGA in applying to Knapsack Problem

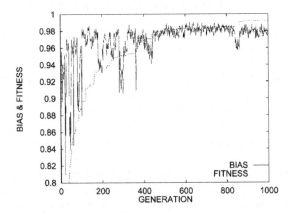

Fig. 3. The change of *Bias* in one of the subpopulations of SPGA in applying to

building block consists of 32-bit binary string. Fitness value is obtained when higher order building block is constructed. Optimum value is obtained when all of the 128 loci are set to '1'.

4.1   Experiments

We have two experiments, the evaluation of our migration scheme and the evaluation of cooperative search using multiform subpopulations.

Experiment 1: Migration in APGA We evaluate our migration scheme by applying APGA to R_1 and R_4. The population of 1024 individuals is divided into 4, 8, 16 and 32 subpopulations. Every R_1 trial is performed for 200 generations, and every R_4 trial is performed for 2000 generations. The results are evaluated by the average of 30 times trials.

Experiment 2: Cooperative Search in APGA Using Multiform Subpopulations We compare the single parameter model with the multiform parameters model by applying them to R_4. The population of 1024 individuals is divided into 32 subpopulations. Every R_4 trial is performed for 2000 generations. The results are evaluated by the average of 30 times trials.

In the single parameter model, we set the pair, (generation gap, mutation rate, threshold of Bias K_B), at (0.8, 0.01, 0.9).

In the multiform parameters model, we set the pair, (generation gap, mutation rate), at (0.8, 0.01) and (0.5, 0.05). The pair (0.8, 0.01) emphasizes the crossover and the pair (0.5, 0.05) emphasizes the mutation. And we set the threshold of Bias K_B at (0.9) and (0.8). K_B (0.9) emphasizes the carefully search in each subpopulation and K_B (0.8) emphasizes the global search by positively introducing migrants. We set 4 kinds of character on subpopulations by combining these parameter sets, (generation, gapmutation rate, threshold of Bias K_B) as (0.8,0.01,0.9), (0.8,0.01,0.8),(0.5,0.05,0.9) and (0.5,0.05,0.8).

4.2   Results and Discussion

Fig.4 and Fig.5 show the results of the first experiment. In the four subpopulations case, they converged early generations in the all experimental results. When the number of subpopulations increases and, at the same time, the number of the individuals in each subpopulation decreases, the convergence as the whole population becomes slow. Because the genetic construction of each subpopulation becomes various, since random genetic drift affects each subpopulation strongly. Therefore, our migration scheme is not suitable for the simple problem such as R_1. On the other hand, at the di cult problem such as R_4, our migration scheme is very e cient and good solution is obtained. Because the maintaining the diversity of the genetic construction prevents subpopulations from falling into local optimum solution. And furthermore, each subpopulation searches separate building blocks simultaneously, since subpopulations become

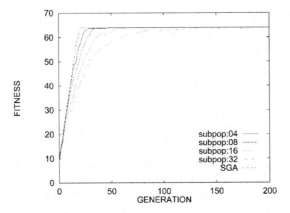

Fig. 4. Experiment 1: The process in applying APGA to Royal Road Function R_1

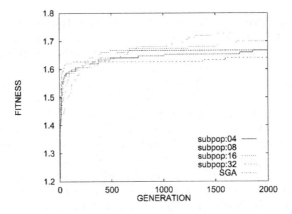

Fig. 5. Experiment 1: The process in applying APGA to Royal Road Function R_4

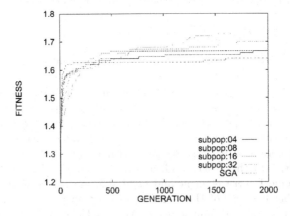

Fig. 6. Experiment 2: The comparison between the single parameter model and the

various by random genetic drift. Therefore, APGA is suitable for the problem which has the strong tendency of building block hypothesis.

Fig.6 shows the result of the second experiment. The multiform parameters model improved the accuracy comparing the single parameter model. We think the reason of this result that multiform subpopulations are allotted different task and cooperate with each other effectively. Unfortunately, we did not make su ciently investigation into multiform parameters model to substantiate the reason of the second experiment's result, we need more consideration about these things.

5   Conclusion

In this research, we proposed Asynchronous Island Parallel GA where multiform subpopulations migrate asynchronously according to each situation. The effect on the combinational optimization problems was verified by applying our algorithm to Knapsack Problem and Royal Road Functions using parallel computer CRAY-T3E. Through these experiments, the following results were obtained.

The migration scheme proposed in this research is effective for the combinational optimization problems. Especially, when our algorithm is applyed to the problem, such as Royal Road Functions, which has the strong tendency of building block hypothesis, it performs effectively by the parallel search of the building blocks. In the search using multiform subpopulations, the search e - ciency becomes worse, but the accuracy improves by maintaining the diversity of each subpopulation's genetic construction.

References

1. R. Tanese, Distributed Genetic Algorithm, in *Proceedings of the Third International Conference on Genetic Algorithms*, pp.434 439, 1989.
2. M. Munetomo, Y. Takai, and Y. Sato,   An E cient Migration Scheme for Subpopulation-Based Asynchronously Parallel Genetic Algorithms, in *Proceedings of the Fifth International Conference on Genetic Algorithms*, pp.649, 1993.
3. M. Ishikawa,T. Toya, and Y. Totoki, Parallel Application Systems in Genetic Processing, in *Proceedings of International Symposium on Fifth Generation Computer Systems*, pp.129 138,1994.
4. S. Tsutsui, and Y. Fujimoto, Forking Genetic Algorithm with Blocking and Shrinking Modes (fGA), in *Proceedings of the Fifth International Conference on Genetic Algorithms*, pp.206 213, 1993.
5. M. Mitchell, S. Forrest, and J. H. Holland, The Royal Road for Genetic Algorithms: Fitness Landscapes and GA Performance, in *Toward a Practice of Autonomous Systems: Proceedings of the First European Conference on Artificial Life*, pp.245 254,1992.
6. M. Mitchell, J. H. Holland, and S. Forrest, When Will a Genetic Algorithm Outperform Hill Climbing?, in *Advances in Neural Information Processing 6*, 1994.

Multiple Sequence Alignment Using Parallel Genetic Algorithms

L.A.Anbarasu[1], P.Narayanasamy[1], and V.Sundararajan[2]

[1] Anna University, Chennai 600 025, INDIA
[2] Center for Development of Advanced Computing, Pune 411 007, INDIA

Abstract. An e cient approach to solve multiple sequence alignment problem is presented in this paper. This approach is based on parallel genetic algorithm(PGA) that runs on a networked parallel environment. The algorithm optimizes an objective function weighted sums of pairs which measures alignment quality. Using isolated independent subpopulations of alignments in a quasi evolutionary manner this approach gradually improves the "tness of the subpopulations as measured by an objective function. This parallel approach is shown to perform better than the sequential approach and an alternative method, clustalw. An investigation of the parameters of the algorithm further con"rms the better performance.

1 Introduction

Simultaneous alignment of many DNA or Protein sequences is an important tool in molecular biology. Multiple alignments are used to study molecular evolution, to help predict the secondary or tertiary structure of new sequences, RNA folding and gene regulation. Basically, there have been two approaches to solving the problem of multiple sequence alignment: rigorous optimization by dynamic programming and heuristic algorithms.

Extending dynamic programming for pairwise sequence alignment to multiple alignment of N sequences is limited to small numbers of short sequences [8]. It requires memory space for N- dimensional array and calculation time of the order of the Nth power of the sequence length. However, using Carrillo and Lipman algorithm [3], the Multiple Sequence Alignment(MSA) program attempts to reduce the search space to a relatively small area [7]. Even with this reduction, it is limited to ten sequences at most. Therefore, all of the methods capable of handling larger problems in practical timescales make use of heuristics.

The most widely used heuristic approach is the 'progressive alignment' of Feng and Doolittle [4]. In this approach, the sequences are aligned in an order imposed by some estimated phylogenetic tree. It first aligns the most closely related sequences, gradually adding in the more distant ones. Some of the most widely used multiple alignment programs like ClustalW [13], Mutal and Pileup are based on this algorithm. This approach has the great advantage of speed and simplicity as well as reasonable sensitivity. The main drawback of this approach is the 'local minimum' problem that stems from the greedy nature of the algorithm. Stochastic heuristics such as simulated annealing or genetic algorithm [5] can be used to avoid this pitfall.

Simulated annealing has been used for multiple alignment but can be very slow and usually only works well as an alignment improver [6]. Genetic algorithms have been used to find globally optimal multiple alignments starting from completely unaligned sequences [9]. The stochastic methods have the advantages of "exibility and lower complexity. They do not have any strong restrictions on the number of sequences to align or the length of those sequences. These methods are very "exible in optimizing any objective functions.

Since genetic algorithm for multiple sequence alignment generally requires a long computation time it is desirable to use parallel genetic algorithms. We have developed a parallel genetic algorithm for multiple sequence alignment that runs on a networked parallel environment. We show that our parallel approach performs better than a sequential genetic algorithm when applied to multiple sequence alignment problem.

The contributions of this paper are:

- comparison of the performance of our algorithm with other sequence alignment methods;
- comparison of the alignment quality of our parallel approach with the sequential genetic algorithm running under same constraints;
- an investigation of the in"uence of some parallelization parameters on the alignment results.

We will use the term PGA to describe an *island genetic algorithm* with isolated independent subpopulations. The rest of the paper is organized as follows: the second section describes the problem formulation of multiple alignment. The parallel approach is discussed in section three. The fourth section gives the implementation details and results. The last section draws the conclusion and summarizes the present work.

2   Problem Formulation

One can define a biosequence multiple alignment as an alignment of the residues of a number of nucleic acid or protein sequences where a *gap character*, - , is used as a spacer so that each sequence has the same number of residues plus gaps in the alignment. A *column* is a set of characters(residues plus gaps), one from each sequence, written one over the other. The multiple alignment is composed of the union of its columns. Each multiple alignment induces a pairwise alignment [7].

Let $S_1, \ldots, S_K$, be the input sequences and assume that K is at least 2. Let be the input alphabet; we assume that   does not contain the character '-', so that a dash can be used to denote the gap in the alignment. Algorithms that construct multiple sequence alignments require a cost model as a criterion for constructing optimal alignment [7].

In the simplest cost model there is a cost function sub: $'\times' \to N$, where $'$ be the input alphabet including the gap character $-$. It can be defined such that $sub(a, b)$ is the cost of substituting a b in the second sequence for an a in the first sequence; also, $sub(-, b)$ is the cost for columns where the first sequence has a gap and the second has a b, and $sub(a, -)$ is the cost for columns where the first sequence has an a and the second has a $-$. The cost of pairwise alignment $A_{i,j}$ induced in a multiple alignment A of width w is

$$c(A_{i,j}) = \sum_{1 \leq k \leq w} sub(A[i][k], A[j][k])$$

With this, the basic *weighted sum of pairs* multiple sequence alignment problem is to minimize the pairwise sum

$$c(A) = \sum_{i<j} W_{i,j} c(A_{i,j})$$

3   Description of PGA

Genetic algorithms are highly suitable for parallelization and different ways exist to parallelize them [12]. Parallel genetic algorithm with isolated subpopulations or *the island genetic algorithms* is used to gain better problem solutions [11]. The population is divided into a few subpopulations or *demes*, and each of these relatively large demes evolve separately on different processors. Exchange between subpopulations is possible via a migration operator. A set of n individuals is assigned to each of N processors, for a total population size of $n \times N$.

Initial subpopulations that consist of randomly constructed alignments are created at each processor. Each processor, disjointly and in parallel, executes the sequential genetic algorithm on its subpopulation for a certain number of generations(*migration interval*). Afterwards, each subpopulation exchanges a specific number of individuals(*migrants*) with its neighbors. We exchange the individual themselves, i.e., the migrants are removed from one subpopulation and added to another. Hence, the size of the population remains the same after migration. The process continues with the separate evolution of each subpopulation for certain number of generations. [9].

3.1   Characteristics of PGA

Representation As DNA or Protein sequence alignment consist of both alphabets and a gap character '-', it's better to represent alignments as it is so that there is no need for any encoding or decoding mechanism. With all input sequences, other important informations such as length of the sequences, number of sequences, score etc. are placed in a structure. Initial subpopulation at each processor is created randomly. It consists of a set of alignments containing only terminal gaps. Alignments are created by choosing a random offset for all the sequences and then moving each sequence to the right, according to its offset.

Fitness function The fitness of each individual in a subpopulation is calculated by scoring each alignment according to the 'weighted sum of pairs' objective function. The overall alignment cost is calculated by adding a substitution cost and gap cost to each pair of aligned residues in each column of the alignment with their weights. We use *pam250* substitution matrix and natural a ne gap penalties for calculating fitness function [1]. Sequence weights are calculated using *rationale 1* method developed by Altschul [2].

Genetic operators In this parallel implementation we used all the operators of a sequential genetic algorithm approach for multiple sequence alignment. A detailed description of these operators can be found in [9] .

Selection

We use overlapping generation technique, where half of the population will survive unchanged, the other half will be replaced by the children during each generation. Individuals are ranked according to their fitness function, and the new children replace the weakest individuals. The expected offspring of an individual is calculated from the fitness. It is used as the probability for each individual to be chosen as a parent. Parent are selected for breeding according to their expected offspring value in spinning wheel.

Crossover

A new alignment is created using crossover operator by combining two different alignment. Both, one-point crossover and uniform crossover are implemented. Two parent alignments are combined through a single exchange in one-point crossover. The first parent is cut straight at some randomly chosen position and the second one is tailored so that the right and the left pieces of each parent can be joined together while keeping the original order of the sequence of amino acids. Any void space that appears at the junction point is filled with null signs. This filling of null signs at junction point forces to design an operator that combines the properties of traditional crossover and those of mutation. The best of the two children produced in this way is kept in the population.

The uniform crossover is designed to promote multiple exchanges between areas of homology. In both the parent, consistent positions are identified first. Two positions are said to be consistent if each column contain the same residue or a null coming from the same gap. Blocks between consistent positions are swapped to create a new alignment.

Block shu ing

A block of residues or a block of gaps can be moved inside an alignment using this operator. A set of overlapping stretches of residues from one or more sequences is called a block of residues. Each subsequence can be of different length but all subsequences must overlap. A block is chosen first by selecting one residue or gap position from the alignment and moved to a specified position.

Gap insertion

The sequences are split into two groups based on an estimated phylogenetic tree. A gap of randomly chosen length is inserted in each of the sequences of one group at a randomly chosen position. A gap of same length is also inserted into all of the sequences of the second group at position that has maximum distance from the first gap insertion.

Block searching

Given a substring in one of the sequences, this operator finds the block to which it may belong in an alignment. Substring of random length at a random position in one of the sequences is compared with all substrings of the same length of other sequences. The best matching one is selected and added to the initial string forming a small profile. Then, best match is located and added to the profile for the remaining sequences. This process continues until a match is identified in all the sequences.

4   Implementation and results

The algorithm has been implemented on PARAM 10000, a parallel machine developed at Center for Development of Advanced Computing(CDAC) [11]. The algorithm is implemented using C language with PVM standard. The results have been achieved with the machines running their normal daily loads in addition to this algorithm.

4.1   Comparison of PGA with other sequence alignment algorithms

A set of four test cases were chosen from Pascarella structural alignment data base [10] . The results of PGA are compared with Clustal w, a well known multiple sequence alignment method [13]. The Clustal w algorithm is based on the greedy approach 'progressive alignment'. It does not explicitly optimize any objective function. Despite these limitations, by choosing an appropriate set of parameters, we evaluated Clustal w score in conditions where it would produce a result as close as possible to the optimization of the weighted sums of pairs objective function.

The results are presented in Table 1 and show that in all four test cases PGA builds an alignment with the better score than Clustal w. PGA is implemented with five subpopulations of size 20 keeping the total population size 100. The run time of PGA is averaged over the runs that led to the presented results.

Table 1. Comparison of PGA with CLUSTAL W

Test Case	Nseq	Length	CLUSTAL W		PGA	
			Score	CPU Time (in secs)	Score	CPU Time (in secs)
Dfr	4	186	21316	5.440	21104	110
Gcr	8	48	39103	4.790	38903	636
Globin	15	169	4248160	13.019	4222846	1178
S protease	15	292	26285660	22.351	25970235	2815

4.2   Investigation on migration parameters

The PGA alternates the maintenance of isolated subpopulations in different environments with the introduction of individuals to new environment. The fitness values of the individuals in the subpopulations will be altered by migrating better individuals between subpopulations. Migration is based on various parameters, such as how often, how much, who, size and the number of neighbor subpopulations. To understand the specific effects of these parameters we have performed several experiments. All the results presented in Table 2 are normalized as the percentage exceeding the best score, with the percentage averaged over five runs. For comparison purposes, we also applied a sequential genetic algorithm(SGA) on the total population size. In all the experiments, the PGA and sequential genetic algorithm were run the same total number of generations. To demonstrate the importance of the migration, we also report the results achieved by PGA with   0 Migrants .

Table 2. Alignment Score with di˜erent numbers of migrants and migration interval. All results are averaged over "ve runs and normalized as percent exceeding the best-known score in Table 1. Thus, the smaller the value, the better the average alignment score

			Migration Interval			
			25 gen.		50 Gen.	
Test case	SGA	Mig	Migrants		Migrants	
		0	1	2	1	2
Dfr	0.062	0.046	0.036	0.037	0.031	0.035
Gcr	0.404	0.272	0.238	0.247	0.221	0.242
Globin	0.163	0.026	0.027	0.030	0.017	0.028
S protease	0.754	0.528	0.329	0.348	0.282	0.320
Average	0.346	0.218	0.158	0.166	0.138	0.156
% SGA	100	63	46	48	40	45

Number of Migrants and Migration Interval The in"uence of migration interval for different numbers of migrants is investigated. Better migrants were chosen, and sent to its right neighbor on a ring topology. Table 2 shows that the sequential approach is outperformed by all parallel variations, including the version without any migration. Thus, the splitting of the total population size into parallel evolving subpopulations increases the probability that at least one of these subpopulations will evolve toward a better result.

Table 2 also shows that a limited migration between the subpopulations further enhances the advantage of the PGA. One migrant to each neighbor in the space of 50 generations resulted in the best parameters when averaged over all the test cases. On the other hand, small migration interval affects the performance of parallel evolving subpopulations. They reduce the genetic diversity between the subpopulations by searching in the limited space of almost same individuals.

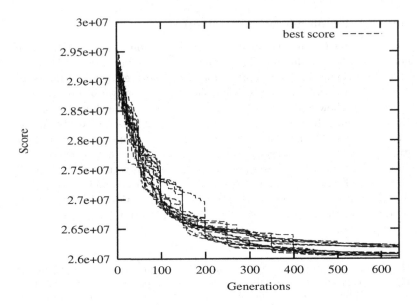

Fig. 1. The convergence of the best alignment score in the individual, parallel evolving subpopulations. Plotted are "ve runs with "ve subpopulation each, i.e. 25 curves with one migrant

Figure 1 shows the convergence behavior of the best individuals in each of the parallel evolving subpopulations for the case of S Protease. All the results were obtained with five subpopulations of size 20 and with one migrants in the space of 50 generations. Plotted are five runs with five subpopulations each, i.e 25 curves. The plot also indicates the importance of migration to avoid premature stagnation by inserting new individuals into a stagnating subpopulation.

5   Conclusions

We presented a PGA for multiple sequence alignment problem. We have shown here that the PGA outperforms the most widely used package Clustal W for all the test cases.The results showed that, when applied to sequence alignment problem, the PGA consistently performs better than a sequential genetic algorithm. A set of experiments has been performed in order to evaluate the effects of migration parameters on the PGA. As a result, a small number of migrants combined with 'moderate' migration interval leads heuristically to the best results. This algorithm can be easily ported on any distributed networked environment. Work is in progress for finding new migration scheme based on the principles of bird migration and improving the performance of PGA using some local search algorithms.

References

1. Altschul, S.F. (1989) Gap costs for multiple sequence alignment. *J. Theor. Biol.,***138**: 297-309.
2. Altschul, S.F., Carroll, R.J. and Lipman, D.J. (1989) Weights for data related by a tree. *Journal of Molecular Biology*, **207**: 647-653.
3. Carrillo, H. and Lipman, D.J. (1988) The multiple sequence alignment problem in biology. *SIAM J. Appl. Math.,***48**: 1073-1082.
4. Feng, D.-F. and Doolittle, R.F. (1987) Progressive sequence alignment as a prerequisite to correct phylogenetic trees. *Journal of Molecular Evolution,***25**: 351-360.
5. Goldberg, D.E. (1989). *Genetic Algorithms in Search, Optimization, and Machine Learning*. New York, Addison-Wesley.
6. Ishikawa, M., Toya, T., Hoshida, M., Nitta, K., Ogiwara, A. and Kaneshia, M. (1993) Multiple alignment by parallel simulated annealing. *Comp. Applic. Biosci.,* **9**: 267-273.
7. Lipman,D.J., Altschul, S.F. and Kececioglu, J.D. (1989) A tool for multiple sequence alignment. *Proc. Natl. Acad. Sci. USA*, **86**: 4412-4415.
8. Needlman, S.B. and Wunch, C.D. (1970) A general method applicable to the search for similarities in the amino acid sequence of two proteins. *J. Mol. Biol.*, **48**: 443-453.
9. Notredame, C. and Higgins, D.G. (1996) SAGA: sequence alignment by genetic algorithm. *Nucleic Acids Res.*, **24**: 1515-1524.
10. Pascarella, S. and Argos, P. (1992) A data bank merging related protein structures and sequences. *Protein Eng.*, **5**: 121-137.
11. Sundararajan, V. and Kolaskar, A.S. (1998) Distributed Genetic Algorithms on PARAM for conformational search. in *Computer Modeling and simulations of Complex Biological systems* Ed. S.Seetharama Iyengar. CRC Press 16-25.
12. Tanese, R. (1987) Parallel genetic algorithms for a hypercube. in *Proceedings of the Second International Conference on Genetic Algorithms and their Applications*, Ed. Grefenstette. Lawrence Erlbaum Associates 177-183.
13. Thompson, J., Higgins, D.G. and Gibson, T.J. (1994) CLUSTAL W: improving the sensitivity of progressive multiple sequence alignment through sequence weighting, position-speci"c gap penalties and weight matrix choice. *Nucleic Acids Res.*, **22**: 4673-4690.

Evolving Logic Programs to Classify
Chess-Endgame Positions

Philip G.K. Reiser and Patricia J. Riddle
philip@cs.auckland.ac.nz

Department of Computer Science
University of Auckland
New Zealand

Abstract. In this paper, an algorithm is presented for learning concept classi"cation rules. It is a hybrid between evolutionary computing and inductive logic programming (ILP). Given input of positive and negative examples, the algorithm constructs a logic program to classify these examples. The algorithm has several attractive features including the ability to explicitly use background (user-supplied) knowledge and to produce comprehensible output. We present results of using the algorithm to tackle the chess-endgame problem (KRK). The results show that using "tness proportionate selection to bias the population of ILP learners does not signi"cantly increase classi"cation accuracy. However, when rules are exchanged at intermediate stages in learning, in a manner similar to crossover in Genetic Programming, the predictive accuracy is frequently improved.

1 Introduction

This work addresses the classification problem in machine learning. That is, given training examples of the form $\{(\mathbf{x}_1, y_1), \ldots, (\mathbf{x}_m, y_m)\}$ for some unknown function $y = f(\mathbf{x})$, where the $\mathbf{x}_i$ values are vectors of the form $\langle x_{i,1}, x_{i,2}, \ldots, x_{i,n} \rangle$, and y values are drawn from a discrete set of classes $\{1, \ldots, K\}$; find a definition of function f such that the y value for any $\mathbf{x}_i$ from the same distribution is accurately predicted, [4].

Evolutionary algorithms (EA) have in the past successfully been used for the classification problem. GABIL [3], and REGAL, [5], for example, create a mapping between logic expressions and fixed-length binary strings. A genetic algorithm then searches the space of strings. To evaluate strings they are mapped to the corresponding logical expression which may then be interpreted. Other work has been done on suitably modifying the operators in genetic algorithms to manipulate logical expressions directly, e.g. SAMUEL, [12], GLPS, [13].

However, as the hypothesis language becomes increasingly expressive, the space of logical expressions that needs to be searched grows combinatorially. There is accumulating evidence that indicates that the performance of evolutionary algorithms can be improved through the introduction of a local search method, [1,7]. A local method progresses by refining an existing solution. Instead of considering the entire search space, a small subset   the solution's neighbour-hood   is examined. This can result in the rapid location of good solutions. However, if all the points in the neighbourhood are inferior, then the algorithm becomes trapped. Unless the local method is perturbed in some way, no fur-ther improvements can be made. Evolutionary algorithms are relatively robust against such local maxima, but are poor at local refinement.

Furthermore, evolutionary algorithms do not easily lend themselves to using domain knowledge explicitly. Typically, they begin *tabula rasa*. The only real alternative is to seed, or bias the initial population of candidate solutions towards likely answers. However, this only makes certain classes of solution less likely, it does not allow solutions to be declared invalid. For example, Wong and Leung's GLPS [13] induces logic programs by evolving a suitably chosen representation such that the syntactic correctness will be guaranteed. However, the algorithm does not easily allow background knowledge to be used to constrain the space of solutions. The semantics of expressions are ignored.

The aim of this work is to combine the local search properties of an in-ductive logic programming algorithm with the global search properties of an evolutionary algorithm. The algorithm presented in this paper uses a common language to express input and output, namely function-free Horn clauses. As a result knowledge can be supplied *a priori* in the form of rules and facts; this knowledge constrains the space of candidate solutions and thus eliminates from consideration solutions known to be inappropriate.

The remaining sections of this paper introduce inductive logic programming; describe EVIL_1, a hybrid ILP-EA algorithm; and finally present an empirical study of learning performance on a chess-endgame problem.

2   Evolutionary Inductive Logic Programming

2.1   Inductive Logic Programming: a Brief Introduction

Inductive logic programming (ILP), [9], is an approach to inducing concept de-scriptions that draws on the foundations of logic programming. The task tackled by ILP is that of developing predicate descriptions given training examples and background knowledge. More specifically, given sets of positive $\mathcal{E}^+$ and negative $\mathcal{E}^-$ examples and relevant background knowledge $\mathcal{B}$, construct an hypothesis $\mathcal{H}$ that is consistent and complete with respect to the training data and background knowledge.

The search through the space of logic programs is structured. A partial order-ing is imposed on the space of hypothesis clauses and this orders hypotheses by generality and allows large parts of the search space to be pruned. For example, if a clause C does not cover a positive example, then none of the specialisations of C need be considered. In practice, however, this strict condition must be relaxed in order to tolerate noise in training data.

Inductive logic programming is an appealing local search method as it allows the easy incorporation of domain specific knowledge. Furthermore, it produces comprehensible solutions. However, as ILP algorithms are typically based on the set covering algorithm, a greedy search algorithm, they are susceptible to local maxima.

2.2   Evolutionary Algorithms

Evolutionary algorithms are domain independent search algorithms inspired by principles of population genetics. Using very simple mechanisms, evolutionary algorithms exhibit complex behaviour that has been harnessed to solve some difficult problems, e.g. [2,6]. However, evolutionary algorithms have certain drawbacks. Domain knowledge cannot be used easily. Furthermore, while such algorithms are good at establishing peaks in discontinuous multimodal objective functions, they have poor local search properties.

2.3   Integrating the EA with ILP

Inductive logic programming and evolutionary algorithms have appealing properties which appear to be complementary. Evolutionary algorithms have good global search properties, whereas inductive logic programming algorithms have good local refinement characteristics. This provokes the question can a concept learning algorithm be constructed that captures both of these properties?

Furthermore, when only a subset of the training set is seen by an ILP algorithm the theories induced are likely to be less accurate than if all the data had been used. However, in most real world applications, data will necessarily only become available gradually, or will be too great to use in one batch for the learner. It is therefore interesting to observe how algorithms perform when only samples of the data are used.

2.4   The EVIL_1 Algorithm

In the approach adopted, an evolutionary algorithm is used to direct the computational effort spent by multiple parallel instances of the ILP algorithm. The evolutionary algorithm maintains a population of agents each comprising of a logical theory (a logic program). The traditional mutation and crossover operators are replaced with the crossover operator used in [11] which in some respects is similar to crossover in Genetic Programming.

Each agent is able to induce logic programs using an ILP algorithm. An agent takes as input a random sample of the training data and induces a theory. This theory is evaluated on a validation set. Those theories with poor predictive accuracy risk extinction, while those with high predictive accuracy are likely to occupy a larger proportion of the population in the next generation. As new rules are discovered they are added to the theory. This augmented theory together with the background knowledge is then used in subsequent trials. The fitness of a theory is measured by determining its predictive accuracy on the validation set[1] comprising of the entire training set. The algorithm is shown below.

---

[1] It should be noted that this is not to be confused with the test set which is used only for evaluation independently of any learning.

---

procedure EVIL_1 **is**
begin
  initialise(Population);
  "tness = accuracy(Population,validation_set);

  while not termination_criterion **loop**
    for each member of population **loop**
      theory = select_parent(Population);
      subset = sample(training_set,sample_size);
      new_theory = induce(background_knowledge, theory, subset);
    end loop
    "tness = accuracy(Population, validation_set);
    new_population = select(population);
    population = new_population;
  end loop
  return "ttest(Population);
end EVIL_1;

The **induce** procedure refers to a call of the inductive logic programming algorithm. The algorithm chosen was Progol, [10].

3 An Empirical Study

The aim of this empirical investigation is to examine the effect on predictive accuracy of (1) applying fitness proportionate selection on a population of ILP algorithms that only use a sample of the training set; and (2) of exchanging rules between ILP algorithms at intermediate stages.

The task domain is the Chess Endgame (KRK) problem, proposed by [8]. This problem is a widely used test problem for ILP systems. The problem may be characterised as follows. There are three pieces left on a chess board: the white king, white rook, and the black king. The objective of the learning algorithm is to discover rules to describe illegal positions when it is white's turn to move, given a set of positive and negative training instances. For example, an illegal position occurs when the black king is in check with white to move. The predicate illegal/6 is the target to be learned, and the attributes of the target predicate are file and rank for white king, white rook and black king respectively. Examples, therefore, take the form illegal(e,3,a,1,e,1) and :- illegal(d,4,g,3,b,5) (where :- denotes negation). These examples correspond to board positions as illustrated in Figure 1. The data comprises of 20000 examples which are split into 10000 training and validation instances and 10000 test instances.

The following background knowledge is also supplied. The adj/2 predicate defines cases where the rank or file represented by the left argument is adjacent

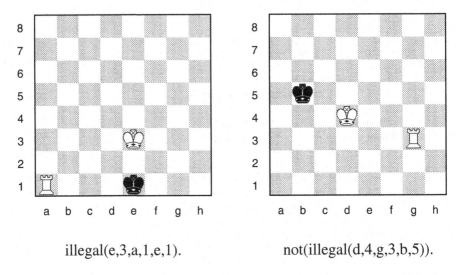

illegal(e,3,a,1,e,1).   not(illegal(d,4,g,3,b,5)).

Fig. 1. Examples of legal and illegal positions.

to that represented by the right argument. The `lt/2` predicate defines pairs of ranks or files, where the left argument is less than the right. Consequently, rules may take the form

```
illegal(A,B,C,D,C,C).
illegal(A,B,C,D,E,F) :- adj(A,E).
```

A population of 10 learning agents are supplied with subsets of the training set and are allowed to induce a hypothesis using the *Progol* inductive logic programming algorithm. In each generation, each agent is supplied with a 0.2% random sample of the training set[2]. Two experiments were conducted.

The first experiment considers the effect of fitness proportionate selection. Two cases are considered: (1) multiple instances of ILP are run batch incrementally; and (2) also with fitness proportionate selection. The predictive accuracy on the test set was examined for both approaches. Figure 2 shows a scatter plot for the test set accuracy of the fitness-proportionate selection case (y-axis) against the no fitness proportionate selection case (x-axis). Points above the line $y = x$ re"ect an improvement in predictive accuracy for the introduction of fitness-proportionate selection. However, the distribution of points indicates that while the introduction of fitness-proportionate selection is not advantageous, it is also not disadvantageous.

The second experiment examined the effect of rule exchange between learners. At certain intervals denoted by the communication period c agents are selected to exchange parts of their clausal theory. In the control case $c = \infty$,

---

[2] The choice of sample size was based on a trade-o" between providing enough data for rules to be found while avoiding excessive run-times.

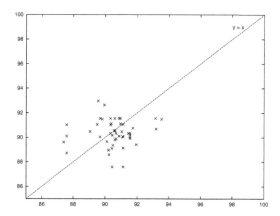

Fig. 2. Fitness-proportionate selection versus no "tness-proportionate selection.

no rule exchange occurs. In the treatment cases, $_c$ = 3, 5 or 10 generations. The following types of rule-exchange were considered. (1) Union: new theories are constructed by taking the union of two parent rule sets; (2) Crossover: new theories are constructed by exchanging rules using the crossover operator described in [11].

Figure 3 shows scatter plots for the test set accuracy of rule exchange using union, and Figure 4 the performance distributions for crossover. The graphs indicate that in the cases where the ILP algorithm performs badly, the introduction of either union or crossover increases predictive accuracy. However, in the cases where the ILP algorithm already performs well, union and crossover have a detrimental effect. The statistical significance of these results were examined using the paired t-test. For union periods 3, 5 and 10, the introduction of union does not result in a statistically significant increase in predictive accuracy, and therefore it may not be reasonably asserted that union improves performance in the chess endgame problem. However, the exchange of rules through crossover with high crossover frequency does result in a statistically significant increase. $_c$ = 3 ($P < 0.0005$); $_c$ = 5 ($P < 0.05$); $_c$ = 10 ($P < 0.1$).

4   Conclusions

A new hybrid evolutionary learning algorithm has been presented that induces first order logic clauses from examples. The algorithm has a number of attractive features. In particular, it allows the use of explicit background knowledge to constrain the space of solutions. In addition, the algorithm is inherently parallel and its output is su ciently expressive to learn relational concepts.

The algorithm's learning properties were examined on the chess endgame (KRK) problem. It was shown that learning with a population of ILP learners, where fitness proportionate selection is used to bias trials towards good theories does not yield an increase in predictive accuracy. When rules are exchanged using a union operation a statistically significant increase is not observed.

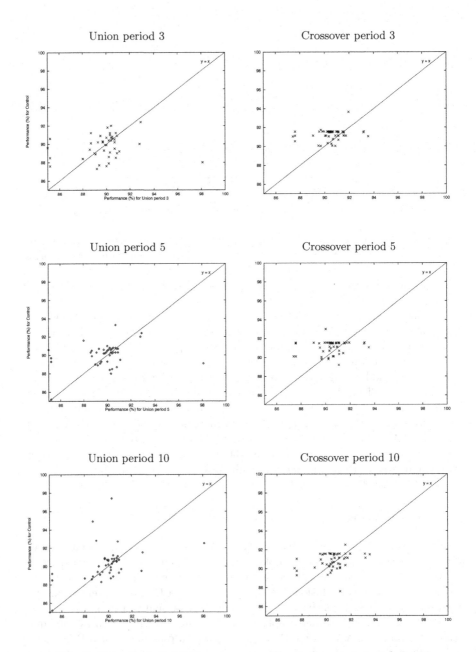

Fig. 3. Union periods 3,5,10   **Fig. 4.** Crossover periods 3,5,10

However, when crossover is used to exchange rules between learners, then a significantly superior predictive accuracy is attained ($P < 0.0005$).

One possible explanation for these results is that the ILP algorithm is based on the greedy algorithm which is susceptible to local minima. Crossover, together with fitness-proportionate selection, serves as a global strategy, which can redirect the ILP algorithm to other areas of the search space.

Areas currently being pursued include a more detailed analysis of rule exchange between inductive learners and the application of evolutionary inductive logic programming to more complex problem domains.

References

1. L. Davis. *Handbook of Genetic Algorithms*. Van Nostrand Reinhold, New York, 1991.
2. Kenneth A. DeJong and William M. Spears. Using genetic algorithms to solve NP-complete problems. In *International Conference on Genetic Algorithms*, pages 124 132, 1989.
3. Kenneth A. DeJong, William M. Spears, and Diana F. Gordon. Using genetic algorithms for concept learning. *Machine Learning*, 13:161 188, 1993.
4. T. G. Dietterich. Machine learning research: Four current directions. *AI Magazine*, 18(4):97 136, 1997.
5. A. Giordana and L. Saitta. Regal: an integrated system for learning relations using genetic algorithms. In *Proceedings of 2nd International Workshop on Multistrategy Learning*, pages 234 249. Morgan Kaufmann, 1993.
6. David E. Goldberg. Genetic and evolutionary algorithms come of age. *Communications of the ACM*, Vol. 37:113 119, March 1994.
7. William E. Hart and Richard K. Belew. Optimization with genetic algorithm hybrids that use local search. In Richard K. Belew and Melanie Mitchell, editors, *Adaptive Individuals in Evolving Populations: Models and Algorithms.*, volume 26, chapter 27, pages 483 496. SFI Studies in the Sciences of Complexity, 1996.
8. S. H. Muggleton, M. Bain, J. Hayes-Michie, and D. Michie. An experimental comparison of human and machine learning formalisms. In *Proc. Sixth International Workshop on Machine Learning*, pages 113 118, San Mateo, CA, 1989. Morgan Kaufmann.
9. Stephen Muggleton. Inductive logic programming. *New Generation Computing*, 8(4):295 318, 1991.
10. Stephen Muggleton. Inverse Entailment and Progol. *New Generation Computing*, 13, 1995.
11. Philip Reiser. *EVIL1*: a learning system to evolve logical theories. In *Proc. Workshop on Logic Programming and Multi-Agent Systems (International Conference on Logic Programming)*, pages 28 34, July 1997.
12. A. C. Schultz and J. J. Grefenstette. Improving tactical plans with genetic algorithms. In *Proceedings of the 2nd International IEEE Conference on Tools for Artificial Intelligence*, number IEEE Cat. No. 90CH2915-7, pages 328 334, Herndon, VA, 6-9 Nov 1990. IEEE Computer Society Press, Los Alamitos, CA.
13. Man Leung Wong and Kwong Sak Leung. Inductive logic programming using genetic algorithms. In J.W. Brahan and G.E. Lasker, editors, *Advances in Artificial Intelligence - Theory and Application II*, pages 119 124, 1994.

Genetic Programming with Active Data Selection

Byoung-Tak Zhang and Dong-Yeon Cho

Arti"cial Intelligence Lab (SCAI)
Dept. of Computer Engineering
Seoul National University
Seoul 151-742, Korea
{btzhang, dycho}@scai.snu.ac.kr
http://scai.snu.ac.kr/

Abstract. Genetic programming evolves Lisp-like programs rather than "xed size linear strings. This representational power combined with generality makes genetic programming an interesting tool for automatic programming and machine learning. One weakness is the enormous time required for evolving complex programs. In this paper we present a method for accelerating evolution speed of genetic programming by active selection of "tness cases during the run. In contrast to conventional genetic programming in which all the given training data are used repeatedly, the presented method evolves programs using only a subset of given data chosen incrementally at each generation. This method is applied to the evolution of collective behaviors for multiple robotic agents. Experimental evidence supports that evolving programs on an incrementally selected subset of "tness cases can signi"cantly reduce the "tness evaluation time without sacri"cing generalization accuracy of the evolved programs.

1 Introduction

Genetic programming (GP) is a method for finding the most fit computer programs by means of artificial evolution. A population of computer programs are generated at random. They are evolved to better programs using genetic operators. The ability of the program to solve the problem is measured as its fitness value.

The genetic programs are usually represented as *trees*. A genetic tree consists of elements from a function set and a terminal set. Function symbols appear as nonterminal nodes. Terminal symbols are used to denote actions taken by the program. Since Lisp S-expressions can be represented as trees, genetic programming can, in principle, evolve any Lisp programs. Due to this powerful expressiveness, GP provides an effective method for automatic programming and machine learning.

One di culty in genetic programming is, however, that it requires enormous computational time. The time for evolution is proportional to the product of population size, generation number, and the data size needed for fitness evaluation. Typical population size for GP ranges from a few hundreds to several thousands [4]. A typical run requires fifty to hundreds of generations. The data size depends on the application. Fitness evaluation takes the most of evolution time in GP since it requires programs to be executed against fitness cases.

In this paper we present two methods for reducing computational costs for genetic programming by evolving programs on a selected subset of given fitness cases. The idea of active data selection in supervised learning was originally introduced in 1991 by one of the authors for e cient training of neural networks [11,7,8]. Motivated by this work Gathercole *et al.* used training subsets for genetic programming [1,2]. Our approach is different from that of Gathercole *et al.* in that we increase the training set incrementally as generation goes on, rather than using the same number of fitness cases. The effectiveness of the presented methods was tested on a multiagent learning problem in which a group of mobile agents are to transport together a large table to the goal position.

The paper is organized as follows. Section 2 describes the multiagent task. Section 3 presents the genetic programming approach with active data selection. Section 4 shows experimental results. Section 5 discusses the result.

2   Evolving Multiagent Strategies Using Genetic Programming

The table transport problem that will be used in our experiments is an example of multi-robot applications [9]. In an $n \times n$ grid world, a single table and four robotic agents are placed at random positions, as shown in Figure 1. A specific location is designated as the destination. The goal of the robots is to transport the table to the destination in group motion. The robots need to move in herd since the table is too heavy and large to be transported by single robots.

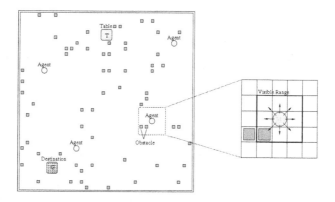

Fig. 1. The environment for multiagent learning.

Table 1. Terminals and functions of GP-trees for the table transport problem.

	Symbol	Description
Terminals	FORWARD	Move one step forward in the current direction
	AVOID	Check clockwise and make one step in the "rst direction that avoids collision
	RANDOM-MOVE	Move one step in the random direction
	TURN-TABLE	Make a clockwise turn to the nearest direction of the table
	TURN-GOAL	Make a clockwise turn to the nearest direction of the goal
	STOP	Stay at the same position
Functions	IF-OBSTACLE	Check collision with obstacles
	IF-ROBOT	Check collision with other robots
	IF-TABLE	Check if the table is nearby
	IF-GOAL	Check if the table is nearby
	PROG2, PROG3	Evaluate two (or three) subtrees in sequence

Each robot i $(i = 1, .., N_{robots})$ is equipped with a control program A_i. If $A_i \neq A_j$ for $i \neq j$, then control programs are said to be *private*. In case of *public* control programs, all instances of A_i are constrained to be the same A.

The robots activate A_i's in parallel to run a team trial. At the beginning of the trial, the robot locations are chosen at random in the arena. They have different positions and orientations. During a trial, each robot is are granted a total of S_{max} elementary movements. The robot is allowed to stop in less than S_{max} steps if it reaches the goal. At the end of the trial, each robot i gets a fitness value which was measured by summing the contributions from various factors.

The objective of a GP run is to find a multi-robot algorithm that, when executed by the robots in parallel, causes e   cient table transport behavior in group. The terminal and function symbols used for GP to solve this problem are listed in Table 1. The terminal set consists of six primitive actions: FORWARD, AVOID, RANDOM-MOVE, TURN-TABLE, TURN-GOAL and STOP. The function set consists of six primitives: IF-OBSTACLE, IF-ROBOT, IF-TABLE, IF-GOAL, PROG2 and PROG3. Each fitness case represents a world of 32 by 32 grid on which there are four robots, 64 obstacles, and the table to be transported. A set of training cases are used for evolving the programs.

All the robots use the same control program. To evaluate the fitness of robots, we made a complete run of the program for one robot before the fitness of another is measured. The fitness value, $f_{ij}(g)$, of individual i at generation g against case j is computed by considering various penalty factors. These include the distance between the target and the robot, the number of steps moved by the robot, the number of collisions made by the robot, the distance between starting and final position of the robot, and the penalty for moving away from other robots. More details can be found elsewhere [9].

The fitness, $F_i(g)$, of program i at generation g is measured as the average of its fitness values $f_{ij}(g)$ for the cases j in the training set:

$$F_i(g) = \frac{1}{S} \sum_{j=1}^{S} f_{ij}(g) \tag{1}$$

where S is the number of fitness cases.

In the following section we present the active data selection method for genetic programming.

3   Genetic Programming with Incremental Data Selection

With each program is associated a small set of initial training cases of size n_0, chosen from the base training set $D^{(N)}$ of size N. Individuals are evolved by the usual genetic programming. In addition, the algorithm has an additional step, i.e. incremental data inheritance (IDI), in which data sets are evolved.

For the initial data population, a small subset of fitness cases, $D(0)$, is chosen from the base training set $D^{(N)}$ of size N:

$$D(0) \subset D^{(N)}, \quad |D(0)| = n_0. \tag{2}$$

After individuals are evolved by the usual evolutionary process (fitness evaluation, selection, and mating to generate offsprings), a portion of training set, (g), is chosen from the previous candidate set $C(g-1)$

$$(g) \subset C(g-1), \quad |\ (g)| = \ , \tag{3}$$

where $C(g-1) = D^{(N)} - D(g-1)$. And it is mixed with the previous training set to make a new training set $D(g)$ for the next generation

$$D(g) = D(g-1) \cup \ (g), \quad D(g-1) \cap \ (g) = \{\}. \tag{4}$$

That is, the sequence of training sets for GP active is

$$D(0) \subset D(1) \subset D(2) \subset ... \subset D(G) = D^{(N)}, \tag{5}$$

where G is the number of maximum generation.

We use a variant of uniform crossover to produce offspring data from their parent data. Two parent data sets, $D_i(g)$ and $D_j(g)$, are crossed to inherit their subsets to two offspring data sets, $D_i(g+1)$ and $D_j(g+1)$. In uniform data crossover, the data of parents' are mixed into a union set

$$D_{i+j}(g) = D_i(g) \cup D_j(g), \tag{6}$$

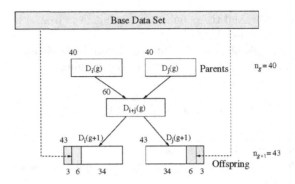

Fig. 2. Uniform data crossover for data inheritance.

which are then redistributed to two offspring:

$$D_i(g+1) \subset D_{i+j}(g)$$
$$D_j(g+1) \subset D_{i+j}(g) \tag{7}$$

where the size of offspring data sets are equal to $n_{g+1} = n_g + $, where ≥ 1 is the data increment size.

To ensure performance improvement, it is important to maintain the diversity of the training data as generation goes on. The diversity of data set $D_i(g)$ is measured by the ratio of distinctive examples:

$$d_i = \frac{|D_{i+j}(g)|}{|D_i(g)|} - 1, \qquad 0 \leq d_i \leq 1 \tag{8}$$

where $d_i = 0$ if the parents have the same data and $d_i = 1$ if parents have no common training examples. To maintain the diversity, a portion   of the diversity factor d_i is used to import examples from the base data set.

$$r_i = \cdot (1 - d_i), \qquad 0 \leq \quad \leq 1. \tag{9}$$

For example, assume that the current parents have data sets, $D_i(g)$ and $D_j(g)$, of size $n_g = 40$ each and $|D_{i+j}(g)| = 60$. Let the parameters be $= 0.3$, $= 3$. Then, we need to generate two training sets of size $n_{g+1} = n_g +   = 43$ for the offspring (Figure 2). The diversity is $d_i = \frac{|D_{i+j}(g)|}{|D_i(g)|} - 1 = 1.5 - 1 = 0.5$ and the import rate is $r_i =   \cdot (1 - d_i) = 0.3 \cdot (1 - 0.5) = 0.15$. The data for each offspring is generated by randomly choosing 34 examples from $D_{i+j}(g)$, 6 examples from $D^{(N)}$ and again $= 3$ examples from $D^{(N)}$. Figure 2 illustrates this process.

4   Experimental Results

Experiments have been performed using the parameter values listed in Table 2. The terminal set and function set consist of six primitives, respectively, as summarized in Table 1. A total of 100 training cases were used for evolving the programs for standard GP runs. GP runs with active data selection used $10 + 3g$ examples out of the given data set, i.e. $n_0 = 10$, $= 3$, for fitness evaluation. For all methods, a total of 100 independent worlds were used for evaluating the generalization performance of evolved programs.

We compared the performance of the GP with active data selection to the GP with random data selection. Results are shown in Figure 3. GPs with IDI and incremental random selection (IRS) achieved better than GP without active selection (GP standard). Figure 4 shows the fitness of three methods with repect to the total number of evaluations. Since the GP with active data selection uses variable data size, we calculated the number of evaluations at generation g by a product of the population size and the data size at generation g. The active GP methods achieved a speed-up factor of approximately two compared with that of the standard GP. The results are summarized in Table 3. Though the GP with active data selection methods used a smaller set of fitness cases, its training and test performance were slightly better than those of the standard GP. Though further experiments are necessary for more definite conclusion, it seems that the active GP has a potential to evolve smaller programs than the standard GP since small data usually tends to require smaller programs. This seems interesting from the Occam's razor principle point of view [10,6].

Table 2. Parameters used in the experiments.

Parameter	Value
Population size	100
Max generation	30
Crossover rate	0.9
Mutation rate	0.1

Table 3. Comparison of time and average "tness values (lower is better) for the standard GP and the GP with active data selection. The values are averaged over ten runs. Also shown are the standard deviation.

Method	Time	Average Fitness	
		Training	Test
GP standard	300000	211.21 ± 9.19	225.64 ± 12.05
GP with IRS	170500	209.60 ± 7.67	219.91 ± 13.11
GP with IDI	170500	195.97 ± 8.41	203.39 ± 10.78

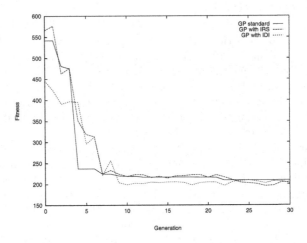

Fig. 3. Comparison of "tness values as a function of generation number.

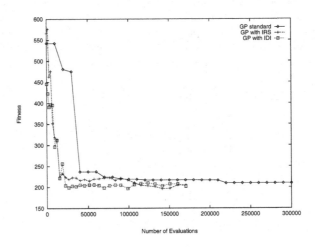

Fig. 4. Comparison of "tness values as a function of the number of function evaluations.

5   Conclusions

We have presented a method for accelerating evolution speed of genetic programming by selecting a subset of given fitness cases. Since the fitness evaluation step is a bottleneck in GP computing time, this method can make an essential contribution to improving the GP performance.

Experimental results have shown that by reducing the fitness cases the evolution speed of GP can be enhanced without loss of generality of the evolved programs. This is especially true for problem settings in which a large amount of fitness cases are available. In this case, the active data selection can exploit the redundancy in the data, while the standard GP blindly re-evaluates all the fitness cases.

Acknowledgements

This research was supported in part by the Korea Science and Engineering Foundation (KOSEF) under grants 96-0102-13-01-3 and 981-0920-350-2.

References

1. Gathercole, C. and Ross, P. 1994. Dynamic training subset selection for supervised learning in genetic programming. In Y. Davidor, H.-P. Schwefel, and R. Männer, (eds.). *Parallel Problem Solving from Nature III*, Berlin: Springer-Verlag, Pages 312-321.
2. Gathercole, C. and Ross, P. 1997. Small populations over many generations can beat large populations over few generations in genetic programming. In J.R. Koza (eds.). *Genetic Programming 1997*. Cambridge, MA: The MIT Press. Pages 111-118.
3. Haynes, T., Sen, S., Schoenefeld, D., and Wainwright, R. 1995. Evolving a team, In *Proc. AAAI-95 Fall Symposium on Genetic Programming* AAAI Press. Pages 23-30.
4. Koza, John R. 1992. *Genetic Programming: On the Programming of Computers by Means of Natural Selection*. Cambridge, MA: The MIT Press.
5. Luke, S. and Spector, L. 1996. Evolving teamwork and coordination with genetic programming. In J.R. Koza (eds.). *Proc. First Genetic Programming Conf.* Cambridge, MA: The MIT Press. Pages 150-156.
6. Soule, T., Foster, J. A., and Dickinson, J. 1996. Code growth in genetic programming. In J.R. Koza (eds.). *Genetic Programming 1996*. Cambridge, MA: The MIT Press. Pages 215-223.
7. Zhang, B. T. 1992. *Learning by Genetic Neural Evolution*, DISKI Vol. 16, 268 pages, ISBN 3-929037-16-6, In "x-Verlag, St. Augustin/Bonn.
8. Zhang, B. T. 1994. Accelerated learning by active example selection, *International Journal of Neural Systems*, 5(1): 67-75.
9. Zhang, B. T. and Cho, D. Y. 1998. Fitness switching: Evolving complex group behaviors using genetic programming. In *Genetic Programming 1998*, Madison, Wisconsin, pp. 431-438, 1998.
10. Zhang, B. T. Mühlenbein, H. 1995. Balancing accuracy and parsimony in genetic programming. *Evolutionary Computation*. 3(1) 17-38.
11. Zhang, B. T. and Veenker, G. 1991. Focused incremental learning for improved generalization with reduced training sets, *Proc. Int. Conf. Artificial Neural Networks*, Kohonen, T. *et al.* (eds.) North-Holland, pp. 227-232.

Evolutionary Programming-Based Uni-vector Field Method for Fast Mobile Robot Navigation

Yong-Jae Kim, Dong-Han Kim, and Jong-Hwan Kim

Dept. of EE, KAIST,
373-1 Kusong-dong, Yusong-gu, Taejon, 305-701, Korea
Tel: +82-42-869-8048, Fax: +82-42-869-8010
{yjkim, dhkim, johkim}@@vivaldi.kaist.ac.kr

Abstract. A novel obstacle avoidance and a "nal position and orientation acquiring methods are developed and implemented for fast moving mobile robots. Most of the obstacle avoidance techniques do not consider the robot orientation or its "nal angle at the target position. These techniques deal with the robot position only and are independent of its orientation and velocity. To solve these problems we propose a novel uni-vector "eld method, which introduces a normalized two-dimensional vector "eld for navigation. To obtain the optimal vector "eld, a function approximator is used, and is trained by evolutionary programming. Two kinds of vector "elds are trained, one for the "nal posture acquisition, and the other for obstacle avoidance. Computer simulations and real experiments are carried out to demonstrate the e˘ectiveness of the proposed scheme.

Keywords: Navigation, Wheeled mobile robots, Uni-vector "eld method, Evolutionary programming, Soccer robots.

1 Introduction

Navigation with obstacle avoidance is one of the key issues to be looked into for successful applications of autonomous mobile robots. Navigation involves three tasks: mapping and modeling the environment, path planning and selection, and path following. The traditional navigation method separates path planning and following, into two isolated tasks. In contrast, in the unified navigation such as potential field method, these two steps are unified in one task [1].

Conventional navigation methods do not consider the robot orientation and its final angle at the target position. For instance, when a robot dribbles a ball in a robot soccer game [2,3] or pushes a load in an industrial field, it is very important to acquire the final robot orientation. Using the conventional methods, a robot has di culties in performing such tasks. Moreover, in the path planning step, the generated path ignores the mechanical properties of the robot.

In this paper, a novel uni-vector field method is proposed for the unified navigation considering the kinematic properties of the robot and the practical application to the fast moving mobile robots. To obtain the optimal uni-vector field, a function approximator and its learning algorithm by evolutionary programming (EP) are proposed. By introducing the uni-vector fields, the performance of the unified navigational approach is improved along with the obstacle avoidance capability. The developed navigation is implemented on a bi-wheel type mobile robot designed for MiroSot [2].

In Sections 2, the kinematic properties of bi-wheel type mobile robot are discussed. In Section 3, a novel uni-vector field navigation method is described as a unified navigation approach, based on EP. Sections 4 and 5 describe computer simulations and experimental results, respectively. Concluding remarks follow in Section 6.

2 Modeling of a Mobile Robot

In this paper, two wheeled mobile robots with non-slipping and pure rolling are considered [4]. The mechanical structure of the mobile robot is shown in Fig.1(a).

The kinematics of the robot can be described using Fig. 1(b). Posture p_s and position p of the robot are defined as

$$
p_s = \begin{bmatrix} x_c \\ y_c \\ \theta_c \end{bmatrix}, \; p = \begin{bmatrix} x_c \\ y_c \end{bmatrix}
\tag{1}
$$

where (x_c, y_c) is the position of the center of robot, and θ_c is the heading angle of the robot with respect to absolute coordinates. Velocity vector S is defined as follows :

$$
S = \begin{bmatrix} v \\ \omega \end{bmatrix} = \begin{bmatrix} \frac{V_R + V_L}{2} \\ \frac{V_R - V_L}{L} \end{bmatrix} = \begin{bmatrix} \frac{1}{2} & \frac{1}{2} \\ -\frac{1}{L} & \frac{1}{L} \end{bmatrix} \begin{bmatrix} V_L \\ V_R \end{bmatrix}
\tag{2}
$$

where v is the translational velocity of the center of robot and ω is the rotational velocity with respect to the center of robot. Equation (2) shows the relation between the velocity vector and the velocities of two wheels, V_L and V_R, where V_L is the left wheel velocity, and V_R is the right wheel velocity.

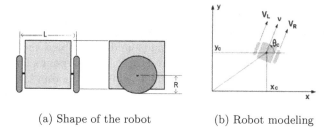

(a) Shape of the robot   (b) Robot modeling

Fig. 1. Shape of bi-wheel type mobile robot and its modeling

3   Uni-vector Field Navigation Method

Potential field method is generally used in robot control. As it is very simple, it is possible to control robots in real time. However, when the regular velocity cannot be maintained or the obstacle is big, the robot is liable to get into oscillation, and its direction cannot be guaranteed at an arriving position [5]. These are due to the approximation of the robot to a point mass. By potential field navigation the robot moves in the direction proportional to a resultant force comprised of an attractive force from the desired position and a repulsive force from the obstacle to be avoided. The resultant force can be considered as a vector field. It is possible to control the robot better with a modified vector field, if we can find the optimal one. In this paper, we introduce a uni-vector field in which the magnitude of vectors is a unity at all the positions.

3.1   Uni-vector field generation

A uni-vector field, N for the robot navigation is defined as

$$N : F \to I \tag{3}$$

where F is the workspace of the robot in $\mathbb{R}^2$ and I is a set of unit vectors with arbitrary direction. While controlling the robot, these unit vectors correspond to the desired robot heading directions. As normalized vectors are used, the uni-vector field N can be represented in terms of its directions, as follows:

$$N : F \to [-\ ,\ ]. \tag{4}$$

Fig. 2 shows an example of the uni-vector field for a desired posture at a point g, where the points and straight lines are uni-vector field, and the trajectories of rectangles are simulated robot paths. The uni-vector field at position p is defined as $N(p)$. It is assumed that the magnitude of vectors in the field is a unity at all points. The angle of the vector at a robot position p is generated by

$$N(p) = \angle pg - n \tag{5}$$

with

$$= \angle pr - \angle pg$$

where n is a positive constant. The shape of the field and the turning motion of the robots vary as per the parameter n and the distance between points g and r. By this equation, we can obtain a uni-vector field at all points for the desired posture at point g. This uni-vector was implemented to the robot soccer system [3] for kicking motion, where the point g was the ball position and the heading position r was adjusted to the desired kicking direction. As shown in Fig. 2, there are ine cient properties in this heuristic uni-vector field. For example, the robot behind the point g follows the long path to approach the final posture.

In order to exploit the vector field N for robot control with better performance, the field has to be adjusted e ciently. A function approximator is introduced in order to achieve the same.

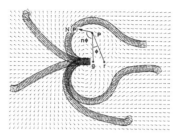

Fig. 2. Heuristic uni-vector "eld for "nal posture at a point g

To start with, a grid of size $n \times m$ is located within the workspace as shown in Fig. 3(a). The shape and density of the grid net can be varied as per the application and the desired accuracy. $p_{i,j}$ is the position of node (i,j) and $N_{i,j}$ represents the field vector at $p_{i,j}$.

The set of field vectors $N_{i,j}$ forms an $n \times m$ matrix, $\{N_{i,j} | 1 \leq i \leq n, 1 \leq j \leq m\}$. The vector associated with an arbitrary position P in F, is calculated with the function approximator as follows:

$$N(p) = \frac{(d_b d_c d_d) N_{i,j} + (d_a d_c d_d) N_{i,j+1} + (d_a d_b d_d) N_{i+1,j} + (d_a d_b d_c) N_{i+1,j+1}}{d_b d_c d_d + d_a d_c d_d + d_a d_b d_d + d_a d_b d_c} \quad (6)$$

with
$$d_a = ||p - p_{i+1,j+1}||, \quad d_b = ||p - p_{i,j+1}||,$$
$$d_c = ||p - p_{i+1,j}||, \quad d_d = ||p - p_{i,j}||$$

where $p_{i,j}$, $p_{i,j+1}$, $p_{i+1,j}$ and $p_{i+1,j+1}$ are the positions of the nodes surrounding the point p as shown in Fig. 3(b). $N(p)$ in (6) represents an intermediate vector for the $N_{i,j}$, $N_{i,j+1}$, $N_{i+1,j}$ and $N_{i+1,j+1}$ vectors. As p approaches $p_{i,j}$, $N(p)$ converges to $N_{i,j}$.

Consequently, by setting the elements of the matrix $\{N_{i,j} | 1 \leq i \leq n, 1 \leq j \leq m\}$ to each of node values, all the vectors in field N can be fully determined. In Section 3.3, the training of the vector field N is discussed.

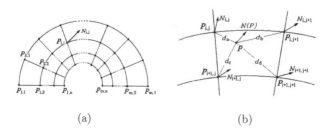

(a)   (b)

Fig. 3. Grid net of the function approximator

3.2   Uni-vector field tracking controller

To apply the vector field method for navigation, a field tracking controller is required. The control inputs to the wheels reduce the error in angle between the robot heading direction and the field vector. The error in angle $_e$, between the robot heading angle $_c$ and the vector orientation $_N$ is given as follows:

$$ _e = \ _c - \ _N. \tag{7} $$

Let us employ the following rotational velocity:

$$ = G(x_c, y_c, \ _c)||p|| + K_\omega sgn(\ _e)\sqrt{|\ _e|} \tag{8} $$

with
$$ G(x_c, y_c, \ _c) = \frac{\partial \theta_N}{\partial x_c} cos \ _c + \frac{\partial \theta_N}{\partial y_c} sin \ _c, $$

where K_ω is a positive constant and sgn is a sign function. Then, $_e$ will become zero within a time $T \geq \frac{2\sqrt{\theta_e(0)}}{K_\omega}$ [6]. $G(x, y, \ _c)$ is the product of the gradient of $_N$ and a unit vector in the direction of $_c$. In other words, it means the variation of $_N$ in the direction of $_c$, at the current position (x, y). The term $G(x, y, \ _c)||p_c||$ refers to the variation of $_N$ of robot center in unit time. Equation (8) represents a kind of sliding mode controller.

3.3   EP and the learning algorithm

To control a fast mobile robot, many conditions should be satisfied, which are di cult to represent. Researchers focus on some of them, based on their interest and the application field. To optimize such a complex system, EP is an e cient tool. The evaluation function is decided based on the elapsed time, the distance from target position, the distance from obstacle, the final orientation of robot heading, and the maximal rotational acceleration.

These criteria are merged to form an evaluation function $f(x)$ as follows:

$$ f(x) = k_t \ t_s + k_d \ | \ _c(t_s) - \ _d \ | + f_t(x) + f_o(x) + f_a(x) \tag{9} $$

where t_s is the elapsed time, and $_d$ is the desired final direction. The evaluation function is used for learning the uni-vector field matrix $\{N_{i,j}|1 \leq i \leq n, 1 \leq j \leq m\}$.

The first term in the evaluation function helps the robot to reach the target point without wasting time, and the second term forces the robot heading to converge to the desired final direction $_d$. The function $f_t(x)$ makes the robot to move to the target point:

$$ f_t(x) = \begin{cases} 0, & \text{if arrived at } p_g \\ T_p + min_{t\in[0,t_s]}(\ |p(t) - p_g| \ ), & \text{otherwise} \end{cases} \tag{10} $$

where $p(t)$ is the position of the robot center at time t, p_g is the target position and T_p is a penalty value that is added when a robot does not arrive at p_g. If the robot does not reach the target position, the evaluation function increases depending on the distance from the robot center to the target point, and the corresponding value $min_{t\in[0,t_s]}(\,|p(t)-p_g|\,)$ added with T_p, gives the $f_t(x)$ value as in equation (10). The function $f_o(x)$ prevents the robot from colliding with an obstacle:

$$f_o(x) = \begin{cases} 0, \text{when not in collision with an obstacle} \\ B_p + max_{t\in\Phi}(\,|p(t)-p_b|\,), \quad \text{otherwise} \end{cases} \quad (11)$$

where B_p is a penalty value, $\subset [0,t_s]$ refers to the time interval during which the robot is within an obstacle boundary, and p_b is the closest point on the obstacle boundary from the robot center. When a robot collides with an obstacle, the $f_o(x)$ function is calculated going by projecting the robot trajectory nearest to the obstacle center. The shortest distance of such a point from the periphery of the obstacle is used in getting the value of the $f_o(x)$ function. The function $f_a(x)$ makes the robot rotational acceleration,   not to exceed its limit $_{max}$:

$$f_a(x) = \begin{cases} 0, \quad\quad\quad\quad \text{when   is within the limit   } _{max} \\ A_p + max_{t\in[0,t_s]}(\,|\ (t) - \ _{max}|\,), \quad \text{otherwise} \end{cases} \quad (12)$$

In computer simulation, the penalty values G_p, B_p, and A_p are taken as 500, 100, and 50, respectively. The value of G_p is greater than the sum of the other two terms in evaluation function, as we assumed that the arrival at the target point is the most important condition to be satisfied in robot navigation.

In the EP algorithm, self-adaptive Gaussian mutation is used. For details on constrained optimization by evolutionary algorithms, the reader is referred to [7].

4   Computer Simulations

Computer simulations were carried out using two kinds of vector fields(for final posture and obstacle avoidance) on a Pentium IBM PC considering the kinematic model of the robot. For each individual, the simulation is carried out 25 times with uniformly distributed random starting positions. Throughout the simulations, the elitist $((\mu + \ ) - EP)$ selection method was used and the grid nets used in following simulations have circular form with size 10×6. The maximum speed of wheels was 100 cm/s, of the center of the robot was 50 cm/s, and the maximal rotational acceleration of robot was 10 rad/sample. The number of individuals was 20, and the number of offsprings was 40.

4.1   Uni-vector field for final posture

In this case, It was assumed that the final position is the center of the field (0,0) and the final orientation is to the right (0 rad). Fig. 4(a), 4(b) and 4(c) show the best vector fields obtained at each generation. Fig. 4(c) shows the constraints are satisfied or traded off.

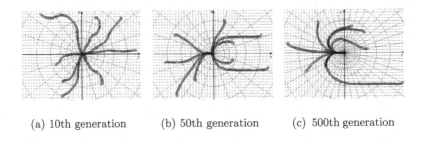

(a) 10th generation   (b) 50th generation   (c) 500th generation

Fig. 4. Simulation results for "nal posture acquisition

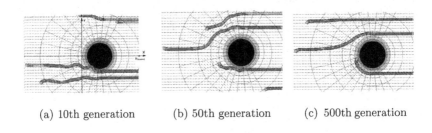

(a) 10th generation   (b) 50th generation   (c) 500th generation

Fig. 5. Simulation results for obstacle avoidance

4.2   Uni-vector field with obstacles

Fig. 5(a), 5(b) and 5(c) show the results for circular obstacle avoidance. The final position is to the right border of each frame. As the generation goes on, the navigation becomes more satisfactory.

5   Experiments

To demonstrate the effectiveness of the proposed scheme, it is implemented in the real robot system. The overall system is composed of a robot, a host computer, a vision system, and a communication system. The vision system detects the position and orientation of the robot and obstacle. Using this vision information, the host computer applies the proposed navigation method to calculate the velocities of the robot wheels. The calculated wheel velocities are transmitted to the robot through the communication system.

The vision system is composed of a TMC-7 CCD camera with a resolution of 320×240 pixel and an image grabber with a processing rate of 30 frames/sec. The vision system in the experimental setup has measurement errors of about 2.4cm for position and 4.83 degree for angle calculations. The host computer is a Pentium processor with 133 MHz clock. The mobile robot is developed for the purpose of playing MiroSot robot-soccer game [3]. The robot size is 7.5

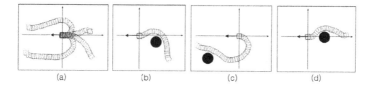

Fig. 6. Experimental results for desired robot postures

cm×7.5 cm×7.5 cm, with a wheel width of 6.5 *cm*. The robot has an AT89C52 micro-controller, two DC motors, and two LM629 motion controllers. In the experiment, a sampling time of 33 ms is used. Other conditions are the same as in simulation. Fig. 6 (a) shows the case of final posture acquiring without an obstacle. Fig. 6 (b), (c), and (d) show the cases with obstacle avoidance. The radius of the obstacle considered is 6cm. The arrows in Fig. 6 show the desired final orientation of the robot. The robots move to the final position and converge to the final heading angle by the short and smooth path without collision. Fig. 6 shows good performance for all cases.

6 Conclusions

A novel navigation method for obstacle avoidance and final posture acquiring method were developed and implemented. This method was obtained introducing a modifiable uni-vector field into the unified navigation. To obtain the optimal vector field, a function approximator and its learning algorithm were proposed. The developed navigation was implemented on a bi-wheel type mobile robot. As seen from both simulations and experiments, the proposed method is useful for fast mobile robot control and for robots performing more complex tasks.

References

1. E. Rimon,   Exact Robot Navigation Using Arti"cial Potential Functions,   IEEE Trans. on Robotics and Automation, Vol. 8, No. 5, pp. 501-518, Oct. 1992.
2. http://www."ra.net/
3. J.-H. Kim (ed.), Special Issue: First Micro-Robot World Cup Soccer Tournament, MiroSot, Robotics and Autonomous Systems, Elsevier, Vol. 21, No. 2, Sep. 1997.
4. G. Camoin, G. Bastin and B. D. Novel,   Structural Properties and Classi"cation of Kinetic and Dynamic Models of Wheeled Mobile Robots,   IEEE Trans. Robotics and Automation, Vol. 12, No. 1, pp. 47-62, Feb. 1996.
5. J. Borenstein and Y. Koren,   Real-time Obstacle Avoidance for Fast Mobile Robots,   IEEE Trans. Syst. Man. Cybern., Vol. 20, No. 4, pp. 1179-1187, 1989.
6. J. Gulder and V. I. Utkin,   Stabilization of Non-holonomic Mobile Robots using Lyapunov functions for Navigation and Sliding Mode Control,   Proc. of the IEEE conf. on Decision and Control, pp. 2967-2972, Dec. 1994.
7. J.-H. Kim and H. Myung,   Evolutionary Programming Techniques for Constrained Optimization Problems,   IEEE Trans. on Evolutionary Computation, pp. 129-140, May 1997.

Evolution with Learning Adaptive Functions

Masayuki Ishinishi and Akira Namatame

Dept. of Computer Science
National Defense Academy
Yokosuka, 239-8686, JAPAN
E-mail: mishi@cs.nda.ac.jp, nama@cc.nda.ac.jp

Abstract. In this paper, we consider a society of economic agents. Economic agents are de"ned as autonomous software entities equipped with the adaptive functions. They have their own adaptive functions de"ned over the market which is governed with the market mechanism. We especially focus the evolutional explanation on how the social competence that provides the motivation for the coordinated behavior can be emerged from the interactions guided by the sel"sh behaviors of economic agents. Especially we need to understand the following basic issues how get the architecture of an agent, as a component of a complex system, suited for evolution, how self-interested behaviors evolve to coordinated behaviors, and how the structure of each goal (adaptive) function can be modi"ed for globally coordinated behaviors. We also show that the concept of sympathy becomes a fundamental element for adaptation and coordinated behavior.

Keywords: emergence of optimal behaviors, market mechanism, economic agent, emotion

1 Introduction

In a large-scale complex adaptive system composed of those many rational agents, two types of strategic behaviors may occur: agents mutually interact and behave to achieve the common goal of the society, while at the same time, each agent also behaves to optimizes its own goal. For an individual rational agent, it behaves to improve its own adaptive function based on its local observation. This ability is based on principles of the individual rationality. By a social goal we mean a goal that is not achievable by any single agent alone but is achievable by a society of agents. The key element that distinguishes a social goal from an agent's individual goal is that they require cooperation. Then how will the evolution of individually rational behaviors proceed to coordinated behavior?

We describe the model of economic agent as the basis for social cooperation learnable through competitive interaction. We call the latter ability as competitive cooperation. Economic agents are driven by their own selfish motivations, and they are selfish in the sense that they only do what they want to do and what they think is in their own best interests, as determined by their own interests. The collective behavior of those agents is determined through the local interactions of their constituent parts. These interactions merit careful study in order to understand the macroscopic properties of collective behaviors . We especially ask the following questions: If agents make decisions on the basis imperfect information about other agents' goals or adaptive funcitons, and incorporate expectations on how its decision will affect other agents' adaptive functions, then how will the evolution of cooperation proceed? How will the structure of adaptive function of each agent should be self-modified for the evolution of social cooperation?

In this paper, we study the evolution of social cooperation without loosing the principle of competition in a society. Social learning is defined as the set of mechanism which utilizes adaptive decision-making of economic agents. In the adaptive decision-making mechanism, each economic agent modifies its own adaptive function by re"ecting its sympathy level to the other members. With the principle of sympathy, It adapts its own decision to based on the current and previous performance. The goal of an agent is determined solely by how that agent affects other members of the society and how the decision of other agents affects its own adaptive function. Adaptive decision-making is facilitated by designing the agents to be somewhat modified selfish interest.

Social learning allows agents to achieve high-level social goals without the need for cooperative planning and communications. Thus, over a time, a society of economic agents will be able to learn to cooperate together at an even higher-level learning of e ciency and adaptability. Under this social learning, cooperation emerges as a side-effect of the adaptive decision-making which lead them to learn the cooperative behaviors without sacrificing that the principle of competition in the society.

2   A Model of Economic Agents

We consider a society of economic agents, $G = \{A_i : i = 1, 2, \ldots, n\}$. Economic agents are defined as autonomous software entities equipped with the adaptive capabilities. They have their own adaptive functions as the function of the market price which is governed with the market mechanism. We define the adaptive function of each agent $A_i \in G$ as

$$U_i(x_1, \ldots, x_i, \ldots, x_n) = x_i P_i\{x_i, x(i)\} \tag{1}$$

where $P_i\{x_i, x(i)\}$ represents the price scheme associated to the activity of agent $A_i \in G$. And x_i represents the level of activity of agent $A_i \in G$, and $x(i) = (x_1, \ldots, x_{i-1}, x_{i+1}, \ldots, x_n)$ represents the set of activities of all agents in G except agent A_i.

As a specific example, we consider the following social price scheme for each agent $A_i \in G$,

$$P_i = a_i - \sum_{j=1}^{n} b_{ij} x_j \tag{2}$$

where $a_i, b_{ij}, i, j = 1, 2, \ldots, n$, are some positive constant.

The competitive solution in which each agent maximizes its own adaptive function simultaneously is given as the solution of the following system of linear equations:

$$(B + B_1)x^\circ = a \tag{3}$$

where B is a $n \times n$ matrix with the (i, j)th element is, $b_{ij}, i, j = 1, 2, \ldots, n$, B_1 is a diagonal matrix with the i-th diagonal element is b_{ii}, and a are the column vectors with the elements, $a_i, , i = 1, 2, \ldots, n$, respectively.

We define the socially optimal behavior as the set of the activities that optimize the summation of the adaptive functions of all agents defined as

$$S(x_1, \ldots, x_i, \ldots, x_n) = \sum_{i=1}^{n} U_i\{x_1, \ldots, x_i, \ldots, x_n\} \tag{4}$$

The socially optimal behaviors is then obtained as the set of the activities satisfying the following equations.

$$S/ x_i = U_i/ x_i + \sum_{j \neq i}^{n} U_j/ x_i = 0, \quad i = 1, 2, \ldots, n, \tag{5}$$

As an example of the quadratic adaptive functions with the linear social price scheme is given in (2), the social optimal solution is obtained as the solution of the following system of linear equations:

$$(B + B^T)x^* = a \tag{6}$$

where B^T is the transpose matrix of B.

We especially consider the case in which the interaction matrix B is symmetric with the diagonal elements are the same, i.e., $b_{ii} = d$ and the off-diagonal elements are, $b_{ij} = b, (0 < b < d), i, j = 1, 2, \ldots, n$. The column vector a also has the same elements, i.e., $a_i = a, i = 1, 2, \ldots, n,$.

The level of adaptation of each agent at competitive equilibrium is obtained as follows:

$$U_i^\circ(n) = a^2 d / \{2d + b(n-1)\}^2 \tag{7}$$

The level of the adaptation as a society, which is defined as the summation of the adaptive level of each agent is then given as

$$G^\circ(n) \equiv \sum_{i=1}^{n} U_i^\circ(n) = a^2 dn / \{2d + b(n-1)\}^2 \tag{8}$$

The level of adaptation of each agent at socially optimal behavior is given as

$$U_i^*(n) = a^2 / 4\{d + b(n-1)\} \tag{9}$$

The levels of the adaptation as a society, which is defined as the summation of the adaptive level of each agent is then given as

$$G^*(n) \equiv \sum_{i=1}^{n} U_i^*(n) = a^2 n / 4\{d + b(n-1)\} \tag{10}$$

Here we are interested in how the adaptiveness of the whole organization may affect if the size of the organization increases, i.e, we will investigate the asymptotic value of the summation of the adaptive functions of each agent in the case that the number of agents increases. By taking the limits of those social adaptive functions with the number of the economic agents, those values converge as follows:

$$\lim_{n \to \infty} G^\circ(n) = 0 \tag{11}$$

$$\lim_{n \to \infty} G^*(n) = a^2/4b \tag{12}$$

This implies that the level of adaptation under competitive behaviors converges to zero, and that of under socially optimal behaviors converge to same constant.

3   Learning of Social Adaptive Function

In the previous section, we showed that the conditions of the individual optimality and the social optimality are different. This implies that if each economic seeks its own optimality the level of adaptation decreases as the number of agents in a society increases. Our question is then stated as follows, how will the evolution of cooperation proceed and how the emergence of cooperation can take place in a society.

We now consider the following modified adaptive function for each agent $A_i \in G$.

$$\overline{U}_i\{x_i, x(i)\} = U_i\{x_i, x(i)\} - {}_i\{x(i)\}x_i \tag{13}$$

The adaptive function of each agent defined in (13) consists of the two terms, the private adaptive function and the social adaptive function. By taking the derivative of the modified adaptive function of (13) by x_i, we obtain

$$\overline{U}_i/ x_i = U_i/ x_i - {}_i(x(i)) \tag{14}$$

we set ${}_i(x(i))$ in (14) as (15), the condition of the individual optimality under the modified adaptive functions is equivalent to the condition of the social optimality defined over the set of the original adaptive functions in (1).

$$_i(x(i)) = - \sum_{j \neq i}^{n} ({}^2 U_j/ x_j x_i) x_j = \sum_{j \neq i}^{n} b_{ji} x_j \tag{15}$$

We term ${}_i(x(i))$ as the level of the symphathy of the i-th economic agent. The symphathy level indicates the level of the in"uence of the decision of i-th agent to the adaptive functions of the other economic agents.

The condition of the individual optimality by considering the symphathy level is given as

$$M_i\{x_i, x(i)\} - {}_i\{x(i)\} = 0 \quad i = 1, 2, \ldots, n. \tag{16}$$

where we denote the derivative of the adaptive function as $M_i\{x_i, x(i)\}$.

The emergence of those social competence as intelligent can take place without any commitment among selfish agents. In a society, economic agents are driven by their own selfish motivations which lead them to learn the rules of decentralized decision-making or the coordinated behaviors.

The process of building up intelligent behaviors and cooperative intentions may be called mutual or social learning [7][12]. Social learning from the social perspective is grounded in the actions of many agents' activities taken together, and it not a matter of individual choice. It is one's actions in relation to those of others (vice versa) that maintain its participation. Social learning is in this sense is the outcome of a web of activity emerged from the mutual interactions among agents. In the model of social learning, two types of learning may occur: the economic agent can learn to cooperate as a group, while at the same time, each agent can also learn its own by adjusting its activity level. Social learning would require the exchange of actions of the other agents.

The dynamic action selection process must be coordinated to achieve globally consistent and good actions. We define the social learning as the adjustment process of each agents' individually economic behavior. The social learning model describes how each agent, without knowing the others' adaptive functions, adjusts its activity level over time and reaches to an equilibrium situation.

Without complete knowledge of other agents, agent needs to infer the strategies, knowledge, plans of other agents. Economic agents can put forward their private knowledge for consideration by other agents based on its own local interactions, and agents would require the exchange of actions with other agents. Learning is then formulated as the web of activity emerged from the mutual interactions among economic agents. With the individual learning capability, each agent modifies its decision based on the current and previous performance in order to optimize its own adaptive function[1]. This adjustment process generates a partial action that governs the actions of the agents .The mutual adjustment process of behaviors is modeled as follows:

$$\begin{array}{l} M_i\{x_i, x(i)\} > {}_i\{x(i)\} \quad then \quad x_i := x_i + {} x_i \\ M_i\{x_i, x(i)\} < {}_i\{x(i)\} \quad then \quad x_i := x_i - {} x_i \end{array} \tag{17}$$

At equilibrium , we have

$$M_i\{x_i^*, x^*(i)\} - {}_i\{x^*(i)\} = 0 \quad i = 1, 2, \ldots, n. \tag{18}$$

The use of directives by an agent to control another can be viewed as a form of incremental behavior adjustment[14]. The adjustment process without any sympathy by setting ${}_i = 0, i = 1, 2, \ldots, n.$, converges a competitive equilibrium.

The mutual adjustment process with the sympathy is modeled specifically as follows:

$$\begin{array}{l} {}_i = x_i(t+1) - x_i(t) \\ = ({}_i/b_{ii})[M_i\{x_i(t), x(i,t)\} - {}_i\{x(i,t)\}] \end{array} \tag{19}$$

where $x(i,t) = (x_1(t), \ldots, x_{i-1}(t), x_i(t), x_{i+1}(t), \ldots, x_n(t))$. The mutual adjustment process is then given as follows:

$$x_i(t+1) = ({}_i/b_{ii})P_i(t) + (1 - {}_i)x_i(t) - ({}_i/b_{ii}) {}_i\{x(i,t)\} \tag{20}$$

We also describe the adjustment process of each agent's symphathy level as follows:

$$_i(t+1) = {}_i[M_i\{x_i(t), x(i,t)\} - {}_ix(i,t)] + {}_i\{x(i,t)\} \tag{21}$$

With the definition the level symphathy in (18), we have the following process for learning:

$$_i(t+1) = {}_i\{P_i(t) - b_{ii}x_i(t)\} + (1 - {}_i)\sum_{j\neq i}^{n} b_{ji}x_j(t) \tag{22}$$

The activity level of each agent should be determined solely by how its decision affects other members in the same society and how the decisions of other agents affect its own adaptive function. However, in the large society, it may di cult for each agent to consider the interactions with other agent. Therefore, we assume the following symmetric condition for mutual interactions.

$$b_{ji}/b_{ii} = k \quad (0 < k \leq 1), j = 1, 2, \ldots, n, j \neq i \tag{23}$$

The mutual adjustment process of behaviors based on goal-seeking with the sympasy is then modeled as follows:

$$_i(t+1) = {}_i\{P_i(t) - b_{ii}x_i(t)\} + (1 - {}_i)b_{ii}k\sum_{j\neq i}^{n} x_j(t) \tag{24}$$

4   Some Simulation Results

The goal of the research is to understand the competitive interactions based on the self-interested motivations which produce purposive and optimal collective behavior. In this section, we address the question of how a society of the economic agents with different internal model can achieve complex collective behaviors as a whole. We especially address the following questions: How will the internal model of each economic agent affect the evolution of their collective behaviors, how will the collective behavior of in economic agents proceed by changing the combination patterns of different types of agents? In order to answer those questions, we did some simulation under the following condition.

(simulate conditions)
(1) number of Agents:30
(2) social price scheme :$a_i = 300, b_{ii} = 1, b_{ij} = 0.1$
(3) initial action of each agentœB!'œ(B5

The following figures show the change of adaptation level over the adaptive time.

(Case1) $_i = 0.1$(slow to adjust the market price) and $_i = 0.1$(low learning speed)

Fig.1 and Fig.2 shows the level of adaptation of an individual and the whole society. Fig.1 shows the level of adaptation under sympathy. Fig.2 shows that the level of adaption without sympathy From this simulation, each individual can increase its adaptation level with sympathy to other agent.

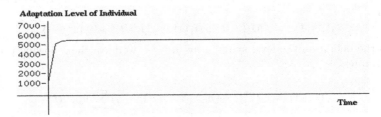

(a) The adaptive level of individual

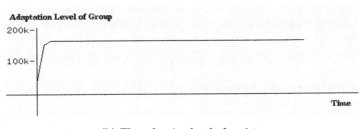

(b) The adaptive level of society

Fig. 1. The change of adaptation level (with sympathy)

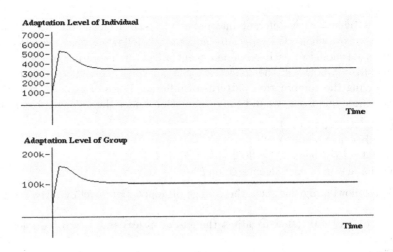

Fig. 2. The change of adaptation level (without sympathy)

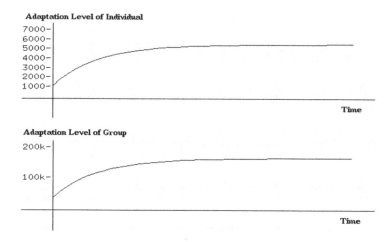

Fig. 3. The change of adaptation level: slow convergence

(Case2) $_i$ = 0.1 (slow to adjust the market price) and $_i$ = 0.1 (high learning speed)

Fig.3 shows the case of the high speed of learning factor of sympathy, and in which the level of adaptation of each agent converges slowly.

5   Conclusion

The goal of the research is to understand the types of simples local interactions which produce complex and purposive group behaviors. We formulated and analyzed the social learning process of independent economic agents. We showed that cooperative behaviors can be realized through purposive local interactions based on each individual goal-seeking. Each economic agents does not need to express its adaptive function, nor to have a priory knowledge of those of others. Economic agent adapts its action both to the actions of other agents.

References

1. Barto,A.G,Sutton, Learning and sequential decision-making , *Learning and Computational Neuro Science,* MIT Press,1991b
2. Basar,T, & Olsder,G., *Dynamic Noncooperative Game Theory,* Academic Press ,1982
3. Brazdil, P.B, Learning in Multi-agent Environments , *Proc. of the Second Workshop on Algorithmic Learning Theory,* pp. 15 29,(1991).
4. Carley,K, & Prietula,M.: Computational Organization Theory, Lawrence Erallbawn, 1994
5. Creps,J,E., An Introduction to Modern Micro Economics,MIT Press, 1991.

6. Fudenberg,D,E,and Tirole.J, Game Theory, MIT Press ,1991.
7. Gasse,L.,Social conceptions of knowledge and action:DAI foundations and open systems semantics, in *Artificial Intelligence,* Vol.47, pp.107 135,1991.
8. Kandori,M,Mailath,G,& Rob.R., Learning, mutation, and long run equilibrium, *Econometrica,* Vol.61,No.1, pp.29 56, 1993.
9. Marschak,J,& Radner,R,: *Theory of Teams,* Yale Univ. Press,1972.
10. Ordeshook,P: *Game Theory and Political Theory,* Cambridge Univ. Press,1987.
11. Shoham,Y: Agent-oriented Programming, *Artificial Intelligence,* Vol.60, pp51 92,1993,
12. Sian. S.E. The Role of Cooperation in Multi-agent Learning Systems , in *Cooperative Knowledge-Based Systems,* Springer-Verlag, pp. 67 84 (1990).
13. R. Sikora, Learning Control Strategies for Chemical Processes : A Distributed Approach, *IEEE Expert,* June, pp. 35 43 (1992).
14. Tenney. R.,& Sandell,N.R., Strategies for Distributed Decision making, *IEEE Trans. Automatic Control,* Vol.AC-19,,pp.236 247,1974.
15. Young,P., The evolution of conventions,*Econometrica,* Vol.61,No.1, pp.57 84, 1993.

Modelling Plant Breeding Programs as Search Strategies on a Complex Response Surface

D.W. Podlich and M. Cooper

School of Land and Food, The University of Queensland, Brisbane, Australia
d.podlich@mailbox.uq.edu.au

Abstract. The concept of an adaptation ("tness) landscape has been used to explain evolutionary processes. The landscape is a response surface for the genetic space de"ned by a genotype-environment system and evolution of populations through natural selection a search for higher peaks in this space. This is an appealing framework for other disciplines interested in issues of search and optimisation. One such application is the genetic improvement of traits in plant breeding. Here, breeding programs can be viewed and analysed as search strategies that are used to explore the surface of an adaptation landscape to "nd higher adaptive positions. The current theoretical framework considers genetic improvement as a hill climbing process on a smooth single peaked adaptation landscape. However, there is strong evidence to suggest that due to the e˜ects of genotype-by-environment (G×E) interactions and epistasis, the landscapes encountered by plant breeders are in fact rugged and multi-peaked. Simulation methodology was used to compare two selection strategies currently used in plant breeding and investigate their capacity to confront the di culties associated with the in"uences of G×E interaction and epistasis: (i) selection of genotypes based on performance in a single environment (mass selection), and (ii) selection of genotypes based on performance in several environments (multi-environment testing). A third selection strategy was proposed for genetic improvement on more complex adaptation landscapes. This selection strategy (shifting search strategy) was based on Wright s Shifting Balance Theory .
bf Keywords: "tness, adaptation, landscape, G×E interaction, epistasis, plant breeding

1 Introduction

Breeding strategies applied to the genetic improvement of plants in agriculture can be considered as search strategies seeking particular combinations of genes (genotypes) to improve traits of commercial significance. The majority of these traits are quantitative and under the control of many genes. For each gene there are alternative forms, referred to as alleles. These alleles combine to generate the different genotypes possible for a single gene at a locus on a chromosome. Combining this variation across genes rapidly generates large numbers of possible genotypes. Therefore, any search for a new genotype is a complex combinatorial problem where the numbers preclude evaluation of all possible genotypes. In addition the expression of the genes is in"uenced by environmental conditions, which vary within a target population of environments (TPE). The genetic variation within the gene pool available to a breeding program and the environmental variation within the TPE combine to generate a complex genotype-environment system. Improved genotypes for this system are sought by applying artificial selection strategies that aim to increase the frequency of genes contributing to enhanced performance of the traits.

Any search for improved genotypes is further complicated by our lack of understanding of the genetic control of these quantitative traits. Theoretical considerations, experimental investigations and experience from applied breeding programs indicate that the relative effectiveness of alternative breeding strategies will depend on the nature of this genetic control. For quantitative traits the importance of both genotype-by-environment (G×E) interactions and gene-by-gene interactions (epistasis) is of particular interest. G×E interactions occur when there is a change in the relative performance of genotypes when the genotypes are exposed to different environmental conditions. Epistasis occurs when the contributions to a trait by the genotypes of one gene are in"uenced by the genotypes of other genes. Both of these sources of interaction complicate the nature of the genotype-environment system and increase the degree of di culty of the search for improved genotypes.

R.A. Fisher and S. Wright debated similar issues in relation to evolution and natural selection [1]. Fisher proposed that a gene can be deemed favourable or unfavourable in terms of its average effect within a genotype-environment system. Therefore, adopting the Fisher model, breeding programs should operate to increase the frequency of the favourable genes. Wright proposed an alternative model where epistasis had a stronger in"uence on the value of genes. He suggested that the relative performance of genotypes can be viewed in terms of the concept of a landscape with multiple peaks. Therefore, with the Wright model it can be argued that breeding programs should operate to exploit local peaks by selecting specific desirable epistatic combinations of genes but at the same time maintain a capacity to search for new higher peaks. Fisher's model, considered in terms of Wright's landscape concept, is a simplification of the shape of the landscape which assumes a single peak. If there was a single peak, breeding programs should operate to climb it as rapidly as possible without allocating resources to search for new peaks. Historically the Fisher model has dominated much of the thinking and principles used in the design of applied breeding strategies.

The availability of powerful tools to investigate the genetic control of traits at the molecular level is contributing to increasing awareness of their complexity. With this awareness the issue of what is an appropriate genetic model for the design of breeding strategies is resurfacing. There is a growing body of evidence suggesting a greater importance of epistasis and G×E interaction than was previously thought. Improving our understanding of the relationship between the structure of the underlying adaptation landscape and the effectiveness of alternative search strategies represented by breeding programs provides a basis for designing and implementing selection strategies that optimise response to selection for different genotype-environment systems. We have used computer simulation to investigate the effectiveness of plant breeding strategies for genotype-environment systems that are in"uenced by both epistasis and G×E interactions [2]. The objective of this paper is to examine the relative e - ciency of plant breeding strategies that take into consideration the in"uence of G×E interactions and epistasis on the relative performance of genotypes for a quantitative trait.

2   Materials and Methods

A computer simulation experiment was conducted using the QU-GENE (QUantitative GENEtics) simulation platform [2]. The QU-GENE simulation platform enables the design of $E(N{:}K)$ models for genotype-environment systems; E is the number of different types of environments in the TPE, N is the number of genes and K is a measure of the level of epistasis in the model. Using the $E(N{:}K)$ notation identifies that different $N{:}K$ genetic models are nested within the different types of environments encountered in the TPE, generating G×E interaction. The $E(N{:}K)$ framework is a more general treatment of Kauffman's [3] NK model and incoporates both the in"uences of G×E interaction and epistasis. The $E(N{:}K)$ model provides "exibility for investigating a wide range of genetic models ranging from smooth single peaked landscapes (no G×E interaction or epistasis: $E = 1; K = 0$) to rugged multi-peaked landscapes (G×E interaction and epistasis: $E > 1; K > 0$).

The architecture of the QU-GENE platform consists of two major components: (i) the engine that is used to define the genetic model (based on a diploid system) for the genotype-environment system, and (ii) the application modules that are used to investigate, analyse or manipulate populations of genotypes within the defined genotype-environment system [2]. The engine generates an $E(N{:}K)$ adaptation landscape by defining the performance values of all possible genotypes in each type of environment. For this simulation experiment, the allocation of performance values to individual genotypes was based on the fitness definition used for the NK model by Kauffman [3]. Here, the fitness (performance) of a genotype in the TPE (W) was defined as:

$$W = \sum_{j=1}^{E} e_j \sum_{i=1}^{N} \frac{w_{ij}}{N}$$

where E is the number of environment types in the TPE, N is the number of genes, e_j is the frequency of occurrence of environment type j in the TPE and w_{ij} is the fitness contribution of the ith gene in environment type j and is drawn (at random) from the uniform distribution between 0 and 1. For each epistatic combination, an independent fitness contribution (w_{ij}) was defined for locus i.

An application module (LANDS) was developed to improve population fitness using three different recurrent selection strategies: (i) mass selection (MASS), (ii) multi-environment testing (MET) and (iii) shifting search strategy (SSS).

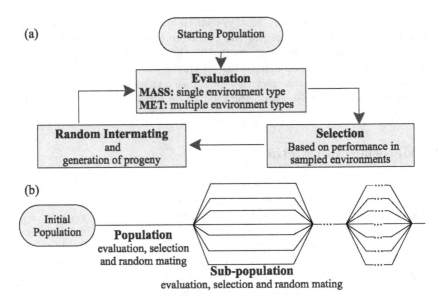

Fig. 1. Schematic outline of three selection strategies (a) mass selection (MASS) and multi-environment trials (MET), (b) shifting search strategy (SSS).

Fig. 1a represents a schematic outline of the MASS and MET selection strategies. Using the individuals generated by the engine as an initial population, recurrent selection proceeds by evaluating the performance of the genotypes, identifying a select group of individuals and randomly intermating the select group to generate a population for the next cycle. For MASS selection, the evaluation of genotypes was based on performance in a single environment type sampled at random from the TPE. For MET selection, the evaluation of genotypes was based on performance in multiple environment types sampled at random from the TPE. The third selection strategy (SSS) was based on Wright's [4] 'Shifting Balance Theory' (Fig. 1b). As with the MET selection strategy, the population of genotypes was evaluated in multiple environment types, a select group of genotypes identified and randomly intermated. However, these cycles of population improvement were interspersed with phases of subdivision. Here, the population was divided into smaller sub-populations where evaluation, selection and intermating were independently conducted. After a number of cycles these sub-populations were combined into a single population where the process was continued as for the MET strategy.

Using the LANDS module, the performance of three selection strategies (MASS, MET, SSS) were evaluated for $E(N{:}K)$ landscapes with increasing complexity. Genotype-environment systems based on 20 genes ($N = 20$), eight levels of K ($K = 0, 1, ..., 7$) and four levels of E ($E = 1, 2, 5, 10$) were considered, resulting in 32 different $E(N{:}K)$ models. For each model, 250 independent runs

(10 different starting populations; 25 runs of each) were conducted for each selection strategy. Each run was conducted for 50 cycles using a population of 500 genotypes (starting populations constructed to have a fitness level of 0.5) with the top 20% selected at each cycle. During the subdivision phases of the SSS, the population was divided into 20 sub-populations (25 genotypes in each). The subdivision phases were conducted in blocks of five cycles interspersed with blocks of ten cycles of single population improvement (Fig. 1b). For the MASS selection strategy, genotypes were evaluated in a single environment type. For the MET and SSS, genotypes were evaluated across ten environments sampled at random from the TPE. The performance of the three selection strategies for each of the $E(N{:}K)$ models was evaluated as the average fitness of the population for the 250 runs over the 50 cycles.

3   Results

The simulation experiment indicated there were significant interactions between the relative efficiency of the three selection strategies and two major parameters of the $E(N{:}K)$ model, E (G×E interaction) and K (epistasis). For smooth single peaked landscapes ($E = 1; K = 0$), all three selection strategies achieved similar response to selection. However, with the introduction of G×E interaction and epistasis into the $E(N{:}K)$ framework, alternative response profiles were observed for the three strategies.

Fig. 2 displays the average performance of the three selection strategies for four levels of G×E interaction ($E = 1, 2, 5, 10$) and no epistasis ($K = 0$). As the level of G×E interaction introduced into the system was increased, the population fitness achieved by the three selection strategies decreased (Fig. 2a d). The relative efficiency of the three selection strategies within levels of E was not constant. For the model containing no G×E interaction, $E(N{:}K)=1(20{:}0)$, the three selection strategies achieved a similar response (Fig. 2a). However, as G×E interaction was introduced (Fig. 2b d), the two selection strategies using multi-environment trials (MET and SSS) were more efficient than the single environment trial (MASS). The level of relative improvement of the MET and SSS strategies increased as the level of E was raised.

Fig. 3 displays the average performance of the selection strategies for four levels of epistasis ($K = 1, 3, 5, 7$) and no G×E interaction ($E = 1$). Here, the MET selection strategy offered no improvement over the MASS selection strategy. However, the strategy based on phases of subdivision (SSS) achieved a higher level of fitness. Furthermore, the level of relative improvement increased with the amount of epistasis (Fig. 3a d). Unlike the smooth curvilinear average fitness response of the MASS and MET selection strategies, the SSS displayed phases of rapid improvement interspersed with cycles of sharp decrease in fitness. The fitness profile of the SSS can be attributed to the different components of the shifting search. Here, the independent searches conducted during the subdivision phases of the SSS enabled smaller sub-populations to explore different regions of the adaptation landscape. Due to the large amount of genetic variability among

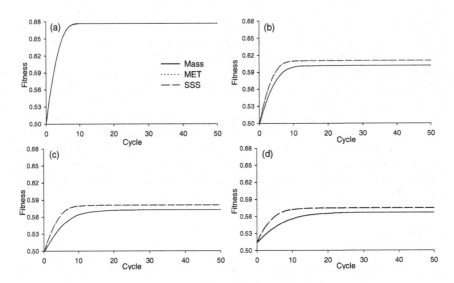

Fig. 2. Response to selection of the MASS, MET and SSS strategies for four levels of E and $K = 0$: (a) $E = 1$, (b) $E = 2$, (c) $E = 5$ and (d) $E = 10$.

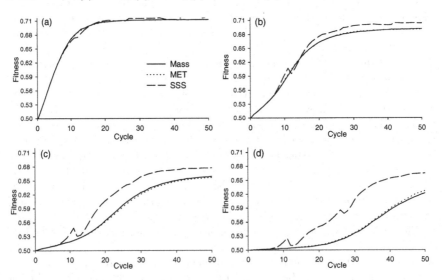

Fig. 3. Response to selection of the MASS, MET and SSS strategies for four levels of K and $E = 1$: (a) $K = 1$, (b) $K = 3$, (c) $K = 5$ and (d) $K = 7$.

sub-populations, the combination of these independent searches into a single population initially reduced population fitness. However, the exposure to alternative regions of the landscape provided an opportunity for the SSS to increase performance relative to the MASS and MET strategies.

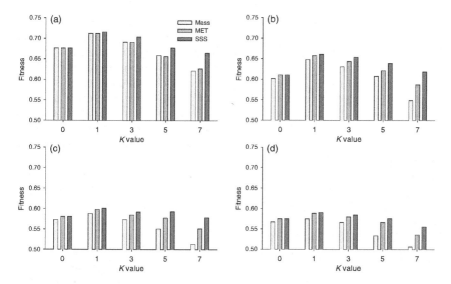

Fig. 4. Response to selection of the MASS, MET and SSS strategies at cycle 50 for four levels of E and "ve levels of K: (a) $E = 1$, (b) $E = 2$, (c) $E = 5$ and (d) $E = 10$.

Fig. 4 displays the average performance of the selection strategies at cycle 50 for combinations of both G×E interaction and epistasis. The three selection strategies achieved an improved fitness level, relative to the starting population (0.5), for all of the $E(N{:}K)$ models considered. However, the introduction and increase in levels of G×E interaction and epistasis in"uenced the relative effectiveness of the selection strategies. For models containing no G×E interaction (Fig. 4a), the MASS and MET strategies achieved similar levels of response for all levels of K. However, the e ciency of the MET strategy increased relative to MASS with the introduction of G×E interaction into the system (Fig. 4a d). For models containing no epistasis (Fig. 4a d; $K = 0$), the MET and SSS strategies achieved similar levels of response for all levels of E. However, the e ciency of the SSS strategy increased relative to MET with the introduction of epistasis into the system (Fig. 4a d).

4   Discussion

As the complexities of the genome are exposed there is an increasing awareness that many of the simplifying assumptions used to mathematically model genotype-environment systems are di cult to sustain. The $E(N{:}K)$ model provides a framework for relaxing many of these assumptions, in particular those related to epistasis and G×E interactions. Plant breeding strategies apply artificial selection to finite samples of genotypes and seek to identify those genotypes with higher performance values for a given genotype-environment system. As the levels of epistasis and G×E interaction increase, the shape of the adaptation landscape on which this search takes place becomes more complex. We are investigating the relative merits of alternative breeding strategies in terms of their ability to search for improved genotypes on these landscapes. An important finding is that directional selection is an extremely powerful search strategy across a wide range of levels of complexity in the genotype-environment systems and their associated adaptation landscapes. For example, in the present study mass selection was capable of making improvement for all of the $E(N:K)$ models considered, albeit gradual for the most complex. However, it is clear that selection strategies which take into account important features of the shape of the adaptation landscape can improve the effectiveness of the search. The use of multi-environment trials (MET and SSS) was more effective than the single environment trial (MASS) as G×E interaction was introduced to the system. This is a common strategy used in applied plant breeding to deal with this source of complexity. The use of the shifting search strategy (SSS) introduced a further improvement to the search over MET as the level of epistasis in the system increased. The role of this sort of search strategy has been discussed in relation to evolution in natural systems but only speculated on in agricultural systems. However, at the global level the "ow of genetic resources from small local breeding programs to the larger breeding programs of the international centres and the subsequent "ow of new germplasm back to the local programs may be viewed as a form of shifting search strategy. This suggestion and the results of our simulation studies identifies avenues for investigation of the e cient use of genetic resources in plant breeding.

While to date we have confined our investigations to random genetic networks, the resulting genotype-environment systems show many emergent properties that are observed in practice when plant breeding programs search real biophysical systems. These parallels, and the limited ability of our current quantitative genetic theory to predict significant genetic improvements for quantitative traits, provide much food for thought in relation to the role of plant breeding in the quest for food security and sustainable agricultural systems.

References

1. Wade, M.J: Sewall Wright: Gene interaction and the Shifting Balance Theory. Oxford Surveys in Evolutionary Biol. **8** 35 62 (1992)
2. Podlich, D.W., Cooper, M.: QU-GENE: A platform for quantitative analysis of genetic models. Bioinformatics. **14** 632 653 (1998)
3. Kau˘man, S.A.: The origins of order, self-organisation and selection in evolution. Oxford University Press, New York (1993)
4. Wright, S.: Evolution and the genetics of populations, Vol 3. University of Chicago Press, Chicago. (1977)

Generating Equations with Genetic Programming for Control of a Movable Inverted Pendulum

Hiroaki Shimooka and Yoshiji Fujimoto

Department of Applied Mathematics and Informatics
Faculty of Science and Technology, Ryukoku University
1-5 Yokoya, Ooe, Seta, Ohtsu, Shiga 520-2194 Japan
fujimoto@math.ryukoku.ac.jp

Abstract. Equations for calculating the control force of a movable inverted pendulum are generated directly with Genetic Programming (GP). The task of a movable inverted pendulum is to control the force given a cart on which a pole is hinged, not only to keep a pole standing but also to move it to an arbitrary target position.

As the results of experiments, intelligent control equations are obtained that can lean the pole toward a target position by pulling the cart in the opposite direction, and then move the cart to the target while keeping the pole standing inversely. They also have the robustness to move the cart with the pole standing to the new target position when the target is changed, even if the cart is moving to the old target position.

The robustness of the problem is experimentally de"ned and the appropriate value of the parsimony factor in GP is identi"ed to obtain control equations with robustness and simplicity as the solutions.

1 Introduction

The pole-balancing problem has been attacked many times previously with methods such as evolutionary fuzzy logics [1] and evolutionary neural networks [2,3]. However, approaches to this problem with Genetic Programming (GP) have hardly been found except in the eleventh chapter of the book Genetic Programming by John Koza [4]. His approach is to evolve equations to determine the direction of the bang-bang force given a cart.

However, the objective of this paper is to evolve an equation with GP that can calculate the magnitude of the driving force of a cart so that it allows the cart to move to given target positions while keeping a pole standing on the cart. It is in contrast to a general pole-balancing problem whose objective is only to keep a pole standing. Moreover, a robustness of a control equation is experimentally defined and evaluated to realize a robust control that is able to respond to the changes of a target position while moving to an old target.

2   Model of Inverted Pendulum

The model of the pole-balancing problem in this study is simulated in two-dimensional space, and no friction of the hinge or sliding of the cart is assumed. The equations of motion given by Anderson [5] are simulated at discrete times. The velocity of the cart and the angular velocity of the pole at time $t+1$ are calculated with the Runge-Kutta approximation method. The position of the cart and the angle of the pole are calculated with the Euler approximation method. For these simulations, the constants are the time step ($t = 0.02$ seconds), the mass of the cart ($m_c = 1.0$ kg), the mass of the pole ($m_p = 0.1$ kg), the pole length ($l = 1.0$ m) and gravity ($g = 9.8$ m/s^2).

3   Applying GP to the Inverted Pendulum

3.1   Function Set and Terminal Set

In this study, the force to control the cart is directly expressed as an equation defined by a tree of S-expression with a function set and a terminal set in GP. For this problem, the function set and the terminal set are prepared as follows.

$$\mathcal{F} = \{+, -, *, \%\},$$
$$\mathcal{T} = \{\ ,\ , x, d, 1.0, 10.0, -1.0\},$$

where $\%$ is the modified division defined by Koza [4]. The parameters of the pole-cart system are , and x, which are the angular velocity, the pole angle, the cart velocity, respectively. Moreover, d is the difference between the cart and the target positions. The function set is the most elemental set of the four arithmetic functions. This is determined by preparatory experiments with larger function sets that additionally include the absolute, square root, exponential and sine functions. In these experiments, the complex functions are rarely used for successful solutions.

The driving force of the cart is calculated at each time step from the status of the pole-cart system by the equation tree consisted of the elements of the function set and the terminal set.

3.2   Fitness Function

The purpose of this study is to search for a control equation which will move the cart to the given target positions while keeping the pole standing. The target position is a variable in the control process. However, it is di cult to define the fitness function that evaluates the control performance in such a dynamic environment with variable target positions.

Therefore, the fitness function is defined as the control problem of moving the cart to a fixed target position while keeping the pole standing. It is defined as a minimum search problem as follows:

$$fitness = \sum_{t=1}^{t_0-1} (\omega_1 |\theta(t)| + \omega_2 |x(t) - T|)$$

$$+ \sum_{t=t_0}^{STEP} (\omega_1 \theta_{max} + \omega_4 x_{max}) + \omega_3 \times s, \tag{1}$$

$$s = \begin{cases} t_s & ((\dot{\theta}^2(t_s) + \theta^2(t_s) + x^2(t_s)) < \epsilon \\ & \text{and } |x(t_s) - T| \leq \delta), \\ STEP & (\text{otherwise}), \end{cases} \tag{2}$$

where T is the target position, ϵ is the small constant to decide the stationary state of the pole, and δ is the allowance for the error between the cart and the target positions. In addition, ω_1, ω_2, ω_3 and ω_4 are weight constants given in Table 1. $STEP$ shows the maximum number of simulation steps, which means that the maximum simulation period is $STEP \times 0.02$ seconds. Moreover, t_0 is the time of the first instant when the condition $|\theta(t_0)| \geq \theta_{max}$ or $|x(t_0)| \geq x_{max}$ is satisfied. The constants are set at $\theta_{max} = 45.0$ degrees, $x_{max} = 15.0$ m, $\epsilon = 10^{-6}$ and $\delta = 10^{-3}$.

Table 1. Weights for the fitness function

Weight	ω_1	ω_2	ω_3	ω_4
Value	0.1	5.0	3.0	10.0

4   Empirical Study

4.1   Empirical Procedure

In this empirical study, the SGPC program developed by Walter Aldern Tackett and Aviram Carmi is used for GP simulations. The main parameters of GP are set at population $= 2{,}100$, maximum generation $= 100$ and parsimony factor $= 0.0, 10.0, 30.0, 50.0, 80.0, 100.0, 150.0$ and 200.0. The paper of Kinner [6] is referred to for the parsimony factor. The reason why the parsimony factor is used is that it works for reducing the number of nodes in a tree in an evolutionary process. It is also because the generalization of an equation tree for the problem may be expected. The tree fitness which includes the parsimony factor is defined by Eq. (3).

$$tree\text{-}fitness = fitness + parsimony\ factor \times No.\ of\ nodes\ in\ a\ tree. \tag{3}$$

In the evaluation, the initial states and the target position are as follows.

$$\theta(0) = 0.0,$$
$$\dot{\theta}(0) = \{2 \theta_{max} + \text{Rnd}(-1.0,\ 1.0)\} \bmod (2 \theta_{max}) - \theta_{max},$$
$$x(0) = 0.0,$$
$$\dot{x}(0) = \text{sign}(\text{Rnd}(-1.0,\ 1.0)) \times 10.0,$$
$$T = 0.0.$$

A simulation is done for $STEP = 2000$, i.e. 40 seconds.

4.2   Empirical Results

The first objective of the experiments is to investigate the robustness of the control equations obtained by evolutions of GP. It is important to examine whether they work in a wide variety of situations. In this study, the robustness of a control equation is regarded as how successfully it controls the driving force to move the cart to a given target position while keeping the pole standing for the initial states of various angular velocities of the pole and various velocities of the cart. The reason is that the pole-cart system has various angular velocities and various cart velocities at the instant the target position is changed on the way of moving to the old target position.

The robustness of a control equation is defined as the success rate in 1,000 simulations of the pole-cart system. Success is defined as controlling the driving force that moves the cart to the fixed target position while keeping the pole standing for the random initial values of the four parameters. The initial values of the parameters have normal distributions, with the variances given in Table 2.

Table 2. Variances of initial values

Parameters	θ	θ	x	x
Variance	2.0	12.0	2.5	4.0

Table 3 shows the results of the evolutionary experiments and the robust tests for each value of the parsimony factors for 20 experiments of GP evolutions. In this table, the hit rate means the rate at which the control equations which satisfy the condition part of Eq. (2) in the simulation process are obtained as solutions of GP evolutions in 20 experiments. The depth and nodes are the average depth and the average number of nodes of the trees obtained as the best solutions in 20 experiments.

Table 3. Results of robust tests for 20 experiments

parsimony factor	hit rate	robustness	depth	nodes
0.0	0.75	0.588	16.20	181.6
10.0	0.90	0.770	12.00	70.8
30.0	0.70	0.615	9.35	42.5
50.0	0.75	0.685	9.45	41.0
80.0	0.70	0.626	8.80	37.7
100.0	0.90	0.824	9.15	31.5
150.0	0.75	0.653	7.85	27.4
200.0	0.65	0.618	5.20	18.6

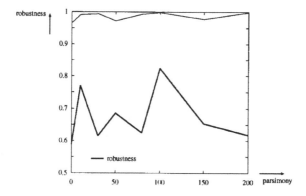

Fig. 1. The effect of parsimony factors on the robustness

Fig. 1 shows the effect of the parsimony factors on the average (indicated by a bold line) and the best (indicated by a thin line) robustness over 20 experiments. In this figure, there is the highest peak when the parsimony factor is 100, although the variations of the best robustness are small. The best global robustness in all experiments is also obtained at the parsimony factor of 100. This means that if the parsimony factor were properly set around 100, solutions with higher robustness would be obtained with the highest probability. That is, it is found that there exists an optimal value of the parsimony factor for the evolution of robustness.

Fig. 2 also shows the effect of parsimony factors on the average number of nodes and the depth of trees for 20 experiments. The number of nodes and the depth of equation trees with the best robustness are also shown for 20 experiments by the thinner line in Fig. 2. In this figure, the average number of nodes and the average depth decrease monotonically, but the depth of equation trees with the best robustness have a peak at the parsimony factor of 100. From this,

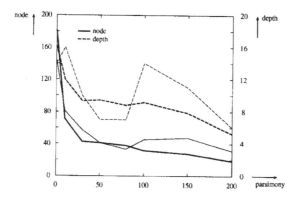

Fig. 2. The effect of parsimony factors on the number of nodes and the depth

it is estimated that the equation tree with higher robustness needs fewer nodes and more depth.

The following Eqs. (4), (5), (6), (7) and (8) are simplified control equations from equation trees with the higher robustness that are obtained in each of 20 evolutionary experiments that has parsimony factors of 10, 30, 80, 100 and 200, respectively.

$$force_1(\ , \ , x, d) = 30 \ + 101 \ + 12\,x + 6\,d - 10 \quad (\ -10 \ +1), \quad (4)$$
$$force_2(\ , \ , x, d) = 54 \ + 118 \ + 54\,x + 5\,d, \quad (5)$$
$$force_3(\ , \ , x, d) = 33 \ + 99 \ + 10\,x + 4\,d + 2 \quad x\,d, \quad (6)$$
$$force_4(\ , \ , x, d) = 40 \ + 88 \ + 8\,x + 3\,d, \quad (7)$$
$$force_5(\ , \ , x, d) = 19 \ + 42 \ + 3\,x + d - \quad (\ +20 \ ). \quad (8)$$

The depths and the numbers of nodes of equation trees from which the above equations are simplified are shown in Table 4.

Table 4. Depths and numbers of nodes of equation trees

Equation No.	(4)	(5)	(6)	(7)	(8)
depth	10	10	7	14	6
nodes	81	57	33	45	31

Eqs. (5) and (7) have the form of a very simple linear combination of parameters: the angular velocity, the pole angle, the cart velocity and the difference between the cart and the target positions. They also form the equations of P-D control. Eqs. (4), (6) and (8) are also simple, although they include quadratic, cubic and biquadratic terms.

The control processes by control Eqs. (4) and (7) are shown in Fig. 3 and 4, respectively. The simulations are executed with two initial values of the cart position for Eq. (4).

$$\text{(i)} \quad x(0) = 10.0, \quad \text{(ii)} \quad x(0) = -10.0.$$

Other parameters are set at 0.0 and the target position is also 0.0.

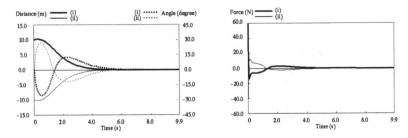

Fig. 3. Transitions of distance, angle and force for Eq. (4)

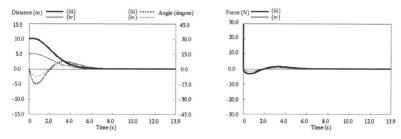

Fig. 4. Transitions of distance, angle and force for Eq. (7)

Because the control equation (7) is an odd function for all parameters of the pole-cart system, simulations are executed for two positive initial values of the cart position shown as follows.

$$\text{(iii)} \quad x(0) = 10.0, \quad \text{(iv)} \quad x(0) = 5.0.$$

Other parameters are set at 0.0 and the target position is also 0.0.

The time elapsed until stationary state are 9.86 seconds in case (i) and 9.52 seconds in case (ii) for Eq. (4) and 13.88 seconds in case (iii) and 12.92 seconds in case (iv) for Eq. (7).

Fig. 3 and 4 show that the equation controlled the driving force so that if the target position is changed to another position when the pendulum is in the stationary state, the cart moves to the target position after leaning the pole toward the target direction by pulling the cart in the opposite direction.

This control pattern is executed even when the pendulum is not in the stationary state, that is, the state moving toward the old target position. This control pattern easily comes to human minds through experiences and learning. However, it has been very di cult for conventional artificial intelligence to obtain an intelligent control pattern without human help. This is one evidence that it is possible to obtain high intelligence by evolutionary processes. Moreover, it is interesting to note that high intelligence is obtained with a very simple linear equation.

5   Conclusions

In this paper, the evolutions with GP are tried to obtain equations for the control of the movable inverted pendulum. In the experiments, robust solutions of equations are obtained that control driving force to move a cart to a given target position while keeping a pole standing.

The robustness for this problem is defined quantitatively and the effectiveness of the parsimony factor for the evolutions of robustness is investigated. As a result, it is found that there exists an optimal value of the parsimony factor for the evolution of robustness. It is also found that solutions of very simple control equations have the intelligence to move the cart to the target position after leaning the pole toward the target direction by pulling the cart in the opposite direction. This study contributes to the evidence that it is possible to obtain high intelligence by evolutionary processes.

Future works are to evolve control equations for the control of a movable inverted pendulum in an environment that contains factors such as the friction of the hinge and cart sliding, and various noises. In addition, future studies will focus on more di cult control problems and investigate deeply how robustness and generalization can be obtained in the evolutionary process.

References

1. C.L. Karr, Design of an Adaptive Fuzzy Logic Controller Using Genetic Algorithm, Proc. of the Fourth Int. Conf. on Genetic Algorithms, pp. 450 457 (1991).
2. D.B. Fogel, Evolving Neural Control Systems, IEEE Expert Vol. 10, No. 3, pp. 23 27 (1995).
3. B. Maricic, Genetically Programmed Neural Networks for Solving Pole-Balancing Problem, Proc. of the 1991 Int. Conf. on Arti"cial Neural Networks, Vol. 2, pp. 1273 1276 (1991).
4. J. Koza, *Genetic Programming*, MIT Press, pp. 289 307 (1992).
5. C.W. Anderson, Strategy Learning with Multilayer Connectionist Representations, Proc. of the 4th Int. Workshop on Machine Learning, pp. 103 114 (1987).
6. K.E. Kinner, Jr., Generality and Di culty in Genetic Programming: Evolving a Sort, Proc. of the Fifth Int. Conf. on Genetic Algorithms, pp. 287 294 (1993).

A Hybrid Tabu Search Algorithm for the Nurse Rostering Problem

Edmund Burke[1], Patrick De Causmaecker, and Greet Vanden Berghe[2]

[1] Department of Computer Science, University of Nottingham, University Park, Nottingham, NG7 2RD, UK, Tel: (0044)(115)9514234, Fax: (0044)(115)9514254, e-mail: ekb@cs.nott.ac.uk

[2] KaHo St.-Lieven, Procestechnieken en Bedrijfsbeleid, Gebr. Desmetstraat 1, 9000 Gent, Belgium, Tel: (0032)(9)2658610, Fax: (0032)(9)2256269, e-mail: patdc,greetvb@kahosl.be

Abstract. This paper deals with the problem of nurse rostering in Belgian hospitals. This is a highly constrained real world problem that was (until the results of this research were applied) tackled manually. The problem basically concerns the assignment of duties to a set of people with di˘erent quali"cations, work regulations and preferences. Constraint programming and linear programming techniques can produce feasible solutions for this problem. However, the reality in Belgian hospitals forced us to use heuristics to deal with the over constrained schedules. An important reason for this decision is the calculation time, which the users prefer to reduce. The algorithms presented in this paper are a commercial nurse rostering product developed for the Belgian hospital market, entitled Plane.

Keywords Nurse rostering, personnel scheduling, tabu search

1 Introduction

In this paper we will discuss the algorithms that have been developed for the commercial nurse rostering system (Plane). The development of Plane was based on an extensive market research in 1993. One of the conclusions was that the requirements of Belgian hospitals cannot be met with a cyclic 'three shift' schedule. Recent research done by the Stichting Technologie Vlaanderen [7] also showed that, instead of a cyclic schedule, the nurses prefer an 'ad-hoc schedule' in which they can express their personal wishes and priorities. Because of the size of the solution space (the scheduling period is usually one month and the number of possible duties per day varies from 6 to 15), the nurse rostering problem tackled by Plane differs a lot from other rostering problems described in the literature. The planning period in [2,3] is restricted to 1 week and in [2,5,6] there are only three different duties to be planned.

Plane can decide (per nurse) which duties can or cannot be performed (according to that nurse's qualification category) when there is not enough personnel available.

Another goal of Plane is the freedom for the user to define a personal cost function modifying predefined constraints, modifying weight parameters, ... The solution method has to be robust enough to cope with widely varying cost functions.

In [3] a constraint programming solution for the nurse rostering problem is presented. Preliminary experiments with Oz showed that it is very hard to calculate monthly schedules that take into account the high number of 'consecutiveness' constraints that Belgian hospitals have to deal with. Also in the mathematical approaches of [4,8], the number of different constraints is much lower than in our problem.

A heuristic method, combining tabu search and algorithms based on manual scheduling techniques proved to be very appropriate for this combinatorial problem in which the calculation speed is as important as the attempt to find a solution that is close to optimal.

2   Plane, nurse rostering software for Belgian hospitals

Plane is a scheduling system developed by Impakt[1] and GET[2] to assist the scheduling of personnel in hospitals for which the demands for every qualification can be determined over a fixed period in time and which have to fulfil a number of constraints, limiting their assignments.

A description of Plane, its problem domain, its system specific and functional requirements can be found in [1]. The first version of Plane was first implemented in a hospital in 1995 but the system is still evolving to cope with the new and more complicated real world problems that keep appearing. So far, several hospitals in Belgium have replaced the very time consuming manual scheduling by this system.

The cost function used in the algorithms is modular and can deal with all constraints matching the types described section 3.2.

3   Problem description

In general, a ward consists of about 20 people, having different qualifications and responsibilities. These people are placed into categories based upon their qualifications and job description such as head nurse, regular nurse, nurse aid, student,... Some of the nurses can replace people from another category (depending upon their qualifications). Each replacement by a person from another category will raise the evaluation function by an amount the user can set.

3.1   Hard constraints

The personnel requirements are expressed in terms of a required number of nurses of every category for every duty during the planning period, which is often one month. These requirements are the only hard constraints in the problem. Optionally, the user can choose to plan the minimum number of required personnel

---

[1] Impakt N.V., Ham 64, B-9000 Gent

[2] GET, General Engineering & Technologie, Antwerpse Steenweg 107, B-2390 Oostmalle

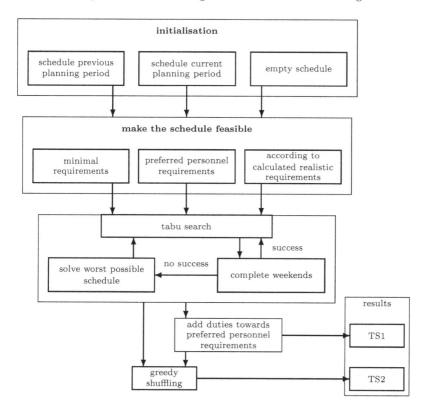

Fig. 1. Diagram of the hybrid tabu search algorithms for the nurse rostering problem

or the preferable number of personnel. A third option is to plan at least the minimal required number of nurses and to add nurses whenever it doesn't increase the evaluation function ('add duties towards preferred personnel requirements' Fig. 1).

3.2   Soft constraints

It is highly exceptional in real world problems to find a schedule that satisfies all the soft constraints, but the aim of the algorithms is to minimise the violations of these constraints. The constraints are all to be specified by the users of the system. Certain general constraints are recommended by hospital regulations (but in certain situations, may need to be ignored). There are other soft constraints that are normally created by an agreement between the head nurse (or personnel manager) and the individual nurses. At this moment there are about 30 (modifiable) constraints. It is usually the case that not all constraints can be satisfied at the same time. When a contradiction between constraints occurs, the personal preferences of staff (such as requests for holidays, requests to work a certain duty on a certain day) are stronger than any other constraint. A detailed list of the constraints in Plane can be found at http://www.impakt.be/plane/indexf.htm.

4   Tabu search algorithm and variants

The entire "ow diagram of the hybrid tabu search algorithms described in this section can be seen in Fig. 1.

4.1   Feasible initial schedule

The first part of the scheduling algorithm is the construction of a feasible initial solution. For practical planning problems three possible strategies are used:

Current schedule: This is especially useful when urgent changes in the schedule are required. In real life this may happen when a scheduled nurse is suddenly ill and has to be replaced and, of course, we do not want to drastically change the schedule for the other people.

Schedule of the previous planning period: this option is useful when the schedule in the previous planning period was of very high quality and the constraints on the current and the previous planning period are similar.

Random initialisation: This is the simplest initialisation, it starts from an empty schedule.

After this initialisation, the schedule has to be made feasible. This is carried out by randomly adding and/or removing duties for every category until the requirements are met.

Although the two first initial schedule constructors may seem very attractive, our experiments show that it is not too di cult for the tabu search algorithm to produce schedules of comparable quality starting from a random initial schedule. Indeed it is often the case that with the two latter initialisations, the algorithm is in a local minimum already and has problems escaping from it.

4.2   Original tabu search algorithm

In the simplest tabu search algorithm, the only move we consider is a move of a duty from one person to another on the same day. The move is not allowed if the goal person is not of the right category or is already assigned to that duty. This will not affect the hard constraints.

For each category (for each iteration) possible moves will be calculated and the move leading to the highest benefit will be performed. If the highest benefit is negative, the move will be performed anyway, unless this move is forbidden by the tabu list. When a move is accepted, an area in the roster around the roster point where the duty comes from and where it is moved to may not be changed. For comparison purposes only, we introduced a steepest descent algorithm in which the neighbourhood of the moves is exactly the same as in the tabu search algorithm. After evaluating all the possible moves in the neighbourhood, the best one will be performed, unless this best move does not improve the schedule, in which case the algorithm stops. These algorithms turned out not to be powerful enough to produce good solutions for complex problems as is shown in the 'steepest descent' and 'tabu search' experiments in Table 1 & 2 (section 5). The tabu search algorithm performs better than the steepest descent algorithm and is therefore used as a local search heuristic in the hybrid algorithms described in section 4.4.

4.3   Some Heuristics for the problem

Here we describe some heuristics that can be employed (in conjunction with the tabu search algorithm) to improve the solution.

Diversification 1: Complete weekend Although the users of the program can assign a cost parameter to this constraint it is very hard to find satisfactory solutions. The problem is that there are so many constraints and the degree of freedom of the problem is so high that it is likely to find solutions satisfying many other constraints but not this one. In the graphical user interface, incomplete weekends really catch the eye, while other constraints such as overtime or too many morning shifts on Mondays,... are not immediately visible. Because it is almost impossible to guarantee good solutions with a certain setting of the parameters, we decided to solve this problem the hard way, by not caring about possible problems for other constraints.

Diversification 2: Consider the worst personal schedule If the complete weekend function (above) has not changed the schedule it can be beneficial to look at the people with the worst schedule (according to the evaluation function). For every person (within the category being scheduled) it is possible to calculate the value of the evaluation function after exchanging a part of the schedule of the people involved. The parts of the schedule always contain full days and the maximum length is half the planning period. After all possibilities have been calculated, which is quite time consuming, the best exchange (chosen at random from equal values) is performed. The result of this process often results in a better solution.

Greedy shuffling: Model human scheduling techniques There was a problem with the results of the tabu search algorithm because sometimes a human could improve the visual result by making a small change. This process calculates all possible 'Diversification 2' (above) moves for every pair of people. After listing the gain in the cost function for every possible exchange, the shu e leading to the best improvement will be performed. Afterwards, the next best improvement in the list is performed, provided none of the people involved were already involved in an earlier shu e. As long there are improving exchanges in the list, they are carried out. The whole procedure starts over again until none of the possible exchanges improves the cost function.

The improvements on the schedule that can be obtained by employing this procedure and tabu search (described below) are considerable but the biggest advantage of this step is that it creates schedules for which it is almost impossible for a human to improve the schedule.

4.4   Hybrid tabu search algorithms

After extensive testing of hybrid versions of the tabu search algorithm and the above heuristics 2 algorithms were developed. The first one produces schedules when a very short calculation time is required (as it often is). The second algorithm needs more calculation time but generates schedules of a considerably higher quality.

Tabu search + diversification: TS1 The aim of this algorithm is to provide reliable solutions in a very short time. In practice this algorithm has proved to be very useful to check whether the constraints are realistic, whether during the holiday periods it will be possible to plan good schedules if every person gets their desired holiday period etc...

The algorithm is constructed quite simply from the original tabu search algorithm. If after a number of iterations no improvement is found, the weekend step is performed. If the weekend step does not result in a different schedule the second diversification step is performed. After this diversification step, the original tabu search algorithm is used again and so on. The calculations stop after a number of iterations without improvement.

Tabu search + greedy shuffling: TS2 This requires more time but the results are considerably better from the human point of view. Anecdotal evidence suggests that the level of satisfaction with schedules produced by this algorithm is actually higher than the cost function indicates. The main reason for this is that after the shu ing step the users cannot easily improve the results.

It is important to do the greedy shu ing step at the end of the calculations because its real aim is to perform the exchanges a human user would perform. It is because of the exhaustive search character of the shu ing that this step takes a lot of time. It is very important to calculate this step until there are no further improvements because otherwise the goal of excluding manual improvements to the schedule might be lost (Greedy shu ing in section 4.3).

5   Test results

The tests in this paper are restricted to planning the minimal requirements (R-min), planning between the minimal and the preferred requirements (R-min-pref), and planning according to the calculated demands (R-calc) as explained in section 3.1 (Hard constraints). For the latter we decided to do the step 'add

Problem 1	R-min		R-min-pref		R-calc	
	Value	Time	Value	Time	Value	Time
steepest descent	2594	1 26	2395	1 37	2657	1 36
tabu search	2435	2 05	2214	2 06	1928	1 59
ts stop crit. x50	1915	40 58	1675	41 21	1534	23 58
ts1	1341	6 00	1089	5 59	929	5 27
ts2	1264	20 15	1011	24 39	809	28 08

Table 1. Value of the evaluation function and results of the steepest descent and variants of the hybrid tabu search algorithm for Problem 1, planning order of the quali"cations as chosen by the customer

Problem 2	R-min		R-min-pref		R-calc	
	Value	Time	Value	Time	Value	Time
steepest descent	1338	44	1338	45	1134	47
tabu search	1189	57	1189	58	933	1 03
ts1	843	3 18	843	3 18	867	2 14
ts2	809	6 25	809	6 25	588	10 19

Table 2. Value of the evaluation function and results of the steepest descent and variants of the hybrid tabu search algorithm for Problem 2, planning order of the quali"cations as chosen by the customer

duties towards preferred personnel requirements' whenever this does not cause a violation of the soft constraints (section 3.2).

In Table 1 and 2, the results of the variants of the tabu search algorithm are compared to the steepest descent algorithm. The test examples Problem 1 and Problem 2 are hard to solve real world problems and in both cases the personal demands make a good schedule almost impossible.

The column 'value' shows the value of the evaluation function (cost parameter per constraint times the extent the constraint is violated). The column 'Time' contains the calculation times on an IBM Power PC RS6000.

The third set of results, where the demands are adapted to the constraints as described in section 3.1 (calculating more realistic demands), are better than the results in the first column. In Problem 2, there was no difference between the minimal and the required demands.

For all the considered examples, the tabu search algorithm performs better than the steepest descent algorithm. We decided to organise the stop criterion for the tabu search algorithm so that the calculation time is of the same order of magnitude as the time required to do steepest descent. Only Table 1 contains the results of the original tabu search algorithm for a longer calculation time.

The behaviour of the hybrid algorithms is better than the behaviour of the normal tabu search algorithm (with a short calculation time). Even considering the calculation time, for use in practice it is worth using the hybrid tabu search algorithm because the degree of confidence the users have in the program is much higher.

6   Conclusion

By automating the nurse rostering problem, the scheduling effort and calculation time are reduced considerably. The evaluation of schedules is very quick for all possible combinations of constraints and the quality of the automatically produced schedules is much higher than the quality of the manual schedules. The users of Plane often place an emphasis on the higher quality of the solution because the system provides an objective schedule in which all nurses are treated equally and in which the number of violated constraints is very low. Combining the simple tabu search algorithm with some specific problem solving heuristics not only guarantees better quality rosters but also satisfies the users of the system to a very high extent because it is almost impossible for experienced planners to improve the results (considering the constraints) manually. For many practical scheduling problems the higher quality of the solutions produced by the hybrid algorithm compared to the simple tabu search algorithm compensates for the increase in calculation time.

References

1. Coppens, P.: Geautomatiseerde personeelsplanning bij het A.Z. Sint-Erasmus. GET info **9** (1995) 1 3
2. Dowsland, K.: Nurse scheduling with Tabu Search and Strategic Oscillation. EJOR (to appear)
3. Meisels, A., Gudes, E., Solotorevski, G.: Employee Timetabling, Constraint Networks and Knowledge-Based Rules: A Mixed Approach. Practice and Theory of Automated Timetabling, First International Conference Edinburgh (1995) 93 105
4. Miller, H., Pierskalla, W., Rath, G.: Nurse Scheduling Using Mathematical Programming. Operations Research **24** (1976) 857 870
5. Okada, M.: Prolog-Based System for Nursing Staʹ Scheduling Implemented on a Personal Computer. Computers and Biomedical Research **21** (1988) 53 63
6. Okada, M.: An approach to the Generalised Nurse Scheduling Problem - Generation of a Declarative Program to represent Institution-Speciʺc Knowledge. Computers and Biomedical Research **25** (1992) 417 434
7. Vanderhaeghe, S.: Dienstroosters in de gezondheidszorg: ongezond? Informatiedossier. Stichting Technologie Vlaanderen (1998)
8. Warner, M., Prawda, J.: A Mathematical Programming Model for Scheduling Nursing Personnel in a Hospital. Management Science **19** (1972) 411 422

Reinforcement Learning:
Past, Present and Future*

Richard S. Sutton

AT&T Labs, Florham Park, NJ 07932, USA,
sutton@research.att.com, www.cs.umass.edu/~rich

Reinforcement learning (RL) concerns the problem of a learning agent interacting with its environment to achieve a goal. Instead of being given examples of desired behavior, the learning agent must discover by trial and error how to behave in order to get the most reward. RL has become popular as an approach to artificial intelligence because of its simple algorithms and mathematical foundations (Watkins, 1989; Sutton, 1988; Bertsekas and Tsitsiklis, 1996) and because of a string of strikingly successful applications (e.g., Tesauro, 1995; Crites and Barto, 1996; Zhang and Dietterich, 1996; Nie and Haykin, 1996; Singh and Bertsekas, 1997; Baxter, Tridgell, and Weaver, 1998). An overall introduction to the field is provided by a recent textbook (Sutton and Barto, 1998). Here we summarize three stages in the development of the field, which we coarsely characterize as the past, present, and future of reinforcement learning.

RL *past*, up until about 1985, developed the general idea of trial-and-error learning—of actively exploring to discover what to do in order to get reward. It was many years before trial-and-error learning was recognized as a significant subject for study different from supervised learning and pattern recognition. RL past emphasized the need for an active, exploring agent, as in the studies of learning automata and of the n-armed bandit problem. Another key insight of RL past was just the idea of a scalar reward signal as a simple but general specification of the goal of an intelligent agent, an idea which I like to highlight by referring to it as the *reward hypothesis*. The learning methods of RL past usually learned only a *policy*, a mapping from perceived states of the world to the action to take. This limited them to relatively benign problems in which reward was immediate and indicated (e.g., by its sign) whether the behavior was good or bad. Problems with delayed reward, or in which the best action much be picked out of several good actions (or the least bad out of several bad actions), could not be reliably solved until the ideas of value functions and temporal-difference learning were introduced in the 1980s.

The transition to RL present ($\approx$ 1985) came about by focusing on *value functions* and on a general mathematical characterization of the RL problem known as *Markov decision processes* (MDPs). The state-value function, for example, is the function mapping perceived states of the world to the expected total future reward starting from that state. Almost all sound methods for solving MDPs (that is, for finding optimal behavior) are based on learning or computing approximations to value functions, and the most efficient methods for doing this all

---

* The slides used in the talk corresponding to this extended abstract can be found at
http://envy.cs.umass.edu/~rich/SEAL98/sld001.htm.

seem to be based on temporal differences in estimated value (as in dynamic programming, heuristic search, and temporal-difference learning). Although finding a policy to maximize reward is still the ultimate goal of RL, RL present is much more focused on the intermediating goal of approximating value, from which the optimal policy can be determined. RL present is also as much about *planning* using a model of the world as it is about learning from interaction with the world. Whether learning or planning optimal behavior, approximation of value functions seems to be at the heart of all efficient methods for finding optimal behavior. The *value function hypothesis* is that approximation of value functions is the dominant purpose of intelligence.

RL future has yet to happen, of course, but it may be useful to try to guess what it will be like. Just as RL present took a step away from the ultimate goal of reward to focus on value functions, so RL future may take a further step away to focus on the structures that enable value function estimation. Principle among these are representations of the world's state and dynamics. It is commonplace to note that the efficiency of all kinds of learning is strongly affected by the suitability of the representations used. If the right features are represented prominently, then learning is easy; otherwise it is hard. It is time to consider seriously how features and other structures can be constructed automatically by machines rather than by people. In RL, representational choices must also be made about states (e.g., McCallum, 1995), actions (e.g., Sutton, Precup, and Singh, 1998) and models of the world's dynamics (Precup and Sutton, 1998), all of which can strongly affect performance. In psychology, the idea of a developing mind actively creating its representations of the world is called *constructivism*. My prediction is that for the next tens of years RL will be focused on constructivism.

References

Baxter, J., Tridgell, A., Weaver, L. (1998). KnightCap: A chess progream that learns by combining TD(λ) with game-tree search. *Pr oceedings of the Fifteenth International Conferenc e on Machine learning*, pp. 28–36.

Bertsekas, D. P., and Tsitsiklis, J. N. (1996). *Neuro-Dynamic Pr ogramming* A thena Scientific, Belmont, MA.

Crites, R. H., and Barto, A. G. (1996). Improving elevator performance using reinforcement learning. In *Advances in Neural Information Pro cessing Systems 9*, pp. 1017–1023. MIT Press, Cambridge, MA.

McCallum, A. K. (1995) Reinforcement Learning with Selective Perception and Hidden State. University of Rochester PhD. thesis.

Nie, J., and Haykin, S. (1996). A dynamic channel assignment policy through Q-learning. CRL Report 334. Communications Research Laboratory, McMaster University, Hamilton, Ontario.

Precup, D., Sutton, R.S. (1998). Multi-time models for temporally abstract planning. *Advances in Neural Information Processing Systems 11*. MIT Press, Cambridge, MA.

Singh, S. P., and Bertsekas, D. (1997). Reinforcement learning for dynamic channel allocation in cellular telephone systems. In *A dvanes in Neural Information Processing Systems 10*, pp. 974–980. MIT Press, Cambridge, MA.

Sutton, R. S. (1988). Learning to predict by the methods of temporal differences. *Machine Learning*, 3:9–44.

Sutton, R. S., and Barto, A. G. (1998). *R einfor cementdarning: An Intr oduction*. MIT Press, Cambridge, MA.

Sutton, R. S., Precup, D., Singh, S. (1998). Betw een MDPs and semi-MDPs: Learning, planning, and representing knowledge at multiple temporal scales. Technical Report 98-74, Department of Computer Science, University of Massach usetts.

T esauro, G. J. (1995). Temporal difference learning and TD-Gammon. *Communic ations of the ACM*, 38:58–68.

Watkins, C. J. C. H. (1989). *L earning fom Delayed Rewards*. Ph.D. thesis, Cambridge University.

Zhang, W., and Dietterich, T. G. (1996). High-performance job-shop scheduling with a time–delay TD(λ) netw ork. In *A dvanes in Neural Information Processing Systems 9*, pp. 1024–1030. MIT Press, Cambridge, MA.

A Reinforcement Learning with Condition Reduced Fuzz Rules

Hiroshi Kawakami[1], Osamu Katai[1], and Tadataka Konishi[2]

[1] Kyoto University, Yoshida-Honmachi, Kyoto 606-8501, JAPAN
{kawakami, katai}@i.kyoto-u.ac.jp
http://www.symlab.sys.i.kyoto-u.ac.jp/indexE.html
[2] Okayama University, 3-1-1 Tsushima-Naka, Okayama 700-8530, JAPAN
konishi@sdc.it.okayama-u.ac.jp

Abstract. This paper proposes a new Q-learning method for the case where the states (conditions) and actions of systems are assumed to be continuous. The components of Q-tables are interpolated by fuzzy inference. The initial set of fuzzy rules is made of all the combinations of conditions and actions relevant to the problem. Each rule is then associated with a value by which the Q-value of a condition/action pair is estimated. The values are revised by the Q-learning algorithm so as to make the fuzzy rule system eˇective. Although this framework may require a huge number of the initial fuzzy rules, we will show that considerable reduction can be done by using what we call Condition Reduced Fuzzy Rules (CRFR) . The antecedent part of CRFR consists of all the actions and the selected conditions, and its consequent is set to be its Q-value. Finally, experimental results show that controllers with CRFRs perform equivalently to the system with the most detailed fuzzy control rules, while the total number of parameters that have to be revised through the whole learning process is reduced and the number of the revised parameters at each step of learning is increased.

Key Words: Q-learning, fuzzy rule, interpolation, reduced condition.

1 Introduction

In case of solving problems with various types of I/O data that are related with each other in complicated manners, extracting embedded rules from these I/O data manually becomes quite complicated and hence is sometimes practically impossible.

Recently, reinforcement learning methods have been successfully applied to various kinds of problems. Among them, Q-learning[1] is one of the widely-used methods, which employs Q-functions for evaluating condition/action pairs. One of the simplest ways to realize a Q-function is to look up a Q-table. Assume an environment that has n conditions for taking m actions. Each cell of the $n + m$ dimensional Q-table holds a value of one of the conditions/actions pairs (Q-value). The values are revised through the whole learning process. Q-table is simple, but its size will explode when applied to practical problems in which continuous-valued conditions and actions are sometimes involved. In addition to this, only a portion of a Q-table is revised at each time of learning, and hence we can not make good use of the continuity of condition/action values. Thus, we will propose a new framework where fuzzy reasoning is introduced to continuously interpolate the Q values.

Q-learning requires only experienced condition/action and rewards combinations. Therefore, Q-learning can be applied to problems where meaningful I/O sets can not be specified beforehand. Thus, fuzzy rules can not be specified beforehand by referring to domain-specific heuristics. Namely, the initial rule set has to be made of all the combinations of conditions and actions. This framework may lead to the explosion of initial rule sets. To cope with this problem, we introduce fuzzy reasoning by the use of condition reduced fuzzy rules to Q-learning.

2   Q-learning with Condition Reduced Fuzzy Rules

2.1   Interpolating Q-tables

For utilizing the continuity of I/O values, many methods for interpolating cells of Q-tables have been proposed. We focus our attention to the methods where CMAC[2] architecture or Fuzzy reasoning[3] is incorporated.

The Cerebellum Model Arithmetic Computer (CMAC) has been introduced to reinforcement learning [2] where a Q-table is represented by multi-layered tables whose partition of the cells is set to be cruder than the original table. Figure 1 illustrates the idea where one dimensional Q-table with 9 cells (Figure 1 (a)) is represented by the combination of three tables with $3 + 4 + 4 (= 11)$ cells (Figure 1 (b)).

In case (a), 9 parameters are associated with these 9 cells, whereas in case (b) 11 parameters are required. Through learning processes, these parameters have to be revised correctly. Thus the increase of total number of parameters seems to be disadvantage of CMAC (b), but CMAC enhances the effect of learning. As shown by the meshed part in Figure 1, only one cell is revised at each step of learning in case (a), whereas the effect of each revision is not limited to one cell in case (b).

Fuzzy reasoning has also been successfully used to interpolate the cells of Q-tables[3]. This method estimates a Q-value for an action by fuzzy reasoning. The antecedent part of each rule consists of conditions and actions, and the consequent shows the Q-value of the rule. The framework of learning process is almost same as the basic Q-learning algorithm[1] except for the way to estimate Q values by using Takagi-Sugeno method[4], the way of selecting an action and the way of learning by revising the Q-value of each fuzzy rule.

2.2   Condition Reduced Fuzzy Rule

We propose fuzzy reasoning with Condition Reduced Fuzzy Rules (CRFR) and incorporate it to Q-learning. The antecedent part of each CRFR consists of all the possible actions and the selected conditions. Table 1 shows parameters for

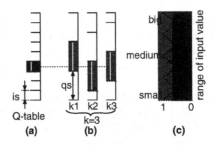

Fig. 1. Interpolating a Q-table (a) by Cerebellar Model (b) or Fuzzy Sets (c)

generating the initial fuzzy rules. Let us assume that each condition and action involve fuzzy sets and that their numbers are uniformly N_f. Then, in case of $Nc + Na = 3$ and $N_f = 5$, the normal form of fuzzy rules will be represented in the following form:

$$\text{if}(X_1 \text{ is } P_{1y_1}) \wedge (X_2 \text{ is } P_{2y_2}) \wedge (X_3 \text{ is } P_{3y_3}) \text{ then } (Q_z = C_z),$$

where P_{xy}, Q_z and C_z denote fuzzy set, Q-variable and its value, respectively. The combination of y_1, y_2 and y_3 such that $1 \leq y_1, y_2, y_3 \leq 5$ yields $125(=5^3)$ fuzzy rules. On the other hand, in case of $Nr + Na = 2$, the CRFR will be given as

$$\text{if}(X_1 \text{ is } P_{1y_1}) \wedge (X_2 \text{ is } P_{2y_2}) \text{ then } (Q_l = C_l)$$
$$\text{if}(X_2 \text{ is } P_{2y_2}) \wedge (X_3 \text{ is } P_{3y_3}) \text{ then } (Q_m = C_m)$$
$$\text{if}(X_1 \text{ is } P_{1y_1}) \wedge (X_3 \text{ is } P_{3y_3}) \text{ then } (Q_n = C_n),$$

where the total number of CRFR is $75(= 3 \times 5^2)$.

Table 1. Parameters for generating initial fuzzy rules

Nc: the total number of conditions
Nr: the number of conditions which are included in each CRFR
Na: the total number of actions
N : the number of fuzzy sets for each condition and action
N_g: the number of fuzzy sets having nonzero grades for an arbitrary input

2.3   Introducing CRFR to Q-learning

The framework of Q-learning with CRFR is given in Table 2. In the experiment described in the next section, the Q-value of a condition/action pair is estimated by the mean value of C_i with weighting by $_i$ $(Q = (\sum_i {}_iC_i)/\sum_i {}_i)$. $_i$ are given by the algebraic product of the grades of its antecedents. The action for the current condition is randomly selected with the probabilities calculated by the Q-values of assumed actions. Each time an action is selected, the Q values of the rules that contributed the process of selecting the action ($\omega_i \neq 0$) are revised. The obtained reward is distributed to each rule so as to ΔC_i be proportional to ω_i, i.e., $C_i = (\sum_i \omega_j \omega_i Q)/(\sum_i \omega_j^2)$.

Table 2. The framework of Q-learning with CRFR

1. Initialize C_i (value of Q_i)
2. repeat forever
   (a) repeat T times
      i. Randomly assume (select) a set of actions.
      ii. Calculate the grade of each rule (ω_i) under the current conditions and assumed actions.
      iii. Estimate the Q-value for the current conditions/actions pair.
   (b) (after the second cycle)
      i. Calculate ΔQ for the last conditions/actions pair by the standard way of Q-learnings, i.e., the equation proposed in [1].
      ii. distribute ΔQ to CRFRs ΔC_i.
   (c) Select and execute one of the assumed (selected) actions.
   (d) Observe the next state and reinforcement signal.

2.4   Comparison of Learning Efficiency

In order to compare the performance of learning algorithms, we examine the total number of the parameters to be revised through the whole learning process, the size of revised parameters at each step of learning and the generality of the following algorithms:
   (a) standard Q-learning (QL)
   (b) Q-learning with interpolation by CMAC (QL+CMAC)
   (c) Q-learning with interpolation by normal Fuzzy Rule (QL+Fuzzy)
   (d) Q-learning with interpolation by CRFR (QL+CRFR)
   In order to examine the number of parameters, we assume that each condition and each action is uniformly partitioned into S regions, and in the case of using fuzzy rules, the number of fuzzy sets (labels) for each condition/action is equal to be N_f.

QL: The total number of parameters is equal to the number of all the combinations of conditions and actions as shown in Table 3 (a). The rule revision at each step of learning is localized to one section.

QL+CMAC: The total number of parameters depends on the number (k) of tables and the width (qs) of their cells. Table 3 (b) shows the number of parameters in case that no redundancy is allowed, i.e., qs is set to be $k \times is$, where is denotes the width of the normal Q-tables cells as shown in Figure 1 (b).

QL+Fuzzy: The total number of parameters depends on the number of consequent parts of the rules. Table 3 (c) shows the number in case of only one parameter is associated with each rule. In order to estimate the number of revised rules at each step of learning, we assume that fuzzy sets are placed like Figure 1 (c). The same number (N_g) of the fuzzy sets will have nonzero values for various values of inputs. Table 3 (c) shows the number under this assumption.

QL+CRFR: Table 3 (d) shows the total number and the revised number of parameters in case (d). They reveal that the total number of parameters is smaller than that in case (c) when $N_f^{(Nc-Nr)} >_{Nc} C_{Nr}$. They also show that the number of revised parameters is larger than that in case (c) when $N_g^{(Nc-Nr)} <_{Nc} C_{Nr}$. We can set Nr such that these two conditions hold simultaneously.

Table 3. Number of parameters in the interpolating methods

	total	revised at each step
(a) QL	S^{Nc+Na}	1
(b) QL+CMAC	$\{\frac{S}{k}\}^{Nc+Na} + (k-1)\{\frac{S}{k}+1\}^{Nc+Na}$	k
(c) QL+Fuzzy	N^{Nc+Na}	N_g^{Nc+Na}
(d) QL+CRFR	$_{Nc}C_{Nr}N^{Nr+Na}$	$_{Nc}C_{Nr}N_g^{Nr+Na}$

3   Experiments and Results

3.1   Experimental Environment

Figure 2 illustrates an experimental problem. Learning methods in this case will yield rules for controlling boats to go around the racing track. The state variables (condition for selecting an action) of this system are the current location (x, y), the velocity (oz, sy), the direction (r) and the angular velocity (w) of the boat, and the action is the combination of operating steering wheel (hnd) and acceleration lever (acc) . In this case, $Nc = 6$, $Na = 2$. The value of T (cf. Table 2. 2. (a)) is set to be 25.

States are calculated by $sx_{(t+1)} = 0.8\, sx_{(t)}+acc\cdot\cos(r_{(t)})$, $sy_{(t+1)} = 0.8\, sy_{(t)}+ acc \cdot \sin(r_{(t)})$, $w_{(t+1)} = 0.8\ _{(t)} + hdl$ and $r_{(t+1)} = r_{(t)} + w_{(t+1)}$. The large time-constant of the boat makes the controlling task di cult.

Fuzzy membership functions are set as shown in Figure 1 (c). Rewards in this case are set to be inversely proportional to the distance between the boat and the nearby local target as shown in Figure 2, and each time a boat collides with a fence, it will be penalized. Penalties are given as rewards with certain minus value.

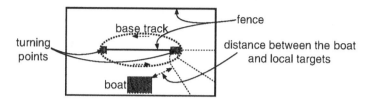

Fig. 2. Experimental problem (boat racing track)

3.2   Comparison with Interpolation Method

In order to compare the performance of each method under the condition that each method requires almost the same number of total parameters, we set S for QL, S for QL+CMAC, k and N_f to be 5, 24, 8 and 5, respectively.

Table 4 shows the number of times the boat could go around the track after 500,000 steps of learning, and also the number' of collisions with the fences. We call the number of control signals for going around the track lap time . Table 4 shows the average lap time and the average number of collisions for one round of the track. The upper part of Figure 3 shows the learning processes of these methods. In the figure, the lap time averaged over 10,000 rounds of QL+CMAC, QL+Fuzzy and QL+CRFR (in the case of $Nr = 4$) are shown by dashed thin line, thin line and thick line, respectively.

The result shows that QL+CMAC could not achieved the performance equivalent to Fuzzy-based methods. The normal QL could not achieve the performance equivalent to other methods.

Table 4. Performance of each interpolating method after 500,000 steps of learning

	Nr	number of parameters		total number		average	
		total ($\times 1,000$)	each revision	rounds	collisions	lap time	collisions
(a) QL		391	1	755	11,109	660.877	14.685
(b) QL+CMAC		465	8	3,470	3,357	144.057	0.967
(c) QL+fuzzy		391	256	4,469	1,328	111.865	0.297
(d) QL+CRFR	6	391	256	4,469	1,328	111.865	0.297
	5	469	768	4,489	1,561	111.358	0.348
	4	234	960	4,584	1,370	109.058	0.299
	3	63	640	4,426	1,774	112.960	0.401
	2	9	240	3,838	4,542	130.268	1.183
	1	1	48	2,179	10,288	229.415	4.721

3.3   Performance of Condition Reduction

The fundamental difference between the proposed method and QL+Fuzzy is the introduction of Nr. QL+Fuzzy can be seen as a specific version of the proposed method where Nr is always set to be Nc. Table 4 shows the results on all the possible values of Nr ($1 \sim Nc$) after 500,000 steps of learning. The lower part of Figure 3 shows the lap time averaged over 10,000 rounds.

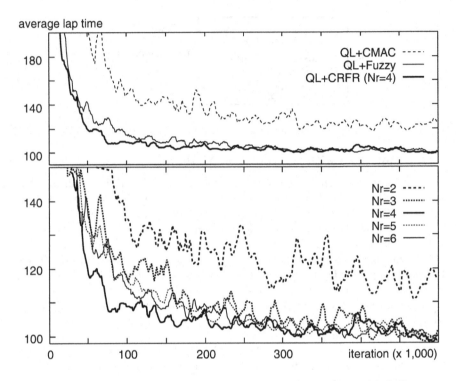

Fig. 3. Comparison the learning process between Interpolating Methods

Generally speaking, it is expected that the rules using all the conditions (the most detailed rules) will yield better performance than the rules with reduced number of conditions. However, Table 4 and Figure 3 reveal that the result with CRFR is equivalent to or even better than those with the most detailed rules. When Nr is set to be 1 or 2, the number of parameters is too small that the controller can not achieve good performance. The ratio of revised number of parameters (at each step) over the total number of parameters ($(N_g/N_f)^{Nr+Nc}$) shows that Nr should be set to be small in order to enhance the effect of each step of learning, but the results show that it is di cult to be set as a small number.

3.4   Robustness to the Complexity of Environments

When other boats are existent in the environment, the controller has to take into account not only their locations (ox_i, oy_i) but also their velocities (osx_i, osy_i) since they are moving. The controller learns a skill for avoiding moving obstacles by receiving the minus rewards when it collides with another boat.

In this case, the relation between conditions and actions are extremely complicated. In the case of two boats are in the environment ($Nc = 10$), even if Nr

is set to be small value, e.g. 3, total parameters and revised parameters at each step of learning are calculated to be 375,000 and 3,840, respectively.

After 500,000 steps of learning, the two boats showed performances almost equivalent to the case where they are trained solely. We also examined the relation between the average lap time and the step of learning, which showed that the two boats attained the level of 120 step/round within 1,500,000 steps. Comparing with the result shown in Figure 3, we can say that the proposed method is not affected by the complexity of environments.

4   Conclusion

We have proposed a method for applying Q-learning to problems where continuous I/O data are involved, where the Learning/Adaptation is done by changing Q-values of each Condition Reduced Fuzzy Rules. The experimental results elucidated the satisfying performance of the proposed method. This method is applicable to the problem where domain-specific heuristics are not known beforehand. Furthermore, we can expect that it will learn novel actions. when we do not intend to utilize the continuity of I/O values, nor to yield symbolic representations, Q-learning may be integrated with other generalization methods, e.g. neural networks[5]. Namely, this method is peculiar in reforming outputs of the proposed systems into human-readable symbolic rules.

References

1. C. Watkins and P. Dayan: Technical Note: Q-learning. Machine Learning **8**-3/4 (1992) 279 292
2. R. S. Sutton: Generalization in Reinforcement Learning: Successful Examples Using Sparse Coarse Coding. Advances in Neural Information Processing Systems **8**, MIT Press (1996)
3. T. Horiuchi, A. Fujino, O. Katai and T. Sawaragi: Fuzzy Interpolation-Based Q-Learning with Pro"t Sharing Plan Scheme. Proc. of the 6th IEEE International Conference on Fuzzy Systems (FUZZ-IEEE 97) **3** (1997) 1,707 1,712
4. M. Sugeno: Fuzzy Controls. Nikkan kogyo Sinbun (1988), (in Japanese)
5. L. J. Lin: Self-improving reactive agents based on reinforcement learning, planning and teaching. Machine Learning **8**-3/4 (1992) 293 321

Generality and Conciseness of Submodels in Hierarchical Fuzzy Modeling

Kanta Tachibana[1] and Takeshi Furuhashi[1]

Nagoya University, Furou-cho Chikusa-ku Nagoya 464 8603, Japan

Abstract. Hierarchical fuzzy modeling is a promising technique to describe input-output relationships of nonlinear systems with multiple inputs. This paper presents a new method of dividing input spaces for hierarchical fuzzy modeling using Fuzzy Neural Network (FNN) and Genetic Algorithm (GA). Uneven division of input space for each submodel in the hierarchical fuzzy model can be achieved with the proposed method. The obtained hierarchical fuzzy models are probable to be more concise and more precise than those identi"ed with the conventional methods. Studies on e˘ects of the weights on performance indices for the fuzzy model are also shown in this paper.

1 Introduction

Fuzzy modeling[1] is a method to describe the characteristics of nonlinear systems using fuzzy rules. For automatic acquisition of fuzzy rules, combinations of fuzzy logic and neural networks have been studied[2]. The Fuzzy Neural Network (FNN) in [2] is capable of identifying fuzzy rules and tuning the membership functions by means of back propagation learning. This FNN has been applied to the fuzzy modeling of nonlinear systems. Su cient data, which cover whole input space, is hard to obtain from the actual plant with many input variables. Hierarchical fuzzy modeling method using multiple FNNs[3] was proposed. Each sub model in the hierarchical fuzzy model has a smaller number of input variables, and it does not need many data to describe the input-output relationships in the sub space.

Karr et al. [4] proposed a combination of fuzzy logic and Genetic Algorithm (GA). GA finds fuzzy rules using the payoff for the success/failure of its actions. GA was applied to identification of hierarchical structure of fuzzy model[5] from given input-output pairs of data. The authors[6] have applied GA to selection of input variables of FNN hierarchical model. This method is very effective in the case where the plant has a strong nonlinearity. GA can find appropriate sets of input variables and a proper number of membership functions for each selected input variable from many candidates. The authors have also proposed a fuzzy modeling method which realized uneven division of input spaces using the FNN[8], and have applied the method to the hierarchical fuzzy modeling.

This paper presents a new hierarchical fuzzy modeling method using the FNN and GA. The proposed method can find fuzzy submodels with unequally divided input space.

2 Hierarchical Fuzzy Modeling Using FNN

2.1 Fuzzy neural network

The FNN presented by the authors is a multi-layered back-propagation (BP) model with a specially designed structure for easy extraction of fuzzy rules from the trained NN. This paper uses Type I of the FNNs in [2]. Fig. 1(a) shows an example of the FNN.

This is a case where the FNN has two inputs x_1 and x_2, one output y and three membership functions for each input. The Back Propagation (BP) learning algorithm can be applied to modify the connection weights w_c, w_g, and w_b. From this network, the following simplified fuzzy inference can be extracted:

$$R^i : \text{if} x_1 \text{is} A_{i,1} \text{and} x_2 \text{is} A_{i,2} \text{then} y = b_i (i = 1, 2, \cdots, n) \tag{1}$$

$$\mu_i = A_{i,1}(x_1) A_{i,2}(x_2) \tag{2}$$

$$\widehat{\mu}_i = \frac{\mu_i}{\sum_k \mu_k} \tag{3}$$

$$y^* = \sum_{i=1}^{n} \widehat{\mu}_i b_i \tag{4}$$

where R^i is the i-th fuzzy rule. $A_{i,1}$, $A_{i,2}$ are labels of membership functions, b_i is a singleton in consequence, n is the number of fuzzy rules, μ_i is the truth value of R^i, $\widehat{\mu}_i$ is the normalized truth value, and y^* is the inferred value.

Fig. 1(b) shows an example of membership functions in the antecedent formed in (A)-(D)-layers. The connection weights w_c, w_g determine the positions and slopes of the sigmoid functions f in the units in (C)-layer, respectively. Each membership function consists of one or two sigmoid functions. The outputs of the units in (D)-layer are the values of membership functions. The products of these values are the inputs to the units in (E)-layer and the outputs of the units are the normalized truth value in the antecedent $\widehat{\mu}_i$ in eq.(3). The output of the unit in (F)-layer is the sum of the products of the connection weights w_b

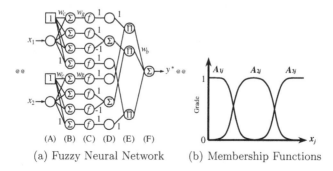

(a) Fuzzy Neural Network   (b) Membership Functions

Fig. 1. Fuzzy Neural Network

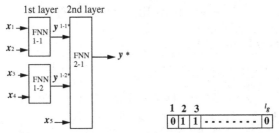

(a) Hierarchical Fuzzy Model (b) Example of Chromosome

Fig. 2. Hierarchical fuzzy model using FNNs and chromosomes

and the normalized truth values. The connection weights w_b correspond to the singletons in the consequence b_i in eq.(1). The output in (F)-layer is, therefore, the inferred value y^* in eq.(4).

Since the center-of-gravity method is used in (E)-layer, the updating method of connection weights, i.e. BP algorithm, needs some modifications. The learning algorithm for the FNN is well described in [2].

The feature of this FNN is that fuzzy rules can be extracted easily from the trained FNN. Three layered neural network can identify the input-output relationships. However, it is hard to extract rules from the three layered neural network.

2.2 Procedure of Hierarchical Fuzzy Modeling

Fig. 2 shows an example of hierarchical fuzzy model which consists of FNN sub-models. The figure shows a case where the model has 5 inputs $(x_1, x_2, x_3, x_4, x_5)$, one output (y), a two level hierarchical structure. In Fig. 2, y^{1-1^*}, y^{1-2^*}, y^* are the inferred values of the fuzzy sub-models. In the 1st layer, the fuzzy model with the inputs x_1 and x_2, and the model with x_3 and x_4 are lined in parallel. The outputs of these models are y^{1-1^*} and y^{1-2^*}, respectively. These two fuzzy sub-models in the 1st layer greatly contribute to the input-output relationships of the system. The input variable x_5 is used for a small adjustment of the model. This fuzzy model reduces the number of divisions of each input space by constructing sub-models in a hierarchical manner. This reduction of divisions prevents the model from over-fitting. The obtained fuzzy model, therefore, has the generalities.

The authors have proposed a hierarchical fuzzy modeling method using the FNNs and GA[3,6]. Each sub-model was built by the FNN and a proper set of input variables and sets of membership functions for the sub-model were selected by GA. A hierarchical structure was constructed by finding proper sub-models one by one.

This paper proposes a new hierarchical fuzzy modeling method which realizes uneven division of input space. GA is utilized to find an appropriate set of input variables. A model having the selected variables is generated by the proposed uneven division method of input space and it is tuned by the FNN learning. The procedure of this hierarchical fuzzy modeling is as follows:

1. The input-output data are divided into two groups A, B whose statistical characteristics are nearly the same. The group A constitutes training data, and the group B is used as a test set. The model identified from the data of group A is called model A. The number of layer h is initially set at 1.

2. Using GA and the FNN, a sub-model is identified. A combination of input variables is encoded into a chromosome as shown in Fig. 2(b). The number of genes l_g is the same as that of the whole candidates of input variables. If the value of a gene is 1, the corresponding input variable is used for the model. If it is 0, the input variable is not selected. The evolution of individuals is carried out by the following procedure:

   (a) Chromosomes are initialized to have 0 in each gene. The number of chromosomes is n_g. The binary number in each gene is "ipped to 1 with the probability of p_i.

   (b) Chromosomes are evaluated. The chromosome determines a combination of input variables to be used for the sub-model. The division process of the input space to be described in subsection 2.3 is carried out. In this process, the identification of singletons in the consequent parts of FNN is done with the data of group A. The performance index F used in this fuzzy modeling process is given by

$$F = \frac{\sum_{i=1}^{n_B} \left(y_i^{BA} - y_i^B \right)^2}{n_B} + kS \qquad (5)$$

   where n_B is the number of the data of group B, y_i^B is the output data of group B, y_i^{BA} is the inferred value of model A with data B, and S is the number of subspaces. The first term evaluates the generality of the identified model, and the second term is a criterion for the conciseness of the model. Coe   cient k adjust the weights on the generality and the conciseness.

   An appropriate division of input space for each input variable is obtained as described in subsection 2.3.

   (c) Individuals are ranked with this performance index. The worst n_w chromosomes are replaced with copies of better chromosomes.

   (d) Crossover and mutation operations are applied to the population. Crossover is applied to the whole population except for one elite at the rate of p_c. Parents are randomly selected, and one point crossover with randomly selected crossover point is applied. Mutations are applied to each gene of all the chromosomes except for that of the elite chromosome at the rate of p_m.

   (e) Stop if the performance of the elite chromosome does not improve during m_{end} generations. Otherwise, go to step (b).

   The next step is fine tuning of the acquired model by the back propagation learning of the FNN[9]. The membership functions in the antecedent as well the singletons in the consequence of the best model found in the above process are modified to obtain a better model. For the stopping condition of this learning, the following criterion is used:

$$C = \sqrt{\sum_{i=1}^{n_A} \left(y_i^A - y_i^{AA}\right)^2 + \sum_{i=1}^{n_B} \left(y_i^B - y_i^{BB}\right)^2} \\ + \sqrt{\sum_{i=1}^{n_A} \left(y_i^{AB} - y_i^{AA}\right)^2 + \sum_{i=1}^{n_B} \left(y_i^{BA} - y_i^{BB}\right)^2} \tag{6}$$

where n_A and n_B are the numbers of data groups A, B, respectively; y_i^A and y_i^B are the outputs of data A and data B, respectively; y_i^{AA} and y_i^{BB} are the inferred value of model A with data A and that of model B with data B, respectively; y_i^{AB} and y_i^{BA} are the inferred value of model B with group A and that of model A with group B, respectively. The first term on the right hand side in eq.(6) is the precision of the model, and the second term is the criterion for evaluation of the generalities of the model.

This identified model is called model h-1 and its output is denoted by y^{h-1^*}. The model h-k means that it is the k-th model in the h-th layer.

3. If the number of remaining input variables that are not used in the model h-1 is more than two, another model to compensate the error of model h-1 is identified using GA. This error is used as the teaching signal for the next model. Some of the remaining input variables would be selected. The fine tuning of the acquired model is, then, carried out. The model is denoted by model h-2. If more variables remain, model h-3 for the compensation of the error of model h-2 will then be identified. This modeling is repeated until the number of remaining input variables becomes less than two. The model h-1 will be used for the identification of the models in the succeeding layer. The outputs of the models h-2, -3, $\cdots$ will be the candidates for the input variables of the models in the next layer.

4. Fuzzy modeling in the next layer is done using the sub-models identified in the previous layer. The output of model h-1 is always used. A combination of this output y^{h-1^*} and some of the outputs of models h-2, -3, $\cdots$ as well as the input variables not used in model h-1 is chosen by GA. The acquired model is denoted by $(h+1)$-1.

5. The evaluation criterion C of model h-1 and model $(h+1)$-1 are compared. If the latter value is less, repeat the procedure from (3). If not, stop. Since the input variables which are used in the previous layer are not used in the succeeding layers, the acquired structure is simple.

2.3   Unequal Division of Input Space

Unequal division of input space for the fuzzy modeling is described in this section. The input space is divided so that the variations of data outputs across the subspaces are minimized. The procedure of input space division is as follows:

1. If the given data have I input variables, I dimensional input space is to be divided. The input space initially has no division, i.e. the number of

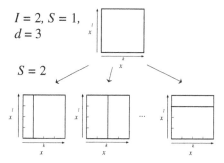

Fig. 3. Division of input space

subspaces S equals 1. Figure 3 shows a case where two inputs x_k, x_l are given. The top figure shows the initial division of input space. A fuzzy model with one rule is made with an FNN, trained, and evaluated under the criterion F in eq.(5). The training of the FNN here is only to adjust the singleton in the consequence for e cient training.

2. Input space is divided. S is increased by 1, i.e. $S = S+1$. Number of possible division points on each axis d is given a $priori$. Figure 3 shows that it has three possible division points, $d = 3$. There are $I \times S \times d$ possible division points in this case. Each division is evaluated as shown in the figure with the criterion given by

$$V = \sum_{s}^{S} v_s \qquad (7)$$

V is the accumulation of variation of data outputs in each subspace. The variation in a subspace s is expressed as:

$$v_s = \frac{\sum_{j}^{n_s}(y_j - \bar{y}_s)^2}{n_s}, \bar{y}_s = \frac{\sum_{j}^{n_s} y_j}{n_s} \qquad (8)$$

where n_s is the number of data in the subspace s, y_j and $\bar{y}_s$ are the data output and the average of the data outputs in this subspace, respectively. The division with the smallest V value is selected. An FNN with S rules is generated, trained, and evaluated. The training of the FNN is only to adjust the singletons in the consequence for e cient training.

3. If F is not improved, stop. The model obtained before the above step is selected as the final fuzzy model. If it is improving, step 2 is repeated. Figure 4 shows an example of unequal division of the input space x_k, x_l, and the membership functions constructed by the FNN.

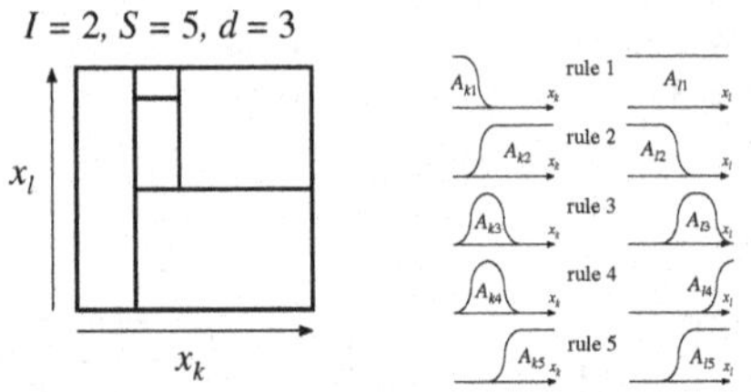

$I = 2,\ S = 5,\ d = 3$

(a) Unequal division (b) Membership functions

Fig. 4. Obtained division and membership functions

3   Numerical Experiment

Numerical experiments are discussed in this section. Model 1-1 was identified with the coe cient k in eq.(5) varied from 10^{-9} to 1. The object nonlinear system was given by the following equation:

$$
\begin{aligned}
y &= (-4 + x_0^{0.5} + x_1^{-1})^2 + 5\sin(x_2 + x_3) \\
&\quad + \exp(1 + x_4 + x_5) \\
&= (-4 + x_{10})^2 + 5\sin(x_{11}) + \exp(1 + x_{12})
\end{aligned}
\tag{9}
$$

$$
\begin{aligned}
&x_6 = x_0^{0.5}, \qquad x_7 = x_1^{-1}, \qquad\qquad x_8 = x_1^{-2}, \\
&x_9 = x_0^{0.5}x_1^{-1},\ x_{10} = x_0^{0.5} + x_1^{-1},\ x_{11} = x_2 + x_3, \\
&x_{12} = x_4 + x_5
\end{aligned}
\tag{10}
$$

where x_0 to x_5 were input variables. x_6 to x_{12} were arranged input variables expressed by eq.(10). x_{13} was used as a dummy variable, that had no relationship with y. The number of candidates of inputs l_g was 14. The ranges of input variables are shown in Table 1. The ranges were decided so that the input variables in"uenced the output nearly equally.

Table 1. Range of variable

variable	range
x_0	$\{0, 1, \cdots, 20\}$
x_1	$\{0.5, 0.7, \cdots, 1.5\}$
x_2, x_3	$\{-1.0, -0.9, \cdots, 5.0\}$
x_4	$\{0.0, 0.1, \cdots, 0.5\}$
x_5	$\{-1.5, -1.4, \cdots, 0.5\}$
x_{13}	$\{0, 1, \cdots, 17\}$

Eighteen sets of eighty pairs of input-output data were generated. The input-output data were normalized within the range $[0, 1)$ for the fuzzy modeling. The parameters of GA were set as follows: $n_g = 20$, $n_s = 2$, $p_i = 0.1$, $p_c = 0.85$, $p_m = 0.01$ and $m_{end} = 10$. The number of possible dividing point d was set at 9.

Two of the eighteen sets were used each for A and B group, i.e. tainning data and test data respectively, in an experiment. Nine experiments were done.

The input variables of the model 1-1 identified by the proposed method were x_{10} and x_{11}. The input space was divided into 7 subspaces. Fig.5(a) shows the divisioin of input space obtained with the proposed method. The mean square error (MSE) for test data was 0.0199.

The model 1-1 identified with the conventional method in [7] also had the same combination of input variables, x_{10} and x_{11}, and the number of membership functions were 6 for x_{10} and 7 for x_{11}. The number of subspaces was 42. Fig.5(b) shows the division of input space with the conventional method. The MSE was 0.0108. Obtained models are summerized in Table 2.

Table 2. Comparison of the models 1-1

	proposed method	conventional method
selected variables	x_{10}, x_{11}	x_{10}, x_{11}
mean square error	0.0199	0.0108
number of rules	7	42

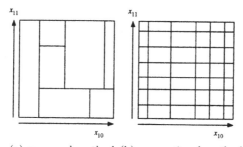

(a) proposed method (b) conventional method

Fig. 5. Division of Input Space

4   Conclusion

This paper presented a hierarchical fuzzy modeling with FNN and GA. The proposed method generated more precise and concise model than the one by the conventional method. Numerical experiments show that the weights on the performance indices affect the generality and the conciseness of obtained submodel. These weights can control the characteristics of the obtained model. Various models can be generated as candidates for the model by changing the coe - cient.

References

1. T. Takagi and M. Sugeno, Fuzzy Identi"cation of Systems and Its Applications to Modeling and Control , IEEE Trans. on Syst., Man, and Cybern., Vol.15, No.1, pp.116 132, 1985.
2. S. Horikawa, T. Furuhashi and Y. Uchikawa, On Fuzzy Modeling Using Fuzzy Neural Networks with the Back-Propagation Algorithm , IEEE Trans. on Neural Networks, Vol.3, No.5, 801 806, 1992.
3. S. Nakayama, T. Furuhashi, Y. Uchikawa, A Proposal of Hierarchical Fuzzy Modeling Method , Journal of Japan Society of Fuzzy Theory and Systems, vol.5, no.5, pp.1155-1168, 1993.
4. C.L. Karr, L. Freeman, D. Meredith, Improved Fuzzy Process Control of Spacecraft Autonomous Rendezvous Using a Genetic Algorithm , SPIE Conf. on Intelligent Control and Adaptive Systems, pp.274-283, 1989.
5. K. Shimojima, T. Fukuda, Y. Hasegawa, Self-tuning Fuzzy modeling with Adaptive Membership Function, Rules, and Hierarchical Structure Based on Genetic Algorithm , Fuzzy Sets and Systems, Vol.71, No.3, pp.295-309, 1995.
6. S. Matsushita, A. Kuromiya, M. Yamaoka, T. Furuhashi, and Y. Uchikawa, Determination of Antecedent Structure of Fuzzy Modeling Using Genetic Algorithm , Proc. of 1996 IEEE Int l Conf. on Evolutionary Computation (ICEC 96), pp.235-238, 1996.
7. K. Tachibana, T. Hasegawa, T. Furuhashi, Y. Uchikawa, Y. Fujime, M. Yamaguchi, A Proposal of Allocation of Membership Functions for Fuzzy Modeling , The 13th Fuzzy System Symposium, pp.87-90, 1997.
8. K. Tachibana, T. Furuhashi, A Hierarchical Fuzzy Modeling Using Fuzzy Neural Networks which Enable Uneven Division of Input Space , The 14th Fuzzy System Symposium, pp.305-308, 1998.

Using Evolutionary Programming to Optimize the Allocation of Surveillance Assets

V. William Porto

Natural Selection, Inc.
3333 N. Torrey Pines Ct., Suite #200
La Jolla, CA 92037   USA
Tel (619) 455-6449   FAX (619) 455-1560

Abstract. An intelligent surveillance planning system must allocate available resources to optimize data collection with respect to a variety of operational requirements. In addition, these requirements often vary temporally (i.e., targets of interest move, priorities change, etc.), requiring dynamic reoptimization on-the-fly. Allocation of surveillance resources has typically been accomplished either by human planners, (for small problems of very limited complexity) or by deterministic methods (typically producing suboptimal solutions which are incapable of adapting to dynamic changes in the environment). The method presented here solves these problems by using evolutionary programming to optimize the simultaneous and coordinated scheduling of multiple surveillance assets. The problem of allocating unmanned aerial vehicles (UAVs) to acquire temporally variable, time-differential intelligence data is addressed. Imposition of realistic constraints ensures solution feasibility in real-world problems. This implementation can be modified to optimize solutions for a suite of different surveillance asset types, such as manned vehicles and satellites.

1 Introduction

Airborne reconnaissance involves allocating a limited number of surveillance assets to a set of 'targets of interest'. Although aerial surveillance is often accomplished by means of human pilots, there are times when other intelligence gathering methods are required. Unmanned aerial vehicles (UAVs) provide the capability to gather intelligence in areas where inherent danger/threats would present an unacceptable risk to human pilots. In addition, they can often operate more covertly than manned aircraft. Whether under human or autonomous control, the goal is to obtain the desired information within the imposed constraints: available fuel capacity, turning rates, desired sensing/imaging requirements, etc. In most cases the surveillance asset is required to return to its original base, in effect completing a 'tour' of the assigned targets of interest. Hence, the problem is analogous to a set of multiple constrained traveling salesman problems (TSP) solved in parallel, albeit with notable differences due to the specific problem domain.

Time-differential imagery is important to reconnaissance as it is often the change in an image (e.g., movement of targets) which is of interest to the analyst. Thus, in this TSP it is necessary to revisit a target of interest on a periodic basis to obtain time-differential images. When multiple surveillance assets are available, their flight paths may be optimized over and around the targets of interest cooperatively, i.e., desired imaging schedules are met via a combination of assets. The problem can be formulated as a simultaneous tour assignment for a set of UAVs such that the solution optimizes the mission goals. Importantly, this formulation permits combining both UAVs and overhead assets (i.e., satellites) within one optimization framework, as opposed to solving the problems separately (and perhaps, suboptimally). Providing for simultaneously optimizing allocation of multiple asset types represents a capability that was not possible with prior methods.

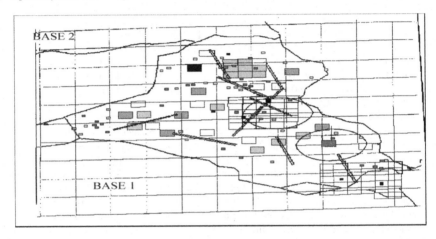

Fig 1. Geographic plot of a multi-target UAV reconnaissance scenario with targets of interest color coded by priority. Elliptical regions define threat zones.

In the real world, no intelligence gathering system operates in a completely covert manner. Lack of covert operation often poses a significant risk to reconnaissance vehicles. UAVs are often tasked to fly over hostile territories. Surface-to-air missile (SAM) sites pose a threat to any flying object within range of the missile. Minimizing threat exposure is important since the UAV may have to return to its base intact for its reconnaissance information to be usable. Potential threats from SAM sites are generally known with some degree of precision so their presence can be incorporated into a path evaluation function. Fig. 1 shows a typical scenario with a target-rich environment (targets of opportunity are indicated by various sized shaded rectangular shapes). A set of spatio-temporal paths for multiple UAVs (based at two geographically separate locations) must be planned over this hostile environment. In this example, over 100 targets of opportunity must be imaged within the desired surveillance time, fuel, and acceptable threat exposure constraints.

2 Background

This problem belongs to the class of NP-complete problems. The search space of candidate solutions for even small sized problems is too large for direct enumeration. Given N surveillance platforms and K targets, there are $[N/2*(K-1)!]$ potential solutions. Applicable feasibility constraints reduce this somewhat, but for a typical problem with only 5 UAVs and 100 targets, there exist over 2.3 x 10^{156} possible solutions. Branch and bound techniques [8] are applicable for reducing the size of the search space, but typically they only reduce the number of possible search paths by a few orders of magnitude.

Chief among the known approaches to solving this problem is the ubiquitous greedy method wherein targets are first prioritized then assigned for imaging. Assignment proceeds through the list until all available resources (e.g., fuel) are exhausted. This method forms the basis for the rank-trimming (RT) algorithm. Targets are first ranked using a target value function. UAVs are then assigned to visit the rank-ordered targets with respect to the desired target imaging periodicity. Because of the heuristic UAV and target assignment strategy, this rarely results in an optimal solution. Variations of this technique include scheduling each UAV according to a 'best-fit' metric which attempts to maximize utilization (total imaging time).

Methods for solving the TSP for a single entity range from neural network algorithms [6] to techniques incorporating variants of evolutionary computation [3], [4]. Blanton and Wainwright [2] solved a related multiple vehicle routing problem (VRP) using an order-based genetic algorithm. Their approach optimized assignment of routes for multiple vehicles visiting a set of customers in prescribed time windows, given a single start/terminal point for all vehicles. Although similar in concept, the formulation did not allow for multiple visits to any site, utilized fixed time windows, and required all vehicles to choose tours constructed from a set of defined (i.e., geographically fixed) paths.

All of the aforementioned methods have deficiencies in one or more of the following areas: 1) generation of optimal solutions for multiple, cooperative, time-coordinated entities, 2) creating integrated solutions for multiple asset types (i.e., overhead sensors), 3) incorporating revisitation (re-imaging) of target sites for time-differential surveillance information, and 4) scalability to larger (real-world) problem sizes.

Porto and Fogel [7] demonstrated the use of evolutionary programming (EP) [5] as an optimization technique to generate optimal cooperative behaviors for multiple vehicles with respect to a set of mission goals. Complex, interactively intelligent behaviors which optimized vehicle routes, firing capabilities, and variable action sequences were generated. The evolved vehicle routes were only constrained by terrain and the physical dynamics of the vehicles. Obvious similarities between evolving cooperative behaviors and the assignment of flight tours for multiple surveillance assets inspired confidence that EP is well suited for solving this problem.

3 Technical Approach

There are several key aspects to developing a successful evolutionary optimization solution to this problem. First, a suitable representation must be defined. The chosen formulation represents the tour for each UAV as an ordered sequence of targets to image. The tour for each UAV is a unique list instantiation. Flexible (and more realistic) cooperation between multiple UAVs is achieved by incorporating individually variable UAV tour start times. Starting and ending points in the list are constrained to be the initial base of the vehicle. Replication of targets in these lists allows for multiple revisits of targets (time-differential re-imaging). The number of replications necessary, R, can be defined as follows:

$$R = F_t / K_{min} \tag{1}$$

where F_t is the maximum possible flight (or surveillance) time over all UAVs, and K_{min} is the smallest desired imaging periodicity. This representation is also extensible to include overhead assets with potentially variable imaging schedules. Once the list sequences are created, evaluation consists of calculating the number of targets imaged, adjusted by priority, with respect to desired imaging periodicities. Similarly, constraints (i.e., remaining fuel and survivability) can be evaluated by sequential checks through the cumulative flight distance and exposure through threat zones.

Path sequences for each UAV are aggregated into a single solution that is evaluated as a whole. Due to re-imaging requirements as well as cooperative capabilities (when incorporating multiple UAVs), individual UAV path sequences cannot be evaluated independently. Evolutionary programming provides an efficient optimization method for this problem. Because EP optimizes total behaviors instead of individual parts, it is well suited to exploit the inherent interdependence of the UAV imaging schedules.

4 Implementation

Four separate phases of flight (each with a unique but constant flight speed) are modeled, including ramp-up/down, ingress (to the surveillance area), steady-state flight, and egress (flight back to the base). Associating a specific starting base for each UAV allows optimizing for multiple UAVs launched from a variable number of bases. Fuel consumption rates are a function of the specific phase of flight. No fuel penalty is imposed for changing direction. Refueling is not permitted during flight.

Targets of interest are modeled as stationary geographic points in space with assigned priorities, desired imaging periodicities, and image qualities. Required imaging times are a function of both target size and required image quality. Since the angle of inspection (imaging angle) is not currently modeled in this study (it is assumed that UAV images can be taken directly over targets), UAV tours can be specified efficiently as point-to-point paths. Additionally, the time to the first (closest) target is assumed to be greater than the time required to reach an operational imaging altitude.

Direct routing of UAVs to and from a set of predefined targets leads to paths that may intersect threat zones. Way-points which can delineate paths around an object are incorporated to address this problem. These 'pseudo-targets' have the same structure as regular targets except that their imaging times, priorities, and revisitation periodicities are all ignored. In this way, the addition (or deletion) of appropriate way-points in the tours allows the model to permit maneuvering around threat zones.

Probability of survival is a function of the length of time a UAV spends traveling through threat zones. Threat zones are modeled as 3-D cylindrical regions extending through the UAV vertical flight envelope. Any path intersecting a threat zone boundary is assigned a probability of kill, Pk, proportional to the length of the path in the zone. A path intersecting a threat zone through its center (maximal exposure to the threat) is assigned a zero survival score. Path segments not intersecting threat zones are survivable with probability one (mechanical failures are not modeled). The cumulative survival probability over the entire flight tour for UAV_j can then be expressed as follows:

$$Ps_j = \prod_{i=1}^{M} (1 - \alpha_{i,j}\, Pk_{i,i})$$ (2)

where

M = total number of threats in the scenario
R_i = kill radius of threat i
C_j = chord length of UAV_j passing by threat i
$Pk_{i,j}$ = probability of threat i killing UAV_j
  = $C_{j,i} / 2R_i$
$\alpha_{i,j} \in \{0,1\}$ denotes the vulnerability of UAV_j to threat i

Each pass of a UAV through a threat zone is treated as an independent event allowing paths to intersect threat zones multiple times in a single tour. In addition, feasibility constraints dictate that all UAVs must have sufficient fuel to return to their bases. At least one target is assumed to be within the range (including return) of each originating base point. UAV tours with zero survivability are feasible but have zero fitness score. No advantage is gained for returning to base with more than the minimum fuel load.

4.1 Mutation

Given the sequential target-list problem representation, numerous mutation operators are possible which span the range of small to large jumps through the search space. Unless otherwise specified, random selection of list entries indicates selection with equal probability for all outcomes. The mutations operators implemented are:

1) Swap two adjacent randomly selected targets in the list.
2) Swap two non-adjacent randomly selected targets.
3) Move a randomly selected target to the bottom of the list.
4) Add/Delete a way-point to/from the list at a randomly selected point.
5) Modify a randomly selected way-point by random alteration of its position.
6) Alter the starting launch time for a randomly selected UAV.

The mutation operator which adds a new pseudo-target (way-point) to the list utilizes the position(s) of adjacent target points in the list. New pseudo-target positions are randomly generated within a bounding circle with radius equal to the distance between adjacent target points in the list. Mutation of pseudo-target locations is accomplished by adding a random variable $N(0,1)$ in $\Re^2$. Mutation of initial UAV launch times uses addition of a $N(0,1)$ random variable to the existing starting time.

4.2 Constructing a Feasible Solution

Construction of initial list sequences is accomplished by one of three methods: 1) list sequence generation via random selection, 2) sequence generation based upon ranked target priorities (greedy method), and 3) sequence generation as read from file. Thus, heuristic solutions can be incorporated allowing for direct comparison with existing resource allocation methods. After creating the target-list sequences, solution construction proceeds by selective inclusion of targets into a feasible tour. Feasibility constraints are checked as each target (or way-point) entry is read from the list. Available fuel (a critical constraint) is constantly updated throughout this process. If no constraints are violated, the target is added to the tour and the next potential target point is examined. Upon violation of any constraint, the potential target is skipped, and the next target in the list is examined. Since targets are replicated N times in each list, solutions are generated which allow UAVs to visit a target more than once.

4.3 Fitness Evaluation

Solution fitness is evaluated after constructing tours for all available UAVs. The fitness function, which addresses the requirement for time differential target imaging, is defined by calculating user satisfaction as a function of time. User satisfaction at time t_k can be expressed as follows:

$$S(t_k) = \sum_{i=0}^{N} (Tv_i * Ps_j) \tag{3}$$

where target value for the ith target, imaged by UAV$_j$ is defined as:

$$
\begin{aligned}
Tv_i &= \alpha * Pr_i + \beta * A_i \\
N &= \text{total number of targets in the scenario} \\
Pr_i &= \text{priority of target } i \\
A_i &= \text{normalized area of target } i \\
Ps_j &= \text{cumulative survival probability of UAV}_j \\
\alpha, \beta &\in [0.0, 1.0]
\end{aligned}
\tag{4}
$$

The fitness function, summed over the entire time of the desired surveillance period is

$$F = \sum S(t_k) \tag{5}$$

The formulation of Eq. 3 allows for implementing the fitness function calculation over various time resolutions by discretizing over different time periods. This facilitates inclusion of the concept of an acceptable time-window for imaging a target with respect to its previous imaging time. Incorporating survival probabilities results in a penalty function for targets imaged by UAVs whose paths intersect threat zones.

5 Experiments and Results

Experiments with a variable number of threat zones, target distributions, target priorities, and desired image periodicities were performed. Six UAVs were simulated, each with identical physical capabilities. Forty targets were (uniformly) randomly distributed in the (10,000 geographic units squared) searchable domain. Target priorities (in the range of [1-10]) and target areas, $A_i \in \{2x2, 5x5, \text{or } 10x10$ geographic units} were randomly selected using a uniform distribution. In all tests, a 24 hour surveillance period was used, and each UAV was capable of reaching the farthest target in the search area and returning to base within its available fuel limit. When used, three threat zones with a radius of 50 geographic units) were modeled.

EP without self-adaptation of mutation parameters was used with a of 100 parents, each generating 5 offspring per parent per generation. Selection of mutation operators was from a uniform random distribution. After scoring each candidate solution, tournament selection probabilistically culled the least-fit members from the population (tournament size 10). The RT greedy algorithm was used to initialize the starting population. This provided a performance benchmark for comparison with the evolved solutions (indicated by the initial fitness values at generation 0 in Fig. 2). Results presented below were averaged over all 20 runs for statistical validation.

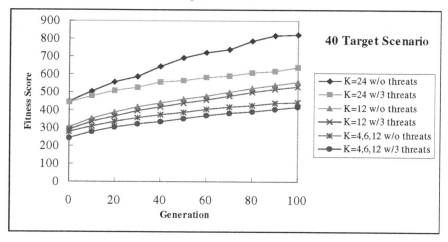

Fig. 2. Graph showing evolved fitness scores vs. generation (averaged over 20 runs).

Algorithmic performance with no requirement for revisiting target sites (all target periodicities, K, set equal to 24 hours) was tested in scenarios with and without threat zones. Evolved solutions quickly exceeded the performance of the RT method both without and in the presence of threat zones. The average number of added way-points (per UAV) in the solution for the no-threat zone scenario was less than one indicating evolution of relatively efficient solutions. Complexity of evolved solutions (as measured by the number of way-points added to a solution) increased with the introduction of threat zones, to an average of 6.4 per UAV.

Next, re-imaging requirements for all targets were set with periodicity K=12 hours. Results of this more constrained problem showed lower overall fitness scores as expected due to the imposed re-imaging constraints. Interestingly, the number of way-points in the no-threat tests increased to an average of 11.4 per UAV. Analysis indicated the additional maneuvering manipulated total flight times to increase the satisfaction of imposed target revisitation schedules. Finally, solutions for scenarios with targets of interest with multiple periodicities were also evolved. Each target was assigned one of three periodicities (K=4, 6, or 12 hours) selected from a uniform distribution. Again, significant improvements over the existing RT solutions were obtained (> 50% increase in user satisfaction) after relatively few generations.

6 Conclusion

Results of this evolutionary programming approach demonstrate performance that is significantly better than that obtained with current typical algorithms. Solutions for realistic numbers of surveillance assets, targets, and threats are possible within a few hours of computational time. Convergence to optimal or near-optimal solutions on problems with a realistic number of targets is now within the capabilities of modern computers. The inherent design of the EP algorithm is also well suited for implementation on parallel processing machines. This research provides a means for optimizing the allocation of multiple UAVs with respect to the reconnaissance goals and environmental constraints. Perhaps of greatest importance is the ability to incorporate other surveillance platforms and sensor types into the simulation. The list-based object-oriented design facilitates this extensibility. Future research will include increasing model fidelity and integration with other sensor suites (i.e., satellite assets).

References

1.   Aho, A.V., Hopcroft, J.E., and Ullman, J.D., (1974) *The Design and Analysis of Computer Algorithms*, Reading, MA: Addison-Wesley, pp. 364-404
2.   Blanton, J.L. Jr. and Wainwright, R.L. (1993) "Multiple Vehicle Routing with Time and Capacity Constraints using Genetic Algorithms," *Proc. of the Fifth International Conference on Genetic Algorithms*, Stephanie Forrest ed., San Mateo, CA: Morgan Kaufmann, pp. 452-459
3.   Dorigo, M. and Gambardella, L.M., (1997) "Ant Colony System: A Cooperative Learning Approach to the Traveling Salesman Problem," *IEEE Trans. on Evolutionary Computation*, Vol. 1, No. 1, pp. 53-66
4.   Fogel, D.B. (1988) "An Evolutionary Approach to the Traveling Salesman Problem," *Biological Cybernetics*, Vol 60:2, pp. 139-144
5.   Fogel, L.J., Owens, A.J., and Walsh, M.J. (1966) *Artificial Intelligence through Simulated Evolution*, New York, NY: John Wiley
6.   Hopfield, J.J, and Tank, D.W., (1985) "Neural Computation of Decisions in Optimization Problems," *Biological Cybernetics*, Vol. 52, pp. 141-152
7.   Porto, V.W., and Fogel, L.J. (1997) "Evolution of Intelligently Interactive Behaviors for Simulated Forces," *Proceedings of the Sixth International Conference on Evolutionary Programming*, P.J. Angeline, R.G. Reynolds, J.R. McDonnell, and R. Eberhart (eds.), Berlin: Springer Verlag, pp. 419-429
8.   Sedgewick, R. (1983) *Algorithms*, Reading, MA: Addison Wesley, pp. 513-524

Applying the Evolutionary Neural Networks with Genetic Algorithms to Control a Rolling Inverted Pendulum

Naoki Kaise and Yoshiji Fujimoto

Department of Applied Mathematics and Informatics,
Faculty of Science and Technology,
Ryukoku University.
1-5 Yokoya, Ooe, Seta, Ohtsu, Shiga 520-2194 Japan
fujimoto@math.ryukoku.ac.jp

Abstract. Genetic Algorithms (GA) are applied to evolutionary neural networks to control a rolling inverted pendulum. The task of a rolling inverted pendulum is to control the driving force of a cart on which one side of a pole is jointed by a rotary shaft in order to roll the pole up from the initial state of hanging down and to keep the pole standing reversely. The controller is a multilayer perceptron (MLP) with three layers whose weight coe cients are evolved and optimized by GA.

Experiments for evolving the weights of two types of MLPs are conducted and their results are compared. Simultaneously, the e˘ect of the weight ranges of neural networks on evolutionary results is investigated. In these evolutionary experiments, MLPs are generated that successfully control the driving force of the cart to roll the pole up and stand it inversely. MLPs also gain the intelligent control patterns with a few swings that correspond to the variations in the maximum driving force of the cart.

1 Introduction

The pole-balancing problem has been attempted many times previously with various control methods including PID control, nonlinear control, fuzzy control, and neural networks [1,2,3]. The target of these attempts is to "nd the control rules that make a pole stand up at a certain position from the initial state of pole angles between $-\pi/2$ and $\pi/2$ when the angle of the upright pole is assumed to be zero.

In this paper, our target is to get an MLP (multilayer perceptron) or a feed-forward neural network to control the driving force of a cart in order to make a pole stand up at a certain position from the hanging state (i.e. the pole angle is π or $-\pi$). This control problem requires two types of control. The "rst one is to control the driving force required to roll the pole up to the upright position and the second one is to control the force needed to keep the pole standing up. It is supposed that it is di cult to implement these two types of control into an MLP. Thierens [4] attacked this problem with evolutionary neural networks whose weights are restricted to ensure the second type of control.

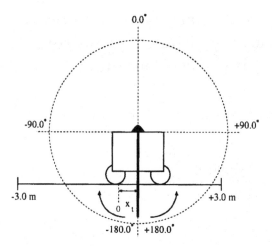

Fig. 1. A pole-cart system

In this paper, two types of MLPs with no restrictions are evolved to "nd solutions for this problem and the effect of the range of weights in neural networks on evolutionary results is investigated. In addition, many MLPs with intelligent control patterns are found by evolution in the experiments that have four values of the maximum driving force.

2   Evolutionary System

2.1   The System Structure

The diagram of the evolutionary system is shown in Fig. 2. GA transfers a set of weights to an MLP as an individual in order to evaluate it. An MLP calculates the driving force at each time step from the state parameters of an inverted pendulum. The inverted pendulum simulator calculates the status at the next time step from the driving force and the current status using the equations of motion. The evaluator observes the transition of status and calculates the "tness value with a "tness function and return it to GA. This cycle for the evaluation of an individual is repeated as many times as the population size. GA evolves the population of the weight sets using these "tness values.

2.2   Simulation of a Rolling Inverted Pendulum

The model of the pole-cart system in this study is simulated in two-dimensional space and no friction of the rotary shaft or cart sliding is assumed. The equations of motion given by Anderson [5] are simulated at discrete times. The velocity x of the cart and the angular velocity θ of the pole at time $t+1$ are calculated with the Runge-Kutta approximation method. The position x of the cart and the angle θ of the pole are calculated with the Euler approximation method. For this simulation, the constants are the time step ($\Delta t = 0.02\ seconds$), the mass of the cart ($m_c = 0.5\ kilograms$), the mass of the pole ($m_p = 0.1\ kilograms$), the pole length ($l = 0.5\ meters$) and gravity ($g = 9.8\ m/sec^2$).

The initial states of the cart position, the cart velocity and the pole angular velocity are set at 0.0. The pole angle is de"ned as 0 degrees when the pole is standing upright on the cart and the range of the angle is between -180 degrees($-\pi$) and 180 degrees (π). The initial state of the angle is set at 180 degrees which means the pole is in the hanging state.

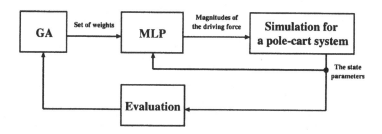

Fig. 2. Evolution system of inverted pendulum controls

2.3 MLP Architectures

The architecture of an MLP has three layers. The structure of a three layer-perceptron is expressed by a triplet $(n_i\text{-}\,n_h\text{-}\,n_o)$ where n_i, n_h, and n_o are the number of inputs, the number of neurons in the hidden layer and the number of neurons in the output layer, respectively. Two types of MLPs (5 - 5 - 1) and (6 - 5 - 1) are prepared. Furthermore, the following sigmoid function is introduced to output the value for the range between -1 and +1.

$$f(v) = \tanh v. \tag{1}$$

The driving force of the cart is given by the following equation:

$$force(x_{(t)}, x_{(t)}, \theta_{(t)}, \theta_{(t)}) = f_{NN} \times F_{max}, \tag{2}$$

where f_{NN} is the output of an MLP and F_{max} is the constant which determines the maximum force.

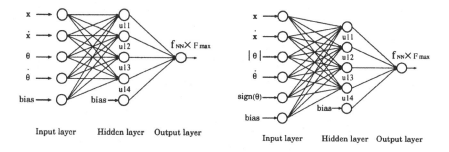

Fig. 3. Architecture of MLP(5-5-1)   **Fig. 4.** Architecture of MLP(6-5-1)

3 Application of GA

The Genetic Algorithm applied to this problem is the basic model of the Forking Genetic Algorithm [6], in which parents and o˘spring are selected together by the best N selection method.

The weights of an MLP that form an individual are coded by a 15-bit Gray code. The movable range of the cart is limited to -3.0 m and 3.0 m. When the cart is moving in this range, the "tness function is de"ned as follows:

$$fitness = \frac{1}{STEP} \sum_{t=0}^{STEP} (\theta_{(t)}^2 + \alpha|x_{(t)}|), \tag{3}$$

where $STEP$ is the maximum number of simulation steps and α is the weight constant. If the cart runs outside of the range limit, the position of the cart and the angle of the pole are "xed at the point when the cart runs outside the range. This "tness function tends to keep the pole at the position 0.0.

4   Empirical Study

The objectives of this study are to verify the possibility of evolving a neural network which realize the complex controls mentioned above, to investigate the e˘ect of varying the neural network weight range on evolutionary results, and to observe control patterns when the maximum driving force is varied between 20N(Newton), 10N, 3N, and 1N, respectively. The weights are encoded by a 15-bit Gray code and are converted to real values with three ranges of Range A (-16.384 $\sim$ 16.383), Range B (-4.09600 $\sim$ 4.09575), and Range C (-1.6384 $\sim$ 1.6383). The experiments are conducted with the combined conditions of these maximum driving forces and weight ranges, and the GA parameters of population size = 400, crossover rate = 1.0, mutation rate = 0.002 and maximum trials = 100,000.

4.1   Experiments and Results

Tables 1 and 2 show the results of experiments for two neural network architectures: (5-5-1)model and (6-5-1)model, respectively. In these tables, Trials is the average number of trials when a solution is found in 20 experiments; No. of Swings is the

Table 1. Results of evolutions with the (551) model

Weight range	F_{max}	Trials	No. of Swings	Success rate	Force Freq.
Range A	20	79069	2	1/20	high
-16.384	10	2680	0.5	1/20	high
$\sim$	3	10331	2.5	15/20	high
16.383	1	13417	5	1/20	low
Range B	20	-	-	0/20	-
-4.09600	10	2563	1.5	4/20	high
$\sim$	3	-	-	0/20	-
4.09575	1	-	-	0/20	-
Range C	20	-	-	0/20	-
-1.6384	10	-	-	0/20	-
$\sim$	3	-	-	0/20	-
1.6383	1	-	-	0/20	-

Table 2. Results of evolutions with the (651) model

Weight range	F_{max}	Trials	No. of Swings	Success rate	Force Freq.
Range A	20	43531	0	1/20	high
-16.384	10	64018	0	9/20	high
~	3	22270	1.5	11/20	high
16.383	1	44384	2	17/20	high
Range B	20	-	-	0/20	-
-4.09600	10	34815	0	7/20	high
~	3	29179	1.5	9/20	low
4.09575	1	69340	2	10/20	low
Range C	20	28013	0.5	1/20	high
-1.6384	10	11548	0.5	4/20	low
~	3	12798	2.5	2/20	low
1.6383	1	42880	3	4/20	low

number of swings contained in the control pattern of the best solution found in 20 experiments; Success Rate is the number of times that the solution is obtained in 20 experiments; and Force Freq. indicates whether the frequency of the on-oˇ control is high or low.

In the standard (5-5-1) model of Fig. 3, input signals are the position and velocity of the cart and the angle and angular velocity of the pole. In the (6-5-1) model of Fig. 4, the input signals are the same as those of the (5-5-1) model, except that the parameter of the angle θ is separated into the sign and the absolute value of the angle in order to reduce the discontinuity of the angle parameter.

Comparing the results of Table 1 and 2, it is clear that the success rates of the (6-5-1) model are better than ones of the (5-5-1) model in almost all experiments based on the combined parameters of the maximum driving forces and weight ranges. In the (5-5-1) model, it is supposed that the discontinuous cliˇ of the angle parameter makes more di cult the evolution of neural networks. On the other hand, the success rate tend to decrease as the maximum driving force increases. It is supposed that the large driving force makes it di cult to stabilize the pole at the inverted position, though it makes it easy to roll the pole up.

4.2   Control Patterns of ENN

The control patterns of the evolutionary neural networks with the (6-5-1) model that are obtained as the solutions of four maximum driving forces in the cases of Range A and C are shown in Figures 5 to 12 by simulations of motion.

In the case of Range A, when the maximum driving force is 20N or 10N, the pole stands up in a single roll without swing by a strong force as shown in Fig. 5 and Fig. 6. However, when the maximum driving force is 3N, the pole stands up after one swing and a half. Similarly, when the maximum driving force is 1N, the pole stands up after two swings. In the case of Range C, similar control patterns are observed. These control patterns show that the kinetic energy to stand the pole is accumulated by swings, because the force is not su ciently strong to make the pole stand up in a single roll. This idea comes easily to human minds through experiences and learning. However, it has been almost impossible for conventional arti"cial intelligence to obtain an intelligent solution of this problem without human help. These experiments corroborate that it is possible to obtain high intelligence through evolution.

228   Naoki Kaise and Yoshiji Fujimoto

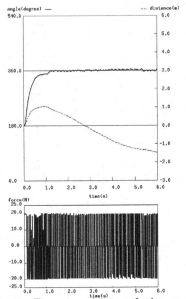

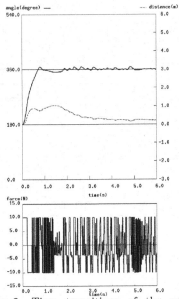

Fig. 5. Time transitions of the angle, the position, and the force[$f_{NN} \times 20N$(6-5-1 Range A)]

Fig. 6. Time transitions of the angle, the position, and the force[$f_{NN} \times 10N$(6-5-1 Range A)]

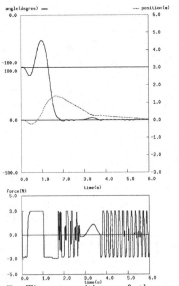

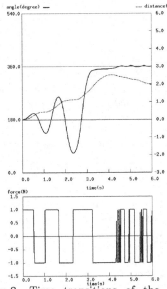

Fig. 7. Time transitions of the angle, the position, and the force[$f_{NN} \times 3N$(6-5-1 Range A)]

Fig. 8. Time transitions of the angle, the position, and the force[$f_{NN} \times 1N$(6-5-1 Range A)]

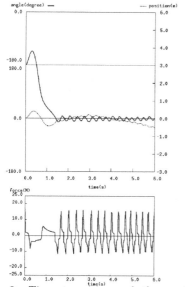

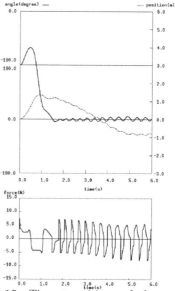

Fig. 9. Time transitions of the angle, the position, and the force$[f_{NN} \times 20N(6\text{-}5\text{-}1$ Range C$)]$

Fig. 10. Time transitions of the angle, the position, and the force$[f_{NN} \times 10N(6\text{-}5\text{-}1$ Range C$)]$

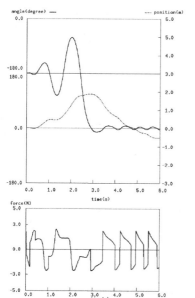

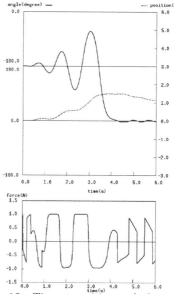

Fig. 11. Time transitions of the angle, the position, and the force$[f_{NN} \times 3N(6\text{-}5\text{-}1$ Range C$)]$

Fig. 12. Time transitions of the angle, the position, and the force$[f_{NN} \times 1N(6\text{-}5\text{-}1$ Range C$)]$

In the case of Range A, the control patterns are an on-o˘ control with high frequency as shown in Figures 5 to 8. Because a strong force is needed for the pole to stand up in a single roll, the neural networks with larger weights survive on the evolutionary process. However, the neural networks with larger weights can hardly make the driving force small. Therefore, it is guessed that they select the on-o˘ control with high frequency to stabilize the pole at the inverted position. For practical use, a driving force with a high frequency on-o˘ control is irrelevant. In the case of Range C, the control patterns are very similar except that the nonlinearity of the sigmoid functions is reduced by small weights. As the results imply, it is supposed that neural networks with small weights tend to select control patterns with swings as shown in Figures 9 and 10. Although the frequency of semi on-o˘ control lessens, the stabilization performance worsens as shown in Figures 9 to 12.

5   Conclusions

This study on applying evolutionary neural networks to control a rolling inverted pendulum con"rm that it is possible for a machine to obtain a higher intelligence by evolution that is hardly obtained by control theories and conventional arti"cial intelligences without human help. The intelligent MLPs are evolved by GA which have sophisticated control patterns with the di˘erent number of pre-swings, based on the magnitudes of the maximum driving force. The two types of MLPs are compared for the evolutionary performance, and it is found that the (6-5-1) model, which has a continuous angle parameter, achieves better performance. The e˘ect of the weight range of neural networks on the control patterns is made clear through these experiments.

Future works are to evolve MLPs with more robust and smoother control, to analyze the functions of the MLPs obtained as solutions, and to evolve weights and architectures of neural networks together [7].

References

1. M.O. Odetayo, D.R. McGregor: Genetic Algorithm for Inducing Control Rules For A Dynamic System, Proc. of the 3rd Int. Conf. on Genetic Algorithms, pp. 177-182, 1989.
2. F. Pasemann: Pole-Balancing with Di˘erent Evolved Neurocontrollers, Proc. of the 7th Int. Conf. on Arti"cial Neural Networks, pp. 823-829, 1997.
3. A.P. Wieland: Evolving neural network controllers for unstable systems, Proc. of IJCNN-91-Seattle: Int. Joint Conf. on Neural Networks, pp. 667-673, 1991.
4. D. Thierens, etc.: Genetic Weight Optimization of a Feedforward Neural Network Controllers, Proc. of the Int. Conf. in Austria on Arti"cial Neural Nets and Genetic Algorithms, pp. 658-663, 1993.
5. C.W. Anderson: Strategy Learning with Multilayer Connectionist Representations, Proc. of the 4th Int. Workshop on Machine Learning, pp. 103-114, 1987.
6. S. Tsutsui, Y. Fujimoto, and Ashish Ghosh: Forking Genetic Algorithms: GAs with Search Space Division Schemes, Evolutionary Computation, Vol. 5, No. 1, pp.61-80, 1997.
7. Xin Yao: A Review of Evolutionary Arti"cial Neural Networks, Int. Journal of Intelligent Systems, Vol. 8, No. 4, pp. 539-567, 1993.

Evolving Cooperative Actions Among Heterogeneous Agents by an Evolutionary Programming Method

Takayuki Fujinaga, Kousuke Moriwaki, Nobuhiro Inuzuka, and Hidenori Itoh

Nagoya Institute of Technology, Gokiso-cho, Showa-ku, Nagoya 466-8555, Japan
E-mail: {fujisan, moriw, inuzuka, itoh}@ics.nitech.ac.jp

Abstract. We studied a baggage carriage problem, in which agents try to carry baggage from a pile to their base, evolving a data structure, called n-BDD, expressing action strategy of the agents. Through this problem we consider emergence of cooperation among heterogeneous agents, or each agent has a particular ability, which is di˘erent each other. We formalize heterogeneity by de"ning forte actions and foible actions of agents. Emergence of cooperation was observed by simulation. Di˘erent types of agents are emerged to behave di˘erent way. We also observed that agents in a type branch to have two di˘erent roles.

1 Introduction

Cooperation among a group is a subject in the field of multi-agent systems. There are two ways of cooperation by many agents. One is to share a task by agents, and every agent plays the same role. We call this way homogeneous cooperation. The other is to play a particular role by each agent, that is, the right man in the right place. The way should be called heterogeneous cooperation.

A number of approaches to emerge cooperative interactions among agents are investigated. H.Yanco et al[1] tries to emerge cooperation among mobile robots by learning non-verbal communication. Reinforcement learning was also used to acquire social action of agents[2] and decision policy in multi-agent systems[3]. Some researches mimic natural creatures, such as ants and bees, to organize social behavior among agents[4,5] and apply the behavior to real robots[6].

In order to study evolution of heterogeneous cooperation, we use a group of agents which are heterogeneous. That is, some agents of a group have different ability from others. Target of this paper is to observe evolution of heterogeneous cooperation that is re"ected by the heterogeneity. For this purpose we use a data structure, called n-BDD, to express action strategy of agents. It was first proposed by Moriwaki et al. [7] and we have demonstrated its applicability[8,9].

We give a goal to a set of heterogeneous agents with an environment, and expect them to evolve their appropriate behavior there. This evolution is not obvious, because agents' abilities do not relate with their behavior directly. They have to find their appropriate behavior only through their experience. In this paper, we give an environment where agents can accomplish their work without their cooperation but they can do more e ciently with cooperation.

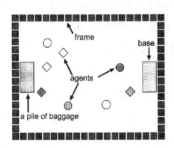

Fig. 1. Field of the problem.

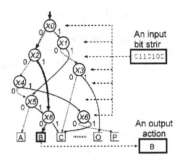

Fig. 2. Deciding action by n-BDD.

2 Baggage carriage problem

In this problem, there are two kinds of agents defined later, a base and a pile of baggage. Each agent tries to find a pile of baggage, to take baggage there, and to find a base where the baggage should be put on.

Agents work on a field which is shown in Fig. 1. The field is a two-dimensional plane with a grid, and enclosed by a frame. Agents can not go out of this frame. There is a pile of baggage at the left of field and a base at the right. In the figure an agent is shown as a circle or a diamond to denote two different types of agents. The difference of the two types will be described in the next section. Shadowed agents show ones carrying baggage.

We expect emergence of roles of agents. Some agents may work to lift up baggage and to hand to others. Some agents may receive baggage and carry to the base. Another may put down baggage received from the carrier to the base.

3 Definition of agents in our problem

Input and output of agents An agent is formalized as a machine that takes an input string and outputs an action by using a strategy which is evolved. The outline is shown in Fig. 2. Input strings re"ect the environment surrounding the agent. On the field every time step an agent takes an input string, calculates its action and does it. An agent can see objects in their surrounding 13×13 square in the grid. These informations are coded in an input bit string:

$$P = (X0, X1, X2, X3, X4, X5, X6).$$

We call the square a visual scope of an agent. Each bit of $X1, \cdots, X6$ in the bit string P for an agent will be one (1) when there is an object in the visual scope of the agent as described in Table 1. A bit will be zero (0) otherwise. $X0$ gives information of self-status of an agent. It will be one (1) if the agent has baggage.

An agent takes an action from the sixteen actions described in Table 2. The algorithm to execute each action is omitted because of the length of paper.

Table 1. Meanings of each input bit.

Input bits	The case where the bit is 1
$X0$	Has baggage.
$X1$	A pile of baggage is in the visual scope.
$X2$	A base is in the visual scope.
$X3$	An agent of the same type is in the visual scope.
$X4$	An agent of the opposite type is in the visual scope.
$X5$	An agent of the same type with baggage is in the visual scope.
$X6$	An agent of the opposite type with baggage is in the visual scope.

Table 2. Actions of agents.

Actions / Descriptions	Actions / Descriptions
Ⓐ / Approaches a pile of baggage.	🄸 / Takes baggage.
Ⓑ / Goes away a pile of baggage.	🄹 / Puts baggage.
Ⓒ / Approaches a base.	Ⓦ / Gets baggage from an agent of the same type.
Ⓓ / Goes away a base.	
Ⓔ / Approaches an agent of the same type.	Ⓥ / Hands baggage to an agent of the same type.
Ⓕ / Goes away from an agent of the same type.	Ⓦ / Gets baggage from an agent of the opposite type.
Ⓖ / Approaches an agent of the opposite type.	Ⓥ / Hands baggage to an agent of the opposite type.
Ⓗ / Goes away from an agent of the opposite type.	Ⓐ / Walks at random.
	Ⓟ / Does nothing.

Table 3. Steps consumed for actions by agents.

	take (I)	put (J)	transport (A to H, K to P)
Type-A (Truck)	70 steps	70 steps	1 steps
Type-B (Lift)	1 step	1 step	7 steps

Strategies to decide actions We used a data structure n-BDD to encode action strategies, which gives an action shown in Table 2 from an input bit string consisting of input bits described in Table 1. Each agent has an n-BDD and obeys an action strategy encoded in it. This data structure gives an e cient calculation of actions and a good framework for evolution as explained in Appendix. Thick arrows in Fig. 2 shows an n-BDD giving the action B from an bit string.

A group of agents To focus on cooperation, we evaluate work of agents by total points accomplished by all of agents in the field. Eight agents, including four type-A and four type-B agents, which are explained later, make a group and behave in the field. The points is also used as a fitness for evolution.

We can also use another fitness, a point accomplished by only an individual agent. We do not take this idea, however, because the effectiveness of total points is investigated and evidenced in [9] as fitness of group.

4   Heterogeneous ability of agents

To give heterogeneous ability of agents, we define forte actions and foible actions for each agent. A forte action is an action which an agent can take with consumption of only small amount of energy or with a short length of time. A foible action is an action which an agent can take with consumption of large energy or with a large length of time.

We can formalize the heterogeneity of agents by giving sets of forte actions and foible actions. Then we define forte and foible actions of two different agents by time lengths for actions:

Type-A agents (Truck agents) We give type-A agents characteristics like dump trucks. They are good at bringing baggage, although they are not good at lifting up and down baggage. So, actions to transport baggage (Actions A to H and K to P with input bit 1 in $X0$) are forte actions. An action to take baggage (Action I) and an action to put on (Action J) are foible.

Type-B agents (Lift agents)   Type-B agents have characteristics of lifts. They have converse abilities to Type-A agents. So, actions to take (Action I) and to put (Action J) baggage are forte actions, and actions to transport (Action A to H and K to P with input bit 1 in X0) are foible.

Table 3 gives time lengths (steps) consumed by the actions.

5   Evolution with an Evolutionary Method

To evolve cooperation among agents we use an evolutionary method, of which Fig. 3 shows an outline. In the algorithm fifty initial groups, each consisting of eight agents, are prepared by generating randomly. Every group is evaluated through execution on the simulator during 500 time steps. Each group is given the following value as its fitness.

$$\text{fitness} = \text{(the total number of pieces of baggage taken from the pile)}$$
$$+2\text{(the total number of pieces of baggage put on the base)}$$

To accomplish the goal to bring baggage to the base, the second term of the above expression is su cient for fitness. However, we add the first term to have effective evolution at the initial stage of evolution.

The groups evaluated are transfered to the next generation based on the elite strategy (Fig. 3). The ten best groups are transfered as is. The ten worst groups are thrown away. The other thirty with copies of the best ten, i.e. forty groups, are modified by genetic operations and make the next generations with the ten best groups. We used genetic operations with probability 0.5 for mutation, 0.25 for insertion and deletion. The genetic operations are described in Appendix.

6   Experimental results

In this section we show experimental results and give analyses of the results.

Analysis of fitness of group   Fig. 4 shows the transition of fitness of the best group at each generation. The graph shows the average of the fitness of 50 trials. The fitness of group increased with the passage of generations by agent's learning. In special, we can see rapid increase of fitness around 1200th generation. This is observed in many cases and explained in the later.

Analysis of ranges where agents act   We divide the field into the four field ranges s1, s2, s3 and s4 as shown in Fig. 5, to analyze the positions in the field where each agent is in large portion of their time. We can expect differences according to roles of agents in the problem and also to the types of agents.

Fig. 6 shows histograms of agent's positions during 500 step simulations through generations. Each histogram is for each agent, Trucks #1 to #4 and Lifts #1 to #4. A histogram consists of 15 small histograms for every 200th generation range and for the best group at the generation. The number of steps when an agent at the generation is in a field range is plotted in the histogram.

From histograms we can observe that Lift agents are in the field ranges adjacent to the pile of baggage or to the base. On the other hand, Truck agents are in every range. This tendency becomes clear according as generations pass, especially after 1200th generation. The rapid increase of fitness at 1200th generation may relate to this phenomena. We also observe that the four Lift agents branch to two groups. Lifts #1 and #2 are mostly in the field range adjacent to the pile of baggage and others are in the range adjacent to the base.

Analysis of handing actions   In Fig. 7 we analyze handing actions from an agent to another. We categorize handing actions by types of sender agents and receiver agents. The categories are described in Fig. 7.

Fig. 7 shows histograms of the numbers of actions happened in each category and in each field range. As according generations pass, only category #2 handings are happened. They are happened only in field ranges s1 and s4. This observation is reasonable for expected cooperation.

Fig. 8 shows n-BDDs of representative agents obtained. We can see that Truck agents does not have nodes for actions to take and put baggage, while Lifts have them. Nodes of Truck are for transport and handing actions and they are chosen by careful conditions. Lifts have fewer nodes and are specialized for their functions. The two different roles of Lifts are also seen in the difference in their structure. Lift #1 has node I and Lift #4 has J.

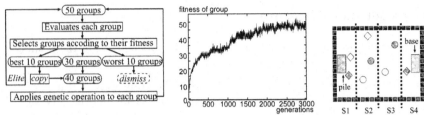

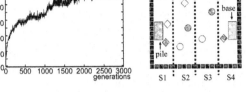

Fig. 3. A generation loop in the algorithm.

Fig. 4. Fitness of group.

Fig. 5. Field ranges.

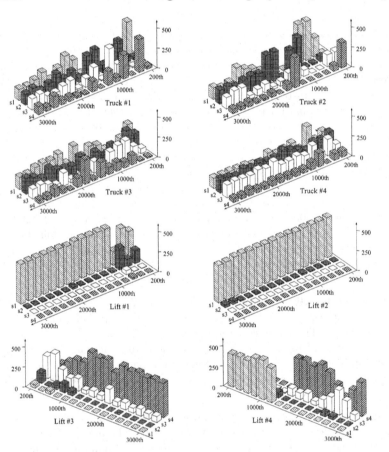

200th to 3000th : generations, s1 to s4 : "eld ranges,
0 to 500   : the number of steps when agents is in the "eld range.

Fig. 6. Histograms of agent s positions.

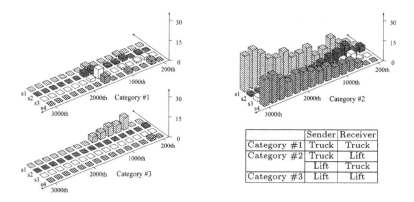

	Sender	Receiver
Category #1	Truck	Truck
Category #2	Truck	Lift
	Lift	Truck
Category #3	Lift	Lift

200th to 3000th : generations, s1 to s4 : "eld ranges,
0 to 30 : the times of handing actions in each categories in the "eld ranges.

Fig. 7. Histograms of handing actions by agents.

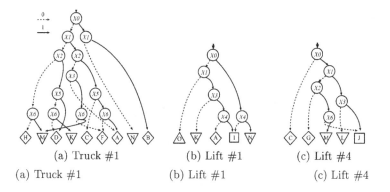

(a) Truck #1   (b) Lift #1   (c) Lift #4

(a) Truck #1   (b) Lift #1   (c) Lift #4

Fig. 8. n-BDD structures of representative agents evolved.

7   Conclusions

Our observation is summarized: (1) Each type of agents works in a particular
field range. (2) Handing actions are done between different types of agents, and
(3) are done around the pile of baggage and the base. (4) Lift agents branches
into two groups. A group works near the pile and the other works near the base.
(5) The tendency of these observations increases according as generations pass.

We conclude that each agent found their individual role, and each agent
selects forte work for e ciency. The right man in the right place is emerged.
The cooperation emerged includes two different type of branching of agent's
roles. First, the two different types of agents, Trucks and Lifts, became to play
two different roles as shown in Fig. 6. Second, the Lift type agents branch to
play their roles in the two different field ranges as shown in Fig. 6 and 7.

Though this paper, we showed the possibility of emerging cooperative works in heterogeneous agents by using n-BDD and its genetic operations. Other evolutionary methods should also be compared in the future work. We characterized agent's abilities by the consumption steps of actions. Investigation by changing the consumption steps also remains for the future work.

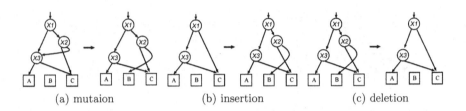

(a) mutaion   (b) insertion   (c) deletion

Fig. 9. Genetic operations for n-BDDs.

Appendix n-BDD and genetic operations

A BDD is a graphical notation of logical functions. A BDD has only two kinds of terminal nodes labeled true or false, but an n-BDD can have more than two labels and gives a value from any set of values. Genetic operations, mutation, insertion and deletion are defined to operate n-BDD as gene.

Mutation changes a direction of an edge to a randomly selected node. The node must be subordinated by the node which the edge rises. Because of this restriction a loop and a cycle are never caused. Insertion inserts a new decision node on a randomly selected edge. Either of 0-edge or 1-edge of the new decision node is randomly selected to point to the node which pointed before. The other edge becomes to point to a subordinate node randomly selected. Deletion deletes a randomly selected decision node. The edge pointing to the deleted node becomes to point to one of the nodes which pointed by deleted node before.

References

1. H. Yanco and L. A. Stein, An Adaptive Communication Protocol for Cooperating Mobile Robots , From animals to animats 2, The MIT Press, pp.478-485, 1993.
2. M. J. Mataric, Learning to Behave Socially , From animals to animats 3, The MIT Press, pp.453-462, 1994.
3. N. Ono and K. Fukumoto, Multi-agent Reinforcement Learning: A Modular Approach , Proc. of 2nd Int l Conf. on Multi-Agent Systems, pp.252-258, 1996.
4. R. Beckers, O. E. Holland and J. L. Deneubourg, From Local Actions to Global Tasks: Stigmergy and Collective Robotics , Arti"cial Life IV, pp.181-189, 1994.
5. A. Hiura, T. Kuroda, N. Inuzuka, K. Itoh, M. Yamada, H. Seki and H. Itoh, Cooperative Behavior of Various Agents in Dynamic Environment , J. Computer and Industrial Engineering Vol.33, Nos.3-4, pp.601-604, 1997

6. D. McFarland, Towards Robot Cooperation , From animals to animats 3, The MIT Press, pp.440-444, 1994.

7. K. Moriwaki, N. Inuzuka, M. Yamada, K. Itoh, H. Seki and H. Itoh, Self Adaptation of Agent s Behavior using GA with n-BDD , Proc. 5th IEEE Int l Workshop on Robot and Human Communication, pp.96-101, 1996.

8. K. Moriwaki, N. Inuzuka, M. Yamada, H. Seki and H. Itoh, A genetic Method for Evolutionary Agents in a Competitive Environment , in Soft Computing in Engineering Design and Manufacturing, pp.153-162, Springer, 1997.

9. T. Suzuki, K. Moriwaki, N. Inuzuka, H. Seki and H. Itoh, Allotment of Individual Roles Among Evolutionary Agents in Pursuit Problem , Proc. 10th Australian Joint Conf. on AI Workshop on Evolutionary Computation, pp.66-83, 1997.

Cooperative Works for Welfare Agent Robot and Human Using Chaotic Evolutionary Computation

Toru Yamaguchi[1], Makoto Sato[1], Tomohiro Takagi[2], and Hideki Hashimoto[3]

[1] Department of Information Science Faculty of Engineering Utsunomiya University
2753 Ishii-machi, Utsunomiya-shi, Tochigi-ken, 321-8585, Japan
[2] Department of Computer Science Meiji University
1-1-1 Higashi-Mita, Tama-ku, Kawasaki 214, Japan
[3] University of Tokyo Institute of Industrial Science
7-22-1 Roppongi, Minato-ku, Tokyo-to, 106, Japan
msato@sophy.is.utsunomiya-u.ac.jp

Abstract. This paper proposes a multi-agent system that carries out cooperative works. To achieve such works, Fuzzy Associative Memory Organizing Unit Systems (FAMOUS), Chaotic FAMOUS (CFAMOUS), and Conceptual Fuzzy Sets (CFS) are employed. With the proposed system, each agent robot can decide its own behavior for the situation in its environment. We apply this system for a Welfare Agent Robot System and carry out simulations.

1   Introduction

Recently, the population of old people has been increasing while at the same time the number of people nursing the elderly has been decreasing. This actual problem will perhaps require the robots to nurse the elderly in place of humans. From such a viewpoint, we are trying to achieve cooperative works with a welfare agent robot system (i.e., a walking support robot system), where robots cooperate with humans and also with other robots.

Accordingly, we propose a multi-agent algorithm; each robot decides its own movement to create a certain formation (line style or circle style). We construct the system using the same robot control used in part FAMOUS, CFAMOUS, and CFS. This control part drives both (1) and (2) below.

(1) A robot determines its own movement by following the general instructions of a human and the situation in its environment, without detailed instructions from a human.
(2) When the robot cannot cope with a problem by using existing knowledge without the instructions of a human, the robot creates new knowledge to avoid trouble.

Experimental results have shown the effectiveness of the welfare agent robot system.

2   Multi-agent Systems for Welfare Agent Robots

In this paper, we regard a welfare agent robot as a walking support robot, such that the robot is equipped with a stick and walks with humans. **Figure 1** shows an image of a welfare agent robot system.

Each agent robot works cooperatively with other agent robots and with humans. The agent robots brain consists of (a)a local feedback block, (b)a microscopic knowledge block, and (c)a macroscopic knowledge block.

(a) Local feedback block: Analyzes information from a camera and sends transfer orders to the robot.
(b) Microscopic knowledge block: Determines the goal coordinates where the robot will move to.
(c) Macroscopic knowledge block: Judges whether the configuration of the robot is right or not.

We construct the robot control block by using the Russmussen model, which is familiar as an e cient model for constructing an intelligent model. We construct the control block of the welfare agent robot by using FAMOUS, CFAMOUS, and CFS (mentioned in Sections 2.1 and 2.2).

The agent robots have standard formations (mentioned in Section 2.3). By defining these, the agent robots are able to do cooperative works in various scenes.

2.1   FAMOUS and CFAMOUS

FAMOUS[1] achieves fuzzy associative inference by constructing fuzzy knowledge on an associative memory. **Figure 2** illustrates this system, which uses fuzzy rules as fuzzy knowledge. FAMOUS adopts BAM (Bidirectional Asso

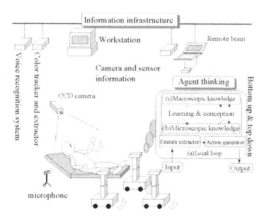

Fig. 1. Image of a welfare agent robot system.

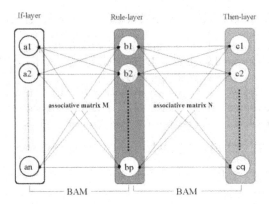

Fig. 2. Construction and fuzzy rules of FAMOUS

ciative Memory)[2], giving it bidirectional retrieval capabilities. Therefore, the system can retrieve the most appropriate pattern to fit the input conditions, by bottom-up and top-down processing conveying active values. (A regular associative matrix is used for the BAM associative matrix.) Furthermore, the system can extract knowledge from active values in post re"ection movements, because it has familiar, clear-cut knowledge expression capabilities.

The associative inference performed on FAMOUS features the following.

1) Bidirectional conversion is possible between oral expressions and feature-value pattern-like images.
2) Macroscopic elements can be analyzed into microscopic elements.

CFAMOUS adopts chaotic retrieval in the process of retrieval of FAMOUS. For our part, we use a chaotic abrupt descending method for chaotic retrieval. This method allows chaotic occurrences in the minimal energy area, by applying a periodically variable non-lineal resistance, in order to scatter the dynamics formula for movement on the energy curved surface of the neural network. CFAMOUS presents the following two functions.

1) From among stored patterns, the system dynamically retrieves patterns within a range close to the input patterns.
2) If no patterns are stored, the system retrieves effective new patterns in terms of meaning.

The second function means that multiple patterns retrieved chaotically from patterns not stored may include possibly effective patterns in terms of meaning. In other words, CFAMOUS can evaluate the effectiveness of such retrieved patterns, since knowledge is clearly expressed on each node of the network with meaningful fuzzy labels.

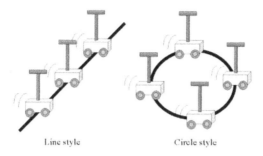

Line style   Circle style

Fig. 3. Robot formations.

These functions enable CFAMOUS to create new knowledge based on existing knowledge stored in the associative memory. Therefore, creativity (support) is possible by adopting CFAMOUS.

2.2   CFS

Fuzzy sets provide strong notations for representing real world concepts, which are essentially vague. However, they do have problems caused by the restrictions of numerical membership functions, restrictions of logical expressions, lack of context dependency, etc. These problems relate to the representation of the meaning of a concept.

In this paper, we propose Conceptual Fuzzy Sets (CFS)[3], fuzzy sets of a new type that conform to Wittgenstein's ideas[4] on the meanings of concepts. A CFS is achieved as an associative memory, combining a long-term memory and a short-term memory, thereby reducing the complexity of knowledge representation. In addition to solving the above problems, CFS provides a simple formula for knowledge representation and a procedure for using this knowledge. We introduce an inductive method for constructing CFS based on neural network learning. The effectiveness of CFS and of the learning method are illustrated through their application to the recognition of facial expressions.

CFS represents the meanings of concepts in multiple layers. The meaning of a concept is translated into an expression indicated by the distribution of activation in each layer. Propagations arise from the activation of the concept. In contrast, the activation of a lower concept determines the activation of an upper concept, it corresponds to recognition or understanding.

2.3   Robot Formations

As shown in **Figure 3**, we propose two robot formations. For the line style formation, all agent robots line up at regular intervals on a line, for example, two agent robots and a human in the center.

In the case of the circle style formation, all agent robots line up at regular intervals on a circle. When there are three agent robots, the three construct an equilateral triangle. With four, a square is constructed.

3   Simulations and Robot Experiments

3.1   Pre requisite

The system consists of a tracking block, sensor data computing block, and robot control block. The tracking block is composed of a CCD camera, color tracker, and color extractor. This block computes the center of gravity of the robot based on color information, and assumes it to be the robot's position. Then it outputs the coordinate values for a two-dimensional coordinate system. These coordinate values are transferred to the computer every 1/60th of a second. Processing is done on a hardware basis. In addition, as shown in **Figure 4**, a visual field to the robot is assumed.

3.2   Robot Control Block

Figure 5 shows CFS representing an action of the welfare robot. The environmental information of a robot through the CCD camera or infrared ray sensor is analyzed. At the lower layer, other information, e.g., the positions of other robots and the unit number of all robots in the visual field are input, in order to determine the movement direction and migration length of the robot.

At the upper layer, the inputs include 1) the difference from the closest robot and the distance from the farthest robot, and 2) the difference from the robot of the right side center piece and the angle of the robot of the left side center piece. The outputs here are the movement direction and the migration length adjustment to the result of the lower layer. Finally, the result of the lower layer and the result of the upper layer are integrated.

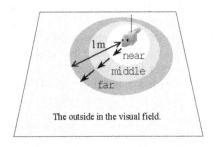

Fig. 4. Robot sense of distance.

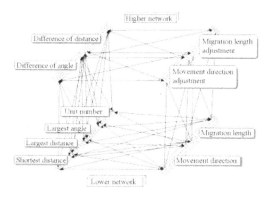

Fig. 5. CFS representing a welfare robot

3.3   Simulation Experiments

To verify the effectiveness of the control rule used in this paper, we experimented with two cases, i.e., only using the lower control rule of CFS and using CFS. **Table 1** shows the results of a circle style formation experiment and a line style formation experiment. In both experiments, the left side of the table used CFS and the right side used only the lower control rule.

Table 1 Circle Style Formation and Line Style Formation.

Circle style formation				Line style formation			
CFS		lower rule		CFS		lower rule	
Ave	Sim	Ave	Sim	Ave	Sim	Ave	Sim
36	4	45	5	30	3	34	4
41	13	32	11	38	4	43	5
42	8	50	18	41	4	44	5
39	7	33	24	30	3	35	4
27	3	27	3	39	4	42	5
18	2	18	2	57	9	56	8
36	4	40	5	20	2	17	2
9	1	8	1	30	3	34	4
59	31	87	12	39	4	43	5
27	3	28	8	29	3	34	4
33.4	7.6	36.8	8.9	35.3	3.9	38.2	4.6

Ave: average of each robot's migration length
Sim: simulation time

In **Figure 6**, first, three robots are placed at random positions. Then, a human sends an order to them to arrange themselves in a single row. All of the robots get the same order. The human, however, does not issue any small

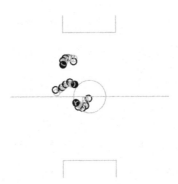

Fig. 6. Simulation result of line style formation with three robots.

indication for each robot. These robots judge where to go by themselves and then move. Finally, they reach for the correct position independently.

In **Figure 7**, first, four robots are placed at random positions. When they get an order from a human to arrange themselves circularly, they reach for the four corners.

From the unit number of the robots placed first, when a difference emerges from an increase in the number, then the formation of the robots changes. As shown in **Figure 8**, four robots are placed first and later one robot is added. Because of the addition, the formation of the robots changes from a square to a positive pentagon.

3.4   Robot Experiments

We apply knowledge obtained by simulation to real robot experiments. In the experiments, we use two robots and create formations of the two robots and one

Fig. 7. Simulation result of circle style formation with four robots.

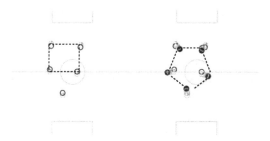

Fig. 8. Simulation result of circle style formation with four robots and "ve robots.

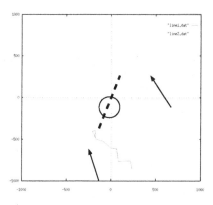

Fig. 9. Experimental result of line style formation with a person and two robots.

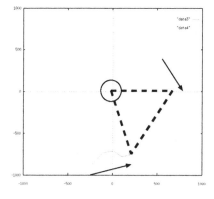

Fig. 10. Experimental result of circle style formation with a person and two robots.

person. In **Figure 9**, the person is in the center of a field (of length 1m by width 1m), and the two robots arrange themselves at both sides to make a line style formation.

In **Figure 10**, the person is in the center of a field (of length 1m by width 1m), and the two robots move to make a circle style formation.

4   Formation Movements using Chaotic Evolutionary Computation

It is necessary to work cooperatively to maintain a formation style. For example, when two persons walk together, they generally walk side-by-side to maintain their formation. When turning, the outside person walks faster, while the inside person slows down.

We apply these concepts to two robots moving in parallel. Each of the robots obtains knowledge based on chaotic retrieval using the proposed method.

In the case of formation movements, the robot control block is switched to another control block, i.e., one representing formation movements. Two robots will have the same control block using CFS. The low-level layer maintains such fundamental action rules as going forward and turning left or right. The high-level layer maintains steering and speed control rules and another rule to maintain a constant distance from the other agent when both are moving together. Chaotic retrieval is applied to the steering and speed control of this high-level layer. Then, it becomes possible to obtain rules on how to move together in parallel, by conceiving and adjusting the steering degree and moving speed. **Figures 11 and 12** show two real robots moving side-by-side while maintaining a regular interval.

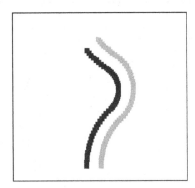

Fig. 11. Simulation locus of two robots moving side-by-side.

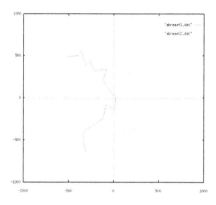

Fig. 12. Experimental result of Figure 11.

5   Effectiveness of Soft DNA

In a system in which a large number of agents work, it is good for all agents to share roles. To produce cooperative works, we have a proposal of a new method (under discussion).

We call this new method Soft DNA (Soft computing oriented Data driven fuNctional scheduling Architecture)[5] . Soft DNA aims to imitate the idea of the developmental process, such as the body plans in actual life based on biological DNA (DeoxyriboNucleic Acid).

In biological DNA, the genes called Homeo box genes dynamically control the body development of an individual in actual life based on the concentrations of proteins in cells. The control architecture called soft DNA dynamically controls the development of intelligence in each agent based on environmental information, in order to achieve dynamic cooperation. Biological DNA has sets of genes that are related to each body part such as the head, chest, abdomen, and tail. These sets of genes are each called a homeo box.

Similarly, soft DNA has boxes of intelligence (made by soft computing, i.e., associative memories, neural networks, fuzzy logic, chaos, and so on) that are related to various environments, a suitable box of intelligence is developed according to the environmental information available as shown in **Figure 13**.

Soft DNA has boxes characterized as a set of roles, e.g., a search robot, transportation robot, or construction robot.

All agent robots have the same soft DNA and can switch their own roles dynamically.

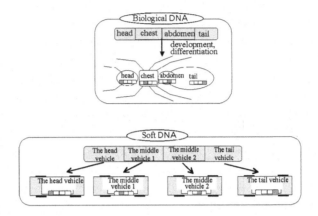

Fig. 13. Biological DNA and Soft DNA

We are trying to apply soft DNA to a multi-agent robot system. As an example, when it was applied to an intelligent transport system (ITS), the average of the vehicular gap error improved about 1/4.

6   Conclusions

This paper proposed a multi-agent system that carries out cooperative works. To achieve cooperative works, we proposed fuzzy sets of a new type named Conceptual Fuzzy Sets (CFS). By using FAMOUS and CFS, each agent robot has become able to determine its own behavior for the situation in its environment. We applied this system to a welfare agent robot system and showed the usefulness of CFS. In addition, we showed the possibility of soft DNA as a new method.

References

1. T.Yamaguchi, Fuzzy Associative Memory System, Journal of Japan Society for Fuzzy Theory and Systems, Vol.5, No.2, 245-260, (1993)(in Japanese).
2. T. Takagi, T. Yamaguchi and M. Sugeno, Conceptual Fuzzy Sets, International Fuzzy Engineering Symposium 91, PART II, pp.261-272, (1991).
3. Tomohiro Takagi, Toru Yamaguchi and Makoto Sato, Multi-Modal Information Integration by Conceptual Fuzzy Set for Interactive Systems, IEEE Int. Conf. on Fuzzy Systems (FUZZ-IEEE 98), pp.738-743, (1998).
4. Wittgenstein, Philosophical Investigations, Basil Blackwell, Oxford, (1953).
5. Naoki Kohata, Toru Yamaguchi, Takanobu Baba and Hideki Hashimoto, Chaotic Evolutionary Parallel Computation on Intelligent Agents, Journal of Robotics and Mechatronics(accepted), (1998).

Evolutionary Computation for Intelligent Agents Based on Chaotic Retrieval and Soft DNA

Naoki Kohata[1], Makoto Sato[1], Toru Yamaguchi[1], Takanobu Baba,
and Hideki Hashimoto[2]

[1] Department of Information Science, Faculty of Engineering, Utsunomiya University
7-1-2 Youtou, Utsunomiya 321-8585, Japan
[2] Institute of Industrial Science, University of Tokyo
7-22-1 Roppongi, Minato-ku, Tokyo 106-8558, Japan

Abstract. This paper proposes a chaotic evolutionary computation algorithm instead of conventional GA (Genetic Algorithm) for such intelligent agents as welfare robots which assist humans. This evolutionary computation is realized by applying chaotic retrieval and Soft DNA(Soft computing oriented Data driven fuNctional scheduling Architecture) on associative memories. We apply this evolutionary computation to multi-agent robots which move abreast and ITS(Intelligent Transport System). Essentially, the process of this evolutionary computation is parallel processing. Therefore, we implement its parallel processing algorithm on A-NET (Actors NETwork) parallel object-oriented computer, and show the usefulness of parallel processing for proposed evolutionary computation.

1 Introduction

Recently, evolutionary computation models on Alife (Artificial life) have been researched by computer[1]. Nowadays, its typical approach method is GA (Genetic Algorithm). Conventional GA is an algorithm based on traditional Darwinism. On the other hand, in recent years, new theories of evolution except Darwinism have been advocated. Nakahara et al. have advocated virus theory of evolution, and explain rapid evolution which can not be explained by mutation and natural selection[2]. Yomo et al. have advocated evolution based on competitive coexistence, and argue that evolution is not simple optimization because of interaction among life[3]. In any case, it is certain that evolution of actual life is not such simple processes as conventional GA. Above all, we think there are not only genetic factors but also other factors (e.g., cultural factor) in evolutionary process of brain or its intelligence. In addition, it is said that evolution is irreversible process which does not enable the life to become again the exactly same life as it used to be. It seems to us that there is chaos in this complexity of evolution.

Therefore, we propose evolutionary computation of intelligence by chaotic dynamics and Soft DNA (Soft computing oriented Data driven fuNctional scheduling Architecture) as shown in Fig.1[4]. We explain this evolutionary computation and Soft DNA in the following chapter.

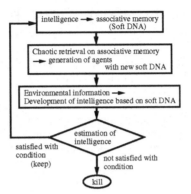

Fig. 1. Evolutionary computation of intelligence by chaotic dynamics

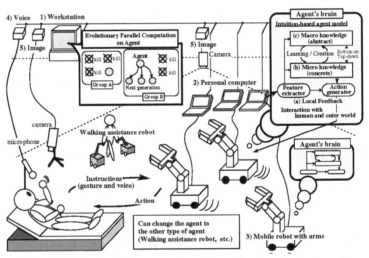

Fig. 2. Welfare intelligent agents and intuition-based agent model

On the one hand, in the society which is filled with old people, the welfare agent robots which assist the old or the sick people are requested as shown in Fig.2. The welfare robots have to move in a suitable formation, in cooperation with other agents, humans and the outer environment. We have to acquire the knowledge of cooperative work e ciently. Therefore, we apply the proposed evolutionary computation to the multi-agent robots which move abreast as an example of cooperative work in welfare robots and we also apply this evolutionary computation to ITS (Intelligent Transport System). The brain of this

welfare robot is constructed by the intuition-based agent model as shown in
Fig.2. This agent model consists of hierarchical fuzzy knowledge that uses associative memories[5], and it imitates human creativities in order to adapt itself
to its environmental changes, conceiving new ideas based on current knowledge
by chaotic retrieval. Each hierarchical part retrieves the knowledge based on
fuzzy associative inference on associative memories. Essentially, this inference in
each part is parallel processing, and these hierarchical parts also work in parallel. Furthermore, a large number of agents work in parallel on a multi-agent
model and its evolutionary computation. Therefore, we undertook parallel processing according to these parallel properties in the brain and in nature. We
implement a parallel processing algorithm on A-NET(Actors NETwork) parallel
object-oriented computer[8], and show its usefulness.

2   Soft DNA and its Evolutionary Computation

2.1   Soft DNA

We propose a new method for development of intelligence in order to realize dynamic cooperation in the intelligent agents. We call this new method Soft DNA
(Soft computing oriented Data driven fuNctional scheduling Architecture) . Soft
DNA aims to imitate the idea of the developmental process, such as the body
plans in actual life based on biological DNA(DeoxyriboNucleic Acid). Fig.3 shows
the image of soft DNA compared with biological DNA. In biological DNA, the
genes called Homeo box genes dynamically control the body development of
an individual in actual life based on the concentrations of proteins in cells. The
control architecture called soft DNA dynamically controls the development
of intelligence in each agent based on environmental information, in order to
achieve dynamic cooperation. Biological DNA has sets of genes that are related
to each body part such as the head, chest, abdomen, and tail. These sets of
genes are each called a homeo box. Similarly, soft DNA has boxes of intelligence
(made by soft computing, i.e., associative memories, neural networks, fuzzy logic,

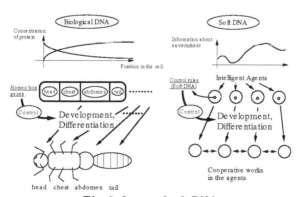

Fig. 3. Image of soft DNA

chaos, and so on) that are related to various environments, and a suitable box of intelligence is developed according to the environmental information.

2.2 Evolutionary Computation on Soft DNA

The proposed soft DNA consists of some boxes which are made by associative memory system named FAMOUS(Fuzzy Associative Memory Organizing Units System)[5]. We use CFAMOUS(Chaotic FAMOUS) to carry out evolutionary computation on soft DNA. We simulate the proposed evolutionary computation in parallel on A-NET parallel computer which is explained in the next chapter.

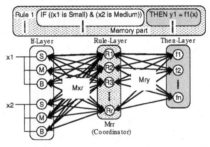

Fig. 4. Fuzzy associative memory organizing units system

FAMOUS (Fig.4) represents fuzzy knowledge using several BAMs (Bi-directional Associative Memories) [7]. This system performs fuzzy associative inference that causes an input pattern to approach the nearest pattern using top-down and bottom-up processing (i.e., network reverberation). This propagates the activation values of each node. CFAMOUS applies the chaotic retrieval to the retrieval process of the memorized patterns in FAMOUS. The chaotic steepest descent method (CSD method)[6] is used as chaotic retrieval method. This method chaotically itinerates among the local minimums in the energy function of the neural network. CFAMOUS has two functions. First, memorized patterns near the external input pattern are dynamically retrieved and this range is restricted by one parameter which defines the degree of system nonlinearity. Second, non-memorized and valid patterns can be retrieved as well as memorized ones. We explain the proposed evolutionary computation at the 6th chapter in detail.

3   The A-NET parallel computer

Baba et al. have been proceeding with development and research of an A-NET (Actors NETwork) parallel computer[8]. A-NET has a parallel object-oriented total architecture, and allows users to describe parallel programs naturally by using A-NETL(A-NET Language). The node processor on this computer consists of a processing element(PE), a local memory, and a router, and optional network topologies have been provided. A-NETL(A-NET Language) is a parallel object-oriented language which describes parallel programs naturally. A unit of parallel processing on A-NETL is an object. An object consists of data and procedure(method). On A-NETL, each object cooperatively sends or receives messages and processes them in parallel.

4   Multi-agent robots which move abreast

We will explain multi-agent robots which move abreast as a fundamental example of cooperative work in welfare robots. When two people walk together, they generally keep in step with one another. When turning, the outside person walks faster, while the inside person slows down. We have applied this conception to two robots which move abreast as shown in Fig.5. In this model, a robot understands its situation, i.e., where the robot is, and it then carries out chaotic retrieval to adapt itself to its situation.

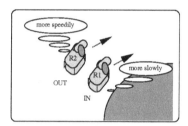

Fig. 5. Multi-agent robots which move abreast

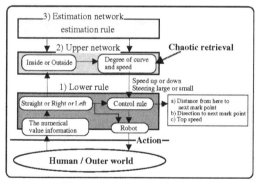

Fig. 6. Robot control block

The robot control block is shown in Fig.6. This control block is constructed based on the proposed agent model shown in Fig.2. The upper network of this figure has the knowledge to adapt itself to the change in its situation. The

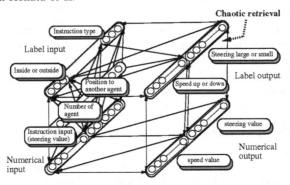

Fig. 7. Lower rule and upper network using CFS (Conceptual Fuzzy Set)

output of the lower rule depends on this knowledge. The robots estimate their movement in the estimation network. These networks are realized by associative memory network based on FAMOUS or CFAMOUS. More concretely, the lower rule and the upper network are constructed by CFS (Conceptual Fuzzy Set)[9] as shown in Fig.7. This CFS is constructed by hierarchical network applying (C)FAMOUS. The bottom of this figure shows the lower rule. The top shows the upper network. In the lower rule, the left is the numerical value input and the right is the numerical value output. The outputs are speed and steering value. In this application, a box of soft DNA is made by the CFS shown in Fig.7. New soft DNA is created by chaotic retrieval on this CFS network. Each intelligence as box of soft DNA can evolve separately according to environmental information such as whether the mobile agent is inside or outside at turning abreast. In order to acquire suitable knowledge(i.e., good soft DNA) in the upper network, we use the proposed evolutionary computation. We create new generation of various agent robots with new knowledge by applying chaotic retrieval in the upper network.

5   ITS(Intelligent Transport Systems)

The ITS are the systems which realize safer and more e cient tra c and transportation by constructing the intelligent automobiles and road environment. For example, the realization of platooning of automobiles has been researched for that purpose. The platooning means platoon (i.e., group) running of automobiles. In platooning, if all platoons or all automobiles run based on the exactly same control knowledge, the tra c system may be a failure as a whole. Therefore, it seems that each platoon or each automobile needs to have the "uctuations of its intelligence in order to do the different movement from the others. If we consider a platoon to be a group of automobile agents, we can apply the proposed evolutionary computation to this platooning. The basic control block is realized by CFS as well as the case of multi-agent robots which move abreast.

In ITS platooning, it seems that desirable intelligence of a automobile should be change according to whether the automobile runs as a head vehicle or as a middle vehicle or as a tail vehicle in the platoon. The situation of each automobile changes dynamically as the current middle vehicle changes to the head vehicle because of division of the platoon. Therefore, we apply evolutionary computation on soft DNA to each ITS automobile and aim to realize the dynamic development of intelligence.

6   Simulation results and discussion

6.1   Multi-agent robot which move abreast

First, we will explain the results of evolutionary computation based on chaotic retrieval and soft DNA in multi-agent robots which move abreast. Second, we will explain the results of parallel processing on agent robots. Fig.8 shows an example of the evolutionary process. The situation of this figure shows the case where the agents are given the Turn Left instruction. First, two agent robots can't move abreast because they move based on the same control value. The evolutionary computation creates new generation of various agents with new knowledge(i.e., the box containing new soft DNA) by applying chaotic retrieval in the agent's brain (i.e., associative memories). The generation consists of the group of the pairs of two agents which intend to move abreast. These pairs are kept or killed based on the estimation about their movement. Finally, the agent with the suitable knowledge(i.e., good soft DNA) to move abreast is kept. Evolutionary computation is performed in the same way for all situations (i.e., for all instructions).

Fig. 8. An example of the evolutionary process

Table 1. The number of pairs of created agents in each instruction before the agent with suitable knowledge is acquired. (The case of parallel algorithm of evolutionary computation)

Instruction	Right & Large	Turn Right	Right & Small	Left & Large	Turn Left	Left & Small
The number of pairs of created agents	26	5	10	27	6	9

Table 1 shows a result in the case of parallel algorithm of evolutionary computation, that is, it shows the number of pairs of created agents in each instruction before the agent with suitable knowledge is acquired. Each knowledge item is acquired by creating the about 14 pairs of agents on average. In this parallel evolutionary process, each knowledge is created separately, that is, plural pairs of

Table 2. The number of pairs of created agents in each instruction before the agent with suitable knowledge is acquired. (The case of serial algorithm of evolutionary computation : Total number is 67)

Instruction	Right & Large	Turn Right	Right & Small	Left & Large	Turn Left	Left & Small
The number of pairs of created agents	26	9	2	22	5	3

agents are created and perform evolutionary computation concurrently. Finally, all knowledges are integrated on the associative memory network of CFAMOUS. This integration of knowledge was realized by utilizing evolutionary computation using CFAMOUS. It is di cult for conventional neural networks to realize this evolutionary parallel computation.

After agent robots had acquired suitable knowledge for all instructions, we verified their movement by means of computer simulation. The results are shown in Fig.9. As shown, the robots move abreast suitably when a series of instructions is given to the robots.

Fig. 9. The movement of robots (Instructions: Turn Left → Right & Small → Right & Large)

Table 2 shows a result in the case of serial algorithm of evolutionary computation, that is, it shows the number of pairs of created agents in each instruction before the agent with suitable knowledge is acquired. In this serial evolutionary process, one pair of agents repeats evolutionary computation serially to acquire all suitable knowledges.

In parallel algorithm, the maximum number of created pairs is 27 at the Left & Large instruction as shown in Table 1. The processing time of parallel algorithm is directly proportional to this number (27). In serial algorithm, the total number of created pairs through all situations is 67 from Table 2. The processing time of serial algorithm is directly proportional to this total number (67). Therefore, the parallel algorithm of evolutionary computation is about 2.5 times faster than its serial algorithm from the viewpoint of the number of pairs of created agents.

We also realized parallel program which simulates the associative inference and the movement of robots in multi-agent robots which move abreast in parallel, and implemented it on A-NET parallel computer. The simulation results show that the parallel program is about 11 times faster than conventional serial program.

6.2   ITS(Intelligent Transport Systems)

We apply the proposed evolutionary computation on soft DNA to the platooning of ITS (Intelligent Transport System). In this application, each box of soft DNA is made by the CFS. and each box develops the intelligence for each role such as the roles of a head vehicle, a middle vehicle and a tail vehicle in the platoon according to environmental information. We show the soft DNA is useful for the realization of dynamic cooperation by simulations. Furthermore, we show the proposed evolutionary computation improves the control performance about distance between vehicles in the ITS platooning. Simulation result showed that the average error between the ideal distance and the actual one improved about 1/4 by the evolved soft DNA.

7   Conclusion

This paper proposed an evolutionary computation algorithm by chaotic dynamics and Soft DNA instead of conventional GA (Genetic Algorithm) for such intelligent agents as welfare robots which assist humans. This evolutionary computation was realized by applying chaotic retrieval on associative memories. We applied this evolutionary computation to multi-agent robots which move abreast. Essentially, the process of this evolutionary computation is parallel processing. Therefore, we implemented its parallel processing algorithm on A-NET (Actors Network) parallel object-oriented computer, and showed the usefulness of parallel processing for proposed evolutionary computation.

References

1. T. Hoshino: Dream and Distress of Alife, SHOUKABOU (1994) (in Japanese).
2. H.Nakahara and T.Sagawa: Virus theory of evolution, HAYAKAWASYOBOU (1996) (in Japanese).
3. W.-Z.Xu, A.Kashiwagi, T.Yomo and I.Urabe: Fate of a mutant emerging at the initial stage of evolution, Researches in Population Ecology, 38(2), pp231-237 (1996).
4. N.Kohata, T.Yamaguchi, Y.Wakamatsu and T.Baba: Evolutionary Parallel Computation based on Chaotic Retrieval and Creation, Proceedings of the 4th International Conference on Soft Computing (IIZUKA 96), Vol.2, pp.638-641 (1996).
5. T.Yamaguchi: Fuzzy Associative Memory System, Journal of Japan Society for Fuzzy Theory and Systems, Vol.5, No.2, 245-260 (1993) (in Japanese).
6. J.Tani: Proposal of Chaotic Steepest Descent Method for Neural Networks and Analysis of Their Dynamics, Trans.IEICE, Vol. J74-A, No.8, pp1208-1215 (1991).
7. B.Kosko: Adaptive Bidirectional Associative Memories, Applied Optic, Vol.26, No.23, pp.4947-4960(1987).
8. T.Baba, T.Yoshinaga, Y.Iwamoto and D.Abe: The A-NET *Working* Prototype: A Parallel Object-Oriented Multicomputer with Recon"gurable Network, Proc. Int. Workshop on Innovative Architecture for Future Generation High-Performance Processors and Systems, IEEE Computer Society Press, pp.40-49 (1998).
9. T.Takagi, T.Yamaguchi and M.Sugeno: Conceptual Fuzzy Sets, International Fuzzy Engineering Symposium 91 (IFES 91), Vol.2, pp.261-272 (1991).

A Study of Bayesian Clustering of a Document Set Based on GA

Keiko Aoki, Kazunori Matsumoto, Keiichiro Hoashi,
and Kazuo Hashimoto

{keiko, matsu, hoashi, kh}@lab.kdd.co.jp
KDD Laboratories Inc.,
2-1-15 Ohara Kamifukuoka-Shi, Saitama 356-8502, Japan

Abstract. In this paper, we propose new approximate clustering algorithm that improves the precision of a top-down clustering. Top-down clustering is proposed to improve the clustering speed by Iwayama et al, where the cluster tree is generated by sampling some documents, making a cluster from these, assigning other documents to the nearest node and if the number of assigned documents is large, continuing sampling and clustering from top to down. To improve precision of the top-down clustering method, we propose selecting documents by applying a GA to decide a quasi-optimum layer and using a MDL criteria for evaluating the layer structure of a cluster tree.

Keywords: Document Retrieval, Beysian Clustering, Minimum Description Length Criteria, Genetic Algorithm

1 Introduction

Recently, Document retrieval based on similarity is becoming a new active research area. Iwayama et al. proposed a hierarchical clustering method for document retrieval based on similarity. They call the algorithm Hierarchical Bayesian Clustering (HBC)[1]. When the number of documents is N, the required time for a simple exhaustive search method is $O(N)$. When a prearranged cluster is used, required time is $O(\log N)$. However the calculation amount to make a cluster is $O(N^2)$, therefore it is extremely di cult to make a cluster of a large number of documents by conventional systems. Then they proposed an approximate clustering technique for applying HBC to large number of document sets. The basic idea of the approximation is to decrease processing time in deciding a layer by computing the similarity from selected documents instead of all documents. However, in Iwayama's proposed method, the layer is not always optimum because documents are selected at random.

We propose to select documents by applying a genetic algorithm (referred to hereafter as GA)[2] to deciding a quasi-optimum layer and using a MDL criteria for evaluating the layer structure of a cluster tree. Our method gives better accuracy than Iwayama's method, because the layer structure of a cluster tree constructed by our method is quasi-optimum. The advantage of the GA based algorithm is that it is known to converge speed compared with other optimal methods.

In this paper, we report speed comparison results between our method and a strict clustering technique, and also report evaluation results of precision compared to Iwayama's method.

2   Strict Clustering by HBC

HBC uses evaluation parameters which take account of word appearance frequency. It is known that compared to a general clustering method such as that of Ward[3], the clustering precision of HBC is higher[4]. Here, the detailed clustering algorithm of HBC and Iwayama's approximate clustering algorithm will be described.

2.1   HBC Algorithm

In this method, the measurement of nearness is posterior probability $P(c_i|d_{test})$, the probability that the test document d_{test} is classified into a cluster c_i. T=t means that a randomly selected term T from the document d_{test} is equal to t.

$$P(c_i|d_{test}) = P(c_i) \sum_t \frac{P(T = t|c_i)P(T = t|d_{test})}{P(T = t)} \tag{1}$$

Probabilities on the right-hand side of this equation are estimated as follows:

- $P(T = t|d_{test})$: relative frequency of a term t in a test document d_{test}.
- $P(T = t|c_i)$: relative frequency of a term t in a cluster c_i.
- $P(T = t)$: relative frequency of a term t in the entire set of training documents.
- $P(c_i)$: relative frequency of documents that belong to c_i in the entire set of training documents.

HBC constructs a cluster hierarchy (also called dendrogram) from bottom to top by merging two clusters at a time. At the beginning, each document belongs to a cluster whose only member is the document itself. For every pair of clusters, HBC calculates the increase of posterior probability after merging the pairs and selects the pair that results in the maximum increase, and those clusters are merged to form a new cluster.

To see the details of this merge process, consider a merge step k+1($0 \le k \le N - 1$). By the step k+1, a data collection of N data $D = \{d_1, d_2, ..., d_{N_D}\}$ has been partitioned into a set of clusters $C_k = \{c_1, c_2, ...\}$. That is, each datum $d_i \in D$ belongs to a cluster $c_j \in C_k$. The overall posterior probability at this point becomes

$$P(C_k|D) = \prod_{c_j \in C_k} \prod_{d_i \in c_j} P(c_j|d_i) \tag{2}$$

The set of clusters C_k is updated as follows:

$$C_{k+1} = C_k - \{c_x, c_y\} + \{c_x \cup c_y\} \tag{3}$$

After the merge, the posterior probability is inductively updated as follows:

$$P(C_{k+1}|D) = P(C_K|D)\frac{\prod_{d_i \in c_x \cup c_y} P(c_x \cup c_y|d_i)}{\prod_{d_i \in c_x} P(c_x|d_i) \prod_{d_i \in c_y} P(c_y|d_i)} \tag{4}$$

When clustering is performed with the above algorithm, the number of calculations of evaluation values of the posterior probability is:

$$_N C_2 + \sum_{k=1}^{N-2} k = (N-1)^2 = O(N^2) \tag{5}$$

Hence when a large number of documents is handled, cluster generation becomes more di cult as the number of documents increases.

2.2   Iwayama's Approximate Clustering Method

Iwayama et al proposed approximate clustering techniques called top-down clustering , where the cluster tree is generated from top to down[5]. The algorithm of top-down clustering is,

1. Selects S-documents from document set $|D|$, randomly.
2. Classifies S-documents with strict clustering, and make a seed cluster.
3. Assigns $|D| - S$ non-selected documents to the nearest leaf node of the seed cluster tree.
4. If the size of document set assigned to a single leaf is reasonable to treat with a strict clustering method, construct a tree, otherwise, continue to select documents and cluster that document set.

The clustering time becomes twice faster than that of strict clustering method. However, in Iwayama's proposed method, the layer is not always optimum because documents are selected at random.

3   Proposed Clustering Method

Now, we shall discuss the technique that we propose, an evaluation function for finding an optimum document set by this method, and the GA technique we use.

3.1   Algorithm of proposed method

To improve the precision of Iwayama's clustering method, we propose the following method, combining conventional strict clustering with top-down clustering using GA. Assume that the total number of documents to be clustered is N, and the number of documents within a range which can be handled by a strict clustering method is M.

procedure GA-clustering()
    all documents are assigned to a root document set (D_{root});
    D_{root} is registered as cue-Q;
    while (Q is not empty) {
        a document set D_p at the head of Q is extracted;
        if (the number of documents $D_p < M$)
            HBC(D_p); /* clustering of D_p by HBC */
        else {
            $D_d = $ Select(D_p);
            /* document set D_d, constructed from M documents considered to be optimum,
            which are extracted from D_p.
            The coding lengths of cluster is minimized based on an MDL criteria (see **3.2**).
            A genetic algorithm is used for the analytical search (see**3.3**).*/
            HBC(D_d);
            The remaining document sets $(D_p - D_d)$ are assigned to the nearest
            leaf $(L_i \in C_d)$;
            Document sets assigned to the $D_i = L_i$;
            if(number of documents $D_i > 0$)
                D_i is added to Q;
        }
    }
endproc

3.2 Evaluation function for finding an optimum document set

To extract document set D_d including M documents considered to be optimum from a document set D, we make a cluster using that document set and use a coding length of a cluster tree as a basis. Herein, as the MDL criteria is used, a document set which minimizes the coding length of a tree is considered to be optimum.

The coding length (L) is calculated as the sum of the description length (L_1) required to write the tree, and the description length (L_2) for the probabilistic distribution of documents assigned to leaf nodes.

The coding of a tree follows the universal coding principle[6]. The tree is queried in a pre-ordered manner[7] and it outputs 1 when an internal node is encountered, and outputs 0 when a leaf node is encountered. In this case, if the number of leaf nodes is k, the number of internal nodes is $k-1$, and the coding length L_1 becomes $2k-1$.

The documents for evaluation are assigned to the nearest leaf nodes. If the number of documents assigned to a leaf node i is n_i, and the probability that a document assigned to n_i is selected from all assigned documents is p_i, the description length L_2 is given by equation (6).

$$L_2 = -\sum_{i}^{k} n_i \log p_i = -\sum_{i}^{k} n_i \log \frac{n_i}{\sum_j n_j} \tag{6}$$

As the number of documents for evaluating the tree (referred to hereafter as R) is extracted at random from $D - D_d$, R is independent of D or D_d.

3.3   GA for finding optimum document sets

Regarding the ploblem of finding an optimum document set, there is no method to define suitable initial value for the next search. GA is suitable for this problem, because GA performe multi-point sampling in parallel. Thus, we apply GA to find a cluster having a minimal coding length.

In this algorithm, a gene represents a document in the target documents, and a value of 1 means selected for evaluation whereas 0 means not selected. A genotype denotes a combination of selected documents. The whole number of genes in a genotype, therefore, is equal to the number of target documents, and the number of genes having a value of 1 is equal to that of the selected documents.

Here, the following model is used.

- **Scaling**: power scaling ($f' = f^2$)
- **Selection crossing**: Fitness proportional strategy and elite storage strategy
- **Crossing and Mutation**: In this method, instead of pairing two parents, a given proportion of bits($Crossing$) of parents of which the number is equal to a generation gap, is replaced by random bits.
- **Generation model**: Continuous generation model

If the number of document sets is N and the number of extracted documents is M, the merge frequency in the GA-clustering of **3.1** is as follows. The merge frequency of strict clustering of M extracted document sets is $(M - 1)^2$. Merge frequency per document to assign to a leaf node is 2 log M where   is a number depending on the degree of balance of the tree, and is in the vicinity of 1 when the balance is good. The frequency of GA-clustering is N/M where (≤ 1) also depends on the balance of the tree. The number of genes to be evaluated per GA-clustering is $N_{pg} + N_{pg}R_g(N_g - 1)$ where N_g, N_{pg}, R_g are respectively number of generations, number of genes per generation and generation gap. From the above, it is seen that the total frequency of merges is approximately:

$$((M - 1)^2 + 2R \quad \log(M))(N_{pg} + N_{pg}R_g(N_g - 1)) \ \frac{N}{M} = O(N) \qquad (7)$$

4   Estimation of Clustering Speed and Precision

Here, we shall show how much the proposed method improves clustering speed and precision.

4.1   Experimental Environment and Measurement Parameters

Sun UltraEnterprise 450 (Solaris 2.6, 512MB) is used. We used patent data all of which have a reasonably large document length. We used 21 patents for search input, and had a professional organization conduct a search for similar patents. We used other patents which we sampled at random from the same period, and all of the patents found by this organization as a target document set.

4.2   Experimental results: speed

We fixed the parameters relating to GA as follows, and examined the relation between number of documents and processing speed.

M (number of documents extracted)	16
R (number of documents assigned to leaf nodes)	128
N_g (number of generations)	10
N_{pg} (number of genes per generation)	10
R_g (generation gap)	10
$Crossing$ (number of bits to be changed)	3

Table 1 shows measured results for processing speed for HBC which is strict clustering and the proposed method when the number of documents is varied. It is seen that almost all of the processing time is taken up by merging clusters.

Table 1. Processing Time

Number of documents		50	100	250	500	1000	2500
HBC	Merge part	10.47	43.16	303.97	1,172.64	4,378.84	25,044.56
(sec)	Total	39.45	72.88	380.27	1,572.07	7,509.49	72,306.67
Proposed	Merge part	604.04	3,183.04	6,230.81	7,150.97	13,896.17	52,608.81
method(sec)	Total	1,747.34	4,555.79	7,929.94	11,692.47	28,267.38	92,279.07

Fig. 1 shows the merge frequency of clusters and the time required to merge clusters for different numbers of documents. Strict clustering refers to HBC, GA based clustering refers to the proposed method, the horizontal axis shows numbers of documents and the vertical axis shows merge frequency and merge time. From this it is found that whereas according to the conventional method the merge frequency increases in direct proportion to N^2, in the proposed method it is directly proportional to N up to N = 250.

When M is small compared to N, there is a larger proportion of clustering using GA. Hence in the proposed method when N = 500, there is a sharp rise in the number of gene evaluations and the merge frequency appears to sharply increase. However it is expected that although the merge frequency increases overall when the value of M is increased, the change-over point will be slightly later.

4.3   Experimental results: precision

To determine the search precision, we found the Recall/Precision considering the patents cited by the professional organization to be correct answers. The search covered 250 patents including all the patents which were correct answers found by inputting the above 21 patents.

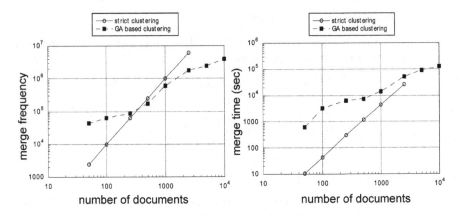

Fig. 1. Merge Frequency and Merge Time

The experimental results are shown in Fig. 2. Exhaustive is the result of a exhaustive search without using a cluster, top-down is the result of a search corresponding to Iwayama's top-down approximation algorithm when clustering was performed by extracting M documents at random using GA, GA based is the result when clustering was performed with 16 generations and 50 genes. As a result, the proposed method achieves a higher precision than a top-down approximation search.

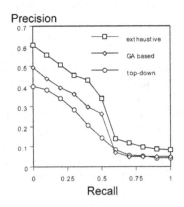

Fig. 2. Measured results of clustering precision

5 Conclusions

In this paper, we measured clustering performance using the proposed method. It was found that according to the proposed method, the number of merges of clusters was reduced from $O(N^2)$ to $O(N)$, and the time required for one merge could be maintained substantially constant regardless of N.

Also, we determined precision by Recall/Precision to verify that there was no deterioration of precision due to increased speed. As a result, it was found that the precision of the proposed method is higher than that of top-down approximation clustering which is a type of approximation clustering proposed by Iwayama et al, and that GA functioned effectively.

References

1. Makoto IWAYAMA, Takenobu TOKUNAGA: A Probabilistic Model for Text Categorization: Based on a Single Random Variable with Multiple Values. Proceedings of 4th Conference on Applied Natural Language Processing, pp.162-167, 1994.
2. Goldberg, D.E.: Genetic Algorithms in Search, Optimization, and Machine Learning, Addison-Wesley(1989).
3. Yutaka TANAKA, Kazuaki Wakimoto: Statistical Analysis of Large Volumes of Information. Modern Mathematics Society, 1983.
4. Makoto IWAYAMA, Takenobu TOKUNAGA: Hierarchical Bayesian Clustering for Automatic Text Classi"cation. Proceedings of IJCAI-95, pp.1322-1327, 1995.
5. IWAYAMA, TOKUNAGA, SAKURAI: Large-Scale Clustering for Document Search. 3rd Annual Meeting of Institute of Language Processing of Japan (March 1997), pp. 245-248, 1997.
6. ITOH, KAWABATA: Universal Data Compression Algorithm using Parameter Dispersion and Estimation Amount. 8th Conference on Information Theory and Applied Research, p.239-244, 1985.
7. Aho, Hopcroft, Ullman: The Design and Analysis of Computer Algorithms. p.54, Addison-Wesley Pub. Co., 1974.
8. AOKI, MATSUMOTO, HASHIMOTO: Evaluation of Clustering Methods for Large Volumes of Documents. 56th Meeting of the Institute of Information Processing of Japan ("rst semester, 1998), 3-100, 1998.

An Evolutionary Approach in Quantitative Spectroscopy

Phil Husbands[1] and Pedro P.B. de Oliveira[2]

[1] COGS, University of Sussex, UK
philh@cogs.susx.ac.uk
[2] Universidade do Vale do Para'ba, Brazil
pedrob@univap.br

Abstract. This paper describes investigations into using evolutionary search for quantitative spectroscopy. Given the spectrum (intensity × frequency) of a sample of material of interest, we would like to be able to infer the make-up of the material in terms of percentages by mass of its constituent compounds. The problem is usually tackled using regression methods. This approach can have various di culties. We have cast the problem as an optimisation task. Using a hybrid of distributed genetic algorithm with a local search around the best individual of the population, very good results have been found, even with noise, for a number of di erent instances of the problem, with variations in the range between 6 and 16 constituent compounds. The stochastic optimisation approach shows great promise in overcoming many of the problems associated with the more standard regression techniques.

Keywords: Genetic algorithm, quantitative spectroscopy.

1 Introduction: The Problem

Given the spectrum (intensity × frequency) of a sample of material of interest, we would like to be able to infer the make-up of the material in terms of percentages by mass of its constituent compounds. This is illustrated in Figure 1.

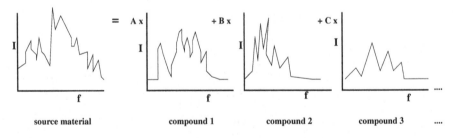

Fig. 1. The problem. Given the spectra, what is the make-up of the source material in terms of the percentages by mass of its constituent compounds?

This important problem in quantitative spectroscopy, occurring widely in medicine and the chemical industries, is o cially referred to as *quantitation*. A useful route into solving the problem comes in the form of the Beer Lambert Law [1,3]. Simply stated, it claims that when a sample is placed in the beam of a spectrometer, there is a direct and linear relationship between the amount (concentration) of its constituent(s) and the absorbance of the sample (the amount of energy it absorbs). It follows directly from this that the source material's spectrum is a linear combination of its constituents' spectra. This law forms the basis of nearly all chemometric methods for spectroscopic data. If the constituent compounds' spectra are known, then we can cast the problem as an optimal line fitting exercise of a special kind. Essentially the constituents' spectra are used as basis functions. The problem is to find the coe cients, a_i, in the following equation (the spectra have all been normalised to equate to the same reference concentration): *source spectrum* $= \sum_{i=1}^{N} a_i \times spectrum_i$, where $0 \le a_i \le 1$.

There are several different versions of this problem. The simplest is where the set of N constituent compounds is known. The problem is to find the proportions of each in the source material. In the second version of the problem the number of constituent compounds is not known. However, the set of compounds from which the constituents might be drawn is known. In the third and hardest version of the problem neither the number of constituents or the full set from which they might be drawn is known. In all version of the problem spectrum noise must be taken into account. We will concentrate on the first version of the problem for the rest of this paper.

The standard way of tackling the problem is to use one of the data fitting techniques based on regression ([7,6]). Although varying in complexity and scope, there is not one single method that is undeniably the best across all possibilities of spectral analysis. All in all, the more sophisticated the method, the more mathematical and complicated it becomes, often introducing mathematical artifacts that may compromise the quality of solution, and the speed of execution.

A typical problem that all these methods can produce unreliable solutions for, will involve a fairly large number of constituent compounds (> 15), with extensively overlapping spectra, where many of the compounds make up a similarly small fraction of the whole (about 1%)   typically there will be singularities in the analytic solutions [8].

However, the quantitation problem can be alternatively cast as an optimisation problem. Namely, find the set of a_is that minimises the difference between the source spectrum and that composed of the constituent spectra multiplied by their respective a_is. In general, the search space will be very large and complex, so simple gradient methods are unlikely to do well.

This paper describes our investigations into using stochastic search (hybrid GA/local search) to tackle the problem. As far as we know, this is the first time the quantitation problem has been treated as an optimisation task. Evolutionary search has been used on data fitting problems before (e.g. [5]), but not on this kind of task with complex non-analytic basis functions and strong constraints.

The evolutionary computation approach being developed is intended as an alternative approach to quantitative spectroscopy, one that avoids the drawbacks of the standard methods, while bringing the additional promise of being able to address problems that affect even the current best methods, for instance their very weak ability to handle samples with constituents not present in the original calibration mixtures. Evolutionary computation seems to be a natural way to tackle the latter problem, with its ability to handle variable-length genotypes that would represent the concentrations of a variable number of constituents.

It would be desirable to compare the evolutionary method with current techniques for this problem. However, since much of the software is proprietary and linked to special apparatus, this comparison was left as the next stage of the research. The aim of the present work is to establish whether or not evolutionary computation can be used at all. If it can find accurate solutions to hard instances of the problem, it must be considered a serious new candidate for this important class of problems.

2   The Encoding

A solution to the problem as outlined in the previous section is clearly a set of a_is, the proportion by mass of the constituents of the source material. A direct encoding for use with a GA could just be a string of N real numbers representing the a_is. However, the a_is are all interrelated by the constraint $\sum_{i=1}^{N} a_i = 1$, which just re"ects the obvious fact that the sum of all proportions by mass must equal unity. This constraint would invalidate nearly all solutions created by simple versions of GA operators, such as crossover and mutation, acting on a direct encoding. In the direct encoding we effectively have maximum epistasis. This means that either an indirect encoding must be found or appropriate genetic operators must be developed.

For this initial study a simple indirect encoding was devised for use with simple cheap genetic operators. In this encoding a genotype is a string of real numbers: genotype $= x_1\ x_2\ x_3\ ...\ ...\ x_N$ where, $0 \leq x_i \leq 100$ (any upper limit could be used, 100 having been chosen for convenience). This is the only constraint on the values of x_i. Figure 2 illustrates how this is decoded into a candidate solution.

First the x_is are mapped onto the real interval [0, 100]. The constituent fractions, the a_is, are then allocated as the sub-interval to the right of each x_i position on the line interval. The rightmost x_i is treated differently; the sub-interval to the its right is calculated by wrapping round to the leftmost x_i; in this way it is guaranteed that the constraint mentioned above is obeyed.

This encoding was found to work well. A normalised encoding, where the a_is were calculated from N x_is, directly encoded on the genotype as reals in the range [0,100], by dividing each x_i by the sum of all x_is on the genotype, was found to work well   but not as well as the encoding presented here.

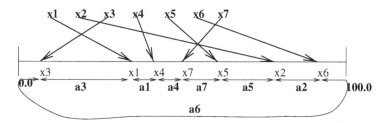

Fig. 2. Decoding the genotype. First the x_is are mapped onto the real interval $[0,100]$, then the a_is are given by the sub-interval to the right of x_is position on the line. The full interval is treated as circular with the end wrapping round to the beginning.

3   Cost Function

Let us assume that a spectrum S is represented by a discrete set of m points, as follows: $S = \{s_1, s_2, s_3, \ldots, s_m\}$. Hence, both the spectra of target materials and of the constituent compounds are stored as sets of m points; in the study presented below synthetic data was used, generated as sets of $m = 500$ points. A candidate solution spectrum, $\widetilde{S}$, is built up from the set of a_is through the relation $\widetilde{S} = \{\sum_{j=1}^{N} a_j \times \widetilde{s}_{ji}\}$, $i = 1, 2, 3, \ldots, m$, where $\{\widetilde{s}_{j1}, \widetilde{s}_{j2}, \widetilde{s}_{j3}, \ldots, \widetilde{s}_{jm}$ $) = \widetilde{S}_j$ is the spectrum of the jth constituent compound. The cost of a solution is just the squared difference between the target spectrum $(\hat{S})$ and the candidate spectrum $(\widetilde{S})$, that is: $C(\widetilde{S}) = \sum_{i=1}^{m} (\hat{s}_i - \widetilde{s}_i)^2$. Minimisation of this function will provide a set of a_is that can account for the observed spectrum. Whether or not it is the right set will depend on whether or not there is a many to one mapping to sets of a_is to spectra. Investigating this question was an important part of this research and it shall be discussed again in Section 5.

4   Implementation

The problem was tackled with the encoding and cost functions as described above, using a distributed GA with local selection similar to that detailed in [2], with a population of size 225 distributed over a 15x15 toroidal grid.

Recalling that the genotypes are just strings of real numbers (that is, genotype $= x_1 \, x_2 \, x_3 \, \ldots \ldots \, x_N$), simple one point crossover was used with a probability of 0.9. Three forms of mutation were used. **Type 1:** a gene, x_i, was mutated by adding to it a random number from a uniform distribution over the range $[-10.0, 10.0]$. The probability of a gene mutating was set at $1.0/N$, where N is the number of genes. **Type 2:** if a gene was to be mutated there was a 1 in 10 chance that the random number added to it was taken from a uniform distribution over the range $[-40.0, 40.0]$. If a mutation event of either of these two kinds caused a gene value to exceed 100.0 or become negative, its value was calculated by treating

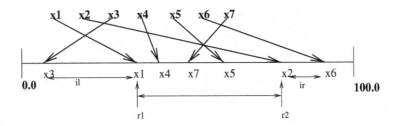

Fig. 3. Coupled mutation. The set of x_is making up the genotype are ordered. Two random points in this set, r1 and r2, are chosen. The whole of the section of the set between r1 and r2 is moved to the right/left (50% chance) by some random fraction of the subinterval immediately to the right/left (ir/il).

the range of possible values [0.0, 100.0] as a circular interval as described earlier. Referring to Figure 2, the effect of this kind of mutation is to slide the relevant gene up or down the line interval. This means that a single mutation is likely to only affect a small number (usually 2) of a_is given the decoding scheme used. **Type 3** is a little more complicated and shall be referred to as *coupled mutation*. Its workings are illustrated in Figure 3. It is a problem specific operator that proved to be very powerful.

In order to achieve the operation illustrated in the diagram, each of the x_is between the random points r1 and r2 are each increased or decreased by the same amount. This means that the subintervals in this section of the ordered set are not altered. Hence, the a_is specified by this part of the ordered set are unchanged. Only the intervals above and below the specified section are altered; one increases by exactly the same amount the other decreases. This has the effect on the solution of randomly choosing two constituent compounds and increasing the proportion of one while decreasing the proportion of the other by the same amount. Although type 1 and type 2 mutations can also have this effect it is less likely that every possible 'coupling' will be 'tweaked' in this way. Type 3 mutation was applied with a probability of 0.2 per genotype. Coupled mutation was also used as the operator at the heart of the local search algorithm incorporated into the GA. Heuristically motivated problem specific encodings and operators are becoming more and more popular in GA application [4], and can often produce significant improvements in performance. After every pseudo-generation a simple local search algorithm   using the coupled mutation operator was run (200 times) on the fittest individual in the population. If a better solution was found using this algorithm, it replaced the original best solution and the GA continued running. The addition of this local search was found to be quite effective, speeding up the search, particularly in the early stages. Run by itself, it produced fairly poor results.

5   Results

A number of synthetic problems were randomly generated by means of random reference constituent spectra. The number, height and width of peaks were chosen randomly (but setting the value of the highest possible peak). The proportion of the constituents in the target compound were then randomly generated and the resulting linear sum of spectra (the target material spectrum) was created. In this way a large number of test problems were created with varying numbers of constituent compounds and also with varying amounts of noise introduced into the data. In all of the problems the number of constituents were known, as well as the set of constituents.

Using this setup, very good results were consistently found. The problems used between 6 and 16 constituent compounds. Note that a problem size of 16 is considered to be very large in this area. The distributed GA incorporating local search on the best individual was able to consistently find solutions with almost zero cost in terms of spectrum difference   these *always* turned out to be correct to two or three sig. figs. on *all* the compound percentages.

A number of baseline experiments were carried out on the problems detailed below. Random search was applied to each. Not surprisingly, it only ever found very poor solutions. Local gradient descent was also tried. The coupled mutation operator described earlier was exhaustively run in small steps on all pairs of a_is in a solution. This created the set of nearest neighbours. The best of these was moved to until no further progress was made. This was much better than random search and often found fairly good solutions. However, they were never down in the very low regions the GA was able to reach. Lastly, running the GA without the local search generally resulted in good solutions. However, they were not as reliably excellent as with the local search in combination with the GA.

No noise. The first set of experiments involved problems of size 6, 8, 12 and 16 where there was no noise on the spectral data. Results are shown in the first half of Table 1. A single random problem was generated for each size and 25 runs of 300 generations were performed on each of these. The left-hand columns of the table show the cost of the worst, average and best solutions found. This cost is just the spectra difference measure used in the cost function detailed earlier. The right-hand columns show the corresponding differences between the set of constituent percentages in the target and those given by the solution. This difference (referred to as *composition error*), is the root mean square difference between the vector of a_is given in the solution $(\widetilde{a}_i)$ and the actual percentages $(\widehat{a}_i)$, that is: $Error = \sqrt{\sum_{j=1}^{N} \left(\widehat{a}_i - \widetilde{a}_i \right)^2}$.

We can see that both sets of errors are reduced to very low values. The good news is that reducing the spectra difference (the only thing available from observable data) does result in solutions that give the constituent percentages to a very high level of accuracy (2 or 3 sig. figs.). The important thing to know is that once the composition error goes below about 0.08, the solutions are almost exactly correct; above this level some of the percentages are not quite right. There is a very strong correlation between where the solution costs (spectra difference)

Number of Components	25 runs on 1 random problem						1 run on 25 random problems					
	Spectrum error			Composition error			Spectrum error			Composition error		
	Worst	Avg.	Best	Worst	Avg.	Best	Worst	Avg.	Best	Worst	Avg.	Best
6	5.3	2.6	1.0	0.08	0.04	0.02	5.5	2.5	1.0	0.1	0.05	0.02
8	7.2	3.2	1.0	0.09	0.04	0.02	6.8	3.2	0.0	0.09	0.05	0.02
12	10.2	7.3	1.0	0.13	0.06	0.04	11.4	7.8	1.0	0.17	0.08	0.03
16	12.5	7.4	1.0	0.18	0.07	0.04	13.9	7.4	1.0	0.19	0.07	0.04

Table 1. *In the first half of the table, a different random problem, of the appropriate size, was generated for each row; the results given are taken from 25 runs on the single problem, and refer to the best solution found in a single run. In the second half of the table, for each row, 25 random problems were generated, of the appropriate size; the results given are taken from a single run of each of the 25 problems, and refer to the best solution found in a single run. Each run lasts 300 generations.*

go below about 12.0 and where the accuracy of the constituent percentages becomes extremely high. If this had not been the case the method would not be applicable. Results from the first half of Table 1 show that the method is reliable every single run gave a very accurate solution.

The second half of Table 1 gives results averaged over single runs of 25 problems each for the four different sizes. Again the results are very good. These sets include very difficult problems such as 16 constituent compounds where most are only present in amounts between 0.5% and 1.0% and a few dominate the mixture with much higher percentages (something like 35% or 50%). Even in these cases the evolutionary method finds solutions where *all* the percentages are correct to a fraction of a percent of the true value. It is important to note that these results are far more accurate than standard methods are able to achieve.

Noise. The second set of experiments involved adding noise to the spectral data, making them unreliable. Amounts of 2% and 5% noise were added to the problem from the first half of Table 1. Every time a spectrum was used in an evaluation its points were randomly moved within these limits giving a slightly different version every time. Each evaluation was repeated 5 times and the average cost was used in the selection algorithm. As can be seen in Table 2, the results are a little worse than with no noise, but not much. The important thing is that the best solutions are still accurate in terms of the percentages of the constituents. The fact that this method inherently uses the whole spectrum, helps in averaging out the effects of noise. This is a very promising result as all real data is noisy.

6   Conclusions

This paper has described initial investigations into casting the spectroscopy quantitation problem as an optimisation task and tackling it with stochastic search. Results are very promising. The method can find very accurate solutions

Number of Components	2% Noise						5% Noise					
	Spectrum error			Composition error			Spectrum error			Composition error		
	Worst	Avg.	Best	Worst	Avg.	Best	Worst	Avg.	Best	Worst	Avg.	Best
6	7.4	4.6	1.7	0.1	0.06	0.03	10.1	5.5	1.9	0.3	0.1	0.06
8	9.2	5.1	1.0	0.13	0.05	0.03	11.2	6.2	1.3	0.18	0.12	0.06
12	11.3	7.4	1.0	0.15	0.08	0.05	13.3	8.4	2.0	0.21	0.18	0.06
16	12.8	7.7	1.0	0.19	0.08	0.04	13.8	8.6	2.0	0.22	0.16	0.05

Table 2. *These results are for the same problem as in the first half of Table 1, but with 2% and 5% noise added. See text for further details.*

to large hard noisy problems, and appears to be general. It is conceptually simpler than the standard methods used and does not appear to suffer from the problems that plague many of these methods (unreliable solutions for certain classes of problem, or solutions that are di cult to interpret).

As already mentioned, an alternative normalised encoding was also tried. However, empirical evidence showed that the results were a little worse with this alternative decoding scheme. Importantly, very good results were only achieved for both encodings as long as a coupled mutation operator was used. Hence, the heuristically motivated coupled mutation appears to be a key issue in the success of the approach described. Future work will tackle problems where the number of constituents are not known in advance.

ACK.: This work was supported by grants from FAPESP (96/7200-8), The British Council (SPA/126/881) and CNPq (300.465/95-5). We thank P.Bargo for conversations on spectroscopy and M.T.Pacheco for suggesting the problem.

References

1. J. J. Baraga. PhD thesis, Massachusetts Institute of Technology, 1992.
2. R. Collins and D. Je˜erson. Selection in massively parallel genetic algorithms. In R. K. Belew and L. B. Booker, editors, *Proceedings of the Fourth Intl. Conf. on Genetic Algorithms, ICGA-91*, pages 249 256. Morgan Kaufmann, 1991.
3. Galactic Industries Corporation. *http://www.galactic.com/galactic/Science/algo.htm*. Web Site, 1996.
4. C. Kappler, T. Back, J. Heistermann, A.V. Velde, and M. Zamparelli. Refueling of a nuclear power plant: Comparison of a naive and a specialized mutation operator. In *Proc. of PPSN IV*, volume LNCS, 1141, pages 829 838. Springer, 1996.
5. J. Koza. *Genetic Programming: On the programming of computers by means of natural selection*. MIT Press, 1992.
6. E.H. Malinowski and D.G. Howery. *Factor Analysis in Chemistry*. John Wiley, 1980.
7. H. Mark. *Analytical Chemistry*, 58:2814, 1986.
8. W. Press, W. Vetterling, S. Teukolsky, and B. Flannery. *Numerical recipes in C (2/e)*. CUP, 1992.

Evolutionary Recognition of Features from CAD Data

Yasuhiro Tsujimura and Mitsuo Gen

Department of Industrial and Information Systems Engg.
Ashikaga Institute of Technology
268-1 Ohmae-cho, Ashikaga 326-8558, Japan
Phone: +81(284)62-0605 Fax: +81(284)64-107
E-mail: tujimr@ashitech.ac.jp

Abstract. This paper proposes a method based on evolutionary computation for recognizing features of CAD data. Feature-based chromosome scheme is developed in which its locus corresponds to two features of CAD data provided by using the Boundary Representation method. The e ciency of the proposed method is shown through experimental results.

Keywords. CALS (Continuous Acquisition and Lifecycle Support), Evolutionary Computation, CAD (Computer Aided Design), Boundary Representation Method

1 Introduction

Recently, a lot of companies integrate CAD/CAM system to enhance the product quality and productivity, and to reduce overall product life cycle cost. However, practical CAD data are usually very large and complex, so integration of a CAD/CAM system to a practical production system is very di cult due to a di culty to store such large actual CAD data in a computer system.

To eliminate the di culty, possible common data in all the CAD data are shared. Sharing common data among the large number of CAD data can reduce amount of whole the CAD data. The common data to be shared can be obtained by recognizing features of the CAD data, *i.e.*, the common data are the features themselves. Such a feature recognition problem can be stated as a combinatorial optimization problem, which must consider huge number of combinations [1].

In this paper, we propose a method to recognize features from CAD data using *Evolutionary Computation* (EC) for sharing CAD information [2][3]. In the proposed method, we employ the *Boundary Representation method* to develop feature-based representation scheme. This scheme is based on two kinds of information derived from CAD data by using the Boundary Representation method, and is developed as a suitable one for recognizing the features of CAD data. Furthermore, the e ciency of the proposed method is demonstrated using some simplified CAD data.

2   Boundary Representation of Solid Model

The solid model shown in Figure 1 can be illustrated as Table 1 by using the Boundary Representation method [4]-[6]. The values of *Face Type* (FT) and *Edge Type* (ET) in Table 1 are given by Table 2. *Neighboring Face Loop* (NFL) represents the relationship between the face and neighboring faces.

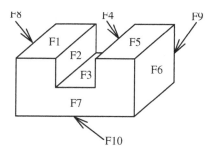

Fig. 1. Solid model

Table 1. Illustration of solid model using Boundary Representation

Face	FT	n_E	NFL (ET)	FS
F1	1	4	F7(1) - F8(1) - F9(1) - F2(1)	1.0
F2	1	4	F7(1) - F1(1) - F9(1) - F3(1)	1.5
F3	1	4	F7(1) - F2(1) - F9(1) - F4(1)	2.0
F4	1	4	F7(1) - F4(1) - F9(1) - F5(1)	1.5
F5	1	4	F7(1) - F5(1) - F9(1) - F6(1)	1.0
F6	1	4	F7(1) - F5(1) - F9(1) - F10(1)	1.0
F7	1	8	F1(1) - F8(1) - F10(1)- F6(1) - F5(1) - F4(1) - F3(1) - F2(1)	1.0
F8	1	4	F7(1) - F1(1) - F9(1) - F10(1)	1.0
F9	1	8	F1(1) - F2(1) - F3(1) - F4(1) - F5(1) - F6(1) - F10(1)- F8(1)	1.0
F10	1	4	F7(1) - F5(1) - F9(1) - F5(1)	1.0

Table 2. Types of Face and Edge

Face	Type	Edge	Type
Plane	1	Straight	1
Cylinder	2	Ellipse	2
Cone	3	Circle	3
Torus	4		
Sphere	5		

Face Score (FS) is used to measure the face complexity based upon the convexity or concavity of the solid model. Face Score can be calculated by equation (1), where *Average Edge Score* (AES) is given by equation (2), and *Angle Score* (AS) is the score of edge for its angle (see Figures 2 and 3).

$$FS = 12 * (ET * AS) + AES \tag{1}$$

$$AES = \frac{\sum (ET * AS)}{n_E} \tag{2}$$

where n_E is the number of edges.

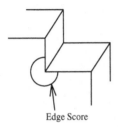

Edge Score

Fig. 2. Concept of Edge Score

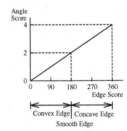

Fig. 3. Illustration of Angle Score

3 Evolutionary Computation Approach

3.1 Chromosome Representation and Initialization

When comparing the target model with a reference model, we must consider all combinations of faces between the target and reference models. In this paper, to deal with such numerous combinations, we use the *random key representation* for encoding [7]. The random key representation encodes a solution with *random numbers.*

The allele tackles a random decimal number from an open interval (0,1). Here, the allele is only used as keys for sorting in descending order. The locus corresponds to two features: FS of each face and the *Average Face Score* (AFS) of NFL (see equation (3)).

$$AFS = \frac{\sum FS \text{ of Neighboring Face}}{The \text{ Number of Neighboring Face}} \tag{3}$$

For example, the solid model shown in Figure 1 can be coded into the feature-based chromosome shown in Figure 4. In Figure 4, the reference list can be obtained by sorting the keys of these features in descending order. The reference list is compared with every reference model stored in database on both FS and

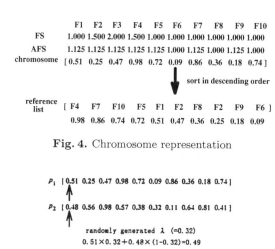

Fig. 4. Chromosome representation

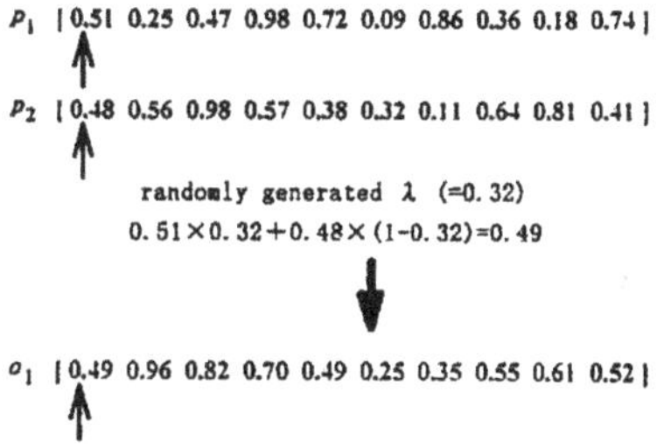

Fig. 5. An example of crossover operation

AFS of NFL, and then one of the reference models which matches the most can be obtained.

The number of genes is as many as the number of faces. Various chromosomes can prepare various orders for comparing the target model with a reference model.

In the initialization phase, *pop_size* (the population size) chromosomes are generated randomly as the initial population.

3.2   Crossover

The *arithmetical crossover* [7] is employed as crossover operator. The arithmetical crossover is defined as a convex combination of two vector. If the constraint set is convex, this operation ensures that children are feasible if both parents are feasible. For a pair of parents p_1 and p_2, the crossover operator can produce two offspring o_1 and o_2 as follows:

$$o_1 = \quad \times p_1 + (1 - \quad) \times p_2$$
$$o_2 = \quad \times p_2 + (1 - \quad) \times p_1$$

where   is randomly generated from (0,1). An example is shown in Figure 5. Note that we choose two chromosomes, which have same length, as the parents.

Changing p_1 and p_2 each other, the other offspring o_2 can be obtained by applying the same manner.

3.3   Mutation

Mutation is designed to perform the *swapping mutation* [7], *i.e.*, it selects two genes randomly in a chromosome and exchanges their positions. An example is shown in Figure 6.

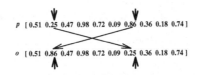

Fig. 6. An example of mutation operation

3.4   Evaluation and Selection

A chromosome (a target solid model) is evaluated by comparing its FS and AFS lists with ones of a reference solid model. If the length of two lists (the number of faces) of the target solid model is different from one of the reference solid model, add dummy variables to the shorter FS and AFS lists to make the lengths of all the lists equal. An example of this adjustment is shown in Figure 7.

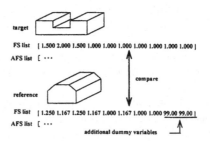

Fig. 7. Adjustment of the lengths of FS and AFS lists

The evolution is controlled by the following evaluation function.

$$Sfs_i = |Rfs_i - Tfs_i| \tag{4}$$

$$Safs_i = |Rafs_i - Tafs_i| \tag{5}$$

$$= \sum_{i=1}^{n_F} S_i \tag{6}$$

$$S_i = \begin{cases} 1 \; ; \; _1 > Sfs_i \text{ and } \; _2 > Safs_i \\ 0 \; ; \text{Both } Sfs_i \text{ and } Safs_i \text{ are dummy variables,} \\ \quad \text{or } (\; _1 \leq Sfs_i \text{ or } \; _2 \leq Safs_i) \end{cases}$$

$$i = 1, 2, \ldots, n_F$$

where Rfs_i is the FS of face i for reference solid models, Tfs_i is the FS of face i for target solid models, $Rafs_i$ is the AFS of face i in NFL for reference solid models, $Tafs_i$ is the AFS of face i in NFL for target solid model,   is the total agreement degree, n_F is the number of faces, and $_1$, $_2$ are threshold values. The total agreement degree   is used as the fitness of a chromosome, and the *roulette wheel approach* [7] is employed at the selection phase.

4   Numerical Experiments

4.1   Experiment 1

In order to verify the basic ability of the proposed method, we tested our method by recognizing a target solid model given in Figure 8 among the reference models shown in Figure 9. There are 6 reference models, and all of them have the same number of faces as the target model $(n_F = 10)$.

The parameters for genetic algorithm, which are the experimentally best tuned values, are set as: population size $pop\_size = 5$, maximum generation $maxgen = 1000$, crossover rate $p_c = 0.2$, mutation rate $p_m = 0.7$, and the threshold values $_1 = 0.1$, $_2 = 0.15$. To verify the robustness of the proposed method, we used such a small population size $(=5)$, even though it restricts the performance of the method.

The result is summarized in Table 3, where the result is obtained by averaging results among 100 runs. In Table 3, a reference model D was recognized as the fittest one with high frequency in 100 runs. Table 3 also includes the results obtained by using EC employing only FS in the evaluation phase.

4.2   Experiment 2

We tested our method using more complex problem, *i.e.*, recognizing a target solid model among the 16 reference models given in Figure 10.

The evolutionary parameters were set as follows: population size $pop\_size = 20$, maximum generation $maxgen = 5000$, crossover rate $p_c = 0.5$, mutation rate $p_m = 0.7$, and the threshold values $_1 = 0.1$, $_2 = 0.15$. We prepared 16 solid models (A∼P) shown in Figure 10. One solid model among the 16 models

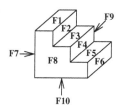

Fig. 8. Target solid model

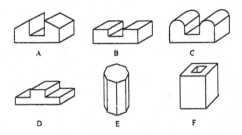

Fig. 9. Reference models

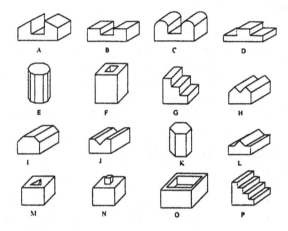

Fig. 10. 16 solid models for the Numerical Experiment

was used as the target model, and the remaining 15 models were used as the reference models. Every A~P models were used as the target.

The results were summarized in Table 4, where each result was obtained as the average among 100 runs. This table shows that the proposed EC-based method could recognize the appropriate model(s) with high probability in most cases.

5   Conclusions

In this paper, we proposed the new feature recognition method of CAD data using EC. And we demonstrated the effectiveness of the proposed method through an experimental result.

The result showed a good ability of our method for feature recognition. For feature study, we will improve the proposed method to deal with more complex solid models.

Table 3. Results of recognition (1)

Result	Using FS and AFS			Using only FS		
	Frequency	Average Fitness	Average Generation	Frequency	Average Fitness	Average Generation
B	24/100	7.00	946.79	-	-	-
D	76/100	8.00	27.25	100/100	10.00	44.56

Table 4. Results of recognition (2)

Target (n_F)	Result (n_F)	Frequency	Average Fitness	Average Generation
A(10)	B(10)	96/100	8.00	413.906
	H(9)	4/100	8.00	94.000
B(10)	P(12)	56/100	8.00	201.964
	A(10)	23/100	8.00	461.783
	G(10)	19/100	8.00	300.579
	J(8)	2/100	7.00	22.500
C(10)	none			
D(10)	H(9)	100/100	7.00	44.280
E(10)	I(8)	100/100	7.00	17.220
F(10)	M(9)	100/100	6.00	51.280
G(10)	P(12)	100/100	10.00	353.190
H(9)	K(8)	53/100	7.00	25.566
	D(10)	42/100	7.00	42.500
	G(10)	3/100	7.00	21.330
	A(10)	1/100	7.00	5.000
	L(8)	1/100	7.00	10.000
I(8)	K(8)	100/100	8.00	75.160
J(8)	K(8)	88/100	7.00	37.318
	B(10)	12/100	7.00	27.583
K(8)	I(8)	100/100	8.00	72.740
L(8)	G(10)	60/100	7.00	277.217
	P(12)	23/100	7.00	287.348
	F(10)	17/100	7.00	154.000
M(9)	F(10)	100/100	6.00	28.310
N(11)	none			
O(11)	none			
P(12)	G(10)	100/100	10.00	134.900

References

1. Chu-Chai Henry Chan: *Artificial Neural-Network-Based Feature Recognition and Grammar-Based Feature Extraction to Integrate Design and Manufacturing*, Ph.D Disser.. Univ. of Iowa. 1994.
2. Yasuhiro Tsujimura. Mitsuo Gen and Masaki Hiji: Feature Recognition of CAD Data Using Evolutionary Computation, *Proc. of 1997 Spring Meeting of JIMA*, pp.164-165. 1997.(in Japanese)
3. Yasuhiro Tsujimura. Mitsuo Gen and Masaki Hiji: Evolutionary Feature Recognition of CAD Data Employing Boundary Representation Method, *Proc. of Third International Symposium on Artificial Life, and Robotics*, pp.39-42, 1998.
4. Nikkei CG ed.: *New Foundation of CAD*, Nikkei BP, 1996.(in Japanese)
5. Mamoru Hosaka and Toshio Sata: *Integrated CAD/CAM System*, Ohm Pub., 1994.(in Japanese)
6. Yukinori Kakazu and Masasi Furukawa: *Shape Disposal Engineering for CAD/CAM/CG*. Morikita Pub., 1995.(in Japanese)
7. Mitsuo Gen and Runwei Cheng: *Genetic Algorithms and Engineering Design*, John Wiley & Sons, New York, 1997.

Modeling Strategies as Generous and Greedy in Prisoner's Dilemma Like Games

Stefan Johansson[1], Bengt Carlsson[1], and Magnus Boman[2]

[1] Department of Computer Science and Business Administration, University of Karlskrona/Ronneby, Soft Center, SE-372 25 Ronneby, Sweden
email {sja, bca}@ide.hk-r.se
[2] Department of Computer and Systems Sciences, Stockholm University and the Royal Institute of Technology, Electrum 230, SE-164 40 Kista, Sweden
email mab@dsv.su.se

Abstract. Four di˜erent prisoner s dilemma and associated games were studied by running a round robin as well as a population tournament, using 15 di˜erent strategies. The results were analyzed in terms of definitions of generous, even-matched, and greedy strategies. In the round robin, prisoner s dilemma favored greedy strategies. Chicken game and coordinate game were favoring generous strategies, and compromise dilemma the even-matched strategy Anti Tit-for-Tat. These results were not surprising because all strategies used were fully dependent on the mutual encounters, not the actual payo˜ values of the game. A population tournament is a zero-sum game balancing generous and greedy strategies. When strategies disappear, the population will form a new balance between the remaining strategies. A winning strategy in a population tournament has to do well against itself because there will be numerous copies of that strategy. A winning strategy must also be good at resisting invasion from other competing strategies. These restrictions make it natural to look for winning strategies among originally generous or even-matched strategies. For three of the games, this was found true, with original generous strategies being most successful. The most diverging result was that compromise dilemma, despite its close relationship to prisoner s dilemma, had two greedy strategies almost entirely dominating the population tournament.

Keywords: games, simulations, evolutionary stable strategies

1 Introduction

In multi agent systems the concept of game theory is widely in use. There has been a lot of research in distributed negotiation [10], market oriented programming [21], autonomous agents [19] and, evolutionary game theory [13] [14].

The evolution of cooperative behavior among self-interested agents has received attention among researchers in political science, economics and evolutionary biology. In these disciplines, it has been used from a social science point of view to explain observed cooperation, while in multi agent systems (MAS) it may be used to try to create systems with a predicted cooperative behavior. In section 2 we look at prisoner's dilemma like games and the Tit-for-Tat (*TfT*) strategy.

In evolutionary game theory [16], the focus has been on evolutionary stable strategies (ESS). The agent exploits its knowledge about its own payoffs, but no background information or common knowledge is assumed. An evolutionary game repeats each move, or sequence of moves, without a memory. In many MAS, however, agents frequently use knowledge about other agents. We look at three different ways of describing ESSs and compare them to MAS. Firstly we treat the ESS as a Nash equilibrium of different strategies. A Nash equilibrium describes a set of chosen strategies where no agent unilaterally wishes to change its choice. In MAS, some knowledge about the other agents should be accessible when simulating the outcome of strategies. This knowledge (e.g., the payoff matrix of another agent, and the knowledge that it maximises its expected utility) makes it hard to predict the outcome of the actual con"ict. Instead of having a single prediction we end up with allowing almost any strategy. This is a consequence of the so-called Folk Theorem (see, e.g., [9], [14]).

A game can be modeled as a strategic or an extensive game. The former is a model of a situation in which each agent choose a plan of action once and for all, and all agents' decisions are made simultaneously while the latter specifies the possible orders of events. All the agents in this paper use strategic strategies, which we classify as generous, even-matched, or greedy. In section 3 the outcomes for 15 different strategies are shown as an example of our classification.

Secondly the ESS can be described as a collection of successful strategies, given a population of different strategies. An ESS is a strategy in the sense that if all the members of a population adopt it, then no mutant strategy can invade the population under the in"uence of natural selection. In an evolutionary context, we can therefore simply calculate how successful an agent will be. The problem is that this is not the same as finding a successful strategy in an iterated game because in this game the agents are supposed to know the history of the moves. Instead of finding the best one, we can try to find a possibly sub-optimal but robust strategy in a specific environment, and this strategy may eventually be an ESS. In section 4 a round robin tournament is held for prisoner's dilemma like games to see what kind of strategy that will do best and population tournaments illustrate what succesful combinations there are.

Thirdly the ESS can be seen as a collection of evolved successful strategies. It is possible to simulate a game through a process of two crucial steps: mutation (changes in the ways agents act) and selection (choice of the preferred strategies). Different kinds of evolutionary computations (see e.g., [11], [12]) have been applied within the MAS society, but the similarities to biology are restricted.[1] In section 5 we introduce noise and the agents become uncertain about the outcome of the game, even if they have complete knowledge about the context.

---

[1] Firstly, EC, use a "tness function instead of using dominating and recessive genes. Secondly, there is a crossover between parents instead of the meiotic crossover.

2   Prisoner's dilemma like games

Prisoner's dilemma [15], [17] was originally formulated as a paradox (in the sense of that of Allais and Ellsberg) where the cooperatively preferable solution for both agents, low punishment, was not chosen. The reason is that the first agent did not know what the second agent intended to do, so he had to guard himself. The paradox lies in the fact that both agents had to accept a high penalty in spite of that cooperation is a better solution for both of them.

The one-choice prisoner's dilemma has one dominant strategy, play defect. If the game is iterated there will be other dominating strategies because the agents have background information about previous moves. The iterated prisoner's dilemma (IPD) is generally viewed as the major game-theoretical paradigm for the evolution of cooperation based on reciprocity.

When Axelrod and Hamilton [4], [3] analyzed the iterated prisoner's dilemma they found that the cooperating *TfT* strategy did very well against more defecting strategies. All agents are interested in maximizing individual utilities and are not pre-disposed to help each other. If an agent cooperates this is not because of an undirected altruism but because of a reciprocal altruism [20] favoring a selfish agent. The *TfT* strategy has become an informal guiding principle for reciprocal altruism [1], [2].

Binmore [5] gives a critical review of the *TfT* strategy and of Axelrod's simulation. He concludes that *TfT* is only one of a very large number of equilibrium strategies and that *TfT* is not evolutionarily stable. On the other hand evolutionary pressures will tend to select equilibrium for the IPD in which the agents cooperate in the long run. In the next section we will look at an alternative interpretation.

3   A simulation example

In a simulation we used the proportions of (C,C), (C,D), (D,C) and (D,D) to analyze the successfulness of a strategy. We have developed a simulation tool in which we let 15 different strategies meet each other The different strategies are described in [7].

The tournament was conducted in a round robin way so that each strategy was paired with each other strategy plus its own twin and a play random strategy. Each game in the tournament was played on average 100 times (randomly stopped) and repeated 5000 times. The outcomes are shown in figure 1 below where the percentage of (C,C), (C,D), (D,C) and (D,D) for each strategy is shown. We will use the proportions of (C,C), (C,D), (D,C) and (D,D) as fingerprints for the strategy in the given environment, independent of the payoff matrix. For some of the strategies this is true without any doubts: Always Cooperate (*AllC*) and Always Defect (*AllD*) have 100 per cent cooperate (C,C)+(C,D) and 100 per cent defect (D,C)+(D,D) respectively. It is possible to look at how the proportions of (C,D) compared to (D,C) form different groups of strategies. *TfT* begins with cooperate and then does the same move as the

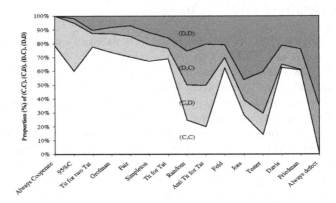

Fig. 1. Proportions of (C,C), (C,D), (D,C) and (D,D) for di˘erent strategies.

other player did last time. This means that (C,D)≈(D,C) for all payoff matrices so the actual values do not matter. It is possible to treat the other strategies the same way because none of them re"ect upon their actual payoff value. We will instead describe the strategies as generous, even-matched or greedy.

1. A generous strategy cooperates more than its partners do. This means that (C,D)>(D,C) i.e. it is betrayed more often than it plays defection against a cooperate agent itself.
2. An even-matched strategy has (C,D)≈(D,C). This group includes the *TfT* strategy, always doing the same as the other strategy.
3. A greedy strategy defects more than its partners do. This means (C,D)<(D,C), i.e., the opposite to a generous strategy.

The basis of the subdivision above is a zero-sum play. The sum of the strategies (C,D) must equal the sum of the strategies (D,C), i.e., if there is a generous strategy there must also be a greedy strategy. The classification of a strategy can change depending on the surrounding strategies. Theoretically a lot of changes are possible making a generous strategy become an even-matched or a greedy strategy, or doing it in a reverse order. What will happen with a particular strategy depends both of the surrounding and the character of the strategy. As an example *AllC* will always be generous while *95%C* will change to a greedy strategy when there are only these two strategies left.

4   Simulating four different games

If we let the letters k, l, m and n be the payoffs for (C,C), (C,D), (D,C) and (D,D) respectively in a symmetric game, the average payoff for a strategy $E_{avg}(strategy)$ is a function of the payoff matrix and the distribution of the payoffs among the four outcomes.

$$E_{avg}(strategy) = p(C,C)k + p(C,D)l + p(D,C)m + p(D,D)n, \qquad (1)$$

$$where\ p(C,C) + p(C,D) + p(D,C) + p(D,D) = 1 \qquad (2)$$

The aim of the simulation is to test how different games behave in a round robin tournament and in a population tournament. We used four different games, prisoner's dilemma (PD), chicken game, coordination game and compromise dilemma games to illustrate the distributions among different strategies (see figure 2). Additional information about the results of the simulations, definitions of the strategies, etc. can be found in [6]. It holds for all the games that (D,D) has

Prisoner's dilemma			Chicken Game			Coordination Game			Compr. Dilemma		
	C	D		C	D		C	D		C	D
	3, 3	0, 4	C	3, 3	1, 4	C	2, 2	0, 0	C	2, 2	2, 3
0, 0	1, 1		D	3, 2	1, 1						

Fig. 2. Payo˘ matrices for prisoner s dilemma, chicken game, coordination game and compromise dilemma.

a lower payoff value than (C,C) and for three of the games that (D,C) has the highest value. In an earlier paper we have examined the differences between PD and chicken game [8]. Compromise dilemma is closely related to chicken game. Coordination game is a game with two dominating strategies, playing (C,C) or playing (D,D). Rapoport and Guyer [18] give a more detailed description of possible 2×2 games.

We ran a round robin tournament with the 15 strategies for the four different games described in figure 2[2]. The greedy strategies *Davis* and *Friedman* are doing well in PD while chicken game and coordinate game favor the generous strategies *AllC* and *Fair* respectively *Tf2T*. Compromise dilemma favored the counter intuitive strategy *ATfT*. In our classification *TfT* is regarded as an even-matched strategy. There is no reason for believing PD to favor more generous strategies than the rest of the games. Finding successful greedy strategies is well in line with the hypothesis that PD, because of the given payoff matrices, is the least cooperative game from the generous strategies point of view. The chicken game is less greedy than PD because it costs more to play defect (0 instead of 1 in the (D,D) case). The most successful strategies *AllC* and *Fair* are both generous. The coordinate game has the highest payoff value for (C,C), but it also has a dominating (D,D) value. The generous *Tf2T* is doing the best but the greedy strategies *Davis* and *Friedman* are also doing well compared to the other games. *Random* and *ATfT*, two strategies with a big proportion of (C,D)+(D,C) are doing very poorly in this game.In compromise dilemma (C,D)+(D,C) have

---

[2] For a full description of the strategies, see [7]

high scores which favor the two even-matched strategies *Random* and *ATfT*[3]. *ATfT* has the biggest proportion of (C,D)+(D,C) making it a winning strategy.

In a population tournament different strategies compete until there is only one strategy left or until the number of generations exceed 10.000. Because of changes in the distribution of strategies between different generations it is not possible to rely on previous descriptions of the strategies. A generous strategy can for example be greedy under certain circumstances. On average it must hold that there is the same amount of greedy strategies as generous ones, forming the even-matched strategies at the position of equilibrium. The population tournament was run 100 times for the four different games. It took between 2100 (compromise dilemma) and 3400 (chicken game) on average to find a winner in the game. At most a single strategy can win all the 100 times, but in our simulation different strategies won different runs. In all, five strategies were not winning a single game namely: *95%C*, *ATfT*, *Feld*, *Joss* and *Tester*. For the compromise dilemma, despite the fact that *ATfT* was the winner in the round robin tournament, the strategy did not win a single game in the population tournament. In the prisoners dilemma there is a change towards the originally more generous strategies *Tf2T* and *Grofman*. This is also true for the coordinate game, which also favors *AllC*, just as in the round robin tournament. For the chicken game the same generous strategies are doing well as in the PD and the coordinate game. The most surprising result is the almost total dominance of two greedy strategies, *Davis* and *Friedman* in compromise dilemma. Both strategies have a large proportion of (D,C) compared to (C,D) in the original round robin tournament. We also found the generous strategies to be more stable in the chicken game part of the matrix.

5   Noisy environment

In the next simulation, we introduced noise on four levels: 0.01, 0.1, 1 and 10%. This means that the strategies change to the opposite move for this given percentage.

In compromise dilemma *Friedman*, a greedy strategy dominates the population when the noise is 1% or below. *ATfT* is the second best strategy and together with *Fair* and *AllD* replace *Friedman* with 10% noise. Unlike the rest of the games there is a mixture of strategies winning each play for 0.1 to 10% noise.

Two greedy strategies are doing well in PD with none or a small level of noise. *Davis* is doing well without noise and *Friedman* with 0.01% noise. *Simpleton*, a generous strategy, is dominating the population when the noise is 0.1% or more.

In chicken game three generous strategies, *Tf2T*, *Grofman* and *Simpleton* are almost entirely dominating the population under noisy conditions. With increasing noise *Tf2T* first disappears then *Grofman* disappears leaving *Simpleton* as a single dominating strategy at 10% noise.

---

[3] Neither of the strategies do have to be even-matched, it depends on the actual surroundings.

Finally in coordination game three generous strategies, *AllC*, *Tf2T* and *Grofman* are winning almost all the games when noise is introduced. With 10% noise *AllC* wins all the games.

6 Conclusions

We investigated four different PD like games in a round robin tournament and a population tournament. The results were analyzed using our classification of generous, even-matched and greedy strategies.

In the round robin tournament we found PD being the game which favored greedy strategy the most. The chicken game and the coordinate game were favoring generous strategies and compromise dilemma even-matched strategies. These results are not consistent with the common idea of treating the PD as the most important cooperating iterated game. We do not find these results surprising because all the used strategies are fully dependent on the mutual meetings.

A more interesting investigation is to figure out what happens in a population tournament. If a strategy is generous, even-matched or greedy it is so only in a particular surrounding and will possibly change when the strategies change. A winning strategy in a population tournament has to do well against itself because there will be lots of copies of that strategy. A winning strategy must also be good at resisting invasion from other competing strategies otherwise it will be impossible to become a single winner.

These restrictions in a population tournament make it natural to look for winning strategies among originally generous or even-matched (i.e. *TfT*) strategies. For three of the games, the PD, the chicken game and the coordination game, this is true with *Tf2T* and *Grofman* winning a big proportion of population games. Contrary to what was advocated by Axelrod and others, *TfT* was not among the most successful strategies.

The most divergent result was that compromise dilemma had two greedy strategies, *Davis* and *Friedman*, almost entirely dominating the population tournament. Both *Davis* and *Friedman* are favoring playing defect against a cooperate agent but unlike *AllD* they are also able to play cooperate against a cooperate agent. Despite a close relationship to the PD, the compromise dilemma finds other, more greedy, successful strategies.

When noise was introduced to the games, chicken game and coordinating game almost entirely favored generous strategies. In PD and even more in compromise dilemma the greedy, *Friedman* strategy was doing well.

We think these results can be explained by looking at the original game matrices. For chicken game (D,D) is doing the worst, favoring generous strategies. Coordination game gives (C,C) the highest results which outscores greedy strategies. PD is, compared to chicken game, less punishing towards (D,D) which allows greedy strategies to become more successful. In compromise dilemma (C,D) and (D,C) have the best scores making a balance between different strategies possible.

Like ESS this description of MAS, as a competition between generous and greedy strategies, tries to find robust strategies that are able to resist invasion by other strategies. It is not possible to find a single best strategy that wins, but it is possible to tell what kinds of strategies which will be successful.

References

1. R. Axelrod. E˜ective choice in the prisoner s dilemma. *Journal of Conflict Resolution*, 24(1):379 403, 1980.
2. R. Axelrod. More e˜ective choice in the prisoner s dilemma. *Journal of Conflict Resolution*, 24(3):3 25, 1980.
3. R. Axelrod. *The Evolution of Cooperation*. Basic Books Inc., 1984.
4. R. Axelrod and Hamilton W.D. The evolution of cooperation. *Science*, 211, 1981.
5. K. Binmore. *Playing Fair: game theory and the social contract*. MIT Press, 1994.
6. B. Carlsson. Evolutionary models in multi-agent systems. Licentiate thesis, Lund University, Department of Cognitive Studies, 1998.
7. B. Carlsson and S.J. Johansson. Generous and greedy strategies. In *Proceedings of Complex Systems '98*, 1998.
8. B. Carlsson and S.J. Johansson. An iterated hawk-and-dove game. In Pagnucco, M. Wobcke, W. and Zhang, C., editors, *Agents and Multi-Agent Systems*, volume 1441 of *Lecture Notes in Artificial Intelligence*, pages 25 37. Springer Verlag, 1998.
9. D. Fudenberg and E. Maskin. The folk theorem in repeated games with discounting or with incomplete information. *Econometrica*, 80(2):274 279, 1986.
10. M.R. Genesereth, M.L. Ginsberg, and J.S. Rosenschein. Cooperation without communication. In Bond and Gasser, editors, *Distributed Artificial Intelligence*, pages 220 226. Kaufmann, 1988.
11. D.E. Goldberg. *Genetic Algorithms*. Addison-Wesley, 1989.
12. J.R. Koza. *Genetic Programming: On the Programming of Computers by Means of Natural Selection*. MIT Press, 1992.
13. K. Lindgren. Evolutionary phenomena in simple dynamics. In Farmer, J. D. Langton, C. G., Taylor, C. and Rasmussen, S., editors, *Artificial life II*. Addison Wesley, 1991.
14. B. Lomborg. Game theory vs. multiple agents: The iterated prisoner s dilemma. In Castefranchi, C. and Werner, E., editors, *Artificial Social Systems*, volume 830 of *Lecture Notes in Artificial Intelligence*. Springer Verlag, 1994.
15. R.D. Luce and H. Rai˜a. *Games and Decisions*. Dover Publications, 1957.
16. J. Maynard Smith. *Evolution and the theory of games*. Cambridge University Press, 1982.
17. A. Rapoport and A.M. Chammah. *Prisoner's Dilemma A Study in Conflict and Cooperation*. The University of Michigan Press, 1965.
18. A. Rapoport and M. Guyer. A taxonomy of 2×2 games. In *Yearbook of the Society for General Systems Research*, pages 203 214. 1966.
19. J.S. Rosenschein and G. Zlotkin. *Rules of Encounter*. MIT Press, 1994.
20. R.L. Trivers. The evolution of reciprocal altruism. *Quarterly Review of Biology*, 46:35 57, 1971.
21. M.A. Wellman. A computational market model for distributed con"guration design. In *Proceedings of AAAI '94*. Morgan-Kaufman, 1994.

Using Genetic Algorithms to Simulate the Evolution of an Oligopoly Game[*]

Shu-Heng Chen[1] and Chih-Chi Ni[2]

[1] AI-ECON Research Group
Department of Economics
National Chengchi University
Taipei, Taiwan 11623
E-mail: chchen@cc.nccu.edu.tw
[2] AI-ECON Research Group
Department of Economics
National Chengchi University
Taipei, Taiwan 11623
E-mail: g2258503@grad.cc.nccu.edu.tw

Abstract. This paper extends the N-person IPD game into a more interesting game in economics, namely, the *oligopoly game*. Due to its market share dynamics, the oligopoly game is more complicated and is in general not an exact N-person IPD game. Using genetic algroithms, we simulated the oligopoly games under various settings. It is found that, even in the case of a three-oligopolist (three-player) game, collusive pricing (cooperation) is not the dominating result.
Keywords: Oligopoly, Cartels, Price Wars, Genetic Algorithms, State-Dependent Markov Chain, Coevolution.

1   Motivation and Introduction

In the past, the *prisoner s dilemma* was frequently applied to the study of *collusive pricing* or *predatory pricing*. However, this application is largely restricted to the *duopoly* industry because most economists are only familar with the 2-person *Iterated Prisoner s Dilemma* (IPD) game. In terms of the *oligopoly* industry, the more relevant one should be the *n-person IPD game*, which economists are less familiar with. Recently, the n-person IPD game was studied in Yao and Darwen (1994). Using *genetic algorithms* (GAs), they showed that *cooperation can still be evolved in a large group, but that it is more di cult to evolve cooperation as the group size increases.* Considering this result as a guideline for the oligopoly pricing probelm, then what the n-person IPD game tells us is that *when the number of oligopolists is small, say 3, it is very likely to see the emergence of collusive*

---

[*] This is a revised version of a paper presented at *The Second Asia-Pacific Conference on Simulated Evolution and Learning* in Canberra, Australia, 24-27 November, 1998. The authors thanks two anonymous referees for helpful comments. Research support from NSC grant NSC. 86-2415-H-004-022 is also gratefully acknowledged.

pricing (cooperation). However, real data usually shows that, even in a three-oligopolist industry, the observed pricing pattern is not that simple. (Midgely, Marks and Cooper, 1996)

- First, while collusive pricing is frequently observed, it is continually interrupte by the occurence of predatory pricing (price wars).
- Second, it is not always true that oligopolists are either *collectively* charging high prices (collusive pricing) or low prices (price wars). In fact, a dispersion of prices can persistently exist, i.e., some firms are charging a higher price, whilst others are charging a lower price.
- Third, the firms who charge a high price may switch to a low price in a later stage, and vice versa.

These features seem to be di cult to be displayed in 3-person IPD games (See Yao and Darwen,ibid, Figure 5). Therefore, one may reasonably conject that *the oligopoly game is not an exact n-person IPD game*. While they share some common features, there are other essential elements which distinguish these two games.

In this paper, we consider the payoff matrix determined by *the market share dynamics* as such an essential element. In Section 2, we propose a very simple oligopoly game with 3 oligopolists. We then in Section 3 show that this setup disqualify the oligopoly game from being an n-person IPD game. Due to the non-equivalence of these two games, we use genetic algrothims to simulate the evolution of oligopoly games in Sections 4 and 5. The simulation results are given in Section 5, followed by concluding remarks in Section 6.

2   The Analytical Model

For simplicity, an oligopoly industry is assumed to consist of three firms, say $i = 1, 2, 3$. At each period, a firm can either charge a high price P_h or a low price P_l. Let a_i^t be the action taken by firm i at time t. $a_i^t = 1$ if the firm i charges P_h and $a_i^t = 0$ if it charges P_l. To simplify notations, let S_t denote the row vector (a_1^t, a_2^t, a_3^t). To characterize the price competition among firms, the *market share dynamics* of these three firms are summarized by the following *time-variant state-dependent Markov transition matrix*,

$$M_t = \begin{bmatrix} m_{11}^t & m_{12}^t & m_{13}^t \\ m_{21}^t & m_{22}^t & m_{23}^t \\ m_{31}^t & m_{32}^t & m_{33}^t \end{bmatrix} \tag{1}$$

where m_{ij}^t, the transition probability from state i to state j, denotes the proportion of the customers of firm i switching to firm j at time period t. Let n_i^t (i=1,2,3) be the number of customers of firm i at time period t, and N_t the row vector $[n_1^t, n_2^t, n_3^t]$. Without loss of generality, we assume that each consumer will purchase only one unit of the commodity. In this case, N_t is also the vector of quantities consumed. With N_t and M_t, the customers of each firm at period $t+1$ can be updated by:

$$N_{t+1} = N_t M_t \tag{2}$$

To see the effect of price competition on the market share dynamics, the transition probabilities m_{ij}^t are assumed to be dependent on the pricing strategy vector S_t. If three firms charge the same price, then M_t is an *identity matrix*. Furthermore, if firm i charges P_h, then it will lose $\frac{\alpha}{2}$ percent of its consumers each to firms j and k, who charge P_l. Furthermore, if firms i and j charge P_h, then they each will lose   percent of their consumers to firm k, who charges P_l.

Given these state-dependent transition matrices, Equation (2) can be rewritten as:

$$N_{t+1} = N_t M_t(S_t), \tag{3}$$

where $S_t = (a_1^t, a_2^t, a_3^t)$ and $a_i^t \in \{0,1\}$.

Equation (3) summarizes the *intra*-industry competition given a number of customers $n_t = \sum_{i=1}^{3} n_t^i$. The next step of our modeling is to endogenize n_t by setting n_{t+1} as a function of S_t. More precisely,

$$n_{t+1} = n_t(1 + \quad), \quad = \quad (S_t) \tag{4}$$

The   (.) function explicitly shows how the market share of the industry can be affected by its pricing strategies S_t. The simple   (.) function considered in this paper is as follows.

$$= \begin{cases} W, & \text{if } \sum_{i=1}^{3} a_i = 0, \\ w, & \text{if } \sum_{i=1}^{3} a_i = 1, \\ c, & \text{if } \sum_{i=1}^{3} a_i = 2, \\ C, & \text{if } \sum_{i=1}^{3} a_i = 3. \end{cases} \tag{5}$$

where $W \geq w \geq c \geq C$.

Given Equations (3)-(5), the objective of oligopolists is to maximize their profits or the present value of the firm, and the profits for a single period is given by Equation (6).

$$_i^s = (P_i^s - C)n_i^s \tag{6}$$

where P_i^s is the price charged by firm i at period s, n_i^s number of customers, and C fixed unit cost. n_i^s can be obtained from Equations (3) - (6).

3   The Oligopoly Game: an N-Perosn IPD Game?

Before proceeding further, let us consider the relevance of the n-person IPD games to the oligopoly game. *Is an oligopoly game necessarily an n-person IPD game?* If not, what is their relation? For simplicity, let us consider the first r periods of an oligopoly game. Here, cooperate (C) means charging high prices for all r periods and defect (D) means charging low prices for all r periods . We first work out the *payo matrix* defined by Yao and Darwen (1994). In our

Table 1. Parameters and Payoˇs

Set	P_H	P_L	C	α	r	D_2	D_1	D_0	C_2	C_1	C_0
1	1.4	1.2	1	0.2	8	3.47	2.07	1.6	3.2	1.33	1.33
2	1.4	1.2	1	0.2	25	13.40	7.10	5	10	1.60	1.60
3	2	1.2	1	0.2	8	3.47	2.07	1.6	8	3.33	3.33
4	2	1.2	1	0.2	25	13.40	7.10	5	25	3.98	3.98

case (3 oligopolists), there are six elements in the payoff matrix, namely C_i and D_i $(i = 0, 1, 2)$. Here, C_i (D_i) denotes the payoff for a specific player who plays C (D) when there are i players acting cooperatively. From Equations (3)-(6), C_i and D_i can be derived. Without losing generality, let us assume that $ = 0$ and $n_1 = n_2 = n_3 = 1$, then the explicit solutions obtained are:

$$\begin{bmatrix} D_2 & C_1 & C_1 \end{bmatrix}' = \begin{bmatrix} (P_L - C)[3r - 2\frac{(1-\alpha)-(1-\alpha)^{r+1}}{\alpha}] \\ (P_H - C)[\frac{(1-\alpha)-(1-\alpha)^{r+1}}{\alpha}] \\ (P_H - C)[\frac{(1-\alpha)-(1-\alpha)^{r+1}}{\alpha}] \end{bmatrix}$$

$$\begin{bmatrix} D_1 & D_1 & C_0 \end{bmatrix}' = \begin{bmatrix} (P_L - C)[r + \frac{1}{2}r - \frac{1}{2}\sum_{j=1}^{r}(1 -)^j] \\ (P_L - C)[r + \frac{1}{2}r - \frac{1}{2}\sum_{j=1}^{r}(1 -)^j] \\ (P_H - C)(\sum_{t=1}^{r}(1 -)^t) \end{bmatrix}$$

$$\begin{bmatrix} C_2 & C_2 & C_2 \end{bmatrix}' = \begin{bmatrix} (P_H - C)r \\ (P_H - C)r \\ (P_H - C)r \end{bmatrix}, \begin{bmatrix} D_0 & D_0 & D_0 \end{bmatrix}' = \begin{bmatrix} (P_L - C)r \\ (P_L - C)r \\ (P_L - C)r \end{bmatrix}.$$

Whether the oligopoly game is an n-person IPD game depends on the following criteria (Yao and Darwen, 1994):

- (1) $D_2 > C_2$, (2) $D_1 > C_1$, and (3) $D_0 > C_0$.
- (4) $D_2 > D_1 > D_0$, and (5) $C_2 > C_1 > C_0$.
- (6) $C_2 > \frac{D_2+C_1}{2}$, and (7) $C_1 > \frac{D_1+C_0}{2}$.

It is not diﬃcult to see that not all of these conditions can be satisfied. For example, in Table 1, four sets of parameters and their associated payoffs are given. The conditions which can be satisfied by these four sets of parameters are summarized in Table 2.

Given the analysis above, we may consider the oligopoly game is a perturbation or a generalization of an n-person IPD game, and it is interesting to see whether the evolution process of the n-person, in particular, the 3-person, IPD game documented by Yao and Darwen (1994) still applies.

Table 2. Parameter Sets and Testing Results

Inequality	Set 1	Set 2	Set 3	Set 4
1. $D_2 > C_2$	>	>	<	<
2. $D_1 > C_1$	>	>	<	>
3. $D_0 > C_0$	>	>	<	>
4. $D_2 > D_1 > D_0$	>,>	>,>	>,>	>,>
5. $C_2 > C_1 > C_0$	>,=	>,=	>,=	>,=
6. $C_2 > 0.5(D_2 + C_1)$	>	>	>	>
7. $C_1 > 0.5(D_1 + C_0)$	<	<	>	<

The sign > in columns 2-5 means the condition is satisifed. Other signs means the condition is weakly violated (=) or strongerly violated (<).

4   Modeling the Adaptive Behavior of Oligopolists with GAs

The main idea of genetic algorithms is to encode the variable one wants to optimize as a binary string and work with it. Following, Midgley et al (1996), we consider the following special class of pricing strategy ,

$$: \quad k \longrightarrow \{0,1\}, \tag{7}$$

where k is the collection of all $\{S_{t-j}\}_{j=1}^{k}$. By this simplification, the oligopolist's memory is assumed to be *nite*.

While, potentially, different choices of k may lead to quite different sets of strategies (Beaufils et al., 1998), the issue concerns us is the smallest value of k which can reasonably replicate the price dynamics of the oligopoly industry, and as we shall see later, setting k to equal 1 is good enough to achieve this goal.

5   Experimental Designs and Results

For all the experiments conducted in this study, P_h is set at 2 , P_l 1.2 and C 1 . Other control parameters of GAs are set according to Tables 3 and 4.

The first experiment is to test whether GA-based oligopolists can achieve a reasonable level of adaptation. For this purpose, we design the experiment *absolute-loyalty-with-no-external-e ects* . In terms of notations, *absolute loyalty* means = 0, and *the absence of external e ects* means = 0. When = = 0, the most profitable pricing strategy for firm i is obviously an unconditional high-price strategy, i.e.,

$$ i = 1, \quad \forall S_t \in \;\; 1, \tag{8}$$

since a lower price will not help the firm to gain any advantages over its competitors or other industries. So, we expect that the GA-based oligopoly industry should converge to a state of a collusive price, i.e., the state $(1, 1, 1)$.

In order to test whether GAs can find out this simple solution, we ran experiment 1 for 1000 periods (125 generations) with the prespecified parameters

Table 3. The Parameters of the GA-based Oligopoly Game

Memory size (k)	1
Number of oligopolists	3
Population size (l)	30
Number of periods in a single play (r)	8 (25)
Selection Scheme	Roulette-wheel selection
"tness function	Pro"ts (π)
Number of generations evolved (Gen)	125 (126)
Number of periods (T)	1000 (3150)
Crossover Style	One-Point Crossover
Crossover rate	0.8
Mutation rate	0.0001
Immigration rate	0.001

Table 4. Experimental Designs and Results

Experiment	r	# of Simulations	α	δ_W	δ_w	δ_c	δ_C	Results
Pilot	8	5	0	0	0	0	0	C(5)
1	25	5	0.2	0	0	0	0	C(2), c(1), NC(2)
2	8	5	0.2	0	0	0	0	C(5)

given in Tables 3 and 4. To facilitate the report of simulations, we need a few more notations. Let W refer to the state *price war* (0,0,0), C the state *collusive price* (1,1,1), w the states which are closer to W and c the states closer to C . Closer is defined in terms of *Hamming distance*. Thus, w includes states (0,0,1), (0,1,0) and (1,0,0), and c includes (1,1,0), (1,0,1), (0,1,1). Since there are 30 pairs of oligopolists in each period of the evolution, to summarize simulation results of S_t in terms of its *distribution*, let p_W^t, p_w^t, p_c^t, and p_C^t denote respectively the percentage of the pairs who, in period t, are in the states labeled with W , w , c , and C respectively. Figures 1.1-1.5 display the time series plot of the distribution of S_t. From Figures 1.1-1.5, we can see that the industry converges to the state C (1,1,1) very quickly.

In Experiment 1, is set to be 0.2. In the meantime, we still assume the absence of external effects, i.e., remains to be zero. In this situation, it is not di cult to see that the best solution is to *form a cartel* and to *jointly charge a high price*. To see how well our GA-based adaptive oligopolists evolve in this scenario, we ran Experiment 1 for 3150 periods (126 generations), and the time series of the distribution of S_t is shown in Figures 2.1-2.5. From Figures 2.2 and 2.5, we can see that, like the Pilot Experiment, p_C^t gradually increases and eventually converges to 1. However, as compared with Figure 1.1-1.5, it can be seen that the convergence speed is *much slower*.

The interesting patterns observed in this experiments are shown in Figures 2.3 and 2.4. In these two simulations, we experience an oscillation between the

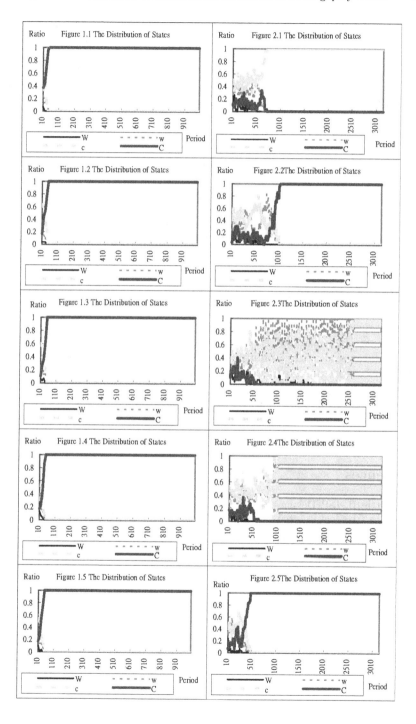

states w and c , i.e., *three rms are continuously charging di erent prices.* This is the second and the third stylized facts of oligopoly industries summarized in Section 1. The emergence of persistenly heterogeneous pricing may be caused by the inconsistency between $D_2 < C_2$ and $D_1 > C_1$ for the first r periods (Table 2). This inconsistency may encourage an early defection, and once that happens, by the path-dependent property, the oligopoly game is further perturbated away from a standard n-person IPD game and may support its own complex dynamics. To see whether or not this conjecture is correct, we design the experiment 2 as shown in Table 4.

The only difference between Experiment 1 and Experiment 2 lies in the choice of the parameter r. The setting has been changed from 25 to 8. By Table 2, this makes the first three inequalities all consistent, i.e., $D_i < C_i, i = 0, 1, 2$. This structure shall punish early defection, and keep the payoff structure unchanged. Then the whole process can be reinforced (an aspect of the path-dependent property). The simulation results, as we have conjected, all converge to the state of collusive pricing.

6   Concluding Remarks

The message revealed in this paper is simple: *the oligopoly game in general is not an n-person IPD game and, in e ect, is more complicated than that.* Therefore, the simulated results can be quite rich in even a 3-person oligopoly game. But, that also bridges the gap between the complexity of the oligopolists' pricing behaviour and the the simplicity of the insight gained from the n-person IPD games. In a word, we think that the oligoply game is a meaningful generalization of the n-person IPD game, and a formal mathematical treatment of it is definitely a direction for future research.

References

1. Beau"ls, B. J.-P. Delahaye and P. Mathieu (1998), Complete Classes of Strategies for the Classical Iterated Prisoner s Dilemma, in V. W. Porto, N. Saravanan, D. Waggen and A. E. Eiben (eds.), *Evolutionary Programming VII*, pp. 32-41.
2. Midgley, D. F., R. E. Marks, and L. G. Cooper (1996), Breeding Competitive Strategies, forthcoming in *Management Sciences*.
3. Yao, X. and P. J. Darwen (1994), An Experimental Study of N-Person Iterated Prisoner s Dilemma Games, *Inoformatica*, Vol. 18, pp. 435-450.

An Evolutionary Study on Cooperation in N-person Iterated Prisoner's Dilemma Game*

Yeon-Gyu Seo and Sung-Bae Cho

Department of Computer Science, Yonsei University
134 Shinchon-dong, Sudaemoon-ku, Seoul 120-749, Korea
[kitestar, sbcho]@candy.yonsei.ac.kr

Abstract. The iterated prisoner s dilemma game has been used to study on the evolution of cooperation in social, economic and biological systems. There have been much work on the relationship of number of players and cooperation, evolutionary strategy learning as a kind of machine learning, and the e˘ect of payo˘ function to cooperation. This paper attempts to reveal that cooperative coalition size depends on payo˘ function and localization a˘ects the evolution of cooperation in the N-player Iterated Prisoner s Dilemma (NIPD). Localization makes individuals to interact or learn with adjacent individuals. Experimental result reports that cooperative coalition size increases as the gradient of the payo˘ function for cooperation becomes steeper than that of defector s payo˘ function or as minimum coalition size gets smaller. It is also shown that localization of interaction is an important factor to a˘ect cooperative coalition.

1 Introduction

The iterated prisoner's dilemma game has been studied for long time. In general, a player in IPD must choose one of the two decisions, defect (D) or cooperate (C). Table 1 shows the payoffs for all the possible combinations of decision. The game is repeated infinitely and none of the players know the end of game. No matter how many players cooperate, anyone of them will earn better payoff by defecting. Therefore, defect may be a rational selection, and all players may get to select D and obtain payoff P. However, if all cooperate, they would get better score than all defect. This is the dilemma for players to face with in the IPD game.

Originally, most of the works were focused on 2IPD. However, 2IPD cannot model such complex problems as social and economic problems in real world. It is the NIPD game that has appeared as more realistic model. Table 2 shows an example of payoff function in NIPD game. The basic principle in 2IPD game is also true for NIPD game: Defect is dominant for each player. In NIPD game, there are many parameters to be considered such as payoff function [3], noise

---

* This work has been supported in part by a grant (975-0900-004-2) from the Korea Science and Engineering Foundation.

[2], population structure [5], localization [4], the shadow of the future [1] [2], the number of players [7]. and so on. Among these parameters, we consider two parameters: payoff function and localization.

Table 1. Payo˘ matrix in 2IPD. T > R > P > S, 2R > T + P

	Cooperate	Defect
Cooperate	R	S
Defect	T	P

The payoff function is generally fixed in the game but there exist many criteria of payoff function in real world, especially in economic and social systems. We examine the effect of payoff function in the first experiment and the second reveals the relationship of cooperative coalition and localization. The latter is divided into two factors: learning and interaction. These factors are reported to affect the emergence of cooperation . This paper uses co-evolutionary strategy learning which has advantage of re"ection of dynamic environment. A genotype has all information which determines a player's next move according to the other player's previous moves as well as his own previous moves.

In Section 2, we discuss relationship of cooperation and payoff functions, and Section 3 focuses on localization. In Section 4, we conduct NIPD game repeatedly with various payoff rules and test the localization effects in learning and interaction.

Table 2. Payo˘ matrix in NIPD.

No. of Cooperator	0	1	$\cdots$	X	$\cdots$	N − 1
Cooperate	C_0	C_1	$\cdots$	C_x	$\cdots$	C_{N-1}
Defect	D_0	D_1	$\cdots$	D_x	$\cdots$	D_{N-1}

2   Payoff Function

In this section, we discuss whether the payoff function is important to cooperative coalition or not. In real society, a selfish and rational individual has a tendency to select action according to payoff that it takes. If there is room for getting more payoff by specified action like as cooperative coaltion in IPD game, an individual might select the collective action to get better result. Thus, we experiment the payoff function as a very important factor in this paper. Generally, the payoff function in NIPD game satisfies the following condition.

$$C_x > C_{x-1}, D_x > D_{x-1}, D_x > C_x, C_{N-1} > D_0$$

The payoff function is a very important factor to determine minimum coalition size [3] [6]. According to Schelling, minimum coalition size means the number of players among which a player obtains any interest, zero or more. Cooperative coalition can emerge above minimum coalition size.

In IPD game, the payoff function is fixed and the payoff of defect is generally higher than that of cooperate, but we can easily find many criteria for payoff function in real world. Therefore, we also examine the linear and quadratic functions for the payoff function which does not belong to payoff rule in NIPD game. This gives us some possibility to observe role of payoff function in depth. Fig. 1 shows some of possible payoff functions. Here, important parameters of the payoff function in the game are the x-intercept and the gradient of C. In the cases of (c) in this figure, as the number of cooperators increases, the payoff of cooperate gets to overrun that of defect. This is not fit for the payoff rule in NIPD game, but there are many similar payoff functions in social and economic systems. We attempt to observe the coalition size by changing the payoff function in NIPD game.

In the case of Fig. 1(a), the larger y-intercept of cooperate, k, is, the smaller the number of cooperators is. In the case of Fig. 1(c), the gradient of defect is steeper than that of C. It can be expected that the result ends up with defect because the payoff is unfavorable to cooperator.

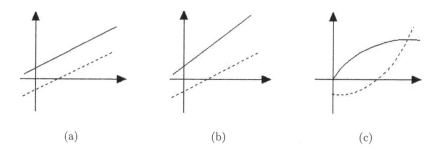

(a)   (b)   (c)

Fig. 1. Payo˜ functions. Solid line is payo˜ function for Defection and dashed line for cooperation. (a) $C_x = 3x - k$ and $D_x = 3x$ (b) $C_x = 2x - k$ and $D_x = 3x + 1$ (c) $C_x = \frac{1}{2}x^2 - k$ and $D_x = \sqrt{2x}$

3   Localization

The emergence of cooperation in the game is strongly affected by the localization of both interaction and learning [4]. Localizing learning means restricting the subset of the population from which players can learn better-performing strategies. Nowak and May [5] study a population of agents distributed on squares on a torus which are only capable of the always defect (AD) and always cooperate (AC) strategies. Each agent interacts with the agents on all eight adjacent squares and imitates the strategy of any better performing one. Cooperative behavior can be sustained in clusters of agents that insulate cooperators from hostile ADs under certain payoffs. Warning and Hoffmann [4] consider localized interaction and learning between agents on torus employing Moore machine to play game.

In order to ascertain the effect of localizing learning and interaction, we make an individual interact and learn with adjacent individuals distributed on torus which is to avoid boundary effect where players in the boundary have an unequal number of neighbors. In many cases, it is not clear why the localization of both learning and interaction should coincide. It is easy to imagine the situation where individuals interact locally while being able to observe what individuals outside their interaction-neighbourhood are doing.

4   Experiments

For the experiments of payoff function and localization, we use population size of 100, crossover rate of 0.6, mutation rate of 0.001, and two-point crossover with elite preserving. In localization, we consider two factors, learning and interaction, which might have different effects on the evolution of coalition size.

4.1   Payoff function

A. $C_x = 3x - k$ and $D_x = 3x$

This case is one of general IPD game. The cooperative coalition size is shown in Fig. 2, according to k. When the number of players is small, cooperative coalition size depends on the number of players: They all cooperate in this experiment. However, as the number of players gets larger, the difference of cooperative coalition size becomes larger according to k. This result indicates that the number of players affects to cooperative coalition.

We can see that cooperative coalition gets lower in Fig. 2(b), as k becomes larger. This result supports that the number of players and y-intercept are important factors to affect cooperation.

B. $C_x = 2x - k$ and $D_x = 3x$

The gradient of payoff function of defect is steeper than that of cooperate. In this case, we can expect all players to defect in any case. However, the result says that high cooperative coalition can appear even in this case. We can see in Fig. 3 that cooperative coalition is stabilized at high level when the number of players is 4 and $k < 3$. In Fig. 3(b), cooperative coalition size is small because the gradient of payoff function and the number of players are adverse to cooperators as the number of players becomes larger. Nevertheless, if the number of players is small and $C_n > D_0$, the cooperation coalition could be stabilized at high level.

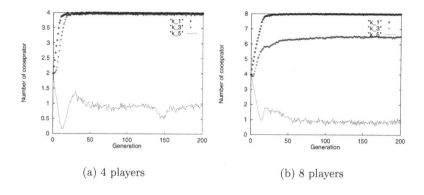

(a) 4 players   (b) 8 players

Fig. 2. $C_x = 3x - k$ and $D_x = 3x$.

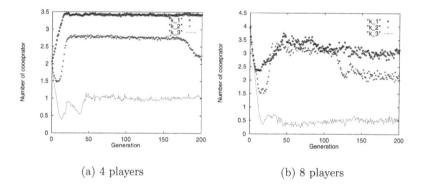

(a) 4 players   (b) 8 players

Fig. 3. $C_x = 2x - k$ and $D_x = 3x$.

C. $C_x = \frac{1}{2}x^2 - k$ and $D_x = \sqrt{2x}$

In this case, if the number of cooperators is large, the payoff of cooperator overruns that of defect. This case makes us to expect cooperative coalition to be stabilized at high level. However, when k is large and the number of players is small, all players defect. It is because the number of players is less than or equal to the minimum coalition size. In this case, the larger the number of players is, the higher cooperative coalition is.

With these experiments, we could get something essential to evolve cooperative coalition to high level. They are payoff for all C and minimum coalition size. If gradient of the payoff for C is steeper than that of all defect, cooperation is stabilized at high level as shown in Fig. 4. Here, minimum coalition size is determined by payoff function. If the minimum coalition size is small, high level of cooperation could emerge [3].

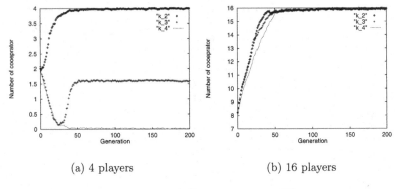

(a) 4 players   (b) 16 players

Fig. 4. $C_x = \frac{1}{2}x^2 - k$ and $D_x = \sqrt{2x}$.

High cooperation level is determined by various factors such as the number of players, the gradient of payoff function, x-intercept, and so on. From the simulations, we can see that the high cooperation level can emerge, as long as the condition such as small number of players, small x-intercept and steep gradient of payoff function for C is satisfied.

4.2   Localization

Experiments have been conducted in two aspects. One is a localizing interaction and the other is a localizing learning. It is not clear that two factors have the same effect on the cooperative coalition.

Localization of interaction High level of localization of interaction can improve cooperativity but it can do that only with localized learning [4]. We experiment localizing interaction and learning, respectively. This paper uses genetic approach to represent strategy and a genotype has all information to determine

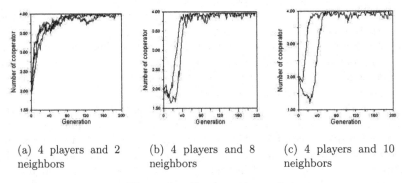

(a) 4 players and 2   (b) 4 players and 8   (c) 4 players and 10
neighbors   neighbors   neighbors

Fig. 5. Localization of inteaction.

the next move. Fig. 5 shows the variations of coalition size in the case of localizing interaction. We can see that cooperative coalition size is large when the level of localization is high.

When local size is small, players gradually cooperate but it takes some time to be stabilized. When the number of neighbours is 8 or 10, players almost defect at first. As time goes on, players turn to keep cooperating. In comparison to the size of 2, it shows somewhat unstable but it takes little time to reach to a stable state.

Localization of learning Just as localizing interaction, localizing learning could be an important factor to improve cooperativity [4]. Experimental results indicate that it is adverse to the evolution to cooperation. It seems that localization of learning prevent the population from evolving to a different state from the initial state. Fig. 6 shows the result.

We can conclude that localization of interaction is very important to affect cooperative coalition size, but the effect of localizing learning produces the ambiguous result to cooperative coalition.

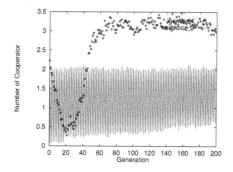

Fig. 6. Localization of learning. Dotted line is for 2 neighbors and large dot is for General case, when the number of players is 4.

5 Concluding Remarks

This paper aims to study on cooperative coalition through experiments of payoff function and localization. In real society, payoff function acts on selection of individuals in economic and social systems. Generally, in IPD game, the payoff function is fixed, but we can easily find many criteria for payoff function in real world. Therefore, we have also considered payoff functions which is not fit for original payoff rule in NIPD game.

A series of simulations reports that payoff function is very important to improve cooperative coalition. The steeper the gradient of payoff function of C is, the higher the level of cooperative coalition is. In this case, the larger the number of players is, the higher the level of cooperative coalition is, especially in case that the gradient of payoff function for C is steeper than that of D.

The localization of interaction also improves the level of cooperative coalition size. If the local size is small, cooperative coalition should be stabilized at high level. However, the effect of local learning is obscure. We could not confirm the effect of localization of learning, which requires much work for further study.

References

1. Axelrod, R.: *The Evolution of Cooperation.* Basic Books, (1984) New York
2. Axelrod, R. and Dion, D.: The further evolution of cooperation. *Science,* **242** (1988) 1385 1389
3. Banks, S.: Exploring the foundation of arti"cial societies: Experiments in evolving solutions to iterated N-player prisoner s dilemma. *ALife IV,* (1994) 337 342
4. Ho˘ mann, R. and Warning, N.: The localization of interaction and learning in the repeated prisoner s dilemma. *Santa Fe Institute Working Paper* no.96-08-064, (1996)
5. Nowak, M. A. and May, R. M.: Evolutionary games and spatial chaos. *Nature,* **359** (1992)
6. Schelling, T. C.: *Micromotives and Macrobehaviour.* New York (1978)
7. Yao, X. and Darwen, P.: The experimental study of N-player iterated prisoner s dilemma. *Informatica,* **18** (1994) 435 450

Simulating a N-person Multi-stage Game for Making a State

Atsushi Iwasaki[1], Sobei H. Oda[2], and Kanji Ueda[3]

[1] Graduate School of Science and Technology, Kobe University, 1-1 Rokkodai-cho, Nada-ku, Kobe 657-8501, Japan(iwasaki@mi-2.mech.kobe-u.ac.jp).
[2] Faculty of Economics, Kyoto Sangyo University, Motoyama, Kamigamo, Kita-ku, Kyoto 603-8047, Japan(oda@cc.kyoto-su.ac.jp).
[3] Faculty of Engineering, Kobe University, 1-1 Rokkodai-cho, Nada-ku, Kobe 657-8501, Japan(ueda@mech.kobe-u.ac.jp).

Abstract. This paper describes how a state emerges and collapses that makes it possible for citizens to do something which they will not do voluntarily. The model is a generalisation of the multi-stage game of Okada and Sakakibara (1991). The general model, its mathematical analysis with condition for simplicity and simulations for more general cases are presented. The results of simulations suggest that sel"sh but rational people may agree to make a state, which grows as the public capital stock accumulates but collapses when the stock reaches a certain level.

1   Introduction

The tragedy of commons is a well-known example of how people fail to cooperate for maintaining the public capital. In the circumstances people may voluntarily make a state that force themselves to construct and maintain the public capital stock. Okada and Sakakibara (1991) presents a multi-stage game to show this possibility. We shall show a more general model and analyse it both mathematically and by simulations.

In Section 2 we shall explain the basic model, which is divided into four sub-games: first each inhabitant announces whether he or she becomes a citizen or an outsider; secondly all citizens propose tax rates, of which the smallest is adopted as the tax rate; thirdly every citizen proposes the rate of the enforcer's salary to the total tax revenue and the person who proposed the minimum ratio is chosen as the enforcer who watches for tax evasion without making private business is elected; last tax payers pay taxes honestly or become tax evaders, whose income from private business will be all confiscated by the enforcer if tax evasion is found by him or her. In Section 3 we shall show how the subgame-perfect Nash equilibrium for a simple case mathematically. In Section 4 we shall show the results of simulations for more general cases, which suggest some inhabitants may make a state, which grows as the public capital stock accumulates but collapses when the stock reaches a certain level.

2 The model

The outline of our model is as follows. There live n inhabitants in a valley irrigated by a canal. Inhabitants make shovels in the winter, dredge the canal in the spring and grow rice in the summer. They exchange all or some of the shovels they made for rice with foreigners living outside the valley, while using the rest of the shovels for dredging the canal. Their non-agricultural income is defined as the rice value of the shovels they made, which may differ from inhabitant to inhabitant according to their skill, while their non-agricultural income is the harvest of rice, which depends on the location of their private rice field as well as the condition of the canal.

For the sake of simplicity, let us assume the following; the non-agricultural income of the ith inhabitant is $_i$, while his agricultural income is $_iK$ where K represents the depth of the canal; if a unit value of shovels are used for dredging the canal, they are all worn out while increasing the depth of the canal by one inch. In other words, if the depth of the canal is $\bar{K}$ at the be beginning of the spring and the ith inhabitant contributes $100t_i$ percent of the shovels he made to the dredge of the canal, the total income of the ith inhabitant is $(1 - t_i)\ _i +\ _i(\bar{K} + \sum_{j=1}^n t_j\ _j)$.

The di culty the valley is faced with is that no one may contribute their shovels to the dredge of the canal even if it can increase every inhabitant's income. This is because th ith inhabitant's contribution to the dredge of the canal is distributed among all inhabitants: it decreases his non-agricultural income by $t_i\ _i$ while increasing the jth inhabitant's agricultural income by $_jt_i\ _i$. In other wards, the valley's income increases in net terms if $1 < \sum_{j=1}^n\ _j$ while the ith inhabitant's total income increases only if $1 <\ _i$. Hence no one contribute if $1 <\ _i$ for all n, even if everyone's income increases if everyone contributes only small portion of his income.

Some organization or the system of monitoring and punishment may be required for making people contribute to the accumulation and maintenance of the public capital stock. In this paper we examine the following scenario or the four-stage game.

Subgame 1

Each inhabitant announces whether he or she becomes a citizen or an outsider. Accordingly the n inhabitants in the valley: {Inhabitant i|i $\in$ N = $\{1, 2, \ldots, n\}$} are divided into $m(0 \leq m \leq n)$ citizens: {Inhabitant i|i $\in$ M $\subset$ N, } and $n - m$ outsiders: {Inhabitant i|i $\in$ L = N $-$ M}, where $M \cup L = N$ and $M \cap L = \emptyset$. The citizens advance towards the following stages to determine their role or duty as well as the penalty which may be imposed on those who do not perform it, while the outsiders can enjoy all benefit from the public capital without making any contribution to its accumulation or maintenance.

Subgame 2

Every citizen announces the acceptable tax rate on non-agricultural income $_i$. The minimum $_i$ is adopted as the tax rate of the state: $^* = \min_{i \in M} {}_i$. (Everyone can virtually dissolve the state by proposing $_i = 0$.)

Subgame 3

Every citizen offers him/herself as the candidate for the enforcer who makes neither shovels nor rice to concentrate on monitoring the other citizens, by declaring the ratio of the enforcer's salary to the tax revenue of the state $_i$. The person who has proposed the minimum $_i$ is elected as the enforcer and has salaries paid accordingly: if $\min_{i \in M} {}_i = {}_e = {}^*$, Inhabitant e is the enforcer, whose salary is $^* \sum_{j \in T} {}_j$ where Inhabitants i ($i \in T$) pay taxes honestly while Inhabitants j ($j \in U$) pay no taxes ($M = \{e\} \cup T \cup U$ and $\{e\} \cap T = T \cap U = U \cap \{e\} = \emptyset$). In addition to the salary, the enforcer can confiscate all non-agricultural income of the tax evaders he or she has found out, whose expected value is ${}^e_{m-1} \sum_{j \in U} {}_j$ as his/her income. Here it is assumed that Inhabitant e can find out each tax evader at the probability of $\frac{e}{l}$ if he or she monitors l citizens.

Subgame 4

The $m - 1$ tax payers make shovels and rice, and pay or do not pay taxes. As the result, Inhabitant i expects the following income:

$$
E_i \begin{cases}
= {}^* {}^* \sum_{j \in T} {}_j + {}^e_{m-1} \sum_{j \in U} {}_j & \text{if } i = e \\
= (1 - {}^*) {}_i + {}_i\{(1 - {}^*) {}^* \sum_{j \in T} {}_j + K\} & \text{if } i \in T \\
= (1 - {}^e_{m-1}) {}_i + {}_i\{(1 - {}^*) {}^* \sum_{j \in T} {}_j + K\} & \text{if } i \in U \\
= {}_i + {}_i\{(1 - {}^*) {}^* \sum_{j \in T} {}_j + K\} & \text{if } i \in L
\end{cases} \tag{1}
$$

3 Game Theoretic Analysis

As to the range of the exogenous parameters: $_i$, $_i$, ${}^i_{m-1}$, K and n and n (where $1 \leq i \leq n$ and $2 \leq m \leq n$), let us assume the following: $0 < {}_i < 1$, $0 < {}_i$, $0 < \frac{i}{l} \leq 1$, $0 \leq K$ and $3 \leq n$. Here the first condition implies that no one voluntarily contributes to the accumulation of the public capital, while the last one is a necessary condition for the emergence of a state; it can readily checked that if a state is made by two persons, the only tax payer's income is - whether he or she honestly pays tax or not - smaller than it would be if he or she were an outsider.

Although we can prove the existence of the unique sub-game perfect Nash equilibrium for our model as well as its mathematical expression under more general conditions, we should here like to mention only simple and symmetric case where the following conditions are satisfied:

1. $_i =$, $_i =$ and $_{m-1}^i =$ for all $1 \leq i \leq n$ and $1 \leq m \leq n$.
2. Every inhabitant knows the structure of the game as well as all the exogenous parameters as common knowledge.
3. In Subgame 3, the enforcer is chosen by lottery if more than one citizens propose the minimum .
4. In Subgame 1, every inhabitant announces whether he or she joins the state or not by turns.

On the first three assumptions we can solve Subgame 4, Subgame 3 and Subgame 4 in this order. In fact * and * are expressed in terms of m, or the number of the citizens M:

if $2 \leq m$, $\max[, \; ^{\hat{\theta}}] < \min[\frac{\epsilon}{1-\beta}, \; _e]$ and $K \leq \frac{(\epsilon m - 1)\gamma}{\beta}$,

$$^* = \max[, \; ^{\hat{\theta}}] \text{ and } ^* = \; ; \tag{2}$$

if $2 \leq m$, $^1 < $ and $0 < \; m - \; - 1$,

$$^* = \text{ and } ^* = \bar{} \; ; \tag{3}$$

if $2 \leq m$, $\max[, \bar{}] < \min[\frac{\epsilon}{1-\beta}, \; ^{\hat{\theta}}, 1]$ and and $0 < \; m - \; - 1$,

$$^* = \min[\frac{}{1-}, \; ^{\hat{\theta}}, 1] \text{ and } ^* = \bar{} \; ; \tag{4}$$

otherwise

$$^* = 0. \tag{5}$$

Here

$$= 1 - \frac{1}{}(1 - \frac{}{_*}) \tag{6}$$

$$\bar{} = \frac{(1 - \; ^*) \; + \; \{ \; (m-1) \; + K\}}{(1 + \;) \; ^*(m-1)} \tag{7}$$

$$^1 = \frac{ + \; K}{m} \tag{8}$$

$$\hat{\theta} = \frac{(\; + \; K) - (1 + \;) \; (m-1)}{(\; - m + 1)} \tag{9}$$

$$_e = \frac{(m-1) \; - \; (\; + \; K)}{(1 - \;)(m-1)} \tag{10}$$

$$\bar{} = \frac{(\; + \; K)}{(\; m - \; - 1)} \tag{11}$$

Hence for every M, every inhabitant's expected income is uniquely determined; for example the expected income of any citizens is determined as $\frac{1}{m} \times$

the enforcer's expected income $+(1 - \frac{1}{m})\times$ the average citizen's income (as is readily checked, every citizen is a honest taxpayers and earns the same income). This assures that when he or she must say whether he or she joins the state, every inhabitant can make backward induction to see which brings him or her in greater income. This assures the existence of the unique subgame-perfect Nash equilibrium.

4 Simulations

The analysis of the previous section suggests that even if the existence of the unique subgame-perfect Nash equilibrium is mathematically proved, its explicit expression is often unattainable or rather complicated. To see how the subgame-perfect Nash equilibrium changes as time passes, simulation is necessary. In fact simulation makes it possible to examine the dynamics of the model with less restrictive conditions. As an example let us show the simulation of cases where non-agricultural income is not common to all inhabitants in this section. To put it concretely, we shall show the results of simulation, assuming the following: $n = 7$; $= 0.9$; $_i = 0.6 + 0.4\frac{i}{n+1}$; $= 0.2$; $K(0) = 0$; $K(t) = K(t-1) + (1 - {}^*(t)) {}^*(t)\sum_{j\in S(t)}$ $_j$. We shall show two cases for these parameters: Case 1 (where inhabitants announce whether they become citizen or an outsider in order of their productivity) and Case 2 (where they announce in the reverse order).

In Figure 1, the left side graphs shows Case 1 while the right side ones describes Case 2.

Figure 1 shows how E_i changes as time passes.

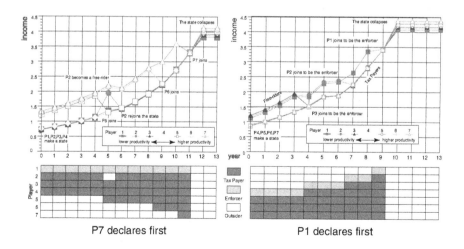

Fig. 1. The dynamics of the state

Since both dynamics are basically the same, let us explain only Case 1.

In Year 0 Inhabitants 1, 2, 3 and 4 make a state and Inhabitant 1, who has the smallest productivity among them is elected to be the enforcer. This is because the value of parameters and the initial condition are such that only a state with four individuals can be formed. Knowing this, Inhabitants 5, 6 and 7 announce that they become outsiders, expecting that the remaining four will make a state.

In Year 5 Inhabitant 5 joins the state. This is because the total income of Inhabitants 1, 2, 3 and 4 can earn if no state is made has increased as the result of the accumulation of the public capital. They will not make a state, which does not make their income lager than it would be if no state is formed. Realises that a state is made if and only if Inhabitant 5 declare that he or she becomes a citizen (on the supposition that Inhabitants 6 and 7 become outsiders), Inhabitant 5 compares the income he or she obtains if no state is formed and what he or she gets if he or she joins the state of Inhabitants 1, 2, 3 and 4 (actually 2 leaves the state, but it has no effect to 5's decision); he or she finds the latter is greater even though it is smaller than his or her income in the previous year.

Inhabitant 6 join the state in Year 9 and Inhabitant 7 also become its citizen in Year 11. The reason they join the state is the same as Inhabitant 5 becomes a citizen in Year 5. It would also be obvious why they become a citizen even though their income temporarily decreases.

An exceptional phenomenon is observed when Inhabitant 5 joins the state: Inhabitant 2 leaves the state. This is because (he or she knows) Inhabitants 5, 4, 3 and 1 make a state; though Inhabitants 4, 3 and 1 do not agree to make a state with Inhabitant 2, they agree to make a state with Inhabitant 5 who has higher productivity. Nevertheless soon (actually in the next year) making a four-person state cannot attract any group of four individuals so that Inhabitant 2 becomes a citizen again to make a five-inhabitant state. Though each of players considers only how his or her maximize his or her payoff in one-shot game, it seems that he or she adapt his or her behavior to Capital Stock in one-shot iterated game. In other words, we can say that players share their roles and cooperate with each other voluntarily.

Now the dynamics of   and   is described in Figure 2: both   and   periodically increase: they repeat a monotonous increase and a sharp fall. Every time the value of either value becomes nearly equal to unity, the number of citizens increases so that (by the reason mentioned above) they can cooperate with a smaller value. This trick can however work only till the capital stock reaches a certain amount.

The dynamics of capital stock is shown in Figure 3: It is only natural that the capital stock monotonously increases in our model where never depreciates. It is also apparent why the speed and the final level of capital accumulation are greater when Inhabitant 1 declares whether he becomes a citizen or not: then those inhabitants with higher productivity become citizens, who pay more taxes to accumulate the capital stock.

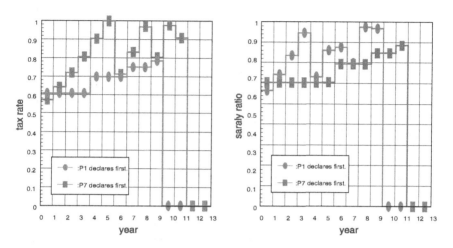

Fig. 2. The dynamics of tax rate and salary ratio

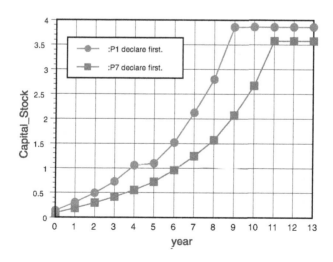

Fig. 3. The dynamics of capital stock

5   Concluding remarks

Though we mentioned very simple cases in the previous sections, we have made
more mathematical analysis and simulations for more general cases. As an example, our model shows there are some cases where some citizens join the state
to evade taxes. This may seem irrational because remaining an outsider is better
than becoming an tax evader who may be charged penalties, but a state may not
be formed without tax evaders who increase the enforcer's expected income. We
are now analysing these cases, which will hopefully deepen our understanding of
the emergence of the state.

Our analysis could be criticised for assuming subgame perfectness, which
is often failed to be realised in experiments (probably because of the lack of
required computational power and/or sticking to fairness; see for example Davis
and Holt (1993). Certainly more realistic cases, in particular such cases where all
or some individuals behave adoptively rather than perfectly rationally, should
be examined. We are actually developing our analysis toward this direction.

We believe that the mathematical analysis of game theory and the evolutionary simulations can be complemental approaches. Although still at an early
stage of our study, we should be grateful if the reader could find this possibility
in our game theoretical analysis with computer simulations

This project Methodology of Emergent Synthesis (JSPS-RFTF96P00702)
has been supported by the Research for the Future Program of the Japan Society
for the Promotion of Science.

References

1. Okada, A. and Sakakibara, K.: The emergence of the state: A game theoretic approach to the theory of social contract, *Economic Studies Quarterly*, vol.42, no.4
   (1991)
2. Davis, D.D. and Holt, C.H.: *Experimental Economics*, Princeton University Press
   (1993)

Learning from Linguistic Rules and Rule Extraction for Function Approximation by Neural Networks

Kimiko Tanaka, Manabu Nii, and Hisao Ishibuchi

Department of Industrial Engineering, Osaka Prefecture University,
Gakuen-cho 1-1, Sakai, Osaka 599-8531, Japan
Phone: +81-722-54-9354   FAX: +81-722-54-9915
E-mail: {kimiko, manabu, hisaoi}@ie.osakafu-u.ac.jp
http://www.ie.osakafu-u.ac.jp/student/ci_lab/ci_lab_e/

Abstract. We have already shown that the relation between neural networks and linguistic knowledge is bidirectional for pattern classi"cation problems. That is, neural networks are trained by given linguistic rules, and linguistic rules are extracted from trained neural networks. In this paper, we illustrate the bidirectional relation for function approximation problems. First we show how linguistic rules and numerical data can be simultaneously utilized in the learning of neural networks. In our learning scheme, antecedent and consequent linguistic values are speci"ed by membership functions of fuzzy numbers. Thus each linguistic rule is handled as a fuzzy input-output pair. Next we show how linguistic rules can be extracted from trained neural networks. In our rule extraction method, linguistic values in the antecedent part of each linguistic rule are presented to a trained neural network for determining its consequent part. The corresponding fuzzy output from the trained neural network is calculated by fuzzy arithmetic. The consequent part of the linguistic rule is determining by comparing the fuzzy output with linguistic values. Finally we suggest some extensions of our rule extraction method.

Key words: Learning of neural networks, hybrid learning, fuzzy neural systems, linguistic knowledge, rule extraction.

1   Introduction

When multi-layer feedforward neural networks are used as information processing systems such as classifiers and function approximators, they are usually handled as black box models. That is, we do not know why a trained neural network produces a particular output (e.g., classification, decision making, and prediction) for a new input vector. Several attempts have been tried to improve the transparency of neural networks. One approach is rule extraction from trained neural networks. In this approach, black box models are explained by extracted rules. Various methods [1-3] have been proposed for extracting non-fuzzy if-then rules and fuzzy if-then rules. Almost all of those approaches were designed for extracting classification rules from neural networks trained for pattern classification problems. In this paper, we discuss the transparency of neural networks trained for function approximation problems. We use linguistic rules, which are fuzzy if-then rules with linguistic interpretation, for explaining neural networks.

Another approach for improving the transparency is the learning of neural networks from experts' knowledge. We have already shown that neural networks can be trained by fuzzy if-then rules [4]. In our learning method, neural networks are trained by simultaneously utilizing linguistic knowledge and numerical data. Based on our former studies on the fuzzy rule extraction [3] and the learning from fuzzy if-then rules [4], we have shown that the relation between neural networks and linguistic knowledge is bidirectional for pattern classification problems [5]. In this paper, we illustrate the bidirectional relation between neural networks and linguistic knowledge for function approximation problems.

2   Learning from Linguistic Rules

Our problem in this section is to train a neural network for approximately realizing an unknown nonlinear function with n inputs and a single output. For this task, we use a standard three-layer feedforward neural network [6] with n input units, n_H hidden units and a single output unit.

We assume that we have a set of input-output pairs obtained from the unknown nonlinear function as training data. We denote the training data as $(\mathbf{x}_p, y_p), p = 1, 2, \ldots, m_{\text{Data}}$ where $\mathbf{x}_p = (x_{p1}, x_{p2}, \ldots, x_{pn})$ is an n-dimensional input vector, y_p is the corresponding output value, and m_{Data} is the number of the given input-output pairs. We also assume that we have linguistic knowledge about the unknown nonlinear function. We denote the linguistic knowledge as the following linguistic rules:

$$\text{Rule } R_q : \text{If } x_1 \text{ is } A_{q1} \text{ and } \ldots \text{ and } x_n \text{ is } A_{qn} \text{ then } y \text{ is } B_q, \ q = 1, 2, \ldots, m_{\text{Rule}}, \quad (1)$$

where R_q is the label of the q-th linguistic rule, A_{qi}'s $(i = 1, 2, \ldots, n)$ are antecedent linguistic values such as *small* and *large* , B_q is a consequent linguistic value, and m_{Rule} is the number of the given linguistic rules. We assume that the meaning of each linguistic value is specified by its membership function. That is, we handle linguistic values as fuzzy numbers. In Fig.1, we show membership functions of typical linguistic values.

In the learning of the neural network, the given linguistic rules in (1) are handled as fuzzy input-output pairs $(\mathbf{A}_p, B_p), p = 1, 2, \ldots, m_{\text{Rule}}$ where $\mathbf{A}_p = (A_{p1}, \ldots, A_{pn})$ is a fuzzy vector. Since real numbers can be viewed as a special case of fuzzy numbers, the given numerical data $(\mathbf{x}_p, y_p), p = 1, 2, \ldots, m_{\text{Data}}$ are also handled as fuzzy input-output pairs. This means that two kinds of available information (i.e., numerical data and linguistic knowledge) are handled in a single framework as fuzzy input-output pairs. In this paper, we denote the linguistic knowledge $(\mathbf{A}_p, B_p), p = 1, 2, \ldots, m_{\text{Rule}}$ and the numerical data $(\mathbf{x}_p, y_p), p = 1, 2, \ldots, m_{\text{Data}}$ as $(\mathbf{A}_p, B_p), p = 1, 2, \ldots, m$ where $m = m_{\text{Rule}} + m_{\text{Data}}$. From the above discussion, we can see that our problem is to train the neural network by the fuzzy input-output pairs $(\mathbf{A}_p, B_p), p = 1, 2, \ldots, m$. When the fuzzy vector $\mathbf{A}_p = (A_{p1}, \ldots, A_{pn})$ is presented to the neural network, the input-output relation of each unit can be written as follows [4]:

Input units: $O_{pi} = A_{pi}, \quad i = 1, 2, \ldots, n,$ (2)

Hidden units: $O_{pj} = f(\sum_{i=1}^{n} w_{ji} \cdot O_{pi} + \,_j), \quad j = 1, 2, \ldots, n_H,$ (3)

Output unit: $O_p = f(\sum_{j=1}^{n_H} w_j \cdot O_{pj} + \,),$ (4)

where w_{ji} and w_j are connection weights, $_j$ and $\,$ are biases, and $f(\cdot)$ is the sigmoidal activation function: $f(x) = 1/\{1 + \exp(-x)\}$. Our neural network architecture in (2)-(4) is the same as the standard three-layer feedforward neural network [6] except that the input and output of each unit are fuzzy numbers. As in various studies on fuzzified neural networks [7,8], the fuzzy input-output relation of each unit is defined by fuzzy arithmetic [9] and numerical calculation is performed by interval arithmetic [10] on the level sets of fuzzy numbers.

In the learning of the neural network, we have to define a cost function to be minimized. We measure the difference (or distance) between the actual fuzzy output O_p and the fuzzy target B_p using their h-level sets as

$$d(B_p, O_p) = \sum_h ([B_p]_h^L - [O_p]_h^L)^2/2 + \sum_h ([B_p]_h^U - [O_p]_h^U)^2/2,$$ (5)

where $[\cdot]_h^L$ and $[\cdot]_h^U$ are the lower limit and the upper limit of the h-level set $[\cdot]_h$ of a fuzzy number, respectively.

In the same manner as the back-propagation algorithm [6], a learning algorithm can be derived for adjusting the connection weights and biases from the cost function in (5). For details of the derivation, see Ishibuchi et al.[4,8].

3   Computer Simulations

Let us illustrate the learning from numerical data and linguistic knowledge by computer simulations on a simple numerical example. As an unknown nonlinear

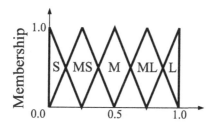

Fig. 1. Membership functions of typical linguistic values. (S:*small*, MS:*medium small*,

function, we used the following one:

$$y = f(\mathbf{x}) = (x_1^{3.5} + x_2^{3.5})^2/4. \tag{6}$$

This nonlinear function is depicted in Fig. 2 (a). As numerical data, we generated 200 input-output pairs by randomly specifying input vectors $\mathbf{x}_p = (x_{p1}, x_{p2})$, $p = 1, 2, \ldots, 200$ in the input space (i.e., the unit square $[0, 1] \times [0, 1]$). First we trained a three-layer feedforward neural network with two input units, five hidden units, and a single output unit using the 200 input-output pairs. We employed the standard back-propagation algorithm [6] with the momentum term (the learning rate and the momentum constant were specified as 0.25 and 0.9, respectively). The shape of the output from the trained neural network after 10000 epochs is shown in Fig. 2 (b). From the comparison between Fig. 2 (a) and Fig. 2 (b), we can see that the neural network could approximately realize the unknown nonlinear function very well.

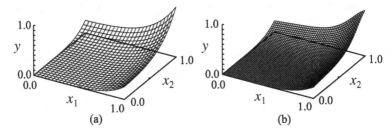

Fig. 2. Learning from numerical data. (a) Unknown function. (b) Result of the learning from numerical data.

Next we trained the same neural network using only 100 input-output pairs whose first input values are less than 0.5 (i.e., $x_1 < 0.5$). The shape of the output from the trained neural network is shown in Fig. 3 (a). Since the given numerical data were not su cient, the neural network could not approximate well the unknown function in this case. Finally we trained the same neural network using the 100 input-output pairs and the following linguistic knowledge:

> If x_1 is *large* and x_2 is *small* then y is *medium small*,
> If x_1 is *large* and x_2 is *large* then y is *large*,

where the membership function of each linguistic value is shown in Fig. 1. It should be noted that these two linguistic rules are not su cient to describe the unknown nonlinear function in Fig. 2 (a). In Fig. 3 (b), we show the shape of the output from the neural network trained by the insu cient numerical data and the insu cient linguistic knowledge. As we can see from Fig. 3 (b), we obtained a good approximation result because these two kind of information were simultaneously utilized in the learning of the neural network.

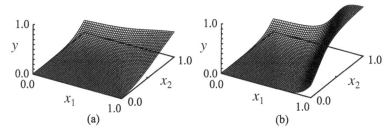

Fig. 3. Learning from numerical data and linguistic knowledge. (a) Result of the learning from insu cient numerical data. (b) Result of the simultaneous learning from numerical data and linguistic knowledge.

4   Linguistic Rule Extraction

Our task in this section is to extract linguistic rules from trained neural networks. We assume that a trained neural network has already been given. We do not assume any particular network architectures or learning algorithms.

Our linguistic rules to be extracted from the trained neural network are of the same type as in the previous sections. In our rule extraction method, we examine all combinations of antecedent linguistic values. When we have the five linguistic values in Fig. 1 for each of n inputs, the total number of possible combinations of antecedent linguistic values is 5^n. For extracting a linguistic rule, first we present a combination of antecedent linguistic values to the trained neural network. The antecedent part of the linguistic rule is specified by these linguistic values. Then we calculate the corresponding fuzzy output from the trained neural network using the fuzzy input-output relation in (2)-(4). Finally the fuzzy output is compared with each linguistic value in order to determine the consequent part of the linguistic rule. The difference (or distance) between the fuzzy output and each linguistic value is measured by (5). The closest linguistic value to the fuzzy output is chosen as the consequent of the linguistic rule. Not only individual linguistic values but also their combinations (e.g., *small* or *medium small*) are considered as a candidate for the consequent of each linguistic rule.

Let us illustrate our rule extraction method by a simple numerical example. In our computer simulation, we used the three-layer feedforward neural network that had already been trained by the back-propagation algorithm in Fig. 2 (b). Our task is to extract linguistic rules from the trained neural network. As

Table 1. Extracted linguistic rules.

x_2	x_1				
	S	MS	M	ML	L
L	MS	MS	MS or M	MS or M or ML	M or ML or L
ML	S	S	S or MS	MS or M	MS or M or ML
M	S	S	S	S or MS	MS
MS	S	S	S	S	MS
S	S	S	S	S	MS

antecedent and consequent linguistic values, we used the five linguistic values in Fig. 1. Thus we examined 25 combinations of antecedent linguistic values, each of which was presented to the trained neural network. In Table 1, we show extracted linguistic rules in the form of a 5×5 rule table.

5   Some Extensions of Rule Extraction Method

Our rule extraction method can be modified in various manners. The following points may be important issues to be discussed for improving our method:

1. Coping with high-dimensional problems.
2. Avoiding the increase in excess fuzziness in fuzzy outputs.
3. Improving the understandability of extracted linguistic rules.

The first issue is the handling of high-dimensional problems. In our rule extraction method in the previous section, we examined all combinations of antecedent linguistic values. Such an exhaustive examination can not be performed in the case of high-dimensional problems due to the curse of dimensionality. One approach to the handling of high-dimensional problems is to extract only general linguistic rules with a few antecedent conditions. Specific linguistic rules with long antecedent parts (i.e., many antecedent conditions) are not extracted in order to decrease the computational load.

The second issue is the increase in excess fuzziness included in fuzzy outputs obtained by the feedforward calculation in neural networks. This undesirable phenomenon is the same as the increase in excess width in interval arithmetic. It is known in interval arithmetic that the excess width can be decreased by subdividing intervals into multiple subintervals [10]. Such a subdivision method can be utilized for decreasing the excess fuzziness included in fuzzy outputs from neural networks. In the numerical calculation of the fuzzy outputs, h-level sets of linguistic inputs are subdivided into multiple subintervals. This is illustrated in Fig. 4. Since sharper fuzzy outputs are obtained by subdividing h-level sets of linguistic inputs as in Fig. 4, the consequent part of extracted linguistic rules can be specified more precisely. Table 2 shows examples of extracted linguistic rules using a subdivision method in Fig. 4 (a). Linguistic rules in Table 2 were extracted from the trained neural network used in the previous section. From the comparison between Table 1 with no subdivision and Table 2, we can see that the fuzziness of the consequent linguistic values of the extracted rules was decreased by the subdivision method.

The third issue is the understandability of extracted linguistic rules. It is a time-consuming task for human users to manually examine extracted linguistic rules when hundreds of rules are extracted. In this case, we can use genetic algorithms for selecting a small number of significant linguistic rules from a large number of extracted rules. GA-based rule selection methods have been proposed for selecting a small number of linguistic rules for pattern classification problems [11,12]. While those methods can not be directly applied to function approximation problems, we can use the same coding method and genetic operations.

The definition of a fitness function and a rule generation procedure should be modified in the application to function approximation problems. Extracted linguistic rules from the trained neural network are used as candidate rules for the rule selection. A fitness function is defined by two terms: the fitting ability of selected rules to training data and the number of selected rules.

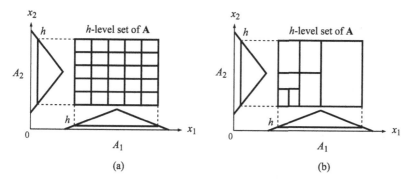

Fig. 4. Examples of subdivision methods. (a) Simple subdivision. (b) Hierarchical subdivision.

Table 2. Extracted linguistic rules using a subdivision method.

x_2	x_1				
	S	MS	M	ML	L
L	MS	MS	MS	M	ML or L
ML	S	S	S or MS	MS or M	M
M	S	S	S	S or MS	MS
MS	S	S	S	S	MS
S	S	S	S	S	MS

6 Conclusion

In this paper, we illustrated the bidirectional relation between neural networks and linguistic knowledge for function approximation problems. That is, we outlined two research directions: the learning of neural networks from linguistic knowledge and the linguistic rule extraction from trained neural networks. We also suggested some extensions of our rule extraction method. The learning from linguistic knowledge and the linguistic rule extraction can be utilized to improve the transparency of neural networks, which are usually handled as black box models. The main characteristic of our approach is that neural networks are linguistically explained.

In this paper, we described the bidirectional relation between linguistic knowledge and multi-layer feedforward neural networks with the sigmoidal activation function. Since RBF networks can be viewed as a kind of fuzzy rule-based systems [13,14], this bidirectional relation is much more straightforward in RBF networks. That is, a single basis function can be viewed as a fuzzy if-then rule.

While such straightforward relation exists, the linguistic interpretation of each fuzzy if-then rule represented as a basis function is not always easy.

Acknowledgement

This research was partially supported by Yazaki Memorial Foundation for Science and Technology.

References

1. Andrews, R., Diederich, J., and Tickele, A. B.: Survey and critique of techniques for extracting rules from trained arti"cial neural networks, *Knowledge-Based Systems*, vol. 8, no. 6. (1995) 373 389.
2. Hayashi, Y.: A neural expert system with automated extraction of fuzzy if-then rules and its application to medical diagnosis, In Lippmann, R. P., Moody J. E., and Touretzky, D. S. (eds.). *Advances in Neural Information Processing Systems 3*. Morgan Kaufmann, San Mateo, USA. (1991) 578 584.
3. Ishibuchi, H., and Nii, M.: Generating fuzzy if-then rules from trained neural networks: Linguistic analysis of neural networks, *Proc. of ICNN'96*. Washington D. C. (1996) 1133 1138.
4. Ishibuchi, H., Fujioka, R., and Tanaka, H.: Neural networks that learn from fuzzy if-then rules, *IEEE Transactions on Fuzzy Systems*, vol. 1, no. 2. (1993) 85 97.
5. Ishibuchi, H., Nii, M., and Turksen, I. B.: Bidirectional bridge between neural networks and linguistic knowledge: Linguistic rule extraction and learning from linguistic rules, *Proc. of FUZZ-IEEE'98*. Anchorage, USA (1998) 1112 1117.
6. Rumelhart, D. E., McClelland, J. L., and the PDP Research Group.: *Parallel Distributed Processing*. MIT Press, Cambridge. (1986).
7. Buckley, J.J., and Hayashi, Y.: Fuzzy neural networks: A survey, *Fuzzy Sets and Systems*, vol. 66, no. 1. (1994) 1-13.
8. Ishibuchi, H., Morioka, K., and Turksen, I. B.: Learning by fuzzi"ed neural networks, *International Journal of Approximate Reasoning*, vol. 13, no. 4. (1995) 327 358.
9. Kaufmann, A., and Gupta, M. M.: *Introduction to Fuzzy Arithmetic*. Van Nostrand Reinhold, New York. (1985).
10. Moore, R. E.: *Methods and Applications of Interval Analysis*. SIAM Studies in Applied Mathematics. Philadelphia. (1979).
11. Ishibuchi, H., Nozaki, K., Yamamoto, N., and Tanaka, H.: Selecting fuzzy if-then rules for classi"cation problems using genetic algorithms, *IEEE Trans. on Fuzzy Systems*, vol. 3, no. 2. (1995) 260 270.
12. Ishibuchi, H., Murata, T., and Turksen, I. B.: Single-objective and two-objective genetic algorithms for selecting linguistic rules for pattern classi"cation problems, *Fuzzy Sets and Systems*, vol. 89, no. 2. (1997) 135 150.
13. Jang, J. S. R. and Sun, C. T.: Functional equivalence between radial basis function networks and fuzzy inference systems, *IEEE Trans. on Neural Networks*, vol. 4, no. 1. (1993) 156 163.
14. Nie, J. and Linkens, D. A.: Learning control using fuzzi"ed self-organizing radial basis function network, *IEEE Trans. on Fuzzy Systems*, vol. 1, no. 4. (1993) 280 287.

Can a Niching Method Locate Multiple A ttractors Embedded in the Hopfield Netw ork?

Akira Imada[1] and Keijiro Araki[2]

[1] Graduate School of Information Science
Nara Institute of Science and Technology
8916-5 Takayama, Ikoma, Nara, 630-01 Japan
akira-i@is.aist-nara.ac.jp

[2] Department of Computer Science and Computer Engineering
Graduate School of Information Science and Electrical Engineering
Kyusyu University
6-1 Kasuga-koen, Kasuga, Fukuoka, 816 Japan
araki@c.csce.kyusyu-u.ac.jp

Abstract. W e apply evolutionary computations to the Hopfield's neural network model of associative memory. In the model, a number of
patterns can be stored in the network as attractors if synaptic weights
are determined appropriately. So far, we have explored *weight space* to
search for the optimal weight configuration that creates attractors at the
location of patterns to be stored. In this paper, on the other hand, we
explore *pattern space* to search for attractors that are created by a fixed
weight configuration. All the solutions in this case are *a priori* known.
The purpose of this paper is to study the ability of a niching genetic
algorithm to locate these multiple solutions using the Hopfield model as
a test function.

1   INTR ODUCTION

Associative memory is a dynamical system which has a num ber of stable states
with a domain of attraction around them (Koml ós et al. 1988). If the system
starts at any state in the domain, it will converge to the stable state. Hopfield (1982) proposed a fully connected neural network model of associative memory in which information is stored by being distributed among neurons.

The Hopfield model consists of N neurons and N^2 synapses. Each neuron
state is either active $(+1)$ or quiescent (-1). When an arbitrary N-bit *bipolar
pattern*, a sequence of $+1$ and -1, is given to the network as an initial state,
the dynamical behavior of neuron states afterwards are characterized by the
strengths of the N^2 synapses. The synaptic strengths are called *weights* and the
weight from neuron j to neuron i is denoted as w_{ij} in this paper. Provided the
synaptic weights are determined appropriately, network can store some num ber
of patterns as attractors. Hopfield employed the so-called Hebbian rule (Hebb,
1949) to prescribe the weights. That is, to store p bipolar patterns ξ^ν:

$$\xi^\nu = (\xi_1^\nu, \cdots, \xi_N^\nu), \quad \nu = 1, \cdots, p,$$

X. Yao et al. (Eds.): SEAL'98, LNCS 1585, pp. 325-332, 1999.

the weight values are determined as:

$$w_{ij} = \frac{1}{N} \sum_{\nu=1}^{p} \xi_i^\nu \xi_j^\nu \quad (i \neq j), \quad w_{ii} = 0.$$

An instantaneous state of a neuron is updated asynchronously (one neuron at a time) as:

$$s_i(t+1) = sgn\left(\sum_{j \neq i}^{N} w_{ij} s_j(t)\right),$$

where $s_i(t)$ is a state of the i-th neuron at time t. If an initial state converges to one of the stored patterns ξ^ν as an equilibrium state, then the pattern is said to be *recalled*. Furthermore, if an initial state chosen from the stored patterns remains unchanged from the beginning, then the pattern is said to be stored as a *fixed point*.

In analyzing the Hopfield model, there have been basically two different approaches: one is to explore *pattern space* searching for attractors under a specific weight configuration, and the other is to explore *weight space* searching for an appropriate weight configuration that stores a given set of patterns. To be more specific, the former is an analysis of the Hamiltonian energy as a function of all the possible configurations of bipolar pattern given to the network, where the synaptic weights are pre-specified using a learning algorithm, usually the Hebb's rule, so that the network stores a set of p given patterns. In this context, the model for $p = 1$ corresponds to the Mattis model of spin-glass (Mattis 1976), in which the Hamiltonian energy has two minima, while the model for infinitely large p corresponds to the Sherrington-Kirkpatrick model (1975), in which the synaptic weights become Gaussian random variables. Analyses of the former type have been made in between these two extreme cases (see Amit, 1989). The latter analysis was addressed by Gardner (1988). She discussed the optimal weight configurations for a *fixed* number of given patterns in terms of the volume of the solutions in weight space, suggesting that the volume shrinks to vanish when p approaches to $2N$. In short, the former approach searches for the optimal pattern configurations which minimize the Hamiltonian energy *in pattern space with the weights being fixed*, while the latter searches for the weight configurations *in weight space* that optimally store a set of given *fixed patterns*.

So far, we have studied the model with the latter approach. We have explored fitness landscapes of the model *defined on weight space*, and have found many solutions that store more patterns or store them with larger basin of attractions than, e.g., the Hebbian synaptic weights (Imada et al. 1997a, 1997b). Now, our interest is on the number and distribution of these solutions over the whole weight space, which is still an open problem. We think the niching GA is one of the appropriate tools to pursue these problems. However, since the N^2-dimensional *continuous* weight space is much more difficult to wander around than the N-dimensional *discrete* pattern space, we explore here the *pattern space* to see preliminary how our fitness function works under the niching method. In other words, we use the model as a test function of the niching technique in the sense that all solutions are *a priori* known, like in other studies using pure mathematical test functions.

Since we explore the fitness landscape defined on the pattern space in this paper, the fitness function of an arbitrary configuration of N-bit bipolar pattern should be defined. Here we evaluate the fitness of a pattern according to how the instantaneous neurons' states $s_i(t)$ after the pattern is given to the network, are similar to either of the stored patterns. The similarity as a function of time is defined as:

$$m^\nu(t) = \frac{1}{N} \sum_{i=1}^{N} \xi_i^\nu s_i^\nu(t).$$

The temporal average of $m^\mu(t)$ is calculated for each stored pattern, and the maximum value among them is assigned to the input pattern as fitness. Thus, the fitness value f is evaluated as follows:

$$f = \max\{ \frac{1}{t_0} \sum_{t=1}^{t_0} m^\nu(t) \mid \mu = 1, 2, \cdots, p\}.$$

In this paper, t_0 is set to $2N$, twice the number of neurons. Note that the fitness 1 implies the pattern is a fixed point attractor, while fitness less than 1 includes many other cases.

2   Niching Methods

Niching genetic algorithm is a genetic algorithm (GA) (Holland 1975) that was devised to locate multiple solutions simultaneously. To do this, *sharing* (Goldberg & Richardson 1987), for example, derates the fitness value of each individual using *sharing function* which reflects the number of similar individuals in the population. Or *crowding* (De Jong 1975) reduces the number of similar individuals in the population by replacing some of the individuals with new individuals. Here, we employ the *deterministic crowding GA* (Mahfoud 1992) because of its niching capability (Mahfoud 1995) as well as the simplicity for implementation.

In each generation, as neatly summarized by Mahfoud (1995), the current population is reproduced as follows.

(1) Choose two parents, p_1 and p_2, at random, with no parent being chosen more than once.
(2) Produce two children, c_1 and c_2, with uniform crossover (Syswerda 1989).
(3) Mutate the children by flipping bit chosen at random with probability p_m, yielding c_1' and c_2'.
(4) Replace parent with child as follows:
   - IF $d(p_1, c_1') + d(p_2, c_2') > d(p_1, c_2') + d(p_2, c_1')$
       * IF $f(c_1') > f(p_1)$ THEN   replace p_1 with c_1'
       * IF $f(c_2') > f(p_2)$ THEN   replace p_2 with c_2'
   - ELSE

$$* \text{ IF }\quad f(c_2') > f(p_1) \text{ THEN }\quad \text{replace } p_1 \text{ with } c_2'$$
$$* \text{ IF }\quad f(c_1') > f(p_2) \text{ THEN }\quad \text{replace } p_2 \text{ with } c_1'$$

where $d(\zeta_1, \zeta_2)$ is the Hamming distance between two points (ζ_1, ζ_2) in pattern configuration space. The process of producing child is repeated until all the population have taken part in the process. Then the cycle of reconstructing a new population and restarting the search is repeated until all the global optima are found or a set maximum number of generation has been reached.

3 Experimen tal Results

Experiments were carried out on networks with 49 neurons. For a given set of p patterns, a configuration of synaptic weights in a network is calculated by the Hebb's rule. Thus, the network with 49 neurons now stores these p patterns as fixed point attractors, so far as p dose not exceed the storage capacity. Namely, the fitness landscape defined on pattern space has p global peaks exactly at the location of the patterns. Then the deterministic crowding GA searches for these attractors. The parameters of the GA employed in this paper are as follows. The population size is 200; mutation probability p_m is set to 0.05; and the number of iterations is limited to a maximum of 12,000 generations.

To take the bird's-eye view of the landscape, we picked up 240,000 samples randomly from pattern space. The number of samples was chosen to be equal to the typical number of function evaluations of our usual GA implementations. We observed that the fitness values were distributed ranging from 0.01 to 0.95. At first glance, this broad distribution might seem that the search for the optimal solution(s) is not so difficult. In fact, Davis (1990) pointed out that some problems can be solved more easily with a simple hill-climber than genetic algorithms. So, we experimented a random hill climbing on the landscape. Starting at a randomly chosen position in the space, a point is mutated 200 times, and then moves to the highest fitness point among mutants. We repeated a run varying p, but all we observed were early stagnations to a local minimum. The solutions of our problem were not reachable by a simple hill-climber. which satisfies Whitley et al.'s (1995) demand that test functions should be resistant to simple hill climbing searches.

Before applying the deterministic crowding, we also studied the problem with a simple GA where two parents are randomly selected from the best fit 40% of the population, and the worst 60% were replaced with the children produced, with other schemes such as recombination and mutation being the same as those described above. The simple GA founds easily the embedded patterns, but only one of them at a time. The typical result of the best and average fitness versus generation obtained by the simple GA is shown in Figure 1.

Next, we apply the deterministic crowding GA to this problem. We investigated how many of the embedded patterns can be located. For a specific number of patterns p, starting with $p = 2$, we studied 30 runs with varying random number seed at the start of a run. The experiments are iterated with p being

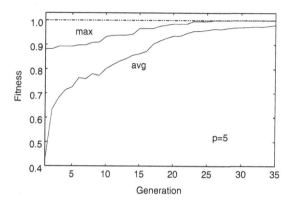

Fig. 1. Best and average fitness versus generation obtained by a simple GA.

incremented if any of the 30 runs locates *all* the embedded solutions. As results, we observed that when $p = 2$, 19 out of 30 runs locate all the embedded patterns; then as p increases, the number of successful runs decreases, i.e., when $p = 3, 4, 5, 6$ the number of successful trials out of 30 runs was 14, 8, 3, 0, respectively. Some examples of the number of individuals that converged on each of the given patterns when a GA run terminated are shown in Table 1.

Table 1. Number of individuals converged to each attractor.

p	#1	#2	#3	#4	#5	#6	total
4	40	96	27	59	-	-	200
4	68	26	24	82	-	-	200
4	109	7	20	64	-	-	200
4	23	52	76	49	-	-	200
4	23	43	78	56	-	-	200
4	18	79	11	92	-	-	200
4	54	8	7	131	-	-	200
4	31	28	38	103	-	-	200
5	85	71	5	34	5	-	200
5	42	54	68	11	25	-	200
5	15	102	26	52	5	-	200
6	33	17	58	50	0	42	200

We can see that all the individuals eventually find some different niches for $p < 6$. Then, how the number of individuals in each of these niches changes as an evolution proceeds? An example is shown in Figure 2. Also the total number of these located solutions are shown in Figure 3, together with a result of a simple GA. The figure shows that all the individuals in the deterministic crowding GA converge to any of the solutions, while the simple GA reaches about half of the solutions.

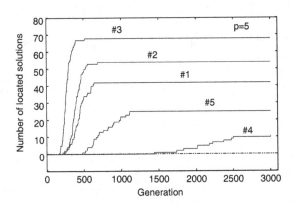

Fig. 2. Number of individuals converged on each niche.

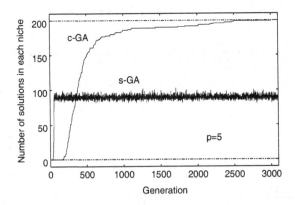

Fig. 3. Number of individuals that reach solutions.

4   Conclusion

We have described an application of the deterministic crowding GA, one of multi-modal function optimization techniques, to the Hopfield model of associative memory. What we concern is to obtain multiple solutions of weigh t configuration in weight space. W e think the deterministic crowding GA is one of the candidates for the purpose. As a preliminary stage, the fitness landscape defined on pattern space instead of weight space was explored in this paper. As expected, we observed that convergence behaviors of the deterministic crowding GA were different from those of a simple GA. The deterministic crowding GA con verges to multiple solutions, while a simple GA converges to one of these solutions. The number of solutions located by the deterministic crowding GA depends on trials. When more than 6 patterns are given, the deterministic crowding GA located only a part of them One possible reason for these results is that the num ber of embedded patterns exceeds the capability of the deterministic crowding GA to make niches on all of them. The other possibility might be due to our fitness evaluation. We are now experimenting with the Hamiltonian energy function for fitness evaluation.

The approach we have taken in this paper, that is, the exploration in pattern space to search for solutions, can be extended in the problem of searching for the solutions in weight space. Needless to say, much remains to be done. The simulations in this paper were made under specific limitations, such as low dimensionality and low cardinality of genes. Under experiments with the network with 49 neurons, the search space to be explored is vertices of the 49-dimensional hyper cube, while the weight space to be explored will be continuous entire region inside the 2401-dimensional hyper cube.

Although the analysis of the fully-connected network model of associative memory is rather classical, man y issues are still unknown. Our goal of applying multi-modal-GA to the model is to address one of these issues, that is, the distribution of solutions in weight space. W e believe these studies using evolutionary algorithms shed new light on the analysis of the model.

Acknowledgemen ts

W e thank Peter Davis at Advanced Telecomm unication Research Institute (ATR) for providing us great insights into the dynamics of the Hopfield neural networks.

References

Amit, D. J. (1989) *Modeling Brain Function: The World of Attr actor Neural Networks.* Cambridge University Press.

Davis, L (1991) *Bit-Climbing, Representation Bias, and Test Suite Design.* Proceedings of the 4th International Conference on Genetic Algorithms, pp.18–23.

De Jong, K. A. (1975) *An Analysis of the Behavior of a Class of Genetic Adaptive Systems.* Ph.D. theses University of Michigan.

Gardner, E. (1988) *The Phase Space of Interactions in Neural Network Models.* Journal of Physics, 21A, pp257-270.

Goldberg, D. E., and J. Richardson (1987) *Genetic Algorithms with Sharing for Multimodal function Optimization.* Proceedings of 2nd International Conference on Genetic Algorithms, pp.41-49.

Hebb, D. O. (1949) *The Organization of Behavior.* Wiley.

Holland, J. (1975) *Adaptation in Natural and Artificial Systems.* The University of Michigan Press.

Hopfield, J. J. (1982) *Neural Networks and Physical Systems with Emergent Collective Computational Abilities.* Proceedings of the National Academy of Sciences, USA, 79, pp2554-2558.

Imada, A., and K. Araki (1997a), *Random Perturbations to Hebbian Synapses of Associative Memory using a Genetic Algorithm.* Proceedings of International Work-Conference on Artificial and Natural Neural Networks. Springer Verlag, Lecture Notes in Computer Science, No.1240, pp398–407.

Imada, A., and K. Araki (1997b) *Evolution of Hopfield Model of Associative Memory by the Breeder Genetic Algorithm.* Proceedings of the 7th International Conference on Genetic Algorithms, pp784–791.

Komlós, J., and R. Paturi (1988) *Convergence Results in an Associative Memory Model.* Neural Networks 1, pp239–250.

Mahfoud, S. W. (1992) *A Comparison of Parallel and Sequential Niching Methods.* Proceedings of the 2nd Parallel Problem Solving from Nature, pp.27–36.

Mahfoud, S. W. (1995) *A Comparison of Parallel and Sequential Niching Methods.* Proceedings of the 6th International Conference on Genetic Algorithms, pp.136–143.

Mattis, D. C. (1976) *Solvable Spin Systems with Random Interactions.* Physics Letters, 56A, pp421–422.

Sherrington, D., and S.Kirkpatrick (1975) *Solvable Model of a Spin Glass.* Physical Review Letters 35, pp1792–1796.

Syswerda, G. (1989) *Uniform Crossover in Genetic Algorithms.* Proceedings of the 3rd International Conference on Genetic Algorithms, pp2–9.

Whitley, D., K. Mathias, S. Rana, and J. Dzubera (1995) *Building Better Test Functions.* Proceedings of the 6th International Conference on Genetic Algorithms, pp239–246.

This article was processed using the LaTeX macro package with LLNCS style

Time Series Prediction by Using Negatively Correlated Neural Networks

Yong Liu and Xin Yao

Computational Intelligence Group, School of Computer Science
University College, The University of New South Wales
Australian Defence Force Academy, Canberra, ACT, Australia 2600
{liuy,xin}@csadfa.cs.adfa.oz.au

Abstract. Negatively correlated neural networks (NCNNs) have been proposed to design neural network (NN) ensembles [1]. The idea of NCNNs is to encourage diˇerent individual NNs in the ensemble to learn diˇerent parts or aspects of a training data so that the ensemble can learn the whole training data better. The cooperation and specialisation among diˇerent individual NNs are considered during the individual NN design. This provides an opportunity for diˇerent NNs to interact with each other and to specialise. In this paper, NCNNs are applied to two time series prediction problems (i.e., the Mackey-Glass diˇerential equation and the chlorophyll-a prediction in Lake Kasumigaura). The experimental results show that NCNNs can produce NN ensembles with good generalisation ability.

1   Introduction

Many real-world problems are too large and too complex for a single monolithic system to solve alone. There are many examples from both natural and artificial systems which show that a composite system consisting of several subsystems can reduce the total complexity of the system while solving a di cult problem satisfactorily. The success of neural network (NN) ensembles in improving classifier's generalisation is a typical example [2]. However, designing NN ensembles is a very di cult task. It relies heavily on human experts and prior knowledge about the problem. This paper describes a cooperative learning algorithm which can create negatively correlated neural networks (NCNNs) automatically [1,3].

The idea behind NCNNs is to encourage different individual networks to learn different parts or aspects of a training data so that the whole system can learn the training data better. NCNNs are trained simultaneously rather than independently or sequentially. Simultaneous training provides an opportunity for individual NNs to cooperate and specialise.

NCNNs have been tested on a number of benchmark problems, including regression and classification problems [1,3]. In all these problems, both the input and the output are independent of time. This paper describes NCNNs' application to the time series prediction problems, where the input and output change over time. It is assumed that the appropriate response at a particular point in time depends not only on the current input, but also on previous inputs. One artificial and one real-world problems are used in this paper to evaluate the effectiveness and e ciency of NCNNs. The experimental results obtained by NCNNs are better than those obtained by other systems in terms of prediction error. They also illustrate that NCNNs are applicable to a wide range of problems, regardless of whether the input and output are *static* or *time-varying*.

The rest of this paper is organised as follows: Section 2 brie"y describes NCNNs. Section 3 presents the experimental results of NCNNs and discussions. Finally, Section 4 concludes with a summary of the paper and a few remarks.

2   Negative Correlation Learning

The negative correlation learning has been successfully applied to NN ensembles [1,3] for creating NCNNs. The idea of negative correlation learning is to introduce a correlation penalty term into the error function of each individual network in a NN ensemble so that the individual network can be trained simultaneously and interactively. The error function E_i for individual i in negative correlation learning is defined by

$$
\begin{aligned}
E_i &= \frac{1}{N} \sum_{n=1}^{N} E_i(n) \\
&= \frac{1}{N} \sum_{n=1}^{N} \left[\frac{1}{2}(F_i(n) - y(n))^2 + \ p_i(n) \right]
\end{aligned}
\tag{1}
$$

where N is the number of training patterns, $E_i(n)$ is the value of the error function of network i at presentation of the nth training pattern, $F_i(n)$ is the output of network i on the nth training pattern, and $y(n)$ is the desired output of the nth training pattern. The first term in the right side of Eq.(1) is the *empirical risk function* of network i. The second term p_i is a correlation penalty function. The purpose of minimising p_i is to negatively correlate each individual's error with errors for the rest of the ensemble. The parameter $0 \le \ \le 1$ is used to adjust the strength of the penalty.

The penalty function p_i has the form:

$$
p_i(n) = (F_i(n) - F(n)) \sum_{j \ne i} (F_j(n) - F(n))
\tag{2}
$$

where $F(n) = \sum_{i=1}^{M} F_i(n)$ is the output of the NN ensemble on the nth training pattern.

The partial derivative of E_i with respect to the output of network i on nth training pattern is

$$
\begin{aligned}
\frac{E_i(n)}{F_i(n)} &= F_i(n) - d(n) + \ \frac{p_i(n)}{F_i(n)} \\
&= F_i(n) - d(n) + \ \sum_{j \ne i} (F_j(n) - F(n)) \\
&= F_i(n) - d(n) - \ (F_i(n) - F(n))
\end{aligned}
\tag{3}
$$

where we have made use of the assumption that $F(n)$ has constant value with respect to $F_i(n)$. The back-propagation (BP) algorithm has been used for weight adjustments in the mode of pattern-by-pattern updating. That is, weight updating of all the individual networks is performed simultaneously using Eq.(3) after the presentation of each training case. One complete presentation of the entire training set during the learning process is called an *epoch*. The negative correlation learning from Eq.(3) is a simple extension to the standard BP algorithm. In fact, the only modification needed is to calculate an extra term of the form $(F_i(n) - F(n))$ for ith NN.

From Eqs.(1), (2), and (3), we may make the following observations:

1. During the training process, all the individual networks interact with each other through their penalty terms in the error functions. Each network F_i minimises the difference between $F_i(n)$ and $y(n)$ while maxmising the difference between $F_i(n)$ and $F(n)$. That is, negative correlation learning considers errors what all other NNs have learned while training a NN.
2. For $= 0.0$, there are no correlation penalty terms in the error functions of the individual networks, and the individual networks are just trained independently using BP. That is, independent training using BP for the individual networks is a special case of negative correlation learning.
3. For $= 1$, from Eq.(3) we get

$$\frac{E_i(n)}{F_i(n)} = F(n) - y(n) \tag{4}$$

Note that the empirical risk function of the ensemble for nth training pattern is defined by

$$E_{ensemble} = \frac{1}{2}(\ {}_{i=1}^{M}F_i(n) - d(n))^2 \tag{5}$$

The partial derivative of $E_{ensemble}$ with respect to F_i on nth training pattern is

$$\frac{E_{ensemble}}{F_i(n)} = \frac{1}{M}(\ {}_{i=1}^{M}F_i(n) - d(n))$$

$$= \frac{1}{M}(F(n) - y(n)) \tag{6}$$

In this case, we get

$$\frac{E_i(n)}{F_i(n)} \propto \frac{E_{ensemble}}{F_i(n)} \tag{7}$$

The minimisation of the empirical risk function of the ensemble is achieved by minimising the error functions of the individual networks. From this point of view, negative correlation learning provides a novel way to decompose the learning task of the ensemble into a number of subtasks for each individual.

3 Experimental Studies

3.1 The MacKey-Glass Time Series Prediction Problem

The MacKey-Glass time series investigated here is generated by the following differential equation

$$x(t) = \quad x(t) + \frac{x(t - \ )}{1 + x^{10}(t - \ )} \tag{8}$$

where $\ = 0.2$, $\ = -0.1$, $\ = 17$ [4,5]. As mentioned by Martinetz *et al.* [6], $x(t)$ is quasi-periodic and chaotic with a fractal attractor dimension 2.1 for the above parameters.

Experimental setup The input consists of four past data points, $x(t)$, $x(t-6)$, $x(t-12)$ and $x(t-18)$. The output is $x(t+6)$. In order to make multiple step prediction (i.e., $\ t = 90$) during testing, iterative predictions of $x(t+6)$, $x(t+12)$, ..., $x(t+90)$ will be made. During training, the true value of $x(t+6)$ was used as the target value. Such experimental setup is the same as that used by Martinetz *et al.* [6].

In the following experiments, the data for the MacKey-Glass time series was obtained by applying the fourth-order Runge-Kutta method to Eq.(8) with initial condition $x(0) = 1.2$, $x(t - \ ) = 0$ for $0 \le t < \ $, and the time step is 1. The training set consisted of point 118 to 617 (i.e., 500 training patterns). The following 500 data points (starting from point 618) were used as the testing set. The values of training and testing data were rescaled linearly to between 0.1 and 0.9. Such experimental setup was adopted in order to facilitate comparison with other existing work.

The normalised root-mean-square (RMS) error E was used to evaluate the performance of NCNNs, which is determined by the RMS value of the absolute prediction error for $\ t = 6$, divided by the standard deviation of $x(t)$ [4,6],

$$E = \frac{\langle [x_{pred}(t, \ t) - x(t + \ t)]^2 \rangle^{\frac{1}{2}}}{\langle (x - \langle x \rangle)^2 \rangle^{\frac{1}{2}}} \tag{9}$$

where $x_{pred}(t, \ t)$ is the prediction of $x(t + \ t)$ from the current state $x(t)$ and $\langle x \rangle$ represents the expectation of x. As indicated by Farmer and Sidorowich [4], If $E = 0$, the predictions are perfect; $E = 1$ indicates that the performance is no better than a constant predictor $x_{pred}(t, \ t) = \langle x \rangle$.

The ensemble architecture used in the experiments has 20 individual networks. Each individual network is a feedforward NN with one hidden layer. Both hidden node function and output node function are defined by the logistic function

$$(y) = \frac{1}{1 + \exp{(y)}} \tag{10}$$

All the individual networks have 6 hidden nodes. The number of training epochs was set to 10000. The strength parameter was set to 1.0.

Experimental Results and Comparisons Table 1 shows the average results of NCNNs over 50 runs. Each run of NCNNs was from different initial weights. Fig.1 shows the best results of NCNNs on the training and testing set. Table 2 compares NCNNs' results with those produced by EPNet [7], BP learning and the cascade-correlation (CC) learning [8]. It is obvious that NCNNs are able to achieve the generalization performance better than that of others.

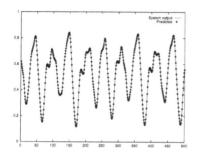 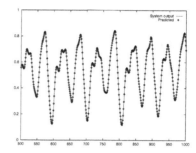

Fig. 1. The Mackey-Glass time series prediction problem. The system s and the best NCNNs outputs on the training set (left). The system s and the best NCNNs outputs on the testing set (right). The time span is $\Delta t = 6$.

For a large time span $t = 90$, NCNNs' results also compare favorably with those produced by Martinetz *et al.* [6] which had been shown to be better than Moody and Darken [9]. For the same training set size of 500 data points, the smallest prediction error achieved by neural-gas networks [6] was about 0.06. The smallest prediction error among 50 runs of NCNNs was 0.0305, while the average prediction error was 0.0458.

	Testing RMS			
	Mean	Std Dev	Min	Max
$\Delta t = 6$	0.0100	0.0006	0.0090	0.0116
$\Delta t = 84$	0.0326	0.0033	0.0273	0.0400
$\Delta t = 90$	0.0367	0.0038	0.0305	0.0458

Table 1. The average results produced by negative correlation learning over 50 runs for the Mackey-Glass time series prediction problem. The Testing RMS in the table refers to the error de"ned by Eq.(9) on the testing set.

	NCNNs	EPNet	BP	CC Learning
$\Delta t = 6$	0.01	0.02	0.02	0.06
$\Delta t = 84$	0.03	0.06	0.05	0.32

Table 2. Generalisation errors comparison among NCNNs, EPNet[7], and BP learning and the cascade-correlation (CC) learning[8] for the Mackey-Glass time series prediction problem. The generalisation error refers to the error de"ned by Eq.(9) on the testing set.

3.2   Chlorophyll-a Prediction

Recknagel [10] has recently proposed to use feed-forward NNs to predict chlorophyll-a in Lake Kasumigaura. The experimental results reported by Recknagel [10] were very promising, although more improvements can be made.

Experimental setup In order to compare our results with previous work, we have followed as closely as possible the previous experimental setup described in [10]. The limnological time series for 10 years between 1984 and 1993, inclusively, were used in our experiments. The experiment was divided into two parts. The first part used the data in 1984 and 1985 as the training data to train the first NN ensemble. Then the NN ensemble was tested on the 1986 data. The second part of the experiment used the data between 1987 and 1992 as the training data to train the second NN ensemble. Then the NN ensemble was tested on the 1993 data. Using the 1986 and 1993 data as the independent testing data was suggested by Recknagel [10] because they represent typical years for blooms of *Microcystis* and *Oscillatoria*, respectively. More details about these data were given in [10].

As a preprocessing step, the original data were rescaled linearly to between 0.1 and 0.9. The input to each individual network consists current 8 input conditions and output conditions in the past seven days. It should be pointed out that Recknagel [10] used a 5-vector input layer which included the current input conditions and those input conditions of present 10, 20, 30, and 40 days previously. The reasons for changing input are to decrease the number of input attributes and make the Chlorophyll-a prediction problem more meaningful in the sense of time series prediction.

The normalised root-mean-square (RMS) error E defined in Eq.(9) for $t = 1$ was used to evaluate the performance of negative correlation learning. The ensemble architecture used in the experiments has 20 individual networks. Each individual network is a feedforward NN with one hidden layer. Both hidden node function and output node function are defined by the logistic function in Eq.(10). All the individual networks have 6 hidden nodes. The number of training epochs was set to 2000 for the first part of the experiment, and 1000 for the second part of the experiment. The strength parameter was set to 1.0.

Experimental Results Table 3 shows the average results of NCNNs over 50 runs for the chlorophyll-a prediction problem. Each run of NCNNs was from different initial weights. Fig.2 shows the best predictions of NCNNs along with the observed values. As can be seen, the predictions of NCNNs are remarkably accurate except the peak magnitudes in 1986 were slightly underestimated. NCNNs also outperformed the standard feedforward NNs for the chlorophyll-a prediction problem [10].

Year		Mean	Std Dev	Min	Max
1983	1984	0.0104	0.0003	0.0099	0.0111
	1986	0.0812	0.0044	0.0740	0.0902
1987	1992	0.0213	0.0005	0.0206	0.0228
	1993	0.1051	0.0016	0.1025	0.1094

Table 3. The average results of RMS errors produced by NCNNs over 50 runs for the chlorophyll-a prediction in Lake Kasumigaura.

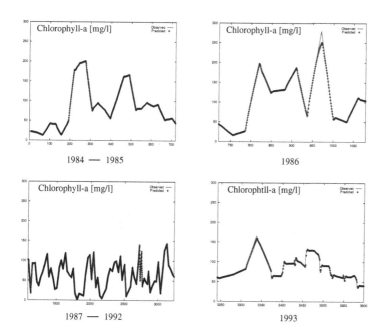

Fig. 2. The observed outputs and the best NCNNs outputs for the chlorophyll-a prediction in Lake Kasumigaura. The time span is $\Delta t = 1$.

4   Conclusions

This paper introduces NCNNs and applies NCNNs to two time series prediction problems, i.e., the Mackey-Glass differential equation and the chlorophyll-a prediction in Lake Kasumigaura. Accurate prediction of chlorophyll-a and other blue-green algae in fresh water lakes can provide ecologists and environmentalists with valuable information for controlling major outbreaks of these algae and protecting the environment. Very good results were obtained by NCNNs in comparison with other algorithms.

NCNNs provide a very promising and competitive alternative to designing NN ensembles manually. However, no special considerations were made in the optimisation of the size of the ensemble in this paper. It would be desirable to develop a learning algorithm which can vary the ensemble size dynamically. Preliminary work on this research has already started.

References

1. Y. Liu and X. Yao, Negatively correlated neural networks can produce best ensembles, *Australian Journal of Intelligent Information Processing Systems*, **4**(3/4), pp.176 185, 1997.
2. X. Yao and Y. Liu, Making use of population information in evolutionary arti"cial neural networks, *IEEE Transactions on Systems, Man and Cybernetics*, **28B**(3),pp.417 425, June 1998.
3. Y. Liu and X. Yao, Simultaneous Learning of Negatively Correlated Neural Networks, *Journal of Artificial Life and Robotics*. Accepted, 1998.
4. J. D. Farmer and J. J. Sidorowich, Predicting chaotic time series, *Physical Review Letters*, Vol. 59, pp.845 847, 1987.
5. M. Mackey and L. Glass, Oscillation and chaos in physiological control systems, *Science*, vol. 197, p. 287, 1977.
6. T. M. Martinetz and S. G. Berkovich and K. J. Schulten, Neural-gas network for vector quantization and its application to time-series prediction, *IEEE Trans. on Neural Networks*, Vol. 4, pp.558 569, 1993.
7. X. Yao and Y. Liu, A new evolutionary system for evolving arti"cial neural networks, *IEEE Transactions on Neural Networks*, Vol.8, no.3, pp.694 713, May 1997.
8. R. S. Crowder, Predicting the Mackey-Glass timeseries with cascade-correlation learning, in *Proc. of the 1990 Connectionist Models Summer School*, pp.117 123, 1990.
9. J. Moody and C. J. Darken, Fast learning in networks of locally-tuned processing units, *Neural Computation*, Vol. 1, pp.281 294, 1989.
10. F. Recknagel, T. Fukushima, T. Hanazato, N. Takamura and H. Wilson, Modelling and Prediction of Phyto- and Zooplankton Dynamics in Lake Kasumigaura by Arti"cial Neural Networks, *Lakes & Reservoirs* (in press).

Animating the Evolution Process of Genetic Algorithms

An Li and Kit Po Wong

Arti"cial Intelligence and Power Systems Research Group
The University of Western Australia
Australia

Abstract. This paper reports the work on the development of an animation system for visualising the optimisation process of the Genetic Algorithm. The description on the requirements and structure of the system is presented. The developed system is applied to visualise some six testing cases. Sequences of animation shots of the evolution process for solving the Branin RCOS problem and the Scha˘er-6 problem are presented. In the latter example, the e˘ect of a solution acceleration technique is also demonstrated. The method of building the visualisation system can be applied to other evolutionary computation techniques.

Keywords: Genetic Algorithm, animation, graphic user interface (GUI), optimisation

1 Introduction

In the areas of science, engineering and economics, there are many optimisation problems, which are highly non-convex and their global optimum solutions are required. Owing to their ability in seeking the global or near-global optimum solution, Genetic Algorithms (GAs) [1,2] have been applied to solving optimisation problems in image processing [3,4], VLSI design [5], robotics systems [6,7], transportation [8,9], and power engineering [10,11,12,13].

Genetic algorithms (GAs) are an adaptive searching technique in the field of evolutionary computation based on the mechanics of natural genetics and natural selection. The success of the application of GAs to an optimisation problem depends on the design of (a) representation of chromosomes, (b) fitness function, (c) method of crossover, (d) mutation operation and (e) measures and techniques to ensure robustness of the GA evolution process for the determination of the optimum solution. Besides these factors, the performances of GAs depend on the parameter settings of the population size, crossover rate and mutation rate.

To ease the design of the components above and to examine the effectiveness of the measures and techniques in (e), a visualisation tool will be very helpful. In such a tool, the evolution processes of GAs need to be animated. While the evolution processes of GAs are di cult to predict particularly during the development phase of the GA-based optimisation algorithms, visualisation of the evolution processes will make the processes transparent. Owing to the transparency provided, deeper insight to the performance of the algorithm under development can be obtained and hence the development time can be shortened.

The animation of the GA evolution process will give aids to determine the appropriateness of the values of the parameter settings, or the appropriate points in the process on which settings of the parameters need to be changed. Furthermore, it will provide a better insight to the distribution and diversity of chromosomes in the population.

While work [14] on a two dimensional data matrix representation of the search space for visualisation purposes has recently been reported, this paper is devoted to the development of an animation system for visualising the evolution of chromosomes during the evolution process. It describes the requirements and structure of the system. The developed system is applied to visualise some six testing cases. Sequences of animation shots of the evolution process for optimising the Branin RCOS problem [15] and the Schaffer-6 problem [15] are presented. In the latter example, the effect of a solution acceleration technique is also demonstrated. The method of building the visualisation system can be applied to optimisation process based on other evolutionary computation techniques.

2   Requirements of animating system

An animating system for the GA evolutionary process should be able to display:
- population of chromosomes;
- distribution of the chromosomes;
- display of search space in two- and three-dimensional space for up-to three variable problems;
- sequential change in the distribution of the chromosomes in a population from one generation to the next;
- crossover action in forming a child chromosome;
- mutation action in forming a child chromosome;
- convergence characteristics of the GA optimisation process;
- background information and relevant terminology.

Moreover, an animating system should have the ability to allow interactive setting of the parameters for executing the evolution process.

3   Design and Structure of the GA Animation System

A system called the Genetic Algorithm Animation System (GAAS) has been designed and developed to fulfil the requirements in Section 2. GAAS is built using the high performance language MATLAB (version 5.2), a sophisticated software package for numeric computation and data visualization. By making use of sophisticated graphic user interfaces (GUIs) provided by MATLAB, GAAS is designed to provide a visually rich environment for conveying information, allowing more intimate interaction between users and machines. Rather than the one-way path from keyboard to video screen, GAAS allows the user to interact directly with the objects on the display. The overall structure of the GAAS is shown in Fig. 1.

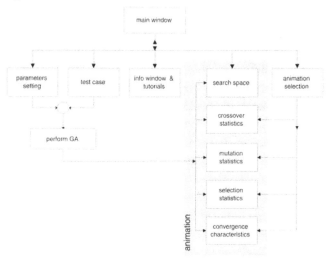

Fig. 1. Block diagram of Genetic Algorithm Animation System

With reference to Fig. 1, when GAAS is initiated, a main window will be displayed. From the main window, the user is allowed to (a) set parameters, (b) select a test case, (c) select the dimension of the search space, (d) access the information on selected test cases, (e) access the tutorials on GA, (f) select the display on genetic operations and convergence characteristics, and (g) execute the animation process. Fig. 2 gives an actual GAAS display of the main window, the parameter setting control panel, test case indicator and menu bar.

GAAS is designed and implemented following a hierarchical structure shown in Fig.3. In GAAS, the main window is the Root Figure object depicted in Fig.3. As shown in Fig. 2, the main window is responsible for taking parameter setting, executing numerical calculation and graphical animation, and initiating the display for tutorials and information. There are a number of key objects developed and built into the main window. The key objects include:

- **2D** (*Radio button*): Enable or disable the display for 2D search space;
- **3D** (*Radio button*): Enable or disable the display for 3D search space;
- **Acceleration** (*Check box*): Enable or disable the acceleration technique;

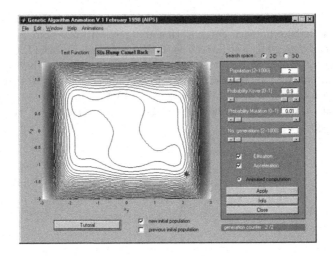

Fig. 2. A sample display of the Genetic Algorithm Animation System

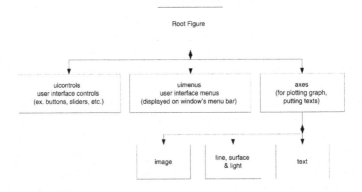

Fig. 3. Hierarchical Structure used in GASS Design

- **Animations** (*User interface menu*): Allow to select pop-up windows for animating crossover, mutation and selection operations. The animation of convergence behavior can also be selected from this object;
- **Animated computation** (*Radio button*): Enable or disable animation;
- **Case Selection** (*Pop-up menu*): Provide 6 build-in test cases including De Jong function 1, De Jong function 2, Schaffer function 6, Schaffer function 7, Six-hump camel back function and Branin RCOS function;
- **Elitism** (*Check box*): Enable or disable the elitism scheme;
- **Info** (*Push button*): Invoke a pop-up window describing selected test case;
- **Tutorials** (*User interface menu*): Allow to select pop-up windows for tutorials on Genetic Algorithms and related technical jargons.

Four pop-up windows have been designed and implemented for animating key genetic operations. These four windows are *Crossover Animation, Mutation Animation, Selection Animation* and *Convergence Animation*. A pop-up help window is also provided and can be invoked from *Tutorials* menu to display the definition for relevant evolutionary computation terms.

In the implementation of GAAS, the object-oriented programming methodology has been used. The implementation details are omitted here.

4   Application Examples

GAAS has been applied to visualise the evolution process of the Standard GA (SGA) in optimising some well-known functions given in [15]. The authors have previously developed a solution acceleration method for improving the performance of SGA. The acceleration method can be found in [16] and it is the acceleration scheme (**a**) described in Reference [17]. This method has been incorporated into the SGA program given in Reference [15] to form the accelerated GA and has also been applied to optimise the functions mentioned above. This section presents the animation shots in the optimisation processes when searching solutions for the Branin RCOS problem. To illustrate the effect of acceleration, the animation results obtained by GAAS for the Schaffer-6 problem are also presented.

(i)   *Solution searching for the Branin RCOS problem*

The objective function, given by Eq. (1), of Branin RCOS problem has the global minimum value of 0.397887 at $(x_1, x_2) = (- , 12.275)$, $(, 2.275)$, or $(9.425, 2.475)$.

$$F(x_1, x_2) = (x_2 - \frac{5.1}{4}\frac{1}{2}x_1^2 + \frac{5}{ }x_1 - 6)^2 + 10(1 - \frac{1}{8})cos(x_1) + 10 \qquad (1)$$

The chromosomes in the initial population spread widely over the search space in terms of the x_1- and x_2- axes as shown in Fig. 4(a). However, it can be observed that there are two initial chromosomes located very close to the third solution point near the bottom-left corner of the figure. This visualisation indicates that the evolution process may be attracted to the third solution point. The distribution of the chromosomes in the 2nd generation in Fig. 4(b) shows that the chromosomes are attracted to the second and the third solution points. A further generation sees the solution process evolves towards the third solution points as shown in Fig. 4(c). The third optimal solution is obtained in the 7th generation. The chromosome distribution at the 20th generation is shown in Fig. 4(d) giving confirmation to the optimal solution. To capture all the optimal solutions, clustering algorithms can be included into the evolution process.

Statistics of the number of mutation performed and the number of times a chromosome has been selected for crossover in the 20th generation are displayed as shown in Figs. 4(e) and (f). In the Fig. 4(e), a bar represents a chromosome and a black bar represents a mutated chromosome. In Fig. 4(f), the digits in the odd columns give the index of a chromosome. In the even columns, the digit summarised the number of times the chromosome has been selected for crossover while the symbol 'x' indicates no selection.

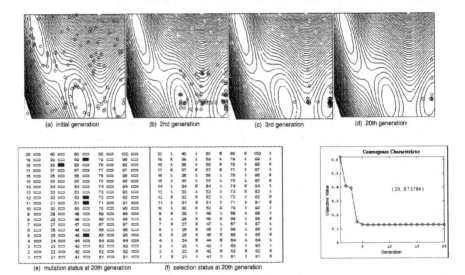

(a) initial generation   (b) 2nd generation   (c) 3rd generation   (d) 20th generation

(e) mutation status at 20th generation   (f) selection status at 20th generation

Fig. 4. Evolution process and statistics in solving the Branin RCOS problem

Fig. 5.

Convergence Characteristic

Fig. 5 shows the convergence characteristics of the process. From the statistics of chromosome selection, crossover and mutation given in the animation widows such as shown in Fig. 4 and the convergence characteristic given in Fig. 5, the user will be able to examine the effectiveness of the evolutionary process at any generation and hence evaluate the appropriateness of the settings of the GA parameters and the performances of the various genetic operations.

(ii)   *Solution searching for the Scha er-6 problem*

To demonstrate the visualisation of the acceleration effect in [16,17], the Schaffer-6 problem is solved here. The objective function is given in eqn. (2) and the global minimum value is zero at $(x_1, x_2) = (0, 0)$.

$$F(x_1, x_2) = 0.5 + \frac{sin^2(\sqrt{x_1^2 + x_2^2}) - 0.5}{(1 + 0.001(x_1^2 + x_2^2))^2} \qquad (2)$$

The evolution of a population of chromosomes through the first four generations with and without the acceleration scheme is shown in Figs. 6 and 7. In these figures, the vertical axis is for the value of the objective function and the other two axes are for x_1 and x_2. Without the acceleration, as shown in Figs. 6(a)-(d), the chromosomes hop around in the searching space without getting close to the optimum point. However, in Figs. 7(a)-(d) when solution acceleration is enabled, the chromosomes move rapidly towards the optimum point immediately after the 1st generation, the optimum point is almost reached at the 4th generation by the fittest chromosome. The same phenomenon was observed when the problem was solved by separate executions of the accelerated GA algorithm.

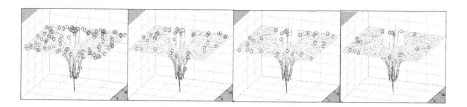

Fig. 6. Evolution process without acceleration in solving the Schaffer-6 problem

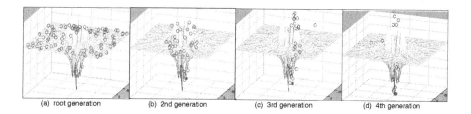

(a) root generation   (b) 2nd generation   (c) 3rd generation   (d) 4th generation

Fig. 7. Evolution process with acceleration in solving the Schaffer-6 problem

5   Conclusions

A GA animation system, GAAS, has been designed and developed using the object-oriented programming methodology. The structure and facilities of GAAS have been reported. The multiple-window displays that the system provides enable a clear visualisation of the evolution process of GA and statistics of some of the important GA operations. Two optimisation problems, Branin RCOS and Schaffer-6, have been used to demonstrate the usefulness of the developed animation system. This system will be very useful for education purposes and for advancing the research into robust evolutionary algorithms. Further development of GAAS is currently undertaken to include more functions and facilities.

References

1. J.H. HOLLAND. *Adaption in Natural and Artificial Systems*. Ann Arbor: University of Michigan Press, 1975.
2. D.E. Goldberg. *Genetic Algorithms in Search, Optimisation and Machine Learning*. Addison-Wesley, 1989.
3. V.R. MANDAVA, FITZPATRICK M., and D. R. PICLENS. Adaptive search space scaling in digital image registration. *IEEE Transactions on Medical Imaging*, 8(3):251 262, 1989.
4. J. LUI, Y.Y. TANG, and CAO Y.C. An evolutionary autonomous agents approach to image feature extraction. *IEEE Trans. on Evolutionary Computation*, 1(2):141 158, 1997.
5. J. LIENIG. A parallel genetic algorithm for performance-driven vlsi routing. *IEEE Trans. on Evolutionary Computation*, 1(1):29 39, 1997.
6. J. K. PARKER and D.E. Goldberg. Inverse kinematics of redundant robots using genetic algorithm. *Proceedings, IEEE International Conference on Robotics and Automation*, pages 271 276, 1989.
7. J. XIAO, Z. MICHALEWICZ, L. ZHANG, and K. TROJANOWSKI. Adaptive evolutionary planner/navigator for mobile robots. *IEEE Trans. on Evolutionary Computation*, 1(1):18 28, 1997.
8. G.A. VIGNAUX and Z MICHALEWICZ. A genetic algorithm for the linear transportation problem. *IEEE Trans. on Systems, Man and Cybernetics*, 21(2):321 326, 1989.
9. S.R. THANGIAH, K.E. NYGARD, and P. L. JUELL. Gideon: a genetic algorithm system for vehicle routing with time windows. *Proceedings, 7th IEEE Conference on AI Applications*, pages 322 328, 1991.
10. K.P. WONG and WONG Y.W. Genetic and genetic/simulated-annealing approaches to economic dispatch. *IEEE Trans. on Systems, Man and Cybernetics*, 1994.
11. K.P. WONG, A. LI, and M. Y. LAW. Development of constrained genetic-algorithm load-"ow method. *IEE Proc.-Gener. Transm. Distrib.*, 144(2):91 99, March 1997.
12. D.C. WALTER and G.B. SHEBLE. Genetic algorithm solution of short term hydro-thermal scheduling with valve point loading. *IEEE PES Summer Meeting, Seattle, SM 414-3 PWRS*, 1992.
13. R.R. BISHOP and G.G. RICHARDS. Identifying induction machine parameters using a genetic opimization algorithm. *IEEE Proceedings, Section 6C2*, pages 476 479, 1990.
14. T.D. COLLINS. Understanding evolutionary computing: A hands on approach. *IEEE Proc. International Conference on Evolutionary Computation, Anchorage, Alaska*, pages 564 569, 1998.
15. Z. MICHALEWICZ. *Genetic algorithms + data structures = evolution programs*, 3rd rev. extended ed. Springer-Verlag, 1996.
16. K.P. WONG and A. LI. A technique for improving the convergence characteristic of genetic algorithms and its application to a genetic-based load "ow algorithm. *Simulated Evolution and Learning, JH Kim, X. Yao, T. Furuhasi (Eds), Lecture Notes in Artificial Intelligence 1285*, pages 167 176, 1997.
17. K.P. WONG and A. LI. Virtual population and solution acceleration techniques for evolutionary optimisation algorithms. *Proc. The 2nd Asia Pacific Conference on Simulated Evolution and Learning (SEAL98), Canberra, Australia*, 24-27 November 1998.

Analysis on the Island Model Parallel Genetic Algorithms for the Genetic Drifts

Tatsuya NIWA* and Masaru TANAKA**

Information Science Division
Electrotechnical Laboratory
1 1 4 Umezono Tsukuba-shi Ibaraki, 305-8568 JAPAN.
phone: +81-298-54-5866, fax: +81-298-54-5841

Abstract. In our former paper, we have investigated the relation among the mean convergence time, the population size, and the chromosome length of genetic algorithms (GAs). Our analyses of GAs make use of the Markov chain formalism based on the Wright-Fisher model, which is a typical and well-known model in population genetics. The Wright-Fisher model is characterized by 1-locus, 2-alleles, "xed population size, and discrete generation. For these simple characters, it is easy to evaluate the behavior of genetic process. We have also given the mean convergence time under genetic drift. Genetic drift can be well described in the Wright-Fisher model, and we have determined the stationary states of the corresponding Markov chain model and the mean convergence time to reach one of these stationary states. The island model is also well-known model in population genetics, and it is similar to one of the most typical model of parallel GAs, which require parallel computer for high performance computing. We have also derived the most e˘ective migration rate for the island model parallel GAs with some restrictions. The obtained most e˘ective migration rate is rather small value, i.e. one immigrant per generation, however the behaviors of the island model parallel GAs at that migration rate are not revealed yet clearly. In this paper, we discuss the mean convergence time for the island model parallel GAs from both of exact solution and numerical simulation. As expected from the Wright-Fisher model s analysis, the mean convergence time of the island model parallel GAs is proportional to population size, and the coe cient is larger with smaller migration rate. Since to keep the diversity in population is important for c˘ective performance of GAs, the convergence in population gives a bad in"uence for GAs. On the other hand, mutation and crossover operation prevent converging in GAs population. Because of the small migration rate makes converging force weak, it must be effective for GAs. This means that the island model parallel GAs is more e cient not only to use large population size with parallel computers, but also to keep the diversity in population, than usual GAs.

Keywords: Markov chain, population genetics, genetic drift, Wright-Fisher model, island model parallel genetic algorithms.

---
* <niwa@etl.go.jp>
** <mtanaka@etl.go.jp>

1   Introduction

Genetic Algorithms (GAs) are adaptive methods based on the genetic processes of biological organisms which were introduced by Holland [6]. They successed to solve many problems of search, optimization, and machine learning [4]. It is natural to study behaviors of GAs theoretically, because we want to know performances of GAs compared with other methods and that how GAs converge good solutions; it is expected that situations are different from random search methods. Then many researchers have studied GAs theoretically [2][12][13]. One of the interesting topics in the finite population of GAs is the genetic drift.

In population genetics and GAs, genetic drift is well known phenomenon. In [1][3][7], genetic drift has been studied with computer simulations. Kimura gave the mathematical analysis for the population genetics through diffusion models [8].

In [11], we derived the most e cient mutation rate for standard GAs and the most e cient migration rate for island model parallel GAs. In this paper, we discuss the mean convergence time for the island model parallel GAs. This paper is organized as follows. Section 2 is a review of our former researches [10][11] in order to understand the later sections, and it is devoted to analyze the mean convergence time and the stationary state on the Wright-Fisher model which is a model of simple GAs. In section 3 we consider the island model parallel GAs, which is often used in parallel GAs. For the details of our analyses on the Markov chain model, see [14].

2   Genetic Drifts and the Wright-Fisher Model

Let the population consist of fixed n individuals which have only one locus, in other words, the length of chromosome is one for each. There are only two different alleles ('0' and '1') in the locus, and the state is denoted as the number of '1's in the population. This is the well known genetic model as   Wright-Fisher model   in biological population genetics field (e.g. [5]).

Genetic drift is the random " uctuation of gene frequencies subjected by probabilistic transition from generation to generation in finite population size. It tends to localize genes to particular genes (convergent states of Markov chain). This tendency is against mutation, which makes genes disperse to various genes. In this section, we consider the mean convergence time of the Wright-Fisher model without mutation using standard Markov chain analysis.

In this case, the convergence of the Wright-Fisher model is driven by genetic drift. The model has only two alleles, i.e. 0 and 1. In general case, i.e. more than two alleles, we pick up a particular allele to use the Wright-Fisher model. If a total population size is n, then the state of the population is uniquely specified by the number of 0s, so we define the state as the number of 0s.

2.1 Mean Convergence Time for the Wright-Fisher Model

The mean convergence time of simple GAs is proportional to the population size. In [1][3][7], the effects of genetic drift to the mean convergence time have been studied with numerical experiments. It is shown that the mean convergence time is proportional to the population size of a model. Theoreticaly, we can show, in the continuous limit such as the large population limit, the mean convergence time is proportional to the size of population. According to Kimura [8] with some tedious calculations, we have the following relation on the mean convergence time ;

$$\simeq \sum_{j=0}^{\infty} \frac{P_{2j}(1-2p) - P_{2j+2}(1-2p)}{(j+1)(2j+1)} n \tag{1}$$

where $P_*(\cdot)$ are the Legendre polynomials, and p is the gene frequency at the initial state. This shows that the mean convergence time is proportional to the population size. It is too di cult to explain the derivation of eq.(1), see [8] and [14] for detail. As shown in table 1, the theoretical values from eq.(1) coincide with the results from the numerical experiments [1]. Note that the right hand side of eq.(1) is equal to $-2\{p \log p + (1-p) \log(1-p)\}n$.

initial state	theoretical analysis from eq.(1)	numerical analysis from [1]
$p = 1/2$	$1.386n$	$1.4n$
$p = 1/4$	$1.125n$	$1.0n$
$p = 1/8$	$0.754n$	$0.7n$

Table 1. Mean convergence time at large population

2.2 Stationary State for the Wright-Fisher Model

Here we consider the Wright-Fisher model with mutation. Then the transition matrix Q, each element of which is transition probability from state i to state j, is given as

$$Q_{ij} = \binom{n}{j} \left(\mu + \frac{1-2\mu}{n}i\right)^j \left(1 - \mu - \frac{1-2\mu}{n}i\right)^{n-j} . \tag{2}$$

Since the largest eigenvalue of Q is 1, we get the density function of the stationary state by normalizing the eigenvector for the eigenvalue 1 [5]. Making the population size n the infinity, the density function of stationary state is given as [8];

$$\frac{(4n\mu)}{\{(2n\mu)\}^2} \left\{\frac{i}{n}\left(1 - \frac{i}{n}\right)\right\}^{2n\mu-1} . \tag{3}$$

Figure 1 shows the shape of the density function of stationary state in the large population limit. From the eq.(3), we see that the mutation rate $\mu = \frac{1}{2n}$

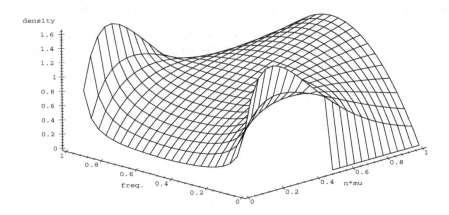

Fig. 1. The density function of the stationary states: the large population limit
$\frac{\Gamma(4n\mu)}{\{\Gamma(2n\mu)\}^2} \left\{ \frac{i}{n}\left(1 - \frac{i}{n}\right) \right\}^{2n\mu-1}$.

makes the density function "at. This shows that this mutation rate makes the GAs work well. Because, if the mutation rate is large, GAs are hard to get stationary results, and if the mutation rate is small GAs become easy to converge to a certain value which might not be an optimal result. When the mutation rate μ is $\frac{1}{2n}$ all of the states have the same probability. At that mutation rate, the density function could be expected to take the same shape as the considered fitness function.

In this consideration, we didn't take the in"uence of the chromosome length into account. This is because, the gene of each locus behaves like described here. Furthermore, since the reciprocal effect spanning plural loci, i.e. epistasis, depends on the problem to be solved, we cannot describe it without knowing the fitness function. But the mutation rate $\mu = \frac{1}{2n}$ could be a standard value.

3   Island Model Parallel GAs

Parallel GAs have been investigated since GAs were introduced. The island model parallel GAs are typical models of parallel GAs [15]. For the island model parallel GAs, the total population is divided into several subpopulations, and one processor is allocated to each subpopulation. Each processor is engaged to run the simple GA independently. Inter-processor communication occurs during the migration phase at regular intervals (i.e. migration interval). During migration, a fixed rate of each subpopulation is selected and sent to another subpopulation. In return, the same number of migrants are received and replace individuals selected according to some criteria.

3.1   Stationary State for the Island Model

In the limit of subpopulation size n tending to infinity, the density function of stationary state is given by [8];

$$\frac{(2nm)\left(\frac{i}{n}\right)^{2nm\bar{x}-1}\left(1-\frac{i}{n}\right)^{2nm(1-\bar{x})-1}}{(2nm\bar{x})\ (2nm(1-\bar{x}))}, \tag{4}$$

where n is the number of individuals in a subpopulation, m is migration rate or the ratio of migrants for each generation in subpopulation, and $\bar{x}$ is the mean value of $\frac{i}{n}$ of whole populations. Figure 2 shows the density function of the stationary states.

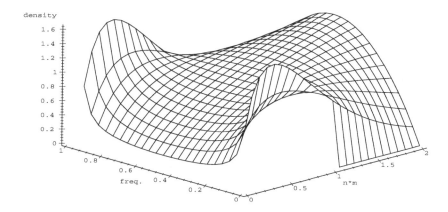

Fig. 2. The density function of the stationary states: the large population limit of island model parallel GAs, where subpopulation size is n, and the mean frequency $\bar{x}$ of whole population is $\frac{1}{2}$; $\frac{\Gamma(2nm)}{\{\Gamma(nm)\}^2}\left\{\frac{i}{n}\left(1-\frac{i}{n}\right)\right\}^{nm-1}$.

From the eq.(4), the migration rate m is twice large as mutation rate μ of the eq.(3) when $\bar{x}$ is $\frac{1}{2}$. That means the migration rate $m = \frac{1}{n}$ makes the density function uniform, similar to the case of $\mu = \frac{1}{2n}$. This implies that the migration rate $m = \frac{1}{n}$, which means one migrant per generation, makes parallel GAs work well. This situation is similar to the case of the mutation rate of standard GAs. However, there are some differences between them; First, mutation is ignored in the eq.(4). Second, we assume $\bar{x}$ (the mean value of $\frac{i}{n}$ of whole populations) is $\frac{1}{2}$. Because of these differences, our expectation would have a little error. In fact, the migration rates used in the several researches on parallel GAs are larger than $\frac{1}{n}$.

Although Manderick et al.[9] tried to determine the most effective migration rate, they could not determine it. Because a small difference of migration rate does not make a meaningful deference in the performance of the island model parallel GAs. Since the smaller migration rate gives less communication overhead cost, we expect the migration rate $\frac{1}{n}$ might drive the island model parallel GAs effectively.

3.2   Mean Convergence Time for the Island Model

For the simple model, i.e. two islands case, we can evaluate the mean convergence time depending on its population size and migration rate by the numerical simulation. As well as the Wright-Fisher model, the mean convergence time is proportional to its population size, and the coe cient decreases by larger migration rate. We set the initial value of this simulation to half of the population for each island.

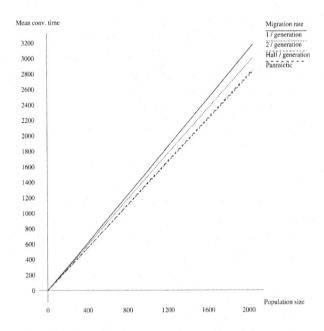

Fig. 3. Mean convergence time vs population size with respect to several migration rates (two islands, population size is in total).

When the population size is small, we can get the exact solution. The number of the states of two islands case is the product of the number of the states of each island. It is too di cult to get the transition matrix in general form. We evaluated the mean convergence time when the population sizes of one island are 2 and 4, i.e. the total population sizes are 4 and 8. As the initial state of

population	migration	simulation	exact solution
2-2	1	6.154	6.167
4-4	1	11.623	11.670
4-4	2	11.240	11.297

Table 2. Mean convergence time for two-island model. Migration represents the number of immigrant per generation.

this simulation, we set the gene frequency of each island to $1/2$. The simulation results almost coincide with the exact solutions, as shown in table 2.

Though the mean convergence time of island model parallel GAs is proportional to population size, the proportional constant is large when the migration rate is small. From the numerical simulation, the proportional constants are 1.54, 1.47, and 1.38, depending on the migration for one per generation, two per generation, and half of island population per generation, respectively. Since the proportional constant of the ordinary (panmictic) GA is 1.386, the migration of half of island population per generation seems to give a similar behavior to panmictic GAs. However, the small migration makes the convergence time long, it would give a good in"uence to GAs.

4   Conclusions

We considered the mean convergence time subjected to genetic drift and gave reference values of mutation and migration. We want to know the performance of GAs compared with other methods. Therefore theoretical and experimental studies of GAs must be performed. The roles of mutation, crossover, and selection must be made clear and controllable. Mutation and crossover are effective to tend to increase the diversity in population. Convergence by reproduction gives the tendency of decreasing the diversity. So we want to know the critical point that is to balance between increasing and decreasing the diversity in population, to make the searching process of GAs effective. Even though the Wright-Fisher model is a very simple model, i.e. 1-locus, 2-alleles, fixed population size, and discrete generation, it has some remarkable features. From figure 1, when the mutation rate has the value $\mu = \frac{1}{2n}$, the density of the stationary states tends to be uniform. Furthermore, in case of island model parallel GAs, the migration rate $m = \frac{1}{n}$ makes the density uniform. Additionally, such small migration rate, as $m = \frac{1}{n}$, increases the convergence time. This means that the island model parallel GAs is more e cient not only to use large population size, but also to keep the diversity in population than usual GAs. These reference values might be a key point to determine the mutation rates and the migration rates.

356   Tatsuya Niwa and Masaru Tanaka

Acknowledgments

The authors would like to give thanks to Dr. H. Nakashima, Director of the Information Science Division, and Dr. H. Asoh, for their continual encouragement and valuable discussions and useful comments.

References

1. H. Asoh and H. Mühlenbein, On the Mean Convergence Time of Evolutionary Algorithms without Selection , *Parallel Problem Solving from Nature 3 (proceedings)*, 1994.
2. A. E. Eiben, E. H. L. Aarts, and K. M. Van Hee, Global Convergence of Genetic Algorithms: a Markov Chain Analysis , *Parallel Problem Solving from Nature (proceedings)*, 4-12, 1990.
3. D. E. Goldberg and P. Segrest, Finite Markov Chain Analysis of Genetic Algorithms , *Proceedings of the 2nd International Conference on Genetic Algorithms*, 1-8, 1987.
4. D. E. Goldberg, *Genetic Algorithms in Search, Optimization & Machine Learning*, Addison-Wesley, Reading, Mass., 1989.
5. D. L. Hartl and A. G. Clark, *Principles of Population Genetics, Second Edition*, Sinauer Associates Inc., 1975.
6. J. H. Holland, *Adaptation in Natural and Artificial Systems*, Univ. of Michigan Press, Ann Arbor, Mich., 1975.
7. J. Horn, Finite Markov Chain Analysis of Genetic Algorithms with Niching , *Proceedings of the 5th International Conference on Genetic Algorithms*, 110-117, 1993.
8. M. Kimura, Di˜usion Models in Population Genetics , *J. Appl. Prob. 1*, 177-232, 1964.
9. B. Manderick and P. Spiessens, Fine-Grained Parallel Genetic Algorithms , *Proceedings of the 3rd International Conference on Genetic Algorithms*, 428-433, 1989.
10. T. Niwa and M. Tanaka, On the Mean Convergence Time for Simple Genetic Algorithms , *Proceedings of the International Conference on Evolutionary Computing '95*, 1995.
11. T. Niwa and M. Tanaka, Analyses of Simple Genetic Algorithms and Island Model Parallel Genetic Algorithm , *Artificial Neural Nets and Genetic Algorithms, Proceedings of the International Conference in Norwich, U.K., 1997*, 224-228, 1997.
12. G. Rudolph, Convergence Analysis of Canonical Genetic Algorithms , *IEEE Transactions on Neural Networks*, Vol.5, No.1, 96-101, 1994.
13. J. Suzuki, A Markov Chain Analysis on a Genetic Algorithm , *Proceedings of the 5th International Conference on Genetic Algorithms*, 146-153, 1993.
14. M. Tanaka and T. Niwa, Markov Chain Analysis on Simple Genetic Algorithm , *ETL-TR-94-13*, 1994.
15. R. Tanese, Distributed Genetic Algorithms , *Proceedings of the 3rd International Conference on Genetic Algorithms*, 434-439, 1989.

A Paradox of Neural Encoders and Decoders or Why Don't We Talk Backwards?*

Bradley Tonkes[1], Alan Blair[1], and Janet Wiles[1][2]

[1] Department of Computer Science and Electrical Engineering
[2] School of Psychology
University of Queensland
QLD 4072 Australia
{btonkes, blair, janetw}@csee.uq.edu.au

Abstract. We present a framework for studying the biases that recurrent neural networks bring to language processing tasks. A semantic concept represented by a point in Euclidean space is translated into a symbol sequence by an encoder network. This sequence is then presented to a decoder network which attempts to translate it back to the original concept. We show how a pair of recurrent networks acting as encoder and decoder can develop their own symbolic language that is serially transmitted between them either forwards or backwards. The encoder and decoder bring di˘erent constraints to the task, and these early results indicate that the con"icting nature of these constraints may be re"ected in the language that ultimately emerges, providing clues to the structure of human languages.

1 Introduction

The study of automata and the languages they can process has a history dating back to Turing [9] and beyond. Entwined with this story is the study of natural languages and of the human mind. The issue is essentially one of constraints. The constraints on an automaton, such as time and space, place bounds on the types of tasks it can perform including the types of languages it can process. Likewise, it is believed that the constraints of the human mind are re"ected in the languages we use, so that by examining the features of language we may better understand the principles that guide human language and thought processes.

Perhaps the best known work relating automata and languages, which also seems highly relevant to natural languages, is Chomsky's hierarchy [1]. Chomsky's hierarchy is a family of language classes that can be recognised by a corresponding family of automata classes. With different restrictions on the automata, different language classes may be processed. This hierarchy was designed with symbolic systems in mind, and it has been suggested that dynamical systems,

---

* We thank Tony Plate and Elizabeth Sklar for helpful discussions. The research was supported by an APA to BT, a UQ Postdoctoral Fellowship to AB and an ARC grant to JW.

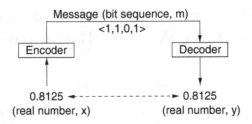

Fig. 1. Getting the point across. Two recurrent networks are used as encoder and decoder for a communication channel. The encoder is presented with a point from a subset of Euclidean space, $x \in U \subset \mathbb{R}^n$, and outputs a sequence of bits, $m \in \Sigma^*, \Sigma = \{0, 1\}$. This sequence of bits is then used as input for the decoder, which outputs a value $y \in \mathbb{R}^n$ after the last bit in the sequence has been processed. If the communication is successful, then y should approximate x. The example shown is using a *numeric encoding*.

including many connectionist models, may bring different biases to language processing tasks relative to their symbolic counterparts [8], necessitating a re-evaluation of the automata/language relationship.

As well as processing constraints, connectionist models also have *learning* constraints. That is, models are limited not only in what they can represent, but in what they can learn. The distinction between learning and representation is important when we consider how human languages have developed. For a natural language to be viable, it must not only be representable by its users, but also learnable by subsequent generations [6]. The learning and representational constraints of the human brain dictate the set of languages humans are able to understand and learn, and consequently the languages that have emerged.

Recurrent neural networks (RNNs) have shown significant promise as computational models of various aspects of the human language processing system. Part of their appeal is the ability to incorporate syntax and semantics into a single model [3]. They have also demonstrated competence in learning a wide range of grammatical structures [7], and often re"ect real-world data on natural language tasks [2,10] and language change [5]. It seems important then, to investigate the constraints of recurrent networks and the way that they in"uence the properties and emergence of language.

This paper is motivated by the observation that communication is essentially a shared task between sender and receiver, in which the kind of language favoured by the sender may not be convenient for the receiver and vice-versa. That is, the constraints of the sender and receiver may be different. The language that ultimately emerges may arise as a compromise between these competing interests.

We consider a simple language task in which two RNNs try to communicate a semantic concept represented by a point in a subset, $U \subset \mathbb{R}^n$ of Euclidean space . One network sends a *message* in the form of a sequence of bits, which the other network decodes back into a point in the same Euclidean space (Fig. 1). In this paper we consider the case where U is the unit interval $[0, 1]$.

While the task is superficially simplistic, it has some interesting properties. The concept is specified in a continuous space with arbitrary precision, whereas the language is a sequence of symbols from a finite alphabet. Unlike studies that have looked at language emergence between symbolic agents over a symbolic channel, this task requires a transformation from a concept described with arbitrary precision in a continuous space to a symbolic language. A trade-off is required between the amount of precision in the concepts and the length of the symbol sequences in the language.

It is possible to accomplish the task by using a numeric encoding interpreting the sequence of bits as its numeric (binary) value. For this numeric code, two possibilities are immediately obvious: either the most significant part of the message can be sent first, or it can be sent last. For example, $0.8125_{10} = 0.1101_2$ may be sent most-significant-bit (MSB) first as $<1, 1, 0, 1>$ or least-significant-bit (LSB) first as $<1, 0, 1, 1>$. This paper investigates the effect that encoder and decoder constraints have on the way that the concept space and message sequence can be related.

In Sect. 2, encoder and decoder networks are each trained separately using a hill-climbing algorithm to perform the task using the numeric code. In Sect. 3, the encoder and decoder are *co-evolved* together and are at liberty to determine their own language . We conclude with some remarks relating the results of the simulations to features of natural language.

2   Simulations 1 and 2: Encoders and Decoders

In the first two series of simulations we investigate the ability of the individual encoders and decoders to perform their respective mappings. In total, four mappings are considered.

1. Encoding a real value to an MSB first binary sequence.
2. Encoding a real value to an LSB first binary sequence.
3. Decoding from an MSB first binary sequence to a real value.
4. Decoding from an LSB first binary sequence to a real value.

2.1   Encoders

The architecture for the encoder is a simple recurrent network (SRN) with additional connections from the output units to the hidden units. Since a real value may require representation by an arbitrarily long binary string, we initially intended that the encoder would output an end-of-sequence symbol once the number had been encoded. Pilot simulations suggested that this encoding was di cult to evolve so the length of sequences was artificially limited.

Given this general architecture, it is relatively straightforward to hand-code a network with a single hidden unit to perform the encoding for an MSB first sequence. Such a network is shown in Fig. 2(a). However, it is not possible to perform the LSB first encoding without a large number of hidden units due

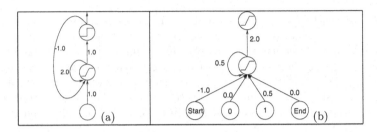

Fig. 2. (a) **MSB encoder:** A RNN that takes a real number between 0 and 1 and encodes it as a numeric string, most signi"cant bit "rst. The hidden unit uses a linear threshold activation function that saturates at -1 and 1, whereas the output units use binary (0.5) threshold units. The input value is presented at the "rst time-step only. (b) **LSB decoder:** A SRN that decodes numeric sequences LSB "rst. The input is wrapped with start and end markers. After presentation of the end marker, the output unit activation corresponds to the appropriate value. Linear (0,1) threshold activations are used on all units.

to the fractal nature of such an encoding. (For messages of n bits, 2^n values $(\frac{0}{2^n}, \frac{1}{2^n}, \ldots, \frac{2^n-1}{2^n})$ may be encoded. For any value, $\frac{k}{2^n}$, the first bit of output is the opposite to that of its neighbours.)

Although a solution could be hand-coded, it was unknown whether it was learnable, so a series of simulations was designed to address this question. Networks were evolved using a simple hill-climbing algorithm to perform both the LSB and MSB mappings. A champion decoder was created with initially random weights. A single mutant was then spawned by randomly perturbing the weights of the champion according to a Gaussian distribution with 0 mean and initially 0.1 variance. If the mutant was able to encode values as well as, or better than the champion, then the mutant became champion and a new mutant was spawned. To evaluate the accuracy with which values were encoded, the strings were decoded with a perfect numeric decoder, and the sum squared error between encoder input and decoder output was calculated.

The values chosen to be encoded were selected by taking a staged learning approach [4]. Initially, only two values, 0 and 0.5, were encoded, and the number of bits that could be sent was accordingly set to 1. Once a network was able to perform this mapping, 2 bits could be sent, encoding 0, 0.25, 0.5 and 0.75. In general, after 2^k numbers could be successfully encoded into k bits, the networks were given 2^{k+1} values to encode into $(k+1)$−bit sequences. The variance was modulated throughout the course of the simulations. Simulations were run for a maximum of 100K generations, or until all 5-bit values could be encoded. Networks with 1, 2, 3 and 5 hidden units were evolved.

2.2   Decoders

SRNs were used as decoders. The task for the these networks was the inverse of the encoders' task with minor variations. Each string presented to a decoder

	MSB First				LSB First			
Hidden units:	1	2	3	5	1	2	3	5
Encoders	11	18	11	7	0	0	0	0
Decoders	0	0	0	0	22	26	30	22

Table 1. Number of networks (of 50 trialed) attaining 5-bit precision in each condition.

was enclosed with start-of-sequence and end-of-sequence inputs, a legacy of the task originally considered for the encoder. The additional inputs did not appear to have a considerable impact on the simulations.

Unlike the encoder, the decoder is capable of decoding either MSB or LSB first, though with some significant differences. Figure 2(b) shows a SRN that decodes LSB first. Although an LSB decoder is able to decode strings of varying lengths with only a single hidden unit, an MSB decoder (not shown) can only decode strings of a fixed length with a single hidden unit. Simulations were carried out in a similar manner to the encoder. A perfect encoder was used to encode values to numeric binary sequences. Decoders were compared by the sum squared error across all presented strings. The same principle of staged learning was applied.

2.3   Results: Encoders and Decoders

Networks of all sizes were able to encode MSB first sequences and decode LSB first sequences of up to 5-bits. No networks could encode more than 2-bit values, LSB first. No networks were able to decode 5-bit sequences MSB first, although one network with 5 hidden units was able to decode 4-bit sequences. The results are broadly summarised in Table 1.

3   Evolving a Language

There is clearly a significant difference between the encoders and decoders. The encoders were only able to learn the MSB first encoding, whereas the decoders preferred learning LSB first sequences. This presents a serious dilemma when we consider the complete system of encoding and decoding (Fig. 1). If the system is to successfully communicate values, then the encoder and decoder must compromise on the nature of the code. An MSB or LSB code will not suffice for the combined system.

Simulations of the complete system were performed under two conditions. In the first, the communication channel reversed the message: whatever was sent first by the encoder was received last by the decoder. This condition allows an MSB code with the encoder encoding MSB first and the decoder decoding LSB first. With the second condition, the order of the message on the communication channel was preserved. In this scenario an MSB code is more difficult, and the

1. Create a champion encoder and decoder.
2. Create a mutant encoder by perturbing the weights of the champion.
3. If the encoding created by the mutant uses a greater variety of strings than the champion, select that mutant.
4. Create a mutant decoder with weights initialised between -1.0 and 1.0.
5. For n iterations, present all inputs of the current precision to the encoder. Train the decoder on the output of the encoder.
6. If the "nal sum squared error of the mutant encoder and decoder across all strings is lower than that of the champions, make the mutants the champions. Furthermore, if the mutants got all strings correct, increase the precision. Return to step (2).

Fig. 3. Evolutionary algorithm for combined encoder/decoder system.

encoder and decoder must develop a code which can be effectively learned and processed by both networks.

Pilot simulations showed that using a hill-climber for both encoder and decoder was intractable. Tests of backpropagation through time (BPTT) on the decoder showed that it was qualitatively similar with respect to the learning task of Sect. 2.2, but faster. Hence, a hill-climber was used for the encoder and BPTT for the decoder. The basic algorithm for the co-evolution of the system is described in Fig. 3.

3.1   Forwards and Reversed

Both the encoder and decoder used two hidden units, with the decoder trained for 1000 epochs. The system was give $n + 2$ bits when communicating n−bit values in the reversed case, and $2n$ bits in the forwards case. The extra bits were found to be necessary for a successful code to develop and have the effect of increasing the proportion of codes that uniquely identify each value.

In the reversed condition, the system was able to create successful codes for 5-bit values. A typical code is shown in Table 2. The code is effectively a sparse numeric code. Although not all binary sequences are used, those that are used are ordered by their numeric values.

The simulations performed with the forwards channel were not nearly as successful as the reversed case. The best observed code, shown in table 2, encoded all 3-bit values. It is apparent that it is neither strictly MSB nor LSB first, since there is no clear ordering of the significance of each bit (less significant bits should tend to show greater sensitivity to changes in the input.)

4   Discussion and Conclusions

The first series of simulations demonstrated the different constraints of the encoder and decoder on the numeric encoding task. Whereas the encoder is only

Input	Reversed			Forwards		
	Message	Flipped	Output	Message	Flipped	Output
0.0000	100111	001101	0.0029	010111	000010	0.0000
0.0625	100100	001110	0.0420			
0.1250	111001	010011	0.1211	010101	000000	0.1194
0.1875	111111	010101	0.1943			
0.2500	110010	011000	0.2738	011101	001000	0.2425
0.3125	110011	011001	0.3136			
0.3750	110000	011010	0.3608	111101	101000	0.3538
0.4375	001001	100011	0.4424			
0.5000	001111	100101	0.4945	111111	101010	0.4977
0.5625	001100	100110	0.5412			
0.6250	000011	101001	0.6105	111110	101011	0.6162
0.6875	000000	101010	0.6577			
0.7500	000001	101011	0.7272	101110	111011	0.7414
0.8125	000111	101101	0.8002			
0.8750	011000	110010	0.8488	101010	111111	0.8761
0.9375	011001	110011	0.9184			

Table 2. Left: Language for the reversed system, 4 bit precision. The code employed is not immediately apparent. Flipping alternate bits of the message (bits 1, 3 and 5) in the third column shows that the messages are, in fact, in numeric order. The bit-"ipping behaviour is a consequence of having negative recurrent weights that oscillate the signi"cance of successive bits. **Right:** The code from a forwards system for 3 bit precision. Flipping the bits of the message results in a code which is almost in numeric order both left-to-right and right-to-left, 0.0 proving the exception in both cases.

able to encode values MSB first, the decoder has a preference for decoding values LSB first. The second series of simulations are pilots and show how the different constraints of the networks may affect the evolved code. In both cases, co-evolution of the encoder and decoder was di cult. The primary cause of this appeared to be the lack of quality information given to direct the encoder's search through a combinatorically large space (functions from values to strings). Encouraging variability in the encoder proved a useful heuristic, since a necessary condition for a successful code is that every value has a unique encoding.

In the reversed condition, the biases of the networks were consistent and produced a numeric code. The system produced the type of encoding expected, given the results of the earlier component simulations. The codes developed in this condition were more sparse than strict numeric codes. Attempting to force a compact encoding on the encoder failed due to the small proportion of appropriate codes within the large search space.

When the message sent by the encoder was not reversed (the forwards case) the networks compromised on the code since neither was able to learn the encoding preferred by the other. Although the simulations did not develop codings to cope with significant levels of precision, they did give indications that the system employed neither MSB nor LSB codes, but instead those that could be read either backwards or forwards.

This is preliminary work and further simulations will be needed to substantiate the combined encoder/decoder study. We have presented a framework for studying the effects of constraints on the processing and emergence of language. The simulations presented here have been abstracted away from real languages, so an important goal of future work is to tie the framework more closely to natural language. A number of extensions for this purpose are immediately obvious including the use of multi-dimensional inputs, more symbols in the language, a non-uniform distribution of inputs and a population of communicators.

However, comparing the results of these initial simulations with human languages shows some interesting parallels. In the unrealistic reversed case, a code develops which resembles a numeric code. In the forwards case, the networks create a code that can be read either forwards or backwards, which is less e cient but meets the constraints of both the encoder and decoder. This is reminiscent of the tendency in human languages towards palindrome-like structure (e.g. N1 N2 N3 V3 V2 V1) which can be parsed in either direction. In further studies we hope to explore how certain features of human languages might have arisen as a compromise between the con"icting constraints of sender and receiver.

References

1. Noam Chomsky. On certain formal properties of grammars. *Information and Control*, 2(2):113 124, 1959.
2. M. H. Christiansen and N. Chater. Toward a connectionist model of recursion in human linguistic performance. To appear: *Cognitive Science*, 1998.
3. J. Elman. Distributed representations, simple recurrent networks and grammatical structure. *Machine Learning*, 7:195 224, 1991.
4. J. Elman. Learning and development in neural networks: The importance of starting small. *Cognition*, 48:71 99, 1993.
5. M. Hare and J. Elman. Learning and morphological change. *Cognition*, 56:61 98, 1995.
6. S. Kirby. Fitness and the selective adaptation of language. In James Hurford, Chris Knight, and Michael Studdert-Kennedy, editors, *Approaches to the Evolution of Language: Social and Cognitive Bases for the Emergence of Phonology and Syntax*. Cambridge University Press, 1998.
7. S. Lawrence, C. L. Giles, and S. Fong. Natural language grammatical inference with recurrent neural networks. To appear: *IEEE Transactions on Knowledge and Data Engineering*, 1998.
8. C. Moore. Dynamical recognizers: Real-time language recognition by analog computers. *Theoretical Computer Science*, 201(1 2):99 136, 1998.
9. A. M. Turing. On computable numbers, with an application to entscheidungsproblem. *Proceedings of the London Mathematical Society, Series 2*, 42:230 265, 1936.
10. J. Weckerly and J. Elman. A PDP approach to processing center-embedded sentences. In *Proceedings of the Fourteenth Annual Conference of the Cognitive Science Society*, Hillsdale, NJ, 1992. Erlbaum.

Continuous Optimization Using Elite Genetic Algorithms With Adaptive Mutations

Aleksandra B. Djurisić[1], Aleksandar D. Rakić[2], E. Herbert Li[1],
Marijan L. Majewski[2], Nenad Bundaleski[3], and Bozidar V. Stanić[4]

[1] Dept. of EEE, University of Hong Kong, Pokfulam Road, Hong Kong
email: dalek@eee.hku.hk, ehli@eee.hku.hk;
Tel: +852-2857-8485 Fax: +852-2559-8738
[2] Department of Computer Science and Electrical Engineering, The University of
Queensland, Brisbane, QLD 4072, Australia; email: rakic@csee.uq.edu.au
[3] Institut of Nuclear Sciences, Vinca, 11000 Belgrade,Yugoslavia
[4] School of Electrical Engineering, P.O.Box 35-54, Belgrade, Yugoslavia

Abstract. The elite genetic algorithm with adaptive mutations is applied to two diˇerent continuous optimization problems: determination of model parameters of optical constants of aluminum and thin "lm optical "lter design. The concept of adaptive mutations makes the employed algorithm a versatile tool for solving continuous optimization problems. The algorithm has been successful in solving both investigated problems. In determination of optical constants of aluminum, excellent agreement between calculated and experimental data is obtained. In application to thin "lm optical "lter design, low-pass "lters designed using this algorithm are clearly superior to "lters designed using the traditional approach.

1 Introduction

Genetic algorithms (GAs) [1] are stochastic global search methods that mimic the concept of natural evolution. Due to the nature of the algorithm, their successful application is mostly restricted to optimization problems whose solution can be conveniently represented in binary form. However, there is a rising interest in applying genetic algorithms to continuous optimization problems. For that reason, various modifications of original GAs have been reported [2,3,4,5,6]. The fact that real-coded GAs are superior to the binary coded ones in continuous optimization has already been recognized [4,5,7,8,9,10]. By representing variables with the real numbers, length of the chromosome is equal to the number of variables and it is significantly smaller than in the case of binary coding. Also, conversion of binary numbers into "oating-point numbers and *vice versa* is avoided. The most important advantages of the real-coded GAs are the absence of the Hamming cliff problem, which is inherent to all binary coded GAs [1,9,10], and the fact that variables cannot be altered in an undesired manner or destroyed in the crossover operation. However, the real coded GAs can in certain cases be blocked from further progress [8]. There has been much work in modifying the real-coded GAs in order to make them as successful in solving continuous optimization problems as they binary counterparts are in solving discrete optimization problems [2,3,9,10].

Main shortcoming in continuous optimization applications of the GAs appears to be the discrete sampling of the solution space, which results in the fact that global minimum can be located only roughly. For obtaining the location of global minimum more precisely a huge number of the chromosomes in the population is required. Several methods have been proposed to overcome this difficulty. Obviously, if new values could be introduced during the optimization procedure, that would reduce the necessary number of chromosomes in the population for finding satisfactory solution of the problem. Since mutation is usually considered to be of less importance than selection and crossover operators [1,8], the work in development of real-coded GAs suitable for continuous optimization was concentrated on devising crossover operators suitable for real numbers [2,3,9,10]. In elite genetic algorithm with adaptive mutations (EGAAM) [11] new values are introduced by mutation operator, while for selection and crossover conventional operators are employed. Adaptive mutations are performed by completely replacing specified percent of entire individuals by new ones, whose variable values are generated in boundaries which are being adaptively narrowed during the optimization. In such a manner, improvement in the precision of locating the minimum is achieved. This algorithm is applied here to two different problems: model parameter determination and thin film optical filter design.

2   Description of the algorithm

We shall give brief description of the employed algorithm. The algorithm uses the "oating point representation [4,5,8], which was proved to be more convenient for continuous optimization problems. In "oating-point chromosome representation, each gene has the value of the corresponding variable $p(k), k = 1, n_v$, w here n_v is the number of variables. Values $p(k)$ in chromosomes of the initial population are given by $p(k) = p_l(k) + (p_u(k) - p_l(k)) \cdot r$, where r is a random number $r \in [0,1]$, and $p_l(k)$ and $p_u(k)$ are initially set boundaries. In such a manner, confinement of variables in the specified domain is achieved insuring that all variables have physical interpretation. Due to the nature of the problem, in design of low-pass optical filter slightly different chromosome representation is used, as follows. Each layer is characterized with two real numbers - material code and layer thickness. Refractive index of the layer is m-th element of the sequence of refractive indexes of available materials, where m is rounded value of material code of the layer.

EGAAM employes the elitist selection mechanism [12,13,14]. In elitist selection, P_s percent of the new generation is produced by selection, and P_c percent is produced by crossover. $N_s = N * P_s$ strings with the best fitness, where N is the number of strings in the population which enter directly the next generation. The $N_c = N * P_c$ strings in the new population are generated by crossover among the parent strings which were chosen fitness proportionally between all the strings in the current population. Crossover is performed by generating a random integer $N_1 \in [n_{min}, n_v]$, where n_v is a number of variables, *i.e.* number of elements in strings, and n_{min} is the minimal number of elements exchanged in the crossover. Then we generate random integers $n_i \in [1, n_{par}]$, $i = 1, N_1$ and swap elements at positions n_i. Adaptive mutations are implemented as follows. In the current generation, average value $\mu(k)$ of parameter $p(k)$ is computed, and P_m percent of the chromosomes in the next generation are formed by generating their genes in the same manner as during the creation of initial population, but in the narrowed boundaries. New boundaries for each parameter are given by $p_{new-u}(k) = p_{old-u}(k) - c \cdot (p_{old-u}(k) - \mu(k))$ and $p_{new-l}(k) = p_{old-l}(k) + c \cdot (\mu(k) - p_{old-l}(k))$, where $\mu(k)$ is the average value of the parameter $p(k)$ in the current population, and c is a predetermined positive number $0 < c < 1$. In such a manner, a specified P_m percent of every generation are entirely new chromosomes. The EGAAM was proved to be superior over the conventional GA on three families of multiminima test functions for 20, 50 and 100 variables [11].

3   Application to modeling the optical constants of aluminum

In this section, the applied Lorentz-Drude (LD) model for the optical dielectric function, which was often employed for modeling the optical constants of metals [15,16] is brie"y discussed. It was shown [17,18] that dielectric constant ( ) can be expressed in the following form

$$( ) = 1 - \frac{\frac{2}{p}}{(+ i_0)} - \sum_{j=1}^{k} \frac{f_j\,\frac{2}{p}}{(\frac{2}{} - \frac{2}{j}) + i_j},$$ (1)

where $_p$ is the plasma frequency, k is the number of interband transitions with frequency $_j$, oscillator strength f_j and lifetime $1/_j$, while $_p = \sqrt{f_0}\,_p$ is associated with intraband transitions with oscillator strength f_0 and damping constant $_0$. The model parameters are determined by minimizing the discrepancy between calculated and experimental dielectric function values, employing the objective function proposed in Refs. [6,11]. To investigate how many significant digits the proposed algorithm obtains for the parameters of the LD model, we have generated values of the dielectric function $_{test}( )$ in the range from 6.3 meV to 15 eV, using the target parameter values given in Table 1. To emulate more realistically a real set of experimental data, we have generated another set of data with the same target parameter values, but with Monte-Carlo generated Gaussian noise which accounts for experimental uncertainties of 0.5% in the re"ectance data calculated from generated dielectric function values. Parameters obtained by EGAAM and conventional GA for both data sets are given in Table I. Mutation in conventional GA is performed by changing the value of parameter $p(k)$ to $p_{mut}(k) = p(k) + sgn * p(k)$, where sgn is a random number in interval [-1,1], while $p(k)$ is the step value for parameter k. It can be observed

Table 1. Target and obtained parameter values, superscript [a] denotes results on data set without noise, while superscript [b] denotes results for the data set with noise.

parameter	Target	EGAAM[a]	GA[a]	EGAAM[b]	GA[b]
F		0.021	1.090	0.782	1.370
f_0	0.700	0.702	0.712	0.702	0.703
Γ_0	0.060	0.061	0.059	0.061	0.061
f_1	0.200	0.194	0.188	0.190	0.188
Γ_1	0.300	0.294	0.280	0.291	0.280
ω_1	0.400	0.401	0.397	0.401	0.402
f_2	0.300	0.308	0.387	0.313	0.378
Γ_2	0.300	0.305	0.354	0.309	0.354
ω_2	1.500	1.502	1.519	1.503	1.519
f_3	0.200	0.191	0.125	0.184	0.114
Γ_3	1.000	1.009	1.252	0.998	0.786
ω_3	2.000	2.026	2.297	2.036	2.196
f_4	0.050	0.050	0.046	0.051	0.064
Γ_4	3.000	3.053	2.956	2.980	3.105
ω_4	4.500	4.519	4.538	4.498	4.341

that EGAAM is clearly superior to GA in terms of how close are the obtained values to the target ones.

There has been considerable interest in the optical properties of aluminum [15,16]. We have chosen to model the optical properties of aluminum as another test of our technique, since it is well known material, ensuring that results can be anticipated in advance. Fig. 1 shows real and imaginary parts of the dielectric function of aluminum as a function of energy. Excellent agreement between calculated and experimental values, with relative rms error of about 6% for ϵ_1 and relative rms error of 3% for ϵ_2, can be observed.

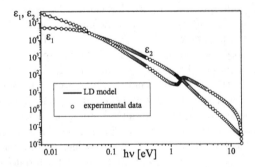

Fig. 1. Real and imaginary parts of the dielectric constant of Al *vs.* energy (solid line - model, open circles - experimental data)

4   Application to thin film filter design

Many electromagnetic applications require devices that exhibit specific frequency dependent properties. One of such structures is an optical filter consisting of dielectric layers. The structure is bounded by air on one side, and by a substrate medium with known refractive index (usually glass) on the other side. The structure is characterized by re"ectance R (fraction of incident energy that is re"ected from the filter). Assuming that the filter is lossless, which is valid for dielectric layers, transmittance T (fraction of incident energy transmitted through the filter) equals $1 - R$ in the case of normal incidence. Design of the optical filter represents choice of the optimal materials of layers and their thicknesses, or just optimal thicknesses if the dielectric properties of two alternating materials are given, in order to obtain the desired frequency dependence of R. GA based filter design algorithms have several advantages compared to classical design procedures [19]. Firstly, GA do not require a crude preliminary design to ensure convergence, since it is not easily trapped in a local optimum, contrary to classical iterative techniques. Secondly, design procedure is independent on the nature of multilayer, as well as the characteristics of incident and substrate media. Finally, the design objective can be changed easily by manipulating the cost function. There are several studies employing GAs in thin film filter design. In [20] real-coded GA was used for optimizing the thicknesses of alternating layers of two given materials, while the objective function measured how closely obtained re"ectance characteristics approaches the desired one over the prescribed frequency band. In [21] similar objective function and real-coded GA were used, while not only thicknesses but also refractive indexes of layers were optimized. However, main shortcoming of this method is that material properties of each layer have continual values within given range, thus giving no guarantee that material with such properties exists. In [22] filter consisting both of dielectric and metal layers was designed. Objective function measured heat trapping e - ciency of the device, while the coding method was binary. Binary coding enabled selection of the material for each layer from the database of available materials.

We shall describe brie"y the theoretical background of transport of electromagnetic wave through a series of dielectric layers with the index of refraction n_I and thickness d_I, placed between the two transparent media with the refractive indexes n_0 and n_y. In the case of one dielectric layer, relation between electric and magnetic fields of the incident (E_I, H_I) and transmitted (E_{II}, H_{II}) waves is [23]

$$\begin{bmatrix} E_I \\ H_I \end{bmatrix} = M \cdot \begin{bmatrix} E_{II} \\ H_{II} \end{bmatrix}; M = \begin{bmatrix} \cos(k_0 h) & i\frac{1}{Y_I}\sin(k_0 h) \\ iY_I \sin(k_0 h) & \cos(k_0 h) \end{bmatrix}. \tag{2}$$

Here, $k_0 = 2\pi/\lambda$ is the wavenumber of the incident electromagnetic wave, $h = n_I d \cos\theta_I$, θ_I is the angle of incidence, and $Y_I = \sqrt{\frac{\epsilon_0}{\mu_0}} n_I \cos\theta_I$. In the case of N layers of dielectrics between two transparent media, we can assign to each layer the matrix in the form of Eq.(2). The connection between electric and magnetic fields before (E_I, H_I) and after (E_{II}, H_{II}) the multilayer structure is described by

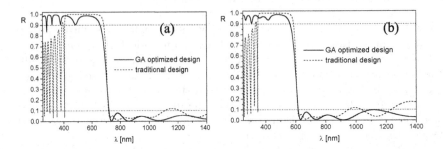

Fig. 2. Re"ectance of the low-pass "lter with cut-o˘ wavelength (a) $\lambda_0 = 750$nm and (b) $\lambda_0 = 600$nm. GA optimized design shows signi"cantly reduced ripple in both the pass band and the stop band

$$\begin{bmatrix} E_{\mathrm{I}} \\ H_{\mathrm{I}} \end{bmatrix} = \left(\prod_{i=1}^{N} M_{\mathrm{I}} \right) \cdot \begin{bmatrix} E_{\mathrm{N+1}} \\ H_{\mathrm{N+1}} \end{bmatrix} = \begin{bmatrix} m_{11} \ m_{12} \\ m_{21} \ m_{22} \end{bmatrix} \cdot \begin{bmatrix} E_{\mathrm{N+1}} \\ H_{\mathrm{N+1}} \end{bmatrix} \tag{3}$$

Coe cient of transmittivity and coe cient of re"ectivity are given by

$$r = \frac{Y_0 m_{11} + Y_0 Y_g m_{12} - m_{21} - Y_g m_{22}}{Y_0 m_{11} + Y_0 Y_g m_{12} + m_{21} + Y_g m_{22}}; t = \frac{2Y_0}{Y_0 m_{11} + Y_0 Y_g m_{12} + m_{21} + Y_g m_{22}} \tag{4}$$

where n_0 and n_g are refractive indexes of the two transparent media, while Y_0 and Y_g are the corresponding admitanses defined in the same manner as the Y_{I} above.

Ratios of the intensities of the transmitted and incident wave and the re-"ected and incident wave, are transmittance $T = tt^*(n_g \cos \ _g)/(n_0 \cos \ _0)$ and re"ectance $R = rr^*$. The multilayer in conventional thin-film optical filters usually consists of alternating layers with high and low refractive index, whose optical thicknesses $h = n_{\mathrm{I}} d \cos \ _{\mathrm{I}}$ equal to one quarter of the chosen wavelength $\ _0$, and there are also some filters with layers where $h = \ _0/8$. Structure of the filter is often denoted with the following: a - air, g - glass, H - layer with high refractive index and L - layer with low refractive index. Conventional low-pass filters have the structure g-(0.5H)L(HL)^{N}(0.5H)-a, where 0.5H denotes the layer with high refractive index whose $h = \ _0/8$.

Region of interest in the low-pass filter is the edge of the pass band, rather then the peak re"ection of the stop band. It is generally desired that (a) the transition edge be as sharp as possible and (b) the transmission zone has re-"ection as close to 0% as possible. Traditionally degree of steepness of the edge is improved by increasing the number of the layers. This, in turn, significantly increases the ripple in the pass band. Departing from the traditional $h = \ _0/4$ layer thicknesses seems to be the only way to achieve both requirements. In

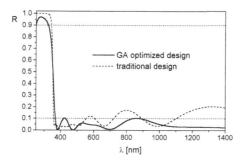

Fig. 3. Re"ectance of the low-pass "lter with cut-o˘ wavelength $\lambda_0 = 350$nm. Pass band ripple is improved, especially in the ling-wavelength region. The peak re"ectance in the stop band is less important feature in these "lters.

EGAAM designed filter, the following objective function was used to achieve the desired re"ectance dependence on wavelength

$$f = \sum_{i=1}^{n_p} 100 \cdot (R_o - R_d)^2 \cdot \exp\left[-\left(\frac{- \quad 0}{2}\right)^2\right] \tag{5}$$

where n_p is the number of points in which we calculate re"ectance, $_0$ cut-off wavelength and R_o and R_d the obtained and the desired re"ectance, respectively. The squared difference between the obtained and desired relectance is multiplied with the Gaussian function to enhance the sharp edge at the cut-off wavelength. In spite of this, EGAAM design still has improved pass band ripple, as compared to the traditional design.

We have compared the frequency characteristics of the re"ectance for the conventional and GA optimized thin film filter design with 15 dielectric layers. The results obtained for the cut-off wavelengths equal 750 nm and 350 nm are shown on Fig. 2 and Fig. 3, respectively. Conventional low-pass filter consists of alternating layers of cryolite and As_2Se_3, which was the most favorable choice for traditional design. GA optimized filter used layers chosen from the list of 16 available materials. It has been found that GA optimized filters tend to preserve the tendency of alternating layers with high and low values of the refractive index, but greater choice of available materials enables finer tuning of the filter characteristics. It can be observed that for all three cut-off wavelengths GA optimized low-pass filters have satisfactory performance in wider spectral range. On the other hand, traditionally designed low-pass filter with $_0 = 750$ nm, has significant ripple in the stop band (especially in the visible range) which can be very important from the application point of view. Its re"ectivity drops to very low values below 400 nm, while GA optimized filter retains high re"ectivity in the entire visible range.

5 Conclusion

Elite genetic algorithm with adaptive mutations (EGAAM) is applied to modeling the optical constants of aluminum and to low-pass thin film optical filter design. In application to determination of model parameters of optical constants it is shown that EGAAM is capable of obtaining more significant digits in model parameter values than its conventional counterpart. Excellent agreement between calculated and experimental data for the dielectric function of aluminum is obtained. In application to low-pass filter design, re"ectance of EGAAM optimized filter is superor over the conventionally designed one in terms of wider spectral range in which the desired characteristics of the filter is achieved.

References

1. D. E. Goldberg, *Genetic algorithms in search, optimization, and machine learning*, (Addison-Wesley, Reading, 1989).
2. M. W. Gutowski, J. Phys. A, Math. Gen., **27**, 7893, (1994).
3. H. Muhlenbein and D. Schlierkamp-Voosen, Evolutionary Computation, **1**, 25, (1993).
4. K. P. Wong and Y. W. Wong, in *Proc. ANZIIS-93, Perth, Western Australia*, pp. 512-516, 1993.
5. K. P. Wong and Y. W. Wong, IEE Proc. Gen. Transm. Distrib., **141**, 507, 1994.
6. A. B. Djurisić, J. M. Elazar and A. D. Rakić, *J.Phys.A Math. Gen.*, **30**, 7849, (1997).
7. A. Chipper"eld and R. Fleming, Control and Computers, **23**, 88, (1995).
8. D. E. Goldberg, *Complex Systems*, **5**, 139, (1991).
9. K. Deb and R. B. Agrawal, *Complex Systems*, **9**, 115, (1995).
10. J. L. Eshelman and J. D. Scha˜er, in *Proc. of Foundations of GA Workshop*, pp.187-202, (1992).
11. A. B. Djurisić, *Opt. Commun.* **151**, 147, (1998).
12. R. Vemuri and R. Vemuri, Elec. Lett., **30**, 1270, (1994).
13. S. H. Clearwater and T. Hogg, Arti"cial intelligence, **81**, 327, (1996).
14. R. R. Brooks, S. S. Iyengar and J. Chen, Arti"cial intelligence, **81**, 327, (1996).
15. A. D. Rakić. Appl. Opt., **34**, 4755, (1995).
16. C. J. Powel, *J. Opt. Soc. Am.*, **60**,78, (1970).
17. H. Ehrenreich, H. R. Philipp, and B. Segall, Phys. Rev., **132**, 1918, (1963).
18. K. Sturm and N. W. Ashcroft, Phys. Rev. B, **10**, 1343, (1974).
19. E. Michielssen and D. S. Weile, in *Genetic Algorithms in Engineering and Computer Science*, edited by G. Winter, J. Periaux, M. Galan and P. Cuesta, John Wiley & Sons, New York, 345-369,(1995).
20. E. Michielssen, S. Ranjithan and R. Mittra, *IEE Proceedings J*, **139**(12), 413, (1992).
21. S. Martin, J. Rivory and M. Shoenauer, *Opt. Comm*,**110**,503,(1994).
22. T. Eisenhammer, M. Lazarov, M. Leutbecher, U. Schoe˜el and R. Sizmann, *Appl. Opt.*, **32**, 6310, (1994).
23. M. Born and E. Wolf, *Principles of Optics*, Pergamon Press, New York, (1964).

Evolutionary Systems Applied to the Synthesis of a CPU Controller

Ricardo S. Zebulum[12], Marco Aurélio Pacheco[23], and Marley Vellasco[23]

[1] CCNR, University of Sussex, Brighton, BN1 9QG UK, e-mail:
ricardoz@cogs.susx.ac.uk
[2] ICA   Ponti"cia Universidade Catolica do Rio de Janeiro   Brasil
[3] Depto de Engenharia de Sistemas e Computaçao, UERJ -RJ, Brasil

Abstract. Our work introduces an evolutionary approach applied to the design of digital circuits. Particularly, we address the case of synthesising a controller for a simple CPU, a case study which has not been tackled by other authors so far. In order to cope with this problem, a novel circuit evaluation strategy has been employed; and new evolvable hardware systems paradigms derive from this technique. We show that the use of this new evaluation approach allows the achievement of smaller circuits and promises to be e˘ective when the problem scales up. Furthermore, our methodology yields novel digital circuits comparing to conventional design.

Keywords: Evolutionary Hardware, Sequential Circuits, CPU control.

1 Introduction

This work applies artificial evolution as a tool for automatic synthesis of digital circuits. Digital design encompasses two major areas, combinational and sequential circuits [1]. Although the majority of the evolutionary systems applications in circuit design have focused on the area of combinational circuits [3], the area of sequential systems promises to be more adequate for evolutionary computation. This stems from the fact that sequential circuits design allows the use of feedback connections, making it more complex for conventional techniques [4].

Our preliminary study on the use of evolutionary computation in sequential circuits design indicated the inability of simple genetic algorithms to handle more complex tasks in the area, a fact observed in combinational design as well. We propose in this work a new kind of evaluation strategy, in which internal points of the evolving digital circuits are assessed together with the circuit output. The authors have selected, as case study, the evolution a CPU controller, since this illustrates a practical application for evolutionary systems.

This article is composed of five additional sections: section 2 brie"y reviews the area of sequential systems design and conventional tools used for that purpose. Section 3 presents the target problem, i.e., the particular architecture of the CPU for which the control circuit will be designed. Section 4 describes our evolutionary approach and section 5 presents the evolved circuit. Finally, section 6 analyses our results.

2   Sequential System Design

Figure 1 illustrates the basic topology of a sequential circuit. It can be seen that a combinational circuit (formed by basic boolean gates) and storage elements are interconnected to form this kind of topology [4]. The sequential circuit receives binary information from its environment via the inputs. These inputs, together with the present state of the storage elements, determine the binary value of the outputs. A sequential circuit is, therefore, specified by a time sequence of inputs, internal states and outputs [4].

SIS is a state of art tool for synthesis and optimisation of sequential circuits [5]. One of the main features of this tool is the exploration of signal dependencies across the memory elements boundaries, instead of optimising logic only within the combinational blocks. However, the design specification must be supplied as a netlist of gates or a finite state machine transition table, which requires a prior knowledge of the system from the user.

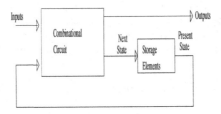

Fig. 1. Block Diagram of a Sequential Circuit (extracted from [4])

3   Target Problem - Random Control Logic Unit

The task of controlling the operations of a microprocessor is a typical example of a sequential circuit task. The control unit enables the CPU to carry out the instruction currently in the instruction register. This is accomplished through the interpretation of the pattern of bits in the instruction register[1], which generates a sequence of actions taking place during the execution of an instruction [1]; the control unit is the circuit that provides this operation. Particularly, the random or hardwired logic control unit is made up of an arrangement of boolean gates and "ip-"ops [4].

In [1], a simple model of CPU is presented and a random logic control unit is designed to allow the execution of eight different instructions. Using this CPU model we propose the task of evolving the control unit, instead of designing it. Figure 2 shows the structure of this primitive CPU; table 1 shows the interpretation of machine-code instructions (note that the fetch cycle occurs for all the eight instructions). There are a total of 16 control signals, which are clustered in 5 groups: Enable signals (E); Clock signals (C); ALU signals; Main Store (MS) signals (Read and Write); and Flip-Flop (FF) signals (Reset and Set). The evolutionary system must generate the signals C_{MAR}, E_{MBR}, E_{IR}, etc, given a particular instruction as input. For further details on the CPU operation, refer to [1].

Time		Enables					Clocks					ALU		MS		FF	
		MBR	IR	PC	DO	ALU	MAR	MBR	IR	PC	DO	F1	F0	R	W	R	S
Fetch	T0	0	0	1	0	0	1	0	0	0	0	x	x	0	0	0	0
	T1	0	0	0	0	0	0	0	1	0	0	x	x	1	0	0	0
	T2	0	0	1	0	0	0	0	0	0	0	1	0	0	0	0	0
	T3	0	0	0	0	1	0	0	0	1	0	x	x	0	0	0	0
	T4	0	1	0	0	0	1	0	0	0	0	x	x	0	0	0	1
Load	T0	0	0	0	0	0	0	0	0	0	1	x	x	1	0	1	0
Store	T0	0	0	0	1	0	0	0	0	0	0	x	x	0	1	1	0
Add	T0	0	0	0	0	0	0	1	0	0	0	x	x	1	0	0	0
	T1	1	0	0	0	0	0	0	0	0	0	0	0	0	0	0	0
	T2	0	0	0	0	1	0	0	0	0	1	x	x	0	0	1	0
Sub	T0	0	0	0	0	0	0	1	0	0	0	x	x	1	0	0	0
	T1	1	0	0	0	0	0	0	0	0	0	0	1	0	0	0	0
	T2	0	0	0	0	1	0	0	0	0	1	x	x	0	0	1	0
Inc	T0	0	0	0	0	0	0	1	0	0	0	x	x	1	0	0	0
	T1	1	0	0	0	0	0	0	0	0	0	1	0	0	0	0	0
	T2	0	0	0	0	1	0	1	0	0	0	x	x	0	0	0	0
	T3	1	0	0	0	0	0	0	0	0	0	x	x	0	1	1	0
Dec	T0	0	0	0	0	0	0	1	0	0	0	x	x	1	0	0	0
	T1	1	0	0	0	0	0	0	0	0	0	1	1	0	0	0	0
	T2	0	0	0	0	1	0	1	0	0	0	x	x	0	0	0	0
	T3	1	0	0	0	0	0	0	0	0	0	x	x	0	1	1	0
BRA	T0	0	1	0	0	0	0	0	0	1	0	x	x	0	0	1	0
BEQ	T0	0	1	0	0	0	0	0	0	Z	0	x	x	0	0	1	0

x = don't care

Table 1 - Interpretation of Machine Code Instructions (Reproduced from [1])

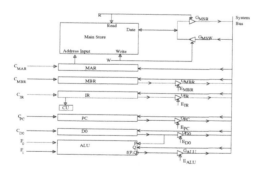

Fig. 2. Block Diagram of a Simple CPU (Reproduced from [1])

4 Problem Modelling

This section describes both the representation and evaluation used within our evolutionary system.

The gate level *representation* [2] has been used to encode each circuit into an integer string. Figure 3 illustrates an example of this kind of representation for a hypothetical output signal. The circuit (phenotype) is constituted by a combinational part (arrangement of boolean gates) and a sequential part (D "ip-"op [1]). The latter provides the means whereby a delayed version of the output signals can be used as feedback for the same or other circuits.

The genotype is made up of blocks of integer numbers or genes that encode the type of each particular logic gate shown in the figure. The genes associated with the gates of the first layer will encode its nature and also the source of the input signals. The cell input signals are chosen among the following signals (Figure 4):

1. Clock signals, supplied by a master-clock and a counter;
2. the three bits of the instruction register that determines the instruction to be executed;
3. and the own output control signals delayed by one clock period.

As there are a total of 16 output signals, the overall system will be made up of 16 cells like the one in the figure.

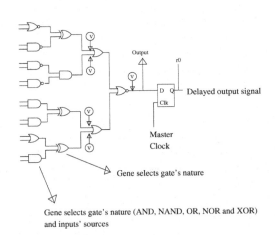

Fig. 3. Gate level representation of a sequential circuit

The *tness evaluation function* was designed to simply count the number of hits in each cell output, comparing to the target output signals. However, this approach proved to be unsuccessful for some output signals. The authors devised a way to overcome the problem by providing additional signals to the fitness evaluation function. These new signals are taken from internal circuit points. Figure 5 illustrates this procedure: circuits (A) and (B) have two internal points and the external output probed. In order to implement this new evaluation strategy, it is necessary to set target functions for the internal points. This has been accomplished through the so-called *OR and NOR evolvable hardware paradigms*, in which the output gates are fixed to either OR (Circuit A) or

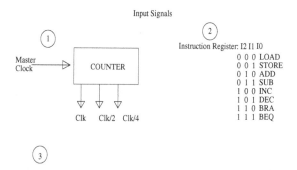

Input Signals

Delayed Output Sugnals: MBR-ENABLE(T - 1), IR-ENABLE(T-1), PC-ENABLE(T-1),
D0-ENABLE(T-1), ALU-ENABLE(T-1), MAR-CLOCK(T-1), MBR-CLOCK(T-1),
IR-CLOCK(T-1), PC- CLOCK(T-1), D0-CLOCK(T-1), F1(T-1),,WRITE(T-1), RESET(T-1),
READ(T-1), SET(T-1) and F0(T-1).

Fig. 4. Inputs available for the evolutionary system

NOR (Circuit B) functions respectively. OR and NOR gates have been chosen
because they simplify the internal points assessment comparing to other gates.
When using the OR paradigm, the internal points' fitness are computed by
taking as target function the own output function to be realised by the circuit,
because the OR gate performs a simple boolean sum. Conversely, when using
the NOR paradigm, the internal points' fitness are calculated by taking as target
function the complement of the output function, since the NOR gate performs
a complemented boolean sum. The circuit shown in Figure 3 illustrates this
strategy as well. Its output gate has been fixed to a NOR boolean function (2
ORs followed by 1 NOR = 1 NOR); five points are then evaluated, the final
output and four internal points.

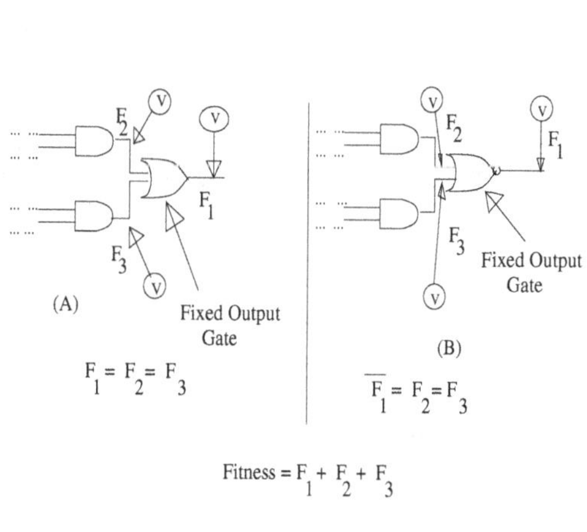

(A)   Fixed Output
             Gate

$F_1 = F_2 = F_3$

(B)

$\overline{F}_1 = F_2 = F_3$

Fixed Output
Gate

Fitness $= F_1 + F_2 + F_3$

Fig. 5. New evaluation strategy

It has been verified that, for some control signals, the OR paradigm brought a significant improvement in performance, whereas the NOR paradigm was more effective for other signals. This improvement stems from the fact that the circuit behaviour is now constrained in its internal points, which makes the search process focus on a smaller set of solutions.

To further improve the GA performance, penalties have been applied to deleterious sub-circuits. For instance, when the output gate is fixed as an OR, the individual fitness is penalized when internal circuit's points produce a '1' output when the target is '0'. This is due to the fact that a '1' will clamp the circuit output to an erroneous value, regardless of the values of the other internal points. A similar method is applied in the NOR paradigm.

5   Results

In order to evolve the whole control system, 16 genetic algorithms have to be executed, one for each circuit output. The authors adopted the following strategy:

1. Run the 16 GAs for each signal, assuming a delay "ip-"op in each circuit output;
2. Find the output signal(s) which was(were) hardest to evolve, and store the delayed output signals used as inputs to this(these) cell(s);
3. Re-run the GA for the other signals, keeping available only the delayed signals used by the circuit(s) representing the signals mentioned in the second item;

The aim of this strategy is to minimise the amount of hardware, by placing a delay "ip-"op only in those signals used as inputs to the cells which have been more diﬃcult to evolve. In our particular case, the evolution of the RESET signal was the most time consuming . The output function of this control signal is depicted in the column R (FF) of Table 1. The OR paradigm has been used and, due to the task complexity, we allowed the GA to use all the available input signals (see Figure 4). Figure 6 shows the evolved circuit as well as its input signals. It has also been verified that the cell could be simplified by taking away a sub-circuit which was not effectively contributing to the final behaviour. The possibility of cutting hardware from the final solution is another advantage of the OR paradigm.

In order to evolve the other signals, we allowed the GA to use only the delayed output signals used as inputs to the RESET circuit. After simplifying the circuit in Figure 6, it can be verified that only 6 out of 16 control signals will need a delay "ip-"op: MBR-Enable, the own Reset signal, PC-Clock, MBR-Clock, D0-Enable and SET (signals with time index T-1).

The graph of Figure 7 compares the evolution of the particular signal ALU-ENABLE when the OR and NOR paradigms are used. The average value of the best genotypes over five executions, along 300 generations for 40 individuals is shown in this graph. It took around 4 minutes to run the executions in a SPARC

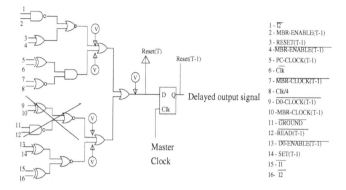

1 - $\overline{I2}$
2 - MBR-ENABLE(T-1)
3 - RESET(T-1)
4 - $\overline{\text{MBR-ENABLE(T-1)}}$
5 - PC-CLOCK(T-1)
6 - $\overline{\text{Clk}}$
7 - $\overline{\text{MBR-CLOCK(T-1)}}$
8 - Clk/4
9 - $\overline{\text{D0-CLOCK(T-1)}}$
10 - MBR-CLOCK(T-1)
11 - $\overline{\text{GROUND}}$
12 - READ(T-1)
13 - $\overline{\text{D0-ENABLE(T-1)}}$
14 - SET(T-1)
15 - $\overline{\text{I1}}$
16 - $\overline{\text{I2}}$

Fig. 6. Circuit evolved to generate the RESET control signal

4 workstation. One of the evolved circuits for the ALU-ENABLE signal is shown in Figure 8. It can be verified that this circuit could be utterly simplified, and there is no need for an output "ip-"op. Due to space limitations, we can not show the other control circuits evolved. The final solutions have been checked using the PSPICE simulator.

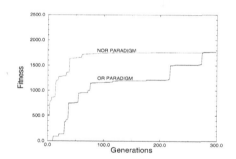

Fig. 7. Average Fitness of the Best Genotypes for the ALU-ENABLE signal using OR and NOR Paradigms

6   Analysis of the Results

We can compare the evolved CPU controller with a human designed one shown in [1]. The evolved circuit uses six additional "ip-"ops, meaning that evolutionary systems does not use the minimum amount of states in the synthesis of the sequential system. In terms of boolean gates, the evolved controller uses around 150 gates, against 90 of the human designed one. Nevertheless, the authors are confident that the amount of hardware can be reduced in further experiments.

Our proposed design approach has the advantage of using minimum designer knowledge of the target system and of achieving novel digital circuits. The former

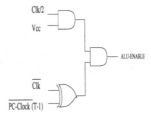

Fig. 8. Circuit evolved to generate the ALU-ENABLE control signal

property reveals an advantage over conventional CAD tools like SIS. The latter property refers to the fact that the evolved circuits depart from the constrained spatial structures observed in conventional circuit design [6]. Two main benefits arise from this feature: the achievement of new design methodologies and the potential of evolutionary tools to handle more complex designs.

The authors have also presented a new evolvable hardware technique, in which internal circuit points are evaluated. This strategy can be generally applied to both combinational and sequential circuits' evolution.

7   Acknowledgements

The authors wish to thank CAPES, Brazilian federal agency, for the support and Dr. Phil Husbands for the collaboration.

References

1. Clements, A., The Principles of Computer Hardware , Oxford University Press, 1991
2. Higuchi, T., Iba, H., Manderick, B., Evolvable Hardware , in Massively Parallel Arti"cial Intelligence (ed. H. Kitano), MIT Press, 1994.
3. Miller, J. F., Thomson, P. and Fogarty, T., Designing Electronic Circuits Using Evolutionary Algorithms. Arithmetic Circuits: A Case Study , chapter 6, in Genetic Algorithms Recent Advancements and Industrial Applications. Editors: D. Quagliarella, J. Periaux, C. Poloni and G. Winter, published by Wiley, 1997 (November).
4. Morris, M., Kime, C. R., Logic and Computer Design Fundamentals , Prentice-Hall International Inc., 1997.
5. Sentovich, E. M., Singh, K. J., Moon, C., Savoj, H., Brayton, R.K., Sangiovanni-Vincentelli, A., Sequential Circuit Design Using Synthesis and Optimization , Proceedings of the IEEE Int. Conf. on Computer Design, pp. 328-333, 1992.
6. Thompson, A., Harvey, I., Husbands, P., Unconstrained Evolution and Hard Consequences , in Towards Evolvable Hardware: An International Workshop, Lausanne, Switzerland, October 2-3, 1995. pages 136-165, edited by E. Sanchez and M. Tomassini, Springer-Verlag LNCS 1062, 1996.

Novel Models in Evolutionary Designing

John S. Gero

Key Centre of Design Computing
Department of Architectural and Design Science
University of Sydney NSW 2006 Australia
john@arch.usyd.edu.au

Abstract. This paper introduces and describes a number of novel models of evolutionary designing beyond that of genetic algorithms and genetic programming treating designing as search. The focus in many of these novel approaches when applied to designing is to add to the range of possible designs which might be able to be produced during an evolutionary process. Four approaches are briefly described: genetic engineering; reverse engineering of emergent features in the phenotypes; developmental biology and generalizing crossover.

1 Introduction

The basic genetic analogy in designing utilises a simple model of the Darwinian theory of improvement of the organism's performance through the "survival of the fittest". This occurs through the improvement of the genotype which goes to make up the organism. This is the basis of most evolutionary systems. Fundamental to this analogy are a number of important operational aspects of the model:

- the design description (structure) maps on to the phenotype
- separation of the representation at the genotype level from that of the design description level
- the processes of designing map on to the evolutionary processes of crossover and mutation at the genotype level
- performances (behaviours) of designs map on to fitnesses
- operations are carried out with populations of individuals.

In designing terms this maps directly onto the method of *designing as search*. We can describe this notion using the state-space representation of computation:

- state space is fixed at the outset
- state space comprises behaviour (fitness) and structure (phenotype) spaces
- genetic operators move between states in structure space, performance evaluated in behaviour space

Designing as search is a foundational designing method but one that is restricted in its application to routine or parametric designing. In such designing all the possible variable which could occur in the final design are known beforehand as are all the behaviours which will be used to evaluate designs. Since the goal is to improve the behaviours of the resulting designs, the processes of designing during search map well onto those of optimization. This sits well with our notion of genetic algorithms and genetic programming. They can be readily viewed as robust optimization methodologies. Genetic algorithms and genetic programming have been used successfully as analogies of designing methodologies.

In this paper we will briefly explore new approaches which can be drawn from nature and humans' intervention in nature as possible sources for fruitful ideas on which to base evolutionary designing methodologies. We will look at four such approaches: genetic engineering, reverse engineering and the genetic analogy, developmental biology and a generalization of the crossover operation.

2 Genetic Engineering in Designing

The practice of genetic engineering in natural organisms involves locating genetic structures which are the likely cause of specified behaviours in the organism [1]. This provides a direct analog with finding significant concepts during the process of designing and giving them a specific primacy. The behaviour of the organism is an observable regularity which maps onto the concept and the structure of the genetic material which causes that behaviour is a representation of that concept, albeit a representation which has to be expressed in the organism for the concept to appear. The practice of genetic engineering is akin to the reverse of synthesis in the sense that one aspect of an already synthesised design is converted into the means by which it could be generated. In fact it is more complex than that since it is the behaviour of the already synthesised design which is the controlling factor but the analogy still holds. Let us examine in a little more detail the concept of genetic engineering [2].

Consider Figure 1 where the population of designs is divided into two groups (it could be more). One group exhibits a specific regularity whilst the other does not. The goal is to locate an "emergent" common structure in the genotypes of those designs which exhibit this regularity. Here "emergent" means that the structure was not intentionally placed there but could be found and represented for later use. Genetic engineering at this symbolic level uses pattern matching and sequence analysis techniques to locate these genetic structures. The process can be summarised as follows:

- locate emergent properties in the behaviour (fitness) space
- produce new genes which generate those emergent properties -> gene evolution
- introduce evolved genes into gene pool.

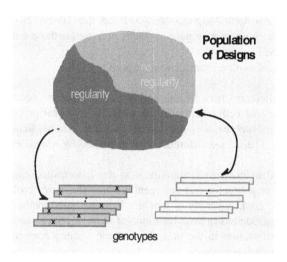

Figure 1. Genetic engineering is concerned with locating groups of genes re gularity, marked as X in the genotypes of those design which exhibit a specific behavioural regularity.

These newly "evolved" genes capture some problem specific characteristics of the genetic representation of the good solutions to that problem. As such they may be able to be re-used in related problems to advantage. Typically each new problem to be solved using optimization techniques is treated anew without taking into account anything which has been learned from previous problems. Genes evolved using genetic engineered provide the basis for learning from previous design episodes and transferring what has been learned to the current design problem.

3 Reverse Engineering and the Genetic Analogy

In the computational model of genetic engineering used in designing the evolved genes are complexes of the original genes. Even when they are mutated they remain complexes of the original genes. As a consequence the boundary of the state space of possible designs is unchanged so that the designs produced are no different to those which could have been produced using the original genes only. In order to produce novel designs, ie designs which could not have been produced using the original genes only, the evolved genes need to be different to simply being complexes of the original genes. In order to "evolve" such genes different processes are required. We can take ideas from reverse engineering in manufacturing and include them in the genetic analogy [3].

The concept is analogically similar to that of genetic engineering in that emergent properties are looked for and new genes which generate those properties are produced, although the processes are different and the result is quite different. The process can be summarised as follows:

- locate emergent design (phenotype rather than fitness) properties
- reverse engineer new genes which can generate those emergent properties → gene evolution
- introduce evolved genes into gene pool.

The critical differences between this and genetic engineering occur in two places in this process. The first difference is in the locus of emergent properties – these are looked for in the phenotype, ie in the designs themselves rather than in their fitnesses or performances. The second difference is in the means by which "evolved" genes are created.

Having located an emergent feature the next step is to reverse engineer a new gene which is capable of producing that emergent feature. This new "evolved" gene is then added to the gene pool. A variety of machine learning-based methods is available for this task. These include inductive substitution of the new representation in the place of the original representation in the design generator, turning constants into variables, and rule-based induction methods.

Evolving genes by reverse engineering is a form of Lamarckism in that characteristics of an organism not directly produced by its genetic makeup are acquired by that organism's genome.

4 Developmental Biology and Designing

Perhaps more interesting is to specifically model phenotypic plasticity to produce a form of pleiomorphism. This would allow for a form of genotype/phenotype environment interaction during the development of the phenotype. A variety of environmental interactions can be proposed to allow for adaptive mapping between genotype and phenotype. Classes of interactions include the following where "f" is some function:

- phenotype = f(genotype, situation), where situation refers to a state of the environment at some time, or
- $phenotype_t$ = f(genotype, $phenotype_{t-1}$);

both in lieu of :
- phenotype = f(genotype).

Example 1

Here the phenotype is made up of components but the components themselves are some function of the path taken to reach that component. A simple path function would be that each component is in some way a function of the components it is connected to, ie:

- phenotype = {$component_1$,... $component_i$,... $component_n$}

Example 2

Here the phenotype is developed over some time intermediate periods from a given genotype, during which various intermediate fitnesses control its development in a pleiomorphic sense, ie:

- phenotype = f(genotype, intermediate fitnesses during development)

Example 3

Here the phenotype, as it develops over some time intermediate periods from a given genotype, does so as a function of its expression at the previous time period. This is a crude model of cell division, ie:

- $\text{phenotype}_t = f(\text{genotype}, \text{phenotype}_{t-1})$.

Models such as these provide opportunities to include both problem- and domain-specific knowledge in the evolutionary process.

5   Generalizing Crossover as an Operator in Designing

Crossover is one of the fundamental genetic operations in evolutionary systems, particularly genetic algorithms and genetic programming. Formally, any genotype, $\mathbf{g}_c$, produced by a crossover operator from genotypes $\mathbf{g}_1$ and $\mathbf{g}_2$ can be written as an interpolation:

$$\mathbf{g}_c(t) = \mathbf{f}(t)\mathbf{g}_1 + (\mathbf{I}\text{-}\mathbf{f}(t))\mathbf{g}_2, \; t = 0,1,...,n$$

where $\mathbf{I}$ is a unit n-dimensional matrix with all diagonal elements equal to 1 and all other elements equal to 0, $\mathbf{f}(t)$ is the n-dimensional matrix obtained from the unit matrix by setting all diagonal elements from the t-th to the n-th to zero, $\mathbf{f}(0)=\mathbf{I}$ and $\mathbf{f}(1)=\mathbf{O}$, where $\mathbf{O}$ is the n-dimensional zero matrix.

From this characterisation the crossover operation can be viewed as a random sampling of interpolating genotypes between two basic points $\mathbf{g}_1$ and $\mathbf{g}_2$ [4]. Note, that this linear matrix interpolation, which corresponds to the standard one-point crossover, is only one of many possible methods of interpolation between two genotypes in genotypic space of the following form:

$$\mathbf{g}_i(t) = \mathbf{c}_1(t)\mathbf{g}_1 + \mathbf{c}_2(n\text{-}t)\mathbf{g}_2,$$

where operators $\mathbf{c}_1(t)$ and $\mathbf{c}_2(n\text{-}t)$ obey the condition $\mathbf{c}_1(0)=\mathbf{I}$ and $\mathbf{c}_1(n)=\mathbf{O}$ and $\mathbf{c}_2(0)=\mathbf{I}$ and $\mathbf{c}_2(n)=\mathbf{O}$. The crossover induced interpolation $\mathbf{g}_c(t)$ is singled out from many other possible interpolations $\mathbf{g}_i(t)$ by the condition that the sum of the Hamming distances from $\mathbf{g}_c(t)$ to $\mathbf{g}_1$ and to $\mathbf{g}_2$ plus a penalty function (any kind of standard optimization penalty function will do) is to be optimized for two sequential coordinates in $\mathbf{g}_c(t)$ one of which coincides with the component of $\mathbf{g}_1$ and the other which the component of $\mathbf{g}_2$.

Different versions of crossover can be constructed by choosing different conditions imposed on the interpolation points.

Since each genotype corresponds to a unique phenotype, the crossover-induced interpolation operation between two genotypes maps onto an interpolation operation between two corresponding phenotypes $\mathbf{p}_1 = M(\mathbf{g}_1)$ and $\mathbf{p}_2 = M(\mathbf{g}_2)$. If $\mathbf{p}_c(t) = M(\mathbf{g}_c(t))$ for $t = 0, 1, \ldots, n$ and assuming that $\mathbf{P}$ is a linear space we can fit a path between $\mathbf{p}_1$ and $\mathbf{p}_2$ and $\mathbf{p}_c(t)$, using the following formula:

$$\mathbf{p}_c(t) = \underline{\mathbf{f}}^c(t)\mathbf{p}_1 + \underline{\mathbf{g}}^c(n-t)\mathbf{p}_2, \quad t = 0, 1, \ldots, n$$

where $\underline{\mathbf{f}}^c(t)$ and $\underline{\mathbf{g}}^c(t)$ are operators which depend continuously on t. Since $\mathbf{p}_c(0) = \mathbf{p}_2$ and $\mathbf{p}_c(1) = \mathbf{p}_1$, the weakest conditions these operators must satisfy are $\underline{\mathbf{f}}^c(0) = \underline{\mathbf{I}}$, $\underline{\mathbf{f}}^c(0) = \underline{\mathbf{O}}$ and $\underline{\mathbf{g}}^c(0) = \underline{\mathbf{I}}$, $\underline{\mathbf{f}}^c(0) = \underline{\mathbf{O}}$ (where $\underline{\mathbf{I}}$ is the unit operator whose application to any phenotypes gives the same phenotype and $\underline{\mathbf{O}}$ is the zero operator whose application to any phenotype gives an empty phenotype). If we use any operators $\underline{\mathbf{f}}(t)$ and $\underline{\mathbf{g}}(t)$ which differ from $\underline{\mathbf{f}}^c(t)$ and $\underline{\mathbf{g}}^c(t)$ but still obey these conditions then this formula will produce interpolation points which differ from those produced by standard genetic crossover.

One way to conceive of this generalization of the crossover operator is to think of the standard crossover operator forcing interpolated results to lie on a surface in phenotypic space $\mathbf{P}$, defined by the bitstring representation of the genotype and the isomorphic mapping between the genotype and the phenotype. Thus, any phenotypes which are a result of this crossover lie on a trajectory which is constrained to lie on this surface as indicated in Figure 2. The generalized crossover in the form of an interpolation generalizes $\mathbf{P}$ to $\mathbf{P}+$ (which is a superspace with respect to $\mathbf{P} \subset \mathbf{P}+$). The generalized crossover consists of interpolating trial points directly in $\mathbf{P}+$ using trial points from $\mathbf{P}$ as the end points of the interpolation. They are shown in Figure 2 with the dotted line. The expectation is that since these end points belong to the established search space $\mathbf{P}$, the exploration due to interpolation in the enlarged $\mathbf{P}^*$ will not distort the consistency and viability of the space $\mathbf{P}$ too much. The critical effect can be noticed in Figure 2, namely that the interpolation in $\mathbf{P}+$ does not lie in $\mathbf{P}$. In addition to interpolation we can now produce extrapolations, shown with arrows in Figure 2. These also lie outside $\mathbf{P}$ and in $\mathbf{P}+$. Hence, these interpolations have the capacity to produce designs outside the original state space. The interpolation process expands the state space of possible designs.

This is significant in designing as it allows for the generation of novel designs, designs which could not been evolved using the standard crossover. Any genotypic representation can be reduced to a bitstring of length n. All possible genotypes lie within the space of 2^n possible designs. Without either increasing the length of the genotype or introducing new members of the alphabet (beyond 0 and 1), it is not possible to expand the state space. The approach introduced here solves this problem by developing a homomorphism between the phenotype and its genetic representation. It does away with the separate bitstring genotype representation, replacing it with this homomorphism after the exploration process. The interpolation and extrapolation processes operate on the phenotype, changing it. As a consequence of this homomorphism a new genotypic representation is constructed each time exploration occurs.

A large number of possible interpolation functions may be used not all of which will produce viable results as there is a close connection between the useful interpolation functions and the representation employed.

P+

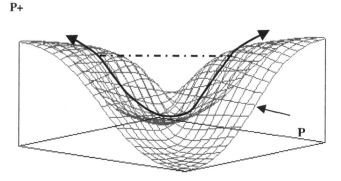

Figure 2. The illustration of the crossover-induced interpolation in **P** and direct interpolation in enlarged space **P+**. The enlarged space **P+** represents the complete 3-d space and the set **P** represents the surface in it. The solid line represents an interpolation in **P**, whilst the dotted line represents an interpolation in **P+** [4].

6   Discussion

The genetic engineering analogy has been applied in designing in a number of disparate ways [5, 6, 7]. The reverse engineering approach has been used with emergent feature detection in state-space search to add to the alphabet of the genotype [8]. The generalization of crossover approach has been used to extend the state-space in designing [4].

The genetic analogy in designing has been based on a model of Darwin's survival of the fittest. This has provided a foundation for a body of important work which has implicitly treated designing as a search method largely akin to optimization. The effect of this in designing terms has been to set up a fixed state-space which is then searched for appropriate solutions. Alternative analogies drawn from genetics, reverse engineering, developmental biology and alternate views of the crossover operation offer the opportunity to change the state-space of possible designs in some cases. In designing this ability to modify the state-space of possible designs in conceptually and practically important.

Designing involves not just finding the best solution from a subset of possible solutions, it also involves determining what the possible solutions might be. A fixed search space does not allow for the exploration of possible solutions. Some of the novel methods described in this paper point to possible direction where such explorations may be modeled.

Acknowledgment

This work has been supported by a number of grants from the Australian Research Council.

References

1. Sofer, W. H.: Introduction to Genetic Engineering, Butterworth-Heinemann, Stoneham (1991)
2. Gero, J. S. and Kazakov, V.: Evolving building blocks for design using genetic engineering: a formal approach. In: Gero, J S (ed.), Advances in Formal Design Methods for CAD, Chapman and Hall, London (1996) 31-50
3. Gero, J. S. and Kazakov, V.: Adaptive expansion of search spaces using emergent features, in J. Slaney, G. Antoniou and M. Maher (eds), AI'98, Griffith University, Brisbane, Australia (1998) 25-36
4. Gero, J. S. and Kazakov, V.: Adapting evolutionary computing for exploration in creative designing. In J. S. Gero and M. L. Maher (eds), Preprints Fourth International Conference on Computational Models of Creative Design, Key Centre of Design Computing, University of Sydney, Sydney, Australia (1998) (to appear)
5. Gero, J. S., Kazakov, V and Schnier, T.: Genetic engineering and design problems. In D. Dasgupta and Z. Michalewicz (eds), Evolutionary Algorithms in Engineering Applications, Springer-Verlag, Berlin (1997) 47-68
6. Gero, J. S. and Ding, L.: Learning emergent style using an evolutionary approach. In B. Varma and X. Yao (eds), ICCIMA'97, Griffiths University, Gold Coast, Queensland, Australia (1997) 171-175
7. Schnier, T. and Gero, J. S.: From Frank Lloyd Wright to Mondrian: transforming evolving representations. In I. Parmee (ed.), Adaptive Computing in Design and Manufacture, Springer, London (1998) 207-219
8. Gero, J. S. and Kazakov, V.: Adaptive expansion of search spaces using emergent features, in J. Slaney, G. Antoniou and M. Maher (eds), AI'98, Griffith University, Brisbane, Australia (1998) 25-36

Co-evolution, Determinism and Robustness

Alan D. Blair[1], Elizabeth Sklar[2], and Pablo Funes[2]

[1] Dept. of Computer Science
and Electrical Engineering
University of Queensland, 4072 Australia
Tel.: +61-7-3365-1195; Fax: +61-7-3365-1999
blair@cs.uq.edu.au
[2] Dept. of Computer Science
Brandeis University
Waltham, MA 02254 USA
Tel.: +1-781-736-3366; Fax: +1-781-736-2741
sklar,pablo@cs.brandeis.edu

Abstract. Robustness has long been recognised as a critical issue for co-evolutionary learning. It has been achieved in a number of cases, though usually in domains which involve some form of *non-determinism*. We examine a deterministic domain   a pseudo real-time two-player game called Tron   and evolve a neural network player using a simple hill-climbing algorithm. The results call into question the importance of determinism as a requirement for successful co-evolutionary learning, and provide a good opportunity to examine the relative importance of other factors.

Keywords: Co-evolution, Neural networks

1 Introduction

In 1982, Walt Disney Studios released a film called <u>Tron</u> which featured a game in a virtual world with two futuristic motorcycles running at constant speed, making only right angle turns and leaving solid wall trails behind them. As the game advanced, the arena filled with walls and eventually one opponent would die by crashing into a wall. This game became very popular and was subsequently implemented on many computers with varying rules, graphic interpretations and configurations.

In earlier work [5] we built an interactive version of Tron (using Java) and released it on the Internet. With this setup, we created a new type of *co-evolutionary* learning where one population consists of software agents controlled by evolving genetic programs (GP) [8] and the other population is comprised of human users. From a human factors standpoint, the fact that this simple game has attracted a large number of users and that many of them return to play multiple games is surprising and significant. From an evolutionary programming standpoint, the fact that the GP players have evolved to embody a robust set of strategies, capable of overcoming a wide range of human behaviours, is noteworthy.

We have been studying co-evolutionary learning environments in several contexts [2,7,3], trying to understand the reasons why this paradigm works very well for some tasks [6,10,11] but poorly for others. In particular, we have developed a minimalist co-evolutionary learning method that consists of a neural network which evolves using a simple hill-climbing algorithm. We have found this to be a useful means for studying the effect of co-evolutionary learning in various task domains.

Previously, we have applied this method successfully to backgammon [9] as well as a simulated robotic hockey game called *Shock* [1]. Tron is similar to these domains in some respects but differs in other, significant, aspects. Backgammon is a *stochastic* domain in which the outcome of each game is in"uenced by random dice rolls as well as choices made by the players. In the Shock domain, each game is started from a different random initial condition. Tron, on the other hand, is totally *deterministic* in the sense that two games played by the same two opponents will necessarily be identical. Since many authors have cited non-determinism as a critical factor in the success of co-evolutionary learning systems, particularly in relation to backgammon, we were interested to apply our hill-climbing procedure to a deterministic domain, hence Tron.

This paper is organised as follows: we first describe the Tron implementation and the network architecture and algorithm. We then detail some of the experiments that were conducted to compare the neural network players with the GP players evolved in the Internet experiment. We conclude with some discussion and ideas for extending this work further.

2   Tron

Our interpretation of Tron abstracts the motorcycles and represents them only by their trails. Players may move past the edges of the screen and re-appear on the opposite side to create a wrap-around, or *toroidal*, game arena. The size of the arena is 256 × 256 pixels. Two players start at positions 128 pixels apart, heading in the same direction. One player is controlled by the computer (e.g. a GP), the other may also be controlled by the computer, or by a human user. The GP players are provided with 8 simple sensors with which to perceive their environment.

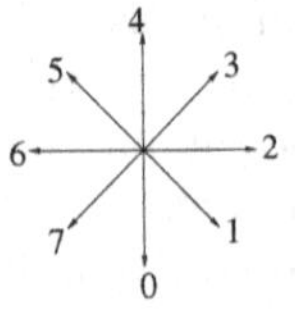

Figure 1   Robot sensors. Each sensor evaluates the distance in pixels from the current position to the nearest obstacle in one particular direction. Every sensor returns a maximum value of 1.0 for an immediate obstacle (i.e. a wall in an adjacent pixel), a lower number for an obstacle further away, and 0.0 when there are no obstacles in sight.

The game runs in simulated real-time, where each player can select one of the following actions: LEFT, RIGHT or STRAIGHT.

In the Internet experiment, data has been collecting since September 1997 and is still accumulating. Over 2500 users have logged into the system and played at least one game. The average number of games played by each human is 53 games; the most games played by one player is 5028. Sixteen players have played over 1000 games.

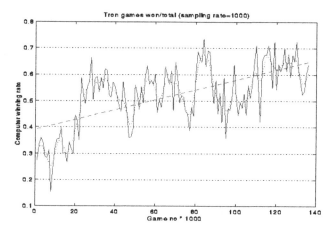

Figure 2   Internet Tron Results.

Our basic measure of performance is the win rate   the percentage of games that the GP players have won in playing against humans. As shown in figure 2, this rate has steadily risen from approximately 30% initially to more than 60% over a period of several months, resulting in a robust GP population capable of beating a wide variety of opponents. This database of players, along with the Java Tron environment, provide an excellent resource for testing and comparison with other methods for training artificial players.

3   Implementation and Results.

In the present work, we develop Tron players controlled by two-layer feed-forward neural networks with 5 hidden units. Each network has 8 inputs   one for each of the sensors described earlier. There are 3 output units, representing each of the three possible actions (as above). Of these, the output unit with the largest activation determines the selected action for the current time step.

We train the network using an evolutionary hill-climbing algorithm in which a *champ* neural network is challenged by a series of *mutant* networks until one is found that beats the champ; the champ's weights are then adjusted in the direction of the mutant:

1. mutant ← champ + gaussian noise
2. mutant plays against champ
3. if mutant beats champ, champ ← $(1 -)$ * champ +   * mutant

Using this neural network architecture, three players were evolved. Network **nn-0** was evolved for 1200 generations, networks **nn-1** and **nn-2** for 50000 generations each. The parameter , which we refer to as the *mutant in uence factor*, was set to 0.5 for **nn-0** and 0.33 for **nn-1** and **nn-2**. The network weights were saved every 100 generations and tested against five of the best GP players hand-picked from our Internet experiment (referred to as GP players 510006, 460003, 480001, 540004 and 400010).[1] Note that the GP players were used purely for diagnostic purposes and had no effect on the evolving networks.

a. versus GP-510006

b. versus GP-460003

c. versus GP-480001

d. versus GP-540004

Figure 3   Network **nn-1**, generation 40500 (darker trail, starting on left)
versus GP players (starting on right)

Many of the GP players exhibit distinctive features, permitting loose characterisation of behaviours. For example, players GP-510006 and GP-460003 follow similar strategies of trying to fill the arena in a contracting spiral, first carving an outline and then gradually moving inward, attempting to reduce the area available to the opponent. They exhibit a consistent inter-line spacing of approximately 12 and 4 pixels, respectively. When confined, both players seem to

---

[1] Note that this numbering is consistent with our previous papers on this work [5]; [4].

panic , making a series of tight turns until either crashing or out-lasting their opponent.

Player GP-480001 often performs a diagonal coat-hanger manoeuvre, turning at angles of 45° or 135° by alternating left and right turns in rapid succession. Player GP-540004 is more aggressive, darting about the space in a seemingly erratic manner looking for opportunities to confine its opponent. Finally, player GP-400010 (shown in figure 4b) seems more defensive, gradually moving outward in a tight spiral pattern with an inter-line spacing of 1 or 2 pixels.

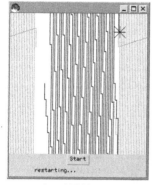
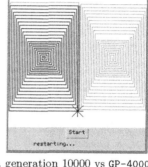

a. generation 20000 vs GP-480001   b. generation 10000 vs GP-400010

Figure 4   Defensive strategies of nn-1 and GP players.

The results of playing every 100th generation network against the five GP players are shown in figure 5, smoothed by aggregation. The performance of network nn-1 can be seen to improve gradually, peaking at around 70% after 40000 generations. In particular, the network sampled at generation 40500 was able to beat all five GP players.

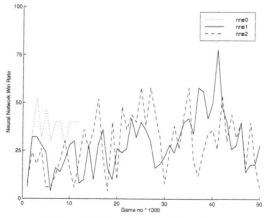

Figure 5   Neural network results.

It is interesting to note that the neural network players do not seem to evolve distinctive features in quite the same way as the GP players (see figure 3).

Figure 6 illustrates the evolution of network nn-1. Each game shown is against GP player 510006. The network makes early mistakes (a), but quickly learns a defensive strategy (b), then changes its behaviour (c), and finally wins again by boxing in its opponent (d).

a. generation 10000

b. generation 20000

c. generation 30000

d. generation 40000

Figure 6   Evolution of Network nn-1 (starting on left),
versus GP-510006 (starting on right)

Network nn-0 (not shown) developed a fragile defensive strategy similar to GP-400010, filling the screen as slowly as possible in a series of expanding spirals. This method works well against GP-400010, an opponent with a similar strategy. It also happens to beat GP-510006 consistently, but loses almost all the time to the other three players.

4 Discussion

Co-evolutionary systems   particularly self-learning hill-climbers   often develop brittle strategies that perform well against a narrow range of opponents but are not robust enough to fend off strategies outside their area of specialisation. This brittleness has been overcome in a number of instances, but usually in domains that involve some form of non-determinism. Even though Tron is a deterministic domain, our self-learning hill-climbers have learned the task well enough to perform capably against a selection of GP players with a variety of different strategies.

The fact that performance oscillates   as measured by our sample of 5 GP players (figure 5)   shows on the one hand that our NN representation for Tron players can be very effective: **nn-1** at generation 40500 beats all the GP opponents. On the other hand, oscillations may indicate that the landscape is deceiving for our hill-climbing algorithm, i.e. going up in one sense may imply going down in another. Further experiments will help us explore these issues.

It is interesting to note that **nn-0**, with a mutant in"uence factor of $= 0.5$, developed a fragile strategy which plays an almost identical game against every opponent, while **nn-1**, with $= 0.33$, developed an ability to react to different opponents in a robust manner. The practice of making only a small adjustment in the direction of the mutant   determined by the parameter   was originally introduced in [9] on the assumption that most of the strategies of the well-tested champion would be preserved, with only limited in"uence from the mutant. However, it may also be that a lower value of   improves the robustness of the champion by exposing it to a greater variety of mutant challengers. Indeed, we conjecture that there may be an optimal value for   which likely varies from one task to another. We plan to explore these issues in further experiments.

In future work we intend to make more extensive studies of Tron and other domains, in the hope of gaining more insight into the role of non-determinism in co-evolutionary learning, and the relative importance of other factors. We also plan to make the neural network players available in the Tron Internet system. Look for them on our web site... `http://www.demo.cs.brandeis.edu/tron`.

Acknowledgements

Thanks to Hugues Juillé for his help in providing the genetic program players, and to Jordan Pollack, Janet Wiles and Brad Tonkes. This research was funded by a University of Queensland Postdoctoral Fellowship and by the O ce of Naval Research under grant N00014-98-1-0435.

References

1. Blair, A. and Sklar, E. (1998). The evolution of subtle manoeuvres in simulated hockey. In *Proc. of SAB-5*.
2. Blair, A. D. and Pollack, J. (1997). What makes a good co-evolutionary learning environment? *Australian Journal of Intelligent Information Processing Systems*, 4(3/4):166 175.
3. Ficici, S. and Pollack, J. (1998). Challenges in coevolution- ary learning: Arms-race dynamics, open-endedness, and mediocre stable states. In *Proc. of ALIFE-6*.
4. Funes, P., Sklar, E., Juillé, H., and Pollack, J. (1997). The inter- net as a virtual ecology: Coevolutionary arms races between human and arti"cial populations. Computer Science Technical Report CS-97-197, Brandeis University.
5. Funes, P., Sklar, E., Juillé, H., and Pollack, J. (1998). Animal- animat coevolution: Using the animal population as "tness function. In *Proc. of SAB-5*.
6. Hillis, W. D. (1992). Co-evolving parasites improve simulated evolution as an optimization procedure. In et al., L., editor, *Proc. of ALIFE-2*, pages 313 324. Addison Wesley.
7. Juillé, H. and Pollack, J. B. (1996). Dynamics of co-evolutionary learning. In *Proc. of SAB-4*, pages 526 534. MIT Press.
8. Koza, J. (1992). *Genetic Programming: On the Programming of Computers by Means of Natural Selection*. MIT Press, Cambridge, MA.
9. Pollack, J. B. and Blair, A. D. (1998). Co-evolution in the successful learning of backgammon strategy. *Machine Learning (to appear)*.
10. Sims, K. (1995). Evolving 3d morphology and behavior by competition. In *Proc. of ALIFE-4*. MIT Press.
11. Tesauro, G. (1995). Temporal di˘erence learning and td-gammon. *Commun. of the ACM 39(3)*.

Co-operative Evolution of a Neural Classifier and Feature Subset

Jennifer Hallinan and Paul Jackway

Cooperative Research Centre for Sensor Signal and Information Processing,
Department of Computer Science and Electrical Engineering,
University of Queensland, St Lucia, QLD 4072,
hallinan@elec.uq.edu.au

Abstract. This paper describes a novel feature selection algorithm which utilizes a genetic algorithm to select a feature subset in conjunction with the weights for a three-layer feedforward network classi"er. The algorithm was tested on the ionosphere data set from UC Irvine, and on an arti"cally generated data set. This approach produces results comparable to those reported for other algorithms on the ionosphere data, but using fewer input features and a simpler neural network architecture. These results indicate that tailoring a neural network classi"er to a speci"c subset of features has the potential to produce a classi"er with low classi"cation error and good generalizability.

Keywords: Genetic algorithm; neural network; classi"cation; ionosphere

1 Introduction

Feature selection is the process of selecting an optimum subset of features from the much larger set of potentially useful features available in a given problem domain [1]. The optimum subset of features which is the aim of the feature extraction algorithm can be defined as the subset that performs the best under some classification system [2], where performs the best is often interpreted as giving the lowest classification error.

The feature selection problem has been investigated by many researchers, and a wide variety of approaches has been developed, including statistical approaches, decision trees, neural networks, and various stochastic algorithms (see [2] for an overview). One approach which has received considerable recent attention is the use of genetic algorithms (GAs) for feature selection.

A GA is an optimization tool inspired by biological evolution. A GA can find near-global optimal parameter values even for poorly behaved functions, given su cient time. As such, its applicability to the optimum feature subset selection problem is apparent, and a number of authors have investigated the use of GAs for feature selection [2,3,4,5].

The actual subset of features which is optimal for a given problem will depend upon the classifier used. In many real-world problems, classes are not linearly separable, and a non-linear classifier, such as a neural net, is required. GAs have been used in combination with neural nets in several ways. They have been used to select feature sets for classification by a neural net trained using conventional learning algorithms (eg [6,7]), and to evolve the weight vector and/or architecture of a neural net (for a review see [8]).

Incorporating the neural net classifier as part of the objective function of the GA requires training a neural net for each fitness evaluation performed by the GA. Due to the stochastic element of neural net training, each net should be trained several times with different initial weights in order to properly assess performance; at least 30 repeats has been suggested in [9]. This makes this approach computationally prohibitively expensive. The solution has usually been to use a simpler, related classifier in the GA [6], or to only partially train a subset of the neural nets in each generation [7,5].

A different approach, described below, is to combine the evolution of the weight vector for a neural net with the selection of a feature subset. In this way it should be possible to use a GA to evolve a nonlinear classifier explicitly tuned to a feature subset, without excessive computational overhead. This combines the advantages of using a small feature set, as discussed above, with those of having a classifier developed specifically for that feature set, and should lead to high accuracy of classification using a small number of features. We decided to see whether such an approach is feasible and whether it could, in fact, lead to the development of an effective, generalizable classifier.

2 Method

The task chosen to test the algorithm was classification of the ionosphere data set from the UCI Repository of Machine Learning Databases [10]. The dataset consists of radar returns from the ionosphere. There are 350 returns, consisting of 34 features, normalized to the range[-1 , 1], with a target value of good or bad , which was recoded for this application as 0 and 1 respectively. The features were originally 17 discrete returns, each comprising a real and an imaginary part. These parts are used as separate features, leading to the final array of 34 features. The data was initially divided into a training set of 200 returns, of which 100 were good and 100 bad, and a test set of 150 returns, of which 123 were good and 27 were bad. This is the partitioning used by [12], who first collected and analyzed the data.

The distribution of good/bad returns in the test set is very uneven . To assess the effect of the partitioning of the data on the classifier developed, a further 5 data partitionings were used. In each case 63 good and 63 bad cases were selected at random from the data set and these 126 cases were used as the training set, with the remaining 124 forming as the test set. This results in a smaller training set, but a test set with a somewhat greater proportion of bad returns.

A three-layer feedforward net was used, with a sigmoid activation function on the hidden and output units. The network had six input units, three hidden units, and a single output unit. The GA could thus select a set of 6 features, or, by setting both the weights from a feature to 0, could select less than 6 features. This choice of network architecture was a compromise between an attempt to make the network as small as possible, reducing the number of parameters to be fitted, and thus the complexity of the problem which the GA is to solve, and the need to make it complex enough to successfully classify the nonlinear input data. Three hidden units were used because they proved to be su cient to solve the problem

experiments with different network architectures indicate that more hidden units, as would be expected, produce a more accurate classifier. However, since the objective of this study was to demonstrate that a very simple classifier can perform well if its inputs are carefully chosen, the simplest successful architecture was used.

Each net was encoded as a single binary string 160 bits long, with each eight bits representing a single integer in the range 0 255 (binary coded decimal). Alternative representations, such as Gray coding, may have advantages in a GA, but were not considered in this study.

Each integer represented either a feature or a weight. The first eight bits represented the first feature, feature 1; the next eight the weight from feature 1 to hidden unit 1; the next eight the weight from feature 1 to hidden unit 2, and so on. The weights associated with a given feature were located close to that feature to facilitate the development of schema during evolution. Features and weights were both coded in eight bits, so that they were both subject to the same chance of mutation and crossover.

Integers representing features were rescaled to lie between 0 and 3 by multiplying by $(3/255)$. The result was rounded, and this integer was interpreted as an index to a particular feature. Integers representing weights were scaled to lie in the range -3.0 to $+3.0$, using $w = (k \times (2 \times 3.0)/255) - 3.0$. This weight range was chosen because it is fairly small and centred around 0.0, which is the centre of the sigmoid activation function used.

The objective function for the GA attempts to minimize the mean squared error of the net over the entire training data set. The fitness of an individual chromosome is $(1 - MSE)$.

The parameter settings used for the GA were achieved by trial-and-error on the training set only. The initial values were taken from [11]. The final configuration was: Population Size 50; Mutation Rate 0.01; Crossover Rate 0.02; Generation Gap 0.5.

Individuals were chosen to reproduce on the basis of their fitness, using Roulette Wheel selection [11] and elitist generational replacement was used, with the fittest 50% of parents and the fittest 50% of offspring making up the next generation.

The GA was run five times on the Sigillito-partitioned training dataset, with a different random number seed each time. The course of training was followed by recording the maximum fitness observed in each generation, and training was stopped when the population appeared to have converged. The fittest individual in the population was then decoded and used to classify the test and training sets. The GA was then run on each of the 5 randomly partitioned data sets, with a random number seed of 1 each time, using the same training methodology.

3   Results and Analysis

The results of the training runs are recorded in Table 1. For each trial, the fittest neural net was used to classify each case in both the training and the test data sets. The optimum threshold for each classifier was selected and the percentage of cases correctly classified using that threshold are recorded in Table 1.

Table 1. Runs of the Neural GA with di˘erent Random Number Seeds

Seed	Max Fitness	Gener- ations	Features Selected	AUC (Train)	AUC (Test)	% Correct (Train)	% Correct (Test)
1	0.901581	687	4,5,7,20,26,28	0.892	0.902	90.5	90.8
345	0.861244	688	4,5,9,9,15,23	0.901	0.808	88.6	90.8
7356	0.892623	609	2,4,5,12,13,14,	0.898	0.947	90.0	93.4
629	0.899525	691	2,4,5,7,9,13,	0.941	0.976	90.0	96.1
30	0.894945	677	4,7,8,9,20,23	0.927	0.859	86.6	90.8
Ave	0.889984					89.1	92.4

The average percentage of cases in the unseen test set classified correctly is 92.4%   somewhat higher than that achieved for the training set, at 89.1%. This implies that the test set is easier to classify than the training set, a conclusion which is supported by [12], who note that bad returns are more diverse than good ones, and hence presumably harder to characterize. Bad returns comprise only 18% of the test set, but form 50% of the training set. When different, and more even, partitionings of the data into training and test sets were used, the average area under the ROC curve on the training set was 0.979, and on the test set was 0.937. This supports the premise that the good returns are easier to classify, and suggests that conclusions about the generalizability of any classifier developed on this data set are limited by this variability.

The accuracy of the nets produced by different runs varied from 86.6% to 90.5% for the training set, and from 90.8% to 96.1% for the test set, indicating that the system is quite robust with respect to initial conditions.

A Receiver Operating Characteristic (ROC) curve was constructed for each set by taking the output of each case in each run and thresholding the entire data set at a number of points between 0 and 1. The proportion of correctly classified good   values (true positives) and incorrectly classified   bad   values (false positives) was computed for each threshold, and these values plotted against each other to give the ROC curves (Fig. 1). A ROC curve provides a concise graphic depiction of the overall performance of a classifier; for any given classifier it is possible to operate at any point on the ROC curve by using the corresponding threshold for classification. The area under the ROC curve may be used as a measure of the power of the classifier. It ranges from 0.5 (no power   random classification) to 1.0 (perfect classification of all cases). The columns labelled AUC   in Table 1 is the area under the ROC curve for that classifier.

The ROC curves in Fig. 1 vary more than the single figure for accuracy would indicate, implying that, although the optimum performance of the classifiers is similar, the overall performance is not so uniform   some feature subsets appear to be more effective than others over a wide range of thresholds.

Fig. 1 also shows the results achieved by Sigillito[12] on this data set. They used a linear perceptron, which achieved an accuracy of 90.7%, a true positive value of 95.9% and a false positive value of 33.3%; a nonlinear perceptron, which achieved an accuracy of 92.0%, a true positive value of 98.4% and a false positive value of 37.0%; and a number of multilayer perceptrons (MLPs) with 3 15 hidden units. The best of these achieved 98% accuracy, with a true positive value of 100% and a false positive rate of 11.1%.

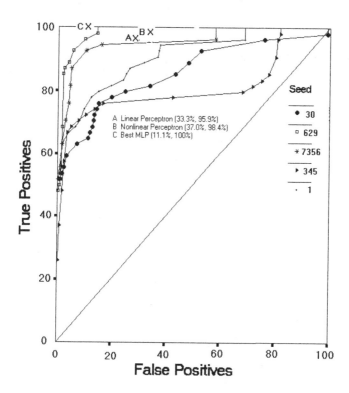

Fig. 1. ROC Curves for 6 Input Neural GA Classi"er. A, B and C mark the results obtained by Sigillito *et al.*(1989) on this data set with varying classi"ers (see text for details)

Fig. 1 illustrates the difference between the point accuracy of a classifier, and its overall performance. While the accuracy achieved by [12] using an MLP with 15 hidden nodes and 34 inputs was considerably better than that achieved by the Neural GA at what we selected as optimum threshold, all their classifiers are operating within the range of the ROC curves for the neural GA. That is, this classifier could operate with equal percentage accuracy with the appropriate tradeoff between true positive and false positive rates.

The variability observed due to different partitionings of the data set makes it di cult to quantify the generalizability of the classifier evolved by this algorithm. In order to overcome this problem, the algorithm was tested on an artificially constructed data set. This consisted of points from a set of multidimensional nested spheres. This problem is clearly non-linearly separable, but is readily visualized by humans. The data set consisted of a two-dimensional, two-class problem. 1,000 points from each class were generated as a training set, a total of 2,000 training cases. An equal number of points was generated for the test set. The spheres are centred on 0.5, with the inner sphere having a radius of 0.25, and the outer forming an annulus of thickness 0.25 around the inner sphere.

Seven features were generated. Features 0 and 1 are the x and y coordinates for the data point. Features 2 ind 5 are random numbers in the range (0,1); feature 3 is half of (feature 0 plus a random number in the range (0,1)); feature 4 is 2/3 of (feature 0 plus feature 1); and feature 6 is half of feature 2 plus feature 5. All feature values are in the range (0,1). The optimum subset of features for this data set is thus (0,1). The neural network consisted of two input nodes, five hidden nodes and a single output node.

Over the course of several runs it became apparent that there was a strong tendency for the GA to converge to either (0,0) or (1,1) as the features selected. These solutions apparently represent local minima in the search space in which the system tended to become trapped, although the correct solution was found occasionally. In order to overcome this, a penalty function was introduced into the fitness function, whereby the SSE for an individual was multiplied by 1.1 for each duplicate feature selected.

The results of five runs of the algorithm on the artificial data are recorded in Table 2.

Table 2. Runs of the Neural GA on Arti"cial Data

Run	Seed	Features Selected	AUC (Train)	AUC (Test)
1	1	1,4	0.999	0.803
2	1234	1,4	1.000	0.999
3	999	0,1	1.000	1.000
4	5869	0,1	1.000	1.000
5	65	0,1	1.000	1.000

In three of the five runs the correct solution was found. On the other two runs the solution found was (1,4); feature 4 is a combination of features 0 and 1, and so provides useful, although noisier, information to the classifier. The classifiers based upon the correct features generalized perfectly to unseen test data, while those based on the noisier features generalized less well.

4 Conclusions

The results achieved with the neural genetic algorithm described above on real data are encouraging, in that they demonstrate that a simple nonlinear classifier, tailored to a feature subset, can perform almost as well as a much more complex classifier utilizing six times as many input features. There is some evidence that many of the features in this data set are not contributing to the true classification, but the more accurate classifier is actually re"ecting idiosyncrasies of the training data set. This is not surprising, given that a three-layer neural net with 20 inputs and three hidden units is attempting to estimate 63 parameters using 200 training exemplars, whereas a 6-input net is fitting only 21 parameters.

On an artifical data set with large amounts of data, the algorithm produces a classifier which selects the most discriminatory features three times out of five, and generalizes well to unseen test data. This suggests that the algorithm can combine feature selection and classifier construction within the limits of the data set.

Feature selection techniques are often applied to data sets having large numbers of features, but relatively few cases. Division of data into training and test (and preferably validation) sets, while essential, further aggravates the situation. In such a situation, the use of a subset of features is highly likely to lead to improved generalizability of a classifier. The algorithm described here permits network architecture to be kept simple, but strongly tailored to a feature subset, to reduce computation and enhance generalizability of the resulting classifier.

References

1. Gose, F., Johnsonbaugh, R. & Jost, S. (1996). *Pattern Recognition and Image Analysis*. Prentice Hall PTR: Upper Saddle River, NJ.
2. Jain, A. & Zongker, D.(1997). Feature Selection: Evaluation, application and small sample performance. *IEEE Transactions on Pattern Analysis and Machine Intelligence* **19**(2): 153 158.
3. Siedlecki, W. & Sklansky, J.(1989). A note on genetic algorithms for large-scale feature selection. *Pattern Recognition Letters* **10**(5): 335 347.
4. Vafaie, H. & DeJong, K. (1993). Robust feature selection algorithms. *Proceedings of the International Conference on Tools with AI*. Boston, Mass.
5. Yang, J. & Honavar, V.(1998). Feature subset selection using a genetic algorithm. *IEEE Intelligent Systems* **13**: 44 49.
6. Brill, F. Z., Brown, D. E. & Martin, W. N.(1992). Fast genetic selection of features for neural network classi"ers. *IEEE Transactions on Neural Networks* **3**(2): 324-328.

8. Yao, X.(1993). A review of evolutionary arti"cial neural networks. *International Journal of Intelligent Systems* **8**(4): 539 577.

9. Setiono, R. & Liu, H.(1997). *Neural-network feature selector. IEEE Transactions on Neural Networks* **8**(3): 654 659.

10. Murphy, P. M. & Aha, D. W. (1992). UCI Repository of Machine Learning Databases, Machine Readable Data Repository, Irvine, CA. University of California, Dept. of Information and Computer Science.

11. Mitchell, M.(1996).An Introduction to Genetic Algorithms. MIT Press: Cambridge, Massachusetts.

12. Sigillito, V. G., Wing, S. P., Hutton, L. V. & Baker, K. B. (1989). Classi"cation of radar returns from the ionosphere using a neural networks. *Johns Hopkins APL Technical Digest,* **10**: 262 266.

Optimal Power Flow Method Using Evolutionary Programming

Kit Po Wong and Jason Yuryevich

Arti"cial Intelligence and Power Systems Research Group
University of Western Australia
Australia

Abstract. This paper reports on an evolutionary programming based method for solving the optimal power "ow problem. The method incorporates an evolutionary programming based load "ow solution. To demonstrate the global optimisation power of the new method it is applied to the IEEE30 bus test system with highly non-linear generator input/output cost curves and the results compared to those obtained using the method of steepest descent. The results demonstrate that the new method shows great promise for solving the optimal power "ow problem when it contains highly non-linear devices.

Keywords: Evolutionary programming, Optimal power "ow, Optimisation

1 Introduction

Recently attempts have been made by power system researchers to develop Evolutionary Computation (EC) based optimisation techniques for solving power system problems. EC is the study of computational systems, which use ideas and get inspiration from natural evolution and adaption. Currently there are three major implementations of the evolutionary algorithms: genetic algorithms (GAs) [1,2], evolutionary programming (EP) [3,4] and evolution strategies [5,6].

In the last five years, the first two EC approaches have been applied to may operating and planning problems in power systems. The GA techniques have been used in the reconfiguration of radial distribution networks, load-"ow [7], economic active power and fuel dispatch [8,9,10], hydrothermal scheduling [11], unit commitment [12,13] and transmission systems [14]. The EP approach has in the last two years gained some momentum and has been applied to economic dispatch [15], economic/environmental dispatch [16], reactive power planning [17] and transmission network expansion planning [18].

The works reported in the literature so far have confirmed that, as an optimisation methodology, EC has global search characteristics and it is "exible and adaptive. Depending on the problem class, it can be very robust. For example, the constrained genetic algorithm based load "ow algorithm [7] has been shown to be robust and has the ability to find the saddle node bifurcation point of

extremely loaded practical systems and abnormal load "ow solutions. Its performance is superior to the conventional Newton Raphson method in these aspects.

The work on GA load "ow has been extended and implemented using the
EP methodology. Based on the work so far developed, this paper reports on the
development of a pure EP based method for solving the optimum power "ow
(OPF) problem [19,20,21], which merges the load "ow and economic dispatch
problems into one. The complexity of the problem is increased due to a larger
set of operational constraints of the generators and transformers in the electrical
networks. Moreover, highly nonlinear generator input/output cost characteristics will increase the complexity of the OPF problem rendering conventional approaches ineffective in obtaining the global optimum solution. An OPF method
based on EC such as the one in this paper will provide a sound basis for further
development, not only to reduce the computational time requirement of the EP
based OPF method, but to include non-linear devices such as FACTs devices.
The OPF evaluations become more and more important under the deregula-
tion of the electricity industry as OPF is an essential component in any power
transmission costing and pricing calculations.

This paper reports a pure EP-based method for solving the OPF problem.
The developed method is tested and validated using the IEEE 30 bus test system. Two study cases are presented in which the generator cost characteristics
are represented by (a) quadratic functions and (b) by mixed quadratic functions
and piece-wise quadratic functions. The convergence characteristics of the new
method in the application studies are presented. The method is shown to be
powerful and promising.

2   Optimum Power Flow Problem

The OPF problem is a combination of the load "ow and economic dispatch problem. The objective of this problem can be stated differently depending on the
aspect of interest. One of the possible objectives of OPF is the minimisation of
the power generation cost subject to the satisfaction of the generation and load
balance in the transmission network as well as the operational limits and constraints of the generators and the transformers. The OPF problem can therefore
be regarded as a constrained minimisation problem which, in general, has the
following formulation:

$$\min f(\mathbf{x}, \mathbf{u}) \tag{1}$$

$$\text{subject to:} \quad g(\mathbf{x}, \mathbf{u}) = 0$$

$$h(\mathbf{x}, \mathbf{u}) \leq 0$$

where $f(\mathbf{x}, \mathbf{u})$ is the objective function in terms of the power production cost,
which depends on the generations levels of the generators. The vector of independent variables $\mathbf{u}$ is given by the active powers of the generators, the voltages
of the PV nodes and transformer tap settings. The vector of dependent variables
$\mathbf{x}$ is given by the voltages of PQ nodes, argument of PV nodes voltages and reactive power generation. The equality constraint in equation set 1 represents the

balance of supply and load at each node in the network, that is the load "ow problem. The inequality constraints represent operational limits of the generators and the tap settings of transformers. In solving the OPF problem, it can be seen that the load "ow problem must also be solved. In the present work, an EP based load "ow method similar to that in [7] is employed.

3   Solving OPF using Evolutionary Programming

The essence of the EP technique can be found in [4,15,16,17,18]. The essential components of the pure EP-based OPF algorithm are given below. Based on these components, an EP based procedure can be established for solving the OPF problem. The procedure is illustrated by the "ow-chart in Fig. 1.

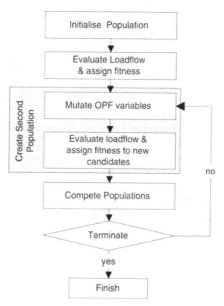

Fig. 1. Flow Chart of EP-based OPF

(a) *Representation of Individuals:* An individual or candidate solution in a population is represented in an array in which the values of the generator active power powers, nodal voltages and transformer tappings are stored. Slack node power is not included in the individual. The active powers of the generators, nodal voltages and transformer tap settings in an individual in the initial population are set randomly within their given ranges. New individuals are formed by mutation.

(b) *Fitness function:* The fitness f_i of individual i, that is the degree of optimality of the candidate solution is evaluated by the following fitness function:

$$f_i = \frac{M}{C_i + \sum_j VP_j + SQ} \tag{2}$$

$$VP_j = \begin{cases} K_v(V_j - 1.0)^2 & \text{if } V_j > V_j^{max} \text{ or } V_j < V_j^{min} \\ 0 & \text{otherwise} \end{cases}$$

$$SQ_j = \begin{cases} K_q(Q_{slack} - Q_{slack}^{max})^2 & \text{if } Q_{slack} > Q_{slack}^{max} \\ K_q(Q_{slack} - Q_{slack}^{min})^2 & \text{if } Q_{slack} < Q_{slack}^{min} \\ 0 & \text{otherwise} \end{cases}$$

In equation (2), C_i is the total cost of active power generation in individual i, $\sum_j VP_j$ represents a penalty applied for any voltage violations, while SQ is a penalty for reactive power violations at the slack node. As the production cost is usually very high, its reciprocal will normally be very small. To obtain better numerical values for the fitness of the individual for comparison purposes, the factor M is used in equation (2) to amplify the value. M is here set to the maximum possible cost of power generation. K_v and K_q are penalty weighting constants.

(c) *Generation of Candidate Solutions:* New individuals are produced by mutating the existing individuals. Let p_i' be the new individual produced from old individual p_i according to:

$$x_{ji}' = x_{ji} + N(0, {}_{ji}^2) \tag{3}$$

where x_{ji}' and x_{ji} are the values of the jth element in p_i' and p_i respectively and $N(0, {}_{ji}^2)$ is a gaussian random number with a mean of zero and a standard deviation of ${}_{ji}$. The expression designed for ${}_{ji}$ is:

$$_{ji} = (x_j^{max} - x_j^{min})((f_{max} - f_i)/f_{max} + a^r) \tag{4}$$

where f_i is the fitness of individual i; f_{max} is the maximum fitness within the population; x_j^{max}, x_j^{min} denote the upper and lower limits of variable j; a is a positive constant slightly less than unity and r is the iteration counter. The term a^r provides a decaying mutation offset the rate of which depends on the value of a [16].

(d) *Selection of a new population by competition:* A resultant population of individuals is formed from the two existing populations. Each of the individuals in the two populations will compete with N_t rival individuals selected randomly in the combined populations and score s_i will be assigned to the individual i, according to:

$$s_i = \sum_{j=1}^{N_t} n_j \tag{5}$$

$$n_j = \begin{cases} 1 & \text{if } f_i > f_r \\ 0 & \text{otherwise} \end{cases}$$

where n_j is the result of a tournament between individuals i and r, f_i and f_r are the fitnesses of the individuals under consideration. If the population size is k, then the k highest ranked individuals will be selected to form the new population form which future generations are evolved.

4   Application Example

The results obtained when the EP-based method is applied to the IEEE 30 bus system are presented in this section. The test system data can be found in [19]. Two study cases are presented, the first case is taken from [19] and uses quadratic generator input/output cost curves which provides a convex solution surface. The second study replaces the generator input/output cost curves for nodes 1 and 2 by piece-wise quadratic curves to simulate different fuels or valve-point loading effects.

All simulations were run on a Pentium Pro 200Mhz computer, the algorithm was written in the C programming language. In all cases the average execution time was 38 seconds. Reactive power limits at all nodes except the slack node are enforced using conventional switching within the load "ow. The population size is set at 20 while in all cases 50 iterations are executed.

(i) *Quadratic Input/Output Curves*

In this study quadratic curves were used to describe the generators. This provides a convex solution surface which is well suited to conventional optimisation techniques such as the method of steepest descent. The data for the generators is given below in Table 1. The EP-OPF was run 100 times and the cost of the final solution in each of the trials is graphed below in Fig. 2. The costs of solutions produced are consistently close to that reported in [19]. The minimum cost being \$802.86 while the average was \$804.42. The details of the minimum solution are provided in Table 3.

To illustrate the convergence of the EP-OPF the average statistics over the 100 trials are plotted in Fig. 3. It can be seen that the EP-OPF converges quite rapidly to the global optimum solution.

The problem was also solved using the SD method of [19] and its convergence is shown on Fig. 3. The SD method performs well on this case as expected, due to the convex nature of the generator input output curves. The final solution returned by the SD method is approximately \$802.40.

Table 1. Unit Input/Output Curves for Case(i)

Bus No.	P_G^{min} MW	P_G^{max} MW	Q_G^{min} MVAr	S_G^{max} MVA	Cost Coefficients		
					a	b	c
1	50	200	-20	250	0.00	2.00	0.00375
2	20	80	-20	100	0.00	1.75	0.01750
5	15	50	-15	80	0.00	1.00	0.06250
8	10	35	-15	60	0.00	3.25	0.00834
11	10	30	-10	50	0.00	3.00	0.02500
13	12	40	-15	60	0.00	3.00	0.02500

$$C_i = a_i + b_i P_i + c_i P_i^2$$

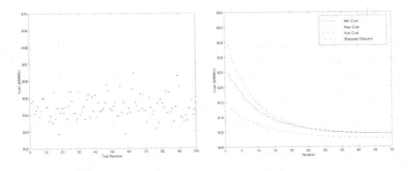

Fig. 2 Solutions for Case(i)   **Fig. 3** Convergence for Case(i)

(ii) *Piece-wise Quadratic Curves*

To simulate the effects of different fuels or valve point loading, the curves describing the generators connected to nodes 1 and 2 were replaced by piece-wise quadratics. The data for these curves is given in Table 2. These curves provide a non-convex solution surface for the problem which will cause more classical solution methods to fail in determining the global optimum.

The algorithm was run 100 times producing a minimum cost of $648.95 and an average cost of $654.81, the data for the minimum solution is given in Table 3. The final costs for the 100 trails are plotted below in Fig. 4. The convergence of the algorithm is also plotted in Fig. 5.

The SD method of [19] was applied to this case also, the convergence is given in Fig. 5. In this case the method fails to find the global optimum solution. With reference to Fig. 5 the jump in cost at iteration 23 is a result of the loading of the unit connected to bus 2 crossing a discontinuity. The gradient information on which the method is based becomes invalid when a discontinuity is crossed and results in the solution converging to a local optimum.

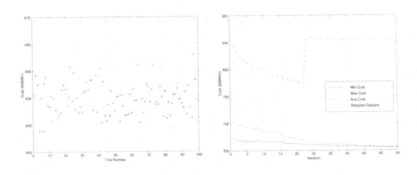

Fig. 4 Solutions for Case(ii)   **Fig. 5** Convergence for Case(ii)

Table 2. Unit Input/Output Curves for Case(ii)

Node	From	To	Cost Coefficients		
No.	MW	MW	a	b	c
1	50	140	55.0	0.70	0.0050
	140	200	82.5	1.05	0.0075
2	20	55	40.0	0.30	0.0100
	55	80	80.0	0.60	0.0200

$$C_i = a_i + b_i P_i + c_i P_i^2$$

Table 3. Solutions for Test Cases

Case	P_2	P_3	P_4	P_5	P_6	V_1	V_2	V_3	V_4	V_5	V_6	t_{11}	t_{12}	t_{15}	t_{36}
EP (i)	46.903	21.210	25.604	12.805	12.145	1.048	1.035	1.007	1.006	1.095	1.068	1.04	0.90	0.98	0.93
SD (i)	52.028	21.095	19.384	13.540	12.734	1.050	1.041	1.007	1.009	1.073	1.054	0.98	0.94	0.94	0.93
EP (ii)	54.936	24.567	33.917	18.630	18.709	1.046	1.057	1.038	1.051	1.025	1.068	0.91	1.09	0.95	1.02
SD (ii)	71.787	14.798	11.669	10.000	12.000	1.006	1.037	1.050	1.010	1.077	1.056	0.98	0.95	0.94	0.93

5 Conclusions

An EP-based method for solving the optimal power "ow problem has been reported and demonstrated through its application to the IEEE30 bus test system. It has been compared to the steepest descent method and has been found to obtain almost identical results in the case where the generator input/output cost curves are quadratic. The new method is however superior when the generator cost characteristics are highly non-linear. The limitations of the new method are (i) that it is not robust enough to guarantee convergence to the global optimum solution in the case of piece-wise quadratic cost functions and (ii) the computational speed is large compared to classical methods.

The EP-based OPF method reported is very promising. Further work is being undertaken to improve the robustness and to reduce its computational requirement.

References

1. J.H. Holland. *Adaption in Natural and Artificial Systems.* Ann Arbor: University of Michigan Press, 1975.
2. D.E. Goldberg. *Genetic Algorithms in Search, Optimisation and Machine Learning.* Addison-Wesley, 1989.
3. L.J. Fogel. Autonomous automata. In *Ind. Res.*, volume 4, pages 14 19, 1962.
4. D.B. Fogel. *Evolutionary Computation: Toward a new Philosophy in Machine Intelligence.* IEEE Press, 1995.
5. I. Rechenberg. *Evolutionsstrategie: Optimierung technischer systeme nach prinzipien der biologischen evolution.* Germany Frommann-Holzboog, 1973.
6. H.P. Schwefel. *Evolution and Optimum Seeking.* Wiley, New York, 1995.
7. K.P. Wong, A. Li, and M.Y. Law. Development of constrained genetic algorithm load "ow method. *IEE Proc. Gener. Transm. and Distrib.*, 144(2):91 99, 1997.

8. D.C. Walter and G.B. Sheble. Genetic algorithm solution of economic dispatch with valve point loading. In *IEEE PES Summer Meeting, Seattle, Paper Number SM 414-3 PWRS*, 1992.

9. K.P. Wong and Y.W. Wong. Genetic and genetic simulated annealing appraoches to economic dispatch. *IEE Proc. Gener. Transm. Distrib.*, 141(5):507 513, 1994.

10. K.P. Wong and Wong S.Y.W. Hybrid genetic/simulated annealing approach to short-term multiple-fuel-constrained generation scheduling. *IEEE Trans. on Power Systems*, 12(2):776 784, 1997.

11. K.P. Wong and Y.W. Wong. Development of hybrid optimisation techniques based on genetic algorithms and simulated annealing. In X Yao, editor, *Progress in Evolutionary Computation, Lectures in Artificial Intelligence*, pages 372 380. 956 Series by Springer-Verlag, 1995.

12. K.P. Wong and Y.W Wong. Thermal generator scheduling using hybrid genetic/simulated-annealing approach. *IEE Proc. Gener. Transm. Distrib.*, 142(4):372 380, 1995.

13. S.A. Kazarlis, A.G. Bakirtzis, and V. Petrdis. A genetic algorithm solution to the unit commitment problem. *IEEE Trans. on Power Systems*, 11(1):372 380, 1995.

14. H. Rudnick, R. Palma, E. Cura, and C. Silva. Economically adapted transmission systems in open access schemes   application of genetic algorithms. *IEEE Trans. on Power Systems*, 11(3), 1996.

15. H.T Yang, P.C. Yang, and C.L. Huang. Evolutionary programming based economic dispatch for units with non-smooth fuel cost functions. *IEEE Trans. on Power Systems*, 11(1):112 117, 1996.

16. K.P. Wong and J Yuryevich. Evolutionary programming-based economic dispatch for environmentally constrained economic dispatch. accepted in 1997 for publication in *IEEE Trans. on Power Systems*.

17. L.L. Lai and J.T. Ma. Application of evolutionary programming to reactive power planning   comparison with non-linear programming approach. *IEEE Trans. on Power Systems*, 12(1), 1997.

18. L.L. Lai, T.J. Ma, Wong K.P., R. Yokoyama, M Zhao, and H. Sasaki. Application of evolutionary programming to transmission system planning. In *Conf. Proc. on Power Systems, Institution of Electrical Engineers Japan*, pages 147 152, 1996.

19. O. Alsac and B. Stott. Optimal load"ow with steady-state security. *IEEE Trans.*, PAS-93:745 751, 1974.

20. R. Ristanovic. Successive linear programming based opf solution. In *Optimal Power Flow: Solution Techniques, Requirements and Challenges*, pages 1 9. IEEE Power Engineering Society, 1996.

21. S.M. Shahidehpour and V.C. Ramesh. Non-linear programming algorithms and decomposition strategies for opf. In *Optimal Power Flow: Solution Techniques, Requirements and Challenges*, pages 10 24. IEEE Power Engineering Society, 1996.

Grammatical Development of Evolutionary Modular Neural Networks*

Sung-Bae Cho[12] and Katsunori Shimohara[2]

[1] Dept. of Computer Science, Yonsei University
134 Shinchon-dong, Sudaemoon-ku, Seoul 120-749, Korea
[2] ATR Human Information Processing Research Laboratories
2-2 Hikaridai, Seika-cho, Soraku-gun, Kyoto 619-02, Japan
E-mail: [sbcho,katsu]@hip.atr.co.jp

Abstract. Evolutionary algorithms have shown a great potential to develop the optimal neural networks that can change the architectures and learning rules according to the environments. In order to boost up the scalability and utilization, grammatical development has been considered as a promising encoding scheme of the network architecture in the evolutionary process. This paper presents a preliminary result to apply a grammatical development method called L-system to determine the structure of a modular neural network that was previously proposed by the authors. Simulation result with the recognition problem of handwritten digits indicates that the evolved neural network has reproduced some of the characteristics of natural visual system, such as the organization of coarse and "ne processing of stimuli in separate pathways.

1 Introduction

There are more than hundred publications that report an evolutionary design method of neural networks [1,2,3,4]. One of the important advantages of evolutionary neural networks is their adaptability to a dynamic environment, and this adaptive process is achieved through the evolution of connection weights, architectures and learning rules [4]. Most of the previous evolutionary neural networks, however, show little structural constraints. However, there is a large body of neuropsychological evidence showing that the human information processing system consists of modules, which are subdivisions in identifiable parts, each with its own purpose or function.

This paper takes a module as a building block for evolutionary neural networks previously proposed by [5], and applies a parametric L-system to the development of the network architecture. Each module has the ability to autonomously categorize input activation patterns into discrete categories, and representations are distributed over modules rather than over individual nodes. Among the general principles are modularity, locality, self-induced noise, and self-induced learning.

* This work was supported in part by a grant no. SC-13 from the Ministry of Science and Technology in Korea.

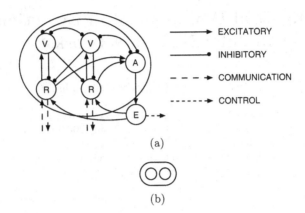

(a)

(b)

Fig. 1. (a) Schematic diagram of the internal structure of a module; (b) Simpli"ed diagram of the module (a).

2   Evolutionary Modular Neural Networks

The basic idea is to consider a module as a building block resulting in local representations by competition, and develop complex intermodule connections with evolutionary mechanism. In computing terms, an evolutionary algorithm maps a problem onto a set of strings, each string representing a potential solution. In the problem at hand, a string encodes the network architecture and learning parameters in tree structure. The evolutionary algorithm then manipulates the most promising strings in its search for improved solutions. This process operates through a simple cycle of stages:

1. creation of a population of tree-structured strings,
2. evaluation of each string,
3. selection of good strings, and
4. genetic manipulation to create the new population of strings.

The activation value of each node in the modular neural network is calculated as follows:

$$e_i = \sum_j w_{ij} a_j(t), \tag{1}$$

where w_{ij} denotes the weight of a connection from node j to node i. The effective input to node i, e_i, is the weighted sum of the individual activations of all nodes connected to the input side of the node. The input may be either positive (excitatory) or negative (inhibitory).

The internal structure of each module is fixed and the weights of all intramodular connections are non-modifiable during learning process (see Fig. 1(a)). In a module, R-node represents a particular pattern of input activations to a module, V-node inhibits all other nodes in a module, A-node activates a positive function of the amount of competition in a module, and E-node activation is a measure of the level of competition going on in a module. The most important feature of a module is to autonomously categorize input activation patterns into discrete categories, which is facilitated as the association of an input pattern with a unique R-node.

The process goes with the resolution of a winner-take-all competition between all R-nodes activated by input. In the first presentation of a pattern to a module, all R-nodes are activated equally, which results in a state of maximal competition. It is resolved by the inhibitory V-nodes and a state-dependent noise mechanism. The noise is proportional to the amount of competition, as measured through the number of active R-nodes by the A-node and E-node. Evolutionary mechanism gives a possibility of change to the phenotype of a module through the genetic operators.

The interconnection between two modules means that all R-nodes in one module are connected to all R-nodes in the other module. These intermodule connections are modifiable by Hebb rule with the following equation:

$$w_{ij}(t+1) = \mu_t a_i \left([K - w_{ij}(t)] a_j - L w_{ij}(t) \sum_{f \neq j} w_{if}(t) a_f \right), \qquad (2)$$

$$\mu_t = d + w_{\mu_E} a_E, \qquad (3)$$

where a_i, a_j and a_f are activations of the corresponding nodes, respectively: $w_{ij}(t)$ is the interweight between R-nodes j and i, $w_{if}(t)$ indicates an interweight from a neighboring R-node f (of j) to R-node i, and $w_{ij}(t+1)$ is the change in weight from j to i at time $t+1$. Note that L and K are positive constants, and a_E is the activation of the E-node. As a mechanism for generating change and integrating the changes into the whole system, we use evolutionary algorithm to determine the parameters in the above learning rule and structure of intermodule connections.

Three kinds of information should be encoded in the genotype representation: the structure of intermodule connection, the number of nodes in each module, and the parameters of learning and activation rules. The intermodule weights are determined by the Hebb rule mentioned at the previous section. In order to represent the information appropriately, a tree-like structure has been adopted. An arc in a tree expresses an intermodule connection, and each node represents a specific module and the number of nodes therein. For more detailed description on the evolutionary modular neural networks, see the recent publication [5].

3   Grammatical Development of MNN

Aristid Lindenmayer introduced a formalism for simulating the development of multicellular organisms, subsequently named L-systems [7], and the vigorous development of the mathematical theory was followed by its applications to the modeling of plants. L-systems are sets of rules and symbols that model growth processes, and there are several variants depending on the properties. This paper adopts one of them, called context-sensitive parametric L-system.

Parametric L-system operates on parametric words, which are strings consisting of letters with associated parameters. The letters belong to an alphabet V, and the parameters belong to the set of real numbers R. A string with letter $A \in V$ and parameters $a_1, a_2, \ldots, a_n \in R$ is denoted by $A(a_1, a_2, \ldots, a_n)$. A formal definition of the context-sensitive parametric L-system is as follows:

Definition 1. *A parametric L-system is de ned as an ordered quadruple $G = (V, \ , w, P)$, where*

- *V is the alphabet of the system,*
- *   is the set of formal parameters,*
- * $\in (V \times R^*)^+$ is a nonempty parametric word called axiom,*
- *$P \in (V \times \quad ^*) \times C(\ ) \times (V \times E(\ )^*)^*$ is a   nite set of productions, where $C(\ )$ and $E(\ )$ denote logical and arithmetic expressions with parameters from , respectively.*

The symbols : and $\rightarrow$ are used to separate the three components of a production: predecessor, condition, and successor. Thus, a production has the format of $lc < pred > rc : cond \rightarrow succ$.

For example, a production with predecessor $B(y)$, left context $A(x)$, right context $C(z)$, condition $x + y + z >= 10$ and successor $U(x + y)V(y + z)$ is written as

$$A(x) < B(y) > C(z) : x + y + z >= 10 \rightarrow U(x + y)V(y + z). \qquad (4)$$

The left context is separated from the predecessor by the symbol $<$, and the predecessor is separated from the right context by the symbol $>$. This production can be applied to the $B(4)$ that appears in a parametric word $\cdots A(3) \ B(4) \ C(5) \cdots$, and replaces $B(4)$ with $U(7)V(9)$.

With this formalism, a basic element of the L-system can be defined as a module or a functional group composed of several modules for modular neural networks. A module is denoted as $A(x, y)$ where A identifies the name, x represents the number of nodes and y means the connection pointer of the module, respectively. Consecutive symbols for modules mean a default forward connection from the former module to the latter module. Positive integer of y means the forward connection and negative one does the backward connection. The functional group is represented by a pair of '[' and ']'. One more addition is a special symbol ',' which is used to represent disconnection between two modules. Fig. 2 shows some of the typical examples of the grammar and structure generated by it.

In order to see how the grammar generates various network structures, assume that we have the following definition of an L-system for modular neural networks.

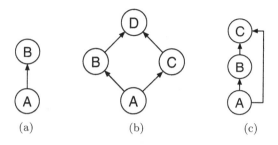

Fig. 2. Some of the typical examples of the network structure generated by the grammar. (a) AB, (b) $A[B,C]D$, (c) $A(x,1)BC$.

- Alphabet $V = \{A, B, C, D, ',' \}$,
- Axiom $= A(100, 0)$,
- Productions:

$$A(x, y) \rightarrow A(x, 1)[B(x/10 - 2, y)B(x/10 + 2, -1)]C(x/10, -1) \quad (5)$$

$$B(x_1, y_1) < B(x, y) > C(x_2, y_2) : x > 10 \rightarrow C(x/2, y)C(x/2, y - 1) \quad (6)$$

$$B(x_1, y_1) < C(x, y) > C(x_2, y_2) : x > 5 \rightarrow [D(x, y), D(x, 0)] \quad (7)$$

The sequence of strings generated by the parametric L-system specified as above is like this:

$$A(100, 0) \rightarrow A(100, 1)[B(8, 0)\mathbf{B(12, -1)}]C(10, -1) \quad (8)$$

$$\rightarrow A(100, 1)[B(8, 0)\mathbf{C(6, -1)}C(6, -2)]C(10, -1) \quad (9)$$

$$\rightarrow A(100, 1)[B(8, 0)[D(6, -1), D(6, 0)]C(6, -2)]C(10, -1) \quad (10)$$

Fig. 3 shows the modular neural networks corresponding to each string generated by the parametric L-system.

4   Simulation Results

In order to confirm the potential of the proposed model, we have used the handwritten digit database of Concordia University of Canada, which consists of 6000 unconstrained digits originally collected from dead letter envelopes by the U.S. Postal Services at different locations in the U.S. The size of a pattern was normalized by fitting to coarse 10×10 grids over each digit. The proportion of blackness in each square of the grid provided 100 continuous activation values for each pattern. Network architectures generated by the evolutionary mechanism were trained with 300 patterns. A fitness value was assigned to a solution by testing the performance of a trained network with the 300 training digits, and the recognition performance was tested on the other 300 digits. Initial population consisted of 50 neural networks of having random connections. Each network

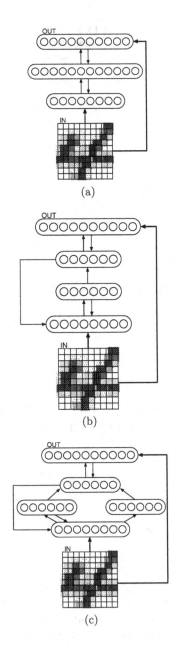

(a)

(b)

(c)

Fig. 3. The sequence of modular neural networks generated by the parametric L-system speci"ed in the text. (a) $A(100,1)$ $[B(8,0)B(12,-1)]$ $C(10,-1)$, (b) $A(100,1)$ $[B(8,0)$ $C(6,-1)C(6,-2)]$ $C(10,-1)$, (c) $A(100,1)$ $[B(8,0)$ $[D(6,-1),D(6,0)]$ $C(6,-2)]$ $C(10,-1)$.

contains one input module of size 100, one output module of size 10, and different number of hidden modules. Every module can be connected to every other module.

From the simulation, we can see that the evolution led to the increase of complexity, and new structures as well as new functionality emerged in the course of evolution: In general, the early networks have simple structures. In the early stages of the evolution some complicated architectures also emerged, but they were disappeared as the search of the optimal solution matured. The earlier good specific solutions probably overfitted some of the peculiar training set with lack of generality.

In the test of generalization capability, for the patterns that are similar to the trained, the network produced the direct activation through a specific pathway. On the contrary, the network oscillated among several pathways to make a consensus for the strange patterns. The basic processing pathways in this case complemented each other to result in an improved overall categorization. Furthermore, the recurrent connections utilized bottom-up and top-down information that interactively in"uenced categorization at both directions.

In order to illustrate the effectiveness of the model proposed, a comparison with traditional neural network has been conducted. Multilayer perceptron has been selected as a traditional neural network, because it is well known as a powerful pattern recognizer. The network is constructed as $100 \times 20 \times 10$, where the number of hidden nodes, 20, has been determined after several trial-and-errors. Table 1 reports the recognition rates of the two methods over ten different sets of the data. As can be seen, the average recognition rate for the proposed method is higher than that for the multilayer perceptron. Furthermore, with the paired t-test, for all the cases no-improvement hypothesis is rejected at a 0.5% level of significance. This is a strong evidence that the proposed method is superior to the alternative method.

Table 1. Comparison of the proposed method with a traditional neural network, multilayer perceptron (MLP), for ten di˘erent data sets.

	Proposed Method	Multilayer Perceptron
1	97.67	95.67
2	97.67	96.33
3	97.33	94.67
4	98.00	96.67
5	96.33	93.67
6	97.00	94.67
7	98.00	96.00
8	97.00	95.67
9	96.67	94.67
10	97.67	95.33
Mean	97.33	95.33
S.D.	0.57	0.92

5   Concluding Remarks

We have described a preliminary design of the modular neural networks developed by evolutionary algorithm and a parametric L-system. It has a modular structure with intramodular competition, and intermodular excitatory connections. We hope that this method can give the modular neural network the scalability in complex problems, similarly to the result of [3]. This sort of network will also take an important part in several engineering tasks exhibiting adaptive behaviors. We are attempting to make the evolutionary mechanism sophisticated by incorporating the concept of co-evolution.

Acknowledgements

The authors would like to thank Dr. Y. Tohkura at NTT Communication Science Laboratories for continuous encouragement, and Mr. S.-I. Lee at Yonsei University for supporting the implementation of the simulation program.

References

1. Harp, S.A.: Towards the genetic synthesis of neural networks. Proc. Int. Conf. Genetic Algorithms. (1989) 360 369
2. Whitley, D., Hanson, T.: Optimizing neural networks using faster, more accurate genetic search. Proc. Int. Conf. Genetic Algorithms. (1989) 391 396
3. Kitano, H.: Designing neural networks using genetic algorithms with graph generation system. Complex Systems. 4 (1990) 461 476
4. Yao, X.: Evolutionary arti"cial neural networks. Int. Journal Neural Systems. 4 (1993) 203 222
5. Cho, S.-B., Shimohara, K.: Evolutionary learning of modular neural networks with genetic programming. Int. Journal Applied Intelligence. 9 (1998) 191 200
6. Whitley, D.: The GENITOR algorithm and selective pressure: why rank-based allocation of reproductive trials is best. Proc. Third Int. Conf. Genetic Algorithms and Their Applications. Morgan Kaufmann. San Mateo, CA. (1989) 116 121
7. Lindenmayer, A.: Mathematical models for cellular interaction in development. Int. Journal Theoretical Biology. 18 (1968) 280 315
8. Prusinkiewicz, P., Hammel, M., Hanan, J., Mech, R.: Visual models of plant development. Handbook of Formal Languages. Springer-Verlag. (1996)

Hybridized Neural Network and Genetic Algorithms for Solving Nonlinear Integer Programming Problem

Mitsuo Gen, Kenichi Ida, and Chang-Yun Lee

Ashikaga Institute of Technology, Ashikaga 326-8558, Japan
{gen ida cylee}@genlab.ashitech.ac.jp

Abstract. Optimization problems such as system reliability design and general assignment problem are generally formulated as a nonlinear integer programming (NIP) problem. Generally, we transform the nonlinear integer programming problem into a linear programming one in order to solve NIP problems. However linear programming problems transformed from NIP problems become a large-scale problem. In principal, it is desired that we deal with the NIP problems without any transformation. In this paper, we propose a new method in which a neural network technique is hybridized with genetic algorithms for solving nonlinear integer programming problems. The hybrid GA is employed the simpelx search method, and the chromosomes are improved to good points by using the simplex search method. The eˇectiveness and e ciency of this approach are shown with numerical simulations from the reliability optimal design problem.

1 Introduction

Neural network (NN) technique is receiving much attention and applied for a variety of optimization problems [3]-[2]. The advantages of neural network technique lie mainly in that the computation is completed in massively parallel architectures and that optimal solutions renewed parameters are adaptively obtained as new equilibrium points under the new environment. However, when we apply neural network techniques for a solving nonlinear integer programming problem, it is di cult to obtain integer solutions.

To solve this problem effectively, we introduced genetic algorithms (GAs) which are very powerful tools for solving such the nonlinear optimization problems and can handle any kind of nonlinear objective function and constraints [8][9]. The method for solving a nonlinear integer programming problem using the neural network technique and the genetic algorithm (NIP/NN-GA) was recently proposed by Gen *et al.* [9]. The NIP/NN-GA method is used Neural Network and GA method to obtain the best solution. In this method, Neural Network is used for finding initial soulutions of the GA. However, if we deal with the large-scale problems, the NIP/NN-GA method has many combination for the solution. In this paper, we propose the new method in which the neural network technique is hybridized with the genetic algorithm combined with the simplex search method for solving NIP problems. Simplex search method is one of the direct search methods, and makes calculations very time-consuming and great accuracy in the final solution is desired. And the effectiveness and e ciency of this approach is shown with numerical simulations from the large-scale problem in which the proposed method is obtained the best solutions faster than the NIP/NN-GA method.

2 Nonlinear Integer Programming Model

The NIP problem which maximizes a nonlinear objective function $f(x)$ subject to m constraints and n decision variables, is formulated as follows:

NIP :

$$\text{max} \quad f(x) \tag{1}$$

$$\text{s. t.} \quad g_i(x) \leq b_i, \quad i = 1, 2, \cdots, m \tag{2}$$

$$x = [x_1 x_2 \cdots x_n], \quad x_j \geq 0, \quad j = 1, 2, \cdots, n : \text{integer}$$

where $g_i(x)$ is the ith inequality constraint, b_i is right-hand side constant of the ith constraint and x_j is the jth decision variable which takes integer value.

3 Methods for solving NIP problem

3.1 NP/NN method

We consider that the NIP problem has no integer restrictions, because the neural network technique is an approximate method suitable for a continuous values, *i.e.*, we solve the NP problem [5]. We can easily transform the above to the minimization prolbem by multiplying objective function by -1.

We can construct the energy function based on the penalty function method for solving the NP problem. The penalty function method transforms the constrained optimization problem into the unconstrained optimization one. In order to solve the NP problem, we construct the following energy function [2]:

$$E(x, \ ) = -f(x) + \frac{}{2} \left[\sum_{i=1}^{m} ([b_i - g_i(x)]_-)^2 + \sum_{j=1}^{n} ([x_j]_-)^2 \right] \tag{3}$$

where > 0 is penalty parameter, $[b_i - g_i(x)]_- = \min\{0, b_i - g_i(x)\}$ and $[x_j]_- = \min\{0, x_j\}$. Minimizing the energy function (3) leads to the system of ordinary differential equations as follows:

$$\frac{dx}{dt} = -\mu \nabla_x E(x, \ ) \tag{4}$$

where $\mu > 0$ is called learning parameter.

3.2   Genetic Algorithms

Representation and Initialization Let x_k denote the kth chromosome in a population as follows:

$$x_k = [x_{k1} \cdots x_{kj} \cdots x_{kn}], \qquad k = 1, 2, \cdots, pop\_size$$

where pop_size means population size. The initial integer solution vectors are randomly created within the region of the real-valued solutions obtained by the neural network technique. The revised width is a parameter to limit the range for creating the initial solution vectors.

Evaluation We evaluate the original objective function of the NIP problem as follows:

$$\text{eval}(x_k) = \begin{cases} f(x_k); & g_i(x_k) \leq b_i \quad (i = 1, 2, \cdots, m) \\ -M; & \text{otherwise} \end{cases}$$

where M is a positive large integer as a penalty in the case of violating the constraints.

Genetic Operators

(1)**Crossover:** For each pair of parents x_1 and x_2, the crossover operator will produce two children x' and x'' as follows:

$$x' = \lfloor c_1 x_1 + c_2 x_2 + 0.5 \rfloor, \qquad x'' = \lfloor c_2 x_1 + c_1 x_2 + 0.5 \rfloor$$

where, $x_1, x_2 \geq 0$ and $c_1 + c_2 = 1$.

(2)**Mutation:** We set the revised width, and then select a mutating position at random. Finally, we exchange the selected value for the revised value.

(3)**Selection:** We select the better chromosomes among parent and offspring by evaluation value. The number to be selected is pop_size and let these chromosomes enter the next generation. Duplicate selection is prohibited.

3.3   Simplex Search Method

The implementation of simplex search algorithm requires only two types of calculations: (1)generation of a regular simplex given a base point and appropriate scale factor, and (2) calculation of the re"ected point. The first of these calculations is readily carried out, since it can be shown from elementary geometry that given an n-dimensional starting or base points $x^{(0)}$ and a scale factor , the other n vertices of the simplex in n dimensions are given by

$$x_j^{(i)} = x_j^{(0)} + _1 \quad \text{if } i = j \tag{5}$$

$$= x_j^{(0)} + _2 \quad \text{if } i \neq j, \quad \text{for } i, j = 1, 2, ..., n \tag{6}$$

where,

$$\alpha_1 = \left[\frac{(n+1)^{1/2} + n - 1}{n\sqrt{2}}\right], \qquad \alpha_2 = \left[\frac{(n+1)^{1/2} - 1}{n\sqrt{2}}\right]$$

The choice $\alpha = 1$ leads to a regular simplex with sides of unit length. The second calculation, re"ection through the centroid, is equally straightforward. Suppose $\boldsymbol{x}^{(p)}$ is the point to be re"ected. Then the centroid of the remaining n points is

$$x_j^{(c)} = \frac{\sum_{i=0, j \neq i}^n x_j^{(i)}}{n}, \quad j = 1, 2, ..., n \tag{7}$$

All points on the line from $\boldsymbol{x}^{(p)}$ through $\boldsymbol{x}^{(c)}$ are given by

$$\boldsymbol{x}^* = \boldsymbol{x}^{(p)} + \gamma (\boldsymbol{x}^{(c)} - \boldsymbol{x}^{(p)}) \tag{8}$$

Here, $\gamma = 2$ will yield the desired new vertex point. Thus,

$$\boldsymbol{x}^* = \lfloor 2\boldsymbol{x}^{(c)} - \boldsymbol{x}^{(p)} + 0.5 \rfloor \tag{9}$$

4   Proposed Algorithms for solving NIP problem

Now, we show the overall procedure for solving the NIP problem as follows:

Step 1: Set learning parameter μ, penalty parameter λ, the initial solutions $x_j(0)$, the step size δ and permissive error ε.

Step 2: Initial search by the neural network technique:

    2-1:   Construct the energy function $E(\boldsymbol{x}, \lambda)$ for solving the NP problem.

    2-2:   Construct the system of ordinary differential equations from $E(\boldsymbol{x}, \lambda)$ and then solve it by using Runge-Kutta method.

    2-3:   If $|x_j(t + \delta) - x_j(t)| < \varepsilon$, round off to initial solutions and go to Step 3.

Step 3: Set population size pop_size, crossover rate p_c, mutation rate p_m, maximum generation $maxgen$ and the revised width rev.

Step 4: Optimal search by the genetic algorithm:

    4-1: Generate the initial population

    Decide the range of the decision variables which we round to a decimal point and the revised width, and then, generate the initial populations.

    4-2: Evaluation

    Calculate the evaluation function.

    4-3: Genetic Operations

        4-3-1:   Crossover (arithmetical crossover)

        4-3-2:   Mutation (one-point mutation)

        4-3-3:   Selection (elitist selection)

    4-4: Reorganization of population

        4-4-1: Generate a regular simplex for each selected chromosome by

$$\text{if } i = j \text{ then } x_j^{(i)} = x_j^{(0)} + \alpha_1, \text{ else } x_j^{(i)} = x_j^{(0)} + \alpha_2 \text{ for } i, j = 1, 2, ..., n.$$

4-4-2: Calculate the centroid vector by which each chromosome is re-"ected. Centroid of the remaining n points is

$$x_j^{(c)} = \frac{\sum_{i=0, i \neq j}^{n} x_j^{(i)}}{n}, \quad j = 1, 2, ..., n.$$

4-4-3: Re"ect all genes through centorid $x^{(c)}$.

$$x^* = \lfloor 2x^{(c)} - x^{(p)} + 0.5 \rfloor$$

where, $\quad x^{(p)} = \mathrm{argmax}\{\mathrm{eval} f(x^{(i)}) \mid i = 0, 1, ..., n\}$

4-4-4: If the evaluation value of the re"ected chromosome get better than those of the selected chromosomes from Step 4-3-3, put it into the population of the next generation.

4-5: Termination condition

If the generation is equal to number of maximum generation, then go to Step 5. Otherwise, go to Step 4-2.

Step 5: Output the solution.

5   Numerical Examples

In this section, numerical examples as a NIP problem are solved by the proposed method and we make comparative study for the simple GA, NIP/NN-GA method and proposed method.

5.1   Example 1:

We consider the following NIP problem with 5 decision variables and 3 constraints [11]:

$$\max f(x) = \prod_{j=1}^{5} \{1 - (1 - R_j)^{x_j}\}$$

$$\text{s. t.} \sum_{j=1}^{5} p_j x_j^2 \leq 100$$

$$\sum_{j=1}^{5} c_j \{x_j + \exp(x_j/4)\} \leq 175$$

$$\sum_{j=1}^{5} w_j x_j \exp(x_j/4) \leq 200, \qquad x_j \geq 1, \quad j = 1, \cdots, 5 : \text{integer}$$

where the coe cients for this problem is shown in Table 1.

Table 1. Coe cients for Example 1

j	1	2	3	4	5
R_j	0.80	0.85	0.90	0.65	0.75
p_j	1	2	3	4	2
c_j	7	7	5	9	4
w_j	7	8	8	6	9

We relax the NIP problem into the NP problem to apply neural network technique and construct the energy function from it. According to the gradient method for the energy function $E(x, \ )$, we can transform the system of ordinary differential equations. When the initial values and the parameters for the initial search are $\mu = 1000$, $= 5000$, $x_1^{(0)} = \cdots = x_5^{(0)} = 1$, $= 0.01$, $= 0.001$, the search result in $x_1 = 2.5641$, $x_2 = 2.3410$, $x_3 = 2.19344$, $x_4 = 3.1850$, $x_5 = 2.77524$. Next, we create the initial population based on the obtained solutions and set revised width for GA. We set the parameters of the genetic algorithm as

Table 2. Simulation Results for Example 1 with 20 times performance

	Simple GA	NIP/NN-GA	Proposed method
best	0.874107	0.904489	0.904514
worst	0.704481	0.890721	0.894232
average	0.783321	0.900031	0.901274

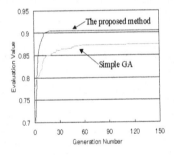

Fig. 1. Convergence of the proposed method and the Simple GA mehtod for Example 1

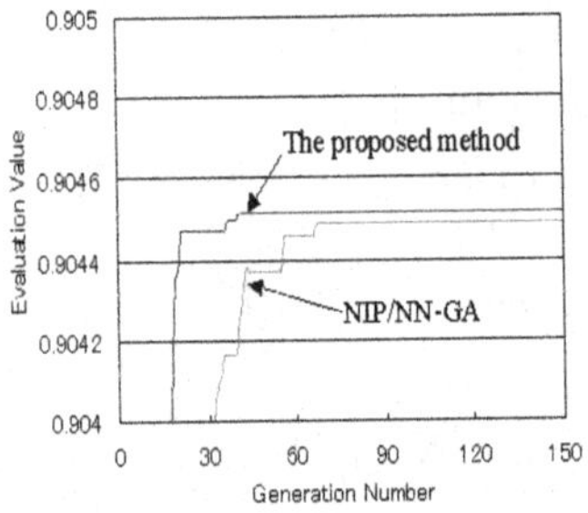

Fig. 2. Convergence of the proposed method and the NIP/NN-GA method for Example 1

follows: the population size is 20, crossover rate is 0.5, mutation rate is 0.2, the maximum generation is 150 and revised width is 3. The optimal solution for this problem is $[x_1 \ x_2 \ \cdots \ x_5] = [3 \ 2 \ 2 \ 3 \ 3]$ and the objective function is 0.904514.

Figure 1 and 2 show the convergence process of the proposed method, NIP/NN-GA method and the simple GA run by 20 times. In Fig. 1 and Fig. 2, the proposed method and the NIP/NN-GA method are obtained the solutions better than the simple GA. And then, the proposed method(NIP/NN-hGA) is obtained the best solutions faster than the NIP/NN-GA method shown in Fig. 2.

5.2   Example 2:

Now, we have another NIP problem with 15 decision variables and 2 constraints:

$$\max \quad f(\boldsymbol{x}) = \prod_{j=1}^{15}\{1 - (1 - R_j)^{x_j}\}$$

$$\text{s. t.} \quad \sum_{j=1}^{15} c_j x_j \le 400$$

$$\sum_{j=1}^{15} w_j x_j \le 414, \qquad x_j \ge 1, \quad j = 1, 2, \cdots, 15 \ : \ \text{integer}$$

Table 3. Coefficients for Example 2

j	1	2	3	4	5	6	7	8	9	10	11	12	13	14	15
R_j	0.90	0.75	0.65	0.80	0.85	0.93	0.78	0.66	0.78	0.91	0.79	0.77	0.67	0.79	0.67
c_j	5	4	9	7	7	5	6	9	4	5	6	7	9	8	6
w_j	8	9	6	7	8	8	9	6	7	8	9	7	6	5	7

Table 4. Simulation Results for Example 2 with 20 times performance

	Simple GA	NIP/NN-GA	Proposed method
best	0.92023	0.94471	0.944819
worst	0.84744	0.93296	0.94383
average	0.89305	0.94432	0.94450

where the coefficients for this problem is shown in Table 3. By the same way, we relax the NIP problem into the NP problem to apply neural network technique. After constructing the energy function and its ordinary differential equations, we can obtain the following solutions to use initial values of the hybridized GA with the neural network technique:

$$x_1 = 2.717, \quad x_2 = 3.707, \quad x_3 = 4.367, \quad x_4 = 3.385, \quad x_5 = 3.059$$
$$x_6 = 2.497, \quad x_7 = 3.514, \quad x_8 = 4.299, \quad x_9 = 3.514, \quad x_{10} = 2.645$$
$$x_{11} = 3.450, \quad x_{12} = 3.578, \quad x_{13} = 4.232, \quad x_{14} = 3.450, \quad x_{15} = 4.232$$

We set the parameters of the genetic algorithm as follows: the population size is 20, crossover rate is 0.4, mutation rate is 0.3, the maximum generation is 2000 and revised width is 2. The optimal solution for this problem is $[x_1 \ x_2 \cdots x_{15}] = [3\ 4\ 5\ 3\ 3\ 2\ 4\ 5\ 4\ 3\ 3\ 4\ 5\ 5\ 5]$ and the objective function is 0.944819 while

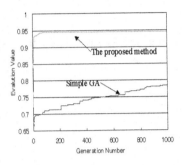

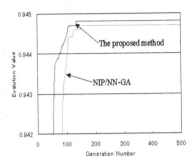

Fig. 3. Convergence of the proposed method and the Simple GA mehtod for Example 2

Fig. 4. Convergence of the proposed method and the NIP/NN-GA method for Example 2

6 Conclusion

In this paper, we proposed the new method in which neural network technique was hybridized with the genetic algorithm for a solving nonlinear integer programming problem. The hybrid GA employs the simplex search method thereby incorporating a local search mechanism to complement the global search capabilities of traditional GAs. In the results of the simulation, the proposed method is obvious that the chromosome is improved as every generation. And then, the NIP/NN-hGA method proposed results in one of practical tools to solve the nonlinear integer programming problems.

Acknowledgment: This research work was partially supported by the International Scientific Research Program (No. 10044173: 1998.4-2001.3), Grant-in-Aid for Scientific Research by the Ministry of Education, Science and Culture of the Japanese Government.

References

1. Gen, M.: Reliability Optimization by 0-1 Programming for a System with Several Failure Modes , pp.252-256 in Rai, S. & D. P. Agrawal eds: *Distributed Computing Network Reliability*, IEEE Comp. Soc. Press, 1990.
2. Cichocki, A. & R. Unbehauen: *Neural Networks for Optimization & Signal Processing*, John Wiley & Sons, New York, 1994.
3. Gong, D., M. Gen, G. Yamazaki & W. Xu: Neural Network Approach for General Assignment Problem , *Proc. of IEEE International Conference on Neural Networks*, pp.1861-1866, 1995.
4. Gong, D., M. Gen, G. Yamazaki & W. Xu: Lagrangian ANN for Convex Programming with Linear Constraints , *Computers & Ind. Engg.*, Vol.32, No. 2, pp.429-443, 1997.

5. Gen, M., K. Ida, & H. Omori: Method for Solving System Reliability Optimization Problem Using Neural Network   , *Journal of Japan Industrial Management
   Association*, Vol. 48, No.5, pp.271-276, 1997 (in Japaneses).
6. Ida, K., M. Gen, Y. Ota, & H. Omori: Method for Solving Linear Programming
   Problem Using Neural Networks   , *The Transactions of the Inst. of Elect., Inform.
   & Communication Engienrs A*, Vol. J80-A, No.1, pp.298-301, 1997 (in Japaneses).
7. Gen, M. & R. Cheng:*Genetic Algorithms & Engineering Design*, John Wiley &
   Sons, New York, 1997.
8. Yokota, T. , M. Gen & Y. Li: Genetic Algorithm for Non-linear Mixed Integer
   Programming Problems & Its Applications , *Computers & Ind. Engg.*, Vol. 30, No.
   4, pp.905-917, 1996.
9. Gen, M., K. Ida & R. Kobuchi: Neural Network Technique and Genetic Algorithm for Solving Nonlinear Interger Programming Problem , *Proceedings of the
   Australia-Japan Joint Workshop on Intelligent & Evolutionary Systems*, pp.95-105,
   1997.
10. Skeel, R. D. & J. B. Keiper: *Elementary Numerical Computing with MATHEMAT-
    ICA*, McGraw-Hill, New York, 1993.
11. Ravi,V., B. S. N. Murty & P. J. Reddy: Nonequilibrium Simulated Annealing-
    Algorithm Applied to Reliability Optimization of Complex Systems , *IEEE Trans-
    actions on Reliability*, Vol. 46, No. 2, 1997.

Evolution of Gene Coordination Networks

Thomas Philip Runarsson and Magnus Thor Jonsson

Department of Mechanical Engineering, University of Iceland
Hjardarhagi 2-6, 107 Reykjavik, Iceland.
Internet: tpr@verk.hi.is, magnusj@verk.hi.is

Abstract. A new model for the incorporation of learning with simulated evolution is presented. The model uses gene coordination networks to control gene expression. Alleles at a locus compete for expression by matching up to the network. Reinforcement is achieved through choice dynamics where gene expression will be decided by competing environmental states. The result is a epistasis model containing both plasticity and mean loci. Solutions obtained are adaptive in the sense that any changes in the environment will bring about a spontaneous self-organization in the pattern of gene expression resulting in a solution with (near) equivalent "tness. Additionally the model makes the search for structures through neutral or near neutral mutation possible. The model is tested on two standard job-shop scheduling problems which demonstrate the novelty of the approach.

1 Introduction

The paper discusses an evolutionary algorithm for adaptive search and optimization. The algorithm evolves plastic solutions capable of immediate self-organization in the event of an environmental change. If a gene is deleted other genes will alter their expression so that a solution with (near) equivalent fitness is obtained. This is accomplished through local gene interaction networks that coordinate gene expression. Genes regulate each other's activity directly or through their products via these networks. Here the gene coordination networks are modelled by simple feed-forward neural networks. An analogy is drawn between the neural network and a network of interactions among information macromolecules responsible for gene coordination (Zuckerkandl, [1997]).

There are two reasons why we should be interested in a system of this type. The first is its role in the search for structures. Due to the plastic nature of individuals, mutations may have little or no in"uence on their fitness. Neutral mutations like these could play an important role in search through random drift due to finite population numbers (Kimura, [1968]). Secondly adaptive solutions may be desirable for critical applications where sudden changes in the environment must be met with a compromise solution immediately.

The next section describes in detail the gene coordination network and how it regulates gene expression. Section 3 discusses how this network may be incorporated in an evolutionary algorithm which then is used in the simulation examples in section 4 on two standard job-shop scheduling benchmarks. The paper concludes with a discussion.

2   Gene Coordination

The gene coordination network's task is to determine which gene is to be expressed as a function of the environmental state of the genome. As genes are expressed their products change the environment. Through the environment or directly genes are capable of regulating the activity of other genes. There is no predetermined environmental problem for which there is a solution, the genome *constructs* the environment and hence determines both the solution and problem simultaneously (Lewontin, [1982]). The construction and reconstruction of their environments is, however, constrained by what they already are. The genome alters its environment based on patterns of the world which are presented to the gene coordination network. The network consists of nodes and connections. The nodes are simple processing units whose activation is the weighted sum of their input from the environment and from other nodes. Knowledge is stored in the connections among the processing units and learning takes place through the adjustment of their connection strengths.

Each environmental state and corresponding response could be considered in isolation by the network if an absolute value judgement were given. The response strength, gene activity, would then be an intervening variable reinforced by some function of the individuals fitness. In essence the network would be attempting to predict the resulting individual's fitness based on the current environmental state and actions taken. Formulating reinforcement in isolation is, however, not a simple procedure. It is believed that choice procedures may provide a better measure of the effects of reinforcement. The measures of 'absolute values' are just a result of choice dynamics (Williams, [1994]). This is the approach taken here, where gene expression is the result of choices made from a set of competing environmental states.

In fig. 1 a section of the genome model, depicted as a genetic string, is illustrated. Two different loci (l and m) are shown. Each locus is occupied by alternative forms of a gene which are known as alleles of one another. An individual is imagined to contain multiple alleles. In general, however, living organisms have only two alleles although a greater variety exists within the population. In our

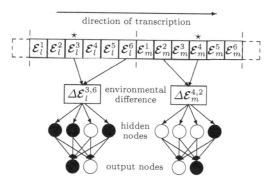

Fig. 1. Genome model. Competing alleles at loci l and m where ($\star$) marks the currently successful allele.

model multiple alleles will compete for the right to be expressed but only two of them at a time. The competition is resolved by the gene coordination network which is modelled by a feed-forward neural network. As for any connectionist model we must make assumptions about the number of nodes, arrangement of connectivity and their interaction with the environment. Since the network is a competitive or choice network the input will be the difference between two competing environmental states associated with the alleles. An array of environment state differences at locus l is denoted by $\mathcal{E}_l^{i,j} = \mathcal{E}_l^i - \mathcal{E}_l^j$, where allele i is competing with allele j. The environmental differences are connected to a hidden layer of nodes which are connected to two output nodes as shown in the figure. The activations of the two output nodes $\mathcal{O}_{\text{lhs}}$ and $\mathcal{O}_{\text{rhs}}$ are real numbers between 0 and 1. The node with the higher activity wins. Having two output nodes allows us to instruct the network when the two choices are equivalent. For each competition performed two separate inquiries are made as to whether an allele should be chosen over the currently successful one. The results must be consistent and if the challenge of allele j is to be successful over allele i then: $\mathcal{O}_{\text{lhs}}^{i,j} < \mathcal{O}_{\text{rhs}}^{i,j}$ and $\mathcal{O}_{\text{lhs}}^{j,i} \geq \mathcal{O}_{\text{rhs}}^{j,i}$ must be satisfied where $\mathcal{E}^{i,j} = - \mathcal{E}^{j,i}$. If the above inequality does not hold then allele i remains successful. With no useful information available from the environment the network may respond in a contradictory manner and the successful gene will hold its position independently of changes in the environment. To achieve this the model must remember which allele was expressed previously at that locus. Loci which are sensitive to the environment are known as *plasticity loci* and those insensitive to the environment *mean loci*. A genome containing only plasticity loci has been labelled the *pleiotropy* model by Scheiner ([1998]). The pleiotropy model is a special case of the *epistasis* model which contains also mean loci.

Two types of perturbations are possible at a given locus. The first is a *minimal perturbation* where a previously expressed allele is forgotten and therefore will not hold through to the next generation. If the locus is a plasticity locus then it is likely that the allele will regain its position. If, however, the locus is a mean locus the allele will loose its position. The second is a *structural perturbation* where the gene coordination network itself is modified. This may be a modification of the network architecture or the connection strengths. Viewed in this manner a structural perturbation may constitute learning. The names for these perturbations are taken from Kauffman ([1991]). Additionally, a previously expressed allele and/or other alleles may be deleted (removed from a locus) and others added.

3   Evolving Gene Coordination

The genome is represented by a string containing M loci as shown in fig. 1. The string is transcribed systematically from left to right processing one locus at a time. Within each locus there exist m alleles. Random competitions are held where alleles compete with the currently successful one for its right to be expressed. The competitions continue until a maximum number is reached or a time   has elapsed. The competitions are decided by the gene coordination network as discussed in the previous section. Each locus will be represented by a data structure containing a neural network for gene regulation and a list of competing alleles. The data structure may also hold information about which allele was previously expressed, training history for the network, etc. In the model presented here the previously expressed allele will be remembered and in the next generation be the default successful allele. If, however, this allele happens to be illegal in the following generation, a random legal allele is selected as the default which then other alleles must compete with.

There are a number of possible methods for evolving the connection strengths of the gene coordination networks. In this paper the networks will be trained using supervised learning with backpropagation. Training data for learning is sampled from the current population. During transcription the environmental states associated with the expressed alleles are recorded in the loci data structure. Once the genome has been expressed completely, its total fitness will be known. From a population of N unique individuals a training set of the size $N \times (N-1)$ can be sampled. Should there be any useful information in this data the network may learn it and hopefully generalize this knowledge.

New individuals may be formed using standard recombination operators. Loci may be exchanged between two or more individuals using one, two or multiple crossover sites. Mutation will play an important role in maintaining a diverse environment. Minimal perturbations will attempt to knock out successful alleles. It is expected that minimal perturbation will have less in"uence on plasticity loci. Structural perturbation will randomly reset the connection strengths for the gene coordination networks and will permanently damage loci. It is also possible to view the training of a network as a more complex structural perturbation. If the new networks perform well, regardless of whether the training data used was sensible, we expect it to be selected for. The evolutionary algorithm used in the following section for our simulations may be summarized as follows:

1. Initialize population and networks randomly.
2. Loop through the following steps until the termination criteria is met:
   (a) Transcribe loci by performing m random competitions at each locus with the successful allele. Record allele transcribed and corresponding environmental state. Compute individual s "tness and store elite individual.
   (b) Select individuals from the current population using tournament selection to form the new population for the next generation.
   (c) Train gene coordination networks in the new population at loci which have not been trained before with a probability P_l. The P_l parameter will essentially dictate the initial rate of learning. Training samples are taken from the old population. When a network has been trained a training "ag T for that locus is set to *false*.
   (d) If the elite has been lost inject a copy into the new population (elitist).
   (e) Shu e new population and perform a two point crossover in order to exchange loci between selected individuals. The probability of crossover is P_c.
   (f) Perform a minimal perturbation with probability P_m by exchanging the currently successful allele at a locus by another randomly chosen allele. Perform a structural perturbation with probability P_s by randomly resetting the connection strengths for a network at a random locus. In both cases set the training "ag T to *true*.

4   Computational Results

In this section the evolutionary algorithm described in the previous section will be tested on two well studied job-shop scheduling problems. The problem is an NP hard optimization problem and has been extensively studied. There exist over a hundred different rules for building job schedules and so it is interesting to observe what type of rules emerge in the networks. The redundant nature of the problem also makes it an interesting test case. The goal is to assign jobs on machines such that the overall production time, the makespan, is minimal. The order by which a job may be processed on the machines is predetermined. Schedules are formed by systematically assigning one job after the other at its earliest convenience. In our experiments each allele denotes a unique job. So for a problem with n_j jobs and n_m machines there will be n_j alleles competing at each locus in the string of length $n_j \times n_m$. Alleles corresponding to jobs that have been completed are illegal and will not compete for expression.

The test problems taken from Muth and Thompson ([1963]) are of sizes 6×6 and 10×10. The optimal makespans are known and are 55 and 930 respectively. As a schedule is being constructed a number of features of the solution become available. These are the environment states which may be associated with a job (allele). For the simulation performed three environment states are used: the time a job is available, the time it may be expected to finish and the total time still needed to complete the entire task (work remaining). These environment states are used as input data for the gene coordination network which has one hidden layer with 6 nodes. For the training of the network the output pattern used is $f_i \leq f_j$ for the left output node and $f_i \geq f_j$ for the right output node, where f is the global fitness value. Note that these are Boolean operators and that the problem is one of minimization. A sample size, twice the size of the

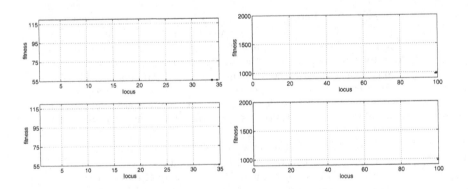

Fig. 2. Perturbation results for the 6×6 (left) and 10×10 (right) problems. The top "gure shows the "tness at a locus which has had its successful allele deleted and all loci to the right of it have been structurally perturbed. The bottom "gure shows the "tness at a locus which has only had its successful allele deleted at that point.

population, is extracted as discussed in the previous section. Samples for which $\mathcal{E} = 0$ are ignored.

The training algorithm used is the gradient decent backpropagation with momentum and adaptive learning rate (Demuth and Beale, [1997]). The log-sigmoid transfer function returns the activations of the nodes squashed between 0 and 1. A network is trained for 100 epochs and if it survives it may be trained further in some future generations. A population size of 30 is used for the 6×6 problem and 50 for the 10×10 problem. These are small population sizes, especially for the larger problem, but are su   cient for our purposes. The probability for crossover is $P_c = 1$, for learning $P_l = 0.2$ and for minimal perturbations $P_m = 1/(\text{string-length})$. The probability of structural perturbation for the smaller problem was none. For the larger problem it was found to be useful to add a very slight chance (0.01%) of a structural perturbation and an increase in minimal perturbations. Thirty independent runs were taken for each problem. For the 6×6 problem the optimal solution was found within 40 generations. The larger problem was stopped after 200 generations since the solutions have essentially converged. The results varied from a makespan of 960 to 990.

Results for a typical solution found for the two problems will be presented. To test the plasticity of the solutions found all loci are systematically perturbed by deleting the successful allele and putting another in its place. This can be done in $m - 1$ different ways at each locus. The result of this is that on average 50% of the loci are immune to the perturbation for the 6×6 problem. Either other loci performed its function or another phenotype was produced which gave the same global fitness value. Fig. 3 (left) shows six different solutions resulting from

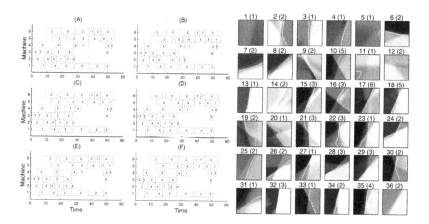

Fig. 3. Gantt charts (left) and network landscapes (right). The left shows six di˜erent solutions obtained due to perturbation by deletion for the 6×6 job-shop problem s elite solution. The right the choice landscapes for the gene coordination networks per locus. The locus number is given above each map with the number of time the network has been trained during its evolution over the generations in parenthesis.

these perturbations. The bottleneck remains on the same machine but some job orders have changed. The means by which a solution is constructed as well as the problem itself are redundant. The bottom plot in fig. 2 shows which loci are most immune to the perturbation by deletion. Regions that are in the start of the string are more susceptible to damage. This is reasonable since they must essentially predict much further into the future. To eliminate the possibility that this is a result of some other factors, such as the constraining of the solution space, all networks to the right of the damaged locus were structurally perturbed. The result of this is shown in the top plot in fig. 2 and illustrates how the fate of the last m loci is determined independent of the network when $M - m$ loci have been expressed.

Fig. 3 (right) shows the choice landscape for the 6×6 problem where the difference in the work remaining has been set to zero. The horizontal axis is the difference in time of completion and the vertical axis when a job is available. On both axis the scale is from -50 to 50. The landscape is the difference between the two output nodes, $\mathcal{O}_{\text{lhs}} - \mathcal{O}_{\text{rhs}}$. The darker regions are positive values whereas the lighter are negative. The network for example at locus 24 will prefer a job (allele) with a sooner completion time and later availability, but at locus 34 early completion time is preferred regardless of availability. In general scheduling jobs with earlier completion times are preferred. Some of the nets are contradictory which will make their corresponding loci a mean loci. Examples of these are the first and the last locus. It is understandable that the last locus could be a mean locus since its fate is always decided. The first loci has one environment state always equal to zero. When we examine the choice landscapes also with respect to the work remaining, we find that most loci are of the plasticity type.

The same perturbations by deletion were performed on a 10×10 solution. The result was that on average 60% of the loci were immune to deletion. The results are depicted in fig. 2 (right). When an arbitrary gene is deleted, how many genes alter their expression pattern? The single perturbation brings about a cascade of change in the patterns of gene activation. If the mutations are neutral the resulting solution   the phenotype   remains the same or the phenotype has changed but its fitness remains unchanged. In fig. 4 the number of genes which alter their expression is plotted against the locus where the deletion occurred. Only the cases where the equivalent elite fitness was obtained is shown. Commonly it su ces that just one additional gene changes its expression to compensate for the damage. Changes for up to 19% of the string are also observed.

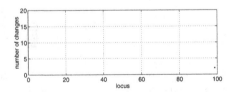

Fig. 4. Expression changes. The "gure shows how many genes have changes their expression as a function of locus where the successful allele was deleted.

5   Discussion

In this paper we have presented a general epistasis model for adaptive search and optimization. The development of the model is like creating a language whose rules have not been formalized and where there is no priori definition of 'purpose' or 'sense'. As the gene coordination networks evolve their meaning develops alongside or with it. Gene expression is controlled by these networks, where two alleles are matched up at a time. This is a contingent process.

It is commonly regarded that in genetic systems information storage lies in the gene frequency within the population. A more e cient means of storing knowledge can, however, be achieved through biological networks. Formulating gene expression as an 'intelligent' process introduces new possibilities for the role of learning in di cult search problems and introduces naturally problem domain knowledge to the evolutionary algorithm.

Further studies of the effects of different learning procedures and learning rate is currently being investigated. The importance of neutral and nearly neutral mutations as pathways toward new structures also needs further studies. Preliminary results suggest that an increase in the rate of minimal perturbation may be beneficial in this case. Additionally, the effect of adding perturbation by deletion during evolution (a removal of competing alleles), which will produce individuals with a varying number alleles, would be a natural extension of the evolutionary approach presented here.

Acknowledgement

The first author would like to thank professor Einar Arnason for helpful discussions and comments. This work has been supported by the Research Council of Iceland and the Research Fund of the University of Iceland, hereby gratefully acknowledged.

References

1997. Demuth, H. and Beale, M.: *Neural Network Toolbox – User's Guide Version 3.0.* The Mathworks Inc. MA (1997)

1986. Kau˘man, S.A.: Developmental logic and its evolution. *BioEssays* **6**:2 (1986) 82 87

1991. Kau˘man, S.A.: Antichaos and adaptation. *Scientific American* **265**:2 (1991) 64 70

1968. Kimura, M.: Evolutionary rate at the molecular level. *Nature* **217** (1968) 624 626

1982. Lewontin, R.C.: Organism and environment in *Learning, Development and Culture*, H.C. Plotkin (ed), John Wiley & Sons Ltd. New York (1982) 162

1963. Muth, J.F. and Thompson, G.L.: *Industrial Scheduling*, Prentice Hall, New Jersey (1963)

1998. Scheiner, S.M.: The genetics of phenotype plasticity. VII. Evolution in a spatially-structured environment. *Journal of Evolutionary Biology* **11**:3 (1998) 303 320

1994. Williams, B.A.: Reinforcement and choice in *Animal Learning and Cognition*, N.J. Mackintosh (ed), Academic Press Inc., London (1994) 81 108

1997. Zuckerkandl, E.: Neutral and nonneutral mutations: the creative mix-evolution of complexity in gene interaction systems. *Journal of Molecular Evolution* **44**:(Suppl 1) (1997) S2 S8

Adaptive Simulation: An Implementation Framework

Richard Hall, Binh Pham, and John Yearwood

Research Centre for Intelligent Tele-Imaging
School of Information Technology and Mathematical Sciences
University of Ballarat, P.O. Box 663, Ballarat, 3353
Facsimile: +61 (03) 53 279 289
Email:(r.hall,b.pham,j.yearwood)@.ballarat.edu.au

Abstract. We present an approach to adaptive simulation based upon a strati"ed representation of the behaviour of entities. In previous simulation models, the adaptation of an entity s behaviour is de"ned prior to runtime, as the conditions they might encounter are completely speci"ed. While entities are custom-made to function properly for particular situations, their behaviour could be inappropriate in other situations. We propose a behavioural model of adaptation which enables entities to modify their behaviour for a large variety of situations, and describe the implementation of the model for two simulations in a biological context. Application areas range from environmental simulation and ecological planning to psychological modelling and navigation simulation.

1 Introduction

Designers of computer simulations aim to accurately represent the entities from a specific domain within the real-world, and these simulated entities do not need to function in other domains. In contrast, our aim is to simulate the capacity of biological organisms to dynamically adapt their behaviour to different domains. Adaptation is defined as the process of becoming adjusted to new conditions [11], and is important to three areas within computer science: artificial life, case-based reasoning and intelligent agents. *Arti cial life* simulates the interactive behaviours of large populations of organisms, where each entity's behaviour is locally defined in their specification [7]. However, each entity's behaviour is usually derived from an original set of behaviours, and is thus constrained to operate in situations for which the original behaviours were designed.

Case-Based Reasoning (CBR) simulates adaptation within the memory of one individual over time, with the basic unit of memory called a 'case'. Three types of adaptation have been investigated: additive, indexing, and case. *Additive* adaptation simply refers to the addition of a new case into memory, and has been compared to experiential learning [14]. *Indexing* adaptation modifies the index structures of memory with the aim of optimising case retrieval e ciency [8]. *Case* adaptation occurs when cases in memory which are similar to an input case are modified to find a solution to an input case [13]. Current CBR research focuses on encapsulating large amounts of expert knowledge about a domain within cases for specialised domains such as cooking [4], and law [1]. CBR thus attempts to simulate the problem-solving reasoning process of an expert about a particular area of knowledge through the adaptation of information, and is not concerned with the adaptation of these individuals' behaviour in new situations.

Intelligent Agents researchers, while not in complete agreement about what constitutes the notion of agency [17], have proposed mentalistic characteristics for agents which are useful for considering adaptation with a biological metaphor. These mentalistic characteristics have been represented in the specification of entities in various explicit and implicit combinations. An *explicit mentalistic representation* (EMR) attempts to model psychological characteristics in the simulated organisms. We consider four characteristics only due to their obvious connection to adaptation: emotions, rationality, memory, and learning.

- *Emotional* states are represented as they can significantly in"uence the behaviour of individuals.
- *Rationality* defines an entity's behaviour as teleological (directed towards a goal). A hierarchy of goals such as Maslow's Model [10] might be included in a mental model.
- *Memory* is required for entities to record past situations. Without it, entities are unable to practically observe even a simple sequence of events. Perceptual aliasing occurs when an entity's behaviour depends upon something from the past as opposed to the present [9].
- *Learning* capability allows an entity to detect recurring sequences of events in their memory which relate to their goals, identify the key events, and act on their knowledge to their own advantage. Such learning has been classed as medium level [5].

An *implicit mentalistic representation* (IMR) relates an entity's perceived world state to an entity's action state, similar to machine learning, so psychological characteristics are not explicitly represented. It has been argued that it would be theoretically possible to create two entities, one with EMR and one with IMR adaptation, and be unable to tell the difference between the two by observing their behaviour [15]. However, it has been shown that it would be practically and computationally infeasible to represent the responses necessary for IMR for all the possible combinations of large numbers of conditions in situations [2]. Nonetheless it is useful for entities to have black box responses for two cases: conditions which are anticipated to occur across a broad range of situations; and for conditions which require adaptation so quickly that the time required for an EMR to process the input would be prohibitive.

In our domain we are investigating the simulation of intelligent interactions and require the behaviour of entities to be appropriate for any conceivable situation. In order to be computationally feasible, all possible situations are structured as much as possible into typical situations with changing parameters. Since Bakhtin [6] argued that the greatest degree of structure occurs when the world is *authored* within the structure of a story, a simulation can be placed conceptually within the context of a story and typical situations can be represented as abstract components of stories [3]. Our domain requires two modular components:

a module capable of authoring situations; and a module capable of representing the behaviour of entities with the capacity to adapt intelligently to any authored situation. The latter is the particular focus of this paper.

In Section 2, we discuss our stratified behavioural model of adaptation which locates the various research efforts in adaptation into a unified framework. Section 3 details the implementation of this model for two simulations of biology, while Section 4 concludes and proposes the future directions of our work.

2   Our Adaptation Model

We now describe our stratified representation of behaviour shown in Figure 1., and relate previous research on adaptation within our structure.

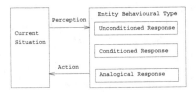

Fig. 1. Conceptual Model of Adaptation

The *Current Situation* describes all objects and events that can be observed by an entity through its perception. An entity is also aware of its own EMR, and other entities will not be aware of these internal states unless they are communicated in some manner. Consequently, each entity perceives a slightly different version of the same current situation. While an entity may not need to continually perceive the state of the world, all entities are in a constant state of action. As Bakhtin asserted, the act of doing nothing is the continous act of choosing not to do something else [6]. We define behaviour for entities by relating what they perceive P of a situation to an act A. The behaviour B of an entity over their lifetime is then a set of these tuples where $t = 0$ is the first moment an entity perceived their environment and acted, and $t = N$ is the current situation.

$$B = \{(P_{t=0}, A_{t=0}), (P_{t++}, A_{t++}), \cdots, (P_{t=--N}, A_{t=--N}), (P_{t=N}, A_{t=N})\}$$

The *Entity Behavioural Type* models the three different sources of behaviour in an entity. Each behavioural type is represented mathematically, and the relationship between these are described.

Traditional simulation creates entities with behaviour which is of the type called *Unconditioned Response* (UR). The behaviour is called unconditioned for two reasons: the rules controlling it are generated before $t = 0$ for an entity; and no modifications are made to the set of behaviours during runtime. Note that both EMR and IMR can produce unconditioned responses. UR can be described mathematically as a set of tuples relating perceived situations P to the actions

A which are optimal as they match some given criteria for situations 0 to N which are created before runtime.

$$UR = \{(P_0, A_0), (P_1, A_1), \cdots, (P_{N-1}, A_{N-1}), (P_N, A_N)\}$$

Note that if every tuple in B maps to a tuple in UR then the entity will behave appropriately for all situations during its lifetime. UR has two advantages for entities: they respond in a specified manner every time to a specific situation; and there is no computational expense associated with training on the "y. However, for an entity to always behave in a correct manner, the complete set of possible world states needs to be known before runtime. With the simulation of biological organisms, unconditioned responses are always appropriate for the situations considered and should have priority over the remaining two response types.

On the other hand *Conditioned Responses* (CR) describes behaviours learnt during runtime that also produce desirable situations for entities, so CR is expressed similarly to UR. Such learning can be likened to situation-based additive adaptation in case-based reasoning, since an entity must be able to recall and store separate cases within some form of memory structure. Since the memory of an entity is finite a maximum size is set for sliding memory window called short term memory M_{ST}. Consider an entity with the ability to remember a limited number J of situations P and correct responses A which they had perceived from $t = 0$ to the current situation $t = N$.

$$M_{ST} = \{(P_{t=J}, A_{t=J+1}), (P_{t=J+1}, A_{t=J+2}), \cdots,$$
$$(P_{t=N-2}, A_{t=N-1}), (P_{t=N-1}, A_{t=N})\}$$

However, storing all of these tuples for multiple entities is computationally expensive, so only the situations which satisfy particular criteria should be remembered. For our biological context, the criteria is the satisfaction of particular goals of entities. We call this filtered memory long term memory M_{LT}, where what has been learnt (CR) is related to the goal G that CR achieves. The long term memory could be indexed by the relative importance I of the goals in a goal hiearchy to facilitate retrieval.

$$M_{LT} = \{(G_0, CR_0), (G_1, CR_1), \cdots, (G_{N-1}, CR_{N-1}), (G_N, CR_N)\}$$
$$\text{where } I(G_0) > I(G_1) > ...I(G_{N-1}) > I(G_N)$$

During the update cycle, M_{ST} should be searched for patterns which an entity could take advantage of, and tuples new to M_{LT} should be added. The best time for elements of M_{ST} to be filtered for M_{LT} is when the process of filtering does not hinder the entity. Psychologists have suggested that this operation may occur in humans during sleep [16].

The disadvantage of CR is the computational expense associated with the creation and maintenance of the dynamic index structure. However, the advantage of CR is that it enables entities to adapt to new situations which do not need to be considered in their specifications, so complete domain knowledge does not need to be integrated into their design. The speed of behavioural response depends on how efficiently the memory is indexed so CR is given less priority than UR. In contrast with analogical response, a 1 to 1 mapping exists between what has been learnt and the current situation so CR is given greater priority.

The behavioural response of an entity can be called an *analogical response* (AR) where no UR or CR exists for the particular situation. Instead of searching for a behaviour which will produce an response which is based on matching an input case to a case in long term memory, a similarity metric is performed between the cases in memory and the input case in an attempt to decide the 'best' behaviour to perform in an intelligent manner. Consider a perceived situation P and correct behaviour A at time X and a long term memory with one goal G_0.

For a perceived situation and correct response $(P_{t=X}, A_{t=X+1})$
and $M_{LT} = \{(G_0, CR_0 = (P_0, A_0), (P_1, A_1), \cdots, (P_{N-1}, A_{N-1}), (P_N, A_N))\}$
then $A_{t=X+1} \equiv A_Q$ where $P_Q \equiv P_{t=X}, \quad (A_Q, P_Q) \in CR_0$

AR can be compared to case adaptation in case-based reasoning, which has been utilised in domains of complex design, and at present we are considering how AR might be useful for entities in the context of simulating a story.

3   Implementation of the Adaptation Model

To demonstrate that our stratified behavioural model was applicable in simulating adaptation in biological environments, we chose to implement two situations which required the behavioural adaptation of entities: the excitation behaviour of bees in the presence of an intruder; and the behaviour of a group of cats who learn that the sound of a tin signifies that they will be fed. These simulations, although simple, could provide the building blocks for more complex examples.

The bee simulation had an UR with both an IMR and EMR. Note that for UR, all of the states which the bees could perceive were specified before runtime. The mental states are not defined when relating perception to action,

$$UR = \{(P_0, A_0), (P_1, A_1), \cdots, (P_{N-1}, A_{N-1}), (P_N, A_N)\}$$

but were defined relating perception to the emotional mental state.

$$UR = \{(P_0, E_0), (P_1, E_1), \cdots, (P_{N-1}, E_{N-1}), (P_N, E_N)\}$$

The cat simulation had some UR and IMR. However the definition of the cat UR is identical to the definition for the bees, so only the method for generating CR through the use of EMR is described. All of the situations that the cats perceive and their responses are stored within their short term memory M_{ST}. When cats are not engaged in moving for a particular period of time, M_{ST} is filtered into long-term memory M_{LT} by considering the recurring sequence of events which precedes the satisfaction of the goal of eating food. A conditioned response is then created which allows the cats to satisfy their goal faster. Goals are only used in analysing the M_{ST} and are not explicitly represented in the CR:

$$CR = \{(P_0, A_0), (P_1, A_1), \cdots, (P_{N-1}, A_{N-1}), (P_N, A_N)\}$$

3.1 Simulation of Adaptation in Bees

Bees change their behaviour in the presence of an intruder, from a calm patrolling state to an angry attacking state [12]. In the simulation a bee detects an intruder at its bee hive and begins to get excited and simultaneously emit an alarm pheremone which increases the pheremone level in the situation. This emission of alarm pheremone then excites other bees who also emit the pheremone. Once the alarm pheremone level exceeds the alarm threshold of an individual bee they become fully excited and attack the intruder.

For our bee representation, each bee had three emotion (E) tuples relating a particular perceived situation in the world to a new situation where their emotions have changed.

P_0 = no intruder E_0 = emotion(calm)
P_1 = detect intruder and emotion(calm) E_1 = emotion(excited)
P_2 = detect intruder and emotion(excited) E_2 = emotion(aggressive)
    and pheremone level $\geq$ alarm

Bees also had four UR tuples. The goals of bees are implicitly represented because the actions of bees protect their hive.

P_0 = no intruder A_0 = patrolling
P_1 = detected intruder and emotion(calm) A_1 = threatening
P_2 = detected intruder and pheremone level $<$ alarm A_2 = release pheremone
    and emotion(calm) and A_1
P_3= detected intruder and pheremone level $\geq$ alarm A_3 = fighting and A_2
    and emotion(aggressive) and A_1

The class relationship diagram of the bee simulation is shown in Figure 2.

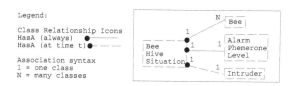

Fig. 2. Bee Simulation Class Diagram

3.2 Simulation of Adaptation in Cats

In the simulation of feeding cats the cats learn that the cats' owner S hitting a tin of cat food implies that S has put out food for them. The situation is divided into two partitions known as *Kitchen* and *Lounge Room* respectively. The cats prefer the room which is warmer so on the basis of warmth alone the cats will

spend the majority of their time in the Lounge Room. Each time S puts out
food they then hit the tin of cat food. If the cats do not come to the kitchen
S picks them up and carries them. After a few times of being carried the cats
learn that the sound of the tin implies that food is available in the kitchen. The
class relationship diagram of the cat simulation is shown in Figure 3.

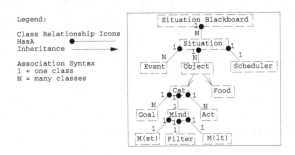

Fig. 3. Cat Simulation Class Diagram

The cats were given two UR type behaviours which enabled them to cope
with situations where conditions existed simultaneously by using an EMR with
goals. The goal importance I determined which tuple had priority.

$$UR_{cat} = \{(P_0, G_0, A_0), (P_1, G_1, A_1)\} \text{ where } I(G_0) > I(G_1)$$
$$P_0 = \text{detect food } G_0 = \text{satisfy hunger } A_0 = \text{eat food}$$
$$P_1 = \text{detect cold } G1 = \text{satisfy warmth } A_1 = \text{move to warmer place}$$

During the simulation, the cats updated their long term memory while all of
their goals were satisfied. By examining their short term memory of events the
cats realised that the best time to move to the kitchen for food was when the
sound of the tin was heard. Thus

$$M_{LT} = \{(G_0, CR_0 = (P_0, A_0))\} \text{ where}$$
$$P_0 = \text{detect tin sound } A_0 = \text{move to food place}$$

4   Conclusion

Previously, entities in simulations had all the important domain knowledge embedded into their specifications. However, these entities are unable to function
optimally in other situations, simply because they are not designed to do so.

We presented a theoretical adaptation model based upon a stratification of
behavioural responses which enabled entities to adapt to new situations. Our
model was implemented in two simulations which demonstrated different elements of implicit and explicit mentalistic representations. The work presented
is important to the development of our wider area of study- story authoring-
which is currently being implemented.

Computer simulations have been attempted for a long period of time, and entities within these simulations often embody large amounts of complex and specific domain knowledge. One can envisage the benefits of cross-domain interations which adaptation capabilities would make possible for entities.

References

1. Ashley K.: Distinguishing - a reasoner s wedge. In Proceedings of the Ninth Annual Conference of the Cognitive Science Society. Cognitive Science Society. L. Erlbaum. Hillsdale N.J. 1987 737-747
2. Ginsberg M.: Universal Planning: An (Almost) Universally Bad Idea. AI Magazine. Winter 1989 v10 n4. 40-44
3. Hall R., Pham B., Yearwood J.: Design Of An Arti"cial Life Simulation System Based On The Concept of MetaStories. University of Ballarat Research Report Series. 98/2
4. Hammond K.: Case-based planning using planning as a memory task. Perpsectives in Arti"cial Intelligence. Academic Press. Boston MA. 1989
5. Harrison N.: How to design e˜ective text-based open-learning: a modular course. New York. McGraw- Hill. 1991
6. Holquist M.: Dialogism: Bakhtin and His World. Routledge. London 1990
7. (ed) Langton, C.: Arti"cial Life. The Proceedings of an Interdisciplinary Workshop on the Synthesis and Simulation of Living Systems. Sept 1987. Los Alamos. New Mexico
8. Leake D., Plaza E.: Case-Based Reasoning Research and Development. Second International Conference on Case-Based Reasoning. ICCBR-7. Providence. RI. USA. July 1997
9. Lin L-J., Mitchell T.: Memory Approaches To Reinforcement Learning in Non-Markovian Domains. Technical Report CMU-CS-92-138. Carnegie Mellon University. Pittsburg. 1992
10. Maslow A.: Motivation and personality. New York. Harper s Psychological Series. 1954
11. The Concise Oxford Dictionary. Ninth Edition. Clarendon Press. Oxford. 1995
12. Staniford G., Paton R.: Simulating Animal Societies with Adaptive Communicating Agents. In Intelligent Agents : ECAI-94 Workshop on Agent Theories, Architectures, and Languages. Amsterdam, the Netherlands, August 8-9. 1994. 145-159
13. Riesbeck C., Schank R.: Inside Case-Based Reasoning. Hillsdale. N.J. L. Erlbaum. 1989
14. Schank R., Abelson R.: Scripts, Plans, Goals and Understanding. L. Erlbaum. Hillsdale. N.J.
15. Schoppers, M.: Universal Plans for Reactive Robots in Unpredictable Domains. In Proceedings of the Tenth International Joint Conference on Arti"cial Intelligence. Menlo Park. California. 1987. 1039-1046
16. Smith, C. Sleep States and Memory Processes. Journal of Behavioural Brain Research. 1995 Jul-Aug: Vol 69(1- 2) 37-145
17. (eds) Wooldridge M., Jennings, N.: Intelligent Agents : ECAI-94 Workshop on Agent Theories, Architectures, and Languages. Amsterrdam. the Netherlands. August 8-9. 1994

A Model of Mutual Associative Memory for Sim ulations of Evlution and Learning

Yoshida Akira(akira-yo@is.aist-nara.ac.jp)

Graduate School of Information Science, Nara Institute of Science and Technology
8916-5 Takayama, Ikoma, Nara, 630-0101 Japan

Abstract. Evolution could be assumed as a natural reinforced learning. We tried simulations of Mutual-association with varying population size to investigate evolution and learning. Mutual associative memory is our extension from hetero-association or temporal-association of the Associative Memory by J.J.Hopfield[1]. Mutual Associative Memory is used as memory of organism for the tool to investigate evolution and learning. Genetic Algorithms are used to evolve the weights of mutual associative memory. We got the result that evolution of learning can be observed when organisms change rule itself during their lifetime.

1 Introduction

Mutual associative model typically associate the pattern to be stored with different patterns. W e name the word "mutual associative memory" as an extended concept from so called hetero-association of simple perceptron. Our m utual associative memory uses fully connected neural net work instead of multi-layer networks with back-propagation and observe the evolution and the capacity of learning using genetic algorithms.

Mechanism of mutual associative memory is implemen ted by adjusting the weights, which means the degree of how much effect the synapses give to the neurons connected by the synapses to each other. This weight or the degree of effect is called "weights of connection" or "connection matrix" since it is usually represented with matrix. W e call the adjustment of weights of connection "learning" or "remem brance" of the neural network. And we call the learning(adjustment) of weights of connection during organism's lifespan "Mutual Association" of the neural network. Increment of the capacity of being able to mutually associate over many generations is called "Evolution of Learning".

We have proposed a toy model of m utual associative memory on a few papers[2][3]. Now the models became more natural and the sim ulation time became shorter since varying population size by death of organism was added to our Genetic Algorithms. W e call the mutual associative memory an organism or an individual after this since we assume the m utual associative memory as an organism which have the ability of learning in a virtual environment.

2 Mutual Associativ e Memory

The model of m utual associative memory use genetic algorithms to evolve the functions of recalling memories and m utually associating memories or experiences. We think that genetic algorithm could be a model of reinforcemen t learning nature have been executing for more than three billion y ears over. The selection of parents and the reproduction of offsprings in the genetic algorithm correspond to the single yes/no reinforcemen t signal in reinforcement learning.

Figure 1 shows our meaning and concepts of the words "Mutual Association". In auto-association the recalled pattern(output) is same as the input pattern, on the contrary the output is distinct from the input in hetero-association. These two associations deal with only known patterns. Third and fourth association also deal with unknown patterns. We want to call third association in which the input is an unknown pattern and the output is a known pattern "Learning unknown" or simply "Learning". Fourth association in which the input is a known pattern or an unknown pattern and the output is a new unknown pattern is called "Creating".

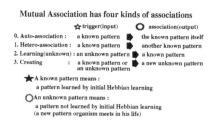

Fig. 1. Concept of Mutual Association

2.1 Evolution of Mutual Association

(1) The initial weight matrices(w_{ij}^0) are made by Hebbian rule or all zero. Hebbian rule determines the elemen ts of the weight matrix as follows:

$$w_{ij}^0 = \frac{1}{N} \sum_{\mu=1}^{p} \xi_i^\mu \xi_j^\mu + \frac{\lambda}{N} \sum_{\mu=1,\nu=1}^{p} \xi_i^\nu \xi_j^\mu$$

where p means the n umber of patterns to be stored, ξ_i^μ is the i-th bit of the μ-th initial patterns. λ is a constant that governs the relative strength of first and second terms. The second term specifies the fixed pairs bet ween initial patterns(ξ^ν and ξ^μ) for $f_h(5)$ and $f_b(7)$.

(2) N chromosomes which have a fixed length from 2401 to 4096 alleles are randomly made. They are c hosen randomly from $\{-1, 0, +1\}$, where the probability of selecting either -1 or 0 is set to 0.01 in this paper. Allele -1 means to reverse excitatory/inhibitory connections, and 0 means to remo ve the connection. These alleles(-1 and 0) are used to give a small perturbation to synaptic weights as Sompolinsky wrote[5]. This mak e the initial weight matrices sligh tly asymmetry.

$$w_{ij}^n = w_{ij}^0 + c^n(Ni + j) \quad (i, j = 1, 2, \cdots, N; n = 1, 2, \cdots, 128)$$

where w_{ij}^n denotes (i, j) element of the n-th weight matrix in the population, $c^n(k)$ denotes the k-th allele of the n-th chromosome.

(3) Renew state asynchronously with a discrete time, as follows:

$$S_i(t+1) = sgn(w_{ii}S_i(t) + \sum_{j \neq i}^{N} w_{ij}S_j(t))$$

where $S_i(t)$ is the state of i-th neuron at time t, and sgn is the sign function to be $sgn(x) = 1$ if $x \geq 0$, $sgn(x) = -1$ if $x < 0$. Hopfield set the self-coupling diagonal terms $w_{ii} = 0$. We found when $w_{ii} > 0$ (chaos neural network) auto-association converges extremely fast.

(4) Go to (5), (6) or (7) depending on the kind of mutual association

(5) Evaluate mutual fitness value f_h for hetero-association. At first sum of the similarity between the initial state vectors and varying state vectors over a fixed time T_{max} is calculated as the mutual relation. Then this sum is divided with the product between the number of patterns to be stored p, a certain maximum life time T_{max}, and the number of neurons N.

$$f_h = \frac{\sum_{\mu=1,\nu=1,\mu\neq\nu}^{p} \sum_{t=2}^{T_{max}} \sum_{j=1}^{N} \xi_j^\mu s_j^\nu(t)}{p \cdot T_{max} \cdot N}$$

where ξ_j^μ is the j-th bit of the μ-th initial pattern which takes the value of either -1 or $+1$. $s_j^\nu(t)$ means the state of the j-th neuron at time t when the ν-th initial pattern is given to the network. $f_h = 1$ means all the pairs of ξ^ν and ξ^μ are stored as fixed points. Goto(8)

(6) Evaluate mutual fitness f_l for an unknown patterns as follows:

$$f_l = \frac{\sum_{\mu=1}^{p} \sum_{t=2}^{T_{max}} \sum_{j=1}^{N} \pi_j^\mu s_j^\mu(t)}{p \cdot T_{max} \cdot N}$$

where π_j^μ is the j-th bit of the μ-th unknown pattern. Go to (8).

(7) Evaluate mutual fitness f_c for both known and unknown patterns :

$$f_c = \frac{\sum_{\mu=1,\nu=1,\mu\neq\nu}^{p} \sum_{t=2}^{T_{max}} \sum_{j=1}^{N} \xi_j^\mu \pi_j^\mu s_j^\nu(t)}{p \cdot T_{max} \cdot N}$$

where ξ_j^μ, π_j^μ, and $s_j^\nu(t)$ mean the same as (5) and (6).

(8) Evaluate fitness f_a for auto-association as follows:

$$f_a = \frac{\sum_{\mu=1}^{p} \sum_{t=2}^{T_{max}} \sum_{j=1}^{N} \xi_j^\mu s_j^\mu(t)}{p \cdot T_{max} \cdot N}$$

$f_a = 1$ means all the patterns are stored as fixed points.

(9) Extend or shorten the lifetime of organisms according to the mutual fitness value calculated by (5),(6) or (7). Kill organisms whose remaining days are zero.

(10) Select two parent at random from the upper 40% of the population sorted in descending order. Then recombinations are made with uniform crossing over to generate child chromosomes. Next mutation occur upon the offsprings with mutation rate 0.05. The value of randomly selected allele in chromosome $c^n(k)$ rotates cyclically such as : $+1 \Rightarrow -1 \Rightarrow 0 \Rightarrow +1$

(11) If the highest fitness value (different in the cases which use f_h, f_l, or f_c) reach 1.0 or the number of generation exceeds the upper limit this simulation terminates. If not, above processes from (2) to (10) are repeated.

Mutual associative memory evolve the weight matrix explained at (1) during above processes. The above simulation is a mixture of "learning on an individual level during its life time" and "learning on a population level during evolution".

2.2 Varying population size

We simulated the hetero-association with varying population size. The lifetime(4 generations on average) is extended or shorten according to the value of mutual fitness of an organism. Even 5% natural increase of population would cause an exponential growth of population size if constant decrease of population were not made. Figure 2 (a) shows the increases of hetero fitness with decreasing population down to 64 organisms every 50 generations. Thick zigzag broken line is the change of B-population. Figure 2 (b) shows the result of same simulation with constant population.

We calculated the total population in order to study the relation between the increasing of fitness value and the total population at a certain generation. Figure 2 (c) shows the comparison of them. Here the lines which have "v" at the head are the results with varying population size, and "c" shows the results with constant population. Meanwhile the first column shows total population and the second shows the values of fitness. We can see both the values of B-hetero-fitness with varying population and constant population are nearly equal (**), although total populations of constant population is nearly twice as much as total populations of varying population at both 1000th and 12000th generation(*).

Our models became more natural and the simulation time became shorter since varying population size improved the performance more than double.

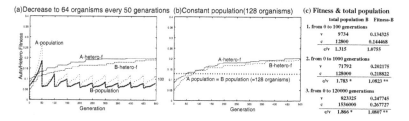

Fig. 2. Varying population size and Constant population

2.3   Hetero-association(associating another known pattern)

W e simulated hetero-associations with learning the pairs between initial patterns
($\lambda > 0$ and $\lambda = 0$ on 2.1(1)) and without learning them. Figure 3(left) shows
the results of simulation using 2.1(5) with varying the values of λ=0 to 3.0.
Organisms remem ber 16 initial patterns, and also 8 pairs between initial patterns
at birth if $\lambda > 0$. Hetero-fitness increases as the value of λ increase from 0 to
1.0 on both generation=0 and 12000. But they begin to decrease slightly when
λ rises more than 1.0 since the memory of initial patterns are gradually lost.

Figure 3(right) shows the same results as the figure 3(left) except it remembers the 4 pairs of initial patterns in the beginning which is half the number
compared with figure 3(left). In figure 3(right) hetero-fitness increases slightly
even when λ become more than 1.0 on both generation=0 and 12000 since the
organism has enough room for storage capacit y.

W e can observe the effect of learning the pairs initially ($\lambda > 0$ in 2.1(1)) become insignificant after long evolution. This can be seen by the curves of mutual
fitness on generation=12000 of figure 3(thick broken lines). Natural reinforcement learning which corresponds to from 2.1(2) to (10) is not inferior to the
compulsory learning the pairs of patterns at his birth.

Figure 4 shows the results of hetero-association started with the values of
λ=0 or 1.0 (left or right) and 12 initial patterns. In the figure 4(left) hetero-
fitness cannot catch up with auto-fitness. But, in the figure 4(right) hetero-
fitness catches up with auto-fitness on near 300th generation and keeps higher
value from near 500th generation. This is the result of smaller n umber of initial
patterns and the value of $\lambda > 0$. The curves of hetero-fitness and auto-fitness
show nearly a line symmetry.

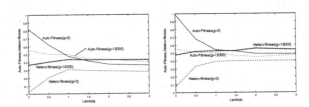

Fig. 3. Hetero-fitness vs λ (N=49,p=16(left),p=8(right))

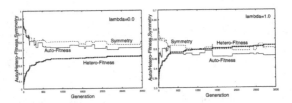

2.4   Learning unknown

Learning may be said to associate a known pattern from a given unknown pattern(see Figure 1 and 2.1(6)). This process may be recognized as the process of learning, for example, new languages. W e can also observe auto-fitness decreases as learning-fitness increases, and the curves of learning-fitness and auto-fitness show nearly a line symmetry.

3   Evolution of learning

Here we try to simulate the evolution of learning capacity using the mutual associative memory. This is the simulation of mutual associative memory with many populations. To be exact, this simulation of evolution of learning is the simulation of "learning with many teachers among many populations". An imaginary language is the target of "Learning". W e also try to simulate one of the "Dynamics to change rule itself" since one of the essence of life is the ability to change itself or open dynamics[6].

W e simulate here the evolution of learning capacity or the evolution of weight matrix for learning no more than tens of w ords. First, we prepare two populations which have evolved their own language separately. Second, two populations begin the communication with one of their languages. The fitness function is the ability to comm unicate to another populations with some language. The survival rule is the same rule as the sim ulation of mutual association. The situation where third medium whic h neither A nor B know is used can be consider. This may mean creating new language.

Figure 5 shows the algorithm of the evolution of learning on the condition that organisms change rule by themselves. They always watch the other populations to see which language-fitness has higher value in order to change the language which they learn next.

Genetic Algorithm Implementation (Evolution of Learning Ability)

Initialize N populations which has 64 ~ 128 organisms
    by learning own language with Heb rule
while (mutual-fitness<1.0 && genaration<12000) do
    evaluate mutual-fitness of N populations
        by comparing with N learning abilities
    select language learning from N languages
    evaluate mutual-fitness of each individual
        by counting how many relations can be memorized
    repeat until the worst 60% in the population are replaced do
        select two individuals randomly from the best 40%
        rennmhine them with uniform crossover to produce offspring
        mutate all the offsprings
    generation++

Fig. 5. The algorithm of evolution of learning the language on the condition that organisms change rule itself

3.1   Evolution when rule never change

W e observe evolution of learning as the interaction among man y populations. Figure 6 shows the result of A population and B population with the same fixed rules. The rules are that A population uses only their language A from the start to the half of their lives, but starts learning the language B from half to the end. B population uses the same rule as A population. The language-fitness is calculated using the expression 2.1(6) : mutual-fitness f_l for the unknown patterns. The figure 6 shows both language-fitness of A and B increase their values as the generation go on. They show nearly same values though the amplitude of B is bigger than A. On the contrary, both fitness of A and B decrease. These results show both A population and B population have more abilities to learn foreign language as the generation go on. The simulations with more than two populations also shows progress as the result of evolution.

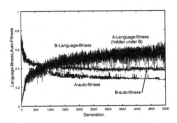

Fig. 6. Competition of language ability by two populations A and B

3.2   Evolution when organisms c hange rule

Here we simulate on the condition that organisms change the rule itself. First is the simulation of evolution when populations change language learning during their own lives. Second is the simulation of evolution when populations change language learning on the start point of each generations.

Figure 7 shows the result of first one. On this simulation all organisms have two kinds of processes in their life times. Organisms learn their own language at first half life, and at second half life they decide to learn what language to learn by comparing the language abilities of other populations. W e can observe evolution on both A-language-fitness and B-language-fitness. A-language-fitness has chaotic bifurcation.

Figure 8 shows the result of same simulation with four populations. Here C-language-fitness shows much higher increase than A, B and D. Sudden twice increases at about 500th and 4000th generation of C-language-fitness attract much attention. These may be happened by mutations.

Second simulation that populations change language learning on the start point of each generation showed no evolution except first 500 generations.

3.3   Creating new medium

Creating new medium means that organisms in vent, for example, a new sign comprehensible only to them. W e tried two simulations with the initializations by Hebbian weight matrix and Zero matrix (see 2.1(1)). The organisms do not learn their native language when we use Zero matrix for the initial weight. The mutual fitness f_c is used here for evaluate comm unication-fitness (2.1(7)).

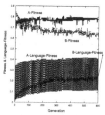

Fig. 7. Two populations A and B change language learning in their life time

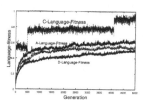

Fig. 8. Four populations change the language learning in their life time

We could observe evolution of communication only when two populations have their native languages. Simulation without native languages showed insignificant increase of their communication-fitness.

4 Conclusion

(1) Genetic algorithms with varying population size improves the performance.
(2) We got a mutual capacity of 14% as a result of evolution of hetero-association.
(3) The cognition between a known pattern and another known pattern is easier than the cognition between a known pattern and an unknown pattern.
(4) Evolution of learning can be observed only when organisms change rule itself during their lifetime
(5) Evolution of communication or making contact with others needs initial knowledge of native language in advance.

References

[1]J.J.Hopfield,"Neural Networks and Physical Systems with Emergent Collective Computational Abilities", Proc. Nat. Acad. Sci.,U.S.A,vol.79,p.2554,1982.
[2]A.Yoshida,"Evolution of learning Capacity by means of Mutual Associative Memory", JCIS'98, Earth Science & Softcomputing, Proc.Vol.1,p439,1998.
[3]A.Yoshida,"Self-Organizing approach of Mutual Associative Memory"(submitted
[4]H.Sompolinsky,"Neural Network with Non-linear Synapses and Static Noise", Phys.Rev.A34 p2571,1986.
[5]Daniel J.Amit,"Modeling Brain Function-The world of attractor neural networks",Cambridge U. P.,1989.
[6]K.Kaneko,"A trial to extend the view of dynamical system", Dynamics and Logic for Understanding Cognition and Behavior of Human,Yukawa Institute, Kyoto U.,1997.

The Application of Cellular Automata to the Consumer's Theory: Simulating a Duopolistic Market

Sobei H. Oda[1], Kouhei Iyori[2], Miura Ken[3], and Kanji Ueda[4]

[1] Faculty of Economics, Kyoto Sangyo University, Motoyama, Kamigamo, Kita-ku, Kyoto 603-8501, Japan (oda@cc.kyoto-su.ac.jp).
[2] Graduate School of Science and Technology, Kobe University, 1-1 Rokkodai-cho, Nada-ku, Kobe 657-8501, Japan (iyori@mi-2.mech.kobe-u.ac.jp).
[3] Graduate School of Science and Technology, Kobe University, 1-1 Rokkodai-cho, Nada-ku, Kobe 657-8501, Japan (miuraken@mbox.kyoto-inet.or.jp).
[4] Faculty of Engineering, Kobe University, 1-1 Rokkodai-cho, Nada-ku, Kobe 657-8501, Japan (ueda@mech.kobe-u.ac.jp).

Abstract. This paper presents a cellular automata model of a duopolistic market with consumers leraning and network externalities. The model produces various dynamics of the market. In particular, if the user cost can locally be di˜erent, it generates such rich dynamics that aggregate models could not explain. The results of simulations also suggest that the long-run consequence of duopolistic competition may crucially depends on the initial condition.

1 Introduction

When you buy an application, you may probably take account of how long you have used it and how many of others will use it. Even if an application with higher performance is available, you may hesitate to change it from the one you are familiar with, suspecting understandably that mastering a new application may require considerable time and effort. You may however abandon the use of your favorite application if increasingly many of your friends and colleagues use another one, fearing naturally that adhering to it may make it di cult to exchange data and programs with them. We should like to examine such markets where consumers consider these things: consumers' learning by doing and network externality, which plays an important role in the so-called information-oriented society.

This paper, which describes a duopolistic market with network externality and consumers' learning by doing, is a generalisation of our previous one (Oda et al [3]) does, which examines the dynamics of a monopolistic market with network externality. In fact both are cellular automata models; what is new in the present work are only the existence of a rivalling product and the dependence of the consumers' reservation prices for products on their past purchasing behaviour. Although consumers do not like move around, their behaviour is in"uenced by their experience so that our model has become similar to the CA+Agent models of (Epstein and Axtell [1]).[1]

We shall explain our model in Section 2 and mention a few results of its simulation in Section 3. Owing to the introduction of consumer's learning and a rivalling product, the dynamics of the market has become much more complex: in addition to the drastic change of the final equilibrium by a small change in the initial condition, it is often observed that the market goes on changing in a complicated   not simple but not random   manner.

2   The model

Let us assume the following.

1. There are M^2 consumers in a closed society. Every consumers has a personal computer for which two operating systems are available. To use an OS, each consumer must make a new or renewal contract at its supplier at the beginning of every week. We designate $X(m, n, t) = 1$ if Consumer m $(m = (m_1, m_2)$, $1 \leq m_1 \leq M$ and $1 \leq m_2 \leq M)$ contracts with the supplier of OSn $(n = 1$ or $2)$ for Week t $(t = 0, 1, 2, \ldots)$ and $X(m, n, t) = 1$ if he or she does not.

2. The utility which Consumer m obtains from using his or her computer for Week t is

$$U(m, t) = \max_{n \in (1,2)} (X(m, n, t)U(m, n, t) +   X(m, 3 - n, t)U(m, 3 - n, t)) \quad (1)$$

where   is a constant while $U(m, n, t)$ represents Consumer m's utility from using OSn alone. Here $0 \leq   < 1$ is assumed because using two operating systems does not brings in twice as much utility as using one.

3. Consumer's utility from using an OS consists of three terms:

$$U(m, n, t) = U_{min} + (U_{max} - U_{min})L(m, n, t) + (1 -)(U_{max} - U_{min})N(m, n, t) \quad (2)$$

where U_{min}, U_{max} and   are given constants $(0 \leq U_{min} \leq U_{max}$ and $0 \leq \leq 1)$. Here the first term of (2) stands for the basic utility that a beginner can readily obtain from standing alone computer usage.

4. The second term of (2) represents the effect of consumers' learning by doing: one can obtain more utility from the same OS as he or she uses it longer. Here

---

[1] The other new point is that each consumer s neighbourhood is probabilistically determined according to the method developed by (Markus and Hess [2]). Yet it does not seem to make signi"cant e˘ects at least in the simulations mentioned in this paper.

$L(m,n,t)$ stands for the skill for using OSn that Consumer m has acquired till time t (the beginning of Week t), which is defined as

$$L(m,n,t) \begin{cases} = L(m,n,0) & \text{for } t = 0 \\ = \displaystyle\sum_{k=1}^{t} (1-)^k \max(X(m,n,t-k), \ X(m,3-n,t-k)) & \text{for } t \geq 1 \end{cases} \tag{3}$$

where   and   are given constants $(0 \leq \ \leq 1)$ while $L(m,n,0)$ are all given as a part of the initial condition $(0 \leq L(m,n,0) \leq 1)$. Here   stands for the speed of skill depreciation, while   represents the substitutability between the two operating systems: the increase of the skill for using an OS by using the other OS alone is 100   percent of its increase by using the OS. Note that the second term of (2) is regarded as the product of the degree of skill accumulation $L(m,n,t)$ and its absolute weight on the total consumer's utility $(U_{max} - U_{min})$, because $0 \leq L(m,n,t) \leq 1$, $\lim_{t\to\infty} L(m,n,t) = 1$ if $X(m,n,0) = X(m,n,1) = \ldots = 1$, and $\lim_{t\to\infty} L(m,n,t) = 0$ if $X(m,n,0) = X(m,n,1) = \ldots = 0$.

5. The third term of (2) stands for the effect of network externality, which is determined by

$$N(m,n,t) = \frac{\sum_{i\in\Omega(m)} \max(X(i,n,t), \ X(i,3-n,t))}{| \ (m)|}. \tag{4}$$

Here   is a given constant $(0 \leq \ \leq 1)$; (m) represents the set of Consumer m's neighbours:

$$(m) = \{\text{Consumer } i| \ \text{dis}(i,m) < R\} \tag{5}$$

where R is a given constants $(1 < R)$; $| \ |$ stands for the number of Consumer m's neighbours. It is tacitly assumed that in our model cells (consumers) are arranged so that those who exchange more information are nearer. That is to say, in our terms neighbours are not those who live in neighbourhood but those who share the same interest.

We can find some similarities in the second and the third term of (2). First, since $0 \leq N(m,n,t) \leq 1$, we can regard the third term as the product of the degree of network externality $N(m,n,t)$ and its absolute weight on the total consumer's utility $(1- \ )(U_{max} - U_{min})$. Secondly,   and   play a similar role: is smaller if consumers can use both operating systems in a more similar way, while   is smaller if users of different operating systems can more easily exchange data and programs. Thirdly, (m) corresponds to   : the former sets the contemporary boundary to network externality while the latter limits the benefit from past experience.

6. Consumers follow a simple adoptive behaviour: they calculate $N(m,n,t)$ on the supposition that $X(i,n,t) = X(i,n,t-1)$ for all $i \in \ (m)$. In other words, at time t Consumer m expects the following utility for Week t:

$$N(m,n,t) \begin{cases} = N(m,n,0) & \text{for } t = 0 \\ = \dfrac{\sum_{i\in\Omega(m)} max(X(i,n,t-1),\gamma X(i,3-n,t-1))}{|\Omega(m)|} & \text{for } t \geq 0 \end{cases} \tag{6}$$

where $N(m, n, 0)$ are given as the other part of the initial condition $(0 \leq N(m, n, 0) \leq 1)$. We also define $U(m, n, t)$ by replacing $N(m, n, t)$ with $N(m, n, t)$ in (2) and $U(m, t)$ by replacing $U(m, n, t)$ with $U(m, n, t)$ in (1). Here we have explained how consumers expect their weekly utility $U(m, t)$ at the beginning of each week.

7. Consumer's cost for using a computer is given by

$$C(m, t) = X(m, 1, t)P_1 + X(m, 2, t)P_2 \tag{7}$$

where P_n represents cost for using OSn. In the next section it will be assumed to be constant for Examples 1, 2 and 3 of the next section while it will be regarded as

$$P(m, n, t) = Q(n, t) + R(m, n, t) \tag{8}$$

for Examples 4, 5, 6 and 7. Here $Q(n, t)$ stands for the rental fee for using OSn while $R(m, n, t)$ represents the consumer m's fees for using OSn applications. The former decreases as the total number of the users of the OS increases, while the latter decreases as the number of the consumer m's neighbours who use the OS:

$$Q(n, t) = Q_{n\min} + (Q_{n\max} - Q_{n\min})x(n, t) \tag{9}$$

$$R(m, n, t) = R_{n\min} + (R_{n\max} - R_{n\min})y(m, n, t) \tag{10}$$

$$x(n, t) = rZ(n, t - 1) + \frac{x(n, t - 1)}{1 + r} \tag{11}$$

$$y(m, n, t) = rW(m, n, t - 1) + \frac{y(m, n, t - 1)}{1 + r} \tag{12}$$

$$Z(n, t - 1) = \frac{\sum_{\text{all } m} X(m, n, t - 1)}{M^2} \tag{13}$$

$$W(m, n, t - 1) = \frac{\sum_{l \in \Omega(m)} X(l, n, t - 1)}{|\Omega(m)|}. \tag{14}$$

Here $Q_{n\max}$, $Q_{n\min}$, $R_{n\max}$, $R_{n\min}$ and r are all given positive constants.

8. At time t Consumer m calculates

$$V(m, n, t) = U(m, t) - C(m, t) \tag{15}$$

for all the four possible combinations of $X(m, 1, t)$ and $X(m, 2, t)$: $(0, 0)$, $(0, 1)$, $(1, 0)$ and $(1, 1)$, and chooses the combination that maximises $V(m, n, t)$ as $(X(m, 1, t), (m, 2, t))$.

3   Simulations

Let us show some results of simulations for the following value of parameters and the set of the initial condition: $M = 50$, $R = 2$, $U_{min} = 0.2$, $U_{max} = 0.4$, $=$ $= 0$, $= 0.5$ and $L(m, n, 0) = 0.5$ for all m and n. In the following figures, black points, gray points and white points represent OS1 users, OS2 users and non-users respectively (no consumer use both operating systems simultaneously in the following examples).

3.1   Examples 1, 2 and 3

These are cases where P_n are given constants ($P_1 = P_2 = 0.25$). Since all the parameters are common to both operating systems, their technical performance is the same. Fail or success totally depends on the distribution of the initial users.

Example $k(1 \leq k \leq 3)$ is more advantageous for OS2 unconditionally than Example $k - 1$. Because the initial distribution of the OS1 users are common to the three examples, while initial OS2 users are chosen so that an OS2 initial user in Example $k(1 \leq k \leq 3)$ is an OS2 initial user in Example $k - 1$. In addition, the initial condition for every example is chosen so that all consumers will user an OS if the initial users of the other OS does not exist.

The long-run consequence of competition is quite understandable: in Example 1 OS1 dominates the whole markets; in Example 2 OS1 and OS2 shares the market; in Example 3 OS2 monopolises the market.

Example 3 seems noteworthy. OS1 users and OS2 users rapidly increase almost at the same rate till every consumer uses either product, but then the former gradually decrease and disappear in the end. Yet neither products' properties nor consumers' behaviour has changed when the market is saturated. Both the rapid diffusion of OS1 and its fade-out are explained by the same value of parameters and the same utility functions.

3.2   Examples 4, 5, 6 and 7

Let us examine cases where the price of the same product may locally be different. Let us assume that $R_{n\max} = R + a$ and that $R_{n\min} = R - a$. Since $R_{n\max} - R_{n\min} = 2a$, the greater a is, the larger P_i can locally differ. Figures 4, 5, 6 and 7 show cases where a equals 0, 0,03, 0.04 and 0.09 respectively (all the other parameters and the initial condition are common to all the four cases).

The dynamics of the distribution of the users of the two OSs (the black-gray patterns in the figures) qualitatively changes according as a increases. For $a = 0$, the black-gray patterns are finally fixed (every consumer goes on using either OS in the long run). For $a = 0.03$, the black and gray belts move rightwards for ever(every consumer continue to change the product he or she buys cyclically). For $a = 0.04$, the dynamics is most interesting: after 300 weeks, winding black and gray stripes (from upper right to lower left) emerge and continue to move (from upper right to lower left) with their shapes changing for 1000 weeks. Then the shifting diagonal stripes suddenly disappear; then no steady changing patterns can apparently be seen even approximately for thousands weeks; then again suddenly the shifting diagonal stripes appear.

For $a = 0.09$, the black-gray patterns change unsteadily at least as long as the simulation is observed. In short, the larger a is, the more di cult it is to predict each consumer's behaviour in the long run.

the number of users

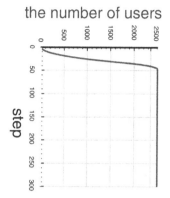

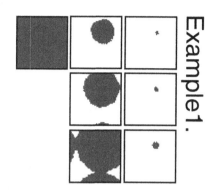

Example1.

the number of users

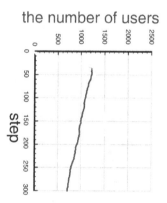

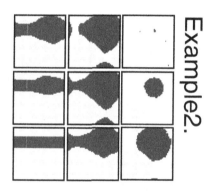

Example2.

the number of users

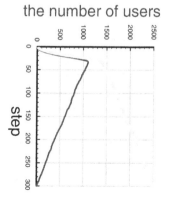

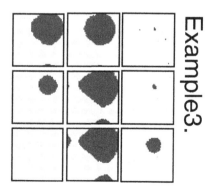

Example3.

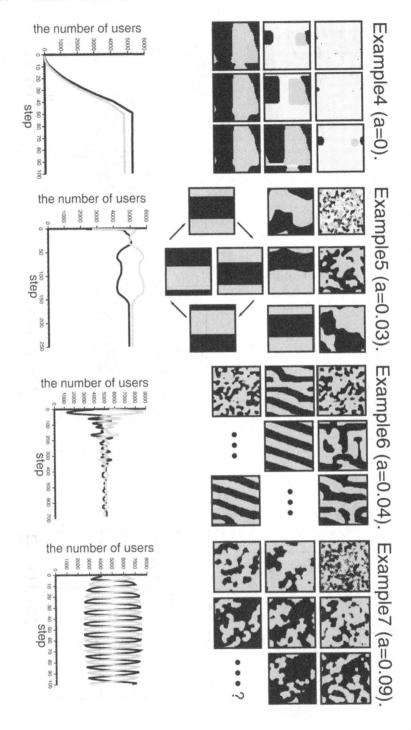

4 Concluding Remarks

Though having made a small number of simulations for very limited combinations of parameters and the initial condition, we have found both results of simulations which could and could not be explained by some aggregate model. This suggests that the cellular automata model of oligopolistic market may have much richer dynamics than the aggregate model describes. We hope that our model and simulations could contribute to connecting individual consumers' interaction and the dynamics of aggregate values in oligopolistic markets.

This project Methodology of Emergent Synthesis (JSPS-RFTF96P00702) has been supported by the Research for the Future Program of the Japan Society for the Promotion of Science.

References

1. Epstein, J.M. and Axtell, R.: Growing Arti"cial Society; Social Science From the Bottom Up. Brooking Institution Press (1996)
2. Markus, M. and Hess, B.: Isotropic cellular automaton for modeling excitable media. Nature **347** (1990) no.6288, 56-58
3. S.H. Oda, K. Miura and K. Ueda.: The application of cellular automata to network externality in consumer s theory: a generalisation of life game. *Artificial Life Five* in Langton, C.G. and Shimohara, K. (ed). MIT Press (1997) 473-480

Object-Oriented Genetic Algorithm Based Artificial Neural Network for Load Forecasting

L.L. Lai[1], H. Subasinghe[1], N. Rajkumar[1], E. Vaseekar, B.J. Gwyn[1], and V.K. Sood[2]

[1] City University, London EC1V 0HB
United Kingdom
http://eeisun5.city.ac.uk
[2] Hydro Quebec, Montreal
Canada

Abstract. This paper illustrates an integrated Computational Intelligence (CI) technique using Arti"cial Neural Networks (ANN) and Genetic Algorithms (GA) for Electric Load Forecasting. A load forecasting model has been developed based on ANN and GA. The model produces a short-term forecast of the load in the 24 hours of the forecast day concerned. Optimum weights and the biases of ANN are found by the Genetic Algorithm. The technique has been tested on data provided by an Italian power company and the results obtained through the application of integrated computational intelligence approach show that this approach is not practical without high computational facilities as this problem is very complex. However, this points to the direction of evolutionary computing being integrated with parallel processing techniques to solve practical problems ...

1 Introduction

An accurate and stable load forecast is essential for many operating decisions taken by utilities. In fact, it is well known that a cheap and reliable power system operation is definitely the result of good short-term load forecasting. The short-term load forecast provides the information to be adopted in the on-line scheduling and security functions of the energy management system, such as unit commitment, economic dispatch and load management. Hence, accurate load forecasting is essential for the optimal planning and operation of large-scale power systems.

Many techniques have been proposed and used for short-term load forecasting. Time-series models based on extrapolation are used for the representation of load behaviour by trend curves. The time series approach, regression approach, state-space models, pattern recognition and expert systems are also some of the other techniques used [1-5].

The time series approach assumes that the load of a time depends mainly on previous load patterns, such as the auto-regressive moving average models and the spectral expansion technique [2]. The regression method utilises the tendency that the load pattern has a strong correlation to the weather pattern. The weather-sensitive portion of the load is arbitrarily extracted and modelled by a pre-determined functional relationship with weather variables. All the above approaches use a large number of complex equations that involve lots of computational time. More recently, artificial neural network (ANN) techniques have been used in many modelling problems [6-10]. One of the most popular training algorithms for feed-forward ANNs is a gradient descent search algorithm, for example, the back-propagation (BP) approach, which tries to minimise the total Mean Square Error (MSE) between actual output and target output of an ANN. This error is used to guide BP's search in the weight space. There have been some successful applications of BP algorithms in various areas. However, drawbacks with the BP algorithm do exist due to its gradient descent nature. It often gets trapped in a local minimum of the error function and is very ine - cient in searching for a global minimum of a function which is vast, multimodal, and non-differentiable. One way to overcome BP's as well as other gradient descent search-based training algorithms' shortcomings, is to consider the training process as the evolution of connection weights towards an optimal (near optimal) set defined by a fitness function. From such a point of view, global search procedures like GAs can be used effectively to train an ANN. Therefore, GA integrated with ANN (GA-ANN) has been implemented for searching a solution. Object Oriented Techniques (OOT) were the framework for integrating ANN and GA. OOT gives us the ability to combine the existing objects (ANN object and GA object) and create new components (GA-ANN).

2   GA and ANN Hybridisation

There are three levels at which GA search procedures can be introduced to ANNs, namely, connection weights and biases, architectures and training algorithms. In here GA has been used to optimise the connection weights and biases of the neural network.

2.1   Optimising ANN Weights Using GA

The GAs training approach is divided into two major steps: the first one is to decide the representation scheme of connection weights, e.g., binary strings and the second one is the evolution itself driven by GA. Different representation schemes and GAs can lead to quite different training performance in terms of training time and accuracy. A typical cycle of the evolution of connection weights with GA is shown in figure 1:

2.2   Representation of Connection Weights

When using GA the most convenient representation is binary, since GA usually uses binary representation (chromosomes) of the problem parameters and binary

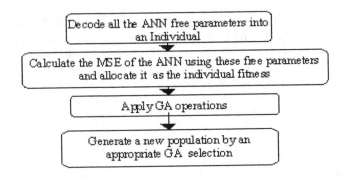

Fig. 1. One Typical cycle of evolution of connection weights with GA

operators for combination. The range of each free parameter depends on the problem complexity and the required resolution of the system parameters.

A key issue here is to decide how much information about an architecture should be encoded into a representation. This includes number of layers and number of neurons in each layer. As the architecture parameters decoded in GA individuals are increased, the computational cost increases. There is a trade off between these two factors as the combination differs for different classes of problems.

2.3   GA and ANN Hybridisation

Interaction between developed ANN and GA components are presented in order to explore possible benefits arising from these combinations, instead of using them individually. Object Oriented Technique gives us the ability to combine the existing developed objects and create new components. In order to perform this task, a through analysis on both objects should be done, including understanding the principles of the hybrid systems, identifying objects which will remain important in the life of the hybrid system and finally identifying the relationships between the different objects and the ways in which the objects interact.

After analysing the system which includes identifying the object interactions, adaptation of classes in the new environment is performed. This task also includes composing ANN free parameters including weights, biases and decoding them into chromosomes. The number of ANN free parameters is calculated as shown in the equation below to form the chromosomes.

$$n_{free} = [(n_{in} \times n_{hid}) + (n_{hid} \times n_{out}) n_{hid} + n_{out}] . \tag{1}$$

where

n_{in} = Number of Nodes in Input Layer
n_{hid} = Number of Nodes in Hidden Layer
n_{out} = Number of Nodes in Output Layer
n_{free} = Number of Free Parameters

Other parameters such as architecture and training algorithms can be added to the chromosomes as an extension. The interaction between ANN and GA objects is performed by message passing. Both ANN and GA instances are created at the beginning of the optimisation procedure and last until the end. The GA object makes calls to ANN object and passes messages to fitness function. The optimisation is processed to find the near optimum global solution for each applied problem. Our experience is that GA-ANN are highly application dependent, the approach is tested on a parabolic function approximation and on electric load forecasting as explained in the following section.

3   GA-ANN Application

3.1   Parabolic Function Approximation

Parabolic function parameters (x and y values) were obtained using MatLab to create training and testing data files. The following system parameters are found to be the best for this problem, namely, population size, ANN free parameters, bits for each parameter, mutation rate, crossover rate, number of inputs to the neural network, number of nodes in the hidden layer and number of outputs which are 200, 16, 10. 0.1, 0.9, 1, 5 and 1 respectively.

Similar network was constructed using BP-ANN for comparison with GA-ANN. Figure 2 shows comparison of BP and GA training schemes' resulting error functions in the first 100 generations during the training.

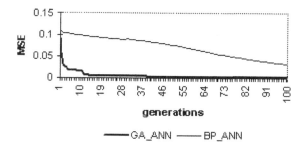

Fig. 2. Comparison between GA and BP during training for 100 Generations

GA-ANN and BP-ANN were further trained to reduce the RMS error in order to obtain better results. Figure 3 shows comparison between BP and GA training scheme's resulting error functions in the first 500 generations during the training. As shown in Figure 2, the GA-ANN system converges much faster than BP-ANN. It means that it finds a near global optimum with no significant difference in computational time between the two training schemes. The GA training scheme shows improvement over the BP in the first 100 generations

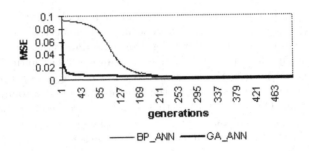

generations

——— BP_ANN ———GA_ANN

Fig. 3. Comparison between GA and BP during training for 500 Generations

and presents a very good convergence. However, when GA generations increase, the convergence speed reduces rapidly. As in Figure 3, BP begins to converge faster than GA after about 220 generations. Figures 4 and 5 show the outputs of GA-ANN and BP-ANN for unseen data with 100 and 500 generations of trained GA-ANN and BP-ANN respectively.

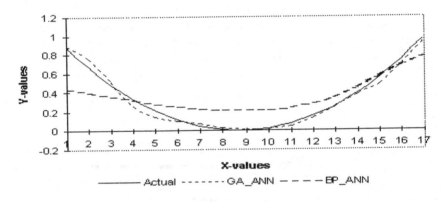

Fig. 4. Comparison between actual, GA-ANN and BP-ANN outputs for unseen data with 100 generations of trained GA-ANN and BP-ANN

3.2   Short-term Load Forecasting

There are 58 inputs to the developed model. The features that are taken into account as input factors in the load forecast system are as follows: two 24-hour load records of day i-1 and i-2 (the forecast day is day i. Six more inputs are the maximum and minimum temperatures of day i, i-1 and i-2. Three other inputs are the binary codes to show seven days of the week. One binary code is dedicated to the holidays or any yearly special occasions that may affect the

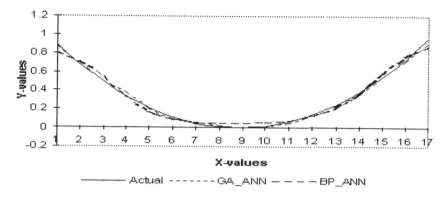

Fig. 5. Comparison between actual, GA-ANN and BP-ANN outputs for unseen data with 500 generations of trained GA-ANN and BP-ANN

forecast. In summary, the designed NN is of the MLP type and is used to learn about the relationship between the 58 inputs and 24 outputs.

The input are:

Hourly loads for two days prior to the forecast day	24
Hourly loads for the day prior to the forecast day	24
Max. and Min. temps for two days prior to the forecast day	4
Max. and Min. temps for the forecast day	2
Day of the week	3 bits
Holiday	1 bit
The outputs are:	
Load forecast for all 24 hours of the day	24

The above values are normalised as indicated by Equation (2).

$$Normalised\ \ Value = \frac{Actual\ \ Value - Min}{Max - Min}. \tag{2}$$

where Max. and Min. are the maximum and minimum of the attribute respectively.

The mean square error (MSE) is used to measure the accuracy of the model. The sigmoid activation function is adopted. The following system parameters are found to be the best for this problem, namely, population size, ANN free parameters, bits for each parameter, mutation rate, crossover rate, number of inputs to the neural network, number of nodes in the hidden layer and number of outputs which are 150, 1269, 16, 0.1, 0.9, 58, 15 and 24 respectively.

The Back-propagation was also used to train another ANN which is then used as a reference to make a comparison between two algorithms. The training Mean Square Error (MSE) of both BP-ANN and GA-ANN for the first 100 generations is shown in Figure 6.

As in Figure 6, it shows that the BP-ANN converges much faster than GA-ANN. It could mean that that it finds a better optimum in less number of iterations. Figure 7 shows the comparison between actual results and GA-ANN outputs for unseen data.

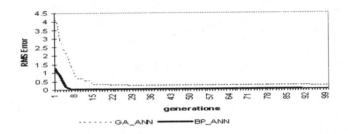

Fig. 6. Comparison between GA-ANN and BP-ANN for 100 generations

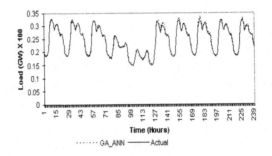

Fig. 7. Comparison between actual and GA-ANN outputs for unseen data

4   Conclusions

The main question is whether the GA-ANN is more e cient than conjugate gradient (e.g. BP) methods. In general GA-ANN gives better solutions for the problems with a small number of parameters. But for systems with a large number of problem parameters it becomes impractical as it increases the computational time and the computational cost. If powerful computer facilities are available, then GA-ANN are generally the preferred method. Parallel GA-ANN is one of the solutions to reduce training time. The OO methodology is a very useful framework in the development of GA-ANN as it reduces the development time. The developed OO models of all algorithms give this "exibility to upgrade and maintain the software constantly and form different configurations. Artificial Neural Network and Genetic Algorithms have been used to design a neural network for short-term load forecasting. The forecasting model has been used to produce a forecast of the load in the 24 hours of the forecast day concerned, using data provided by an Italian powerthe company. The results obtained are promising. In this particular case, the comparison between the results from the GA-ANN and BP-ANN shows that the GA-ANN does not provide a faster solution than the BP-ANN. This could be due to the fact that the initial randomly selected starting point is a poor one. The size of the problem is very large and as such the amount of memory and computation time are large too. This points to the direction of parallel processing techniques being integrated with evolutionary computing to solve complex practical problems.

5   Acknowledgements

The authors would like to express their thanks to M Sforna and M Caciotta of Electric and Automation Department, ENEL Research, Italy for providing the data.

References

1. Gross, G., Galiana, F.D.: Short term load forecasting. Proc. of IEEE, Vol. 75, No. 12, 1987, pp. 1558-1573
2. Hagan, M.T., S M Behr, S.M.: The time series approach to short term load forecasting. IEEE Transactions on Power Systems, Vol. 2, No. 3, 1987, pp. 785 -791
3. Papalexopoulos, A.D., Hesterberg, T.C.: A regression-based approach to short-term load forecasting. IEEE Transactions on Power Systems, Vol. 5, No. 4, 1990, pp. 1535-1547
4. Rahman, S., Bhantnagar, R.: An expert system based algorithm for short-term load forecast. IEEE Transactions on Power Systems, Vol. 3, No. 2, 1988, pp. 392-399
5. Dhdashti, A.S., Tudor, J.R., Smith, M.C.: Forecasting of hourly load by pattern recognition: a deterministic approach. Transactions on Power Apparatus and Systems, Vol. 101, 1982, pp. 900-910
6. Caciotta, M., Lamedica, R., Cencelli, V.O., Prudenzi, A., Sforna, M.: Application of arti"cial neural networks to historical data analysis for short-term electric load forecasting. European Transactions on Electrical Power, Vol. 7, 1997, pp. 49-56
7. Mai"eld, T., Sheble, G.: Short term load forecasting by neural network and a re"ned genetic algorithm. Electrical Power Systems Research, Vol. 31, pp. 9-14.
8. Lai, L.L.,Sichanie, A.G., Rajkumar, N., Styvaktakis, E., Sforna, M., Caciotta, M.: Practical application of object oriented techniques to designing neural networks for short-term electric load forecasting. Proceedings of the Energy Management and Power Delivery Conference, IEEE Catalogue No 98EX137, March 1998, pp. 559-563
9. Heng, E.T.H., Srinivasan, D., Liew, A.C.: Short term load forecasting using genetic algorithm and neural networks. Proceedings of the Energy Management and Power Delivery Conference, IEEE Catalogue No 98EX137, March 1998, pp. 576-581
10. Lai, L.L.: Intelligent system applications in power engineering - evolutionary programming and neural networks. John Wiley and Sons, 1998

Author Index

Lecture Notes in Artificial Intelligence (LNAI)

Lecture Notes in Computer Science